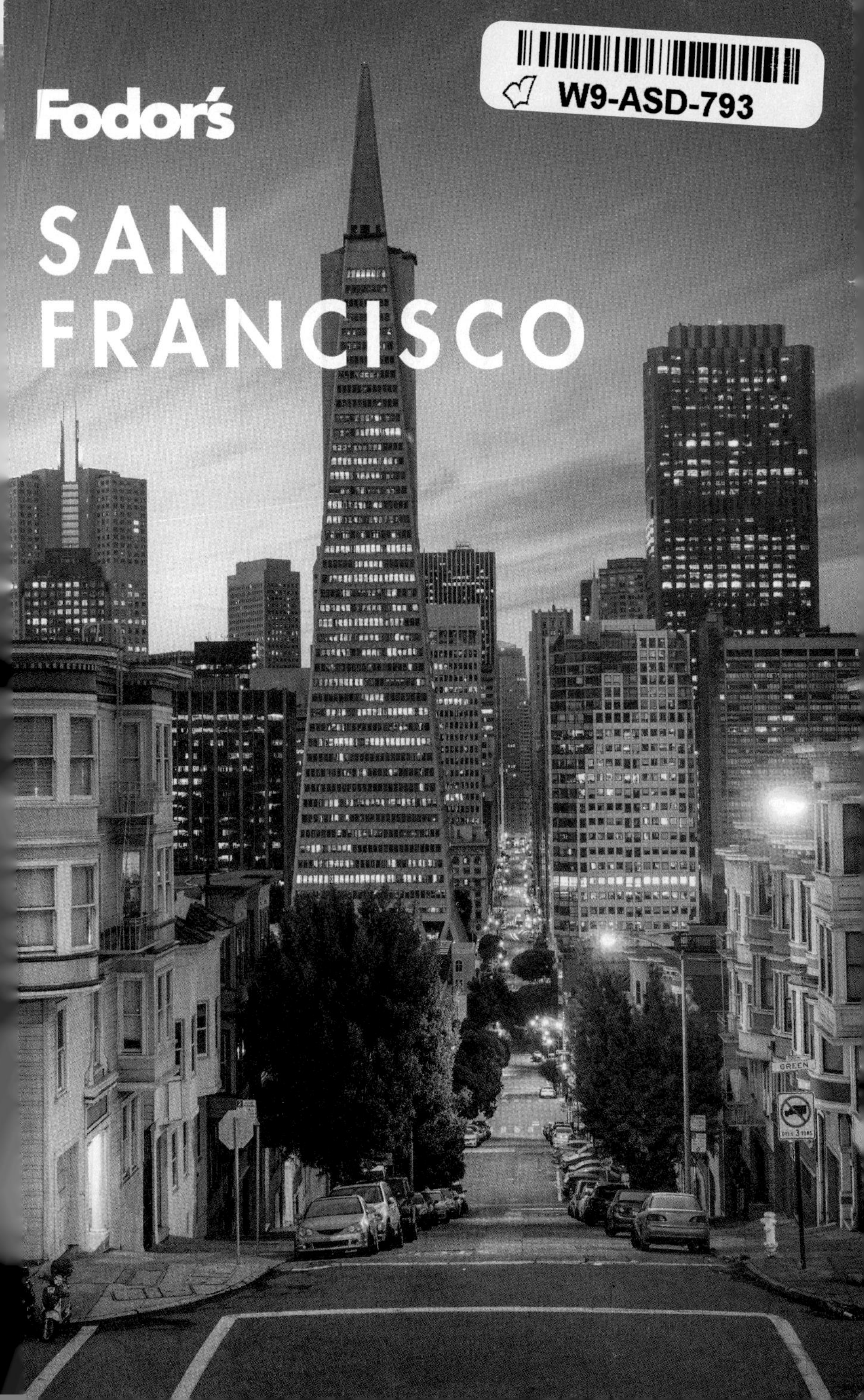
Fodor's
SAN FRANCISCO
GREEN
OVER 3 TONS

Welcome to San Francisco

With its myriad hills and spectacular bay, San Francisco beguiles with natural beauty, vibrant neighborhoods, and contagious energy. From the hipster Mission District to the sassy Castro, from bustling Union Square to enduring Chinatown, this dynamic town thrives on variety. The city makes it wonderfully easy to tap into the good life, too: between San Francisco's hot arts scene, tempting boutiques, parks perfect for jogging or biking, and all those stellar locavore restaurants and cocktail bars, it's the ultimate destination for relaxed self-indulgence.

TOP REASONS TO GO

★ **Foodie heaven:** Top restaurants, hip ethnic favorites, farmers' markets, food trucks.

★ **Distinctive neighborhoods:** Buzzing, walkable streets invite discovery.

★ **Golden Gate Bridge:** Electric orange and towering, this glorious span inspires awe.

★ **Waterfront activities:** Whether you hike, bike, or stroll it, the bay is magnetic.

★ **Accessible art:** From famous street murals to top-notch museums, art is everywhere.

Contents

Fodor's Features

MAPS

Chapter 1

EXPERIENCE SAN FRANCISCO

25 ULTIMATE EXPERIENCES

San Francisco offers terrific experiences that should be on every traveler's list. Here are Fodor's top picks for a memorable trip.

1 Ride a Cable Car

Clatter and jiggle up mansion-topped Nob Hill, then hold on for the hair-raising descent to Fisherman's Wharf, with sun glittering off the bay and Alcatraz bobbing in the distance.

2 Wander Through Chinatown

Have dim sum at Yank Sing, inhale the scented air as you watch the nimble hands at Golden Gate Fortune Cookie Factory, then take in the hundreds of red lanterns at Tin How Temple. *(Ch. 3)*

3 Frolic in Golden Gate Park

San Francisco's green beating heart, a 3-mile long park, stretches from the Haight to the Pacific Ocean and offers museums, gardens, a carousel, and a resident bison population. *(Ch. 9)*

4 See a Classic Film at the Castro Theater

One of the country's last, great independent theaters, this 1922 theater is a hodgepodge of art deco, Spanish, and Asian influences and features a pipe organ to entertain preshow. *(Ch. 10)*

5 Picnic in the Presidio

Almost 50% larger than Golden Gate Park, Presidio is home to a variety of public art, an extensive network of hiking trails, two cemeteries, and Sunday picnic events. *(Ch. 7)*

6 City Lights Bookstore

A city landmark, this independent publisher and former hangout of Beat-era writers remains a vital part of the city's literary scene. Browse three levels of books and local zines. *(Ch. 5)*

7 Old and New at Mission Dolores and Dolores Park

Mission Dolores' 18th-century chapel, with its painted wooden ceiling, is the oldest standing building in the city. Just down the road, Dolores Park is a favorite local hangout. *(Ch. 11)*

8 Gaze at the Palace of Fine Arts

Perched on a swan-filled lagoon near the Marina's yacht harbor, this stirringly beautiful terra-cotta-color domed structure was built in 1915 for an expo and has been a photo op since. *(Ch. 7)*

9 Coit Tower

The tower itself is just okay; it's all about the city and bay views here. Also, it sits at the top of Telegraph Hill's Filbert Steps, a steep stairway through glorious gardens. *(Ch. 5)*

10 Find a Ghost at Alcatraz

Walk the cold cement cellblock of America's most infamous federal pen as you hear about desperate escape attempts and notorious crooks like Al "Scarface" Capone and George "Machine Gun" Kelly. *(Ch. 6)*

11 Eat at the Ferry Building

Find cafés, restaurants, a farmers' market, and merchants peddling everything from wine and olive oil to oysters and mushrooms. Plaza tables offer great people-watching. *(Ch. 6)*

12 See Your Favorite Band at the Fillmore

This is *the* club that all the big names want to play. Catch a show and view the amazing collection of rock posters upstairs, then get free apples and posters on the way out. *(Ch. 12)*

13 Feel the Wind in Twin Peaks

Windswept and desolate, Twin Peaks yields sweeping vistas of San Francisco and neighboring counties. You can get a real feel for the city's layout here. *(Ch. 10)*

14 Dive Into Urban Ruins at the Sutro Baths

Explore the ruins, staircases, and a cave of what was once the largest indoor saltwater swimming pool in the world, to the soundtrack of pounding Pacific waves. *(Ch. 8)*

15 Tonga Room and Hurricane Bar

Since the 1940s this kitschy tiki bar has served up signature mai tais with a backdrop of fake palm trees, a lagoon (bands play pop standards on a floating barge), and faux monsoons. *(Ch. 4)*

16 Walk Across a Rainbow in the Castro

Take your selfies at the rainbow crosswalk at 18th and Castro, walk the Rainbow Honor Walk honoring brave pioneers, and visit the GLBT History Museum. *(Ch. 10)*

17 Mission Murals

Street art is at its most concentrated in the Mission where several small alleys have become magnets for artists creating murals with themes of social justice and Latino heritage. *(Ch. 11)*

18 SFMOMA

With about 150,000 square feet of galleries, SFMOMA is the largest museum in America devoted to modern and contemporary art and as essential a visit as the Louvre or the Met. *(Ch. 3)*

19 Cross the Golden Gate Bridge

Walking the 1.7 miles to Marin County—inches from roaring traffic, steel shaking beneath your feet, and the water 200 feet below—is much more than a superlative photo op (though it's that, too). *(Ch. 7)*

20 Explore Historic North Beach

San Francisco's "Little Italy" is populated with establishments like century-old foccacia purveyors, Liguria Bakery, and a string of Italian joints along Columbus Avenue. *(Ch. 5)*

21 Seward Street Slides

Designed by a 14-year-old kid in the 1970s, the side-by-side steep concrete slides for grown-up kids remain a random pocket of joy in a rapidly changing city. *(Ch. 1)*

22 Vintage Arcade Games at Musée Mécanique

This quirky "museum" has more than 200 antique arcade games from the early days of mechanization, including, coin-operated fortune tellers, moving dioramas, and stereoscopes. *(Ch. 6)*

23 The Redwoods at Muir Woods National Monument

Walking among some of the last old-growth redwoods on the planet, trees hundreds of feet tall and a millennium or more old, is a magical experience. *(Ch. 13)*

24 Stand in Line at Tartine Bakery

Experience loaves of tangy country bread and morning buns dusted with brown sugar, cinnamon, and orange zest at this cult Mission bakery. *(Ch. 11)*

25 Climb the Vallejo Steps

Though very steep, the walk up to Ina Coolbrith Park and beyond is possibly the most pleasurable thing to do while on Russian Hill, rewarding you as it does with glorious views. *(Ch. 4)*

WHAT'S WHERE

1 Union Square and Chinatown. Live fish flopping around on ice; the scent of incense, cigarettes, and vanilla; bargains announced in myriad Chinese dialects—you'll feel like you should've brought your passport.

2 SoMa. Anchored by SFMOMA and Yerba Buena Gardens, SoMa is a once-industrial neighborhood that's in transition. Luxury condos and stylish restaurants abound and cool dance clubs draw the bridge-and-tunnel crowd, but some parts are still gritty.

3 Civic Center. Monumental city government buildings and performing arts venues dominate, but it's also a chronic homeless magnet. Locals love Hayes Valley, the chic little neighborhood west of City Hall.

4 Nob Hill. Topped by staid and elegant behemoths, hotels that ooze reserve and breeding, Nob Hill is old-money San Francisco.

5 Russian Hill. These steep streets hold a vibrant, classy neighborhood that's very au courant. Locals flock

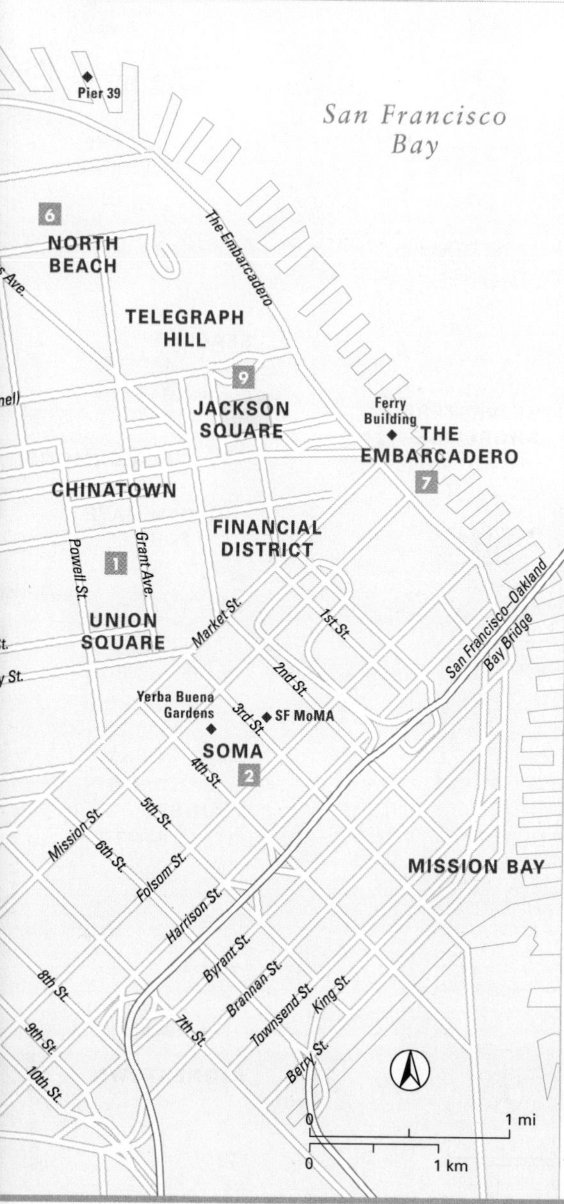

to Polk and Hyde Streets, the hill's main commercial avenues, for excellent neighborhood eateries and fantastic window-shopping.

6 North Beach. The city's small Italian neighborhood makes even locals feel as if they're on holiday. In the morning, fresh focaccia beckons, and there are few better ways to laze away an afternoon than in one of North Beach's cafés.

7 Embarcadero. The city's northeastern waterfront is anchored at the foot of Market Street by the exquisite Ferry Building marketplace. The promenade that starts in back has great views of the bay and the Bay Bridge.

8 The Waterfront. If you wander the shops and attractions of Fisherman's Wharf, Pier 39, and Ghirardelli Square, the only locals you'll meet will be the ones with visitors in tow. Everything here is designed for tourists.

9 Jackson Square. For history buffs and antiques lovers, this upscale corner of the Financial District is a pleasant diversion.

WHAT'S WHERE

10 The Marina. With fine-wine shops, trendy boutiques, fashionable cafés and restaurants, and pricey waterfront homes, the Marina is San Francisco's yuppiest neighborhood. It's also home to the exquisite 1915 Palace of Fine Arts.

11 The Presidio. Locals come to the Presidio, the wooded shoreline park just west of the Marina, for a quick in-town getaway, the spirit lift only an amble on the sand in the shadow of the Golden Gate Bridge can provide.

12 Golden Gate Park. Covering more than 1,000 acres of greenery, with sports fields, windmills, museums, gardens, and a few bison thrown in for good measure, Golden Gate Park is San Francisco's backyard.

13 The Western Shoreline. A natural gem underappreciated by locals and visitors alike, the city's windswept Pacific shore stretches for miles.

14 The Haight. If you're looking for '60s souvenirs, you can find them here, along with some of the loveliest Victorians in town (and aggressive panhandling). Hip locals come for the great secondhand

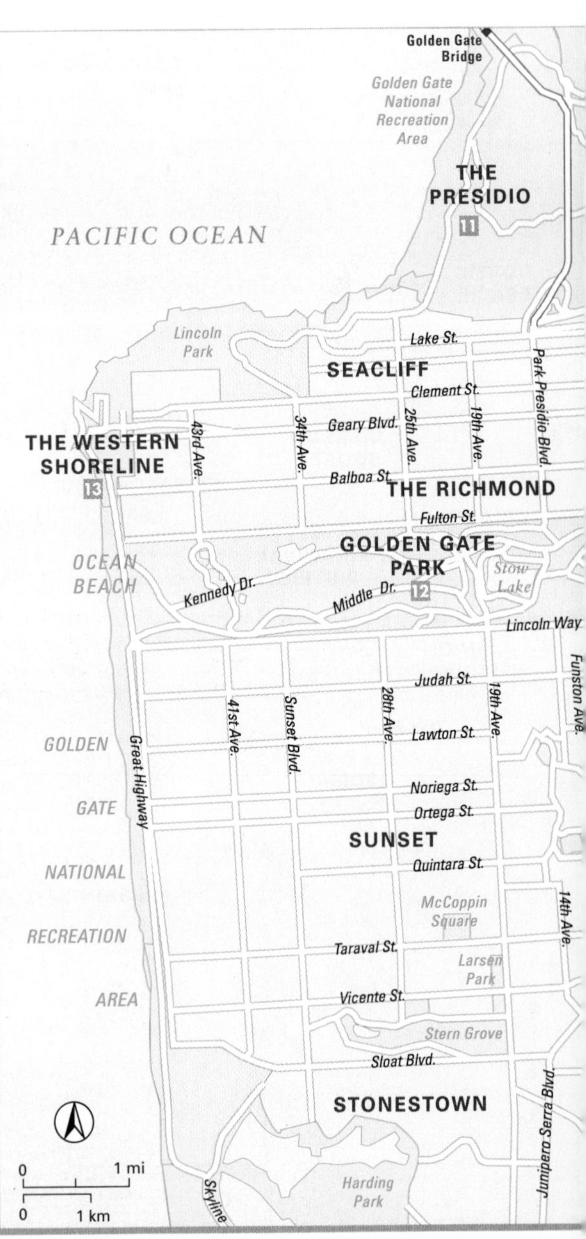

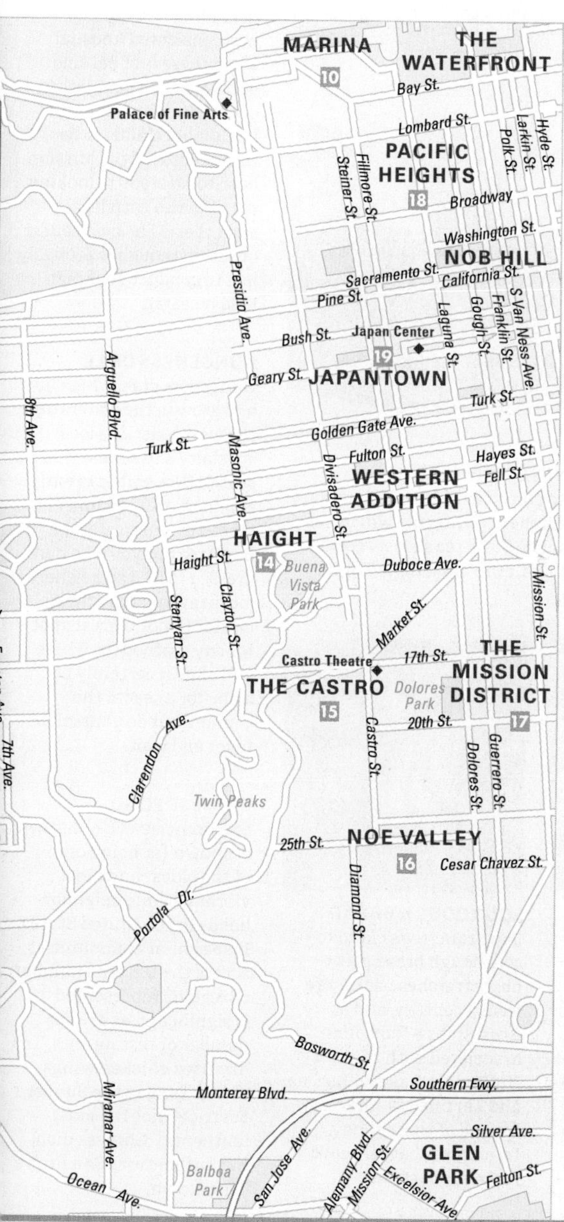

shops, cheap brunch, and low-key bars and cafés.

15 The Castro. Yes, it's proudly rainbow-flag-waving, in-your-face fab, but the Castro is a friendly neighborhood that welcomes visitors of all stripes. Shop the trendy boutiques, and catch a film at the truly noteworthy Castro Theatre.

16 Noe Valley. A cute, pricey neighborhood favored by young families. The main strip, 24th Street, is lined with coffee shops, eateries, and boutiques selling fancy bath products and trendy children's clothing.

17 The Mission District. When the sun sets, people descend on the Mission from all over the Bay Area for destination restaurants, excellent bargain-price ethnic eateries, and the hippest bar scene around.

18 Pacific Heights. This neighborhood has some of San Francisco's most opulent real estate—but in most cases you'll have to be content with an exterior view.

19 Japantown. A tight-knit Japanese American population supports this area, of interest to outsiders mostly for the ethnic shopping and dining opportunities of the Japan Center and the small streets just north.

10 Things to Eat and Drink in San Francisco

MICHELIN-STARRED CUISINE

Few regions have managed to cultivate the level of culinary intensity and creativity of Northern California which has eight three-star restaurants. The Bay Area's most recent three-star designations, Atelier Crenn and Single Thread, are especially hot right now.

LOCAL WINE

San Francisco sits smack dab in wine paradise and you should drink deep. To the north is Napa, Sonoma, and the Russian River Valley. To the northeast lies the Sierra Foothills. To the south, the Central Coast. Tip: Chardonnay is a major product of the area.

SOURDOUGH BREAD

San Francisco's claim to sourdough bread greatness stretches back more than a century, and as a result it's a food often associated with the city. Hit Boudin Bakery, Tartine, and Tartine Manufactory for one of these tangy, fermented loaves. Leave room for pastries!

MISSION BURRITO

Named for San Francisco's Mission District, this burrito has three identifiers: the size (gigantic), the variety of ingredients (including rice, which was considered unusual when these first became popular), and the tightly packed weight. Taqueria La Cumbre claims to be the inventor of the Mission burrito, so if you're looking for a burrito with legacy start there. The best course of action though is probably just to conduct your own field research.

DUNGENESS CRAB

Dungeness crab, which live and grow in the waters off the west coast, is a local specialty and a must if in season (November to early summer). You can find it in many restaurants in the Bay Area but you'd be hard pressed to find somewhere more revered than Swan Oyster Depot, a great spot for any seafood fix. There will almost certainly be a line for a seat at the counter, but do yourself a favor and wait.

CHINESE FOOD

San Francisco's Chinatown is known for being one of the oldest and most vibrant ethnic neighborhoods in the United States. Like similar communities across the U.S., the number of regions represented is significant, as are the number of restaurants. Try dry fried chicken wings at San Tung in the Sunset District—not the most "authentic" Chinese dish, but authentic to San Fran's Chinatown.

Dungeness crab

CIOPPINO
San Francisco's diverse history and incredible confluence of cultures makes for unique dishes like cioppino, which is essentially the Bay Area's own version of bouillabaisse. The dish is credited to Italian immigrants who began fishing California's generous waters. With a broth made from tomatoes and red wine, this seafood-filled soup is worth seeking out. Try Anchor Oyster Bar in the Castro.

BRUT IPA
On the more experimental end of the San Francisco beer spectrum is Brut IPA, a brand new style of beer whose creation is credited to Kim Sturdavant, the brewmaster at Social Kitchen and Brewery. It's extremely unusual to see a truly new style of beer emerge but Brut IPA––which was designed to mimic aspects of champagne–– is pale, hoppy, bone dry, and a true San Francisco original.

LOCAL COFFEE
Local chains like Blue Bottle Coffee (from Oakland) and Philz (from the Mission District) have cult followings across the country. Be sure to support other independently owned coffee shops as you wander: there's no shortage of talent or expertly roasted beans.

OAKLAND'S SOUL FOOD
Thanks to authors like Toni Tipton-Martin and Michael Twitty, America has begun to more fully recognize the incredible cultural debt that is owed to African American cooks. While 3,000 miles from the south, Oakland, which is home to a long-standing and historic African American community, offers some of the best soul food you can find on the west coast. Head to Flip n' Soul or Lena's Soul Food for some classic fried chicken and waffles or fried shrimp and catfish.

10 Best Photo Ops

THE PAINTED LADIES
Familiar to fans of the 1990s' TV show "Full House," the so-called Painted Ladies or Seven Sisters are a row of seven gorgeous and beautifully maintained Queen Ann–style houses just off Alamo Square. Take photos at midday for clear city views.

TWIN PEAKS
These two adjacent peaks are at the near geographic center of San Francisco and at an elevation of 925 feet. Especially pretty (and popular) at sunrise and sunset, you'll find sweeping 180-degree views of the Bay Area, with a great view of downtown San Francisco, the Bay Bridge, and the tips of the Golden Gate Bridge.

THE PALACE OF FINE ARTS
Perched on a swan-filled lagoon near the Marina's yacht harbor, this stirringly beautiful terra-cotta-color domed structure has an otherworldly quality about it. Built in 1915, the palace is a San Francisco architect's version of a Roman ruin, and it's been eliciting gasps for almost a century. It's a popular wedding spot if you like happy couples in your photos.

LANDS END COASTAL TRAIL
This 4-mile trail winds and twists along the rugged cliffs of the San Francisco bay, offering stunning views of the Golden Gate Bridge and surprisingly woodsy forest. At the 1.3-mile mark, turn left at the wooden staircase to explore Mile Rock Beach and the Lands End Labyrinth. On a clear day, you can see the Golden Gate Bridge in the distance.

THE PRESIDIO

As the gateway to the Golden Gate Bridge, San Francisco's 1,500-acre Presidio national park offers incredible views of the bridge and the sprawling vistas that surround it. The Presidio also abuts Baker Beach, a stretch of sand that lies below the park's western cliffs and offers alternative angles of the Golden Gate Bridge, Baker Beach.

MUIR WOODS

John Muir wrote, "Most people are on the world, not in it—have no conscious sympathy or relationship to anything about them..." It's hard not to feel connected as you walk the shaded paths of Muir Woods amid the towering majesty of the redwood forests. It will live on in your memories.

UNION SQUARE

This lively and central location is a great spot to capture cable cars as they rumble by. Also, the towering pillar of Dewey Monument, topped triumphantly by Nike, the Greek goddess of victory, is a legitimately beautiful sculpture. Relax on the steps and soak in/photograph the city.

TREASURE ISLAND

Despite its proximity to downtown San Francisco, the tiny, man-made Treasure Island is generally off the tourist track so your photos won't be crowded with selfie-takers. Set right in the middle of San Francisco Bay, it offers gorgeous views and photos of the San Francisco skyline, especially at night when the skyline is lit up.

HAWK HILL

Located at a high point on the south-facing Marin Headlands, Hawk Hill lies opposite the city and offers views of the Golden Gate Bridge as it enters San Francisco. True to its name, it's also a great spot for nature watching. Hawk Hill is the site of the autumnal raptor migration, and is also a habitat for the Mission Blue Butterfly.

BERNAL HEIGHTS

Pictures of Bernal Heights Hill show a somewhat stumpy-looking hill that rises unenthusiastically above the houses of the surrounding neighborhood. But, pictures taken *from* Bernal Heights Hill offer 360-degree panoramic views. Take a sunset stroll here for stunning San Fran shots.

Under the Radar

KABUKI SPRINGS & SPA
Enter the peaceful lobby and prepare to be transported at the Japanese-style communal baths, a Japantown spa popular with locals of all ages. The extensive menu includes facials, salt scrubs, and mud and seaweed wraps. Enjoy banging the gong if fellow bathers are ruining your zen with chit chat.

PIER 24
Just beneath the Bay Bridge along the Embarcadero, Pier 24 provides a fantastic space for displaying photography of all sizes and styles, and is home to world-class photography exhibitions.

16TH AVENUE STEPS
From the base of this glorious stairway mosaic in the Inner Sunset you can view the beautiful themes, from an underwater theme to dragonflies and butterflies, and a starry night sky. From the top, you have beautiful city views.

EL TECHO DE LOLINDA
In a city where rooftop bars are a rarity (for a reason), this Mission spot offers a retractable roof and heat lamps along with cocktails, street-style food, and panoramic views of the city.

FLEA MARKETS
The Alemany flea market which takes place every Sunday year-round is often overlooked because it's smaller than other area markets. The monthly Treasure Island flea is a much larger, flea market with hundreds of vendors, craftspeople, artists, plenty of free parking, food trucks, and live entertainment.

HIDDEN BOOK CLUB OF CALIFORNIA
A secret haven for book lovers, this club has a collection of more than 10,000 volumes and ephemera, with many books about the history of California and the evolution of printing in the state. You don't have to be a member to attend frequent exhibitions.

PICNIC AT THE WARMING HUT
Walking over the Golden Gate Bridge can be a blustery experience, but head down to sea level and you'll find a port in a storm. The Warming Hut offers warm drinks and gifts and it'sthe perfect spot to stock up on picnic supplies to enjoy while exploring the waterfront.

CHURCH OF 8 WHEELS
You haven't lived until you've roller skated in church, specifically at the former Sacred Heart Church, now a bonafide roller disco for holy and not-so-holy rollers. Friday and Saturday nights are for adults only, with plenty of old-school funk to get your groove on.

POLLY ANN'S AND MITCHELL'S
San Francisco is filled with hip ice cream shops, but two of the older shops (both open for over 50 years) stand out for their unusual offerings. Polly Ann Ice Cream has ice cream flavors like Thai tea, durian, taro, and red bean. Mitchell's offers tropical flavors including langka, lucuma, ube, and buko.

MOUNT DAVIDSON
In the shadow of Twin Peaks, but actually taller, this "mountain" the next hill over is topped with a eucalyptus-filled park. Finding the road up here is tricky (entrance at Dalewood and Myra Ways), but once here you'll have amazing views—while tourists look for parking on Twin Peaks.

What to Watch and Read

THE MALTESE FALCON

There was a time when San Francisco's most notorious antiheroes weren't billionaires in t-shirts, but rather chain-smoking, hard-boiled detectives. In *The Maltese Falcon*, detective Sam Spade criss-crosses an atmospheric 1930s San Francisco to locate a jeweled statue. The novel, written by Dashiell Hammett, is a legendary piece of noir fiction, but the film, which starred an in-his-prime Humphrey Bogart and was nominated for three Oscars, is also a must-watch.

THE JOY LUCK CLUB

San Francisco's Chinatown is one of the largest and most famous immigrant enclaves in the United States and Amy Tan's novel (and the film based on it) provides a glimpse into the lives of four women who emigrated from China and their relationships with their American-born daughters. The film's grounding anchor is San Francisco, the city which ultimately becomes the home of the four matriarchs who tell their stories while playing mahjong.

THE ROCK

Set on Alcatraz, San Francisco's infamous island prison, The Rock sets Nicholas Cage and Sean Connery against a rogue unit of special-forces Marines who threaten to launch rockets filled with nerve gas into the city unless they're paid a ransom of $100 million.

THE MAYOR OF CASTRO STREET

Randy Shilts' biography of gay civil rights icon Harvey Milk is perhaps the most well-regarded and authoritative reckoning of his life to date. Milk was a bombastic, iconic figure whose advocacy and brutal murder permanently shaped the political landscape of not just San Francisco, but the entire United States.

INFINITE CITY: A SAN FRANCISCO ATLAS

Rebecca Solnit offers her own narrative of the city as well as those of collaborating artists, writers, and mapmakers, too. The end result is a fascinating visual representation of San Francisco's many diverse geographical and cultural layers.

MRS. DOUBTFIRE

Robin Williams had a stunning, iconic career, but for people of a certain generation Mrs. Doubtfire is perhaps his most recognizable role. Williams plays a freshly divorced dad in San Francisco who dresses up as an elderly British nanny to care for his children. The beautiful, Victorian-style "Mrs. Doubtfire House," on the corner of Broadway and Steiner in the Pacific Heights neighborhood is a popular attraction.

TALES OF THE CITY

Few books offer such a longitudinal view of a place, but Armistead Maupin's stories started running in serial format in the *San Francisco Chronicle* in 1978, as well as the *San Francisco Observer* in later years, before they were compiled into novels. As a result the books (of which there are now nine) were often grounded in the events of the day so the AIDS epidemic was represented and gay characters played an important and influential role.

GUN, WITH OCCASIONAL MUSIC

Set in San Francisco and Oakland, Jonathan Lethem's compelling, not-quite-dystopian vision of the near-yet-distant future, highlights what San Francisco might become with just a little (okay, a lot) of rampant genetic experimentation.

VERTIGO

One of Alfred Hitchcock's career-defining films, *Vertigo* follows the relationship between a detective-turned-investigator and the woman he was hired to follow.

Filmed on location in San Francisco and the surrounding Bay Area, this film offers a smorgasbord of iconic sights, bringing both presence and authenticity to a captivating story of love, mystery, and murder.

MR. PENUMBRA'S 24-HOUR BOOKSTORE

Robin Sloan's novel about a curiously quirky used-book store in San Francisco does double duty. Not only is it a story of mystery, love, code-breaking, secret societies, and adopted and inherited culture, it's also a narrative about the potential dangers of rapid technological advancement (and of rejecting technology), tribalism, and other issues currently impacting San Francisco.

THE ROOM

Set in San Francisco, *The Room* is widely considered to be one of the worst films ever produced, and for good reason. It's a disjointed mess with atrocious acting, a nonsensical plot, and a script that almost defies belief. However, thanks to its sheer ridiculousness (and raucous midnight screenings at arthouse theaters) both *The Room* and its creator, director, and principal actor Tommy Wiseau have become cult film legends. It's also impossible to mention *The Room* without noting *The Disaster Artist,* the dramatic mockumentary detailing its inception and production, which is also incredibly fun to watch.

SILICON CITY: SAN FRANCISCO IN THE LONG SHADOW OF THE VALLEY

Written by a documentary filmmaker, *Silicon City* interviews a broad swath of San Franciscans, including both older bohemians who are concerned about the changes to their longtime home and technocratic millennials pushing a future tied to rapid growth. McClelland's book delves into the cultural shifts of San Francisco through the eyes of both new and longtime residents and examines how people of differing backgrounds, and philosophies, live side-by-side.

THE CHEZ PANISSE CAFE COOKBOOK

Located in Berkeley, Chez Panisse taught lessons to cooks, chefs, and diners that now seem so obvious—cook with fresh ingredients, eat local meat and produce, and treat your guests like friends. While the ethos of Chez Panisse is deliberately unstuffy, the Chez Panisse Cafe—which sits upstairs from the main dining room—is even looser and a little more bohemian. The *Chez Panisse Cafe Cookbook* captures this and is as much about relationships and culinary philosophy as it is about recipes. If you can't make it to the restaurant itself, this book will help get you there in flavor and in spirit.

ZODIAC

When people think of the San Francisco Bay Area, serial killers don't typically come to mind. This wasn't the case during the late '60s though, when the city and its surrounding areas were terrorized by a person known only as the "Zodiac Killer." Seven people were killed, and the assailant—who to this day remains unknown—sent taunts, cryptic codes, and ciphers to local newspapers, causing both curiosity and panic. Both Robert Graysmith's book and the David Fincher film adaptation chronicle the efforts to catch the Zodiac Killer and are well-received thrillers.

San Francisco with Kids

ON THE MOVE

Adventure Cat Sailing. Them: playing on the trampoline at the bow of this 55-foot catamaran. You: enjoying a drink and the bay sunset on the stern deck.

Cable Cars. This one's a no-brainer. But don't miss the **Cable Car Terminus** at Powell and Market Streets, where conductors push the iconic cars on giant turntables, and the **Cable Car Museum,** where you can see how cable cars work.

F-Line Trolleys. Thomas the Tank Engine fan in tow? Hop on one of the F-line's neat historic streetcars. ■ **TIP→ Bonus: this line connects other kid-friendly sights, like Fisherman's Wharf, Pier 39, and the San Francisco Railway Museum**.

SNEAK IN SOME CULTURE

ODC/San Francisco. Best known for its holiday production of *The Velveteen Rabbit,* the dance troupe also holds other performances throughout the year.

San Francisco Mime Troupe. We know, it sounds lame. But these aren't your father's mimes, or mimes at all. In fact, they're a vocal political theater troupe that gives family-friendly outdoor performances.

Stern Grove Festival. Enjoying a delicious picnic in a eucalyptus grove, your kids might not even complain that they're listening to—gasp—classical music (or Latin jazz or opera).

THE GREAT OUTDOORS

Aquatic Park Beach. Does your brood include a wannabe Michael Phelps? Then head to this popular beach, one of the few places around the city where it's safe to swim. ■ **TIP→ Many other Bay Area beaches have powerful currents that make swimming dangerous.**

Golden Gate Promenade. If your kids can handle a 3.3-mile walk, this one's a beauty—winding from Aquatic Park Beach, through the Presidio, to Fort Point Pier near the base of the Golden Gate Bridge.

Muir Woods. If these massive trees look tall to you, imagine seeing them from 2 or 4 feet lower.

Stow Lake. When feeding bread to the ducks gets old (like that's ever going to happen), you can rent a rowboat or pedal boat.

JUST PLAIN FUN

AT&T Park. Emerald grass, a sun-kissed day, a hot dog in your hand … and suddenly, you're 10 again, too.

Dim Sum. A rolling buffet from which kids point and pick—likely an instant hit.

Fisherman's Wharf, Hyde Street Pier, Ghirardelli Square, and Pier 39. The phrase "tourist trap" may come to mind, but in this area you can get a shrimp cocktail, clamber around old ships, snack on chocolate, and laugh at the sea lions.

Musée Mécanique. How did people entertain themselves before Wii (or TV)? Come here to find out.

San Francisco Zoo. Between Grizzly Gulch, Lemur Forest, and Koala Crossing, you can make a day of it.

Yerba Buena Gardens. Head here for ice-skating, bowling, a carousel, a playground, and the Children's Creativity Museum, a hands-on arts-and-technology center.

LEARN A THING OR TWO

California Academy of Sciences. Dinosaurs, penguins, free-flying rain-forest butterflies, giant snakes … what's not to like?

Exploratorium. A very hands-on science museum, including the full-immersion Tactile Dome.

Top Walking Tours

All About Chinatown. On a delightful behind-the-scenes look at the neighborhood, owner Linda Lee and her guides stop in Ross Alley and at a Buddhist temple. At herbal and food markets, you'll learn the therapeutic benefits of fish stomachs and ponder uses for live partridges. ☎ *415/982–8839* 🌐 *www.allaboutchinatown.com* 🎫 *From $35.*

Chinatown Alleyway Tours. To learn about the modern Chinatown community, join up with one of these young guides. Tour leaders, who all grew up here, discuss Chinatown's history and current social issues. ☎ *415/984–1478* 🌐 *www.chinatownalleywaytours.org* 🎫 *From $23.*

Discover Walks. These free, hour-long tours of Chinatown, Fisherman's Wharf, and North Beach by enthusiastic young locals conveniently happen every day, so you can book one when it suits your schedule. The guides are paid in tips, so be sure to show them some love. Free tours run April through October; the rest of the year paid tours are available by reservation. ✉ *San Francisco* ☎ *415/494–9255* 🌐 *www.discoverwalks.com/san-francisco-walking-tours* 🎫 *Free, gratuity expected.*

Don Herron's Dashiell Hammett Tour. Brush up on your noir slang and join trench-coated guide Herron for a walk by the mystery writer's haunts and the locations from some of Hammett's novels. At four hours for $20, it's one of the best deals going. See the website for tours or arrange one of your own. ✉ *Civic Center* 🌐 *www.donherron.com* 🎫 *$20.*

Local Tastes of the City Tours. If you want to aggressively snack your way through a neighborhood as you walk it, consider hanging with cookbook author Tom Medin or one of his local guides. You'll learn why certain things just taste better in San Francisco—like coffee and anything baked with sourdough—and you'll get tips about how to find good food once you get back home. Along the way, you'll gorge yourself into oblivion: the North Beach tour, for instance, might include multiple stops for coffee and baked goods. ☎ *415/665–0480, 888/358–8687* 🌐 *www.sffoodtour.com* 🎫 *From $69.*

Precita Eyes Mural Walks. For an insider's look at the Mission District's vibrant murals, this is the place to call. The nonprofit organization has nurtured this local art form from the get-go, and the folks here stay on top of the latest additions. ☎ *415/285–2287* 🌐 *www.precitaeyes.org* 🎫 *From $20.*

San Francisco City Guides. An outstanding free service supported by the San Francisco Public Library, these walking tours have themes that range from individual neighborhoods to local history (the gold rush, the 1906 quake, ghost walks) to architecture. Each May and October additional walks are offered. Although the tours are free and the knowledgeable guides are volunteers, it's appropriate to make a $5 donation for these nonprofit programs. Tour schedules are available online, at library branches, and at the San Francisco Visitor Information Center at Powell and Market Streets. ☎ *415/557–4266* 🌐 *www.sfcityguides.org* 🎫 *Free.*

Wok Wiz Chinatown Tour. The late cookbook author and Chinatown booster Shirley Fong-Torres founded Wok Wiz, and her team continues to lead these walks. Conversation topics include folklore and, of course, food. The version called "I Can't Believe I Ate My Way Through Chinatown!" includes breakfast and lunch. ☎ *650/355–9657* 🌐 *www.wokwiz.com* 🎫 *From $35.*

San Francisco Today

San Francisco's roller coaster history often gets summed up by its major moments: the gold rush, the 1906 earthquake, the Barbary Coast, the Summer of Love, the late-20th-century dot-com bubble, and a whole lot of groundbreaking (literally and figuratively) moments between them. As the city wraps up another decade, it's very much in the midst of a polarizing time where it's seeing unprecedented growth and challenges, largely because of the Bay Area's rapidly growing technology-focused economy. Of course, the tried-and-true icons of the city are still as magnificent as ever: the Golden Gate Bridge, the summer fog known to locals as Karl, Lombard Street, "Beach Blanket Babylon," the Painted Ladies. The cable cars are still climbing up and down Nob Hill and Russian Hill — except in fall 2018 when smoke from the tragic Paradise Camp Fire (roughly 2½ hours northeast of the city) forced them to halt service for one of the few times in their long history.

A CHANGING CITY

New residents and longtime city dwellers generally agree at least on one thing: the charming quirkiness and creativity of San Franciscans is one of the chief hallmarks of what makes locals proud to be call this place "home." It can be seen in the arts scene that thrives in both the visual arts and performing arts sectors, led by "Hamilton" taking over the Orpheum Theater for two extended runs and the reopening of beautifully renovated Golden Gate and Curran theaters. At the same time, concerns remain whether artists will be able to afford to live in a city that once was a haven for hard-working but poor writers, painters, and poets.

The latest tech boom has brought a contemporary edge to the city's architecture personality, focusing heavily on environmentally sustainable practices. The city's skyline drastically changed with the 2018 opening of the massive Salesforce Tower, designed by the firm of Pelli Clarke Pelli, and is now the city's tallest skyscraper and the second-tallest building west of the Mississippi River. The soaring orb-like tower simply seems to appear in every view from every angle in the city. Below the building is the Salesforce Park above the Transbay Transit Center, a classic case of urban planners finding a way to add nature and wellness to a needed city construction project. In late 2019, the Golden State Warriors (2018's NBA champions) will move into the state-of-the-art Chase Center in the rapidly growing Mission Bay area. Along with the basketball arena, Mission Bay is witnessing massive construction for the numerous biotech companies and UCSF medical school campus that call the area home. Green-minded apartment buildings are also rising in residential areas across the city, while new hotels like the Proper Hotel San Francisco are revitalizing neglected-but-beautiful old buildings in neighborhoods like Mid-Market.

A HOUSING CRISIS

There is no way to sugarcoat it: San Francisco is a really, really expensive city to live in. According to Zillow, the median rent price is $4,490 and the median home price is $1,374,800. Most one-bedroom apartments now rent for slightly below or above the $4,000 mark, which San Franciscans previously thought was only Manhattan territory. It's not just the homes that cost a lot, either. Many critically praised restaurants have been forced to close because they can't afford to pay landlords exorbitant rents while also serving food at a price that diners deem "fair." In addition, the high home and retail prices have forced many workers and companies to look for new locations/homes farther and farther from San Francisco, eventually deciding to just leave the city altogether. For those workers who still live in the Bay Area and work in San Francisco, the freeways, bridges, and BART rides have become even more congested because residents now have much longer commutes.

There is also no way to sugarcoat the city's homeless problem: it's bad. For a city of such natural beauty, history, and economic success, San Francisco still has its many warts and this is generally the first one noticed by visitors. Latest counts have the city's homeless population at around 7,000 and growing. The circumstances that lead to people being homeless are varied and often tragic, ranging from mental health issues, substance abuse, and economic plight, and the city's acute lack of affordable housing does not help. Many tech companies have employee community service programs to aid the city's street population, and nonprofits, like Code Tenderloin and Glide Memorial Church, have also been instrumental in providing food or job skills to the city's homeless, formerly incarcerated, and down-and-out residents.

WHAT'S NEXT FOR SAN FRANCISCO?

The President of the United States has threatened to cut off federal funding to San Francisco because of its status as a "sanctuary city." Start-ups are succeeding and failing. Restaurants are opening and closing at a blistering rate because while people are ready to spend money, chefs and servers can't afford to live in the city, nor can teachers, bus drivers, police officers, and an endless amount of other vital professions. Will Mayor London Breed be able to deliver on proposals to direct $181 million in available funding to programs for homelessness, affordable housing, behavioral health, and street cleanliness? There are a lot more questions than answers right now.

Free and Almost Free

Despite—or perhaps because of—the astronomical cost of living here, San Francisco offers loads of free diversions. Here are our picks for the best free things to do in the city, in alphabetical order. Also check out 🌐 *sf.funcheap.com* for a calendar of random, offbeat, and often free one-offs.

FREE MUSEUMS AND GALLERIES

- Fort Point National Historic Site
- Octagon House
- San Francisco Cable Car Museum
- San Francisco Railway Museum
- Wells Fargo History Museum

FREE MUSEUM TIMES

The first week of every month brings a bonanza of free museum times.

- Asian Art Museum, first Sunday of every month
- Chinese Historical Society of America, first Sunday of every month
- Contemporary Jewish Museum, first Tuesday of every month
- de Young Museum, first Tuesday of every month
- Legion of Honor, first Tuesday of every month
- Yerba Buena Center for the Arts (galleries), first Tuesday of every month

FREE CONCERTS

- The Golden Gate Park Band plays free public concerts on Sunday afternoon, April through October, on the Music Concourse in the namesake park.
- Stern Grove Festival concerts, held on Sunday afternoon from June through August, ranging from opera to jazz to pop music. The amphitheater is in a beautiful eucalyptus grove, so come early and picnic before the show.
- Yerba Buena Gardens Festival hosts many concerts and performances from May through October, including Latin jazz, global music, dance, and even puppet shows.

FREE TOURS

- The free San Francisco City Guides walking tours are easily one of the best deals going. Knowledgeable, enthusiastic guides lead walks that focus on a particular neighborhood, theme, or historical period, like Victorian architecture in Alamo Square or the bawdy days of the Barbary Coast.
- City Hall offers free tours of its grandiose HQ on weekdays.

MORE GREAT EXPERIENCES FOR $7 OR LESS

- See some baseball at AT&T Park, for free! Go to the stadium's Portwalk, beyond the outfield wall, and you'll have a standing-room view of the game through the open fence.
- Do your own walking tour of the Mission District's fantastic outdoor murals, then grab a bite at a taqueria or food truck.
- Choose a perfect treat at the Ferry Building's fabulous marketplace—maybe a scoop of Ciao Bella gelato or a croissant from Miette—and stroll the waterfront promenade.
- Hike up to the top of Telegraph Hill for sweeping city and bay views.

SAN FRANCISCO'S CABLE CARS

The moment it dawns on you that you severely underestimated the steepness of the San Francisco hills will likely be the same moment you look down and realize those tracks aren't just for show—or just for tourists.

Sure, locals rarely use the cable cars for commuting these days. (That's partially due to the $7 fare—hear that, Muni?) So you'll likely be packed in with plenty of fellow sightseers. You may even be approaching cable-car fatigue after seeing its image on so many souvenirs. But if you fear the magic is gone, simply climb on board, and those jaded thoughts will dissolve. Grab the pole and gawk at the view as the car clanks down an insanely steep grade toward the bay. Listen to the humming cable, the clang of the bell, and the occasional quip from the gripman. It's an experience you shouldn't pass up, whether on your first trip or your fiftieth.

HOW CABLE CARS WORK

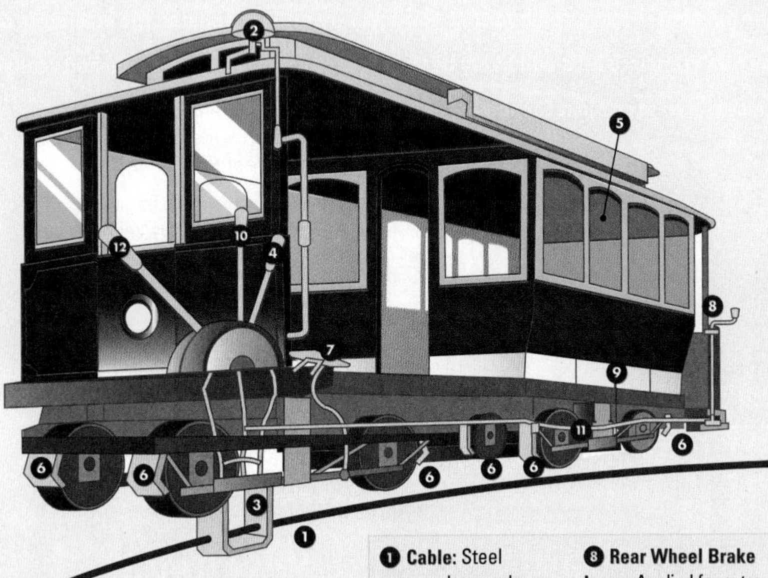

The mechanics are pretty simple: cable cars grab a moving subterranean cable with a "grip" to go. To stop, they release the grip and apply one or more types of brakes. Four cables, totaling 9 miles, power the city's three lines. If the gripman doesn't adjust the grip just right when going up a steep hill, the cable will start to slip and the car will have to back down the hill and try again. This is an extremely rare occurrence—imagine the ribbing the gripman gets back at the cable car barn!

Gripman: Stands in front and operates the grip, brakes, and bell. Favorite joke, especially at the peak of a steep hill: "This is my first day on the job folks . . ."

Conductor: Moves around the car, deals with tickets, alerts the grip about what's coming up, and operates the rear wheel brakes.

❶ **Cable:** Steel wrapped around flexible sisal core; 2 inches thick; runs at a constant 9½ mph.

❷ **Bells:** Used for crew communication; alerts other drivers and pedestrians.

❸ **Grip:** Vice-like lever extends through the center slot in the track to grab or release the cable.

❹ **Grip Lever:** Left-hand lever; operates grip.

❺ **Car:** Entire car weighs 8 tons.

❻ **Wheel Brake:** Steel brake pads on each wheel.

❼ **Wheel Brake Lever:** Foot pedal; operates wheel brakes.

❽ **Rear Wheel Brake Lever:** Applied for extra traction on hills.

❾ **Track Brake:** 2-foot-long sections of Monterey pine push down against the track to help stop the car.

❿ **Track Brake Lever:** Middle lever; operates track brakes.

⓫ **Emergency Brake:** 18-inch steel wedge, jams into street slot to bring car to an immediate stop.

⓬ **Emergency Brake Lever:** Right-hand lever, red; operates emergency brake.

ROUTES

Cars run at least every 15 minutes, from around 6 am to about 1 am.

Powell–Hyde line: Most scenic, with classic Bay views. Begins at Powell and Market streets, then crosses Nob Hill and Russian Hill before a white-knuckle descent down Hyde Street, ending near the Hyde Street Pier.

Powell–Mason line: Also begins at Powell and Market streets, but winds through North Beach to Bay and Taylor streets, a few blocks from Fisherman's Wharf.

California line: Runs from the foot of Market Street, at Drumm Street, up Nob Hill and back. Great views (and aromas and sounds) of Chinatown on the way up. Sit in back to catch glimpses of the Bay. ■ TIP→ **Take the California line if it's just the cable-car experience you're after—the lines are shorter, and the grips and conductors say it's friendlier and has a slower pace.**

RULES OF THE RIDE

Tickets. There are ticket booths at all three turnarounds, or you can pay the conductor after you board (they can make change). Try not to grumble about the price—they're embarrassed enough as it is.

■ TIP→ **If you're planning to use public transit a few times, or if you'd like to ride back and forth on the cable car without worrying about the price, consider a one-day Muni passport. You can get passports online, at the Powell Street turnaround, the TIX booth on Union Square, or the Fisherman's Wharf cable-car ticket booth at Beach and Hyde streets.**

All Aboard. You can board on either side of the cable car. It's legal to stand on the running boards and hang on to the pole, but keep your ears open for the gripman's warnings. ■ TIP→ **Grab a seat on the outside bench for the best views.**

Most people wait (and wait) in line at one of the cable car turnarounds, but you can also hop on along the route. Board wherever you see a white sign showing a figure climbing aboard a brown cable car; wave to the approaching driver, and wait until the car stops.

Riding on the running boards can be part of the thrill.

CABLE CAR HISTORY

HALLIDIE FREES THE HORSES

In the 1850s and '60s, San Francisco's streetcars were drawn by horses. Legend has it that the horrible sight of a car dragging a team of horses downhill to their deaths roused Andrew Smith Hallidie to action. The English immigrant had invented the "Hallidie Ropeway," essentially a cable car for mined ore, and he was convinced that his invention could also move people. In 1873, Hallidie and his intrepid crew prepared to test the first cable car high on Russian Hill. The anxious engineer peered down into the foggy darkness, failed to see the bottom of the hill, and promptly turned the controls over to Hallidie. Needless to say, the thing worked . . . but rides were free for the first two days because people were afraid to get on.

SEE IT FOR YOURSELF

The Cable Car Museum is one of the city's best free offerings and an absolute must for kids. (You can even ride a cable car there, since all three lines stop between Russian Hill and Nob Hill.) The museum, which is inside the city's last cable-car barn, takes the top off the system to let you see how it all works. Eternally humming and squealing, the massive powerhouse cable wheels steal the show. You can also climb aboard a vintage car and take the grip, let the kids ring a cable-car bell (briefly, please!), and check out vintage gear dating from 1873.

■ TIP→ The gift shop sells cable car paraphernalia, including an authentic gripman's bell for $600 (it'll sound like Powell Street in your house every day). For significantly less, you can pick up a key chain made from a piece of worn-out cable.

CHAMPION OF THE CABLE CAR BELL

Each September the city's best and brightest come together to crown a bell-ringing champion at Union Square. The crowd cheers gripmen and conductors as they stomp, shake, and riff with the rope. But it's not a popularity contest; the ringers are judged by former bell-ringing champions who take each ping and gong very seriously.

Chapter 2

TRAVEL SMART

Updated by
Jacob Dean and
Trevor Felch

★ CAPITAL
Sacramento

POPULATION
36,132,147

LANGUAGE
English

$ CURRENCY
U.S. Dollar

AREA CODE
415

⚠ EMERGENCIES
911

DRIVING
On the right

ELECTRICITY
120–220 v/60 cycles; plugs have two or three rectangular prongs

TIME
Pacific Time; 3 hours behind New York.

WEB RESOURCES
www.sftravel.com
www.visitcalifornia.com
www.sfgate.com
www.sfexaminer.com

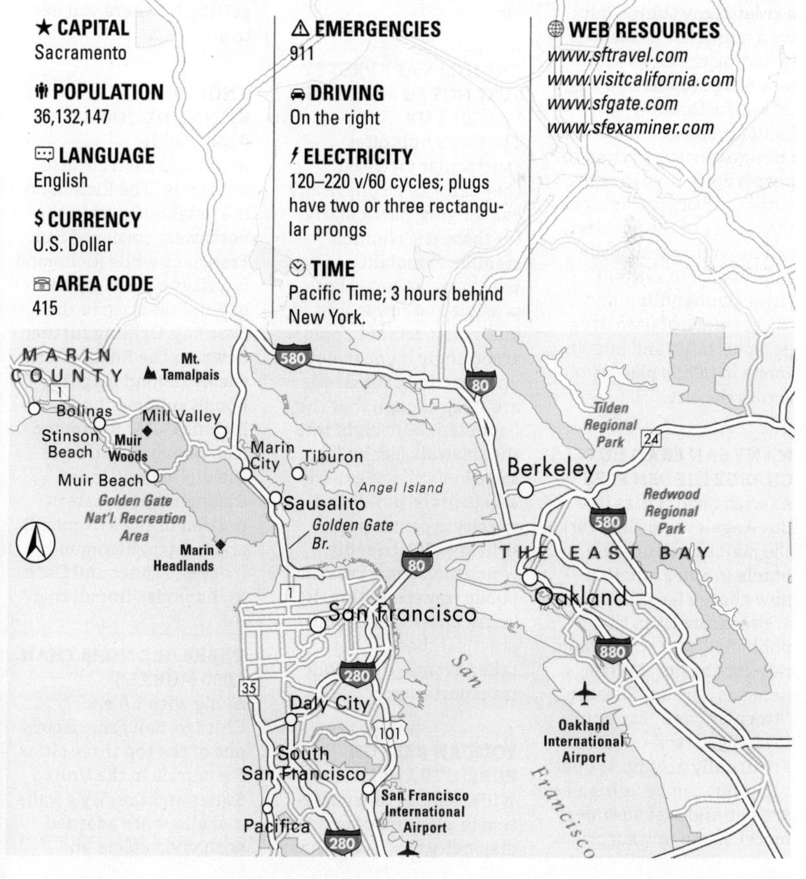

What to Know Before You Go

PACK FOR SAN FRANCISCO NOT CALIFORNIA
California has drawn in many a traveler with visions of beaches and endless sunny days, but the average high in the Bay Area is only 63.8°F and nights tend to drop into the low 50s. So, while it is beautiful, it's not exactly beach weather. Even the summer months are marked by foggy, windy weather.

SAN FRAN HAS THE HIGHEST RATE OF STREET HOMELESSNESS NATIONWIDE
San Francisco is famous for a great many things, but for a multitude of reasons, including the city's acute lack of affordable housing, this unfortunately includes homelessness. The circumstances that lead to people being homeless are varied and often tragic and the reality of the problem can be jarring and upsetting: expect to see tent cities, panhandling, and the presence of used drug paraphernalia and human waste in public places across the city.

MANY SAN FRAN HOTELS CHARGE HIDDEN FEES
As with major cities like Los Angeles and New York, the majority of upscale hotels in San Francisco now charge fees that are separate from the published advertised room rate for the hotel. Often listed as "Urban," "Resort," "Amenity," and "Facility" fees, these tack-on rates are usually around $25 per night but can be as high as $85 per night (sometimes more). Avoid any surprises and ask about such fees before you book or when you are checking in (and feel free to contest them in person and on social media).

THE HILLS ARE PRETTY JUST NOT SO MUCH ON THE WAY UP
The City's hills offer spectacular views but they can also be physically challenging, particularly for those with limited stamina or mobility. Exploring by foot is both possible and rewarding, but it's important to plan accordingly if you're not up for a climb. Some hills are steep enough that they have steps built right into the sidewalk (easier for some but still not exactly a walk in the park!) and the city is committed to being ADA-friendly, which includes accessible public transportation. If you're up to it, pack your practical shoes; if not, take advantage of public transportation.

YOU CAN RELY ON PUBLIC TRANSIT
While public transportation is a feature of every major city, few places have the sheer variety offered by San Francisco. The Bay Area Rapid Transit (BART) system is a mix of both heavy rail and subway and serves San Francisco, Oakland, and a variety of suburban areas. At the same time, San Francisco has hybrid Muni buses, Muni Metro Light Rail, cable cars, historic streetcars, electric trolleys, and a range of privately run options such as taxis, app-based rideshares, electric bicycles, and motorized scooters. Between the public and the private options you will have an easy time getting to where you need to go.

KNOW WHICH RICHMOND YOU'RE RENTING IN
Richmond District, also known as "The Richmond" is a neighborhood in the northwest corner of San Francisco while Richmond is a city 20 miles northeast of San Francisco in the East Bay. Drilling further down on the Richmonds, the Richmond neighborhood's subneighborhoods include Outer Richmond (the western portion of the Richmond), Inner Richmond (the eastern portion of the Richmond), and Central Richmond (between Inner and Outer Richmonds). Got all that?

THERE ARE MORE THAN 1,000 MURALS
Along with LA and Chicago, San Francisco is one of the top three cities for murals in the United States and the city's walls and alleys are adorned with vivid colors and

poignant messages. The Mission alone has almost 500. Some highlights are the Chris Ware mural at 826 Valencia, the multitude of murals in Balmy Alley and Clarion Alley, and the Hidden Garden Steps.

THE PIERS ARE TOURIST TRAPS, BUT THAT'S OKAY
San Francisco's public piers are absolutely, 100% a set of loud and crowded tourist traps. There's a reason the piers are such a famous tourist-magnet—they're kind of awesome! The straight, weatherworn expanse of Fisherman's Wharf is iconic, and Pier 39's basking sea lions and multitude of vendors make it a vibrant and popular destination. Even if you don't think of yourself as the kind of person that these sights would appeal to, give them a shot. Wander along the Embarcadero, stop for some crab legs and oysters along the way, and enjoy one of the most leisurely parts of the city.

SIDETRIPS ARE A MUST
San Francisco is a vibrant and engaging city but you'll be doing yourself a disservice if you only stick to the major tourist neighborhoods. Redwood Regional Park in the Oakland Hills is a less-crowded alternative to Muir Woods National Monument (but it's okay to do both if you have time!); Daly City has some of the best Filipino restaurants in the country; and Berkeley is home not just to a famous university but also a variety of museums, cafés, and legendary restaurants. And don't forget all that incredible wine to be had in nearby Sonoma and Napa.

PRIVATE PARKS ARE PUBLIC
It's a little known fact that cities often require privately owned buildings to provide public spaces. In San Francisco those are known as POPOS (Privately-Owned Public Open Space) and they're all over the city just waiting for you to come sit here, feel like a local, and use the bathroom. These spaces are legally required to be labeled with visible signage indicating both how they can be accessed and what their hours of operation are, but in the off chance those signs are hard to find (or simply aren't there) the San Francisco Planning Department provides a searchable map that lets you see which sites have amenities such as bathrooms, food, tables, and seating.

IT'S NOT CHEAP
San Francisco is not only one of the most expensive cities in the entire world in which to live, it's also expensive to visit. Between the high price of flights, hotels, and meals, if you're budget-conscious you'll need to plan ahead to maximize your resources. Fortunately, it's not that hard to explore cheaply with just a little research. CityPASS bundles together public transit passes and museum tickets for both ease and savings, and the customizable GOCard lets you build your own itinerary from scratch while still saving money. The city's public transportation network also sells unlimited ride day passes, which will help you get around while saving you money.

YOUR DOG IS VERY WELCOME
If you're a dog lover or like to travel with your dog, San Francisco is your city. There are hundreds of acres in and around the city where your pup can romp off-leash. Every neighborhood has one or two parks with sizeable dog-run areas and people are just out and about everywhere with their dogs, socializing with other people with dogs. There are dog-friendly bars; dog-friendly beaches like Baker Beach, Ocean Beach, and Lands End Beach; dog-friendly cabs; dog-friendly gyms, pet-friendly apartment rentals and hotels; dog-friendly wineries in Napa; and lots of dog-friendly walking tours. In April, the annual DogFest is a huge celebration of all things canine in Duboce Park.

Getting Here and Around

Air Travel

The least expensive airfares to San Francisco are priced for round-trip travel and should be purchased in advance. Airlines generally allow you to change your return date for a fee; most low-fare tickets, however, are nonrefundable. (But if you cancel, you can usually apply the fare to a future trip, within one year, to any destination the airline flies.)

Nonstop flights from New York to San Francisco take about 5½ hours, and with the 3-hour time change, it's possible to leave JFK by 8 am and be in San Francisco by 10:30 am. Some flights may require a midway stop, making the total excursion between 8 and 9½ hours. Nonstop times are approximately 1½ hours from Los Angeles, 3 hours from Dallas, 4½ hours from Chicago, 4½ hours from Atlanta, 11 hours from London, 12 hours from Auckland, and 13½ hours from Sydney.

AIRPORTS

The major gateway to San Francisco is **San Francisco International Airport (SFO)**, 15 miles south of the city. It's off U.S. 101 near Millbrae and San Bruno.

Oakland International Airport (OAK) is across the bay, not much farther away from downtown San Francisco (via I–80 east and I–880 south), but rush-hour traffic on the Bay Bridge may lengthen travel times considerably.

San Jose International Airport (SJC) is about 40 miles south of San Francisco; travel time depends largely on traffic flow, but plan on 1½ hours with moderate traffic.

Depending on the price difference, you might consider flying into Oakland or San Jose. Oakland's an easy-to-use alternative, because there's public transportation between the airport and downtown San Francisco. Getting to San Francisco from San Jose, though, can be time-consuming and costly via public transportation. Heavy fog is infamous for causing chronic delays into and out of San Francisco.

GROUND TRANSPORTATION

FROM SAN FRANCISCO INTERNATIONAL AIRPORT

Transportation signage at the airport is color-coded by type and is quite clear. A taxi ride to downtown costs around $60; rideshare companies like Lyft and Uber are a popular option and start around $25 for a shared ride into the city. Airport shuttles are inexpensive and generally efficient. Lorrie's Airport Service and SuperShuttle both stop at the lower level near baggage claim and take you anywhere within the city limits of San Francisco. They charge around $17 each way, depending on where you're going. Lorrie's also sells tickets online; you can print them out before leaving home.

Shuttles to the East Bay, such as Bay-Porter Express, depart from a lot near the lower level; expect to pay between $38 and $47. Inquire about the number of stops a shuttle makes en route to or from the airport; some companies, such as East Bay Shuttle, have nonstop service, but they cost a bit more. Marin Door to Door operates van service to Marin County starting at $40 for the first passenger, and $12 for each additional person. Marin Airporter buses cost $22 (cash only) and require no reservations but stop only at designated stations in Marin; buses leave every 30 minutes, on the half hour and hour, from 5 am to midnight.

You can take BART directly to downtown San Francisco; the trip takes about 30 minutes and costs less than $9. (There are both manned booths and vending machines for ticket purchases.) Trains leave from the international terminal every 15 or 20 minutes, depending on the day or time.

Another inexpensive way to get to San Francisco (though not as convenient as BART) is via two SamTrans buses: No. 292 (50 minutes) and the KX (35 minutes). Fares are $2.25 from SFO, $4 to SFO. Board the SamTrans buses on the lower level.

To drive to downtown San Francisco from the airport, take U.S. 101 north to the Civic Center/9th Street, 7th Street, or 4th Street/Downtown exits. If you're headed to the Embarcadero or Fisherman's Wharf, take I–280 north (the exit is to the right, just north of the airport, off U.S. 101) and get off at the 4th Street/King Street exit. King Street becomes the Embarcadero a few blocks east of the exit. The Embarcadero winds around the waterfront to Fisherman's Wharf.

FROM OAKLAND INTERNATIONAL AIRPORT

A taxi to downtown San Francisco costs around $80; rideshare companies like Lyft and Uber offer rides for around $50. BayPorter Express and other shuttles serve major hotels and provide door-to-door service to the East Bay and San Francisco. SuperShuttle operates vans to San Francisco and Oakland. Marin Door to Door serves Marin County for $50 for the first passenger, and $12 for each additional person.

The best way to get to San Francisco via public transit is to take BART, which is free upon boarding but requires ticket purchase at the Coliseum/Oakland International Airport BART station (BART fares vary depending on where you're going; the ride to downtown San Francisco from here costs $10.20).

If you're driving from Oakland International Airport, take Airport Drive east to I–880 north to I–80 west over the Bay Bridge. This will likely take at least an hour.

FROM SAN JOSE INTERNATIONAL AIRPORT

A taxi to downtown San Jose costs about $20 to $25; a trip to San Francisco runs about $150 to $165. Rideshare companies like Lyft and Uber offer rides to downtown San Jose starting around $12; a trip to San Francisco starts around $55.

To drive to downtown San Jose from the airport, take Airport Boulevard east to Route 87 south. To get to San Francisco from the airport, take Route 87 south to I–280 north. The trip will take roughly two hours.

At $9.75 for a one-way ticket, there's no question that Caltrain provides the most affordable option for traveling between San Francisco and San Jose's airport. However, the Caltrain station in San Francisco at 4th and Townsend Streets isn't in a conveniently central location. It's on the eastern side of the South of Market (SoMa) neighborhood and not easily accessible by other public transit. You'll need to take a taxi or walk from the nearest bus line. From San Francisco it takes 90 minutes and costs $9.75 to reach the Santa Clara Caltrain station, from which a free shuttle runs every 15 minutes (every 30 minutes on nights and weekends), whisking you to and from the San Jose International Airport in 15 minutes.

Boat Travel

Several ferry lines run out of San Francisco. Blue & Gold Fleet operates a number of routes, including service to Sausalito ($11.50 one-way) and Tiburon ($11.50 one-way). Tickets are sold at Pier

Getting Here and Around

39, boats depart from Pier 41 nearby. Alcatraz Cruises, owned by Hornblower Cruises and Events, operates the ferries to Alcatraz Island ($35.50 including audio tour and National Park Service ranger-led programs) from Pier 33, about a half-mile east of Fisherman's Wharf. Boats leave 14 times a day (more in summer), and the journey itself takes 30 minutes. Allow at least 2½ hours for a round-trip jaunt. Golden Gate Ferry runs daily to and from Sausalito and Larkspur ($11.75 and $11 one-way), leaving from Pier 1, behind the San Francisco Ferry Building. The Alameda/Oakland Ferry operates daily between Alameda's Main Street Terminal, Oakland's Jack London Square, and San Francisco's Pier 41 and the Ferry Building ($6.60 one-way); some ferries go only to Pier 41 or the Ferry Building, so ask when you board. Purchase tickets on board.

 Bus Travel

Greyhound serves San Francisco with buses from many major U.S. cities; within California, service is limited to hub towns and cities only. The Greyhound depot is located at the Transbay Temporary Terminal, in the SoMa district. Tickets can be purchased online; seating is on a first-come, first-served basis. Cash, checks, and credit cards are accepted.

 Cable-Car Travel

Don't miss the sensation of moving up and down some of San Francisco's steepest hills in a clattering cable car. Jump aboard as it pauses at a designated stop, and wedge yourself into any available space. Then just hold on.

Tracking Cheap Gas

Determined to avoid the worst prices at the pump? Check the website *www.sanfrangasprices.com*, which tracks the lowest (and highest) gasoline costs in the Bay Area. It also has a handy price-mapping feature and a master list of local gas stations.

The fare (for one direction) is $7. You can buy tickets on board (exact change isn't required but operators can only make change up to $20) or at the kiosks at the cable-car turnarounds at Hyde and Beach Streets and at Powell and Market Streets.

The heavily traveled Powell–Mason and Powell–Hyde lines begin at Powell and Market Streets near Union Square and terminate at Fisherman's Wharf; lines for these routes can be long, especially in summer. The California Street line runs east and west from Market and California Streets to Van Ness Avenue; there's often no wait to board this route.

 Car Travel

Driving in San Francisco can be a challenge because of the one-way streets, snarly traffic, and steep hills. The first two elements can be frustrating enough, but those hills are tough for unfamiliar drivers.

Be sure to leave plenty of room between your car and other vehicles when on a steep slope. This is especially important when you've braked at a stop sign on a steep incline. Whether with a stick shift or an automatic transmission, every car rolls backward for a moment once the brake is released.

So don't pull too close to the car ahead of you. When it's time to pull forward, keep your foot on the brake while tapping lightly on the accelerator. Once the gears are engaged, let up on the brake and head uphill.

■TIP→ **Remember to curb your wheels when parking on hills—turn wheels away from the curb when facing uphill, toward the curb when facing downhill. You can get a ticket if you don't do this.**

Market Street runs southwest from the Ferry Building, then becomes Portola Drive as it rounds Twin Peaks (which lie just south of the giant radio-antennae structure, Sutro Tower). It can be difficult to drive across Market. The major east–west streets north of Market are Geary Boulevard (it's called Geary Street east of Van Ness Avenue), which runs to the Pacific Ocean; Fulton Street, which begins at the back of the Opera House and continues along the north side of Golden Gate Park to Ocean Beach; Oak Street, which runs east from Golden Gate Park toward downtown, then flows into northbound Franklin Street; and Fell Street, the left two lanes of which cut through Golden Gate Park and empty into Lincoln Way, which continues to the ocean.

Among the major north–south streets are Divisadero, which heading south becomes Castro Street at Waller Street and continues just past César Chávez Street; Van Ness Avenue, which heading south becomes South Van Ness Avenue after it crosses Market Street; and Park Presidio Boulevard, which heading south from the Richmond District becomes Crossover Drive within Golden Gate Park and empties into 19th Avenue.

Take the 511

Several transportation organizations—the Metropolitan Transportation Commission, the California Highway Patrol, the California Department of Transportation, and more—pool their data into a free, one-stop telephone (☎ *511*) and Web (🌐 *www.go511.com*) resource for all nine Bay Area counties. The service provides the latest info on traffic conditions, route, and fares for all public transit and has info about bicycle and other transportation. The phone line operates 24/7 toll-free.

GASOLINE

Gas stations are hard to find in San Francisco; look for the national franchises on major thoroughfares such as Market Street, Geary Boulevard, Mission Street, or California Street.

PARKING

San Francisco is a terrible city for parking. In the Financial District and Civic Center neighborhoods parking is forbidden on most streets between 3 or 4 pm and 6 or 7 pm. Check street signs carefully to confirm, because illegally parked cars are towed immediately. Downtown parking lots are often full, and most are expensive. The city-owned Sutter-Stockton, Ellis-O'Farrell, and 5th-and-Mission garages have the most reasonable rates in the downtown area. Large hotels often have parking available, but it doesn't come cheap; many charge in excess of $40 a day for the privilege.

ROAD CONDITIONS

Although rush "hours" are 6–10 am and 3–7 pm, you can hit gridlock on any day at any time, especially over the Bay

Getting Here and Around

Bridge and leaving and/or entering the city from the south. Sunday-afternoon traffic can be heavy as well, especially over the bridges.

The most comprehensive and immediate traffic updates are available through the city's 511 service, either online at 🌐 *www.511.org* (where real-time data shows you the traffic on your selected route) or by calling 511. On the radio, tune in to an all-news radio station such as KQED 88.5 FM or KCBS 740 AM/106.9 FM.

Be especially wary of nonindicated lane changes.

San Francisco is the only major American city uncut by freeways. To get from the Bay Bridge to the Golden Gate Bridge, you'll have to take surface streets, specifically Van Ness Avenue, which doubles as U.S. 101 through the city.

RULES OF THE ROAD

The speed limit on city streets is 25 mph unless otherwise posted. A right turn on a red light after stopping is legal unless posted otherwise, as is a left on red at the intersection of two one-way streets.

Ⓜ Metro/Public Transport

BART TRAVEL

BART (Bay Area Rapid Transit) trains, which run until midnight, travel under the bay via tunnel to connect San Francisco with Oakland, Berkeley, and other cities and towns beyond. Within San Francisco, stations are limited to downtown, the Mission, and a couple of outlying neighborhoods.

Trains travel frequently from early morning until evening on weekdays. After 8 pm weekdays and on weekends there's often a 20-minute wait between trains on the same line. Trains also travel south from San Francisco as far as Millbrae. BART trains connect downtown San Francisco to San Francisco International Airport; the ride costs $8.95.

Intracity San Francisco fares are $1.95; intercity fares are $3.20 to $11.45. BART bases its ticket prices on miles traveled and doesn't offer price breaks by zone. The easy-to-read maps posted in BART stations list fares based on destination, radiating out from your starting point of the current station.

During morning and evening rush hour, trains within the city are crowded—even standing room can be hard to come by. Cars at the far front and back of the train are less likely to be filled to capacity. Smoking, eating, and drinking are prohibited on trains and in stations.

BUS OPERATORS

Outside the city, AC Transit serves the East Bay, and Golden Gate Transit serves Marin County and a few cities in southern Sonoma County.

MUNI TRAVEL

The San Francisco Municipal Railway, or Muni, operates light-rail vehicles, the historic F-line streetcars along Fisherman's Wharf and Market Street, buses, and the world-famous cable cars. Light rail travels along Market Street to the Mission District and Noe Valley (J line), the Ingleside District (K line), and the Sunset District (L, M, and N lines) while also passing through the West Portal, Glen Park, and Castro neighborhoods. The N line continues around the Embarcadero to the Caltrain station at 4th and King Streets; the T-line light rail runs from the Castro, down Market Street, around the Embarcadero, and south past Mission Bay and Hunters Point to Sunnydale Avenue and Bayshore Boulevard. Muni provides 24-hour service on select lines to all areas of the city.

On buses and streetcars the fare is $2.75. Exact change is required, and dollar bills are accepted in the fare boxes. For all Muni vehicles other than cable cars, 90-minute transfers are issued free upon request at the time the fare is paid. These are valid for unlimited transfers in any direction until they expire (time is indicated on the ticket). Cable cars cost $7 and include no transfers *(see Cable-Car Travel)*.

One-day ($23), three-day ($34), and seven-day ($45) Visitor Passports valid on the entire Muni system can be purchased at several outlets, including the cable-car ticket booth at Powell and Market Streets and the visitor information center downstairs in Hallidie Plaza. A monthly ticket is available for $94, and can be used on all Muni lines (including cable cars) and on BART within city limits. The San Francisco CityPass ($89), a discount ticket booklet to several major city attractions, also covers all Muni travel for seven consecutive days.

■ **TIP→ Save money by purchasing your Passports on MuniMobile, the SFMTA's mobile ticketing app.**

Taxi Travel

Taxi service is notoriously bad in San Francisco, and finding a cab can be frustratingly difficult. Popular nightspots such as the Mission, SoMa, North Beach, and the Castro are the easiest places to hail a cab off the street; hotel taxi stands are also an option. If you're going to the airport, make a reservation or book a shuttle instead. Taxis in San Francisco charge $3.50 for the first 0.5 mile (one of the highest base rates in the United States), 55¢ for each additional 0.2 mile, and 55¢ per minute in stalled traffic; a $4 surcharge is added for trips from the airport. There's no charge for additional passengers; there's no surcharge for luggage. For trips farther than 15 miles outside city limits, multiply the metered rate by 1.5; tolls and tip are extra.

That said, San Francisco's poor taxi service was a direct factor in the creation of ride-sharing services such as Uber and Lyft, which are easy to use and prominent throughout the city and its surrounding areas. San Franciscans generally regard taxis as a thing of the past and use ride-sharing on a day-to-day basis. If you're willing to share a car with strangers, a trip within the city can run as low as $4; rates go up for private rides and during peak demand times. These services are especially economical when going to or from the airport, where a shared ride will run you about $25—half the cost of a cab.

Train Travel

Amtrak trains travel to the Bay Area from some cities in California and the United States. The *Coast Starlight* travels north from Los Angeles to Seattle, passing the Bay Area along the way, but contrary to its name, the train runs inland through the Central Valley for much of its route through Northern California; the most scenic stretch is in Southern California, between San Luis Obispo and Los Angeles. Amtrak also has several routes between San Jose, Oakland, and Sacramento. The *California Zephyr* travels from Chicago to the Bay Area, and has spectacular alpine vistas as it crosses the Sierra Nevada range. San Francisco doesn't have an Amtrak train station but does have an Amtrak bus stop at the Ferry Building, from which shuttle buses transport passengers to trains in Emeryville, just over the Bay Bridge. Shuttle buses also connect the Emeryville train station with BART and other points in downtown San Francisco. You can buy a California Rail Pass, which gives you 7 days of travel in a 21-day period for $159.

Caltrain connects San Francisco to Palo Alto, San Jose, Santa Clara, and many smaller cities en route. In San Francisco, trains leave from the main depot, at 4th and Townsend Streets, and a rail-side stop at 22nd and Pennsylvania Streets. One-way fares are $3.75 to $13.75, depending on the number of zones through which you travel; tickets are valid for four hours after purchase time. A ticket is $7.75 from San Francisco to Palo Alto, at least $9.75 to San Jose. You can also buy a day pass ($7.50–$27.50) for unlimited travel in a 24-hour period. It's worth waiting for an express train for trips that last from 1 to 1¾ hours. On weekdays, trains depart three or four times per hour during the morning and evening, only once or twice per hour during daytime non-commute hours and late night. Weekend trains run once per hour, though there are two bullet trains per day, one in late morning and one in early evening The system shuts down after midnight. There are no onboard ticket sales. You must buy tickets before boarding the train or risk paying up to $250 for fare evasion.

Before You Go

Passport

All visitors to the United States require a valid passport that is valid for six months beyond your expected period of stay.

Immunizations

There are no immunization requirements for visitors traveling to the United States for tourism.

U.S. Embassy/Consulate

A total of 36 Consulates-General and 33 Honorary Consulates have offices in the San Francisco Bay Area.

When to Go

You can visit San Francisco comfortably any time of year. Possibly the best time is September and October, when the city's summerlike weather brings outdoor concerts and festivals. The climate here always feels Mediterranean and moderate—with a foggy, sometimes chilly bite. The temperature rarely drops below 40°F, and anything warmer than 80°F is considered a heat wave. Be prepared for rain in winter, especially December and January. Winds off the ocean can add to the chill factor. That old joke about summer in San Francisco feeling like winter is true at heart, but once you move inland, it gets warmer. (And some locals swear that the thermostat has inched up in recent years.)

Packing

Walking Shoes. A pair of comfortable walking shoes is your must-pack item. This is a walking city, with notoriously steep and uneven streets, and if you fail to pack for it, your feet will pay. If you are planning to hike Mount Diablo or the Dipsea Trail (both highly recommended), you will need a pair of hiking boots or shoes with good treads.

A Good Raincoat. San Francisco is in California, but it doesn't adhere to your idea of California weather. It does stay mild year-round but it is a peninsula surrounded by water on three sides so you will want to plan for foggy mornings,

Sweaters. San Francisco weather can be a bit unpredictable. One minute you could be comfortable, and the next, shivering with the cold. Having a sweatshirt or sweater with you at all times will alleviate this.

Scarf. Lightweight and easy layers offset those sudden chills. In spring or Indian Summer (September to November), you can bring a lightweight one but you will want warmer options for the rest of the year.

Backpack. A lightweight daypack is handy to tote those layers around in along with sunscreen, a hat (the sun *does* often come out), and a change of shoes if you are planning a variety of activities, that is, hiking, sightseeing, and then drinks.

Wine bottle protectors. If your visit to San Francisco allows time to visit Napa and Sonoma's amazing vineyards, you may want to plan for the reality that you will want to bring a few bottles of wine home with you. Protect those previous liquid souvenirs (and everything in your suitcase) with bubble-wrap wine-bottle protectors.

Essentials

Lodging

RESERVATIONS

Reservations are always advised, especially during the peak seasons—from August through November, during the Oracle Convention week in fall, and weekends in December. Celebrations like Chinese New Year (late January or early February), Mother's Day and Bay to Breakers (mid-May), and gay pride (June) also require reservations.

FACILITIES

When pricing accommodations, always ask what facilities are included and what entails an additional charge. One big unexpected extra might be parking fees, which are off the charts in San Francisco. A seemingly expensive hotel that provides free parking and a hearty breakfast, for instance, can end up costing you less than one that charges for parking and breakfast. All the hotels listed have private baths, central heating, and private phones unless otherwise noted. Many places don't have air-conditioning, but you probably won't need it. Even in September and October, when the city sees its warmest days, the temperature rarely climbs above 70°F.

Nearly all hotels have Wi-Fi available, and though many offer the service for free, some charge for quicker connections, multiple devices, or both. Larger hotels often have video or high-speed checkout capability. Pools are a rarity, but most large properties have gyms or health clubs, and sometimes full-scale spas; hotels without facilities usually have arrangements for guests at nearby gyms, sometimes for a fee. At the end of each review, we state whether any meals (and in San Francisco, this means breakfast) are included in the room rate. Mirroring a trend elsewhere in the country, some hotels no longer provide room service, so if that's an amenity you require, be sure to inquire.

PARKING

Several properties on Lombard Street and in the Civic Center area have free parking (but not always in a covered garage). And, occasionally hotel package deals include parking. Hotels in the Union Square and Nob Hill areas charge $30 to $70 per day for garage parking; many hotels charge extra fees for SUVs. Some bed-and-breakfasts have limited free parking available, but many don't, requiring you to park on the street. Depending on the neighborhood, this can be easy or quite difficult, so ask for realistic parking information when you call. Some hotels offer a choice of valet parking with unlimited in-out privileges or self-parking. The cost is generally less for the latter in part because no tip is involved. Given the expense of parking, and the ease of getting around San Francisco on public transportation, you may well want to leave the car at home or wait to rent one until you're ready to leave town.

PRICES

San Francisco hotel prices rank among the highest in the country. Weekend rates for double rooms in high season average about $250 a night citywide except during large conventions such as Oracle's and Salesforce's, when even the humblest downtown lodgings command $500 or more. At other times, even in high season, decent lower-cost accommodations are relatively plentiful, especially in comparison to New York, Washington, and other big cities. Most hotels price rooms dynamically, with rates for dates a few days forward or months down the line fluctuating from hour to hour depending on availability—if you have your heart set on a particular property and its prices are high for your desired dates, it's wise to check back often either online or by phone.

Where Should I Stay?

	Neighborhood Vibe	Pros	Cons
Union Square/ Downtown	Union Square is a hub for visitors; you'll find a wide range of choices—and prices—for lodging.	Excellent shopping. Home to the theater district, great transit access to other neighborhoods.	Often crowded and noisy. Many panhandlers. Close to Tenderloin, a still-seedy part of town. Take cabs at night.
SoMa	Square one for the business set. Offers luxury high-rises, old classics, and a few bargains.	Near the museums and Yerba Buena Gardens. Steps from the convention center. Many fine eateries.	Construction in the area may mean traffic snarls. As with many changing neighborhoods, street life takes many forms. Be cautious walking around at night.
Financial District	A mini Midtown Manhattan where properties cater to business travelers.	Excellent city and bay views, which are spectacular by night. Easy access to restaurants and nightclubs.	Some streets are iffy at night. Hotels are on the pricey side. Many businesses close at night and on weekends.
Nob Hill	Synonymous with San Francisco's high society, this area contains some of the city's best-known luxury hotels.	Many hotels boast gorgeous views and notable restaurants. Easy access to Union Square and Chinatown.	Hotels here will test your wallet, while the area's steep hills may try your endurance.
Civic Center/Van Ness	A wide mix of lodgings scattered throughout this area.	Many cultural offerings and government offices surround this central hub. Not too far from Union Square.	Away from touristy areas. A large homeless population lives in the area.
Fisherman's Wharf/ North Beach	Mostly chain hotels by the wharf; lodgings get funkier and smaller in North Beach.	Near attractions like Ghirardelli Square and Pier 39. Cable-car lines and bay-cruise piers are nearby.	City ordinances limit wharf hotels to four stories, so good views are out. Very touristy.
Pacific Heights/Cow Hollow/The Marina	A few tony accommodations in quietly residential Pacific Heights. Mostly motels along Lombard Street, a busy traffic corridor.	Away from the more tourist-oriented areas; visitors have a chance to explore where locals eat and shop. Lots of free parking.	Getting downtown can be challenging via public transportation. Some complain of the fraternity-like bar scene.

Essentials

You'll sometimes, but not always, find a hotel's best rates on its website. If looking for a same-day room, check out apps such as Hotel Tonight or access the last-minute pages of Expedia and other travel sites for the best deals. Whenever you're making a reservation, inquire about special rates and packages. The lodgings we list are the cream of the crop in each price category.

WHAT IT COSTS

	$	$$	$$$	$$$$
HOTELS	under $150	$150–$249	$250–$350	over $350

Communications

INTERNET

The city of San Francisco offers free Wi-Fi service in selected parks and areas in and around the city. For a detailed list of locations visit *www6.sfgov.org.* All public libraries also provide Internet access and most hotels have a computer stationed in the lobby with free (if shared) high-speed access for guests. Some hotels can charge a small fee to provide a high-speed connection in the room, others offer it free of charge. In addition, many cafés throughout San Francisco, Marin County, and the East Bay offer free Wi-Fi, but a few continue to charge a fee. For a list of free Wi-Fi spots in San Francisco, check *www.openwifispots.com.*

Shopping

Each neighborhood has its own distinctive finds, whether it's 1960s housewares, cheeky stationery, or vintage Levi's. If shopping in San Francisco has a downside, it's that real bargains can be few and far between. Sure, neighborhoods such as the Lower Haight and the Mission have thrift shops and other inexpensive stores, but you won't find many discount outlets in the city, where rents are sky-high and space is at a premium.

Serious shoppers head straight to Union Square, San Francisco's main shopping area and the site of most of its department stores, including Macy's, Neiman Marcus, Barneys, and Saks Fifth Avenue. Nearby are such platinum-card international boutiques as Yves Saint Laurent, Cartier, Emporio Armani, Gucci, Hermès, and Louis Vuitton.

Seasonal sales, usually in late January and late July or August, are good opportunities for finding deep discounts on clothing. The *San Francisco Chronicle* and *San Francisco Examiner* advertise sales. For smaller shops, check the free *SF Weekly,* which can be found on street corners every Wednesday. Sample sales are usually held by individual manufacturers, so check your favorite company's website before visiting.

Nightlife

After hours, the city's business folk and workers give way to costume-clad partygoers, hippies and hipsters, downtown divas, frat boys, and those who prefer something a little more clothing-optional. Downtown and the Financial District remain pretty serious even after dark, and Nob Hill is staid, though you can't beat views from penthouse lounges, the most famous being the Top of the Mark (Hopkins). Nearby North Beach is an even better starting point for an evening out.

Always lively, North Beach's options include family-friendly dining spots, historic bars from the city's bohemian past (among them Jack Kerouac's old haunts), and even comedy clubs where stars such as Robin Williams and Jay Leno cut their teeth. In SoMa there are plenty of places to catch a drink before a Giants game and brewpubs to celebrate in afterward. SoMa also hosts some of the hottest dance clubs, along with some saucy gay bars. While Union Square can be a bit trendy, even the swanky establishments have loosened things up in recent years.

Heading west to Hayes Valley, a more sophisticated crowd dabbles in the burgeoning "culinary cocktail movement." Up-and-coming singles gravitate north of here to Cow Hollow and the Marina. Polk Street was the gay mecca before the Castro and still hosts some wild bars, but things get downright outlandish in the Castro district. Indie hipsters of all persuasions populate the Mission and Haight districts by night. Keep in mind, though, that some of the best times San Francisco has to offer are off the beaten path. And a good party can still be found in even the sleepiest of neighborhoods, such as Bernal Heights and Dogpatch.

Sports bars and hotel bars tend to be open on Sunday, but others may be closed. A few establishments—especially wine bars and restaurant bars—also close on Monday.

Performing Arts

The heart of the mainstream theater district lies on or near Geary Street, mostly west of Union Square, though touring Broadway shows land a little farther afield at big houses like the Orpheum and Golden Gate. But theater can be found all over town. For a bit of culture shock, slip out to eclectic districts like the Mission or Haight, where smaller theater companies reside and short-run and one-night-only performances happen on a regular basis.

The city's opera house and symphony hall present the musical classics, and venues like the Fillmore and the Warfield host major rock and jazz talents, but the city's extensive festival circuit broadens the possibilities considerably. Stern Grove is the nation's oldest summer music festival that remains free to this day; Noise Pop is the premier alt-rock showcase putting such acts like Modest Mouse on the map; and Hardly Strictly Bluegrass is a beloved celebration of bluegrass, country, and roots music, attracting hundreds of thousands of attendees from all over the nation every year.

Activities

Bikers and hikers traverse the majestic Golden Gate Bridge, bound for the Marin Headlands or the winding trails of the Presidio. Runners, strollers, and cyclists head for Golden Gate Park's wooded paths, and water lovers satisfy their addictions by kayaking, sailing, kite-surfing, and even swimming, in the bay and along the rugged Pacific coast.

Prefer to watch from the sidelines? The Giants (baseball) are San Francisco's professional sports team; the A's (baseball) and the Golden State Warriors (basketball) play in Oakland; and the 49ers (football) are based in Santa Clara. But the city has plenty of other periodic sporting events to watch, including that roving costume party, the Bay to Breakers race in May. For events listings and local perspectives on Bay Area sports, pick up a copy of the *San Francisco Chronicle* (🌐 *www.sfgate.com*) or the *San Francisco Examiner* (🌐 *www.examiner.com*).

BIKING

San Francisco is known for its treacherously steep hills, so it may be surprising to see so many cyclists. This is actually a great city for biking—there are ample bike lanes, it's not hard to find level ground with great scenery (especially along the water), and if you're willing to tackle a challenging uphill climb, you're often rewarded with a fabulous view—and a quick trip back down.

RUNNING

San Francisco is spectacular for running. There are more than 7 miles of paved trails in and around **Golden Gate Park**; circling **Stow Lake** and then crossing the bridge and running up the path to the top of Strawberry Hill is a total of 2½ miles. An enormously popular route is the 2-mile raised bike path that runs from Lincoln Way along the ocean, at the southern border of Golden Gate Park, to Sloat Boulevard, which is the northern border of the San Francisco Zoo. (Stick to the park's interior when it's windy, as ocean gusts can kick up sand.) From Sloat Boulevard you can pick up the **Lake Merced** bike path, which loops around the lake and the golf course, to extend your run another 5 miles.

The paved path along the **Marina** provides a 1½-mile (round-trip) run along a flat, well-paved surface and has glorious bay views. Start where Laguna Street meets Marina Boulevard, then run west along the Marina Green toward the Golden Gate and St. Francis yacht clubs, near the docks at the northern end of Marina Boulevard. On weekends beware: you'll have to wind through the crowds—but those views are worth it. You can extend your Marina run by jogging the paths through the restored wetlands of Crissy Field, just past the yacht harbor, then up the hill to the Golden Gate Bridge.

The *San Francisco Bike Map and Walking Guide (see Bicycling)*, which indicates hill grades on city streets by color, is a great resource. Online, check the **San Francisco Road Runners Club** site (🌐 *www.sfrrc.org*) for some recommended routes and links to several local races.

SPECTATOR SPORTS

San Francisco has several professional sports teams.

San Francisco 49ers

FOOTBALL | The state-of-the-art Levi's Stadium, 45 miles south of San Francisco, has more than 13,000 square feet of HD video boards. Home games usually sell out far in advance. **Ticketmaster** (*www.ticketmaster.com*) and **StubHub** (*www.stubhub.com*) are sources for single-game tickets. ✉ *Levi's Stadium, 4900 Marie P. DeBartolo Way, from San Francisco, take U.S. 101 south to Lawrence Expressway and follow signs, Santa Clara* ☎ *800/745–3000 Ticketmaster, 866/788–2482 StubHub!, 415/464–9377 Santa Clara stadium* 🌐 *www.49ers.com.*

San Francisco Giants

BASEBALL/SOFTBALL | Three World Series titles (2010, 2012, and 2014) and the classic design of Oracle Park lead to sellouts for nearly every home game the National League team plays. ✉ *Oracle Park, 24 Willie Mays Plaza, between 2nd and 3rd Sts., SoMa* ☎ *415/972–2000, 800/734–4268* 🌐 *sanfrancisco.giants.mlb.com.*

Safety

San Francisco is generally a safe place for travelers who observe all normal urban precautions. Use common sense and, unless you know exactly where you're going, steer clear of certain neighborhoods late at night, especially if you're walking alone. Below are certain areas to stay on alert, or avoid:

The Tenderloin. Thought to be named for a cut of steak, this neighborhood west of Union Square and above Civic Center can be a seedy part of town, with drug dealers, homeless people, hustlers, and X-rated joints. It's roughly bordered by Taylor, Polk, Geary, and Market Streets. Avoid coming here after dark, especially if you're walking.

Western Addition. Past incidents of gang activity have made this neighborhood somewhat sketchy. Don't stray too far off Fillmore Street.

Civic Center. After a show here, walk west to Gough Street; and avoid Market Street between 6th and 10th.

Some areas in Golden Gate Park. These include the area near the Haight Street entrance, where street kids often smoke and deal drugs, and around the pedestrian tunnels on the far west end of the park.

Like many large cities, San Francisco has many homeless people. Although most are no threat, some are more aggressive and can persist in their pleas for cash until it feels like harassment. If you feel uncomfortable, don't reach for your wallet.

Tipping

Tipping Guidelines for San Francisco	
Bartender	About 15%, starting at $1 a drink at casual places
Bellhop	$1–$5 per bag, depending on the level of the hotel
Hotel concierge	$5 or more, if he or she performs a service for you
Hotel doorman, room service, or valet	$3–$4
Hotel maid	$5 a day (either daily or at the end of your stay, in cash)
Taxi driver	15%–20%, but round up the fare to the next dollar amount
Tour guide	10% of the cost of the tour
Waiter	18%–20%, with 20% being the norm at high-end restaurants

A Waterfront Walk: The Ferry Building to Fisherman's Wharf

One of the great pleasures of San Francisco is a stroll along the bay, with its briny scent, the cry of the gulls, and boats bobbing on the waves. The flat, 2-mile walk along the Embarcadero from the Ferry Building offers a chance to take in some of the city's blockbuster sights, along with spectacular bay vistas.

THE FERRY BUILDING: FOODIE MECCA

Standing sentry at the foot of Market Street, the **Ferry Building** offers organic, seasonal delights from such local treasures as Cowgirl Creamery and Prather Ranch Meat Company. Take your picnic to a bench out back and take in the bay and the Bay Bridge.

EMBARCADERO: NEW LIFE FOR OLD PIERS

Heading north on the Embarcadero as the piers go up in number, watch for a mélange of historical info on black-and-white pillars, engraved in the sidewalk, and on plaques. These line **Pier 1,** where the giant paddle wheeler *San Francisco Belle* docks. **Pier 7** juts out far into the bay; an evening stroll here is lovely (if chilly) under the street lamps.

Just two blocks beyond at Pier 15 is the city's excellent hands-on science museum, the **Exploratorium.**

NORTH BEACH DETOUR: LEVI'S AND COIT TOWER

Near Pier 17, a left on Union and a right on Battery leads to **Levi Strauss headquarters,** where visitors can shop for jeans or peruse artifacts such as miners' jeans from the 1880s. Back across Battery, **Levi's Plaza** is one of the most manicured parks in town.

Consider heading west on Filbert or Greenwich and ascending one of the steep staircases clinging to **Telegraph**

A Waterfront Walk: The Ferry Building to Fisherman's Wharf

WHERE TO START:

In front of the Ferry Building.

TIME/LENGTH:

30–60 minutes at a moderate pace, without stops. With a picnic and park breaks, this walk could be a three-hour affair. The total distance is 2 miles.

WHERE TO STOP:

At the cable-car turnaround or resting your feet at the Buena Vista.

BEST TIME TO GO:

Sunny days are best for strolling the waterfront. Start off at the Ferry Building in the morning, ideally on a Saturday, when farmers' market stalls fill the plaza. The street-theater scene from Pier 39 to Fisherman's Wharf is liveliest on weekends, too.

WORST TIME TO GO:

Rain puts a huge damper on this walk, which is all about being outside. Weekends are bustling, but they can mean large crowds at the big-ticket attractions—Alcatraz and Fisherman's Wharf.

GETTING AROUND:

If you're driving, park at the north end—it's much cheaper—and do the walk backward from north to south. Pedicabs will offer rides along the way, and the F-line is always available for the weary.

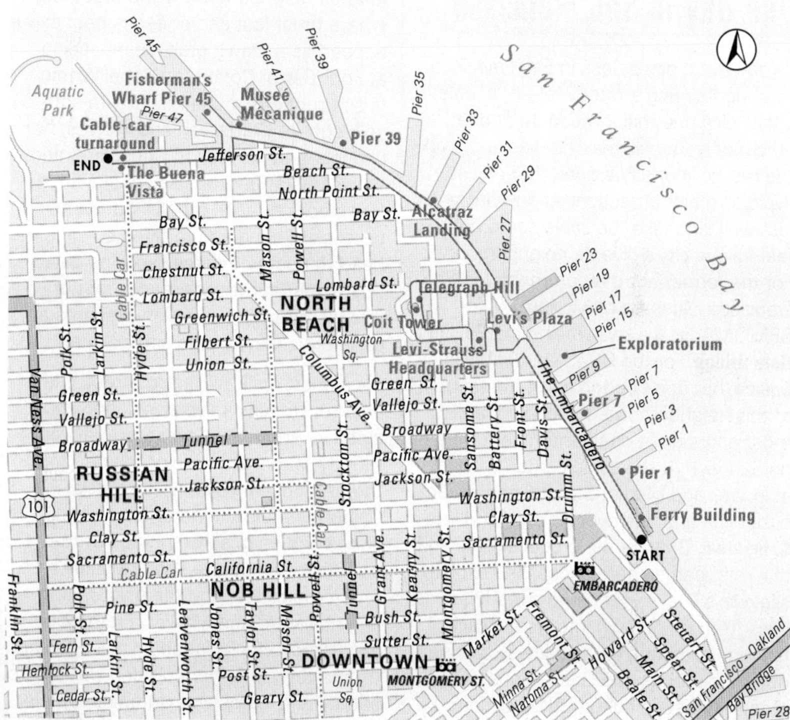

Hill for spectacular views and a peek into the lush stairway gardens along the way up to **Coit Tower.** Then return down the stairs to continue along the Embarcadero.

EMBARCADERO NORTH END: TOURIST SAN FRANCISCO

Continuing north up the Embarcadero, **Alcatraz Landing** (Pier 33) is a good spot to pick up souvenirs even if you're not taking the highly recommended tour. **Pier 39** is just around the corner, with its cornucopia of souvenir vendors; thankfully, sea lion–watching is still free.

A few blocks farther north is **Fisherman's Wharf,** at Pier 45. Bypass the wax museum and make a beeline for the fabulous vintage arcade **Musée Mécanique** (at the foot of Taylor Street). For crab- and bunny-shape sourdough loaves, stop by Boudin Bakery, just down Taylor on Jefferson.

LAST STOP: HISTORIC VESSELS AT THE HYDE STREET PIER

Follow the towering masts to the foot of Hyde Street and the collection of exquisitely restored ships there. Afterward, head up Hyde to the **cable-car turnaround,** where you can grab an Irish coffee at the **Buena Vista.**

Great Itineraries

One Day in San Francisco

If you have a day or less in San Francisco, your sightseeing strategy is very simple: either pick one major museum or one attraction you really want to see and work the rest of your day around that *or* just avoid all major attractions altogether, and just walk and take the cable car to get a feel for the city's diverse neighborhoods. For the former, we'd recommend the San Francisco Museum of Modern Art (or SFMOMA, as it's known) and the **Golden Gate Bridge.** For the latter, start in **Union Square,** but don't be too early: the focus of this neighborhood is shopping, and most doors don't open until 10 am (11 am on Sunday). At the cable-car turnaround at Powell and Market Streets, hop aboard either line and ride over Nob Hill and into **Chinatown.** Browse the produce stalls and markets, peruse herb shops, and explore alleyways. Have your camera ready as you pass from Chinatown into **North Beach,** the old Italian quarter: Broadway looking down Columbus and Grant is one of the most interesting cultural intersections of the city. Walk Columbus Avenue—stopping for espresso, of course—then head toward Coit Tower up Filbert Street, which becomes the Filbert Steps, one of the city's many stairways. Keep your eyes—and ears—open for **Telegraph Hill** 's famous wild parrots. Take in the views at the top and the tower's WPA-era murals of California's history, then head back into North Beach for dinner or cocktails.

Three Days in San Francisco

DAY 1

With more time, you have a chance both to see the sights, eat all the amazing food, and really get to know the city. The **Mission** neighborhood is the first stop, where breakfast and coffee is best experienced as a crawl: grab a cappuccino at Four Barrel Coffee, a "Rebel Within" (a scrumptious muffin filled with soft-yolk egg) at Craftsman and Wolves, hot chocolate at Dandelion Chocolate, and croissants at Tartine. They're all within five blocks of each other. With some pastries in hand and fortified by caffeine, head to nearby **Dolores Park,** The park's southwest corner offers your first of many steep climbs. It also presents a panoramic view of the city skyline.

It's a short walk to Castro Street, the heart of the city's gay population and culture, where it's never too early for Bloody Marys at Harvey's (named for the first openly gay elected official in California). Allow time to browse the shops and snap some photos of the classic movie palace **Castro Theatre's** ornate marquee, and the giant rainbow flag at Castro and Market. From here, it's a steep climb but short mileage-wise trek to the city's "it" corridor, Divisadero and its chic cafés and vintage shops. At Hayes Street, hang a right and ahead is **Alamo Square Park,** with the backdrop of the beautifully painted Painted Ladies Victorian homes, made famous by the TV show "Full House." This is *the* view of San Francisco.

It's all downhill from here ... at least until the late afternoon. Stroll down the hill along Hayes Street and check out the sleek boutiques of "Hayes Valley." Lunch just a few blocks away at Zuni Café, a fine-dining staple that defines "California Cuisine."

Back on your feet, continue down Market Street, San Francisco's "Champs-Elysée" that sadly is also one of its more struggling corridors with the evident street life. There are many important sights to see here including the Twitter headquarters and it's must-photograph "@Twitter" sign at Market and 10th Street. Walk one block off Market Street to admire the magnificent **City Hall** and its grand rotunda. Catch a ride here to the beautiful Dragon's Gate entrance to **Chinatown** at Grant and Bush Street. Continue along Grant Street to Columbus Avenue and admire North America's oldest Chinatown. Hang a left at Columbus and after crossing Broadway, Chinatown evolves into the city's "Little Italy", North Beach. The Italian influence continues to dwindle but can be found in cozy espresso cafés like Mario's Bohemian Cigar Store Cafe overlooking Washington Square Park. After a much-needed espresso jolt, get ready for another steep climb up **Telegraph Hill,** home of a community of parrots and Coit Tower with its mesmerizing views at the top.

Back down the hill, immediately backtrack on Columbus Avenue to Comstock Saloon, a delightful ode to the early-20th-century Barbary Coast era of the city with high-quality classic cocktails. The pineapple-enriched Pisco Punch is a must as it supposedly was invented in San Francisco. Wrap up the day with dinner at Mister Jiu's, the city's game-changing contemporary Chinese restaurant by chef Brandon Jew. Everything is stellar and has an intriguing spin, but be sure to start with the prawn toast and sea urchin *cheong fun*.

DAY 2

Start in Union Square and admire the grand outdoor plaza that could fit in any European capital. It's surrounded by the city's luxury department stores and the 97-foot Victory Monument column commemorating Commodore George Dewey's victory against the Spanish fleet at Manila in 1898 resides in the center. Right off of the square is Sears Fine Food, an all-day slice of Americana that is known for one thing: irresistible petite Swedish pancakes that come 18 to an order. Give your legs a rest this morning and take the Powell-Hyde cable car that weaves up and down Nob Hill and Russian Hill from its loading spot by Union Square. After the requisite selfies dangling from the outdoor poles, get off the cable car at Lombard Street. This flower-adorned curvy street is best viewed in the morning before there are more tourists than flowers. When you're ready, walk a block or two away and request a car and head to Pier 33, where the **Alcatraz** boats leave. Generally, 2½ to 3 hours is a good amount of time for the boat ride and tour of "The Rock," a federal prison until the '60s. **■TIP→ Avoid disappointment and secure Alcatraz tickets in advance online.**

Back on the mainland, walk along the **Embarcadero,** a former elevated freeway turned palm tree-lined thoroughfare along the Bay that is the defacto official venue for San Francisco joggers and stroller walking. For lunch, head to the **Ferry Building,** which is indeed the public transit ferry terminal, in addition to being a spectacular food hall filled with all sorts of delicious vendors and artisans showcasing why the Bay Area is one of the greatest places to eat in the world. The options can be daunting, so start with a grilled cheese sandwich at Cowgirl Creamery, chocolates by Recchiuti, ice cream at Humphry Slocombe and a pastry at Vive la Tarte. As a bonus, if it's Tuesday, Thursday, or Saturday, the city's most extensive farmers' market gathers outside the building.

Spend the late afternoon in the sprawling **San Francisco Museum of Modern Art (SFMOMA),** the city's magnificent museum of modern art that is a 460,000-square-foot behemoth with more than 1,000 works. You won't make it through all the galleries, so be sure to start with highlights like the third-floor sculpture garden with a living wall and signature works by the likes of Wayne Thiebaud, Andy Warhol, and Alexander Calder's "mobiles." If you want to linger a little longer here, dine at SFMOMA's in-house restaurant, In Situ

Finally, take a short car ride up steep Nob Hill to the two grande dame hotels of the city, the Fairmont and the Huntington. Their two bars are San Francisco classics for wildly different reason. The Big 4 in the Huntington is all about piano music, dim lighting, an old-school vibe, and stiff classic cocktails. The Fairmont's Tonga Room is as kitsch as it gets with its lagoon and ultra tiki atmosphere. The mai tais aren't so bad, either. Choose one for a nightcap. Or both.

DAY 3

After exploring the city's urban and residential sides, this final day is all about nature. If it's a weekend, get a head start on the brunch crowds by racing out toward the Pacific. Then, enjoy San Francisco's "unofficial official meal" at Outerlands, a surfer-cool, reclaimed wood-paneled restaurant that is often cited at the city's best brunch. If it's a weekday, Outerlands still has a terrific breakfast and lunch menu that isn't too different from weekend brunch. Walk a few blocks to Ocean Beach and enjoy the sea salt-kissed air. If there were more time today, the walk all the way to **Golden Gate Bridge** is one of the most stunning in the country, ... but it would take several hours. Take a car to Baker Beach, just to the western edge of the bridge. The views from here of the bridge are magnificent, even dreamy. Afterward, climb up the steep Battery to Bluffs trail, hang a left on Lincoln Boulevard, follow the trail along the road for another gorgeous Golden Gate overlook, and follow the trails to the Golden Gate Bridge's parking lot. The views from the bridge are beautiful, but the experience can take a lot of time ... and is frightening if you are even vaguely afraid of heights. Today, bypass the popular walk across the bridge and follow the steps down to "Fort Point" at its base. The walk from here to Crissy Field, an expansive grassy area that used to be a military airfield, is one of the more spectacular in the whole Bay Area. There are two bridges in view, the skyline, and lots of fresh air ... yes, welcome to California. End the walk at the Palace of Fine Arts, an elegant, colossal monument built in 1915 for the Panama-Pacific Exposition.

One final neighborhood, dinner, and drink: use the "Mrs. Doubtfire home" as the starting address at 2640 Steiner Street. This is the heart of Pacific Heights, the city's deep pockets district with splendid mansions and views on each block. Walk down nearby Fillmore Street and admire the price tags and high-end boutiques. Cross Geary Street and duck into Fat Angel for one of the highly rated local beers on tap to experience San Francisco's fascination with craft beer. Then, for your final dinner, head to the wildly inventive State Bird Provisions, to enjoy a feast of globe-spanning contemporary creations served dim sum-style. **TIP→ Make reservations at State Bird Provisions at least a month in advance.**

Contacts

Air Travel

Oakland International Airport (*OAK*). ✉ *1 Airport Dr., Oakland* ☎ *510/563–3300* 🌐 *www.oaklandairport.com.* **San Francisco International Airport (*SFO*).** ✉ *McDonnell and Links Rds.* ☎ *800/435–9736, 650/821–8211* 🌐 *www.flysfo.com.* **San Jose International Airport (*SJC*).** ✉ *1701 Airport Blvd., San Jose* ☎ *408/392–3600* 🌐 *www.flysanjose.com.*

Boat Travel

INFORMATION

Alameda/Oakland Ferry. ☎ *877/643–3779* 🌐 *sanfranciscobayferry.com.* **Alcatraz Cruises.** ☎ *415/981–7625* 🌐 *www.alcatrazcruises.com.* **Blue & Gold Fleet.** ☎ *415/705–8200* 🌐 *www.blueandgoldfleet.com.* **Ferry Building Marketplace.** ✉ *1 Ferry Bldg., at foot of Market St. on Embarcadero* ☎ *415/983–8030* 🌐 *www.ferrybuildingmarketplace.com* **Golden Gate Ferry.** ☎ *415/923–2000* 🌐 *www.goldengateferry.org.*

Bus Travel

Greyhound. ✉ *Transbay Temporary Terminal, 200 Folsom St., at 1st St., SoMa* ☎ *415/495–1569* 🌐 *www.greyhound.com.*

Metro/ Public Transport

BART TRAVEL

Bay Area Rapid Transit (*BART*). ☎ *510/465-2278* 🌐 *www.bart.gov.*

MUNI TRAVEL

San Francisco Municipal Transportation Agency (*Muni*). ☎ *311, 415/701–3000* 🌐 *www.sfmta.com.*

Taxi Travel

Flywheel Taxi. ☎ *415/970–1303* 🌐 *flywheeltaxi.com.* **Luxor Cab.** ☎ *415/282–4141* 🌐 *www.luxorcab.com.* **National Veterans Cab.** ☎ *415/321–8294* 🌐 *sfnationalcab.sftaxischool.com/index.html.* **Yellow Cab.** ☎ *415/333–3333* 🌐 *yellowcabsf.com.*

Train Travel

Amtrak. ☎ *800/872–7245* 🌐 *www.amtrak.com.* **Caltrain.** ☎ *800/660–4287* 🌐 *www.caltrain.com.* **San Francisco Caltrain station.** ✉ *700 4th St., near Townsend St.* ☎ *800/660–4287.*

Visitor Information

San Francisco Visitor Information Center. ✉ *Hallidie Plaza, lower level, 900 Market St., at Powell St., Union Sq.* ☎ *415/391–2000* 🌐 *www.sftravel.com.*

METRO AREA

Marin Convention & Visitors Bureau. ✉ *1 Mitchell Blvd., Suite B, at Redwood Hwy., San Rafael* ☎ *415/925–2060, 866/925–2060* 🌐 *www.visitmarin.org.* **San Jose Convention & Visitors Bureau.** ✉ *408 S. Almaden Blvd., near Balbach St., San Jose* ☎ *800/726–5673, 408/295–9600* 🌐 *www.sanjose.org.* **Visit Berkeley Information Center.** ✉ *2030 Addison St., Suite 102, Berkeley* ✣ *1 block north of Downtown Berkeley BART station* ☎ *800/847–4823, 510/549–7040* 🌐 *www.visitberkeley.com.*

STATE

California Travel and Tourism Commission. ☎ *877/225–4367, 916/444–4429* 🌐 *www.visitcalifornia.com.* **California Welcome Center.** ✉ *Pier 39 , Beach St. and the Embarcadero , Bldg. B, 2nd level* ☎ *415/981–1280* 🌐 *www.visitcwc.com.*

Chapter 3

UNION SQUARE AND CHINATOWN

Updated by
Denise M. Leto

Sights	Restaurants	Hotels	Shopping	Nightlife
★★★☆☆	★★★☆☆	★★★★★	★★★★★	★☆☆☆☆

NEIGHBORHOOD SNAPSHOT

TOP REASONS TO GO

- **Ross Alley, Chinatown:** Breathe in the scented air as you watch the nimble hands at Golden Gate Fortune Cookie Factory, then kick back with a cocktail at Li Po around the corner, rumored to be haunted by the ghost of an opium junkie still looking to score.
- **Return to noir San Francisco:** Have a late martini lunch under the gaze of the Maltese Falcon at John's Grill, then swing through the lobby of the Flood Building and nod to the other Maltese Falcon there.
- **Shop the square:** Prime your credit cards and dive right in, from Bloomie's to the boutiques of Maiden Lane.
- **Tin How Temple:** Climb the narrow stairway to this space with hundreds of red lanterns, then step onto the tiny balcony and take in the alley scene below.
- **Elevator at the St. Francis:** Ride a glass elevator to the sky (or the 32nd floor) for a gorgeous view of the cityscape, especially in the evening when the lights come up.

PLANNING YOUR TIME

Set aside at least an hour to scope out the stores and sights in and around Union Square—or most of the day if you're a shopper—but don't bother arriving before 10 am, when the first shops open. Sunday is a bit quieter.

Give yourself at least two hours to tour compact Chinatown. If possible, come on a weekday (it's less crowded) and before lunchtime (busiest with locals). You won't need more than 15 or 20 minutes at any of the sights themselves, but exploring the shops and alleys is, indeed, the whole point.

GETTING THERE

- In these two neighborhoods, cars equal hassle. Traffic is slow and parking is pricey. Take advantage of the confluence of public transit at Powell and Market Streets: buses, Muni light-rail vehicles and BART (Powell Street Station for both), cable cars, and F-line streetcars run here.
- It's an easy walk to Chinatown from Union Square, and both Powell lines of the cable-car system pass through.

The Union Square area bristles with big-city bravado, while just a stone's throw away is a place that feels like a city unto itself, Chinatown. The two areas share a strong commercial streak, although manifested very differently. In Union Square—a plaza but also the neighborhood around it—the crowds zigzag among international brands, trailing glossy shopping bags. A few blocks north, people dash between small neighborhood stores, their arms draped with plastic totes filled with groceries or souvenirs.

Union Square

The city's finest department stores put on their best faces in Union Square, along with such exclusive emporiums as Tiffany & Co. and Bulgari, and such big-name franchises as Nike, the Apple Store, H&M, Barney's, and Uniqlo. Visitors lay their heads at several dozen hotels within a three-block walk of the square, and the downtown theater district is nearby. Union Square is shopping-centric; nonshoppers will find fewer enticements here.

Lotta's Fountain

FOUNTAIN | Saucy gold rush–era actress, singer, and dancer Lotta Crabtree so aroused the city's miners that they were known to shower her with gold nuggets and silver dollars after her performances. The peculiar, rather clunky fountain was her way of saying thanks to her fans. Given to the city in 1875, the fountain became a meeting place for survivors after the 1906 earthquake. Each April 18, the anniversary of the quake, San Franciscans gather at this quirky monument. An image of redheaded Lotta herself, in a very pink, rather risqué dress, appears in one of the Anton Refregier murals in Rincon Center. ☒ *Traffic triangle at intersection of 3rd, Market, Kearny, and Geary Sts., Union Sq.*

KEY
Sights
Restaurants
Hotels
Union Square
NOB HILL
UNION SQUARE
TENDERLOIN
Sacramento St.
California St.
Pine St.
Bush St.
Sutter St.
Post St.
Geary St.
O'Farrell St.
Ellis St.
Eddy St.
Turk St.
Market St.
Taylor St.
Jones St.
Leavenworth St.
Mason St.
Powell St.
Cyril Magnin St.
5th St.
Stevenson St.
Cushman St.
Huntington Park
Cable Car
Frank St.
Vine Ter.
Nob Hill Circle
Hooker Al.
Mulford Al.
Touchard St.
Fella Pl.
D. Hammett St.
Joice St.
Pratt Pl.
Burritt St.
Delta Pl.
Cosmo Pl.
Colin Pl.
Shannon St.
Elwood St.
Harlem Al.
Antonio St.
Steveloe Pl.
Wagner Al.
Opal Pl.
Union Square
POWELL ST.
Old U.S. Mint

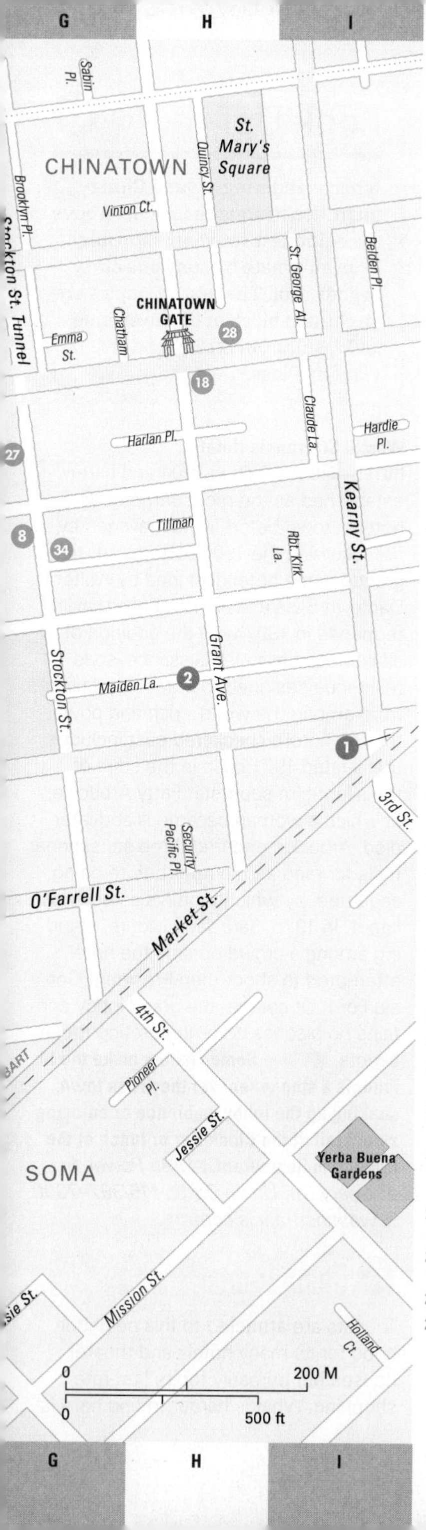

G H I

CHINATOWN
St. Mary's Square
Sabin Pl.
Quincy St.
Brooklyn Pl.
Vinton Ct.
Stockton St. Tunnel
St. George Al.
Belden Pl.
CHINATOWN GATE
Chatham
Emma St.
Claude La.
Hardie Pl.
Harlan Pl.
Kearny St.
Tillman
Rbt. Kirk La.
Grant Ave.
Stockton St.
Maiden La.
3rd St.
Security Pacific Pl.
O'Farrell St.
Market St.
4th St.
BART
Pioneer Pl.
Jessie St.
Yerba Buena Gardens
SOMA
Mission St.
Holland Ct.
0 200 M
0 500 ft

G H I

Sights

1 Lotta's Fountain I5
2 Maiden Lane H5
3 Union Square............ F5
4 Westin St. Francis Hotel F5

Restaurants

1 Farallon E4
2 Katana-Ya............... D5
3 Kin Khao E7
4 Liholiho Yacht Club A4
5 M.Y. China F8

Hotels

1 Axiom Hotel San Francisco........... F8
2 Beresford Arms......... B5
3 The Cartwright Hotel Union Square............ E4
4 Chancellor Hotel on Union Square......... E4
5 The Clift Royal Sonesta Hotel C6
6 Cornell Hotel De France................ E3
7 Golden Gate Hotel D3
8 Grand Hyatt San Francisco Union Square........... G4
9 Hilton San Francisco Union Square........... D7
10 Hotel Abri................ E7
11 Hotel Adagio C6
12 Hotel Beresford.......... C4
13 Hotel Bijou............... E8
14 Hotel Diva............... D5
15 Hotel Emblem E4
16 Hotel G E5
17 Hotel Nikko San Francisco............ E7
18 Hotel Triton H3
19 Hotel Union Square...... F7
20 Hotel Zeppelin San Francisco.......... D5
21 The Inn at Union Square............ E4
22 JW Marriott San Francisco Union Square........... D4
23 Kensington Park Hotel E4
24 Kimpton Sir Francis Drake Hotel.............. F4
25 King George Hotel E6
26 The Marker San Francisco........... C6
27 Mystic Hotel............ G3
28 Orchard Garden Hotel..................... H2
29 Orchard Hotel F3
30 Parc 55 San Francisco, a Hilton Hotel.............. E8
31 Petite Auberge C3
32 San Francisco Marriott Union Square............ F4
33 Staypineapple San Francisco........... B6
34 Taj Campton Place San Francisco.......... G4
35 Villa Florence............ F6
36 Warwick San Francisco........... C5
37 Westin St. Francis F5
38 White Swan Inn......... D3

Maiden Lane

BUILDING | Known as Morton Street in the raffish Barbary Coast era, this former red-light district reported at least one murder a week during the late 19th century. Things cooled down after the 1906 fire destroyed the brothels, and these days Maiden Lane is a chic, designer-boutique-lined pedestrian mall stretching two blocks, between Stockton and Kearny Streets. Wrought-iron gates close the street to traffic most days between 11 and 5, when the lane becomes an alfresco hotspot dotted with a patchwork of umbrella-shaded tables. At **140 Maiden Lane** is the only Frank Lloyd Wright building in San Francisco, fronted by a large brick archway. The graceful, curving ramp and skylights of the interior, which houses exclusive Italian menswear boutique Isaia, are said to have been his model for the Guggenheim Museum in New York. ⊠ *Between Stockton and Kearny Sts., Union Sq.*

Union Square

PLAZA | Ground zero for big-name shopping in the city and within walking distance of many hotels, Union Square is home base for many visitors. The Westin St. Francis Hotel and Macy's line two of the square's sides, and Saks, Neiman-Marcus, and Tiffany & Co. edge the other two. Four globular contemporary lamp sculptures by the artist R. M. Fischer preside over the landscaped, 2½-acre park, which has a café with outdoor seating, an open-air stage, and a visitor-information booth—along with a familiar kaleidoscope of characters: office workers sunning and brown-bagging, street musicians, shoppers taking a rest, kids chasing pigeons, and a fair number of homeless people. The constant clang of cable cars traveling up and down Powell Street helps maintain a festive mood. ⊠ *Bordered by Powell, Stockton, Post, and Geary Sts., Union Sq.*

Look Up!

When wandering around Chinatown, don't forget to look up! Above the chintziest souvenir shop might loom an ornate balcony or a curly pagoda roof. The best examples are on the 900 block of Grant Avenue (at Washington Street) and at Waverly Place.

Westin St. Francis Hotel

HOTEL—SIGHT | Built in 1904 and barely established as the most sumptuous hotel in town before it was ravaged by fire following the 1906 earthquake, this grande-dame hotel designed by Walter Danforth Bliss and William Baker Faville reopened in 1907 with the addition of a luxurious Italian Renaissance–style residence designed to attract loyal clients from among the world's rich and powerful. The hotel's checkered past includes the ill-fated 1921 bash in the suite of the silent-film superstar Fatty Arbuckle, at which a woman became ill and later died. Arbuckle endured three sensational trials for rape and murder before being acquitted, by which time his career was kaput. In 1975, Sara Jane Moore, standing among a crowd outside the hotel, attempted to shoot then-President Gerald Ford. Of course, the grand lobby contains no plaques commemorating these events. ■ TIP→ **Some visitors make the St. Francis a stop whenever they're in town, soaking up the lobby ambience or enjoying a cocktail at the Clock Bar or lunch at the Oak Room Restaurant.** ⊠ *335 Powell St., at Geary St., Union Sq.* ☎ *415/397–7000* 🌐 *westinstfrancis.com.*

Restaurants

Tourists are attracted to this neighborhood for its many hotels and theater houses but primarily for its first-rate shopping. What is harder to find here is

Union Square is the city's epicenter of high-end shopping.

authentic San Francisco eating (locals dislike battling the crowds). But if you know where to look, you can find good places tucked away into narrow side alleys or in the lobbies of hotels.

Farallon

$$$$ | **SEAFOOD** | Even though San Francisco is right on the Bay, it can be surprisingly hard to find great menus that focus on fish, but this white-linen restaurant delivers with platters of fruits de mer shucked right at the raw bar and sustainably caught pan-roasted fish. The main dining room is a 1920s original with Spanish Gothic influences and a domed hand-painted ceiling, while the bar—a busy happy hour spot—is more modern, with jelly-fish chandeliers and kelp-covered columns. **Known for:** freshly shucked shellfish; sustainably caught fish; happy hour oysters. 💲 *Average main: $37* ✉ *450 Post St., Union Sq.* ☎ *415/956–6969* 🌐 *www.farallonrestaurant.com.*

Katana-Ya

$ | **JAPANESE** | Head downstairs to this hole-in-the-wall ramen house for some of the most authentic noodles in town, served until 2 am. Hand-drawn pictures of specials punctuate a colorful interior with too-close tables and a couple of stools around the bar. **Known for:** great ramen; long waits; just the right amount of spice. 💲 *Average main: $16* ✉ *430 Geary St., Union Sq.* ☎ *415/771–1281* 🌐 *www.katanayausa.com.*

★ **Kin Khao**

$$$$ | **THAI** | Casual eaters of Americanized Thai food probably won't recognize much at this modern, low-lit restaurant, but travelers to Thailand—the chef-owner is a native—will likely see a few familiars on the short, focused menu. Ingredients are sourced—more accurately, tracked down with dedication—from regional purveyors to create such dishes as *yum kai dao*, a spicy fried egg salad, which runs with yolk and is spiked with cilantro, and dry-fried *kua kling* ribs, bursting with curry and chili flavors. **Known for:** authentic dishes with explosive flavors; one Michelin star; solid cocktails. 💲 *Average main: $32* ✉ *55 Cyril Magnin*

Union Square Backstory

The heart of San Francisco's downtown since 1850, Union Square takes its name from the violent pro-Union demonstrations staged here before the Civil War. At center stage, Robert Ingersoll Aitken's *Victory Monument* commemorates Commodore George Dewey's victory over the Spanish fleet at Manila in 1898. The 97-foot Corinthian column, topped by a bronze figure symbolizing naval conquest, was dedicated by Theodore Roosevelt in 1903 and withstood the 1906 earthquake.

After the earthquake and fire of 1906, the square was dubbed "Little St. Francis" because of the temporary shelter erected for residents of the St. Francis Hotel. Actor John Barrymore (grandfather of actress Drew Barrymore and a notorious carouser) was among the guests pressed into volunteering to stack bricks in the square. His uncle, thespian John Drew, remarked, "It took an act of God to get John out of bed and the United States Army to get him to work."

St., corner of Mason and Ellis Sts., Union Sq. ✣ *Located off lobby of Parc 55 Hotel* ☎ *415/362–7456* 🌐 *kinkhao.com.*

★ **Liholiho Yacht Club**

$$$$ | **MODERN AMERICAN** | Inspired but not defined by the chef's native Hawaii, Ravi Kapur's lively restaurant is known for big-hearted, high-spirited cooking, including contemporary riffs on poke and Spam, but also squid served with crispy tripe, and beef ribs with kimchi chili sauce. The dining room and front bar area are perpetually packed, and dominated by an enormous photo of a beaming woman who happens to be none other than the chef's mother. **Known for:** Hawaiian-inspired food; giant mains that serve two to four people; lively buzz. $ *Average main: $40* ✉ *871 Sutter St., Union Sq.* ☎ *415/440–5446* 🌐 *www.lycsf.com* ⏲ *Closed Sun. No lunch.*

M.Y. China

$$$ | **CHINESE** | Hand-pulled noodles are the real star at celebrity chef Martin Yan's show palace, a swank restaurant on the fourth floor of Market Street's Westfield Mall with Chinese opium bottles on display and a megaton bronze bell from China as the bar centerpiece. Whether Yan is there, you'll be sure to watch his cooks stretch, twist, toss, and drop noodles into a beef short-rib soup flavored with star anise; a Dungeness crab menu highlights six styles of Chinese cooking. **Known for:** hand-pulled noodles; celebrity chef; exhibition kitchen. $ *Average main: $25* ✉ *Westfield Mall, 845 Market St., Union Sq.* ☎ *415/580–3001* 🌐 *tastemychina.com.*

Hotels

Scores of hotels—populated by first-time visitors, corporate travelers, and savvy globetrotters—surround Union Square, which is a central shopping district (plus, unfortunately, a large population of San Francisco's homeless). Easy access to public transportation, attractions, the Financial District, and Moscone Center convention activity has influenced major hotel chains to set up shop here, but you'll also find boutique hotels, several inns, and, a few blocks off Union Square, some value options.

★ **Axiom Hotel San Francisco**

$$ | **HOTEL** | Green, pet-friendly, and equipped with fiber-optic wireless Internet, the tech-oriented Axiom—a splashy refresh of a 1908 hotel—nimbly provides a boutique experience business and leisure travelers applaud. **Pros:** tech-friendly amenities; polite, intuitive, efficient staff; on-site café open morning to night. **Cons:** smallish rooms; somewhat congested area; some guests find street people intimidating. *Rooms from: $299 28 Cyril Magnin St., at 5th and Market Sts., Union Sq. 415/392–9466 www.axiomhotel.com 155 rooms No meals.*

Beresford Arms

$$ | HOTEL | FAMILY | Fancy molding and 10-foot-tall windows grace the red-carpeted lobby of this brick Victorian listed on the National Register of Historic Places. **Pros:** moderately priced; suites with kitchenettes and Murphy beds are a plus for families with kids; three blocks from Union Square. **Cons:** no a/c; cramped standard rooms; can be noisy at night. *Rooms from: $189 701 Post St., Union Sq. 415/673–2600, 800/533–6533 www.beresford.com 95 rooms Breakfast.*

The Cartwright Hotel Union Square

$$ | HOTEL | A relatively inexpensive Union Square–area option (look for online specials), this 1913 Edwardian is part of the Best Western chain's Premier Collection, and it retains a period feel, especially in the tile-floor lobby with fireplace and adjoining wood-paneled bar. **Pros:** good price for a great location; free Wi-Fi; staff that cares. **Cons:** small rooms; small baths; uninspired decor. *Rooms from: $255 524 Sutter St., Union Sq. 415/421–2865, 800/780–7234 www.cartwrightunionsquare.com 114 rooms No meals.*

Chancellor Hotel on Union Square

$$$ | HOTEL | Built to accommodate visitors to the 1915 Panama-Pacific International Exposition, this favorite of budget travelers has cable car views from its modest lobby. **Pros:** free Wi-Fi; good value for Union Square; friendly staff, some of whom have worked here for decades. **Cons:** small bathrooms; noise from cable cars; no a/c (ceiling fans). *Rooms from: $269 433 Powell St., Union Sq. 415/362–2004, 800/428–4748 www.chancellorhotel.com 137 rooms No meals.*

The Clift Royal Sonesta Hotel

$$$ | HOTEL | The entrance to this 1915 classic is so nondescript, you could walk right past without a hint of what's inside—a seriously sexy hotel that attracts hipsters, music-industry types, and celebrities. **Pros:** discreet and helpful staff; surreal interior design; close to public transportation, shopping, and theaters. **Cons:** street noise (book on upper floors to avoid); pricey during major conventions; aesthetic too over-the-top for some guests. *Rooms from: $309 495 Geary St., Union Sq. 415/775–4700 sonesta.com/sanfrancisco 372 rooms No meals.*

★ Cornell Hotel de France

$ | HOTEL | In their six-story, 1910 structure, hosts Claude and Micheline Lambert have created a bit of Paris a few blocks from Union Square, with rooms individually decorated with pastel colors, a stenciled ceiling, and prints of works by Picasso, Chagall, Klimt, and other European artists. **Pros:** a bit of Paris in San Francisco; updated bathrooms; special packages and discounts. **Cons:** several blocks from the center of things; surrounding area mildly dodgy after dark; small lobby. *Rooms from: $149 715 Bush St., Union Sq. 415/421–3154 www.cornellhotel.com 48 rooms Breakfast.*

★ Golden Gate Hotel

$ | B&B/INN | FAMILY | Budget seekers looking for accommodations around Union Square will enjoy this four-story Edwardian with bay windows, an original birdcage elevator, hallways lined with historical photographs, and rooms decorated with antiques, wicker pieces, and Laura Ashley bedding and curtains. **Pros:** friendly staff; spotless rooms; good location if you're a walker. **Cons:** some rooms share a bath; resident cat and dog, so not good for guests with allergies; some rooms on small side. 💲 *Rooms from: $185* ✉ *775 Bush St., Union Sq.* ☎ *415/392–3702, 800/835–1118* 🌐 *www.goldengatehotel.com* *23 rooms* *Breakfast.*

Grand Hyatt San Francisco Union Square
$$$ | HOTEL | FAMILY | Location is the main draw at this hotel, where rooms done in warm autumnal tones, with textured custom furniture, original artwork, and teak beds, are showing their age but still offer high-tech features: windows can be blacked out from your bed, and you can stream from your mobile or other device to a swiveling flat-screen. **Pros:** stellar views from upper floors; good-size workstations; weekend deals. **Cons:** small bathrooms; corporate feel; some rooms dated. 💲 *Rooms from: $289* ✉ *345 Stockton St., Union Sq.* ☎ *415/398–1234* 🌐 *sanfrancisco.grand.hyatt.com* *685 rooms* *No meals.*

Hilton San Francisco Union Square
$$ | HOTEL | This is the largest hotel in California—sometimes the lobby feels like downtown at rush hour—and many rooms in the silvery tower enjoy views that rank among San Francisco's finest. **Pros:** super views; outdoor pool—a rarity in this area; full-service on-site restaurant Urban Tavern. **Cons:** area is dodgy after dark; there can be a wait at check-in; some rooms show wear. 💲 *Rooms from: $239* ✉ *333 O'Farrell St., Union Sq.* ☎ *415/771–1400* 🌐 *www.hiltonsanfranciscohotel.com* *1,919 rooms* *No meals.*

Hotel Abri
$$ | HOTEL | Near Union Square shops, theaters, and restaurants, this appealing hotel has small but tastefully appointed rooms with smart TVs, iPod docking stations, comfortable bedding, and fancy bath products. **Pros:** tasteful rooms; lively on-site Italian restaurant and bar, Puccini & Pinetti; near the Powell Street cable-car turnaround, shops, and eateries. **Cons:** most rooms have showers only; on-street parking nearly impossible; $35 "urban fee" for amenities not all guests require. 💲 *Rooms from: $229* ✉ *127 Ellis St., Union Sq.* ☎ *866/823–4669, 415/392–8800* 🌐 *www.hotel-abri.com* *91 rooms* *No meals.*

Monument to San Francisco

In front of the Grand Hyatt hotel at 345 Stockton Street gurgles an intricate bronze fountain depicting whimsical bas-relief scenes of San Francisco. It's one of many local public works by San Francisco sculptor Ruth Asawa. Look closely at this one and you can find an amorous couple behind one of the Victorian bay windows.

Hotel Adagio
$$ | HOTEL | The Spanish-colonial facade of this 16-story theater-row hotel complements its chic interior, with decent-size rooms in hues of fog, spring grasses, and Merlot grapes. **Pros:** Marriott-run property with boutique-hotel charm; close to theater district on a bus route; good drinks and scene at lobby bar, the Mortimer. **Cons:** street noise; area can be dodgy at night; adjacent to a popular outdoor bar. 💲 *Rooms from: $249* ✉ *550 Geary St., Union Sq.* ☎ *415/775–5000, 800/228–8830* 🌐 *www.hoteladagiosf.com* *171 rooms* *No meals.*

Hotel Beresford
$$ | HOTEL | For many budget travelers the Beresford's pluses—reasonable prices, central location, and sightseeing assistance—outweigh minuses that include the small rooms, outdated decor, and no air-conditioning. **Pros:** reasonably priced; close to Union Square; free Wi-Fi. **Cons:** no a/c; small rooms; traditional decor can be stuffy. 💲 *Rooms from: $165* ✉ *635 Sutter St., Union Sq.* ☎ *415/673–9900,*

800/533–6533 🌐 *www.beresford.com* 🛏 *114 rooms* 🍽 *Breakfast.*

Hotel Bijou

$$ | **HOTEL** | Fresh off a 2018 remodel, this boutique hotel bordering the Tenderloin impresses with gorgeous art-deco styling in touches such as floor-to-ceiling gold-painted steel peacock screens and starburst tile in the lobby. **Pros:** near downtown; helpful staff; beautiful (but pricey) on-site bar/restaurant. **Cons:** borders a dicey neighborhood; small rooms; there are better values in this price range. 💲 *Rooms from: $359* ✉ *111 Mason St., at Eddy St., Union Sq.* ☎ *415/771–1200, 800/771–1022* 🌐 *www.hotelbijou.com* 🛏 *65 rooms* 🍽 *No meals.*

Hotel Diva

$$ | **HOTEL** | Entering this magnet for urbanites craving modern decor requires stepping over footprints, handprints, and autographs embedded in the sidewalk by visiting stars; in the rooms, designer carpets complement mid-century-modern chairs and brushed-steel headboards whose shape mimics that of ocean waves. **Pros:** contemporary design; in the heart of the theater district; accommodating staff. **Cons:** few frills; tiny bathrooms (but equipped with eco-friendly bath products); many rooms are small. 💲 *Rooms from: $209* ✉ *440 Geary St., Union Sq.* ☎ *415/885–0200, 800/553–1900* 🌐 *www.hoteldiva.com* 🛏 *130 rooms* 🍽 *No meals.*

Hotel Emblem

Inspiration is everywhere at intimate Hotel Emblem, refurbished and rebranded in 2019 with a literary theme that celebrates San Francisco's Beat poets, from its lobby wall of books and poetry-laced carpet to in-room libraries and typewriters. **Pros:** fun, creative vibe; excellent Union Square location; amenities available by request include essential oil diffusers, coloring books, and bath bombs. **Cons:** $25 nightly amenity fee ; expensive parking; some rooms on the small side. 💲 *Rooms from: $* ✉ *562 Sutter St., Union Sq.* ☎ *415/433–4434* 🌐 *www.viceroyhotelsandresorts.com/en/emblem* 🛏 *96 rooms* 🍽 *No meals.*

Hotel G

$$$ | **HOTEL** | Both homey and innovative, the Hotel G's tiled lobby floors, large windows, and high ceilings (giving even the smallish standard rooms an airy feel) pay homage to the building's century-plus history, while smart TVs, Bluetooth radios, Nespresso machines, and Wi-Fi keep it firmly in the present. **Pros:** fun design; on-site dining and drinking; great central location. **Cons:** street noise; wooden or concrete flooring can be loud; $30 amenity fee catches some guests off guard. 💲 *Rooms from: $270* ✉ *386 Geary St., Union Sq.* ☎ *877/828–4478* 🌐 *www.hotelgsanfrancisco.com* 🛏 *149 rooms* 🍽 *No meals.*

★ **Hotel Nikko San Francisco**

$$$ | **HOTEL** | **FAMILY** | Known for impeccable service and satin-smooth style, this youngish grande dame takes its visual cues from traditional kimonos and Japanese calligraphy. **Pros:** polished multilingual staff; tastefully designed rooms; large indoor pool. **Cons:** slightly formal vibe doesn't work for some travelers; obligatory $25 fee for fitness center and pool use makes some travelers feel nickel-and-dimed; so-so surrounding neighborhood. 💲 *Rooms from: $299* ✉ *222 Mason St., Union Sq.* ☎ *415/394–1111, 800/248–3308* 🌐 *www.hotelnikkosf.com* 🛏 *532 rooms* 🍽 *No meals.*

Hotel Triton

$$ | **HOTEL** | With a fresh top-to-bottom 2018 redesign and a location at the convergence of Chinatown, the Financial District, and Union Square, this boutique anchor attracts a design-conscious crowd. **Pros:** arty environs; good location; room service from next-door Café de la Presse. **Cons:** rooms and baths are on the small side; hallways feel cramped; $25 obligatory fee for fitness center access, Wi-Fi, and lobby beverages. 💲 *Rooms from: $279* ✉ *342*

Grant Ave., Union Sq. ☎ 415/394–0500, 877/793–9931 🌐 www.hoteltriton.com 🛏 140 rooms 🍴 No meals.

Hotel Union Square

$$ | HOTEL | The design-centric interiors of this hotel erected for the 1915 Panama-Pacific International Exposition evoke art-deco style but feel strictly contemporary. **Pros:** stylish rooms; central location; updated rooms. **Cons:** at 120–170 square feet, Economy Petite rooms are small indeed; street noise can be loud at night; $30 "daily facility fee" for Wi-Fi, wine reception, bottled water in guest rooms. 💲 *Rooms from: $239 ✉ 114 Powell St., Union Sq. ☎ 415/397–3000 🌐 www.hotelunionsquare.com 🛏 131 rooms 🍴 No meals.*

★ **Hotel Zeppelin San Francisco**

$$$ | HOTEL | A frothy homage to 1950s Beat writers, 1960s hippies and rockers, and other local agents of change, the hip Hotel Zeppelin appeals to a youngish crowd with high-tech amenities and an inviting, sometimes boisterous, game room with shuffleboard, Skee-Ball, and other entertainments. **Pros:** plucky design; communal lobby and game room; responsive concierge reachable by text for advice or requests. **Cons:** smallish rooms; some guests find pace too frenetic; service can seem too informal. 💲 *Rooms from: $250 ✉ 545 Post St., Union Sq. ☎ 415/563–0303, 888/539–7510 🌐 www.hotelzeppelin.com 🛏 196 rooms 🍴 No meals.*

The Inn at Union Square

$$$ | B&B/INN | Built in 1922 and smartly renovated in 2017, this six-story inn is strictly 21st century, with amenities that include high-quality bath products, soft robes, free high-speed Wi-Fi, and in-room service tablets. **Pros:** comfortable rooms; lounges with complimentary snacks; chocolates and bottles of water delivered at turndown. **Cons:** some rooms can be noisy; interiors feel stuffy; cramped hallways. 💲 *Rooms from: $309 ✉ 440 Post St., Union Sq. ☎ 800/288–4346 🌐 www.unionsquare.com 🛏 30 rooms 🍴 Breakfast.*

JW Marriott San Francisco Union Square

$$$$ | HOTEL | Bullet elevators whisk guests skyward from the third-floor marble lobby to contemporary guest rooms outfitted with business-oriented clientele in mind. **Pros:** large rooms; luxurious bathrooms; public spaces updated in 2018. **Cons:** lacks character; service is polite but not particularly warm; expensive parking. 💲 *Rooms from: $362 ✉ 500 Post St., Union Sq. ☎ 415/771–8600 🌐 www.jwmarriottunionsquare.com 🛏 344 rooms 🍴 No meals.*

Kensington Park Hotel

$$ | HOTEL | Built in the 1920s in a Moorish and Gothic style, this former Elks Club retains its period feel and features, with rich marble and dark-wood accents, crystal chandeliers, vaulted ceilings, and antique furnishings in the lobby and vintage touches in the comfortable guest rooms. **Pros:** friendly personal service; unbeatable location; period feel. **Cons:** some rooms have street noise; rooms average 220 square feet; bathrooms are small. 💲 *Rooms from: $220 ✉ 450 Post St., Union Sq. ☎ 415/788–6400, 800/553–1900 🌐 www.kensingtonparkhotel.com 🛏 93 rooms 🍴 No meals.*

Kimpton Sir Francis Drake Hotel

$$$ | HOTEL | Beefeater-costumed doormen welcome guests into the ornate high-ceilinged lobby of this 1928 landmark whose rooms are equipped with 21st-century tech amenities but evoke the hotel's heyday with regal headboards and plush white comforters. **Pros:** first-rate Powell Street location; Starlight Room skyline bar and popular drag show; bathrooms updated in 2018. **Cons:** small rooms and baths; slow elevators; dated room decor. 💲 *Rooms from: $299 ✉ 450 Powell St., Union Sq. ☎ 415/392–7755, 800/546–7866 🌐 www.sirfrancisdrake.com 🛏 416 rooms 🍴 No meals.*

King George Hotel

$$ | **HOTEL** | With its compact rooms pleasantly refreshed in 2018 and the addition of the Mason Social Club, a lively, Union Jack–theme bar/living room/game room, the King George has upped its game to match its service and hospitality, points of pride since the hotel's 1914 opening. **Pros:** convenient to Union Square and SoMa; rooms often at a very good rate; updated guest rooms and marble bathrooms. **Cons:** low ceilings in hallways; location on the edge of the Tenderloin unnerves some guests; baths and some closets are minuscule. *Rooms from: $249 334 Mason St., Union Sq. 415/781–5050, 800/288–6005 www.kinggeorge.com 153 rooms No meals.*

The Marker San Francisco

$$ | **HOTEL** | Behind a cheery 1910 Beaux-Arts facade and with public spaces smartly updated in 2018, The Marker delivers a comfortable experience amid the theater district. **Pros:** self-parking option at garage across street; local art in public spaces; on-site Italian bar/restaurant Tratto. **Cons:** close to sketchy Tenderloin neighborhood; some discount-rate rooms very small; bar/restaurant service can be overly casual. *Rooms from: $229 501 Geary St., Union Sq. 415/292–0100, 844/736–2753 www.jdvhotels.com/the-marker-san-francisco 208 rooms No meals.*

Mystic Hotel

$$$ | **HOTEL** | Chef-hotelier Charlie Palmer serves up art and style at this historic property that survived the 1906 earthquake. **Pros:** online specials especially off-season; historic property; artsy decor. **Cons:** smallish rooms (but large suites have soaking tubs); city noise; no a/c and poor air circulation. *Rooms from: $279 417 Stockton St., Union Sq. 415/400–0500 www.mystichotel.com 82 rooms Breakfast.*

★ Orchard Garden Hotel

$$ | **HOTEL** | Feel virtuous and eco-friendly while enjoying a junior terrace room with private outdoor space and views of downtown at this service-oriented boutique hotel close to the Financial District and Chinatown. **Pros:** close to the Financial District and Chinatown; rooftop deck with sweeping city views; capable service. **Cons:** pricey during high season; lacks character of older establishments; minimalist aesthetic won't appeal to all travelers. *Rooms from: $235 466 Bush St., Union Sq. 415/399–9807 www.theorchardgardenhotel.com 86 rooms No meals.*

Orchard Hotel

$$$ | **HOTEL** | Unlike many of the area's other boutique hotels that occupy century-old buildings, the Orchard was built in 2000—though the marble lobby, with dramatic architectural embellishments like arched openings, vaulted ceilings, and stone floors, evokes another era. **Pros:** cutting-edge technology; sizable rooms; green pedigree. **Cons:** can be pricey (but look for deals on hotel website); uphill from Union Square; area outside hotel safe but a tad grungy. *Rooms from: $289 665 Bush St., Union Sq. 415/362–8878, 888/717–2881 www.theorchardhotel.com 113 rooms No meals.*

Parc 55 San Francisco, a Hilton Hotel

$$$ | **HOTEL** | One of the largest hotels in town, the Parc 55 brims with activity, but its size is by no means overwhelming. **Pros:** close to public transportation, shops, and restaurants; guests can access amenities, including rooftop pool, at adjacent Hilton; Michelin-starred Thai restaurant. **Cons:** the immediate area can be seedy at night; panhandlers abound; street parking is a challenge. *Rooms from: $250 55 Cyril Magnin St., near 5th and Market Sts., Union Sq. 415/392–8000 www.parc55hotel.com 1,078 rooms No meals.*

Petite Auberge

$$$ | **B&B/INN** | The provincial room decor of Petite Auberge—bright flowered wallpaper and an armoire that compensates for little or no closet space—pleases Francophiles seeking Old World charm. **Pros:** old-world charm; complimentary evening wine and hors d'oeuvres and breakfast buffet; personalized service. **Cons:** guests staying front of house complain of street noise; a bit of a climb from Union Square; limited amenities. *Rooms from: $299 ✉ 863 Bush St., Union Sq. ☎ 415/928–6000, 800/365–3004 🌐 www.petiteaubergesf.com 26 rooms 🍴 Breakfast.*

San Francisco Marriott Union Square

$$ | **HOTEL** | Business travelers appreciate the 30-floor Marriott's attention to their needs with easily accessible plugs, movable desks, ergonomic chairs, and laptop connectors to flat-screen TVs—and its prime location near shopping, restaurants, nightspots, and public transportation. **Pros:** convenient location; in-room pull-out sofas and roll-away bed options a plus for families with children; generally solid service. **Cons:** noisy street; lacking in atmosphere; not worth it if not on sale. *Rooms from: $229 ✉ 480 Sutter St., Union Sq. ☎ 415/398–8900, 866/912–0973 🌐 www.marriott.com/hotels/travel/sfous 500 rooms 🍴 No meals.*

★ **Staypineapple San Francisco**

$$ | **HOTEL** | Three blocks west of Union Square and loaded with high- and low-tech amenities, this Pineapple Hospitality boutique property delivers value in a stylish package, starting with the lobby's paintings and sculptures and the giant black-and-white paintings above the adjacent bar. **Pros:** bright-yellow decor; loaded with amenities and extras like loaner bikes and afternoon pineapple cupcakes; fun vibe. **Cons:** many rooms are small; some visitors find hotel's neighborhood intimidating after dark; $30 amenity fee to cover Wi-Fi and "extras." *Rooms from: $239 ✉ 580 Geary St., Union Sq. ☎ 415/441–2700, 800/227–4223 🌐 www.staypineapple.com/union-square-san-francisco 93 rooms 🍴 No meals.*

Taj Campton Place San Francisco

$$$$ | **HOTEL** | Beauty and highly attentive service remain the hallmarks of this top-tier hotel, whose rooms are elegantly decorated in a contemporary Italian style, with sandy earth tones and handsome pearwood paneling and cabinetry. **Pros:** discreet, attentive service; Michelin-starred French-influenced Cal-Indian restaurant ; abundant natural light. **Cons:** pricey (but worth it); smallest rooms 250 square feet; $30 obligatory resort fee a surprising annoyance to many guests. *Rooms from: $425 ✉ 340 Stockton St., Union Sq. ☎ 415/781–5555, 866/332–1670 🌐 www.tajcamptonplace.com 110 rooms 🍴 No meals.*

Villa Florence

$$$ | **HOTEL** | A stylish refuge amid the Powell Street whirlwind, this boutique hotel welcomes guests to rooms that feel comfortable, upbeat, and expansive—gray and white predominate, with magenta accents and gold-veined mirrors. **Pros:** easy access to shopping, theater, and public transportation; business meeting room named for Machiavelli (imagine the possibilities); stylish rooms updated in 2017. **Cons:** excess fees for amenities; noise from cable cars; crowded street. *Rooms from: $269 ✉ 225 Powell St., Union Sq. ☎ 415/397–7700, 877/564–2086 for reservations 🌐 www.villaflorence.com 189 rooms 🍴 No meals.*

Warwick San Francisco

$$ | **HOTEL** | The handsome, if small, rooms at this 1913 theater district hotel evoke an aristocratic feel with geometric wallpaper, black-and-white framed historic photos curated by the San Francisco Public Library, and ornate wooden furnishings. **Pros:** artsy rooms with historic photos; gorgeously appointed on-site cocktail bar and paella restaurant well above par for a hotel; good online rates.

Cons: older property with thin walls; small rooms; some guests complain of street noise. *Rooms from: $237* *490 Geary St., Union Sq.* *415/928–7900* *warwickhotels.com/san-francisco* *74 rooms* *No meals.*

Westin St. Francis

$$$$ | **HOTEL** | The survivor of two major earthquakes, some headline-grabbing scandals, and even an attempted presidential assassination, this richly appointed and superbly located grande dame dating to 1904 is comprised of the landmark building, renovated in 2018, and a modern 32-story tower whose glass elevators reveal Union Square views from the upper floors. **Pros:** prime Union Square location; great views from some rooms; Chateau Montelena wine-tasting room. **Cons:** rooms in original building can be small; public spaces lack the panache of days gone by; no dinner at on-site Oak Room Restaurant. *Rooms from: $356* *335 Powell St., Union Sq.* *415/397–7000, 800/917–7458* *www.westinstfrancis.com* *1,195 rooms* *No meals.*

White Swan Inn

$$$ | **B&B/INN** | A cozy library with a crackling fireplace and comfortable chairs and sofas is the heart of this inviting English-style bed-and-breakfast, a sister property to the French-style Petite Auberge next door. **Pros:** cozy antidote to nearby chain hotels; nice lounge and patio area; caring staff members. **Cons:** thin walls can make for noisy rooms; nearby streets can feel gritty at night; some rooms in need of an update. *Rooms from: $288* *845 Bush St., Union Sq.* *415/775–1755, 800/999–9570* *www.whiteswaninnsf.com* *26 rooms* *Breakfast.*

Nightlife

Known mostly for high-end shopping and the surrounding theater district, the square has its own share of nightlife. You'll find places pouring interesting cocktails, a good mix of locals and tourists, and nods to nightspots and eras past.

BARS

Harry Denton's Starlight Room

BARS/PUBS | Forget low-key drinks—the only way to experience Harry Denton's is to cough up the cover charge and enjoy the opulent, over-the-top decor. Red velvet booths and romantic lighting help re-create the 1950s high life on the 21st floor of the Sir Francis Drake Hotel. Sunday brunch brings a popular drag show, and the small dance floor is packed on Friday and Saturday nights. Jackets are preferred for men. *Sir Francis Drake Hotel, 450 Powell St., between Post and Sutter Sts., Union Sq.* *415/395–8595* *starlightroomsf.com.*

Le Colonial

BARS/PUBS | Down an easy-to-miss alley off Taylor Street is what appears to be a two-story plantation house in the center of the city. Without being kitschy, the top-floor bar successfully evokes French-colonial Vietnam, thanks to creaky wooden floors, Victorian sofas, a patio with potted palms, and tasty French-Vietnamese food and tropical cocktails. You'll find local jazz bands playing early in the week, but come the weekend this is a full-on DJ-driven dance party. *20 Cosmo Pl., off Taylor St., between Post and Sutter Sts., Union Sq.* *415/931–3600* *www.lecolonialsf.com.*

Pacific Cocktail Haven

BARS/PUBS | PCH for short, this neighborhood hangout with a convivial aura and industrial-chic decor hits all the right notes. Plus the well-chosen and unique ingredients mean there's a little something for everyone, and the glassware is as dazzling as the elixirs inside. **TIP→ The must-try cocktail is the Oh Snap!, a concoction of gin, sugar snap peas, citrus, and absinthe.** *580 Sutter St., at Mason St., Union Sq.* *415/398–0195* *pacificcocktailsf.com* *Closed Sun.*

Redwood Room

BARS/PUBS | Opened in 1933 and updated by designer Philippe Starck in 2001, this lounge at the Clift Hotel is a San Francisco icon. The entire room is paneled with the wood from a single redwood tree, giving the place a rich, monochromatic look. The gorgeous original art-deco sconces and chandeliers still hang, but bizarre video installations on plasma screens also adorn the walls. Young scenesters swarm in on the weekends; for maximum glamour, visit on a weeknight. ✉ *Clift Hotel, 495 Geary St., at Taylor St., Union Sq.* ☎ *415/929–2372 for table reservations, 415/775–4700 for hotel* 🌐 *www.clifthotel.com.*

Performing Arts

THEATER

American Conservatory Theater

THEATER | One of the nation's leading regional theater companies presents about eight plays a year, from classics to contemporary works, often in repertory. The season runs from early fall to late spring. In December ACT stages a beloved version of Charles Dickens's *A Christmas Carol.* ✉ *415 Geary St., Union Sq.* ☎ *415/749–2228* 🌐 *www.act-sf.org.*

Curran Theater

THEATER | Fresh from a makeover, some of the biggest touring shows come to this local gem, which has hosted classical music, dance, and stage performances since its 1925 opening. Shows are of the long-running Broadway musical variety, such as *Stomp* and *The Book of Mormon,* and the seasonal *A Christmas Carol.* ✉ *445 Geary St., at Mason St., Union Sq.* ☎ *415/358–1220* 🌐 *www.sfcurran.com.*

EXIT Theatre

THEATER | *The* place for absurdist and experimental theater, this three-stage black-box venue also presents the annual **Fringe Festival** in September. ✉ *156 Eddy St., between Mason and Taylor Sts., Tenderloin* 🌐 *www.theexit.org.*

Shopping

Serious shoppers head straight to Union Square, San Francisco's main shopping area and the site of most of its department stores, including Macy's, Neiman Marcus, Barneys, and Saks Fifth Avenue. Nearby are such platinum-card international boutiques as Yves Saint Laurent, Cartier, Emporio Armani, Gucci, Hermès, and Louis Vuitton.

The **Westfield San Francisco Centre,** anchored by Bloomingdale's and Nordstrom, is notable for its gorgeous atriums and top-notch dining options.

■ TIP→ Most retailers in the square don't open until 10 am or later, so there isn't much advantage to getting an early start unless you're grabbing breakfast nearby. If you're on the prowl for art, be aware that many galleries are closed on Sunday and Monday.

ART GALLERIES

Hang Art

ART GALLERIES | A spirit of fun imbues this inviting space that showcases local and emerging artists. Prices range from a few hundred dollars to several thousand, making it an ideal place for novice collectors to get their feet wet. ✉ *567 Sutter St., 2nd fl., near Mason St., Union Sq.* ☎ *415/434–4264* 🌐 *www.hangart.com.*

Hespe Gallery

ART GALLERIES | Priced between $3,000 and $50,000, the paintings and sculptures here by mid-career artists, many of them Californians, are primarily representational. Owner Charles Hespe is an instantly likable art enthusiast who delights buyers and browsers. ✉ *251 Post St., Suite 420, between Stockton St. and Grant Ave., Union Sq.* ☎ *415/776–5918* 🌐 *www.hespe.com.*

CLOTHING

Cable Car Clothiers

CLOTHING | This classic British menswear store, open since 1939, is so fully stocked that a whole room is dedicated to hats, pants are cataloged like papers in file cabinets, and entire displays showcase badger-bristle shaving brushes. **■ TIP→ The cable-car logo gear, from silk ties to pewter banks, makes for dashing souvenirs.** ✉ *110 Sutter St., Suite 108, Union Sq.* ☎ *415/397–4740* 🌐 *www.cablecarclothiers.com.*

★ Levi's

CLOTHING | A San Francisco icon, founded in 1853, Levi's offers every style, size, color, and cut of 501s at its massive flagship store. You can even get a custom fitting if you book ahead of time. ✉ *815 Market St., at 4th St., Union Sq.* ☎ *415/501–0100* 🌐 *www.levi.com.*

★ Margaret O'Leary

CLOTHING | If you can only buy one piece of clothing in San Francisco, make it a hand-loomed cashmere sweater by this Irish-born local legend. The perfect antidote to the city's wind and fog, the sweaters are so beloved by San Franciscans that some of them never wear anything else. Pick up an airplane wrap for your trip home. Another store is in Pacific Heights, at 2400 Fillmore Street. ✉ *1 Claude La., at Sutter St., just west of Kearny St., Union Sq.* ☎ *415/391–1010* 🌐 *www.margaretoleary.com.*

ELECTRONICS

Apple Store San Francisco

CAMERAS/ELECTRONICS | Apple's flagship San Francisco store is a two-level open-aired tech temple to Macs and the people who use them. Play with iPhones, laptops, and hundreds of geeky accessories, then watch a theater presentation or attend an educational workshop. ✉ *300 Post St., at Stockton St., Union Sq.* ☎ *415/486–4800* 🌐 *www.apple.com.*

Top Local Shops

Apple Store San Francisco. The company's flagship store has all the latest products.

Britex Fabrics. Pilgrimage-worthy fabric store adored by creative types.

Levi's. San Francisco is the home to Levi's, easily the most well-known brand of jeans which has been in operation since 1853.

Margaret O'Leary. Knitwear like no other; it'll last for decades.

Vital Tea Leaf. For an authentic Chinese tea-drinking experience.

FURNITURE, HOUSEWARES, AND GIFTS

Samuel Scheuer

GIFTS/SOUVENIRS | A San Francisco staple since the 1930s, this decadent shop draws designers and other fans for its luxurious bed and bath items and linens. The pretty tablecloths, runners, napkins, fragrant candles, and luxurious bath accessories are popular gifts. *340 Sutter St., between Grant Ave. and Stockton St., Union Sq.* ☎ *415/392–2813* 🌐 *www.scheuerlinens.com.*

Williams-Sonoma

HOUSEHOLD ITEMS/FURNITURE | Behind striped awnings and a historical facade lies the massive mother ship of the Sonoma-founded kitchen-store empire. La Cornue custom stoves beckon you inward, and two grand staircases draw you upward to the world of dinnerware, linens, and chefs' tools. Antique tart tins, eggbeaters, and pastry cutters from the personal collection of founder Chuck Williams line the walls. ✉ *340 Post St., between Powell and Stockton*

Sts., Union Sq. ☎ 415/362–9450 ⊕ www.williams-sonoma.com.

HANDICRAFTS

★ Britex Fabrics

TEXTILES/SEWING | Walls of Italian wool in deep rich colors, yards of Faille striped silk, and neat stacks of fresh cotton prints await your creative touch. A San Francisco institution for more than 60 years, the two-story Britex also sells more than 75,000 varieties of buttons as well as thread and trim. If sewing is your thing, this will be a visit to paradise. ✉ *117 Post St., between Grant Ave. and Stockton St., Union Sq.* ☎ *415/392–2910* ⊕ *www.britexfabrics.com.*

JEWELRY

Shreve & Co.

JEWELRY/ACCESSORIES | Along with gems in dazzling settings, San Francisco's oldest retail store—it's been in business since 1852—carries watches by Jaeger-LeCoultre and others. On weekends well-heeled couples scope out hefty diamond engagement rings. ✉ *150 Post St., at Grant Ave., Union Sq.* ☎ *415/421–2600* ⊕ *www.shreve.com.*

Chinatown

A few blocks uphill from Union Square is the abrupt beginning of dense and insular Chinatown—the oldest such community in the country. When the street signs have Chinese characters, produce stalls crowd pedestrians off the sidewalk, and whole roast ducks hang in deli windows, you'll know you've arrived. (The neighborhood huddles together in the 17 blocks and 41 alleys bordered roughly by Bush, Kearny, and Powell Streets and Broadway.) Chinatown has been attracting the curious for more than 100 years, and no other neighborhood in the city absorbs as many tourists without seeming to forfeit its character. Join the flow and step into another world. Good-luck banners of crimson and gold hang beside dragon-entwined lampposts and pagoda roofs, while honking cars chime in with shoppers bargaining loudly in Cantonese or Mandarin.

Sights

Chinatown Gate

BUILDING | This is the official entrance to Chinatown. Stone lions flank the base of the pagoda-topped gate; the lions, dragons, and fish up top symbolize wealth, prosperity, and other good things. The four Chinese characters immediately beneath the pagoda represent the philosophy of Sun Yat-sen (1866–1925), the leader who unified China in the early 20th century. Sun Yat-sen, who lived in exile in San Francisco for a few years, promoted the notion of friendship and peace among all nations based on equality, justice, and goodwill. The vertical characters under the left pagoda read "peace" and "trust," the ones under the right pagoda "respect" and "love." The whole shebang telegraphs the internationally understood message of "photo op." Immediately beyond the gate, dive into souvenir shopping on Grant Avenue, Chinatown's tourist strip. ✉ *Grant Ave. at Bush St., Chinatown.*

Chinese Culture Center

ARTS VENUE | Chiefly a place for the community to gather for calligraphy and tai chi workshops, the center operates a gallery with interesting temporary exhibits by Chinese and Chinese-American artists. Excellent political, historical, and food-focused walking tours of Chinatown depart from the gallery; call the center or visit its website for details. ✉ *Hilton Hotel, 750 Kearny St., 3rd fl., Chinatown* ☎ *415/986–1822* ⊕ *www.cccsf.us* 🎫 *Center and gallery free (donations suggested), tour $40* ⏲ *Closed Sun.*

Golden Gate Fortune Cookie Factory

FACTORY | **FAMILY** | Follow your nose down Ross Alley to this tiny but fragrant cookie factory. Two workers sit at circular

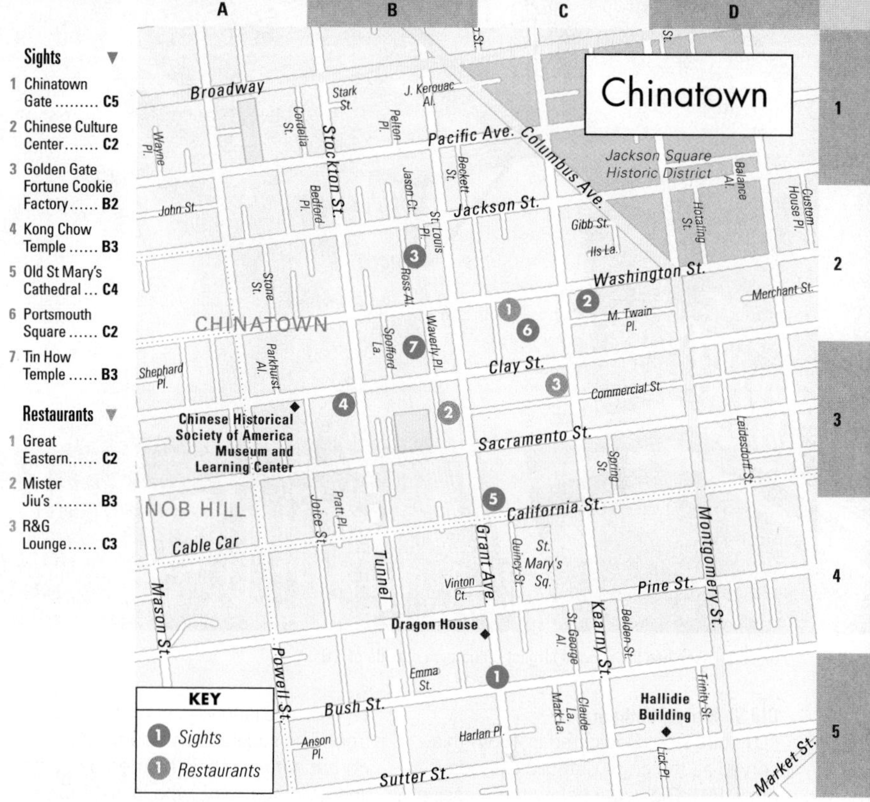

motorized griddles and wait for dollops of batter to drop onto a tiny metal plate, which rotates into an oven. A few moments later out comes a cookie that's pliable and ready for folding. It's easy to peek in for a moment, and hard to leave without a few free samples. A bagful of cookies—with mildly racy "adult" fortunes or more benign ones—costs less than $5. ✉ *56 Ross Alley, between Washington and Jackson Sts., west of Grant Ave., Chinatown* ☎ *415/781–3956* 🎫 *Free.*

Kong Chow Temple

RELIGIOUS SITE | This ornate temple sets a somber, spiritual tone right away with a sign warning visitors not to touch *anything*. The god to whom the members of this temple pray represents honesty and trust. Chinese stores and restaurants often display his image because he's thought to bring good luck in business. Chinese immigrants established the temple in 1851; its congregation moved to this building in 1977. Take the elevator up to the fourth floor, where incense fills the air. You can show respect by placing a dollar or two in the donation box and by leaving your phone stowed. Amid the statuary, flowers, and richly colored altars (red wards off evil spirits and signifies virility, green symbolizes longevity, and gold connotes majesty), a couple of plaques announce that "Mrs. Harry S. Truman came to this temple in June 1948 for a prediction on the outcome of the election ... this fortune came true." **■ TIP→ The temple's balcony has a good view of Chinatown.** ✉ *855 Stockton St., 4th fl., Chinatown* ☎ *415/788–1339* 🎫 *Free.*

San Francisco has the second largest Chinatown outside of Asia.

Old St. Mary's Cathedral

RELIGIOUS SITE | Dedicated in 1854, this served as the city's Catholic cathedral until 1891. The verse below the massive clock face beseeched naughty Barbary Coast boys: "Son, observe the time and fly from evil." Across the street from the church in **St. Mary's Square,** a statue of Sun Yat-sen towers over the site of the Chinese leader's favorite reading spot during his years in San Francisco. **TIP→ A surprisingly peaceful spot, St. Mary's Square also has a couple of small, well-kept playgrounds, perfect for a break from the hustle and bustle of Chinatown.** ✉ *660 California St., at Grant Ave., Chinatown* 🌐 *oldsaintmarys.org.*

Portsmouth Square

PLAZA | Chinatown's living room buzzes with activity. The square, with its pagoda-shape structures, is a favorite spot for morning tai chi; by noon dozens of men huddle around Chinese chess tables, engaged in competition. Kids scamper about the square's two grungy playgrounds. Back in the late 19th century this land was near the waterfront. The square is named for the USS *Portsmouth,* the ship helmed by Captain John Montgomery, who in 1846 raised the American flag here and claimed the then-Mexican land for the United States. A couple of years later, Sam Brannan kicked off the gold rush at the square when he waved his loot and proclaimed, "Gold from the American River!" Robert Louis Stevenson, the author of *Treasure Island,* often dropped by, chatting up the sailors who hung out here. Some of the information he gleaned about life at sea found its way into his fiction. A bronze galleon sculpture, a tribute to Stevenson, anchors the square's northwest corner. A plaque marks the site of California's first public school, built in 1847. ✉ *Bordered by Walter Lum Pl. and Kearny, Washington, and Clay Sts., Chinatown.*

★ Tin How Temple

RELIGIOUS SITE | Duck into the inconspicuous doorway, climb three flights of stairs, and be assaulted by the aroma of incense in this tiny, altar-filled room.

Continued on page 87

CHINATOWN

Chinatown's streets flood the senses. Incense and cigarette smoke mingle with the scents of briny fish and sweet vanilla. Rooflines flare outward, pagoda-style. Loud Cantonese bargaining and honking car horns rise above the sharp clack of mah-jongg tiles and the eternally humming cables beneath the street.

Most Chinatown visitors march down Grant Avenue, buy a few trinkets, and call it a day. Do yourself a favor and dig deeper. This is one of the largest Chinese communities outside Asia, and there is far more to it than buying a back-scratcher near Chinatown Gate. To get a real feel for the neighborhood, wander off the main drag. Step into a temple or an herb shop and wander down a flag-draped alley. And don't be shy: residents welcome guests warmly, though rarely in English.

Whatever you do, don't leave without eating something. Noodle houses, bakeries, tea houses, and dim sum shops seem to occupy every other storefront. There's a feast for your eyes as well: in the market windows on Stockton and Grant, you'll see hanging whole roast ducks, fish, and shellfish swimming in tanks, and strips of shiny, pink-glazed Chinese-style barbecued pork.

CHINATOWN'S HISTORY

Sam Brannan's 1848 cry of "Gold!" didn't take long to reach across the world to China. Struggling with famine, drought, and political upheaval at home, thousands of Chinese jumped at the chance to try their luck in California. Most came from the Pearl River Delta region, in the Guangdong province, and spoke Cantonese dialects. From the start, Chinese businesses circled around Portsmouth Square, which was conveniently central. Bachelor rooming houses sprang up, since the vast majority of new arrivals were men. By 1853, the area was called Chinatown.

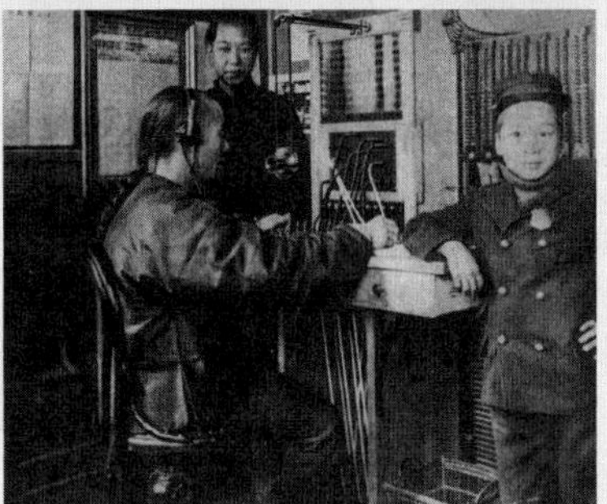

The Street of Gamblers (Ross Alley), 1898 (top). The first Chinese telephone operator in Chinatown (bottom).

COLD WELCOME

The Chinese faced discrimination from the get-go. Harrassment became outright hostility as first the gold rush, then the work on the Transcontinental Railroad petered out. Special taxes were imposed to shoulder aside competing "coolie labor." Laws forbidding the Chinese from moving outside Chinatown kept the residents packed in like sardines, with nowhere to go but up and down—thus the many basement establishments in the neighborhood. State and federal laws passed in the 1870s deterred Chinese women from immigrating, deeming them prostitutes. In the late 1870s, looting and arson attacks on Chinatown businesses soared.

The coup de grace, though, was the Chinese Exclusion Act, passed by the U.S. Congress in 1882, which slammed the doors to America for "Asiatics." This was

Chinatown's Grant Avenue.

Women and children flooded into the neighborhood after the Great Quake.

the country's first significant restriction on immigration. The law also prevented the existing Chinese residents, including American-born children, from becoming naturalized citizens. With a society of mostly men (forbidden, of course, from marrying white women), San Francisco hoped that Chinatown would simply die out.

OUT OF THE ASHES

When the devastating 1906 earthquake and fire hit, city fathers thought they'd seize the opportunity to kick the Chinese out of Chinatown and get their hands on that desirable piece of downtown real estate. Then Chinatown businessman Look Tin Eli had a brainstorm of Disneyesque proportions.

He proposed that Chinatown be rebuilt, but in a tourist-friendly, stylized, "Oriental" way. Anglo-American architects would design new buildings with pagoda roofs and dragon-covered columns. Chinatown would attract more tourists—the curious had been visiting on the sly for decades—and add more tax money to the city's coffers. Ka-ching: the sales pitch worked.

PAPER SONS

For the Chinese, the 1906 earthquake turned the virtual "no entry" sign into a flashing neon "welcome!" All the city's immigration records went up in smoke, and the Chinese quickly began to apply for passports as U.S. citizens, claiming their old ones were lost in the fire. Not only did thousands of Chinese become legal overnight, but so did their sons in China, or "sons," if they weren't really related. Whole families in Chinatown had passports in names that weren't their own; these "paper sons" were not only a windfall but also an uncomfortable neighborhood conspiracy. The city caught on eventually and set up an immigration center on Angel Island in 1910. Immigrants spent weeks or months being inspected and interrogated while their papers were checked. Roughly 250,000 people made it through. With this influx, including women and children, Chinatown finally became a more complete community.

A GREAT WALK THROUGH CHINATOWN

■ Start at the Chinatown Gate and walk ahead on Grant Avenue, entering the souvenir gauntlet. (You'll also pass Old St. Mary's Cathedral.)

■ Make a right on Clay Street and walk to Portsmouth Square. Sometimes it feels like the whole neighborhood's here, playing chess and exercising.

■ Head up Washington Street to the Old Chinese Telephone Exchange building, now the EastWest Bank. Across Grant, look left for Waverly Place. Here Free Republic of China (Taiwanese) flags flap over some of the neighborhood's most striking buildings, including Tin How Temple.

■ At the Sacramento Street end of Waverly Place stands the First Chinese Baptist Church of 1908. Just across the way, the Clarion Music Center is full of unusual instruments, as well as exquisite lion-dance sets.

■ Head back to Washington Street and check out the many herb shops.

■ Follow the scent of vanilla down Ross Alley (entrance across from Superior Trading Company) to the Golden Gate Fortune Cookie Factory. Then head across the alley to Sam Bo Trading Co., where religious items are stacked in the narrow space. Tell the owners your troubles and they'll prepare a package of joss papers, joss sticks, and candles, and tell you how and when to offer them up.

■ Turn left on Jackson Street; ahead is the real Chinatown's main artery, Stockton Street, where most residents do their grocery shopping. Vegetarians will want to avoid Luen Fat Market (No. 1135), with tanks of live frogs, turtles, and lobster as well as chickens and ducks. Look toward the back of stores for Buddhist altars with offerings of oranges and grapefruit. From here you can loop one block east back to Grant.

In 1852, Day Ju, one of the first three Chinese to arrive in San Francisco, dedicated this temple to the Queen of the Heavens and the Goddess of the Seven Seas, and the temple looks largely the same today as it did more than a century ago. In the entryway, elderly ladies can often be seen preparing "money" to be burned as offerings to various Buddhist gods or as funds for ancestors to use in the afterlife. Hundreds of red-and-gold lanterns cover the ceiling; the larger the lamp, the larger its donor's contribution to the temple. Gifts of oranges, dim sum, and money left by the faithful, who kneel mumbling prayers, rest on altars to different gods. Tin How presides over the middle back of the temple, flanked by one red and one green lesser god. Take a good look around, since taking photographs is not allowed. ✉ *125 Waverly Pl., between Clay and Washington Sts., Chinatown* 🎫 *Free, donations accepted.*

Old Chinese Telephone Exchange

In a time when we rely on our smartphones to remember numbers for us, it's wild that the workers at the Old Chinese Telephone Exchange (743 Washington Street) were required to memorize each subscriber's name. Per the San Francisco Chamber of Commerce in 1914: "These girls respond to calls that are given (in English or one of five Chinese dialects) by the name of the subscriber instead of by his number—a mental feat that would be impossible for most high-schooled American misses."

Restaurants

Once you step beneath the gateway on Grant Avenue and meander the alleyways, into the restaurants and bakeries along Jackson, Clay, and Washington Streets, you might be surprised at what you'll find. A food market, along Stockton, is a riot of exotic fruits, vegetables, and other delicacies. Restaurants feature the cuisine of (mostly) China's Guangdong Province, or Cantonese style. A lot of the Chinese, though, have moved out and into the Richmond and Sunset neighborhoods. This is a trek from downtown, set against the breakers and not the bay, but if you want the real deal, venture there. Not far from Chinatown is also Little Saigon, in the Tenderloin—many restaurants are run by ethnic Chinese who emigrated from Vietnam.

Great Eastern

$$ | CHINESE | FAMILY | Dine here for fresh, simply prepared Cantonese-style cuisine, especially the seafood—it hails from tanks that occupy a corner of the street-level main dining room—as well as kid favorites such as stir-fried noodles, cashew chicken, and fried rice. The dim sum starts at 10 am, but there aren't any carts—you order off a paper sheet, and the dumplings come out of the kitchen piping hot. **Known for:** fresh-from-the-tank seafood; Cantonese food; dim sum. 💲 *Average main: $22* ✉ *649 Jackson St., Chinatown* ☎ *415/986–2500* 🌐 *www.greateasternsf.com.*

Mister Jiu's

$$$ | CHINESE | Brandon Jew's ambitious, graceful restaurant offers the chef's contemporary, farm-to-table interpretation of Chinese cuisine, including options such as hot-and-sour soup garnished with nasturtiums and pot stickers made with Swiss chard and local chicken. The elegant dining room—accented with plants and a chrysanthemum chandelier—provides beautiful views of Chinatown, while the menu breathes new life into it. **Known for:** modern Chinese food; cocktails; one Michelin star. 💲 *Average* *main: $36* ✉ *28 Waverly Pl., Chinatown* ☎ *415/857–9688* 🌐 *www.misterjius.com* ⏲ *Closed Sun. and Mon. No lunch.*

R&G Lounge

$$ | CHINESE | FAMILY | Salt-and-pepper Dungeness crab is a delicious draw at this bright, three-level Cantonese eatery that draws a packed crowd for its crustacean specialties—crab portions are easily splittable by three—and dim sum. A menu with photographs will help you sort through other HK specialties, including Peking duck and shrimp-stuffed bean curd, and much of the seafood is fresh from the tank. **Known for:** fresh-from-the-tank crab; Cantonese specialties; extensive menu. [$] *Average main: $20* ✉ *631 Kearny St., Chinatown* ☎ *415/982–7877* 🌐 *www.rnglounge.com.*

The intersection of Grant Avenue and Bush Street marks the gateway to Chinatown. The area's 24 blocks of shops, restaurants, and markets are a nonstop tide of activity. Dominating the exotic cityscape are the sights and smells of food: crates of bok choy, tanks of live crabs, cages of live partridges, and hanging whole chickens. Racks of Chinese silks, colorful pottery, baskets, and carved figurines are displayed chockablock on the sidewalks, alongside fragrant herb shops where your bill might be tallied on an abacus. And if you need to knock off souvenir shopping for the kids and coworkers in your life, the dense and multiple selections of toys, T-shirts, mugs, magnets, decorative boxes, and countless other trinkets make it a quick, easy, and inexpensive proposition.

ANTIQUES

Dragon House

STORE/MALL | A veritable museum, the store sells authentic, centuries-old antiques like ivory carvings and jade figures (including a naughty statue or two). ✉ *455 Grant Ave., Chinatown* ☎ *415/421–3693.*

CLOTHING

Old Shanghai

STORE/MALL | Hand-painted robes, formal dresses, and jackets are sold here, along with chic Asian-inspired gifts and smaller items that make great souvenirs. ✉ *645 Grant Ave., Chinatown* ☎ *415/986–1222* 🌐 *www.oldshanghaionline.com.*

FOOD AND DRINK

★ **Vital Tea Leaf**

FOOD/CANDY | Tea enthusiasts will feel at peace in this bright, spacious, hardwood-floor haven for sipping. You'll find more than 400 different varieties of tea here, and the staff is extremely knowledgeable on the health benefits of each and every one. ✉ *1044 Grant Ave., between Jackson St. and Pacific Ave., Chinatown* ☎ *415/981–2388* 🌐 *www.vitaltealeaf.net.*

FURNITURE, HOUSEWARES, AND GIFTS

The Wok Shop

HOUSEHOLD ITEMS/FURNITURE | The store carries woks, of course, but also anything else you could need for Chinese cooking—bamboo steamers, ginger graters, wicked-looking cleavers—plus accessories for Japanese cooking, including sushi paraphernalia and tempura racks. ✉ *718 Grant Ave., at Sacramento St., Chinatown* ☎ *415/989–3797* 🌐 *www.wokshop.com.*

Chapter 4

SOMA AND CIVIC CENTER

Updated by
Andrea Powell

Sights	Restaurants	Hotels	Shopping	Nightlife
★★★☆☆	★★★☆☆	★★★★☆	★☆☆☆☆	★★★★☆

NEIGHBORHOOD SNAPSHOT

GETTING THERE

For most SoMa visitors who stick close to the area around Yerba Buena Gardens and the Moscone Center, getting here is a matter of walking roughly 10 minutes from Union Square, less from Market Street transit.

It's best to reach the Civic Center by Muni light rail, bus, or F-line. Hoofing it from Union Square takes you through the occasionally seedy Tenderloin neighborhood, and is a bit of a trek.

After dark, it's best to take a cab or other ride service for both of these neighborhoods.

TOP REASONS TO GO

■ **SFMOMA:** Explore the vast trove of modern masterpieces at this recently expanded museum, one of the 'largest in the country dedicated to modern art.

■ **Asian Art Museum:** Stand face-to-face with a massive gold Buddha in one of the world's largest collections of Asian art.

■ **Club-hopping in SoMa:** Shake it with the cool, friendly crowd that fills SoMa's dance clubs until the wee hours, and all weekend long at the EndUp.

■ **Yerba Buena Gardens:** Gather picnic provisions and choose a spot on the grass in downtown's oasis.

■ **Hanging out at Patricia's Green:** Grab a cup of coffee or an ice cream—Blue Bottle and Smitten Ice Cream are just around the corner—and head to the narrow swath of park that serves as hopping Hayes Valley's living room.

■ **SFJAZZ:** Experience the amazing acoustics at Hayes Valley's intimate temple to jazz.

PLANNING YOUR TIME

■ You could spend all day museum-hopping in SoMa. Allow at least two hours for gigantic SFMOMA. An hour each should do it for the Museum of the African Diaspora, the Contemporary Jewish Museum, and the Yerba Buena Center for the Arts, a little less than that for the smaller museums.

■ SoMa after dark is another adventure entirely. More interested in Merlot or megaclubs than Matisse? Start here around 8 pm for dinner, then move on to a bar or dance spot. *See Where to Eat and Nightlife for our top recommendations.*

■ Plan on spending at least two hours at the Asian Art Museum and no more than a half hour at City Hall. Except for these two mainstays, you'll have little reason to visit the Civic Center area unless you have tickets to the opera, symphony, or other cultural event. Hayes Valley and its shops and boutiques merit a leisurely one-hour look-see.

To a newcomer, SoMa (short for "south of Market") and the Civic Center may look like cheek-by-jowl neighbors—they're divided by Market Street. To locals, though, these areas are separate entities, especially since Market Street itself is considered such a strong demarcation line. Both neighborhoods have a core of cultural sights, as well as their share of sketchy blocks. North of the Civic Center lies the western section of the Tenderloin neighborhood, while to the east is hip Hayes Valley.

SoMa

SoMa is less a neighborhood than a sprawling area of wide, traffic-heavy boulevards lined with office skyscrapers and ultrachic condo high-rises. Aside from the fact that many of them work in the area, locals are drawn to the cultural offerings, destination restaurants, and concentration of bars and restaurants. In terms of sightseeing, gigantic and impressive SFMOMA tops the list, followed by the specialty museums of the Yerba Buena arts district.

SoMa was once known as South of the Slot (read: the Wrong Side of the Tracks) in reference to the cable-car slot that ran up Market Street. Ever since gold-rush miners set up their tents here in 1848, SoMa has played a major role in housing immigrants to the city.

The most recent influx of techies (and their money) is changing the neighborhood again: the skid row of 6th Street, between Market and Mission Streets, now coexists with trendy bars and cafés that cater to Twitter's workforce; once a scary section of SoMa, the neighborhood is trying hard to rebrand itself as Mid-Market.

Sights

Contemporary Jewish Museum
MUSEUM | Daniel Libeskind designed the postmodern CJM, whose impossible-to-ignore diagonal blue cube juts out of a painstakingly restored power substation. A physical manifestation of the Hebrew phrase *l'chaim* (to life), the cube

A
B
C
D
E
F
1
2
3
4
5
6
7
8
9
KEY
BART station
Sights
Restaurants
Hotels
0
350 M
0
1,000 ft
101
Broadway
Bernard St.
Pacific Ave.
John St.
Stockton St.
CHINATOWN
Jackson St.
Cable Car Barn
Washington St.
Pleasant St.
NOB HILL
Huntington Park
Clay St.
Lafayette Park
Sacramento St.
Cable Car
California St.
Larkin St.
Hyde St.
Pine St.
Bush St.
POLK GULCH
Jones St.
Taylor St.
Mason St.
Sutter St.
Post St.
Geary St.
O'Farrell St.
Powell St.
Geary St.
Polk St.
Larkin St.
Leavenworth St.
Ellis St.
Franklin St.
O'Farrell St.
Eddy St.
Gough St.
Cleary Ct.
Ellis St.
TENDERLOIN
Turk St.
Eddy St.
Van Ness Ave.
Turk St.
Market St.
Jefferson Square
Golden Gate Ave.
Hyde St.
Stevenson St.
Jessie St.
McAllister St.
Fulton St.
Minna St.
CIVIC CENTER
CIVIC CENTER
HAYES VALLEY
Grove St.
8th St.
Julia St.
7th St.
Hayes St.
Market St.
9th St.
Mission St.
Octavia Blvd.
Linden St.
Fell St.
Laguna St.
10th St.
Washburn St.
Grace St.
Tehama St.
Clementina St.
Folsom St.
11th St.
Lily St.
Van Ness Ave.
Minna St.
Natoma St.
Dore St.
Ringold St.
Page St.
Rose St.
Brady St.
Howard St.
Lafayette St.
Haight St.
Gough St.
12th St.
Kissling St.
9th St.
Otis St.

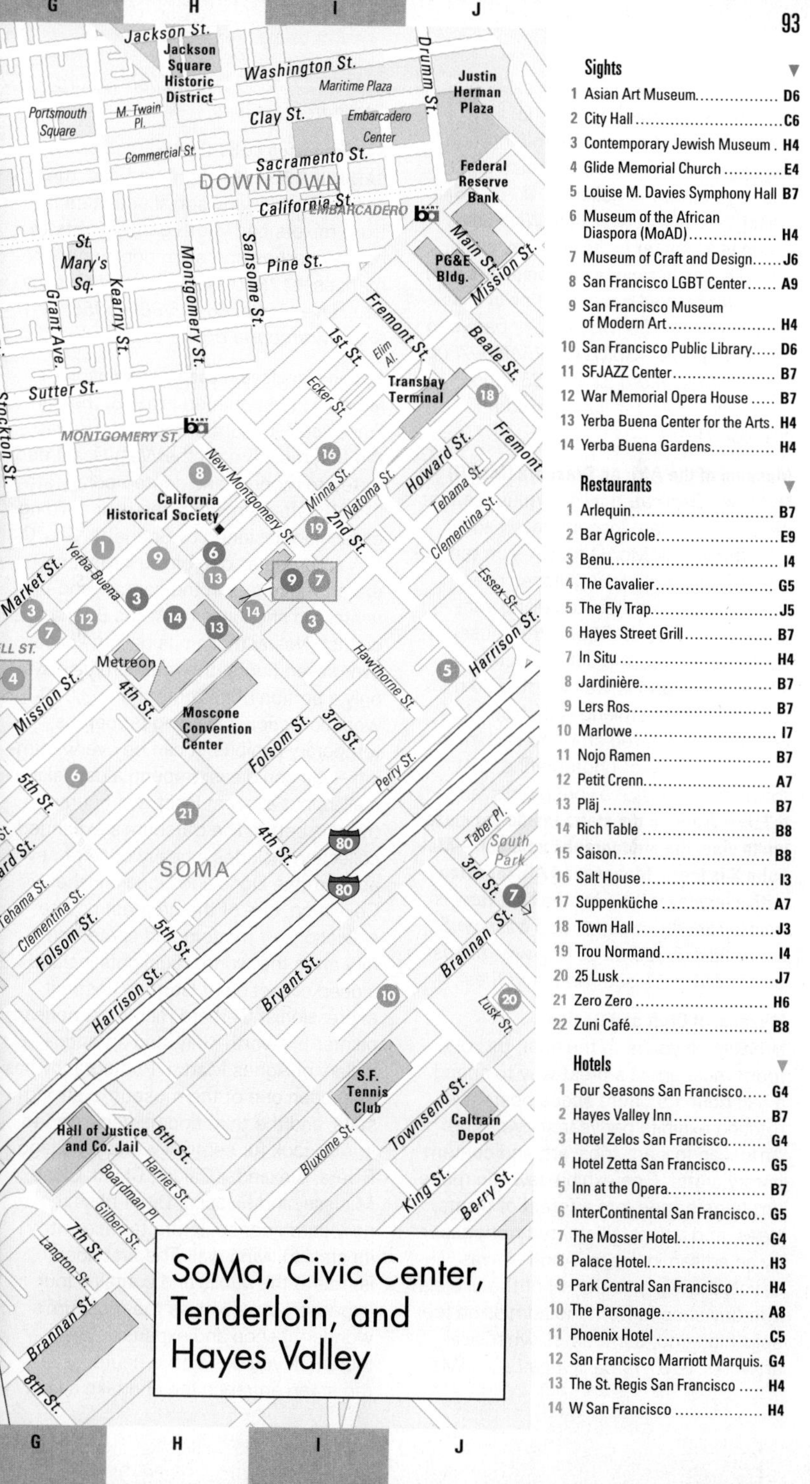

SoMa, Civic Center, Tenderloin, and Hayes Valley

Sights

1 Asian Art Museum ... **D6**
2 City Hall ... **C6**
3 Contemporary Jewish Museum ... **H4**
4 Glide Memorial Church ... **E4**
5 Louise M. Davies Symphony Hall **B7**
6 Museum of the African Diaspora (MoAD) ... **H4**
7 Museum of Craft and Design ... **J6**
8 San Francisco LGBT Center ... **A9**
9 San Francisco Museum of Modern Art ... **H4**
10 San Francisco Public Library ... **D6**
11 SFJAZZ Center ... **B7**
12 War Memorial Opera House ... **B7**
13 Yerba Buena Center for the Arts. **H4**
14 Yerba Buena Gardens ... **H4**

Restaurants

1 Arlequin ... **B7**
2 Bar Agricole ... **E9**
3 Benu ... **I4**
4 The Cavalier ... **G5**
5 The Fly Trap ... **J5**
6 Hayes Street Grill ... **B7**
7 In Situ ... **H4**
8 Jardinière ... **B7**
9 Lers Ros ... **B7**
10 Marlowe ... **I7**
11 Nojo Ramen ... **B7**
12 Petit Crenn ... **A7**
13 Pläj ... **B7**
14 Rich Table ... **B8**
15 Saison ... **B8**
16 Salt House ... **I3**
17 Suppenküche ... **A7**
18 Town Hall ... **J3**
19 Trou Normand ... **I4**
20 25 Lusk ... **J7**
21 Zero Zero ... **H6**
22 Zuni Café ... **B8**

Hotels

1 Four Seasons San Francisco ... **G4**
2 Hayes Valley Inn ... **B7**
3 Hotel Zelos San Francisco ... **G4**
4 Hotel Zetta San Francisco ... **G5**
5 Inn at the Opera ... **B7**
6 InterContinental San Francisco .. **G5**
7 The Mosser Hotel ... **G4**
8 Palace Hotel ... **H3**
9 Park Central San Francisco ... **H4**
10 The Parsonage ... **A8**
11 Phoenix Hotel ... **C5**
12 San Francisco Marriott Marquis. **G4**
13 The St. Regis San Francisco ... **H4**
14 W San Francisco ... **H4**

may have obscure philosophical origins, but Libeskind created a unique, light-filled space that merits a stroll through the lobby even if current exhibits don't entice you into the galleries. ■ **TIP→ San Francisco's best Jewish deli, Wise Sons, operates a counter in the museum, giving you a chance to sample the company's wildly popular smoked trout or a slice of chocolate babka.** ✉ *736 Mission St., between 3rd and 4th Sts., SoMa* ☎ *415/655–7800* 🌐 *www.thecjm.org* 🎟 *$14; $5 Thurs. after 5 pm, free 1st Tues. of month* 🕒 *Closed Wed.*

Museum of the African Diaspora (MoAD)

MUSEUM | Dedicated to the influence that people of African descent have had all over the world, MoAD focuses on temporary exhibits in its four galleries over three floors. With floor-to-ceiling windows onto Mission Street, the museum fits perfectly into the cultural scene of Yerba Buena and is well worth a 30-minute foray. Most striking is its front-window exhibit: a three-story mosaic, made from thousands of photographs, that forms the image of a young girl's face. ■ **TIP→ Walk up the stairs inside the museum to view the photographs up close—Malcolm X is there, Muhammad Ali, too, along with everyday folks—but the best view is from across the street.** ✉ *685 Mission St., SoMa* ☎ *415/358–7200* 🌐 *www.moadsf.org* 🎟 *$10* 🕒 *Closed Mon. and Tues.*

Museum of Craft and Design

MUSEUM | If you're in the area, this one-room museum is a great way to spend a half hour. Its bright space hosts five rotating exhibits per year showcasing American folk art, tribal art, and contemporary crafts. One exhibit saw the museum transformed into a forest of plants, trees, and a river, all created from paper by an artisan in Japan. Another was devoted entirely to the art of the ukulele. The tiny shop in front (no admission fee) sells high-end, sometimes whimsical artworks. ✉ *51 Yerba Buena La., SoMa* ☎ *415/227–4888* 🌐 *https://sfmcd.org/* 🎟 *$8, free 1st Tues.*

San Francisco LGBT Center

GATHERING PLACES | Night and day, the center hosts many social activities, from mixers and youth game nights to holiday parties and slam poetry performances. ✉ *1800 Market St., at Octavia St., Hayes Valley* ☎ *415/865–5555* 🌐 *www.sfcenter.org.*

★ **San Francisco Museum of Modern Art**

MUSEUM | First opened in 1935, the San Francisco Museum of Modern Art was the first museum on the West Coast dedicated to modern and contemporary art. In 2016, after a major three-year building expansion designed by Snøhetta, SFMOMA emerged as one of the largest modern art museums in the country and the revitalized anchor of the Yerba Buena arts district. Nearly tripling its gallery space over seven floors, the museum displays only a portion of its more than 33,000-work collection, including numerous temporary exhibits. It can be overwhelming—you could easily spend a day taking it all in, but allow at least two hours; three is better. The museum's expanded collection includes a heavy dose of new art from the Doris and Donald Fisher Collection, one of the greatest private collections of modern and contemporary art in the world. Highlights include a deep collection of German abstract expressionist Gerhard Richter, American painter Ellsworth Kelly, and a tranquil gallery of Agnes Martin. Photography has long been one of the museum's strong suits, and the third floor is dedicated to it. Also look for seminal works by Diego Rivera, Alexander Calder, Chuck Close, Matisse, and Picasso. Don't miss the new third-floor sculpture terrace with its striking living wall. The first floor is free to the public and contains four large works, as well as the museum's wonderful shop and expensive restaurant. If you don't have hours, save the steep entrance fee and take a spin through here. Ticketing, information, and one gallery are on the second floor; save time and reserve timed tickets online. Daily guided tours—a quick 20 minutes or 45 minutes—are an excellent way to get a foothold in this expansive space. And if you start to fade, grab a cup of Sightglass coffee at the café on the third floor; another café/restaurant is located by the fifth-floor sculpture garden. ✉ *151 3rd St., SoMa* ☎ *415/357–4000* 🌐 *www.sfmoma.org* 🎟 *$25.*

Yerba Buena Center for the Arts
ARTS VENUE | You never know what's going to be on display at this facility in Yerba Buena Gardens, but whether it's an exhibit of Mexican street art (graffiti to laypeople), innovative modern dance, or a baffling video installation, it's likely to be memorable. The productions here, which lean toward the cutting edge, tend to draw a young, energetic crowd. **TIP→ Present any public library card or public transit ticket to receive a 10% discount.** ✉ *701 Mission St., SoMa* ☎ *415/978–2787* 🌐 *www.ybca.org* 🎟 *Galleries $10, free 1st Tues. of month* ⏲ *Closed Mon.*

Yerba Buena Gardens
CONVENTION CENTER | **FAMILY** | There's not much south of Market Street that encourages lingering outdoors—or indeed walking at all—with this notable exception. These two blocks encompass the Yerba Buena Center for the Arts, the Metreon, and newly renovated Moscone Convention Center, but the gardens themselves are the everyday draw. Office workers escape to the green swath of the East Garden, the focal point of which is the memorial to Martin Luther King Jr. Powerful streams of water surge over large, jagged stone columns, mirroring the enduring force of King's words that are carved on the stone walls and on glass blocks behind the waterfall. Moscone North is behind the memorial, and an overhead walkway leads to Moscone South and its rooftop attractions. **TIP→ The gardens are liveliest during the week and especially during the Yerba Buena Gardens Festival, from May through October (www.ybgfestival.org), with free performances of everything from Latin music to Balinese dance.**

Atop the Moscone Convention Center perch a few lures for kids. The historic Looff carousel (*$4 for two rides*) twirls daily 10–5. The carousel is attached to the Children's Creativity Museum (*415/820–3320, creativity.org*), a high-tech, interactive arts-and-technology center (*$13*) geared to children ages 3–12. Just outside, kids adore the excellent slides, including a 25-foot tube slide, at the play circle. Also part of the rooftop complex are gardens, an ice-skating rink, and a bowling alley. ✉ *Bordered by 3rd, 4th, Mission, and Folsom Sts., SoMa* 🌐 *yerbabuenagardens.com* 🎟 *Free.*

Restaurants

Hip SoMa covers a large area that swings from chic residential lofts and 19th-century warehouses–turned–trendy eateries to slightly dingy sidewalk scenes, particularly near the police station and in the higher numbers (7th through 10th nearer to Market). It has the rowdy ballpark and the genteel South Park within its fold. And restaurants near here fuel the mostly young and single local crowd who work in tech (Pinterest, Yelp, Twitter, and Adobe are nearby and so is the train to Silicon Valley). Also, interesting chef-owned restaurants are finding their footing here, like Benu, Saison, and Bar Agricole.

Bar Agricole
$$$ | **MODERN AMERICAN** | Thanks to celebrated bartender/owner Thad Vogler, this sleek LEED-certified spot is a haven for cocktail hounds. Be sure to enjoy the creative libations, but don't neglect the terrific food, either. **Known for:** cocktails; green design; California-Mediterranean

cuisine. $ *Average main: $30 ✉ 355 11th St., SoMa ☎ 415/355–9400 🌐 www.baragricole.co.*

★ Benu

$$$$ | MODERN AMERICAN | Chef Corey Lee's three-Michelin-star fine-dining mecca is a must-stop for those who hop from city to city, collecting memorable meals. Each of the tasting menu's courses is impossibly meticulous, a marvel of textures and flavors. **Known for:** high-end dining; tasting menu; good service. $ *Average main: $310 ✉ 22 Hawthorne St., SoMa ☎ 415/685–4860 🌐 www.benusf.com ⏲ Closed Sun. and Mon. No lunch.*

The Cavalier

$$$ | MODERN BRITISH | British pub grub gets a Nor Cal makeover at this Anna Weinberg–Jennifer Puccio production. Like the pair's other collaborations (Marlowe, Park Tavern, Leo's Oyster Bar), it's insanely popular and loud, yet deliciously comforting. **Known for:** Brit-inspired food; cocktails; lively atmosphere. $ *Average main: $30 ✉ Hotel Zetta, 360 Jessie St., SoMa ☎ 415/321–6000 🌐 thecavaliersf.com.*

The Fly Trap

$$$ | MEDITERRANEAN | The pistachio meatballs put this place on the San Francisco culinary map. It continues to attract SoMa crowds with Cal-Med fare like moroccan cauliflower and flatbread with roasted pear and gorgonzola. **Known for:** Mediterranean-influenced food; cocktails. $ *Average main: $25 ✉ 606 Folsom St., SoMa ☎ 415/243–0580 🌐 flytrapsf.com ⏲ Closed weekends. No lunch.*

★ In Situ

$$$ | CONTEMPORARY | Benu chef Corey Lee's restaurant at SFMOMA is an exhibition of its own, with a rotating menu comprised of dishes from 80 famous chefs around the world. You might taste David Chang's sausage and rice cakes, Rene Redzepi's wood sorrel granita, or Wylie Dufresne's shrimp grits. **Known for:** global influences; originality; museum location. $ *Average main: $30 ✉ 151 3rd St., SoMa ☎ 415/941–6050 🌐 insitu.sfmoma.org ⏲ Closed Tues. and Wed. No dinner Mon.*

Marlowe

$$$ | AMERICAN | Hearty American bistro fare and hip design draw crowds to this Anna Weinberg–Jennifer Puccio production. The menu boasts one of the city's best burgers, and the dining room gleams with white penny tile floors and marble countertops. **Known for:** burgers; strong drinks; festive atmosphere. $ *Average main: $27 ✉ 500 Brannan St., SoMa ☎ 415/777–1413 🌐 www.marlowesf.com.*

Saison

$$$$ | MODERN AMERICAN | This Michelin-starred restaurant always begs the question, what exactly do you get for $298 per person? The answer is a culinary adventure of many courses, prepared by a crew overseen by chef Joshua Skenes, who tease the deepest flavors from premium ingredients. **Known for:** splurgy dining; unique, inventive menu. $ *Average main: $298 ✉ 178 Townsend St., SoMa ☎ 415/828–7990 🌐 www.saisonsf.com ⏲ Closed Sun. and Mon.*

Salt House

$$$ | MODERN AMERICAN | A boisterous Financial District crowd packs this high-ceiling, brick-lined dining space that housed a printing press back in 1896. Rusted girders, chandeliers fashioned from old postcard racks, an elevated mezzanine-level dining room (with only 6 tables up there), make the space a stunner, along with the open kitchen and large windows fronting Mission Street. $ *Average main: $26 ✉ 545 Mission St., SoMa ☎ 415/543–8900 🌐 www.salthousesf.com ⏲ No lunch weekends.*

Town Hall

$$$ | MODERN AMERICAN | American fare with a Southern flair is the headline at owners Doug Washington and Mitchell and Steven Rosenthal's power broker's pit stop. Barbecue gulf shrimp, juicy fried chicken, and butterscotch-chocolate *pot de crème* highlight a menu that has enough variety to satisfy nearly everyone, and portions to satisfy almost every appetite. **Known for:** hearty food; lunchtime scene. *Average main: $30 342 Howard St., SoMa 415/908–3700 www.townhallsf.com No lunch weekends.*

★ Trou Normand

$$$ | MODERN AMERICAN | Thad Vogler's second endeavor (Bar Agricole was the first) delivers a fun boozy evening in stunning surroundings. Located off the lobby of the art deco–era Pacific Telephone building, it excels at house-cured salami and charcuterie and classic cocktails. **Known for:** house-made charcuterie; cocktails. *Average main: $28 140 New Montgomery St., SoMa 415/975–0876 www.trounormandsf.com.*

25 Lusk

$$$$ | MODERN AMERICAN | Tucked off an alley, this sleek two-story (plus rooftop) bastion of American cuisine serves a hefty helping of glamour with its food. The lights are low, the wines are well chosen, and the menu serves dishes that range from club sandwiches to caviar. **Known for:** sexy ambience; top-notch ingredients; rooftop restaurant. *Average main: $20 25 Lusk St., SoMa 415/495–5875 www.25lusk.com.*

Zero Zero

$$ | ITALIAN | You can visit this popular and comfortable California-Italian place almost any time of day, whether you're craving a thin-crust "Cali-politan" pizza for lunch or house-made pasta for dinner. Ingredients are fresh and seasonal, and portions are affordable and easy to share. **Known for:** thin-crust pizza; lively bar. *Average main: $24 826 Folsom St., SoMa 415/348–8800 www.zerozerosf.com.*

Hotels

SoMa's burgeoning lodging scene, spawned by the Moscone Convention Center, AT&T Park, and the conglomeration of museums and high-end eateries, includes some of the city's greenest chain operations, and boutique hotels are opening that cater to techie conventioneers. In SoMa, you won't want to take leisurely evening strolls, as the streets can occasionally get seedy after dark.

Four Seasons Hotel San Francisco

$$$$ | HOTEL | Occupying floors 5 through 17 of a skyscraper, the Four Seasons delivers subdued elegance in rooms with contemporary artwork, fine linens, floor-to-ceiling windows that overlook Yerba Buena Gardens or downtown, and bathrooms with deep soaking tubs and glass-enclosed showers. **Pros:** near museums, galleries, restaurants, shopping, and clubs; terrific fitness facilities; luxurious rooms and amenities. **Cons:** pricey; rooms can feel sterile. *Rooms from: $569 757 Market St., SoMa 415/633–3000 www.fourseasons.com/sanfrancisco 277 rooms No meals.*

Hotel Zelos San Francisco

$$$ | HOTEL | A high-style haven on the top five floors of the green-tiled 1907 Pacific Building, the Zelos offers a luxurious oasis above the busiest part of town, with spacious rooms decked out in muted alligator-pattern carpeting, earth-toned drapes, and sleek furniture echoing a 1930s sensibility. **Pros:** snappy design; convenient to public transit including cable cars; complimentary snack bar. **Cons:** rates soar during large conventions; too much of a scene for some guests; some rooms have no street views. *Rooms from: $295 12 4th St., SoMa 415/348–1111, 888/459–3303 hotelzelos.com 202 rooms No meals.*

★ Hotel Zetta San Francisco

$$$ | HOTEL | With a playful lobby lounge, the London-style Cavalier brasserie, and slick-yet-homey tech-friendly rooms, this trendy redo behind a stately 1913 neoclassical facade is a leader in the SoMa hotel scene. **Pros:** tech amenities and arty design; in-room spa services; noteworthy fitness center. **Cons:** lots of hubbub and traffic; no bathtubs; aesthetic mildly too frenetic for some guests. *Rooms from: $315 55 5th St., SoMa 415/543–8555 hotelzetta.com 116 rooms No meals.*

InterContinental San Francisco

$$$ | HOTEL | The arctic-blue glass exterior and subdued, Zen-like lobby may mimic an airport concourse, but it's merely a prelude to expansive, spectacularly thought-out guest rooms supplied with all the ultramodern conveniences sophisticated travelers expect. **Pros:** well-equipped gym; near Moscone Center; destination restaurant. **Cons:** decor short on character; borders a rough area; a few blocks off the major tourist path. *Rooms from: $275 888 Howard St., SoMa 415/616–6500, 800/496-7621 www.intercontinentalsanfrancisco.com 550 rooms No meals.*

The Mosser Hotel

$$ | HOTEL | A compatible pairing of contemporary decor and original 1913 architectural elements entices a budget-minded clientele to this family-owned eight-floor hotel just south of Market Street. **Pros:** convenient, lively location; lowest-priced rooms a bargain for downtown; coffee, tea, and muffins served free in the morning. **Cons:** some rooms share a bath; rooms are a bit cramped; service can be brusque. *Rooms from: $188 54 4th St., SoMa 415/986–4400, 800/227–3804 www.themosser.com 166 rooms No meals.*

Palace Hotel, San Francisco

$$$$ | HOTEL | When it opened in 1875, the Palace was the world's largest and most luxurious hotel, but it needed to be completely rebuilt after the 1906 earthquake and fire. **Pros:** oozes history; well-trained staff; state-of-the-art fitness center and indoor lap pool. **Cons:** smallish rooms with even smaller baths; west-facing rooms can be warm and stuffy; street noise (ask for an upper-floor room). *Rooms from: $399 2 New Montgomery St., SoMa 415/512–1111, 888/627–7196 www.sfpalace.com 556 rooms No meals.*

Park Central San Francisco

$$$$ | HOTEL | Rising 36 stories over the bustling downtown and SoMa areas, this hotel revels in views from the right, airy rooms with floor-to-ceiling windows. **Pros:** good location; clean rooms; beautiful city views from higher rooms. **Cons:** some street noise; lots of convention and corporate business types; daily facilities fee. *Rooms from: $499 50 3rd St., SoMa 415/974–6400, 877/222–6699 www.parkcentralsf.com 641 rooms No meals.*

San Francisco Marriott Marquis

$$$ | HOTEL | The distinctive design of the 40-story Marriott has been compared to a parking meter and a jukebox, but the guest rooms, decorated in tasteful neutrals, satisfy the business set with ergonomic chairs, wide desks, and a host of technological amenities. **Pros:** stunning views from upper-floor rooms; in the cultural district; staffed full-service business center. **Cons:** pricey parking; frenetic lobby; rooms fill quickly during conferences. *Rooms from: $239 780 Mission St., SoMa 415/896–1600, 888/236–2427 www.marriott.com/sfodt 1,500 rooms No meals.*

★ The St. Regis San Francisco

$$$$ | HOTEL | Across from Yerba Buena Gardens and SFMOMA, the luxurious and modern St. Regis is favored by celebrities such as Lady Gaga and Al Gore. **Pros:** excellent views; stunning lap pool; luxe spa. **Cons:** expensive rates; small front-desk area; cramped space for passenger unloading. *Rooms from: $382 125 3rd St., SoMa 415/284–4000 www.stregis.com/sanfrancisco 260 rooms No meals.*

W San Francisco

$$$ | HOTEL | FAMILY | Chic, urban, and compact, the W's colorful guest rooms come with such homey comforts as upholstered window seats, pillow-top mattresses, goose-down comforters and pillows, and sleek baths. **Pros:** sophisticated digs; in the heart of the cultural district; locally-sourced snacks and exciting cocktails at TRACE restaurant and the Living Room Bar. **Cons:** on-the-go vibe not for everyone; at a busy intersection; area's street people unsettle some guests. *Rooms from: $341* ✉ *181 3rd St., SoMa* ☎ *415/777–5300* 🌐 *www.wsanfrancisco.com* *404 rooms* *No meals.*

Nightlife

In modern, industrial SoMa you'll find everyone from loyal Giants fans celebrating with locally made brews at 21st Amendment to the gay biker crowd that explodes onto the patio of the Lone Star Saloon, with everyone else apt to wind up at one of The Stud's diverse dance parties. The headliners head to Slim's or the DNA Lounge.

BARS

City Beer Store

BARS/PUBS | Called CBS by locals, this friendly tasting room-cum-liquor mart has a wine-bar's sensibility. Perfect for connoisseurs and the merely beer curious, CBS stocks hundreds of different bottled beers, and more than a dozen are on tap. The indecisive can mix and match six-packs to go. ✉ *1148 Mission St., between 7th and 8th Sts., SoMa* ☎ *415/503–1033* 🌐 *www.citybeerstore.com.*

The Hotel Utah Saloon

MUSIC CLUBS | This funky spot—off the beaten path of the area's nightlife—presents a mix of local bands and young national touring acts performing rock, indie pop, alt-country, and everything in between. The low-ceiling performance space is small, with a few tables grouped around the stage. Be sure to grab a club sandwich or Utah burger from the bar before the show. The bar area takes up about half of this joint and is just as popular as the music. Monday is open-mike night. ✉ *500 4th St., at Bryant St., SoMa* ☎ *415/546–6300* 🌐 *www.hotelutah.com.*

MoMo's

BARS/PUBS | This stylish American restaurant and trendy bar has an outdoor patio perfect for sunny days; it's a popular pre- and postgame bar. The individual pizzas are tasty—and big enough to share. ✉ *760 2nd St., at King St., SoMa* ☎ *415/227–8660* 🌐 *www.sfmomos.com.*

Pied Piper Bar

BARS/PUBS | The Palace Hotel's clubby, wood-paneled watering hole takes its name from the Maxfield Parrish mural *The Pied Piper of Hamelin,* which covered most of the wall behind the bar for a century. Until 2013, that is, when the hotel management put it up for auction (tsk, tsk) before backing down after locals on up to the mayor howled in protest. The painting then went to a restorer before eventually returning to the bar, which draws an upscale clientele for two-olive martinis, Manhattans, and other trad libations. ✉ *The Palace Hotel, 2 New Montgomery St., off Market St., SoMa* ☎ *415/512–1111* 🌐 *www.sfpalace.com/pied-piper-bar-and-grill.*

Terroir

WINE BARS—NIGHTLIFE | The focus at this quaint wine bar is on natural (and mostly old-world) vintages, though it's not impossible to find local offerings, too. And while the space may be small, the selection is not: hundreds of different wines, stacked all along the walls, compete for your attention. Don't let the owners' French accents intimidate you: the staff here is helpful. Terroir serves a small selection of artisanal cheeses and charcuterie to pair with the wines. **TIP→ Go on a weekday and head to the candlelit loft above the bar. It's the best**

seat in the house. ✉ *1116 Folsom St., at 7th St., SoMa* ☎ *415/558–9946* 🌐 *www.terroirsf.com.*

Thirsty Bear Organic Brewery

BREWPUBS/BEER GARDENS | This eco-friendly brewpub is the perfect pit stop for those on a budget who don't want to compromise. Thirsty Bear is the only certified organic brewery within the city limits, and the beers here are handcrafted variations on traditional styles. ■ **TIP→ If you can't decide which beer to start with, sample all on tap.** The bar's tapas menu features seasonal meats and produce (mostly local) and sustainably harvested seafood. The upstairs pool hall is ideal for large groups. ✉ *661 Howard St., at Hawthorne St., SoMa* ☎ *415/974–0905* 🌐 *www.thirstybear.com.*

21st Amendment Brewery

BARS/PUBS | This popular brewery is known for its range of beer types, with multiple taps going at all times. In the spring, the Hell or High Watermelon—a wheat beer—gets rave reviews. ■ **TIP→ Serious beer drinkers should try the Back in Black, a black IPA-style beer this brewpub helped pioneer.** The space has an upmarket warehouse feel, though exposed wooden ceiling beams, framed photos, whitewashed brick walls, and hardwood floors make it feel cozy. It's a good spot to warm up before a Giants game and an even better place to party after they win. ✉ *563 2nd St., between Bryant and Brannan Sts., SoMa* ☎ *415/369–0900* 🌐 *www.21st-amendment.com.*

View Lounge

BARS/PUBS | Art-deco-influenced floor-to-ceiling windows frame superb views on the 39th floor of the San Francisco Marriott. You won't feel out of place here just getting a drink or two rather than dinner. It can get crowded here on weekends. ✉ *San Francisco Marriott Marquis, 780 Mission St., between Mission and Market Sts., SoMa* ☎ *415/442–6003* 🌐 *sfviewlounge.com.*

CABARET

AsiaSF

CABARET | Saucy, sexy, and fun, this is one of the best places in town for a drag-show virgin. The entertainment, as well as the gracious food service, is provided by some of the city's most gorgeous transgender women who strut in impossibly high heels on top of the catwalk bar, vamping to tunes like "Cabaret" and "Big Spender." The creative Asian-influenced cuisine is surprisingly good. ■ **TIP→ Go on a weekday to avoid the bachelorette parties.** Make reservations, or risk being turned away. ✉ *201 9th St., at Howard St., SoMa* ☎ *415/255–2742* 🌐 *www.asiasf.com.*

DANCE CLUBS

DNA Lounge

DANCE CLUBS | The music changes nightly at the venerable DNA Lounge, and one of the highlights is **Bootie.** Every Saturday night, this popular mash-up unites hard-core and indie rockers, hip-hop devotees, and emo fans. Three bars and dance floors on two levels mean that DNA is rarely uncomfortably crowded. ■ **TIP→ The action spills into the pizza joint next door, so you don't have to stop dancing if you suddenly get hungry.** ✉ *375 11th St., between Harrison and Folsom Sts., SoMa* ☎ *415/626–1409* 🌐 *www.dnalounge.com.*

The EndUp

DANCE CLUBS | Sometimes 2 am is way too early. And with a 12-hour dance party starting at 10 pm on Saturday, the EndUp is by far SF's most popular after-hours place, with possibly the best sound system in the city. ■ **TIP→ Said system is cranked. Even the cool kids wear earplugs.** It's open from 10 pm Saturday until 4 am Monday, and generally 10 pm–4 am weekdays. It can be a bit of a meat market, but this San Francisco institution doesn't adhere to any particular scene. ✉ *401 6th St., at Harrison St., SoMa* ☎ *415/646–0999.*

Mezzanine

DANCE CLUBS | If you like megaclubs, then you'll dig this industrial-chic two-story club, which doubles as a gallery and performance venue. Live acts have included Questlove, the Dandy Warhols, and Def Jux artists. The crowd is generally mixed, straight and gay. If the jam-packed dance floor (which can accommodate nearly 1,000 people) overwhelms you, head upstairs to the quietish mezzanine lounges to converse or to ogle the sexy crowd. ✉ *444 Jessie St., near 5th St., SoMa* ☎ *415/625–8880* 🌐 *www.mezzaninesf.com.*

111 Minna Gallery

CAFES—NIGHTLIFE | Gallery and coffee shop by day, bar–dance club by night, this warehouse space on a small side street just south of Mission Street is usually populated by the trendy art crowd. Dance events typically take place on Friday and Saturday from 9 pm until 2 am, though the bar opens around 5. ✉ *111 Minna St., between 2nd and New Montgomery Sts., SoMa* ☎ *415/974–1719* 🌐 *www.111minnagallery.com* ⏲ *Gallery closed weekends.*

GAY NIGHTLIFE

Lone Star Saloon

BARS/PUBS | This watering hole is popular with bikers, bears, and the men who love them. The inside bar has an old-style-tavern feel, with a pool table and a long wooden bar you half expect the bartender to sling a beer down. Weekend "Beer Busts" unfold on the great outdoor patio bar. Expect a big crowd on a sunny day. The scene here isn't particularly female-friendly, and the action can get steamy during events like gay-pride day or the Folsom Street Fair. ✉ *1354 Harrison St., near 9th St., SoMa* ☎ *415/863–9999* 🌐 *www.lonestarsf.com.*

SF Eagle

BARS/PUBS | This spacious indoor-outdoor leather bar is a holdover from the days before AIDS and SoMa's gentrification. The Sunday-afternoon "Beer Busts" (3 pm–6 pm) remain a high point of the leather set's week, and Thursday nights are given over to live music. This remains a welcoming place for people from all walks of life. ✉ *398 12th St., at Harrison St., SoMa* 🌐 *www.sf-eagle.com.*

The Stud

BARS/PUBS | Glam trans women, gay bears, tight-teed pretty boys, ladies and their ladies, and a handful of straight onlookers congregate here to dance to live DJ sounds and watch world-class drag performers on the small stage. The entertainment is often campy, pee-your-pants funny, and downright fantastic. Each night's music is different—from funk, soul, and hip-hop to '80s tunes and disco favorites. ✉ *399 9th St, at Harrison St., SoMa* ☎ *415/863–6623* 🌐 *www.studsf.com* ⏲ *Closed Mon.*

MUSIC CLUBS

Slim's

MUSIC CLUBS | National touring acts—mostly along the pop-punk and hard- and alt-rock lines but including metal and bluegrass—are the main draws at this venue, which also serves as a popular SoManightclub. Co-owner Boz Scaggs helps bring in the crowds and famous headliners like Dressy Bessy and Dead Meadow. ✉ *333 11th St., between Harrison and Folsom Sts., SoMa* ☎ *415/255–0333* 🌐 *www.slimspresents.com.*

Performing Arts

DANCE

★ **Alonzo King LINES Ballet**

DANCE | Since 1982 this company has been staging the fluid and gorgeous ballets of choreographer and founder Alonzo King, sometimes in collaboration with top-notch world musicians such as Zakir Hussain and Hamza El Din. Ballets incorporate both classical and modern techniques, with experimental set design, costumes, and music. The San Francisco seasons are in spring and

Oracle Park: Where Giants Tread

The size of Oracle Park hits you immediately—the field, McCovey Cove, and the Lefty O'Doul drawbridge all look like miniature models. At just under 13 acres, the San Francisco Giants' ballpark is one of the country's smallest. After Boston's Fenway, Oracle Park has the shortest distance to the wall; from home plate it's just 309 feet to the right field. But there's something endearing about its petite stature—not to mention its location, with yacht masts poking up over the outfield and the blue bay sparkling beyond.

From 1960 to 2000 the Giants played at Candlestick Park, which was in one of the coldest, windiest parts of the city. (Giants' pitcher Stu Miller was famously "blown off the mound" here during the 1961 All-Star Game.)

In 2000 the Giants played their first game at Oracle Park (then called Pacific Bell Park and later SBC Park and AT&T Park). All told, $357 million was spent on the privately funded facility, and it shows in the retro redbrick exterior, the quaint clock tower, handsome bronze statues, above-average food, and tiny details like baseball-style lettering on no-smoking signs. There isn't a bad seat in the house and the park has an unusual level of intimacy and access. Concourses circle the field on one level, and in some ticketed areas you can stand inches from players as they exit the locker rooms. At street level, non-ticket-holders can get up close outside a gate in right field. The giant Coke bottle and mitt you see beyond the outfield are part of the Coca-Cola Fan Lot playground. Diehards may miss the grittiness of Candlestick, but it's hard not to love this park. It still feels new but has an old-time aura and has become a San Francisco institution. Park tours are led daily at 10:30 and 12:30 and cost $22.

The Famous "Splash Hit"

Locals show up in motorboats and inflatable rafts with fishing nets, ready to scoop up home-run balls that clear the right field wall and land in McCovey Cove. Hitting one into the water isn't easy: the ball has to clear a 25-foot wall, the elevated walkway, and the promenade outside. Barry Bonds had the first splash hit on May 1, 2000.

Getting There

Parking is pricey ($30 and up), and 2,300 spaces for nearly 42,000 seats doesn't add up. Take public transportation. Muni lines N and T (to CalTrain/Mission Bay and Sunnydale, respectively) stop right in front of the park, and Muni bus lines 10, 30, 45, and 47 all stop within a few blocks. Or you can arrive in style—take the ferry from Jack London Square in Oakland (🌐 *www.sanfranciscobayferry.com*).

fall. ✉ *26 7th St., SoMa* ☎ *415/863–1180* 🌐 *www.linesballet.org.*

Margaret Jenkins Dance Company

DANCE | Founded in 1973, this nationally acclaimed modern dance troupe sometimes performs with popular local musicians such as the Kronos Quartet and the Paul Dresher Ensemble. Jenkins's highly gestural style sometimes suggests the influence of the late Merce Cunningham, one of her collaborators in the 1960s. ✉ *301 8th St., Studio 200, SoMa* ☎ *415/861–3940 for tickets* 🌐 *www.mjdc.org.*

Robert Moses' Kin Dance Company

DANCE | Founded in 1995 by choreographer Robert Moses and known for its provocative themes, the Kin makes a study of race, class, culture, and gender with the use of eclectic movements, such as jazz, hip-hop, and ballet. ✉ *301 8th St., Suite 200, SoMa* ☎ *415/252–8384* 🌐 *www.robertmoseskin.org.*

MOVIE THEATERS

San Francisco Cinematheque

FILM | In the spotlight are experimental film and digital media. Cinematheque hosts screenings throughout the city, but most are at the Yerba Buena Center for the Arts. ✉ *SoMa* ☎ *415/552–1990* 🌐 *www.sfcinematheque.org.*

PERFORMING ARTS CENTERS

Yerba Buena Center for the Arts

ARTS CENTERS | Across the street from the San Francisco Museum of Modern Art and abutting a lovely urban garden, this performing arts complex schedules interdisciplinary art exhibitions, touring and local dance troupes, music, film programs, and contemporary theater events. You can depend on the quality of the productions at Yerba Buena. Film buffs often come here to check out the San Francisco Cinematheque (*www.sfcinematheque.org*), which showcases experimental film and digital media. And dance enthusiasts can attend concerts by a roster of city companies that perform here, including Smuin Ballet/SF (*www.smuinballet.org*), ODC/San Francisco (*www.odcdance.org*), the Margaret Jenkins Dance Company (*www.mjdc.org*), and Alonzo King's Lines Ballet (*www.linesballet.org*). The Lamplighters (*www.lamplighters.org*), an alternative opera that specializes in Gilbert and Sullivan, also performs here. ✉ *3rd and Mission Sts., SoMa* ☎ *415/978–2787* 🌐 *www.ybca.org.*

On the Horizon 

The **Mexican Museum** will add a new building to the Yerba Buena cultural zone: four floors to house its 17,000 works and topped by a condo tower. Work is underway at the site on Mission Street and 3rd Street. The museum, accredited as a Smithsonian affiliate, is scheduled to open in late 2020.

See 🌐 *www.mexicanmuseum.org* for updates.

Shopping

The South of Market district, once the bastion of light industry, is still framed by warehouses, but today it's best known for its trendy pockets of quaint restaurants, edgy clubs, and airy art spaces, not to mention home to the offices of major tech companies like Dropbox, Twitter, and Airbnb. A smattering of antiques and other dealers occupy some of the former warehouse spaces, and there are a few clothing outlets. At the other end of the spectrum is the massive Metreon Shopping Center. At the corner of 4th and Mission Streets, it has a few shops of note, among them Chronicle Books, along with a 16-screen cinema and a slew of eateries.

ART GALLERIES

Arthaus

ART GALLERIES | This one-story gallery south of Market provides an intimate space for both local and New York artists to display their contemporary work. Gallery owners Annette Schutz and James Bacchi are very approachable and include a diverse range of mediums as well as rotating shows beneath their roof. ✉ *228 Townsend St., between 3rd and 4th Sts., SoMa* ☎ *415/977–0223* 🌐 *www.arthaus-sf.com* 🕐 *Closed Sun. and Mon.*

★ **Berggruen Gallery**

ART GALLERIES | Twentieth-century European and American paintings, including Bay Area figurative works, are displayed throughout two airy floors at this well-respected gallery established in 1970. Some recent exhibitions have included the works of Robert Kelly and Isca Greenfield-Sanders. Look for thematic shows here, too; past exhibits have had titles such as Summer Highlights and Four Decades. ✉ *10 Hawthorne St., at Howard St., SoMa* ☎ *415/781–4629* 🌐 *www.berggruen.com.*

Crown Point Press

ART GALLERIES | What started as a print workshop in 1962 now includes studios as well as a large, airy gallery where etchings, intaglio prints, engravings, and aquatints by local and internationally renowned artists are displayed. ✉ *20 Hawthorne St., between 2nd and 3rd Sts., SoMa* ☎ *415/974–6273* 🌐 *www.crownpoint.com* 🕙 *Closed Sun.*

Hackett Mill

ART GALLERIES | This gallery prides itself on its friendly staffers who will educate you about the art or leave you alone, whichever you prefer. Some of the artists here include Conrad Marca-Relli, Esteban Vincente, Kenzo Okada, and Robert De Niro Sr. The specialties here are American modern, postwar abstract expressionist, and Bay Area figurative art. ✉ *145 Natoma St., Suite 400, SoMa* ☎ *415/362–3377* 🌐 *www.hackettmill.com.*

SF Camerawork

ART GALLERIES | This nonprofit organization mounts thematic exhibits and has a well-stocked bookstore and a reference library. The lecture program includes noted photographers and critics. Admission is free. ✉ *1011 Market St., 2nd fl., at 6th St., SoMa* ☎ *415/487–1011* 🌐 *www.sfcamerawork.org* 🕙 *Closed Sun. and Mon.*

Varnish Fine Art

ART GALLERIES | Jen Rogers and Kerri Stephens's gallery specializes in thought-provoking works such as those by San Francisco–based artist Brian Goggin, known for his public art piece *Defenestration.* Ransom and Mitchell, two other noteworthy locals the gallery represents, blend photography and set design together to create a truly surreal visual experience. This gallery is open by appointment only. ✉ *16 Jessie St., Suite C120, near 1st St., SoMa* ☎ *415/433–4400* 🌐 *www.varnishfineart.com.*

BOOKS

Alexander Book Company

BOOKS/STATIONERY | The three floors here are stocked with literature, poetry, and children's books, with a focus on hard-to-find works by men and women of color. ✉ *50 2nd St., between Jessie and Stevenson Sts., SoMa* ☎ *415/495–2992* 🌐 *www.alexanderbook.com* 🕙 *Closed Sun.*

★ **Chronicle Books**

BOOKS/STATIONERY | This local beacon of publishing produces inventively designed fiction, cookbooks, art books, and other titles, as well as diaries, planners, and address books—all of which you can purchase at two different airy and attractive spaces. The other store is located at 680 2nd Street, near Oracle Park. ✉ *Metreon Westfield Shopping Center, 165 4th St., near Howard St., SoMa* ☎ *415/369–6271* 🌐 *www.chroniclebooks.com.*

FOOD AND DRINK

Blue Bottle Coffee

FOOD/CANDY | The revered microroaster's practitioners brew their sacred beans in a $20,000 siphon bar from Japan with halogen-lighted glass globes that resemble a science experiment. A stop here makes for a perfect reprieve from shopping. ✉ *66 Mint Plaza, off Mission St., SoMa* ☎ *510/653-3394* 🌐 *www.bluebottlecoffee.com.*

Bluxome Street Winery

WINE/SPIRITS | Wineshops exist all over the city, but this is the only winery within city limits. Grapes are brought in from Russian River Valley, and all production takes place on site, reviving an industry that was once thriving a hundred years ago in SoMa before Napa and Sonoma took it over. Come to the tasting room to sample light summery rosés, rich Pinot Noirs, or refreshing Sauvignon Blancs. ✉ *53 Bluxome St., near 4th St., SoMa* ☎ *415/543–5353* 🌐 *www.bluxomewinery.com.*

K&L Wine Merchants

WINE/SPIRITS | More than any other wine store, this one has an ardent cult following around town. The friendly staffers promise not to sell what they don't taste themselves, and weekly events—on Friday from 5 pm to 6:30 pm and Saturday from noon to 3 pm—open the tastings to customers. The best-seller list for varietals and regions for both the under- and over-$30 categories appeals to the wine lover in everyone. ✉ *855 Harrison St., near 4th St., SoMa* ☎ *415/896–1734* 🌐 *www.klwines.com.*

The Wine Club

WINE/SPIRITS | The large selection and great prices make up for this wineshop's bare-bones ambience. At the self-serve wine bar you can taste wines for a modest fee, a great boon if you want to try before you buy. Wine paraphernalia, including wineglasses, books, openers, and decanters, are also sold here. ✉ *953 Harrison St., between 5th and 6th Sts., SoMa* ☎ *415/512–9086* 🌐 *www.thewineclub.com.*

FURNITURE, HOUSEWARES, AND GIFTS

Mscape Modern Interiors

GIFTS/SOUVENIRS | The shop sells sleek furniture and accessories, such as low-slung couches with nary a curve in sight, and a variety of wall beds. Many items can be custom ordered. ✉ *521 6th St., near Bryant St., SoMa* ☎ *415/543–1771* 🌐 *mscapesf.com.*

JEWELRY AND COLLECTIBLES

★ **San Francisco Museum of Modern Art Museum Store**

JEWELRY/ACCESSORIES | The shop is known for its large selection of watches and jewelry, as well as artists' monographs and artful housewares. Posters, calendars, children's art sets and books, and art books for adults round out the merchandise. ✉ *151 3rd St., between Mission and Howard Sts., SoMa* ☎ *415/357–4035* 🌐 *museumstore.sfmoma.org.*

Activities

BASEBALL

San Francisco Giants

BASEBALL/SOFTBALL | Three World Series titles (2010, 2012, and 2014) and the classic design of Oracle Park lead to sellouts for nearly every home game the National League team plays. ✉ *Oracle Park, 24 Willie Mays Plaza, between 2nd and 3rd Sts., SoMa* ☎ *415/972–2000, 800/734–4268* 🌐 *sanfrancisco.giants.mlb.com.*

Civic Center

The eye-catching, gold-domed City Hall presides over this patchy neighborhood bordered roughly by Franklin, McAllister, Hyde, and Grove Streets. The optimistic "City Beautiful" movement of the early 20th century produced the Beaux Arts–style complex for which the area is named, including City Hall, the War Memorial Opera House, the Veterans Building, and the old public library, now the home of the Asian Art Museum. The wonderful Main Library on Larkin Street between Fulton and Grove Streets is a modern variation on the Civic Center's architectural theme.

The Civic Center area may have been set up on City Beautiful principles, but illusion soon gives way to reality. The buildings are grand, but many of the city's most destitute residents eke out an existence on the neighborhood's streets and plazas. Still, areas of interest on either side of City Hall include the Asian Art Museum, the Main Library, United Nations Plaza, the War Memorial Opera House, Davies Symphony Hall, and ACT's Strand Theater. Tickets to a show at one of the grand performance halls are the main reason many venture here, and major city events like the Pride parade and Giants' victory celebrations draw big crowds; the Asian Art Museum and City Hall are worthy sightseeing stops, too.

Sights

★ Asian Art Museum

MUSEUM | You don't have to be a connoisseur of Asian art to appreciate a visit to this museum whose monumental exterior conceals a light, open, and welcoming space. The fraction of the Asian's collection on display (about 2,500 pieces out of 18,000-plus total) is laid out thematically and by region, making it easy to follow historical developments.

Begin on the third floor, where highlights of Buddhist art in Southeast Asia and early China include a large, jewel-encrusted, exquisitely painted 19th-century Burmese Buddha, and clothed rod puppets from Java. On the second floor you can find later Chinese works, as well as pieces from Korea and Japan. The joy here is all in the details: on a whimsical Korean jar, look for a cobalt tiger jauntily smoking a pipe, or admire the delicacy of the Japanese tea implements. The ground floor is devoted to temporary exhibits and the museum's wonderful gift shop. During spring and summer, visit the museum on Thursday evenings for extended programs and sip drinks while a DJ spins tunes. ✉ *200 Larkin St., between McAllister and Fulton Sts., Civic Center* ☎ *415/581–3500* 🌐 *www.asianart.org* 🎫 *$25, free 1st Sun. of month; $10 Thurs. 5–9* 🕓 *Closed Mon.*

City Hall

GOVERNMENT BUILDING | This imposing 1915 structure with its massive gold-leaf dome—higher than the U.S. Capitol's—is about as close to a palace as you're going to get in San Francisco. The classic granite-and-marble behemoth was modeled after St. Peter's Basilica in Rome. Architect Arthur Brown Jr., who also designed Coit Tower and the War Memorial Opera House, designed an interior with grand columns and a sweeping central staircase. San Franciscans were thrilled, and probably a bit surprised, when his firm built City Hall in just a few years. The 1899 structure it replaced had taken 27 years to erect, as corrupt builders and politicians lined their pockets with funds earmarked for it. That building collapsed in about 27 seconds during the 1906 earthquake, revealing trash and newspapers mixed into the construction materials.

City Hall was spruced up and seismically retrofitted in the late 1990s, but the sense of history remains palpable. Some noteworthy events that have taken place here include the marriage of Marilyn Monroe and Joe DiMaggio (1954); the hosing—down the central staircase—of civil-rights and freedom-of-speech protesters (1960); the murders of Mayor George Moscone and openly gay supervisor Harvey Milk (1978); the torching of the lobby by angry members of the gay community in response to the light sentence given to the former supervisor who killed both men (1979); and the registrations of scores of gay couples in celebration of the passage of San Francisco's Domestic Partners Act (1991). In 2004, Mayor Gavin Newsom took a stand against then-current state and federal law by issuing marriage licenses to same-sex partners.

On display in the South Light Court are city artifacts including maps, documents, and photographs. That enormous, 700-pound iron head once crowned the *Goddess of Progress* statue, which topped the old City Hall building until it crumbled during the 1906 earthquake.

Across Polk Street from City Hall is **Civic Center Plaza,** with lawns, walkways, seasonal flower beds, a playground, and an underground parking garage. This sprawling space is generally clean but somewhat grim. Many homeless people hang out here, so the plaza can feel dodgy. ✉ *Bordered by Van Ness Ave. and Polk, Grove, and McAllister Sts., Civic Center* ☎ *415/554–6023 recorded tour info, 415/554–6139 tour reservations* 🌐 *sfgov.org/cityhall/city-hall-tours* 🎫 *Free* ⏲ *Closed weekends.*

★ Louise M. Davies Symphony Hall

ARTS VENUE | Fascinating and futuristic-looking, this 2,739-seat hall is the home of the San Francisco Symphony. The glass wraparound lobby and pop-out balcony high on the southeast corner are visible from outside, as is the Henry Moore bronze sculpture that sits on the sidewalk at Van Ness Avenue and Grove Street. The hall's 59 adjustable Plexiglas acoustical disks cascade from the ceiling like hanging windshields. Concerts range from typical symphonic fare to more unusual combinations, such as performers like Al Green and Arlo Guthrie. Scheduled tours (about 75 minutes) on Mondays take in Davies and the nearby War Memorial Opera House. ✉ *201 Van Ness Ave., Civic Center* ☎ *415/552–8338* 🌐 *www.sfwmpac.org* 🎫 *Tours $7.*

San Francisco Public Library

LIBRARY | Topped with a swirl like an art-deco nautilus, the library's seven-level glass atrium fills the building with light. Local researchers take advantage of centers dedicated to gay and lesbian, African-American, Chinese, and Filipino history. ■ **TIP→ The sixth-floor San Francisco History Center has fun exhibits of city ephemera, including—a treat for fans of noir fiction—novelist Dashiell Hammett's typewriter.** ✉ *100 Larkin St., at Grove St., Civic Center* ☎ *415/557–4400* 🌐 *sfpl.org.*

War Memorial Opera House

ARTS VENUE | After San Francisco's original opera houses were destroyed in the 1906 quake, architect Arthur Brown Jr. was comissioned to design this stunning American Renaissance-style buildling. Taking its name as a tribute to the city's soldiers lost in World War I, the War Memorial Opera House was inaugurated in 1932 with a performance of *Tosca.* It has since played host to two major historic events: the drafting of the United Nations charter in 1945, and the ceremony six years later in which the U.S. restored sovereignty to Japan. Modeled after its European counterparts, the building has a vaulted and coffered ceiling, marble foyer, two balconies, and a huge silver art-deco chandelier that resembles a sunburst. The San Francisco Opera performs here from September through December and in summer; the opera house hosts the San Francisco Ballet from February through May, with December *Nutcracker* performances. ✉ *301 Van Ness Ave., Civic Center* ☎ *415/621–6600* 🌐 *www.sfwmpac.org.*

Nightlife

Lawyers, politicians, and others in the government biz populate this neighborhood by day, and at night the scene tends to remain buttoned-up.

MUSIC CLUBS

Warfield

MUSIC CLUBS | This former movie palace is now one of the city's largest rock-and-roll venues, with folding chairs or standing space (depending on the event) downstairs and theater seating upstairs. The historic venue has booked everyone from Prince and the Grateful Dead to the Pretenders and the Killers. ✉ *982 Market St., at Taylor St., Civic Center* ☎ *415/345–0900* 🌐 *thewarfieldtheatre.com.*

Performing Arts

DANCE

★ San Francisco Ballet

DANCE | For ballet lovers, the nation's oldest professional company is reason alone to visit the Bay Area. SFB's performances, for the past three decades under the direction of Helgi Tomasson, have won critical raves. The primary season runs from February through May. The repertoire includes full-length ballets such as *Don Quixote* and *Sleeping Beauty*; the December presentation of *The Nutcracker* is truly spectacular. The company also performs bold new dances from star choreographers such as William Forsythe and Mark Morris, alongside modern classics by George Balanchine and Jerome Robbins. Tickets are available at the **War Memorial Opera House.** ✉ *War Memorial Opera House, 301 Van Ness Ave., at Grove St., Civic Center* ☎ *415/865–2000* 🌐 *www.sfballet.org.*

MUSIC

★ San Francisco Opera

OPERA | Founded in 1923, this internationally recognized organization has occupied the War Memorial Opera House since the building's completion in 1932. From September through December and June through July, the company presents a wide range of operas, from *Carmen* to an operatic take on *It's a Wonderful Life*. The opera also frequently collaborates with European companies and presents unconventional, sometimes edgy projects designed to attract younger audiences. Translations are projected above the stage during most non-English productions. ✉ *War Memorial Opera House, 301 Van Ness Ave., at Grove St., Civic Center* ☎ *415/864–3330 tickets* 🌐 *www.sfopera.com* ☞ *Box office open Mon. 10–5, Tues.–Fri. 10–6.*

★ San Francisco Symphony

MUSIC | One of America's top orchestras performs from September through May, with additional summer performances of light classical music and show tunes. The orchestra and its charismatic music director, Michael Tilson Thomas, known for his daring programming of 20th-century American works, often perform with soloists of the caliber of Andre Watts, Gil Shaham, and Renée Fleming. The symphony's adventurous projects include its collaboration with the heavy-metal band Metallica. ■ **TIP→ Deep discounts on tickets are often available through Travelzoo, Groupon, and other vendors.** ✉ *Davies Symphony Hall, 201 Van Ness Ave., at Grove St., Civic Center* ☎ *415/864–6000* 🌐 *www.sfsymphony.org.*

PERFORMING ARTS CENTERS

★ War Memorial Opera House

ARTS CENTERS | With its soaring vaulted ceilings and marble foyer, this elegant 3,146-seat venue, built in 1932, rivals the old-world theaters of Europe. Part of the San Francisco War Memorial and Performing Arts Center, which also includes Davies Symphony Hall and Herbst Theatre, this is the home of the San Francisco Opera and the San Francisco Ballet. ✉ *301 Van Ness Ave., at Grove St., Civic Center* ☎ *415/621–6600* 🌐 *www.sfwmpac.org.*

THEATRE

New Conservatory Theatre Center

THEATER | This three-stage complex focuses on contemporary gay- and lesbian-themed works like *Avenue Q*, as well as other events, including educational plays and classes for young people. ✉ *25 Van Ness Ave., between Fell and Oak Sts., Civic Center* ☎ *415/861–8972* 🌐 *www.nctcsf.org.*

Shopping

The Civic Center is often abuzz with protests, performances, and political rallies. Come here to get a glimpse of the mayor or pick up some fresh produce at the twice-weekly farmers' market.

FARMERS' MARKETS

Heart of the City Farmers' Market

OUTDOOR/FLEA/GREEN MARKETS | Twice a week (Wednesday and Sunday) vendors sell heaps of cheap produce, along with baked goods, potted herbs, and the occasional live chicken. It can get busy; come before 3pm for the largest selection. ✉ *United Nations Plaza, along Market St., Civic Center* ☎ *415/558–9455* 🌐 *heartofthecity-farmersmar.squarespace.com.*

FURNITURE, HOUSEWARES, AND GIFTS

Sur la Table

HOUSEHOLD ITEMS/FURNITURE | Everything the home chef could need is here, along with round aspic cutters, larding needles, and other things many cooks never knew existed. The store hosts cooking classes and jaw-dropping demonstrations. ✉ *Westfield San Francisco Centre, 845 Market St., between 4th and 5th Sts., Civic Center* ☎ *415/814–4691* 🌐 *www.surlatable.com.*

Tenderloin

Stretching west of Union Square and north of Civic Center, the Tenderloin could be the city's poster child for urban challenges: low-income families huddle in tiny apartments; single-room-occupancy hotels offer shelter a step up from living on the street; drug dealing and prostitution are common; and very few green spaces break up the monotony of high-rises. So why in the world would anyone go out of the way to come here? Well, exceptional Vietnamese food, for one thing, but these days more than just the great *pho* is luring people to the Tenderloin. Trendy watering holes and coffee shops are springing up, with a handful of intrepid hipsters moving into the hood after them. The Tenderloin may be on its way to becoming the next Mission, but for now it remains a gritty slice of San Francisco.

Little Saigon

The best Vietnamese food in the city can be found along Larkin Street between Turk and O'Farrell Streets, where Vietnamese Americans own most of the businesses. Marketing types call this corridor Little Saigon; locals associate it with the Tenderloin.You can find cheap, often fantastic food here, particularly *pho* (beef-broth noodle soup). Check out Turtle Tower for pho and Saigon Sandwich for *bánh mì* (Vietnamese sandwiches).

TIP→ Some parts of the Tenderloin are more dangerous than others, and a single street can change from block to block. Little Saigon's Larkin Street corridor is relatively safe during the day, as are most streets north of Eddy (an area that realtors insist on calling the TenderNob for its proximity to Nob Hill). Avoid the last two blocks of Turk Street and Golden Gate Avenue before they meet Market Street.

Sights

Glide Memorial Church

RELIGIOUS SITE | For a rockin' gospel concert and an inclusive, feel-good vibe, head to Glide, where Reverend Cecil Williams, a bear of a man and a local celeb do-gooder, leads a hand-clapping, shout-it-out, get-on-your-feet "celebration." The diverse crowd—gay and straight, all colors of the rainbow, religious and not—is large and enthusiastic. You might recognize the church from the Will Smith film *The Pursuit of Happyness.* ✉ *330 Ellis St., at Taylor St., Tenderloin* ☎ *415/674–6000* 🌐 *www.glide.org.*

Restaurants

A land of dive bars, package-liquor stores, panhandlers, and … some of the best pho and bánh mì in the city, this seedy district of low rents encompasses Little Saigon. Locals know to come here for great cheap eats, including not just Vietnamese but naans and masalas. This is San Francisco's rougher neighborhood—one of the last holdouts.

Lers Ros

$$ | THAI | Skip the "same old" pad thai and try something new at this authentic Thai standby. Thai herb sausage and papaya salad with salted egg are good appetizers to share, while the pork belly with crispy rind and basil leaves and *duck larb* (meat salad) come packed with flavor and heat. **Known for:** authentic Thai; extensive menu; postdrinking hangout. *$ Average main: $15 ✉ 730 Larkin St., Tenderloin ☎ 415/931–6917 ⊕ www.lersros.com.*

Hotels

Between Union Square, Nob Hill, and the Civic Center, the Tenderloin contains some hip boutique hotels and happening bars (plus some of the best Vietnamese and Thai food in the region). Be advised that many transients live here; the streets can feel seedy even during the day.

Phoenix Hotel

$$ | HOTEL | A magnet for the boho crowd, the Phoenix is retro and low-key, with colorful furniture, white bedspreads, and original pieces by local artists, as well as modern amenities like flatscreen TVs. **Pros:** mellow staffers set boho tone; cheeky design, hip restaurant/bar; free parking. **Cons:** somewhat seedy location; no elevators; can be loud in the evening. *$ Rooms from: $230 ✉ 601 Eddy St., Tenderloin ☎ 415/776–1380, 800/248–9466 ⊕ www.phoenixsf.com ⇨ 44 rooms 🍴 No meals.*

Nightlife

This neighborhood is best known for its grit and realism, but despite this The Loin is centrally located and, depending on your reservation time at Bourbon & Branch, the perfect place to start (or end) your night on the town.

BARS

★ Bourbon & Branch

BARS/PUBS | Bourbon & Branch reeks of Prohibition-era speakeasy cool. It's not exclusive, though: everyone is granted a password. The place has sex appeal, with tin ceilings, bordello-red silk wallpaper, intimate booths, and low lighting; loud conversations and cell phones are not allowed. The menu of expertly mixed cocktails and quality bourbon and whiskey is substantial, though the servers aren't always authorities. **■ TIP→ Your reservation dictates your exit time, which is strictly enforced.** There's also a speakeasy within the speakeasy called Wilson & Wilson, which is more exclusive, but just as funky. *✉ 501 Jones St., at O'Farrell St., Tenderloin ☎ 415/346–1735 ⊕ www.bourbonandbranch.com.*

Divas

BARS/PUBS | In the rough-and-tumble Tenderloin, around the corner from the Polk Street bars, transgenders and their admirers come here for the racy entertainment. Naughty Schoolgirls night (Wednesday) is a major fave. This multilevel space has separate areas for stage performances, dancing, and quiet chats. It's not a drag bar, as there is no sense of irony or camp about the place; the girls here are charming, and the fun is in the titillation. *✉ 1081 Post St., between Larkin and Polk Sts., Tenderloin ☎ 415/474–3482 ⊕ www.divassf.com.*

Edinburgh Castle Pub

BARS/PUBS | Work off your fish-and-chips and Scottish brew with a turn at the dartboard or pool table at this divey pub. It's popular with locals and Brits who congregate at the long bar or in the scattered seating areas, downing single-malt Scotch or pints of Fuller's. The pub holds weekly trivia nights and occasional Scottish cultural events (January's Robert Burns celebration is a favorite). Be aware that the surrounding neighborhood is gritty. ✉ *950 Geary St., between Larkin and Polk Sts., Tenderloin* ☎ *415/885–4074.*

MUSIC CLUBS

Great American Music Hall

MUSIC CLUBS | You can find top-drawer entertainment at this eclectic concert venue. Acts range from the best in blues, folk, and jazz to up-and-coming college-radio and American-roots artists to indie rockers such as OK Go, Mates of State, and Cowboy Junkies. The colorful marble-pillared emporium (built in 1907 as a bordello) also accommodates dancing at some shows. Pub grub is available on most nights. ✉ *859 O'Farrell St., between Polk and Larkin Sts., Tenderloin* ☎ *415/885–0750* 🌐 *www.slimspresents.com.*

Performing Arts

THEATER

SHN Golden Gate Theater

THEATER | This stylishly refurbished movie theater is now primarily a musical house. Touring productions of popular Broadway shows and revivals are its mainstays. ✉ *1 Taylor St., at Golden Gate Ave., Tenderloin* ☎ *888/746–1799* 🌐 *www.shnsf.com.*

★ **SHN Orpheum Theater**

THEATER | The biggest touring shows, such as *Hamilton* and *The Lion King*, are performed at this gorgeously restored 2,200-seat venue. The theater, opened in 1926, is as much an attraction as the shows. It was modeled after a 12th-century French cathedral and is considered one of the most beautiful theaters in the world; the interior walls have ornate stonework, and the gilded plaster ceiling is perforated with tiny lights. ✉ *1192 Market St., at Hyde St and 8th St., Tenderloin* ☎ *888/746–1799* 🌐 *www.shnsf.com.*

Shopping

Notorious for homelessness and panhandlers, this is not a neighborhood you want to get lost in, especially when the sun goes down. That said, there are several lively galleries here.

ART GALLERIES

Jessica Silverman Gallery

ART GALLERIES | Fashion, music, performance, paintings, and photography collide here—literally. Every six to eight weeks a new exhibit enters the space pushing the boundaries of content, concept, and form. The gallery occasionally hosts events with local and international artists. ✉ *488 Ellis St., at Leavenworth St., Tenderloin* ☎ *415/255–9508* 🌐 *jessicasilvermangallery.com* ⏲ *Closed Sun. and Mon.*

Hayes Valley

A chic neighborhood due west of Civic Center, Hayes Valley has terrific eateries, cool watering holes, and great browsing in its funky clothing, home-decor, and design boutiques. Locals love this quarter, but without any big-name draws it remains off the radar for many visitors.

Sights

★ **SFJAZZ Center**

ARTS VENUE | Devoted entirely to jazz, the center hosts performances by jazz greats such as McCoy Tyner, Joshua Redman, Regina Carter, and Chick Corea. Walk by and the street-level glass walls will make you feel as if you're inside; head indoors and the acoustics will knock your socks off. ✉ *201 Franklin St., at Fell St., Hayes Valley* ☎ *866/920–5299* 🌐 *www.sfjazz.org.*

Restaurants

Hayes Valley is home to several hip and haute dining destinations, centered around its main stem, perfect for pretheater dining. The low-key vibe in the wine bars and cafés makes it easy to feel like a local.

Arlequin

$$ | **AMERICAN** | For lunch on the go, don't submit to fast food when you've got Arlequin, the café offshoot of trendy Absinthe. Whatever you choose—breakfast, a hot or cold sandwich, lamb burger, roasted chicken—take it back to the lovely outdoor patio, a surprising oasis that makes Arlequin a standout. *Average main: $14 384 Hayes St., near Gough St., Hayes Valley 415/626–1211 arlequincafe.com.*

Hayes Street Grill

$$$ | **SEAFOOD** | You'll snag a table if you arrive here just as music lovers are folding their napkins and heading off for a show at the nearby Opera House or SFJAZZ Center. Fresh, sustainable, often local seafood lures the faithful here. **Known for:** seafood; preconcert dining; old-school ambience. *Average main: $31 320 Hayes St., Hayes Valley 415/863–5545 www.hayesstreet-grill.com No lunch weekends; closed most Mon.*

Jardinière

$$$$ | **MODERN FRENCH** | Famed chef Traci Des Jardins' restaurant is so sophisticated you may as well be eating at the nearby Opera House. An eye-catching curving staircase leads to an oval atrium, where locals and out-of-towners alike indulge in French-Californian dishes, such as foie gras terrine or sorrel soup. **Known for:** French technique; pre-opera dining; romantic ambience. *Average main: $36 300 Grove St., Hayes Valley 415/861–5555 www.jardiniere.com No lunch.*

Nojo Ramen

$$ | **JAPANESE** | For a little bonhomie before the symphony, it's hard to go wrong with this buzzy (and typically crowded) ramen spot. Noodles are the star of the menu, and deservedly so, but you'll also find izakaya-style small plates and comfort food like chicken teriyaki. **Known for:** ramen with chicken-based (paitan) broth; Japanese comfort foods; long lines. *Average main: $17 231 Franklin St., Hayes Valley 415/896–4587 www.nojosf.com Closed Mon. No lunch.*

Petit Crenn

$$$$ | **FRENCH** | Chef Dominique Crenn's sequel to her Michelin-starred Atelier Crenn is more casual but no less accomplished. Here, the French chef keeps her focus on seafood and vegetables, inspired by her family home on the French coastal region of Brittany and presented as a seven-course prix-fixe menu. **Known for:** seafood focus; seven-course prix-fixe menu; French cuisine. *Average main: $95 609 Hayes St., Hayes Valley 415/864–1744 www.petitcrenn.com Closed Mon.*

Pläj

$$$ | **SWEDISH** | The only Swedish restaurant in San Francisco is tucked behind the lobby of the Inn at the Opera and serves refreshing cuisine—fish pickled, smoked, or cured. Case in point is the beet-cured gravlax, which is complemented by sorrel sorbet and lemon crème fraîche. **Known for:** authentic Swedish cuisine; homemade aquavits (Scandinavian spirits); house-cured fish. *Average main: $30 333 Fulton St., Hayes Valley 415/294–8925 www.plajrestaurant.com No lunch.*

★ Rich Table

$$$ | **MODERN AMERICAN** | Sardine chips and porcini doughnuts are popular bites at co-chefs Evan and Sarah Rich's lively restaurant—and indicative of its creativity. The mains are also clever stunners: try one of the proteins or pastas, like the sea

urchin cacio e pepe. **Known for:** creative food; freshly baked bread; seasonal ingredients. *Average main: $34 199 Gough St., Hayes Valley 415/355–9085 www.richtablesf.com No lunch.*

Suppenküche

$$ | GERMAN | Nobody goes hungry—and no beer drinker goes thirsty—at this lively, hip outpost of simple German cooking in Hayes Valley. When the room gets crowded, which it regularly does, strangers sit together at unfinished pine tables. **Known for:** generous beer selection; authentic German food; lively atmosphere. *Average main: $20 525 Laguna St., Hayes Valley 415/252–9289 www.suppenkuche.com No lunch Mon.–Sat.*

★ Zuni Café

$$$ | MEDITERRANEAN | After one bite of Zuni's succulent brick-oven-roasted whole chicken with Tuscan bread salad, you'll understand why the two-floor café is a perennial star. Its long copper bar is a hub for a disparate mix of patrons who commune over oysters on the half shell and cocktails and wine. **Known for:** famous roast chicken; classic San Francisco dining; power lunches. *Average main: $35 1658 Market St., Hayes Valley 415/552–2522 www.zunicafe.com Closed Mon.*

Hotels

Hayes Valley should be called Hip Valley. Head-turning urbanites stroll past the boutiques, cafés, and high-end eateries day and night. But this wasn't always the case, and there still is a dodgy element to the streets off the main drag. Travelers can find a couple of modest inns atop gourmet eateries.

Hayes Valley Inn

$ | B&B/INN | Offering a cozy, homelike setting in the heart of Hayes Valley, the modest, clean rooms of this hotel come with sinks and vanities; a couple of spotless shared bathrooms are down the hall. **Pros:** continental breakfast included; free Wi-Fi; close to shopping, restaurants, and theater. **Cons:** no in-room bathrooms; no elevator; some street noise. *Rooms from: $130 417 Gough St., Hayes Valley 415/431–9131 www.hayesvalley-inn.com 28 rooms Breakfast.*

Inn at the Opera

$$ | B&B/INN | Within walking distance of Davies Symphony Hall and the War Memorial Opera House, these small rooms with dark wood furnishings cater to season-ticket holders for the opera, ballet, and symphony; they've also been the choice for stars of the music, dance, and opera worlds, from Luciano Pavarotti to Mikhail Baryshnikov. **Pros:** staff goes the extra mile; intimate restaurant; close to performance venues. **Cons:** smallish rooms and bath; sold out far in advance during opera season; difficult parking. *Rooms from: $250 333 Fulton St., Hayes Valley 415/863–8400, www.shellhospitality.com/inn-at-the-opera 48 rooms Breakfast.*

★ The Parsonage

$$ | B&B/INN | The two owners of this 1883 Victorian, a historic landmark, have created a one-of-a-kind bed-and-breakfast steps from the lower Haight and Hayes Valley, with many of the original mantlepieces, fireplaces, and mirrors, and ornate ceiling molding still intact. **Pros:** step back in time and sleep on antique beds; outstanding breakfast; innkeepers treat visitors like houseguests. **Cons:** street parking only; bygone-era feel not for everyone; two-night minimum. *Rooms from: $240 198 Haight St., Hayes Valley 415/863–3699 www.theparsonage.com 5 rooms Breakfast.*

Nightlife

Chic Hayes Valley is known for its wine and cocktail lounges with dark lighting and amazing atmosphere. Look for fine wines at Hôtel Biron, learn a thing or three about rum at Smuggler's Cove, and compete at karaoke at The Mint.

BARS

Absinthe

BARS/PUBS | The popular restaurant's nearly two dozen specialty cocktails—or even just a plain old Manhattan—make a trip just to the bar worthwhile. ✉ *398 Hayes St., at Gough St., Hayes Valley* ☎ *415/551–1590* 🌐 *www.absinthe.com.*

Hôtel Biron Wine Bar and Art Gallery

WINE BARS—NIGHTLIFE | Sharing an alley-like block with the backs of Market Street restaurants, this tiny, cavelike (in a good way) spot displays the work of local artists on its brick walls. The well-behaved twenty- to thirtysomething clientele enjoys the off-the-beaten-path quarters, the wines from around the world, the soft lighting, and the hip music. ✉ *45 Rose St., off Market St. near Gough St., Hayes Valley* ☎ *415/703–0403* 🌐 *www.hotelbiron.com.*

The Mint Karaoke Lounge

BARS/PUBS | A mixed gay-straight crowd that's drop-dead serious about its karaoke—to the point where you'd think an *American Idol* casting agent was in attendance—comes here seven nights a week. Regulars sing everything from Simon and Garfunkel songs to disco classics in front of an attentive audience. Do *not* walk onstage unprepared! Check out the songbook online to perfect your debut before you attempt to take the mike. Hit the ATM before, everything here is cash-only. ✉ *1942 Market St., between Duboce Ave. and Laguna St., Hayes Valley* ☎ *415/626–4726* 🌐 *www.themint.net.*

★ Smuggler's Cove

BARS/PUBS | With the decor of a pirate ship and a slew of rum-based cocktails, you half expect Captain Jack Sparrow to sidle up next to you at this offbeat, Disney-esque hangout. But don't let the kitschy ambience fool you. The folks at Smuggler's Cove take rum so seriously they've even had it made for them from distillers around the world, which you can sample along with more than 550 other offerings, some of them vintage and very hard to find. A punch card is provided so you can try the entire menu (featuring 80-plus cocktails) and remember where you left off without getting shipwrecked. The small space fills up quickly, so arrive early. ✉ *650 Gough St., at McAllister St., Hayes Valley* ☎ *415/869–1900* 🌐 *www.smugglerscovesf.com.*

Sugar Lounge

BARS/PUBS | Just trendy enough, but never pretentious, Sugar has fun cocktails (lemon drops, pink pussycats), good drink specials, and a low-key vibe. This small, narrow neighborhood favorite is perfect for a quiet drink or preshow aperitif. ✉ *377 Hayes St., at Gough St., Hayes Valley* ☎ *415/255–7144* 🌐 *www.sugarloungesf.com.*

Performing Arts

MUSIC

★ SFJAZZ Center

MUSIC | Jazz legends Branford Marsalis and Herbie Hancock have performed at the snazzy center, as have Rosanne Cash and world-music favorite Esperanza Spalding. The sight lines and acoustics here impress. Shows often sell out quickly. ✉ *201 Franklin St., Hayes Valley* ☎ *866/920–5299* 🌐 *www.sfjazz.org.*

SPOKEN WORD AND READINGS

★ City Arts & Lectures

READINGS/LECTURES | Each year this program includes more than 20 fascinating conversations with writers, composers, actors, politicians, scientists, and others. The Sydney Goldstein (formerly the Nourse) Theater, in the Performing Arts Center, is usually the venue. Past speakers have included Salman Rushdie, Ken Burns, and Linda Ronstadt. ✉ *Sydney Goldstein Theater, 275 Hayes St., Haight* ☎ *415/392–4400* 🌐 *www.cityarts.net.*

Shopping

A community park called Hayes Green breaks up a crowd of cool shops just west of the Civic Center. Art galleries and stores selling hip home decor, clothing, shoes, and handcrafted jewelry predominate. The density of unique shops and the absence of chains make Hayes Valley a favorite destination of local shoppers.

BEAUTY

Nancy Boy

PERFUME/COSMETICS | This sparse white-on-white locally owned store sells indulgent skin- and hair-care products, as well as a small selection of natural laundry and cleaning products. ✉ *347 Hayes St., between Franklin and Gough Sts., Hayes Valley* ☎ *415/552–3636* 🌐 *www.nancyboy.com.*

BOOKS

The Green Arcade

BOOKS/STATIONERY | For environmental, political, and sustainable books, look no further. With deep roots in the community, energetic artwork, and an atmosphere that encourages reading, this is a good place to hide away; the comfy chairs and warm vibe make it hard to leave. ✉ *1680 Market St., at Gough St., Hayes Valley* ☎ *415/431–6800* 🌐 *www.thegreenarcade.com.*

Isotope Comic Book Lounge

BOOKS/STATIONERY | For full-frontal nerdity in a chic modern setting, pay a visit to SF's premier comic book lounge. You'll find a great selection of graphic novels and artwork by popular and local artists, as well as lively after-hours events. ✉ *326 Fell St., at Gough St., Hayes Valley* ☎ *415/621–6543* 🌐 *www.isotopecomics.com* ⏲ *Closed Mon.*

CLOTHING: MEN AND WOMEN

Dish

CLOTHING | Many of the women's clothes displayed within this spare space are romantic, minus the frills. Look for the chic dresses of local designer Kathryn McCarron, as well as clothing and accessories by more widely known brands like Rag & Bone and Zoe Chicco. ✉ *541 Hayes St., between Laguna and Octavia Sts., Hayes Valley* ☎ *415/252–5997* 🌐 *www.dishboutique.com.*

Metier

JEWELRY/ACCESSORIES | For boutique shopping that's anything but hit or miss, browse through this unusual selection of jewelry by artists like Arielle de Pinto, Philip Crangi, and Gillian Conroy. The one-of-a-kind rings, charms, and pendants have won this boutique an obsessively loyal following. ✉ *546 Laguna St., between Linden and Hayes Sts., Hayes Valley* ☎ *415/590–2998* 🌐 *www.metiersf.com.*

Ver Unica

CLOTHING | Though you can find a few items from the psychedelic '60s, beautifully preserved fashions from the '40s and '50s are the best reason for visiting. You can even track down purses and hard-to-find vintage shoes to go with that fur-trimmed jacket. ✉ *526 Hayes St., between Laguna and Octavia Sts., Hayes Valley* ☎ *415/621–6259.*

FOOD AND DRINK

Arlequin Wine Merchant

WINE/SPIRITS | If you like the wine list at Absinthe Brasserie, you can walk next door and pick up a few bottles from its highly regarded sister establishment. This small, unintimidating shop carries hard-to-find wines from small producers. Why wait to taste? Crack open a bottle on the patio out back. ✉ *384A Hayes St., near Gough St., Hayes Valley* ☎ *415/863–1104* 🌐 *www.arlequinwinemerchant.com.*

Miette

FOOD/CANDY | There is truly nothing sweeter than a cellophane bag tied with colorful ribbon and filled with malt balls or floral meringues from this Insta-friendly candy and pastry-store. Grab a gingerbread cupcake or a tantalizing macaron or some shortbread. The pastel-color cake stands make even window-shopping a treat. ✉ *449 Octavia Blvd., between Hayes and Linden Sts., Hayes Valley* ☎ *415/626–6221* 🌐 *www.miette.com.*

True Sake

WINE/SPIRITS | Though it would be reasonable to expect a Japanese aesthetic at the first store in the United States dedicated entirely to sake, you might instead hear dance music thumping quietly in the background while you browse. Each of the many sakes is displayed with a label describing the drink's qualities and food-pairing suggestions. ✉ *560 Hayes St., between Laguna and Octavia Sts., Hayes Valley* ☎ *415/355–9555* 🌐 *www.truesake.com.*

FURNITURE, HOUSEWARES, AND GIFTS

Flight 001

GIFTS/SOUVENIRS | Ultrastylish travel accessories—retro-looking flight bags, supersoft leather passport wallets, and luxury toiletries—line the shelves of this brightly lighted shop, which vaguely resembles an airplane interior. High-tech travel gear and a small collection of guidebooks speed you on your way. ✉ *525 Hayes St., between Laguna and Octavia Sts., Hayes Valley* ☎ *415/487–1001* 🌐 *www.flight001.com.*

HANDICRAFTS AND FOLK ART

F. Dorian

CRAFTS | In addition to scarves, jewelry, and other crafts from around the world—a carved wooden candle holder from Ivory Coast is one example—this store carries brightly colored glass and ceramic works by local artisans and decorative pillows. ✉ *370 Hayes St., between Franklin and Gough Sts., Hayes Valley* ☎ *415/861–3191.*

SHOES

Gimme Shoes

SHOES/LUGGAGE/LEATHER GOODS | From the chunky to the sleek, the shoes carried here—including those by Chie Mihara, Red Wing, Del Carlo, and Paul Smith—are top notch. And if $500 seems steep for a pair of black boots, perhaps you haven't seen the perfect pair by Fiorentini + Baker. ✉ *416 Hayes St., at Gough St., Hayes Valley* ☎ *415/864–0691* 🌐 *www.gimmeshoes.com.*

Paolo Shoes

SHOES/LUGGAGE/LEATHER GOODS | Looking for gorgeous handcrafted Italian leather shoes? (Who isn't?) This is *the* place in San Francisco to find them. From knee-high boots to contoured heel pumps, Paolo Iantorno's selection will make your heart miss a beat. The prices might as well; they hover around the $300 mark, but all shoes are made in quantities of 25 or fewer pairs. ✉ *524 Hayes St., between Octavia and Laguna Sts., Hayes Valley* ☎ *415/552–4580* 🌐 *paoloshoes.com.*

Activities

SKATING

Church of 8 Wheels

IN-LINE SKATING/ROLLER SKATING | Dance or roll along to disco-era tunes at this retro-themed skating rink inside an old church. Friday and Saturday daytime is open to anyone; after dark is adults only. ✉ *554 Fillmore St. (at Fell), Hayes Valley* ☎ *415/752–1967* 🌐 *www.churchof-8wheels.com* 🎟 *$10, skate rental $5.*

Chapter 5

NOB HILL AND RUSSIAN HILL

Updated by
Rebecca Flint Marx

Sights	Restaurants	Hotels	Shopping	Nightlife
★★☆☆☆	★★★☆☆	★★★☆☆	★★☆☆☆	★☆☆☆☆

NEIGHBORHOOD SNAPSHOT

TOP REASONS TO GO

■ **Macondray Lane:** Duck into this secret, lush garden lane and walk its narrow, uneven cobblestones.

■ **Vallejo Steps area:** Make the steep climb up to lovely Ina Coolbrith Park, then continue up along the glorious garden path of the Vallejo Steps to a spectacular view at the top.

■ **San Francisco Art Institute:** Contemplate a Diego Rivera mural and stop at the café for cheap organic coffee and a priceless view of the city and the bay. It may be the best—and cheapest—way to spend an hour in the neighborhood.

■ **Cable Car Museum:** Ride a cable car all the way back to the barn, hanging on tight as it clack-clack-clacks its way up Nob Hill, then go behind the scenes at the museum.

■ **Play "Bullitt" on the steepest streets:** For the ride of your life, take a drive up and down the city's steepest streets on Russian Hill. A trip over the precipice of Filbert or Jones will make you feel as if you're falling off the edge of the world.

QUICK BITES

The Boy's Deli. Tucked in the back of a tiny produce market is a counter serving up some of the biggest, juiciest, best sandwiches in town—strictly to go—along with traditional sides. **Known for:** spicy Sandlot sandwich; lunchtime crowd. ✉ *Polk & Green Produce Market, 2222 Polk St., between Green and Vallejo Sts., Russian Hill* ☎ *415/776–3099* 🌐 *theboys-deli.com.*

Swensen's Ice Cream. The original Swensen's has been a neighborhood favorite since it opened in 1948. An antique sign still fronts the tiny shop, but concessions to the times include such ice-cream flavors as green tea and lychee. **Known for:** old-time atmosphere; unusual flavors; traditional ice cream. ✉ *1999 Hyde St., at Union St., Russian Hill* ☎ *415/775–6818* 🌐 *www.swensensicecream.com* 💳 *No credit cards.*

GETTING THERE

■ The thing about Russian and Nob Hills is that they're both especially steep hills. If you're not up for the hike, a cable car is certainly the most exciting way to reach the top. Take the California line for Nob Hill and the Powell–Hyde line for Russian Hill. Buses serve the area as well, such as the 1–California bus for Nob Hill, but the routes run only east–west. Only the cable cars tackle the steeper north–south streets. Driving yourself is a hassle, since parking is a challenge on these crowded, precipitous streets.

PLANNING YOUR TIME

■ Since walking Nob Hill is (almost) all about gazing at exteriors, touring the neighborhood during daylight hours is a must. The sights here don't require a lot of visiting time—say a half hour each at the Cable Car Museum and Grace Cathedral—but allow time for the walk itself. An afternoon visit is ideal for Russian Hill, so you can browse the shops. You could cover both neighborhoods in three or four hours. If you time it just right, you can finish up with a sunset cocktail at a swanky hotel lounge or the retro-tiki Tonga Room.

In place of the quirky charm and cultural diversity that mark other San Francisco neighborhoods, Nob Hill exudes history and good breeding. Topped with some of the city's most elegant hotels, Gothic Grace Cathedral, and private blue-blood clubs, it's the pinnacle of privilege. One hill over, across Pacific Avenue, is another old-family bastion, Russian Hill. It may not be quite as wealthy as Nob Hill, but it's no slouch—and it's got jaw-dropping views.

Nob Hill

Nob Hill was officially dubbed during the 1870s when "the Big Four"—Charles Crocker, Leland Stanford, Mark Hopkins, and Collis P. Huntington, who were involved in the construction of the transcontinental railroad—built their hilltop estates. The lingo is thick from this era: those on the hilltop were referred to as "nabobs" (originally meaning a provincial governor from India) and "swells," and the hill itself was called Snob Hill, a term that survives to this day. By 1882 so many estates had sprung up on Nob Hill that Robert Louis Stevenson called it "the hill of palaces." But the 1906 earthquake and fire destroyed all the palatial mansions except for portions of the James Flood brownstone. History buffs may choose to linger here, but for most visitors, a casual glimpse from a cable car will be enough.

⇨ *For more details on the Cable Car Museum, see the Cable Cars feature in Experience San Francisco.*

Sights

Cable Car Museum

MUSEUM | FAMILY | One of the city's best free offerings, this museum is an absolute must for kids. You can even ride a cable car here—all three lines stop between Russian Hill and Nob Hill. The facility, which is inside the city's last cable-car barn, takes the top off the system to let you see how it all works. Eternally humming and squealing, the massive powerhouse cable wheels steal the show. You can also climb aboard a vintage car and take the grip, let the kids ring a cable-car bell (briefly), and check out vintage gear dating from 1873. *⊠ 1201 Mason St., at Washington St., Nob Hill ☎ 415/474–1887 🌐 www.cablecarmuseum.org 🎫 Free.*

Collis P. Huntington Park

CITY PARK | The elegant park west of the Pacific Union Club and east of Grace Cathedral occupies the site of a mansion owned by the "Big Four" railroad baron Collis P. Huntington. He died in 1900, the mansion was destroyed in the 1906 fire, and in 1915 his widow—by then married to Huntington's nephew—donated the land to the city for use as a park. The Huntingtons' neighbors, the Crockers, once owned the *Fountain of the Tortoises,* based on the original in Rome's Piazza Mattei. ■ TIP→ **The benches around the fountain offer a welcome break after climbing Nob Hill.** ✉ *Taylor and California Sts., Nob Hill.*

Fairmont San Francisco

HOTEL—SIGHT | The hotel's dazzling opening was delayed a year by the 1906 quake, but since then, the marble palace has hosted presidents, royalty, movie stars, and local nabobs. Things have changed since its early days, however: on the eve of World War I, you could get a room for as low as $2 per night, meals included. Nowadays, prices go as high as $18,000, which buys a night in the eight-room, contemporary art–filled penthouse suite. Swing through the opulent lobby on your way to tea (served on weekends from 1:30 to 3:30) at the Laurel Court restaurant; peek through the foyer's floor-to-ceiling windows for a glimpse of the hotel's garden and beehives, where the honey served with tea is produced. Don't miss an evening cocktail (a mai tai is in order) in the kitschy Tonga Room, complete with tiki huts, a sporadic tropical rainstorm, and a floating bandstand. ✉ *950 Mason St., Nob Hill* ☎ *415/772–5000* 🌐 *www.fairmont.com/san-francisco.*

Grace Cathedral

RELIGIOUS SITE | Not many churches can boast an altarpiece by Keith Haring and not one but two labyrinths. The seat of the Episcopal Church in San Francisco, this soaring Gothic-style structure, erected on the site of the 19th-century railroad baron Charles Crocker's mansion, took 14 years to build, beginning in 1927 and eventually wrapping up in 1964. The gilded bronze doors at the east entrance were taken from casts of Lorenzo Ghiberti's incredible Gates of Paradise, which are on the Baptistery in Florence, Italy. A sculpture of St. Francis by Beniamino Bufano greets you as you enter.

The 34-foot-wide limestone labyrinth is a replica of the 13th-century stone maze on the floor of Chartres Cathedral. All are encouraged to walk the 1/8-mile-long labyrinth, a ritual based on the tradition of meditative walking. There's also a granite outdoor labyrinth on the church's northeast side. The AIDS Interfaith Chapel, to the right as you enter Grace, contains a bronze triptych by the late artist Keith Haring and panels from the AIDS Memorial Quilt. ■ TIP→ **Especially dramatic times to view the cathedral are during Thursday-night evensong (5:15 pm) and during special holiday programs.** ✉ *1100 California St., at Taylor St., Nob Hill* ☎ *415/749–6300* 🌐 *www.gracecathedral.org* 🎫 *Free; tours $25.*

InterContinental Mark Hopkins Hotel

HOTEL—SIGHT | Built on the ashes of railroad tycoon Mark Hopkins's grand estate (constructed at his wife's urging; Hopkins

Close-Ups on the Brocklebank

The grand Brocklebank Apartments, on the northeast corner of Sacramento and Mason Streets across from the Fairmont hotel, might look eerily familiar. In 1958 the complex was showcased in Alfred Hitchcock's *Vertigo* (Jimmy Stewart starts trailing Kim Novak here), and in the 1990s it popped up in the miniseries *Tales of the City.*

Walking the Hills

Start a tour of Nob Hill and Russian Hill with a cable-car ride up to **California** and **Powell Streets** on Nob Hill (all lines go here). Walking two blocks east you can pass all the Big Four mansions-cum-hotels on the hill. Peek at the Keith Haring triptych in impressive **Grace Cathedral**; grab a Peet's coffee in the basement café if you need a lift. Next, head down to the **Cable Car Museum** to see the machinery in action. Then make your way to Russian Hill—a cable car is a fine way to reach the peak—to visit some of the city's loveliest hidden lanes and stairways. At **Mason** and **Vallejo Streets**, head up the **Vallejo Steps**, passing contemplative, terraced **Ina Coolbrith Park** and beautifully tended private gardens. Take in the sweeping city and bay view from the top of the hill, then head right on **Jones Street** and duck right under the trellis to wooded and shady **Macondray Lane.** From here it's a six-block hike to crooked **Lombard Street.** If you've still got some steam, be sure to go another block to see **Diego Rivera's mural** and the surprise panoramic view from the **San Francisco Art Institute.**

himself preferred to live frugally), this 19-story hotel went up in 1926. A combination of French château and Spanish Renaissance architecture, with noteworthy terra-cotta detailing, it has hosted statesmen, royalty, and Hollywood celebrities. The 11-room penthouse was turned into a glass-wall cocktail lounge in 1939: the Top of the Mark is remembered fondly by thousands of World War II veterans who jammed the lounge before leaving for overseas duty. Wives and sweethearts watching the ships depart gave the room's northwest nook its name—Weepers' Corner. ■ **TIP→ With its 360-degree views, the lounge is a wonderful spot for a nighttime drink.** ✉ *999 California St., at Mason St., Nob Hill* ☎ *415/392-3434* 🌐 *www.intercontinentalmarkhopkins.com.*

Nob Hill Masonic Center

ARTS VENUE | Erected by Freemasons in 1957, the hall is familiar to locals mostly as a concert and lecture venue, where such notables as Van Morrison and Al Gore have appeared. But you don't need a ticket to check out artist Emile Norman's impressive lobby mosaic. Mainly in rich greens and yellows, it depicts the Masons' role in California history. ✉ *1111 California St., Nob Hill* ☎ *415/776-7457* 🌐 *sfmasonic.com.*

Pacific-Union Club

BUILDING | The former home of silver baron James Flood cost a whopping $1.5 million in 1886, when even a stylish Victorian like the Haas-Lilienthal House cost less than $20,000. All that cash did buy some structural stability. The Flood residence (to be precise, its shell) was the only Nob Hill mansion to survive the 1906 earthquake and fire. The Pacific-Union Club, a bastion of the wealthy and powerful, purchased the house in 1907 and commissioned Willis Polk to redesign it; the architect added the semicircular wings and third floor. (The ornate fence design dates from the mansion's construction.) ✉ *1000 California St., Nob Hill.*

The Stanford Court Hotel

HOTEL—SIGHT | In 1876 trendsetter Leland Stanford, a California governor and founder of Stanford University, was the first to build an estate on Nob Hill. The only part that survived the earthquake was a basalt-and-granite wall that's been restored; check it out from the eastern side of the hotel. In 1912 an apartment house was built on the site of the former estate, and in 1972 the present-day hotel was constructed from the shell of that building. A stained-glass dome tops the carriage entrance. ✉ *905 California St., Nob Hill* ☎ *415/989–3500* 🌐 *www.stanfordcourt.com.*

Restaurants

Nob Hill, the most famous hill in a city of hills, is known for its iconic hotels—the Fairmont, the Mark, the Ritz-Carlton, the Huntington—and for its views. Unfortunately, the food isn't as unparalleled as the scenic outlooks. Real estate is expensive, so it's not the place for chefs to roll the dice on a new venture. But what you will find are hotel dining rooms and established institutions.

★ Acquerello

$$$$ | ITALIAN | Chef-co-owner Suzette Gresham has elicited plenty of swoons over the years with her high-end but soulful Italian cooking. Her Parmesan *budino* (pudding) is a star of the menu, which features both classic and cutting-edge dishes. **Known for:** prix-fixe dining; Parmesan budino; extensive Italian wine list. $ *Average main: $95* ✉ *1722 Sacramento St., Polk Gulch* ☎ *415/567–5432* 🌐 *www.acquerello.com* ⏲ *Closed Sun. and Mon. No lunch.*

★ Sons & Daughters

$$$$ | AMERICAN | The nine-course tasting menu that chef-owner Teague Moriarty serves at his elegant Michelin-starred restaurant serves as a primer for how to do highly seasonal cuisine—and tasting menus—the right way. Each course is nuanced and beautifully executed, whether it's tender grilled squid with a fennel-persimmon mole or a sorrel granita with buckwheat shortbread. **Known for:** changing prix-fixe menu; excellent housemade bread; attentive service. $ *Average main: $145* ✉ *708 Bush St., Nob Hill* ☎ *415/391–8311* 🌐 *www.sonsanddaughterssf.com* ⏲ *No lunch.*

★ Swan Oyster Depot

$$ | SEAFOOD | Half fish market and half diner, this small, slim, family-run seafood operation, open since 1912, has no tables, just a narrow marble counter with about 18 stools. Most people come in to buy perfectly fresh salmon, halibut, crabs, and other seafood to take home. **Known for:** fresh seafood; long lines; rich history. $ *Average main: $18* ✉ *1517 Polk St., Polk Gulch* ☎ *415/673–1101* 💳 *No credit cards* ⏲ *Closed Sun. No dinner.*

Hotels

The steep Nob Hill is alive with hostelries proffering treatment fit for (and provided to) kings, queens, and politicians. Stay here, and at the end of a long day of sightseeing a cable car can whisk you practically to your hotel's doorstep. The dining scene can be a schlep from your hotel, but the allure of sleeping atop San Francisco can erase that inconvenience. Note that many hotels charge "urban fees" or "amenity fees" so you may want to call in advance to ascertain the true daily rate.

Fairmont San Francisco

$$$$ | HOTEL | Dominating the top of Nob Hill like a European palace, the Fairmont indulges guests in luxury—rooms in the main building, adorned in sapphire blues with platinum and pewter accents, have high ceilings, decadent beds, and marble bathrooms; rooms in the newer Tower, many with fine views, have a neutral color palette with bright-silver notes. **Pros:** huge bathrooms; stunning lobby; great location. **Cons:** some older rooms are small; hills can be challenging for those on foot. $ *Rooms from: $459* ✉ *950 Mason St., Nob Hill* ☎ *415/772–5000, 800/257–7544* 🌐 *www.fairmont.com/san-francisco* 🛏 *606 rooms* 🍽 *No meals.*

Hotel Vertigo

$$ | **HOTEL** | Scenes in Alfred Hitchcock's classic thriller *Vertigo* were shot in this ornate hotel (it was a speakeasy during Prohibition), and designer Thomas Schoos has infused the guest rooms with a reckless, whimsical tribute—consider the tangerine highlights and the horse-head lamps, not to mention the classic *Vertigo* swirl logo along the walls. **Pros:** tons of personality; artsy decor; central location. **Cons:** borderline neighborhood; no a/c; no parking garage. *Rooms from: $139 ✉ 940 Sutter St., between Leavenworth and Hyde Sts., Nob Hill ☎ 415/885–6800, 800/553–1900 🌐 www.hotelvertigosf.com 102 rooms No meals.*

★ **The Huntington Hotel**

$$$ | **HOTEL** | Stars from Bogart and Bacall to Picasso and Pavarotti have stayed in this hotel famed for its spacious high-ceilinged rooms and suites, most of which have great views of Grace Cathedral and Huntington Park or the bay and the fog rolling across the city skyline. **Pros:** spacious rooms; first-rate spa with city views; impressive service from greeting to farewell. **Cons:** up a steep hill from downtown; expensive restaurant; ultracontemporary aesthetic doesn't work for some guests. *Rooms from: $250 ✉ 1075 California St., Nob Hill ☎ 415/474–5400 134 rooms No meals.*

InterContinental Mark Hopkins

$$$ | **HOTEL** | The circular redbrick drive of this towering 1926 architectural landmark leads to an opulent, mirrored, marble-floor lobby that's the gateway to luxurious rooms aglow with gold, cream, and yellow tones. **Pros:** spectacular views; steeped in history; last-minute deals often possible online. **Cons:** decor too old-style for some guests; small bathrooms in some rooms and suites; steep climb from Union Square. *Rooms from: $209 ✉ 1 Nob Hill, Nob Hill ☎ 415/392–3434, 800/662–4455 🌐 www.intercontinentalmarkhopkins.com 380 rooms No meals.*

★ **The Ritz-Carlton, San Francisco**

$$$$ | **HOTEL** | A tribute to beauty and attentive, professional service, the Ritz-Carlton emphasizes luxury and elegance, which is evident in the Ionic columns that grace the neoclassical facade and the crystal chandeliers that illuminate marble floors and walls in the lobby. **Pros:** terrific service; beautiful surroundings; Parallel 37 restaurant and Lobby Lounge. **Cons:** expensive; hilly location; no pool. *Rooms from: $538 ✉ 600 Stockton St., at Pine St., Nob Hill ☎ 415/296–7465, 800/542–8680 🌐 www.ritzcarlton.com/sanfrancisco 336 rooms No meals.*

Stanford Court San Francisco

$$$ | **HOTEL** | Railroad baron Leland Stanford's mansion once stood where the Stanford is today, and the warm tones and handsome leather chairs are reminiscent of a grander time. **Pros:** attention to technological detail; classic yet modern; off-season packages. **Cons:** up a steep hill from Union Square and Financial District; many rooms are small; exterior rooms get outside noise. *Rooms from: $300 ✉ 905 California St., Nob Hill ☎ 415/989–3500 🌐 www.stanfordcourt.com 393 rooms No meals.*

Whether you're out on the streets or inside a bar, Nob Hill serves up fantastic city views, the very best of which can be experienced from the Top of the Mark.

BARS

★ **Tonga Room and Hurricane Bar**

BARS/PUBS | Since the 1940s the Tonga Room has supplied its city with high Polynesian kitsch. Fake palm trees, grass huts, a lagoon (three-piece combos play pop standards on a floating barge), and faux monsoons—courtesy of sprinkler-system rain and simulated thunder and lightning—grow more surreal as you quaff the bar's signature mai tais and other too-too fruity cocktails. **■TIP→ Looking for an evening chock-full of bad decision making? Order the Scorpion Bowl and let the drunk dialing begin!** ✉ *Fairmont San Francisco, 950 Mason St., at California St., Nob Hill* ☎ *415/772–5278* 🌐 *www.tongaroom.com.*

Top of the Mark

BARS/PUBS | A famous magazine photograph immortalized the bar atop the Mark Hopkins as a hot spot for World War II servicemen on leave or about to ship out. The view remains sensational. Entertainment ranges from solo jazz piano to six-piece jazz ensembles. Cover charges vary, and shows begin at 6:30 pm weekdays and 9 pm weekends. ✉ *Mark Hopkins InterContinental, 999 California St., at Mason St., Nob Hill* ☎ *415/392–3434* 🌐 *www.topofthemark.com.*

The Wreck Room

BARS/PUBS | Shuffleboard, arcade basketball, a jukebox, and plenty of flat-screen TVs make this spacious yet divey place feel like a time machine back to your college days. On weekends the crowd is a sea of popped collars, baseball caps, and chest bumps, so get there early if you yearn for a turn at one of the games. ✉ *1390 California St., at Hyde St., Nob Hill* ☎ *415/932–6715* 🌐 *www.thewreckroomsf.com.*

Shopping

With superb vistas and European-style shops and eateries, this leafy neighborhood is a favorite destination for Saturday-morning and after-work shoppers.

CLOTHING

Christine Foley

CLOTHING | Discounts of up to 50% apply to the hand-loomed cotton sweaters with fanciful, intricate designs. There's also a large selection of colorful sweaters for children. Pillows, stuffed animals, and assorted knickknacks are also on offer in this small showroom. ✉ *Fairmont Hotel, 950 Mason St., at California St., Nob Hill* ☎ *415/399–9938* 🌐 *www.christinefoley.com.*

Cris

CLOTHING | This upscale designer consignment shop (the locals' best-kept secret) is full of nearly new items for a lot less than new prices. Chloe and Chanel are a couple of the many designers to grace the racks. Not only is this shop brimming with one-of-a-kind tops, dresses, and coats, but it smells like a spring garden. And to top it all off, they include a fresh flower with every purchase. ✉ *2056 Polk St., at Broadway St., Polk Gulch* ☎ *415/474–1191* 🌐 *www.crisconsignment.com.*

SPAS

Nob Hill Spa

SPA/BEAUTY | Warning: after experiencing this serene and luxurious spa's treatments, you'll start to *expect* champagne after your massage. Unique features include the eucalyptus steam bath and a gorgeous infinity pool that overlooks the city through a glass wall. After your treatments, you can hang here all day: relax in the Zen room, get a green-tea body scrub, or just read on the sundeck. Regulars love the 80-minute Nourishing Seaweed facial, the 50-minute Lavender Salt Scrub skin-exfoliation treatment, and the Table Thai massage, 80 minutes of pure indulgence. ✉ *Huntington Hotel, 1075 California St., at Mason St., Nob Hill* ☎ *415/345–2888* 🌐 *www.nobhillspa.com.*

Russian Hill

Essentially a tony residential neighborhood of spiffy pieds-à-terre, Victorian flats, Edwardian cottages, and boxlike condos, Russian Hill has some of the city's loveliest stairway walks, hidden garden ways, and steepest streets—not to mention those bay views. Several stories explain the origin of Russian Hill's name. One legend has it that Russian farmers raised vegetables here for Farallon Islands seal hunters; another attributes the name to a Russian sailor of prodigious drinking habits who drowned when he fell into a well on the hill. A plaque at the top of the Vallejo Steps gives credence to the version that says sailors of the Russian-American company were buried here in the 1840s. Be sure to visit the sign for yourself—its location offers perhaps the finest vantage point on the hill.

Sights

★ Ina Coolbrith Park

CITY PARK | If you make it all the way up here, you may have the place all to yourself, or at least feel like you do. The park's terraces are carved from a hill so steep that it's difficult to see if anyone else is there or not. Locals love this park because it feels like a secret no one else knows about—one of the city's magic hidden gardens, with a meditative setting and spectacular views of the bay peeking out from among the trees. A poet, Oakland librarian, and niece of Mormon prophet Joseph Smith, Ina Coolbrith (1841–1928) introduced Jack London and Isadora Duncan to the world of books. For years she entertained literary greats in her Macondray Lane home near the park. In 1915 she was named poet laureate of California. ✉ *Vallejo St. between Mason and Taylor Sts., Russian Hill.*

Lombard Street

NEIGHBORHOOD | The block-long "Crookedest Street in the World" makes eight switchbacks down the east face of Russian Hill between Hyde and Leavenworth Streets. Residents bemoan the traffic jam outside their front doors, but the throngs continue. Join the line of cars waiting to drive down the steep hill, or avoid the whole mess and walk down the steps on either side of Lombard. You take in super views of North Beach and Coit Tower whether you walk or drive—though if you're the one behind the wheel, you'd better keep your eye on the road lest you become yet another of the many folks who ram the garden barriers. **■ TIP→ Can't stand the traffic? Thrill seekers of a different stripe may want to head two blocks south of Lombard to Filbert Street. At a gradient of 31.5%, the hair-raising descent between Hyde and Leavenworth Streets is one of the city's steepest. Go slowly!** ✉ *Lombard St. between Hyde and Leavenworth Sts., Russian Hill.*

★ Macondray Lane

NEIGHBORHOOD | San Francisco has no shortage of impressive, grand homes, but Macondray Lane is the quintessential hidden garden. Enter under a lovely wooden trellis and proceed down a quiet, cobbled pedestrian lane lined with Edwardian cottages and flowering plants and trees. A flight of steep wooden stairs at the end of the lane leads to Taylor Street—on the way down you can't miss the bay views. If you've read any of Armistead Maupin's *Tales of the City* books, you may find the lane vaguely familiar. It's the thinly disguised setting for part of the series' action. ✉ *Between Jones and Taylor Sts., and Union and Green Sts., Russian Hill.*

San Francisco Art Institute

MUSEUM | The number-one reason for a visit is Mexican master Diego Rivera's *The Making of a Fresco Showing the Building of a City* (1931), in the student gallery to your immediate left inside the entrance. Rivera himself is in the fresco—his broad behind is to the viewer—and he's surrounded by his assistants. They in turn are surrounded by a construction scene, laborers, and city notables such as sculptor Robert Stackpole and architect Timothy Pflueger. *Making* is one of three San Francisco murals painted by Rivera. The number-two reason to come here is the café, or more precisely the eye-popping, panoramic view from the café, which serves surprisingly decent food for a song.

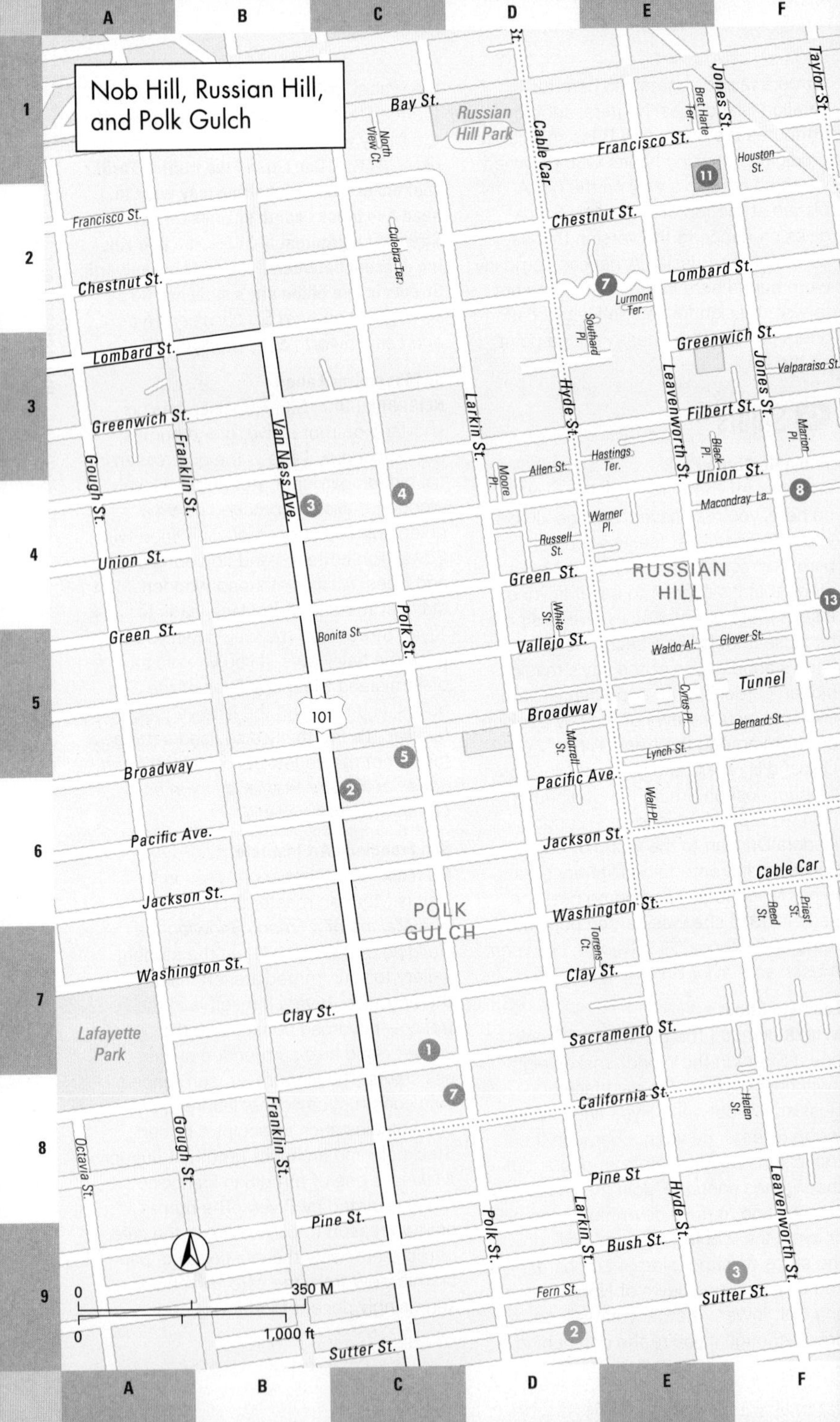
Nob Hill, Russian Hill, and Polk Gulch
A
B
C
D
E
F
1
2
3
4
5
6
7
8
9
Bay St.
Russian Hill Park
North View Ct.
Cable Car
Francisco St.
Bret Harte Ter.
Jones St.
Taylor St.
Houston St.
11
Francisco St.
Chestnut St.
Culebra Ter.
Chestnut St.
Lombard St.
7
Lurmont Ter.
Southard Pl.
Lombard St.
Greenwich St.
Valparaiso St.
Larkin St.
Hyde St.
Leavenworth St.
Filbert St.
Greenwich St.
Van Ness Ave.
Franklin St.
Gough St.
Hastings Ter.
Allen St.
Moore Pl.
Black Pl.
Marion Pl.
Union St.
8
Macondray La.
3
4
Warner Pl.
Russell St.
Union St.
Green St.
RUSSIAN HILL
13
White St.
Green St.
Bonita St.
Polk St.
Vallejo St.
Waldo Al.
Glover St.
Tunnel
Cyrus Pl.
101
Broadway
Bernard St.
Morrell St.
5
Lynch St.
Broadway
2
Pacific Ave.
Wall Pl.
Pacific Ave.
Jackson St.
Cable Car
Jackson St.
POLK GULCH
Washington St.
Reed St.
Priest St.
Torrens Ct.
Washington St.
Clay St.
Clay St.
Lafayette Park
Sacramento St.
1
7
California St.
Helen St.
Octavia St.
Gough St.
Franklin St.
Pine St
Hyde St.
Leavenworth St.
Pine St.
Polk St.
Larkin St.
Bush St.
3
0
350 M
Fern St.
Sutter St.
0
1,000 ft
2
Sutter St.

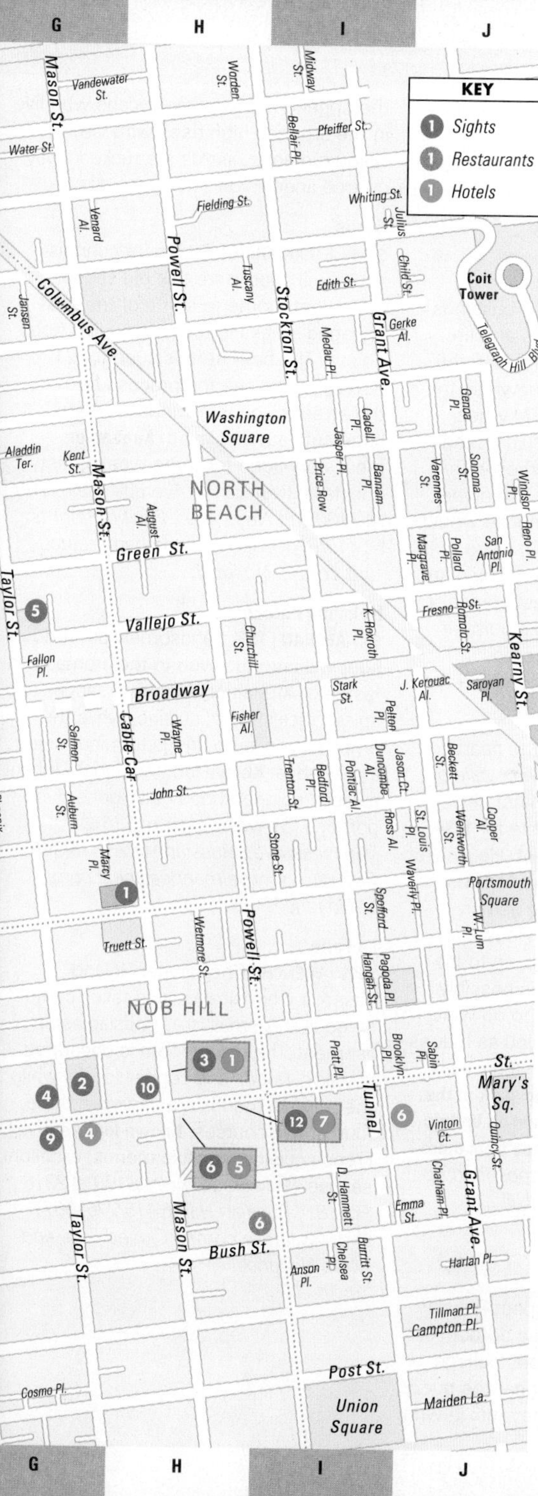

Sights

1 Cable Car Museum G6
2 Collis P. Huntington Park G7
3 Fairmont San Francisco........... H7
4 Grace Cathedral G7
5 Ina Coolbrith Park G4
6 InterContinental Mark Hopkins Hotel H7
7 Lombard Street E2
8 Macondray Lane.................... F4
9 Nob Hill Masonic Center.......... G8
10 Pacific-Union Club................ H7
11 San Francisco Art Institute E2
12 The Stanford Court Hotel H7
13 Vallejo Steps F4

Restaurants

1 Acquerello........................... C7
2 Harris'................................. C6
3 Helmand Palace B4
4 La Folie............................... C4
5 Lord Stanley......................... C5
6 Sons & Daughters I8
7 Swan Oyster Depot................ C8

Hotels

1 Fairmont San Francisco........... H7
2 Hotel Carlton D9
3 Hotel Vertigo F9
4 The Huntington Hotel............. G8
5 InterContinental Mark Hopkins H7
6 The Ritz-Carlton, San Francisco....................... J7
7 Stanford Court San Francisco.... H7

The **Walter & McBean Galleries** (*415/749–4563; Tues. 11–7, Wed.–Sat. 11–6*) exhibit the often provocative works of established artists. ✉ *800 Chestnut St., Russian Hill* ☎ *415/771–7020* 🌐 *www.sfai.edu* 🎟 *Galleries free.*

★ **Vallejo Steps**

BUILDING | Several Russian Hill buildings survived the 1906 earthquake and fire and remain standing. Patriotic firefighters saved what's become known as the **Flag House** (*1652–56 Taylor St.*) when they spotted the American flag on the property and doused the flames with seltzer water and wet sand. The owner, a flag collector, fearing the house would burn to the ground, wanted it to go down in style, with "all flags flying." The Flag House, at the southwest corner of Ina Coolbrith Park, is one of a number of California shingle–style homes in this neighborhood, several of which the architect Willis Polk designed.

Polk drew up the plans for the nearby **Polk-Williams House** (*Taylor and Vallejo Sts.*) and lived in one of its finer sections, and he was responsible for **1034–1036 Vallejo,** across the street. He also laid out the Vallejo Steps themselves, which climb the steep ridge across Taylor Street from the Flag House. Though very steep, the walk up to Ina Coolbrith Park and beyond is possibly the most pleasurable thing to do while on Russian Hill, rewarding you as it does with glorious views. **■TIP→ If the walk up the steps will be too taxing, park at the top of the steps by heading east on Vallejo from Jones and enjoy the scene from there.** ✉ *Taylor and Vallejo Sts., steps lead up toward Jones St., Russian Hill.*

Restaurants

Despite its name, don't expect Russian food here. Instead, this area bordering Nob Hill caters to the postcollege crowds, who want to live near the buzzy Polk and Larkin Streets. They mix in with the upper-crust San Franciscans who live in the art-deco high-rises with views. Many romantic bistros are tucked away on tree-lined Hyde Street.

Harris'

$$$$ | **STEAKHOUSE** | Red-meat connoisseurs will appreciate this old-school restaurant, home to some of the best dry-aged steaks in town, including Kobe rib eye. The beef here is aged for 21 days; you can see the process from the street through a window where large cuts are displayed. **Known for:** steaks dry-aged for three weeks; tasty cocktails; live jazz. $ *Average main: $60* ✉ *2100 Van Ness Ave., Pacific Heights* ☎ *415/673–1888* 🌐 *www.harrisrestaurant.com* ⏲ *No lunch.*

Helmand Palace

$$ | **AFGHAN** | This handsomely outfitted spot will introduce you to the aromas and tastes of Afghan cooking. The sauces and spices recall India's cuisine, while the emphasis on lamb brings to mind Turkey and Greece. **Known for:** traditional Afghani cuisine; neighborhood gem; generous portions. $ *Average main: $16* ✉ *2424 Van Ness Ave., Russian Hill* ☎ *415/345–0072* 🌐 *www.helmandpalacesf.com* ⏲ *No lunch.*

La Folie

$$$$ | **FRENCH** | Chef-owner Roland Passot's whimsical cuisine takes center stage at this small, *très* Parisian establishment. The dining room is decorated in warm woods and copper tones, while the prix-fixe menus are served in three, four, or five courses. **Known for:** creative French cuisine; prix-fixe menus; excellent service. $ *Average main: $100* ✉ *2316 Polk St., Russian Hill* ☎ *415/776–5577* 🌐 *www.lafolie.com* ⏲ *Closed Sun. and Mon. No lunch.*

Polk Gulch

Polk Gulch, the microhood surrounding north–south Polk Street, hugs the western edges of Nob Hill and Russian Hill but is nothing like either. It's actually two microhoods: Upper Polk Gulch, fairly classy in its northern section, runs from about Union Street south to California Street; Lower Polk Gulch, the rougher southern part, continues south from California to Geary or so.

Polk Gulch was the Castro before the Castro. It was the city's gay neighborhood into the 1970s, hosting San Francisco's first pride parade in 1972 and several festive Halloween extravaganzas. The area was once known for transsexual bars and gay prostitution. Today the friendly saloon the Cinch, the last remnant of gay Polk, and stalwart holdovers from that earlier time—among them folksy Grubstake, where you can get a giant burger until 4 am nightly—share space with newer mid-range restaurants, a passel of bars and nightclubs, and some browsable, funky stores, not to mention two great doughnut shops.

Downhill and down-market from its hilltop neighbors, Polk Gulch has been flirting with gentrification for almost a decade, but (female) prostitutes still walk the streets of the Lower Gulch, and the neighborhood feels closer in spirit to the Tenderloin, which it borders. Come to see a lively, scrappy, down-to-earth slice of the city that's forever in transition.

Restaurants

★ Lord Stanley

$$ | **AMERICAN** | Husband-and-wife team Carrie and Rupert Blease bring European training and a Californian sensibility to their sophisticated but approachable Michelin-starred cooking, pairing refined technique with earthy and inventive charm. You may find kimchi dip accompanying *brandade* (creamed cod) beignets, or tender roast duck served with sweet-and-sour cabbage heart. **Known for:** excellent wine list; new interpretations of California cooking; attentive service. *Average main: $35* *2065 Polk St., Polk Gulch* *415/872–5512* *lordstanleysf.com* *Closed Mon. No lunch.*

Hotels

Locals patronize the bars, cheap eats, and nightclubs amid a mildly unsavory section north of Civic Center that straddles Polk Street and Van Ness Avenue. The few hotels on and near these parallel streets tend toward the funky as well, though some are good bargains. The farther north you go, the nicer things get.

Hotel Carlton

$$ | **HOTEL** | "International vintage" aptly describes the collection of textiles, masks, sculptures, and other ephemera decorating this 1927 hotel, whose simply furnished guest quarters have ceiling fans on all floors and good views from the top. **Pros:** decent prices; decor with character; complimentary morning shuttle service to Financial District and Civic Center. **Cons:** on the edge of a seedy area; several blocks from Union Square; can be cold in winter (ask for a space heater). *Rooms from: $139* *1075 Sutter St., Polk Gulch* *415/673–0242, 800/922–7586 for reservations* *www.hotelcarltonsf.com* *161 rooms* *No meals.*

Nightlife

Sassy, vibrant, and even a little crass, Lower Gulch, the southern half of this neighborhood—Polk Street from Geary Street to a little beyond California Street—was the heart of San Francisco's pre-Castro gay mecca. Things mostly settle down north of California in the Upper Gulch section, though even straight bars like Kozy Kar live up to this hood's feisty reputation.

BARS

Amélie

WINE BARS—NIGHTLIFE | A slice of modern French life, this cozy and romantic wine bar is an ideal spot for European oenophiles. Vintage-theater seating is available up front—perfect for mingling with strangers. The prices are reasonable, the pours handsome. ■ **TIP→ Sit at the red-lacquer bar to learn about wine and pick up a French phrase or two.** ✉ *1754 Polk St., at Washington St., Polk Gulch* ☎ *415/292-6916* 🌐 *www.ameliewinebar.com.*

Kozy Kar

BARS/PUBS | Outrageous and full of sexual energy, this tiny space with an even tinier dance floor may be the heterosexual equivalent of San Francisco's gay bar scene. The drinks are stiff, but if they overwhelm you—or you just want to have fun—there's a waterbed for you to lounge on. Cartoons and '80s movies play on various televisions. Pay attention and you'll catch frames of porn mixed in for good measure, but if you miss them, don't worry: the bar and the floors are lined with vintage centerfolds. It may all be on the racy side, but it's never creepy or uncomfortable. ✉ *1548 Polk St., at Sacramento St., Polk Gulch* ☎ *415/346-5699* 🌐 *www.kozykar.com.*

GAY NIGHTLIFE

The Cinch

BARS/PUBS | This Wild West–theme neighborhood bar has pinball machines, pool tables, and a smoking patio. It's not the least bit trendy, which is part of the charm for regulars. ✉ *1723 Polk St., between Washington and Clay Sts., Polk Gulch* ☎ *415/776-4162* 🌐 *www.cinchsf.com.*

Chapter 6

NORTH BEACH

Updated by
Denise M. Leto

Sights	Restaurants	Hotels	Shopping	Nightlife
★★☆☆☆	★★★☆☆	★☆☆☆☆	★★★☆☆	★★★★☆

NEIGHBORHOOD SNAPSHOT

TOP REASONS TO GO

■ **Espresso, espresso, espresso:** Or cappuccino, americano, mocha—however you take your caffeine, this is the neighborhood for it. Hanging out in a café constitutes sightseeing here, so find a chair and get to work.

■ **Colorful watering holes:** The high concentration of bars with character, like Tosca Café and Vesuvio, makes North Beach the perfect neighborhood for a pub crawl.

■ **Filbert Steps:** Walk down this dizzying stairway from Telegraph Hill's Coit Tower, past lush private gardens and jaw-dropping bay views—and listen for the hill's famous screeching parrots.

■ **Grant Avenue:** Check out vanguard boutiques, rambling antiques shops, and cavernous old-time bars, all chockablock on narrow Grant Avenue. The best stuff is crowded into the four blocks between Columbus Avenue and Filbert Street.

■ **Browsing books at City Lights:** Illuminate your mind at this Beat-era landmark. Its great book selection, author events, and keen staff make it just as cool as ever.

QUICK BITES

Liguria Bakery. The Soracco family has been baking focaccia in North Beach for more than a century, and many consider their fresh-from-the-oven bread the neighborhood's best. Arrive before noon: when the focaccia is gone, the bakery closes. **Known for:** excellent focaccia; classic Italian SF bakery. ✉ *1700 Stockton St., at Filbert St., North Beach* ☎ *415/421–3786* ▭ *No credit cards* ⏲ *Closed Sun. and Mon.*

Mario's Bohemian Cigar Store. Intimate, triangular Mario's Bohemian Cigar Store serves up great hot focaccia sandwiches and North Beach–worthy espresso at its few tables and beautiful antique oak bar under old-time posters. On sunny days, take your order across the street to Washington Square for a classic San Francisco picnic. ✉ *566 Columbus Ave., North Beach* ☎ *415/362–0536.*

GETTING THERE

■ The Powell–Mason cable-car line can drop you within a block of Washington Square Park, in the heart of North Beach. The 30–Stockton and 15–3rd Street buses run to the neighborhood from Market Street. Once you're here, North Beach is a snap to explore on foot. Most of it is relatively flat—but climbing Telegraph Hill to reach Coit Tower is another story entirely.

PLANNING YOUR TIME

■ There's no bad time of day to visit this quarter. The cafés buzz from morning to night, the shops along main drags Columbus Avenue and Broadway tend to stay open until at least 6 or 7 pm, and late-night revelers don't start checking their watches until about 2 am. Sunday is quieter, since some shops close (though the iconic City Lights bookstore is open daily, until midnight).

■ Plan to spend a few hours here. It's all about lingering, and the only major "sightseeing" spot is Coit Tower. The walk up to the tower is strenuous but rewarding; if you can tough it, make time for it. If you're driving, keep in mind that parking is difficult, especially at night.

San Francisco novelist Herbert Gold calls North Beach "the longest-running, most glorious, American bohemian operetta outside Greenwich Village." Indeed, to anyone who's spent some time in its eccentric old bars and cafés, North Beach evokes everything from the Barbary Coast days to the no-less-rowdy Beatnik era.

Italian bakeries appear frozen in time, homages to Jack Kerouac and Allen Ginsberg pop up everywhere, and strip joints, the modern equivalent of the Barbary Coast's "houses of ill repute," do business on Broadway. With its outdoor café tables, throngs of tourists, and holiday vibe, this is probably the part of town Europeans are thinking of when they say San Francisco is the most European city in America.

The neighborhood truly was a beach at the time of the gold rush—the bay extended into the hollow between Telegraph and Russian Hills. Among the first immigrants to Yerba Buena during the early 1840s were young men from the northern provinces of Italy. The Genoese started the fishing industry in the newly renamed boomtown of San Francisco, as well as a much-needed produce business. Later, Sicilians emerged as leaders of the fishing fleets and eventually as proprietors of the seafood restaurants lining Fisherman's Wharf. Meanwhile, their Genoese cousins established banking and manufacturing empires.

Once almost exclusively Italian American, today's North Beach has only a small percentage of Italians (many of them elderly), with growing Chinese and San Francisco yuppie populations. But walk down narrow Romolo Place (off Broadway east of Columbus) or Genoa Place (off Union west of Kearny) or Medau Place (off Filbert west of Grant) and you can feel the immigrant Italian roots of this neighborhood. Locals know that the city's finest Italian restaurants are elsewhere, but North Beach is the place that puts folks in mind of Italian food, and there are many decent options to choose from. Bakeries sell focaccia fresh from the oven; eaten warm or cold, it's the perfect portable food. Many other aromas fill the air: coffee beans, deli meats and cheeses, Italian pastries, and—always—pungent garlic.

Sights

★ City Lights Bookstore

STORE/MALL | Take a look at the exterior of the store: the replica of a revolutionary mural destroyed in Chiapas, Mexico, by military forces; the art banners hanging above the windows. This place isn't just doling out best sellers. Designated a city landmark, the hangout of Beat-era

A North Beach Walk

To hit the highlights of the neighborhood, start off with a browse at Beat landmark **City Lights Bookstore.** For cool boutique shopping, head north up **Grant Avenue.** Otherwise, it's time to get down to the serious business of hanging out. Make a left onto **Columbus Avenue** when you leave the bookstore and walk the strip until you find a café table or pastry display that calls your name.

Fortified, continue down Columbus to **Washington Square,** where you can walk or take the 39 bus up **Telegraph Hill** to Coit Tower's views. Be sure to take in the gorgeous gardens along the **Filbert Steps** on the way down. Finally, reward yourself by returning to **Columbus Avenue** for a drink at one of the atmosphere-steeped watering holes like **Tosca** or **Specs.**

writers and independent publishers remains a vital part of San Francisco's literary scene. Browse the three levels of poetry, philosophy, politics, fiction, history, and local zines, to the tune of creaking wood floors.

Back in the day, writers like Ginsberg and Jack Kerouac would read and even receive mail in the basement. Co-founder Lawrence Ferlinghetti cemented City Lights' place in history by publishing Ginsberg's *Howl and Other Poems* in 1956. The small volume was ignored in the mainstream ... until Ferlinghetti and the bookstore manager were arrested for obscenity and corruption of youth. In the landmark First Amendment trial that followed, the judge exonerated both men, declaring that a work that has "redeeming social significance" can't be obscene. *Howl* went on to become a classic.

Stroll Kerouac Alley, branching off Columbus Avenue next to City Lights, to read the quotes from Ferlinghetti, Maya Angelou, Confucius, John Steinbeck, and the street's namesake embedded in the pavement. ✉ *261 Columbus Ave., North Beach* ☎ *415/362–8193* 🌐 *www.citylights.com.*

Coit Tower

BUILDING | Among San Francisco's most distinctive skyline sights, this 210-foot tower is often considered a tribute to firefighters because of the donor's special attachment to the local fire company. As the story goes, a young gold rush–era girl, Lillie Hitchcock Coit (known as Miss Lil), was a fervent admirer of her local fire company—so much so that she once deserted a wedding party and chased down the street after her favorite engine, Knickerbocker No. 5, while clad in her bridesmaid finery. She became the Knickerbocker Company's mascot and always signed her name "Lillie Coit 5." When Lillie died in 1929 she left the city $125,000 to "expend in an appropriate manner ... to the beauty of San Francisco." You can ride the elevator to the top of the tower—the only thing you have to pay for here—to enjoy the view of the Bay Bridge and the Golden Gate Bridge; due north is Alcatraz Island. Most visitors saunter right past the 27 fabulous Depression-era murals inside the tower that depict California's economic and political life, but take the time to appreciate the first New Deal art project supported by taxpayer money.

Lolling around Washington Square, post-espresso, is a fine use of a sunny afternoon.

✉ *Telegraph Hill Blvd. at Greenwich St. or Lombard St., North Beach* ☎ *415/362–0808* 🌐 *sfrecpark.org* 🎫 *Free; elevator to top $9.*

Grant Avenue

NEIGHBORHOOD | Originally called Calle de la Fundación, Grant Avenue is the oldest street in the city, but it's got plenty of young blood. Here dusty bars such as the Saloon and perennial favorites like the Savoy Tivoli mix with hotshot boutiques, odd curio shops and antique jumbles like the vintage map store Schein & Schein, atmospheric cafés such as the boho haven Caffè Trieste, and authentic Italian delis. While the street runs from Union Square through Chinatown, North Beach, and beyond, the fun stuff in this neighborhood is crowded into the four blocks between Columbus Avenue and Filbert Street. ✉ *North Beach.*

Sentinel Building

BUILDING | A striking triangular shape and a gorgeous green patina make this 1907 flatiron building at the end of Columbus Avenue a visual knockout. In the 1970s local filmmaker Francis Ford Coppola bought the building to use for his production company. The ground floor houses Coppola's stylish wine bar, **Café Zoetrope**. Stop in for wines from the Coppola vineyards in Napa and Sonoma, simple Italian dishes, and foodie gifts. ✉ *916 Kearny St., at Columbus Ave., North Beach.*

★ Telegraph Hill

NEIGHBORHOOD | Residents here have some of the city's best views, as well as the most difficult ascents to their aeries. The hill rises from the east end of Lombard Street to a height of 284 feet and is capped by Coit Tower. Imagine lugging your groceries up that! If you brave the slope, though, you can be rewarded with a "secret treasure" San Francisco moment. Filbert Street starts up the hill, then becomes the **Filbert Steps** when the going gets too steep. You can cut between the Filbert Steps and another flight, the **Greenwich Steps,** on up to the hilltop. As you climb, you can pass some of the city's oldest houses and be surrounded by beautiful, flowering

The Birds

While on Telegraph Hill, you might be startled by a chorus of piercing squawks and a rushing sound of wings. No, you're not about to have a Hitchcock bird-attack moment. These small, vivid green parrots with cherry-red heads number in the hundreds; they're descendants of former pets that escaped or were released by their owners. (The birds dislike cages, and they bite if bothered ... must've been some disillusioned owners along the way.)

The parrots like to roost high in the aging cypress trees on the hill, chattering and fluttering, sometimes taking wing en masse. They're not popular with some residents, but they did find a champion in local bohemian Mark Bittner, a former street musician. Bittner began chronicling their habits, publishing a book and battling the homeowners who wanted to cut down the cypresses. A documentary, *The Wild Parrots of Telegraph Hill*, made the issue a cause célèbre. In 2007, City Hall, which recognizes a golden goose when it sees one, stepped in and brokered a solution to keep the celebrity birds in town. The city would cover the homeowners' insurance worries and plant new trees for the next generation of wild parrots.

private gardens. In some places the trees grow over the stairs so it feels like you're walking through a green tunnel; elsewhere, you'll have wide-open views of the bay. The cypress trees that grow on the hill are a favorite roost of local avian celebrities, the wild parrots of Telegraph Hill; you'll hear the cries of the cherry-headed conures if they're nearby. And the telegraphic name? It comes from the hill's status as the first Morse code signal station back in 1853. ✉ *Bordered by Lombard, Filbert, Kearny, and Sansome Sts., North Beach.*

Washington Square

PLAZA | Once the daytime social heart of Little Italy, this grassy patch has changed character numerous times over the years. The Beats hung out here in the 1950s, hippies camped out in the 1960s and early '70s, and nowadays you're more likely to see elderly Asians doing tai chi than Italian folks reminiscing about the old country. You might also see homeless people hanging out on the benches and young locals sunbathing or running their dogs. Lillie Hitchcock Coit, in yet another show of affection for San Francisco's firefighters, donated the statue of two firemen with a child they rescued. ✉ *Bordered by Columbus Ave. and Stockton, Filbert, and Union Sts., North Beach.*

Restaurants

One of the city's oldest neighborhoods, North Beach continues to speak Italian, albeit in fewer households than it did when Joe DiMaggio was hitting home runs at the local playground.

Columbus Avenue, North Beach's primary commercial artery, and nearby side streets boast dozens of moderately priced Italian restaurants and coffee bars that San Franciscans flock to for a dose of strong community feeling. But beware, there are a few tourist traps that are after the college crowd who flock here for cheap drinks then want to fill up on cheap food.

★ Coi

$$$$ | **MODERN AMERICAN** | Although Daniel Patterson no longer presides over the kitchen, under chef Erik Anderson his Michelin three-star restaurant is still a can't-miss destination for exquisite, rarefied dining in a womblike space that features natural linens, soft lighting, and hand-crafted pottery. The eight-course tasting menu focuses on seafood and prizes obsessively sourced, highly seasonal ingredients in dishes such as Dungeness crab with grapefruit, Champagne, and bay leaf. **Known for:** fine dining; seasonal ingredients and fresh seafood; three Michelin stars. *Average main: $275 373 Broadway, North Beach 415/393–9000 www.coirestaurant.com Closed Sun. and Mon. No lunch.*

Maykadeh

$$ | **MIDDLE EASTERN** | The authentic Persian cooking has a large and faithful following of homesick Iranian émigrés and locals in the know who come for lamb specialties with rice served in a warm and attractive dining room. Kebabs, like the chicken *joojeh,* and other marinated meats are great for sharing, and dishes such as *ghorme sabzee,* lamb shank braised with a bouquet of Middle Eastern spices, satisfy heartier appetites. **Known for:** delicious lamb dishes; traditional Persian cooking; succulent kebabs. *Average main: $20 470 Green St., North Beach 415/362–8286 www.maykadehrestaurant.com.*

Molinari Delicatessen

$ | **DELI** | The friendly *paesans* behind the counter have been serving up the most delicious, and quite possibly the biggest, sandwiches in town for more than 100 years in this location alone. Take a number, grab your bread from the bin, and gaze upon the sandwich board, then say a prayer to the patron saint of seating for a spot at one of the three sidewalk tables or head up the street to Washington Square Park for a picnic. **Known for:** huge deli sandwiches; old-time Italian vibe; traditional Italian products. *Average main: $12 373 Columbus Ave., at Vallejo St., North Beach 415/421–2337 www.molinarisalame.com Closed Sun. No dinner.*

Original Joe's

$$$ | **AMERICAN** | Nostalgia isn't just in the decor but also on the menu at this 1937 retro North Beach institution (in this location only since 2012), where you'll find black Formica tabletops, checkerboard floors, red leather booths, and a '50s-era disregard for calorie counts—as well as a perfectly seasoned hamburger steak. Roasted prime rib and six different veal dishes add to the mid-century meat-heavy menu, and the butterscotch pudding is topped with whipped cream and salted caramel. **Known for:** classic Cal-Ital food; meat-heavy menu; retro dining. *Average main: $29 601 Union St., North Beach 415/775–4877 www.originaljoessf.com.*

Park Tavern

$$$ | **AMERICAN** | Offering hearty food in a handsome dining room, this upscale American tavern on pretty Washington Square has been a hit from the day it opened. You can sit at the bar and nibble on delicious things like the deviled eggs (with bacon and jalapeños) or opt for a proper sit-down complete with a twice-baked potato and American Wagyu steak (although the roasted chicken is not to be missed). **Known for:** meaty American food; tasty bar bites; parkside dining. *Average main: $30 1652 Stockton St., North Beach 415/989–7300 www.parktavernsf.com No lunch weekdays.*

Tommaso's

$$ | **PIZZA** | **FAMILY** | San Francisco's first wood-fired brick pizza oven, installed here in 1935, is still here, and the pizzas' delightfully chewy crusts, creamy mozzarella, and full-bodied house-made sauce have kept legions returning for decades. Pair one of the hearty pies with broccoli dressed in lemon juice and olive oil and a bottle of chianti, or tuck into a variety of old-school pasta dishes (think: ravioli, spaghetti, manicotti), and old-school favorite dessert, tiramisu. **Known for:** North Beach institution; legendary pizza;

classic pasta dishes. $ *Average main: $25 ✉ 1042 Kearny St., North Beach ☎ 415/398–9696 🌐 www.tommasos.com ⊗ Closed Mon. No lunch.*

Tony's Pizza Napoletana

$$$ | **PIZZA** | **FAMILY** | Repeatedly crowned the World Champion Pizza Maker at the World Pizza Cup in Naples, Tony Gemignani is renowned here for his flavorful dough and impressive range. The multiple gas, electric, and wood-burning ovens in his casual, modern pizzeria turn out many different pies—the famed Neapolitan-style Margherita, but also Sicilian, Romana, and Detroit styles—while salads, antipasti, homemade pastas, and calzone, round out the menu. **Known for:** World Champion Pizza chef; multiple pizza ovens and pie styles; family dining. $ *Average main: $27 ✉ 1570 Stockton St., North Beach ☎ 415/835–9888 🌐 www.tonyspizzanapoletana.com ⊗ Closed Tues.*

Tosca Cafe

$$$ | **ITALIAN** | The leather booths and chairs are in high demand at this dark and clubby 1919 boho classic, where celebs and local scenesters dine on food that skews Italian. You can eat at the bar, which is first come, first served, or stop by for a cappuccino with local Dandelion chocolate and a shot of bourbon while a jukebox belts out tunes. **Known for:** Italian-American comfort food; tasty cocktails; signature roast chicken for two. $ *Average main: $24 ✉ 242 Columbus Ave., North Beach ☎ 415/986–9651 🌐 www.toscacafesf.com ⊗ No lunch.*

Hotels

The bright lights and frenetic energy of North Beach have long appealed to travelers. Value boutique hotels blend in well with the cafés, delis, clubs, and artsy shops near Washington Square Park. Most accommodations are best for couples or solo travelers, as rooms tend to be petite.

Columbus Motor Inn

$$ | **HOTEL** | **FAMILY** | Close to Chinatown and Fisherman's Wharf, this affordable lodging with basic rooms decked out with oversized pillows, earth-toned bedding, and large flat-screen TVs is a great pick if you have a family and a car to park. **Pros:** free parking; affordable rooms deep-cleaned every three months; lively location. **Cons:** lacks amenities; decor is not stylish; street-facing accommodations can be noisy. $ *Rooms from: $188 ✉ 1075 Columbus Ave., North Beach ☎ 415/885–1492 🌐 www.columbusmotorinn.com 45 rooms No meals.*

Hotel Bohème

$$ | **HOTEL** | This small hotel in historic North Beach takes you back in time with cast-iron beds, large mirrored armoires, and memorabilia recalling the Beat generation—whose leading light, Allen Ginsberg, often stayed here (legend has it that in his later years he could be seen sitting in a window, typing away on his typewriter). **Pros:** North Beach location with literary pedigree; stylish rooms; helpful staff. **Cons:** street parking is scarce; no a/c; small rooms. $ *Rooms from: $195 ✉ 444 Columbus Ave., North Beach ☎ 415/433–9111 🌐 www.hotelboheme.com 15 rooms No meals.*

★ San Remo Hotel

$ | **HOTEL** | **FAMILY** | A few blocks from Fisherman's Wharf, this three-story 1906 Italianate Victorian—once home to longshoremen and Beat poets—has a narrow stairway to the front desk and labyrinthine hallways. **Pros:** inexpensive rates; free Wi-Fi; rooftop penthouse (reserve way ahead) has private bath and deck with Coit Tower views. **Cons:** some rooms are dark; only the penthouse suite has a private bath; parking (discounted fee) is off-site. $ *Rooms from: $144 ✉ 2237 Mason St., North Beach ☎ 415/776–8688, 800/352–7366 🌐 www.sanremohotel.com 64 rooms No meals.*

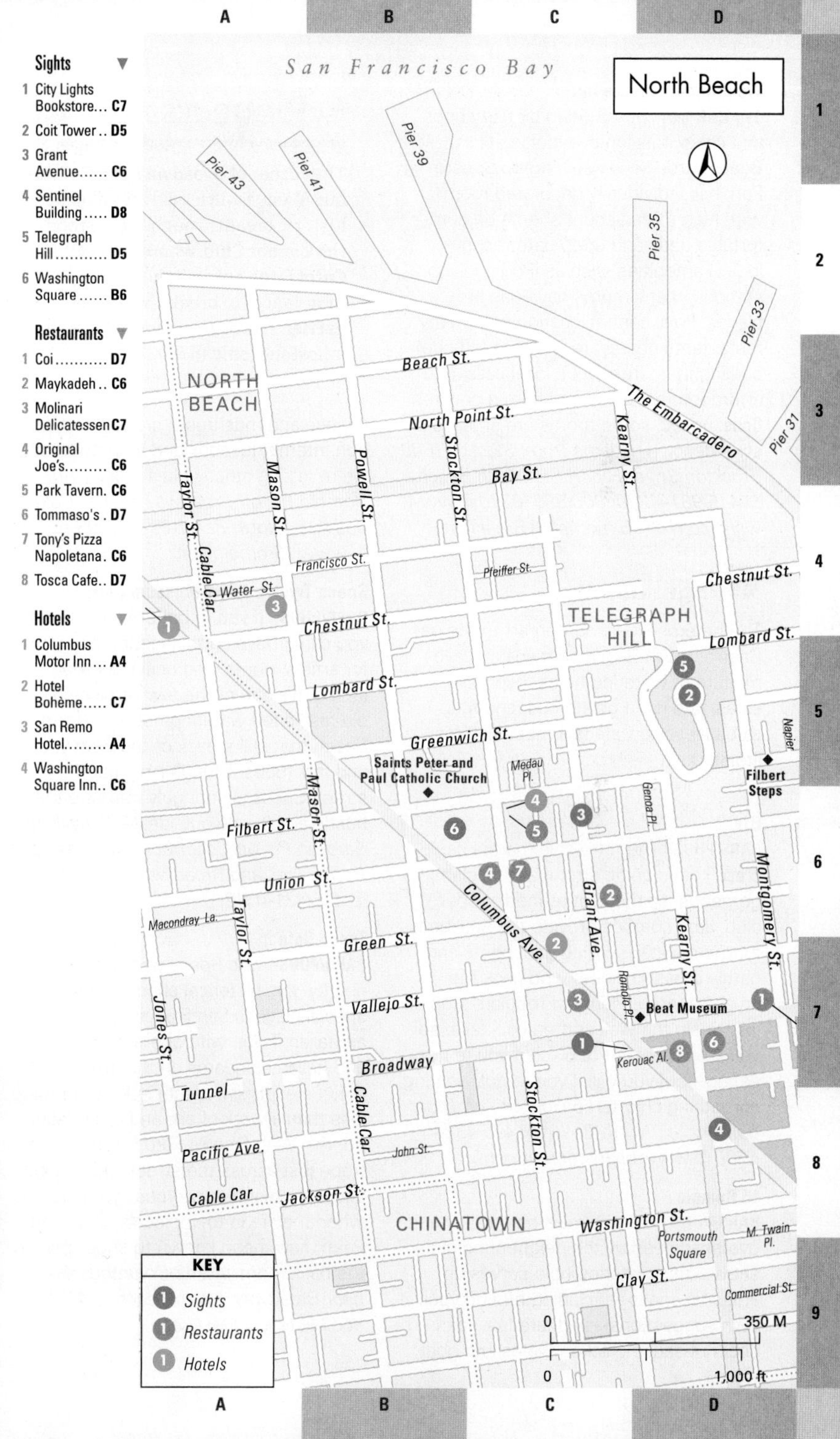

North Beach
Sights
1 City Lights Bookstore... C7
2 Coit Tower .. D5
3 Grant Avenue...... C6
4 Sentinel Building..... D8
5 Telegraph Hill........... D5
6 Washington Square...... B6
Restaurants
1 Coi.......... D7
2 Maykadeh .. C6
3 Molinari Delicatessen C7
4 Original Joe's......... C6
5 Park Tavern. C6
6 Tommaso's . D7
7 Tony's Pizza Napoletana. C6
8 Tosca Cafe.. D7
Hotels
1 Columbus Motor Inn... A4
2 Hotel Bohème..... C7
3 San Remo Hotel......... A4
4 Washington Square Inn.. C6
San Francisco Bay
Pier 43
Pier 41
Pier 39
Pier 35
Pier 33
Pier 31
The Embarcadero
NORTH BEACH
TELEGRAPH HILL
CHINATOWN
Beach St.
North Point St.
Bay St.
Francisco St.
Pfeiffer St.
Water St.
Chestnut St.
Lombard St.
Greenwich St.
Filbert St.
Union St.
Green St.
Vallejo St.
Broadway
Tunnel
Pacific Ave.
Jackson St.
John St.
Washington St.
Clay St.
Commercial St.
Macondray La.
Taylor St.
Mason St.
Powell St.
Stockton St.
Kearny St.
Grant Ave.
Montgomery St.
Jones St.
Columbus Ave.
Cable Car
Medau Pl.
Genoa Pl.
Romolo Pl.
Kerouac Al.
Napier
M. Twain Pl.
Portsmouth Square
Saints Peter and Paul Catholic Church
Filbert Steps
Beat Museum
KEY
Sights
Restaurants
Hotels
0
350 M
0
1,000 ft
A B C D
1 2 3 4 5 6 7 8 9

Washington Square Inn

$$ | **B&B/INN** | Surrounded by fine shops and cafés, this inn overlooking North Beach's tree-lined Washington Square Park has individually decorated rooms with high thread-count sheets on comfortable beds and up-to-date technological amenities such as iPod docking stations; many rooms have gas fireplaces. **Pros:** central location with many restaurants nearby; reasonable (off-site) parking fees; free Wi-Fi, local calls, and afternoon tea, wine, and hors d'oeuvres. **Cons:** no a/c; some rooms are small; old-style decor. *Rooms from: $224 1660 Stockton St., at Filbert St., North Beach 415/981–4220, 800/388–0220 www.wsisf.com 15 rooms Breakfast.*

 Nightlife

The heterosexual counterpart to the gay Castro, North Beach contains a suave mixture of watering holes, espresso cafés, late-night gelato ops, and strip clubs. Vesuvio Cafe is a must-visit for literary fans.

BARS

Bix

BARS/PUBS | The retro-chic martini-bar craze keeps going strong at this glam, gorgeous, spirited yet refined supper club. Jazz combos provide the backbeat for the cocktail-swilling gadabouts and nattily dressed diners who pack the small bar area. Plenty of regulars stop in just to sip the well-crafted cocktails, so you won't feel out of place if you're not eating—but you will if you're not wearing something chic. *56 Gold St., off Montgomery St., North Beach 415/433–6300 www.bixrestaurant.com.*

15 Romolo

BARS/PUBS | Easy to miss on an alley and overshadowed by the neighboring girlie shows, this watering hole serves up artisanal drinks—including riffs off your own suggestions—and fare like spicy coconut-sauce chicken wings and goat cheese and mushroom croquetas. With a non-Internet jukebox and a photo booth, we're talking strictly old school. *15 Romolo Pl., off Broadway east of Columbus Ave., North Beach 415/398–1359 www.15romolo.com.*

O Pioneers! 

The corner of Broadway and Columbus Avenue witnessed an unusual historic breakthrough. Here stood the Condor Club, where in 1964 Carol Doda became the country's first dancer to break the topless barrier. A bronze plaque honors the milestone (only in SF).

Specs Twelve Adler Museum Cafe

BARS/PUBS | If you're bohemian at heart, you can groove on this hidden hangout for artists, poets, and heavy-drinking lefties. It's one of the few remaining old-fashioned watering holes in North Beach that still smack of the Beat years and the 1960s. Though it's just off a busy street, Specs is strangely immune to the hustle and bustle outside. *12 William Saroyan Pl., off Columbus Ave., between Pacific Ave. and Broadway, North Beach 415/421–4112.*

Tosca Café

BARS/PUBS | Like Specs and Vesuvio nearby, this historical charmer holds a special place in San Francisco lore. It has an Italian flavor, with opera, big-band, and Italian standards on the jukebox, an antique espresso machine that's nothing less than a work of art, and red leather booths. With Francis Ford Coppola's Zoetrope just across the street, celebrities and hip film-industry types often stop by when they're in town; locals, like Sean Penn, have been known to shoot pool in the back room. *242 Columbus Ave., near Broadway, North Beach 415/986–9651 toscacafesf.com.*

★ Vesuvio Cafe

BARS/PUBS | If you're hitting only one bar in North Beach, it should be this one. The low-ceilinged second floor of this raucous boho hangout, little altered since its 1960s heyday (when Jack Kerouac frequented the place), is a fine vantage point for watching the colorful Broadway and Columbus Avenue intersection. Another part of Vesuvio's appeal is its diverse clientele, from older neighborhood regulars and young couples to Bacchanalian posses. ✉ *255 Columbus Ave., at Broadway, North Beach* ☎ *415/362–3370* 🌐 *www.vesuvio.com.*

CABARET

★ Club Fugazi

CABARET | The claim to fame here is *Beach Blanket Babylon,* an ever-changing wacky musical send-up of San Francisco moods and mores that has been going strong since 1974, making it the longest-running musical revue anywhere. Although the choreography is colorful, the singers brassy, and the satirical songs witty, the real stars are the comically exotic costumes and famous ceiling-high "hats"—which are worth the price of admission alone. The revue sells out as early as a month in advance. ✉ *678 Green St., at Powell St., North Beach* ☎ *415/421–4222* 🌐 *www.beachblanketbabylon.com.*

COMEDY

Cobb's Comedy Club

COMEDY CLUBS | Stand-up comics such as Bill Maher, Paula Poundstone, and Sarah Silverman have appeared at this club, where you might also see sketch comedy and comic singer-songwriters. No one under 18 is admitted. ✉ *915 Columbus Ave., at Lombard St., North Beach* ☎ *415/928–4320* 🌐 *www.cobbscomedy.com.*

MUSIC CLUBS

Bimbo's 365 Club

MUSIC CLUBS | The plush main room and adjacent lounge of this club, here since 1951, retain a retro vibe perfect for the "Cocktail Nation" programming that keeps the crowds entertained. For a taste of the old-school San Francisco nightclub scene, you can't beat it. Indie low-fi and pop bands such as Mustache Harbor and Tainted Love play here. ✉ *1025 Columbus Ave., at Chestnut St., North Beach* ☎ *415/474–0365* 🌐 *www.bimbos365club.com.*

The Saloon

MUSIC CLUBS | Hard-drinkin' in-the-know locals favor this raucous spot, known for great blues. Built in the 1860s, the onetime bordello is purported to be the oldest bar in the city. This is not the place to order a mixed drink. You've been warned. ✉ *1232 Grant Ave., near Columbus Ave., North Beach* ☎ *415/989–7666* 🌐 *sfblues.weebly.com.*

Shopping

ANTIQUES

Schein & Schein

ART GALLERIES | This tiny spot sells antique maps and engraved prints, many with a local focus, from inexpensive prints to genuine collectors' pieces. Whether you're looking for a chart of the world from the 13th century or a map of the Barbary Coast, this shop just might have it. The helpful owners will enthrall you with their historical anecdotes and vast knowledge. ✉ *1435 Grant Ave., between Green and Union Sts., North Beach* ☎ *415/399–8882* 🌐 *www.scheinandschein.com.*

CLOTHING

AB fits

CLOTHING | The friendly staff can help guys and gals sort through the jeans selection, one of the hippest in the city, from hyperlocal to international brands. Salespeople pride themselves on being able to match the pants to the person. ✉ *1519 Grant Ave., between Filbert and Union Sts., North Beach* ☎ *415/982–5726* 🌐 *abfits.com.*

Knitz & Leather

CLOTHING | Local artisans Julia Relinghaus and Katharina Ernst have been producing one-of-a-kind and custom products of extraordinary craftsmanship for 30 years. Ernst's bold knitted sweaters and accessories and Relinghaus's exquisite, high-quality leather jackets for men and women are expensive but made to last. ✉ *1453 Grant Ave., North Beach* ☎ *415/391–3480.*

FOOD AND DRINK

Graffeo Coffee Roasting Company

FOOD/CANDY | Forget those fancy flavored coffees if you're ordering from this emporium, open since 1935 and one of the best-loved coffee stores in a city devoted to its java. The shop sells dark roast, light roast, and dark roast–decaf beans only. ✉ *735 Columbus Ave., at Filbert St., North Beach* ☎ *415/986–2420* 🌐 *www.graffeo.com.*

Victoria Pastry Co.

FOOD/CANDY | In business since the early 1900s and a throwback to the North Beach of old, this bakery has display cases full of Italian pastries, cookies, and St. Honoré cakes. ✉ *700 Filbert St., between Columbus Ave. and Powell St., North Beach* ☎ *415/781–2015.*

★ XOX Truffles

FOOD/CANDY | The decadent confection comes in 27 bite-size flavors here, from the traditional (cocoa-powder-coated Amaretto) to the unusual (flavored with rum-coconut liqueur and coated with coconut flakes or enrobing a bit of caramel). There's something yummy for everyone, even vegans (soy truffles). ✉ *754 Columbus Ave., between Greenwich and Filbert Sts., North Beach* ☎ *415/421–4814* 🌐 *www.xoxtruffles.com.*

FURNITURE, HOUSEWARES, AND GIFTS

Biordi Art Imports

HOUSEHOLD ITEMS/FURNITURE | An excellent selection of hand-painted Italian pottery, mainly imported from Tuscany and Umbria, has been shipped worldwide by this family-run business since 1946. Dishware sets can be ordered in any combination. ✉ *412 Columbus Ave., at Vallejo St., North Beach* ☎ *415/392–8096* 🌐 *www.biordi.com.*

MUSIC: MEMORABILIA

San Francisco Rock Posters and Collectibles

MUSIC STORES | The huge selection of rock-and-roll memorabilia, including posters, handbills, and original art, takes you back to the 1960s. Also available are posters from more recent shows—many at the legendary Fillmore Auditorium—featuring such musicians as George Clinton and the late Johnny Cash. ✉ *1851 Powell St., between Filbert and Greenwich Sts., North Beach* ☎ *415/956–6749* 🌐 *rockposters.com.*

PAPER AND STATIONERY

Lola of North Beach

BOOKS/STATIONERY | Many of the products at this intimate North Beach store make great San Francisco souvenirs, from Golden Gate Bridge onesies for babies to city-skyline socks for adults. Local artists are well represented. ✉ *1415 Grant Ave., at Green St., North Beach* ☎ *415/781–1817* 🌐 *lolaofnorthbeach.com.*

Chapter 7

ON THE WATERFRONT

Updated by
Denise M. Leto

Sights ★★★☆☆ | Restaurants ★★★☆☆ | Hotels ★★★★☆ | Shopping ★★☆☆☆ | Nightlife ★☆☆☆☆

NEIGHBORHOOD SNAPSHOT

GETTING THERE

The Powell–Hyde and Powell–Mason cable-car lines both end near Fisherman's Wharf. The walk from downtown through North Beach to the northern waterfront is lovely, and if you stick to Columbus Avenue, the incline is relatively gentle. F-line trolleys run all the way down Market to the Embarcadero, then north to the wharf, but a packed trolley or two may pass by before one with room stops.

TOP REASONS TO GO

■ **Ferry Building:** Join locals eyeing luscious produce and foods prepared by some of the city's best chefs at San Francisco's premier farmers' market on Saturday morning.

■ **Alcatraz:** Go from a scenic bay tour to "the hole"—solitary confinement in absolute darkness—while inmates and guards tell you stories about what life was really like on the Rock.

■ **F-line:** Grab a polished wooden seat aboard one of the city's vintage streetcars and clatter down the tracks toward the Ferry Building's spire.

■ **Exploratorium:** Play with the ultimate marble run, touch your way through the pitch-black Tactile Dome, or explore yourself in the Science of Sharing exhibit at the city's beloved hands-on science museum in its spectacular bay-side home.

PLANNING YOUR TIME

■ If you're planning to go to Alcatraz, be sure to buy your tickets in advance, as tours frequently sell out. Alcatraz ferries leave from Pier 33—so there isn't a single good reason to suffer Pier 39's tacky, overpriced attractions. If you're a sailor at heart, though, definitely spend an hour with the historic ships of the Hyde Street Pier.

FERRIES

■ The bay is a huge part of San Francisco's charm, and getting out on the water gives you an attractive and unique (though windy) perspective on the city. ■TIP→ **A ride on a commuter ferry is cheaper than a cruise, and just as lovely.**

■ **Blue & Gold Fleet.** This ferry operator offers bay cruises and, in summer, high-speed RocketBoat rides, as well as commuter service to Oakland, Alameda, Tiburon, Sausalito, Vallejo, and Angel Island. ✉ *Pier 39, Fisherman's Wharf* ☎ *415/705–8200* 🌐 *www.blueandgoldfleet.com.*

■ **Red and White Fleet.** Choose from among the widest range of tour options, including year-round twilight and sunset cruises. ✉ *Pier 43½, Fisherman's Wharf* ☎ *415/673–2900* 🌐 *www.redandwhite.com.*

San Francisco's waterfront neighborhoods have fabulous views and utterly different personalities. Kitschy, overpriced Fisherman's Wharf struggles to maintain the last shreds of its existence as a working wharf, while Pier 39 is a full-fledged consumer circus. The Ferry Building draws well-heeled locals with its culinary pleasures, firmly connecting the Embarcadero and downtown. Between the Ferry Building and Pier 39, a former maritime no-man's-land now houses the relocated Exploratorium, a $90-million cruise-ship terminal, Alcatraz Landing, fashionable waterfront restaurants, and restored, pedestrian-friendly piers.

Fisherman's Wharf

The crack of fresh Dungeness crab, the aroma of sourdough warm from the oven, the cry of the gulls—in some ways you can experience Fisherman's Wharf today as it has been for more than 100 years. Italians began fishing these waters in the 19th century as immigrants to booming Barbary Coast San Francisco. Family businesses established generations ago continue to this day—look for the Alioto-Lazio Fish Company, selling crab fresh off the boat here for more than 70 years, and Castagnola's restaurant, serving Italian food and seafood since 1916.

As the local fishing industry has contracted and environmental awareness has changed fishing regulations, Fisherman's Wharf has morphed. Fewer families make a living off the sea here, fewer fishing boats go out, and more of the wharf survives on tourist dollars. You'll see more schlock here than in any other neighborhood in town: overpriced food

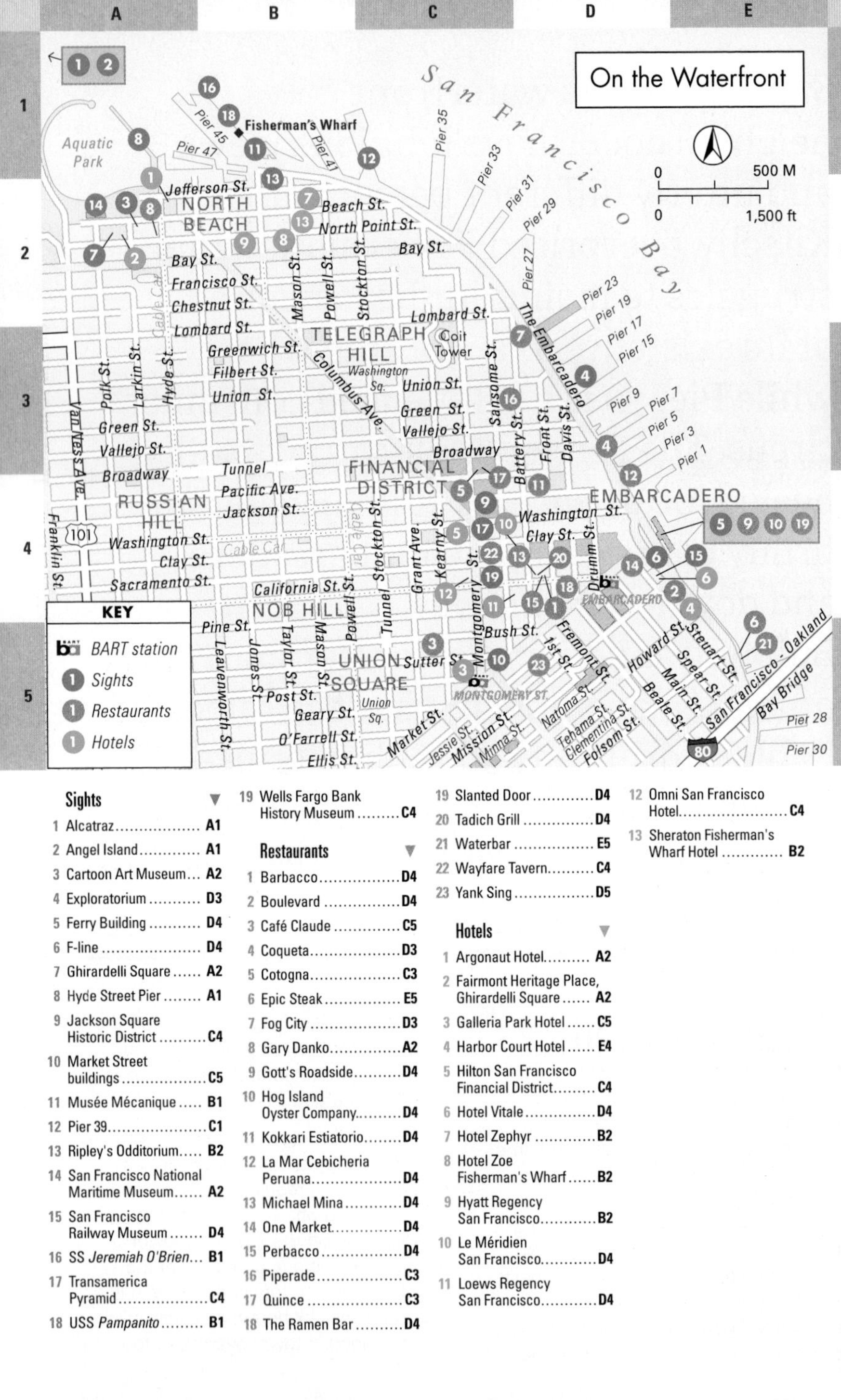

Sights

1 Alcatraz A1
2 Angel Island A1
3 Cartoon Art Museum ... A2
4 Exploratorium D3
5 Ferry Building D4
6 F-line D4
7 Ghirardelli Square A2
8 Hyde Street Pier A1
9 Jackson Square Historic District C4
10 Market Street buildings C5
11 Musée Mécanique B1
12 Pier 39 .... C1
13 Ripley's Odditorium B2
14 San Francisco National Maritime Museum A2
15 San Francisco Railway Museum D4
16 SS *Jeremiah O'Brien* ... B1
17 Transamerica Pyramid C4
18 USS *Pampanito* B1
19 Wells Fargo Bank History Museum C4

Restaurants

1 Barbacco D4
2 Boulevard D4
3 Café Claude C5
4 Coqueta D3
5 Cotogna C3
6 Epic Steak E5
7 Fog City D3
8 Gary Danko A2
9 Gott's Roadside D4
10 Hog Island Oyster Company D4
11 Kokkari Estiatorio D4
12 La Mar Cebicheria Peruana D4
13 Michael Mina D4
14 One Market D4
15 Perbacco D4
16 Piperade C3
17 Quince C3
18 The Ramen Bar D4
19 Slanted Door D4
20 Tadich Grill D4
21 Waterbar E5
22 Wayfare Tavern C4
23 Yank Sing D5

Hotels

1 Argonaut Hotel A2
2 Fairmont Heritage Place, Ghirardelli Square A2
3 Galleria Park Hotel C5
4 Harbor Court Hotel E4
5 Hilton San Francisco Financial District C4
6 Hotel Vitale D4
7 Hotel Zephyr B2
8 Hotel Zoe Fisherman's Wharf B2
9 Hyatt Regency San Francisco B2
10 Le Méridien San Francisco D4
11 Loews Regency San Francisco D4
12 Omni San Francisco Hotel C4
13 Sheraton Fisherman's Wharf Hotel B2

alongside discount electronics stores, bargain-luggage outlets, and cheap T-shirts and souvenirs.

It's enough to send locals running for the hills, but there are things here worth experiencing. Explore maritime history aboard the fabulous ships of the Hyde Street Pier, amuse yourself early-20th-century style with the mechanical diversions at Musée Mécanique, and grab a bowl of chowder or some Dungeness crab from one of the stands along Jefferson Street to get a taste of what made Fisherman's Wharf what it is in the first place. If you come early, you can avoid the crowds and get a sense of the Wharf's functional side: it's not entirely an amusement-park replica.

Sights

Angel Island

ISLAND | For an outdoorsy adventure and some fascinating history, consider a day at this island northwest of Alcatraz. Discovered by Spaniards in 1775 and declared a U.S. military reserve 75 years later, the island was used as a screening ground for Asian, mostly Chinese, immigrants—who were often held for months, even years, before being granted entry—from 1910 until 1940. You can visit the restored Immigration Station, from the dock where detainees landed to the barracks where you can see the poems in Chinese script they etched onto the walls. In 1963 the government designated Angel Island a state park. Today people come for picnics, hikes along the scenic 5-mile path that winds around the island's perimeter, and tram tours that explain the park's history. Blue & Gold Fleet is the only Angel Island ferry service with departures from San Francisco; boats leave from Pier 41. ✉ *Pier 41, Fisherman's Wharf* ☎ *415/435–1915 park information and ferry schedules, 415/705–8200 Blue and Gold Fleet* 🌐 *www.parks.ca.gov/AngelIsland* 🎫 *$20 round-trip.*

Cartoon Art Museum

MUSEUM | Krazy Kat, Zippy the Pinhead, Batman, and other colorful cartoon icons greet you at the Cartoon Art Museum, established with an endowment from cartoonist-icon Charles M. Schulz. The museum's strength is its changing exhibits, which explore such topics as America from the perspective of international political cartoons, and the output of women and African-American cartoonists. Serious fans of cartoons—especially those on the quirky underground side—will likely enjoy the exhibits; those with a casual interest may be bored. The store here carries cool titles to add to your collection. ✉ *781 Beach St., Fisherman's Wharf* ☎ *415/227–8666* 🌐 *www.cartoonart.org* 🎫 *$10* 🕒 *Closed Wed.*

Ghirardelli Square

STORE/MALL | Most of the redbrick buildings in this early-20th-century complex were once part of the Ghirardelli factory. Now tourists come here to pick up the famous chocolate, though you can purchase it all over town and save yourself a trip to what is essentially a mall. But this is the only place to watch the cool chocolate manufactory in action. Placards throughout the square describe the factory's history. ✉ *900 N. Point St., Fisherman's Wharf* ☎ *415/775–5500* 🌐 *www.ghirardellisq.com.*

★ Hyde Street Pier

MARINA | **FAMILY** | If you want to get to the heart of the Wharf, there's no better place to do it than at this pier. Don't pass up the centerpiece collection of historic vessels, part of the **San Francisco Maritime National Historical Park,** almost all of which can be boarded. The *Balclutha,* an 1886 full-rigged three-masted sailing vessel that's more than 250 feet long, sailed around Cape Horn 17 times. Kids especially love the *Eureka,* a side-wheel passenger and car ferry, for her onboard collection of vintage cars. The *Hercules* is a steam-powered tugboat, and the *C.A. Thayer* is a beautifully restored three-masted schooner. Across the street from the pier and a museum in itself is the maritime park's **Visitor Center** (*499 Jefferson St., 415/447–5000; June–Aug., daily 9:30–5:30; Sept.–May, daily 9:30–5*), whose fun, large-scale exhibits make it an engaging stop. See a huge First Order Fresnel lighthouse lens and a shipwrecked boat. Then stroll through time in the exhibit "The Waterfront," where you can touch the timber from a gold rush–era ship recovered from below the Financial District, peek into 19th-century storefronts, and see the sails of an Italian fishing vessel. ✉ *Hyde and Jefferson Sts., Fisherman's Wharf* ☎ *415/561–7100* 🌐 *www.nps.gov/safr* 🎟 *Ships $15 (ticket good for 7 days).*

★ Musée Mécanique

LOCAL INTEREST | FAMILY | Once a staple at Playland-at-the-Beach, San Francisco's early 20th-century amusement park, the antique mechanical contrivances at this time-warped arcade—including peep shows and nickelodeons—make it one of the most worthwhile attractions at the Wharf. Some favorites are the giant and rather creepy "Laffing Sal," an arm-wrestling machine, the world's only steam-powered motorcycle, and mechanical fortune-telling figures that speak from their curtained boxes. Note the depictions of race that betray the prejudices of the time: stoned Chinese figures in the "Opium-Den" and clown-faced African Americans eating watermelon in the "Mechanical Farm." **■ TIP→ Admission is free, but you'll need quarters to bring the machines to life.** ✉ *Pier 45, Shed A, Fisherman's Wharf* ☎ *415/346–2000* 🌐 *museemecaniquesf.com* 🎟 *Free.*

Pier 39

MARINA | FAMILY | The city's most popular waterfront attraction draws millions of visitors each year, who come to browse through its shops and concessions hawking every conceivable form of souvenir. The pier can be quite crowded, and the numerous street performers may leave you feeling more harassed than entertained. Arriving early in the morning ensures you a front-row view of the sea lions that bask here, but if you're here to shop—and make no mistake about it, Pier 39 wants your money—be aware that most stores don't open until 9:30 or 10 (later in winter).

Follow the sound of barking to the northwest side of the pier to view the **sea lions** that flop about the floating docks. During the summer, orange-clad naturalists answer questions and offer fascinating facts about the playful pinnipeds—for example, that most of the animals here are males.

At the **Aquarium of the Bay** (*415/623–5300 or 888/732–3483, www.aquariumofthebay.org; $27.95, hrs vary but at least 10–6 daily*) moving walkways transport you through a space surrounded on three sides by water filled with indigenous San Francisco Bay marine life, from fish and plankton to sharks. ✉ *Beach St. at Embarcadero, Fisherman's Wharf* 🌐 *www.pier39.com.*

Ripley's Odditorium

MUSEUM | Among the two floors of exhibits at this mind-bending museum is a tribute to San Francisco—an 8-foot-long scale model of a cable car made entirely of matchsticks and a replica of the Golden Gate Bridge made of 30,000 toothpicks. ✉ *175 Jefferson St., Fisherman's Wharf* ☎ *415/202–9850* 🌐 *www.ripleys.com/sanfrancisco* 🎟 *$23.*

San Francisco National Maritime Museum

MUSEUM | FAMILY | You'll feel as if you're out to sea when you step aboard, er, inside this sturdy, ship-shape, streamline-moderne structure dubbed the Bathhouse Building. The first floor of the museum, part of the **San Francisco Maritime National Historical Park,** has stunningly restored undersea dreamscape murals and some of the museum's intricate ship models. The first-floor balcony overlooks the beach and has lovely WPA-era tile designs. **■ TIP→ If you've got young kids in tow, the museum makes a great quick, free stop. Then pick up ice cream at Ghirardelli Square across the street and enjoy it on the beach or next door in Victorian Park, where you can watch the cable cars turn around.** ✉ *Aquatic Park, foot of Polk St., Fisherman's Wharf* ☎ *415/447–5000* 🌐 *www.nps.gov/safr* 🎫 *Donation suggested.*

SS *Jeremiah O'Brien*

MILITARY SITE | A participant in the D-Day landing in Normandy during World War II, this Liberty Ship freighter is one of two such vessels (out of more than 2,700 built) still in working order. On board you can peek at the crew's living quarters—bedding and personal items make it look as if they've just stepped away for a moment—and the officers' mess hall. The large display of the Normandy invasion, one of many exhibits on board, was a gift from France. To keep the 1943 ship in sailing shape, the steam engine—which appears in the film *Titanic*—is operated dockside seven times a year on special "steaming weekends." Cruises take place several times a year between May and October, and the vessel is open to visitors daily. ✉ *Pier 45, Fisherman's Wharf* ☎ *415/544–0100* 🌐 *www.ssjeremiahobrien.org* 🎫 *From $20.*

USS *Pampanito*

MILITARY SITE | Get an intriguing, if mildly claustrophobic, glimpse into life on a submarine during World War II on this small, 80-man sub, which sank six Japanese warships and damaged four others. **■ TIP→ There's not much in the way of interpretive signs, so opt for the audio tour to learn about what you're seeing.** ✉ *Pier 45, Fisherman's Wharf* ☎ *415/775–1943* 🌐 *maritime.org/uss-pampanito* 🎫 *From $20.*

Beaches

Aquatic Park

BEACHES | This urban beach, surrounded by Fort Mason, Ghirardelli Square, and Fisherman's Wharf, is a quarter-mile-long strip of sand. The gentle waters near shore are shallow, safe for kids to swim or wade, and fairly clean. Locals—including the seemingly ubiquitous older-man-in-Speedo—come out for quick dips in the frigid water. Members of the **Dolphin Club** and the **South End Rowing Club** come every morning for a swim, and a large and raucous crowd braves the cold on New Year's Day. **Amenities:** restaurants; restrooms; showers. **Best for:** sunsets; swimming; walking. ✉ *San Francisco Maritime National Historical Park, 499 Jefferson St., at Hyde St., Fisherman's Wharf* 🌐 *www.nps.gov/safr.*

Restaurants

To the north of the Ferry Building lies Fisherman's Wharf, a jumbled mix of seafood dining rooms, sidewalk vendors, and trinket shops that visitors religiously trudge through and San Franciscans invariably dismiss as a tourist trap. But even locals may come for a cracked crab.

Gary Danko

$$$$ | **AMERICAN** | This San Francisco classic has earned a legion of fans—and a Michelin star—for its namesake chef's refined and creative seasonal California cooking, displayed in dishes such as pan-seared scallops with parsnip puree, and juniper-crusted venison. The cost of a meal is pegged to the number of courses, from three to five, the wine list is the size of a small-town phone book, and the banquette-lined rooms, with stunning floral arrangements, are as memorable as the food and impeccable service. **Known for:** prix-fixe menu; fine dining; extensive wine list. $ *Average main: $92* ✉ *800 N. Point St., Fisherman's Wharf* ☎ *415/749–2060* 🌐 *www.garydanko.com* ⏲ *No lunch* 🧥 *Jacket required.*

Escape from Alcatraz

Federal-prison officials liked to claim that it was impossible to escape Alcatraz, and for the most part, that assertion was true. For seasoned swimmers, though, the trip has never posed a problem—in fact, it's been downright popular.

In the 1930s, in an attempt to dissuade the feds from converting Alcatraz into a prison, a handful of schoolgirls made the swim to the city. At age 60, native son Jack LaLanne did it (for the second time) while shackled and towing a 1,000-pound rowboat. Every year a couple of thousand participants take the plunge during the annual Escape from Alcatraz Triathlon and Sharkfest Swim. Heck, a dog made the crossing in 2005 and finished well ahead of most of the (human) pack. And since 2006, seven-year-old Braxton Bilbrey remains the youngest "escapee" on record. Incidentally, those reports of shark-infested waters are true, but the sharks are almost never dangerous species.

Hotels

The hub of San Francisco's kitschy tourist trade, Fisherman's Wharf draws families to its chain hotels and smaller properties. Accommodations are generally playful, and many have swimming pools. The downside is that some lodgings lie far from other tourist attractions.

★ Argonaut Hotel

$$$ | HOTEL | FAMILY | The nautically themed Argonaut's spacious guest rooms have exposed-brick walls, wood-beam ceilings, and best of all, windows that open to the sea air and the sounds of the waterfront; many rooms enjoy Alcatraz and Golden Gate Bridge views. **Pros:** bay views; near Hyde Street cable car; toys for the kids. **Cons:** nautical theme isn't for everyone; cramped public areas; far from crosstown attractions. *$ Rooms from: $269 ✉ 495 Jefferson St., at Hyde St., Fisherman's Wharf ☎ 415/563–0800, 866/415–0704 🌐 www.argonauthotel.com ⇨ 252 rooms 🍴 No meals.*

Fairmont Heritage Place, Ghirardelli Square

$$$$ | RENTAL | FAMILY | Located in the former Ghirardelli chocolate factory, one- to-three-bedroom apartments deliver comfort and style, with fully equipped gourmet kitchens, brick walls, plush bedding, laundry facilities, modern furniture in chocolate and lavender hues, and views of Alcatraz and the bay. **Pros:** luxurious and historic; gigantic apartments with many amenities; bay views from most accommodations. **Cons:** a bit of a trek from downtown; expensive; limited food and beverage service. *$ Rooms from: $840 ✉ 950 N. Point St., Fisherman's Wharf ☎ 415/268–9900 🌐 www.fairmont.com/ghirardelli ⇨ 53 rooms 🍴 Breakfast.*

Hotel Zephyr

$$$ | HOTEL | FAMILY | Directly facing Alcatraz with unobstructed bay and island vistas, this Fisherman's Wharf hotel pays tribute to San Francisco's shipyard past. **Pros:** lively decor and views; indoor game room and The Yard outdoor "adult playground"; The Camper grab-and-go food option. **Cons:** touristy area; expensive parking; some housekeeping lapses. *$ Rooms from: $349 ✉ 250 Beach St., Fisherman's Wharf ☎ 415/617–6555, 844/617–6555 🌐 www.hotelzephyrsf.com ⇨ 361 rooms 🍴 No meals.*

Hotel Zoe Fisherman's Wharf
$$$ | **HOTEL** | A smart-looking boutique hotel with guest-room interiors inspired by luxury Mediterranean yachts, the Zoe aims for subtle contemporary elegance in the form of lightly stained woods and soft-brown and cream fabrics and walls. **Pros:** cozy feeling; steps from Fisherman's Wharf; smart-looking contemporary design. **Cons:** congested touristy area; small rooms; resort fee catches some guests off guard. *Rooms from: $249 ✉ 425 N. Point St., at Mason St., Fisherman's Wharf ☎ 415/561–1100, 800/648–4626 🌐 www.hotelzoesf.com 221 rooms No meals.*

Sheraton Fisherman's Wharf Hotel
$$$$ | **HOTEL** | **FAMILY** | It might not look like much from the street, but from the fire pits lining the parking area to the lobby's mood lighting, this Sheraton has a vacation vibe. **Pros:** in the heart of Fisherman's Wharf; fun colors; heated outdoor pool. **Cons:** little bang for a lot of buck; far from downtown and crosstown sights; fee for in-room Wi-Fi on top of hefty resort fee. *Rooms from: $425 ✉ 2500 Mason St., Fisherman's Wharf ☎ 415/362–5500, 888/627–7024 🌐 www.sheratonatthewharf.com 531 rooms No meals.*

Nightlife

Come nightfall, the crowds that throng the northern waterfront during the day tend to thin out, and the nightlife scene here is almost quaint.

BARS

Buena Vista Café
BARS/PUBS | At the end of the Hyde Street cable-car line, the Buena Vista packs 'em in for its famous Irish coffee—which, according to owners, was the first served stateside (in 1952). The place oozes nostalgia, drawing devoted locals as well as out-of-towners relaxing after a day of sightseeing. It's narrow and can get crowded, but this spot provides a fine alternative to the overpriced tourist joints nearby. *✉ 2765 Hyde St., at Beach St., Fisherman's Wharf ☎ 415/474–5044 🌐 www.thebuenavista.com.*

No Uphill Battle

Don't want to get stuck slogging up 20-degree inclines? Then pick up a copy of the foldout *San Francisco Bike Map and Walking Guide* ($4), which indicates street grades by color and delineates bike routes that avoid major hills and heavy traffic. You can pick up a copy in bicycle shops, some bookstores, or at the San Francisco Bicycle Coalition's website (🌐 *www.sfbike.org*).

Activities

BICYCLING

WHERE TO RENT

Bay City Bike
BICYCLING | With four locations in Fisherman's Wharf and one in Haight Ashbury, Bay City Bike isn't hard to find. The shop has an impressive fleet of bikes—many sizes and types—and friendly staff to help you map your biking adventure. *✉ 2661 Taylor St., at Beach St., Fisherman's Wharf ☎ 415/346–2453 🌐 baycitybike.com.*

Blazing Saddles
BICYCLING | This outfitter with multiple locations around San Francisco also offers guided tours—most of which involve biking the Golden Gate Bridge—as well as self-guided options with their app. *✉ 2715 Hyde St., near Beach St., Fisherman's Wharf ☎ 415/202–8888 🌐 www.blazingsaddles.com.*

WHERE TO BIKE

A completely flat, sea-level route, the Embarcadero hugs the eastern and northern bay and gives a clear view of open waters, the Bay Bridge, and sleek high-rises. The route from Pier 40 to Aquatic Park takes about 30 minutes to ride, and there are designated bike lanes the entire way. As you ride west, you'll pass the Bay Bridge, the Ferry Building, Coit Tower (look inland near Pier 19), and historic ships at the Hyde Street Pier. At Aquatic Park there's a nice view of Golden Gate Bridge. If you're not tired yet, continue along the Marina and through the Presidio's Crissy Field. You may want to time your ride so you end up at the Ferry Building, where you can refuel with a sandwich, a gelato, or—why not?—fresh oysters. ■ TIP→ **Keep your eyes open along this route—cars move quickly here, and streetcars and tourist traffic can cause congestion. Near Fisherman's Wharf you can bike on the promenade, but take it slow and watch out for pedestrians.**

BOATING AND SAILING

San Francisco Bay has year-round sailing, but tricky currents and strong winds make the bay hazardous for inexperienced navigators. However, on group sails you can enjoy the bay while leaving the work to the experts.

Adventure Cat Sailing Charters

BOATING | Near Fisherman's Wharf, Adventure Cat takes passengers aboard one of two 55-foot-long catamarans. The kids can play on the trampoline-like net between the two hulls while you sip drinks on the wind-protected sundeck. A 90-minute bay cruise costs $45; sunset sails with drinks and light hors d'oeuvres are $60. ✉ *Pier 39, Dock J, Fisherman's Wharf* ☎ *800/498–4228, 415/777–1630* 🌐 *www.adventurecat.com.*

WHALE-WATCHING

Between January and April, hundreds of gray whales migrate along the coast; the rest of the year humpback and blue whales feed offshore at the Farallon Islands. The best place to watch them from shore is Point Reyes, in Marin County *(see Chapter 14)*.

For a better view, head out on a whale-watching trip. Seas around San Francisco can be rough, so pack motion-sickness tablets. You should also dress warmly, wear sunscreen, and pack rain gear and sunglasses; binoculars come in handy, too. Tour companies don't provide meals or snacks, so bring your own lunch and water. Make reservations at least a week ahead.

California Whale Adventures

WHALE-WATCHING | California Whale Adventures has year-round whale-watching trips (from $100), weekends only, and reservations are highly encouraged. In the fall you can take a great-white-shark tour ($200 per person, weekends only). All trips leave from Fisherman's Wharf. ✉ *Fisherman's Wharf* ☎ *650/579–7777* 🌐 *www.californiawhaleadventures.com.*

Embarcadero

Stretching from below the Bay Bridge to Fisherman's Wharf, San Francisco's flat, accessible waterfront invites you to get up close and personal with the bay, the picturesque and constant backdrop to this stunning city. For decades the Embarcadero was obscured by a terrible raised freeway and known best for the giant buildings on its piers that further cut off the city from the bay. With the freeway gone and a few piers restored for public access, the Embarcadero has been given a new lease on life. Millions of visitors may come through the northern waterfront every year, lured by Fisherman's Wharf and Pier 39, but locals tend to stop short of these, opting instead for the gastronomic pleasures of the Ferry Building. Between the two, though, you'll find tourists and San Franciscans alike soaking up the sun, walking out over the water on a long pier to see the sailboats, savoring the excellent restaurants and old-time watering holes, watching the street performers that crowd Embarcadero Plaza on a sunny day—these are the simple joys that make you happy you're in San Francisco, whether for a few days or a lifetime.

 Sights

Alcatraz

JAIL | FAMILY | Thousands of visitors come every day to walk in the footsteps of Alcatraz's notorious criminals. The stories of life and death on "the Rock" may sometimes be exaggerated, but it's almost impossible to resist the chance to wander the cell block that tamed the country's toughest gangsters and saw daring escape attempts of tremendous desperation. Fewer than 2,000 inmates ever did time on the Rock, and though they weren't the worst criminals, they were definitely the worst prisoners, including Al "Scarface" Capone, Robert "The Birdman" Stroud, and George "Machine Gun" Kelly.

Some tips for escaping to Alcatraz: (1) Buy your ticket in advance. Visit the website for Alcatraz Cruises (*www.alcatrazcruises.com*) to scout out available departure times for the ferry. Prepay by credit card and keep a receipt record; the ticket price covers the boat ride and the audio tour. Pick up your ticket at the "will call" window at Pier 33 up to an hour before sailing. (2) Dress smart. Bring a jacket to ward off the chill from the boat ride and wear comfortable shoes. (3) Go for the evening tour. You'll get even more out of your Alcatraz experience at night. The evening tour has programs not offered during the day, the bridge-to-bridge view of the city twinkles at night, and your "prison experience" will be amplified as darkness falls. (4) Be mindful of scheduled and limited-capacity talks. Some programs are given only once a day (the schedule is posted in the cell house) and have limited seating, so keep an eye out for a cell-house staffer handing out passes shortly before the start time.

The boat ride to the island is brief (15 minutes), but affords beautiful views of the city, Marin County, and the East Bay. The audio tour, highly recommended, includes observations by guards and prisoners about life in one of America's most notorious penal colonies. Plan your schedule to allow at least three hours for the visit and boat rides combined. Not inspired by the prison? Wander around the lovely native plant gardens and (if the tide is cooperating) the tide pools on the north side of the island. ✉ *Pier 33, Embarcadero* ☎ *415/981–7625* 🌐 *www.nps.gov/alca* 🎫 *From $40.*

★ Exploratorium

MUSEUM | FAMILY | Walking into this fascinating "museum of science, art, and human perception" is like visiting a mad-scientist's laboratory. Most of the exhibits are supersize, and you can play with everything. Signature experiential exhibits include the Tinkering Studio and a glass Bay Observatory building, where the exhibits inside help visitors better understand what they see outside. Get an Alice-in-Wonderland feeling in the distorted room, where you seem to shrink and grow as you walk across the slanted, checkered floor. In the shadow room, a powerful flash freezes an image of your shadow on the wall; jumping is a favorite pose. More than 650 other exhibits focus on sea and insect life, computers, electricity, patterns and light, language, the weather, and more. One surefire hit is the pitch-black, touchy-feely Tactile Dome ($15 extra; reservations required): crawl through a course of ladders, slides, and tunnels, relying solely on your sense of touch." ✉ *Piers 15–17, Embarcadero* ☎ *415/528–4444 general information, 415/528–4407 Tactile Dome reservations* 🌐 *www.exploratorium.edu* 🎫 *$30.*

★ Ferry Building

MARKET | The jewel of the Embarcadero, erected in 1896, is topped by a 230-foot clock tower modeled after the campanile of the cathedral in Seville, Spain. On the morning of April 18, 1906, the tower's four clock faces stopped at 5:17—the moment the great earthquake struck—and stayed still for 12 months.

Today San Franciscans flock to the street-level marketplace, stocking up on supplies from local favorites such as Acme Bread, Cowgirl Creamery, Blue Bottle Coffee, and Humphry Slocombe ice cream. Slanted Door, the city's beloved high-end Vietnamese restaurant, is here, along with the well-regarded Hog Island Oyster Company. On the plaza side, the outdoor tables at Gott's Roadside offer great people-watching with their famous burgers. On Saturday morning the plazas outside the building buzz with an upscale farmers' market where you can buy exotic sandwiches and other munchables. Extending south from the piers north of the building all the way to the Bay Bridge, the waterfront promenade out front is a favorite among joggers and picnickers, with a front-row view of sailboats plying the bay. True to its name, the Ferry Building still serves actual ferries: from its eastern flank they sail to Sausalito, Larkspur, Tiburon, and the East Bay. ✉ *Embarcadero at foot of Market St., Embarcadero* ☎ *415/983–8030* 🌐 *www.ferrybuildingmarketplace.com.*

F-line

TRANSPORTATION SITE (AIRPORT/BUS/FERRY/TRAIN) | The city's system of vintage electric trolleys, the F-line, gives the cable cars a run for their money as a beloved mode of transportation. The beautifully restored streetcars—some dating from the 19th century—run from the Castro District down Market Street to the Embarcadero, then north to Fisherman's Wharf. Each car is unique, restored to the colors of its city of origin, from New Orleans and Philadelphia to Moscow and Milan. ■ **TIP→ Purchase tickets on board; exact change is required.** ✉ *San Francisco* 🌐 *www.streetcar.org* 🎫 *$3.*

San Francisco Railway Museum

MUSEUM | **FAMILY** | A labor of love brought to you by the same vintage-transit enthusiasts responsible for the F-line's revival, this one-room museum and store celebrates the city's streetcars and cable cars with photographs, models, and artifacts. The permanent exhibit includes the replicated end of a streetcar with a working cab—complete with controls and a bell—for kids to explore; the cool, antique Wiley birdcage traffic signal; and models and display cases to view. Right on the F-line track, just across from the Ferry Building, this is a great quick stop. ✉ *77 Steuart St., Embarcadero* ☎ *415/974–1948* 🌐 *www.streetcar.org* 🎫 *Free* ⊙ *Closed Mon.*

Restaurants

Locals and visitors alike flock here for gorgeous bay views, a world-class waterfront esplanade, and a Ferry Building that's much better known for its food than its boat rides. Some of the best bakers and cooks in the city have started here or have their satellites here.

Boulevard

$$$$ | **AMERICAN** | Two local restaurant celebrities—chef Nancy Oakes and designer Pat Kuleto—are behind this high-profile, high-priced eatery in the historic 1889 Audiffred Building that's been attracting well-dressed locals and flush out-of-towners for more than 25 years. A striking Belle Époque interior is the setting for sophisticated American food with a French accent, including mains such as grilled king salmon, Angus filet, and truffle-spiked risotto, but save room for one of the dynamite desserts, among them the Valrhona dark-chocolate brioche pudding. **Known for:** sophisticated French-Californian food; generous

Did You Know?

San Francisco is only seven miles long by seven miles wide—which makes it really easy to see a lot in just one day.

portions; excellent desserts. *Average main: $40 1 Mission St., Embarcadero 415/543–6084 www.boulevardrestaurant.com No lunch weekends.*

Coqueta

$$$$ | SPANISH | With its Embarcadero perch, Bay Bridge views, and stellar Spanish tapas, celebrity chef Michael Chiarello's first San Francisco restaurant is a big hit that's equal parts rustic and chic, a lively destination for both small bites and larger meals. Toothpicked *pintxos* (small snacks) like quail egg with Serrano ham are a tasty way to start, but the real draws are the inventive cocktails, luscious paella, and dazzling selection of cured meats. **Known for:** Spanish tapas; water views; creative cocktails. *Average main: $38 Pier 5, on the Embarcadero, near Broadway, Embarcadero 415/704–8866 coquetasf.com No lunch Mon.*

Epic Steak

$$$$ | STEAKHOUSE | "Epic" describes it all, from the outsize dining room and the mile-wide bay view to the slabs of meat grilled over an open fire, and, alas, the prices. For an Epic experience at a fraction of the price, head upstairs to the Quiver bar for the "3 B's," a half-pound burger, a brownie, and a Bud. **Known for:** bay views; steak-house favorites; high prices. *Average main: $67 369 Embarcadero, between Folsom and Harrison Sts., Embarcadero 415/369–9955 www.epicsteak.com.*

Fog City

$$ | AMERICAN | FAMILY | All but hidden on a far-flung stretch of the Embarcadero, this 21st-century diner that's well worth the hike is best known for its updated classics, like a short-rib BLT with kimchi mayo and corn bread that emerges hot from the wood-fired oven. An inviting U-shape bar and tables-with-a-view attract a mix of FiDi locals and tourists who've wandered right into a gold mine. **Known for:** updated diner food; excellent cocktails; views of Battery St. and the Embarcadero. *Average main: $22 1300 Battery St., Embarcadero 415/982–2000 www.fogcitysf.com.*

Gott's Roadside

$ | BURGER | FAMILY | A lunchtime favorite where gleaming metal countertops and hand-lettered boards recall the prime burger era, this Ferry Building stalwart boasts a view of Coit Tower and crowd-pleasing grub. This is a burger chain that cares about details: its dressings are house-made, its patties use freshly ground Niman Ranch beef, and its menu includes a wine list. **Known for:** organic meats; elevated fast food; wine list and good shakes. *Average main: $13 1 Ferry Bldg., Suite 6, Embarcadero 415/318–3423 www.gotts.com.*

Hog Island Oyster Company

$$ | SEAFOOD | A thriving oyster farm north of San Francisco in Tomales Bay serves up its harvest at this raw bar and restaurant in the Ferry Building, where devotees come for impeccably fresh oysters and clams on the half shell. Other mollusk-centered options include a first-rate seafood stew, baked oysters, clam chowder, and "steamer" dishes, but the bar also turns out one of the city's best grilled-cheese sandwiches, made with three artisanal cheeses on artisanal bread. **Known for:** fresh oysters; first-rate seafood stew; busy raw bar. *Average main: $19 Ferry Bldg., Embarcadero at Market St., Embarcadero 415/391–7117 www.hogislandoysters.com.*

La Mar Cebicheria Peruana

$$$$ | PERUVIAN | Right on the water's edge, this casually chic outpost, the chain's first outside Peru, imports real Peruvian flavors to San Francisco. Fresh seafood is a big draw here (though not the only one), including a long list of ceviches, can't-miss *causas* (whipped potatoes topped with a choice of fish, shellfish, or vegetable salads), and everything from grilled fish and shellfish to cilantro-braised lamb shank. **Known for:** fresh seafood; authentic Peruvian food;

tasty empanadas and causas. *Average main: $40 Pier 1½, between Washington and Jackson Sts., Embarcadero 415/397–8880 lamarsf.com.*

One Market

$$$ | AMERICAN | A favorite for business lunches, this white-tablecloth spot caters to suits brokering deals while carving their way through dishes like tender bacon-wrapped pork tenderloin with dandelion greens. Its menu skews seasonal and meaty, and its largish bar, which offers small bites and numerous cocktails, is popular for FiDi happy hour. **Known for:** power lunches; popular happy hour; careful presentation. *Average main: $37 1 Market St., Embarcadero 415/777–5577 www.onemarket.com Closed Sun. No lunch Sat.*

Piperade

$$$ | BASQUE | Longtime San Francisco chef Gerald Hirigoyen serves a rustic French-Basque menu that includes pipérade (cooked peppers and tomatoes served with serrano ham and poached egg) and rack of lamb with cumin and date relish in a sexy, brick-walled dining room. Try a Basque wine from the impressive list, and don't miss the featherweight orange-blossom beignets or the pastry cream–filled gâteau Basque with cherry preserves on the extensive dessert menu. **Known for:** refined Basque and French-inspired cuisine; excellent wine list with plentiful Basque options; often-present chef-owner. *Average main: $29 1015 Battery St., Embarcadero 415/391–2555 www.piperade.com Closed Sun. No lunch Sat.*

Slanted Door

$$$$ | VIETNAMESE | Celebrated chef-owner Charles Phan has mastered the upmarket, Western-accented Vietnamese menu, showcased in a big space with sleek wooden tables and chairs, a big bar, an enviable bay view, and dedicated clientele. His popular dishes, including green-papaya salad, daikon rice cakes, cellophane crab noodles, chicken clay pot, and shaking beef (tender beef cubes with garlic and onion) don't come cheap, but they're made with quality ingredients. **Known for:** upscale Vietnamese food; some of the city's best cocktails; bustling dining room with great bay views. *Average main: $38 Ferry Bldg., Embarcadero at Market St., Embarcadero 415/861–8032 www.slanteddoor.com.*

Waterbar

$$$$ | SEAFOOD | You come for seafood with a view: sky-high aquariums dominate the dining room, and the bay is just beyond, but the biggest attraction is the food: every fin and shell of the sea, from the oak-roasted petrale sole to the grilled steelhead trout, is sustainably sourced. Another highlight is the oyster bar menu, as ample as a wine list, that includes about two dozen varieties daily as well as other fresh shelly things in season. **Known for:** sustainable seafood; ample oyster bar; bay views. *Average main: $39 399 Embarcadero, between Folsom and Harrison Sts., Embarcadero 415/284–9922 www.waterbarsf.com.*

Hotels

Harbor Court Hotel

$$$ | HOTEL | Renovated in 2018, this Spanish Colonial Revival–style Embarcadero hotel has nice touches that enliven the tight guest quarters, from soundproof windows to quirky mathematical wall clocks and brightly colored lumbar pillows adorning beds with Frette linens. **Pros:** convenient quiet location; friendly professional staffers; Bay Bridge and Ferry Building views from some rooms. **Cons:** many rooms are small given the rates; some rooms lack views; fee for amenities they don't require irks some guests. *Rooms from: $279 165 Steuart St., Embarcadero 415/882–1300, 877/989–5861 www.harborcourthotel.com 131 rooms No meals.*

★ Hotel Vitale

$$$$ | HOTEL | FAMILY | The emphasis on luxury and upscale relaxation at this eight-story bay-front property is apparent: limestone-lined baths stocked with top-of-the-line products; the penthouse-level day spa with soaking tubs set in a rooftop bamboo forest; terraces on the fifth, seventh, and eighth floors with great waterfront views. **Pros:** family-friendly studios; great waterfront views; penthouse spa. **Cons:** some rooms feel cramped; "urban fee" adds further expense to an already pricey property; yet another charge for Wi-Fi beyond basic. *$ Rooms from: $385 ✉ 8 Mission St., Embarcadero ☎ 415/278–3700, 888/890–8688 🌐 www.hotelvitale.com 🛏 200 rooms 🍽 No meals.*

Hyatt Regency San Francisco

$$$$ | HOTEL | Renovated in 2016, this waterfront property has a 17-story atrium lobby that starred in several 1970s flicks, most notably the disaster epic The Towering Inferno. **Pros:** elegant design plus grand bay views; near restaurants, shopping, and the Ferry Building; even the smallest rooms a decent size. **Cons:** soaring room rates in high season; geared toward business travelers; lacks intimacy. *$ Rooms from: $429 ✉ 5 Embarcadero Center, Embarcadero ☎ 415/788–1234, 800/233–1234 🌐 sanfranciscoregency.hyatt.com 🛏 804 rooms 🍽 No meals.*

Nightlife

The waterfront's eastern section stays busy at night, not a surprise given its expansive bay views and proximity to Union Square, Chinatown, the Financial District, and SoMa.

BARS

Hard Water

BARS/PUBS | This waterfront restaurant and bar with stunning bay views pays homage to America's most iconic spirit—bourbon—with a wall of whiskeys and a lineup of specialty cocktails. The menu, crafted by Charles Phan of Slanted Door fame, is an ode to New Orleans cuisine and includes spicy pork-belly cracklings, jambalaya, and other fun snacks. *✉ Pier 3, at Embarcadero, Embarcadero ☎ 415/392–3021 🌐 www.hardwaterbar.com.*

Pier 23 Cafe

BARS/PUBS | Beer arrives at your table in buckets at this waterfront bar, which has ample seating at plastic tables on a wooden deck. Although you'd expect to sit elbow-to-elbow with fishermen, you're more likely to share the space with twenty- and thirtysomethings drawn by the beer and food specials. *✉ Pier 23, The Embarcadero, Embarcadero ☎ 415/362–5125 🌐 www.pier23cafe.com.*

SPOKEN WORD AND READINGS

Commonwealth Club of California

READINGS/LECTURES | The nation's oldest public-affairs forum hosts speakers as diverse as Jane Goodall and Bill Gates, covering topics from culture and politics to economics and foreign policy. Events are open to nonmembers, and lectures are broadcast on NPR. *✉ 110 The Embarcadero, Embarcadero ☎ 415/597–6700 🌐 www.commonwealthclub.org.*

Shopping

Four sprawling buildings of shops, restaurants, offices, and a popular independent movie theater—plus the Hyatt Regency hotel—make up the Embarcadero Center, downtown at the end of Market Street. Most of the stores are branches of upscale national chains, such as Ann Taylor and Banana Republic. Also in this area is the Ferry Building, with a focus on local food and other vendors.

FARMERS' MARKETS

★ Ferry Plaza Farmers' Market

OUTDOOR/FLEA/GREEN MARKETS | The partylike Saturday edition of the city's most upscale and expensive farmers' market places baked goods, gourmet cheeses, smoked fish, and fancy pots of jam alongside organic basil, specialty mushrooms, heirloom tomatoes, and juicy-ripe locally grown fruit. Smaller markets also take place on Tuesday and Thursday from April through December. ✉ *Ferry Plaza, at Market St., Embarcadero* ☎ *415/291–3276* 🌐 *www.ferrybuildingmarketplace.com.*

FOOD AND DRINK

★ Cowgirl Creamery Artisan Cheese

FOOD/CANDY | Fantastic organic-milk cheeses—such as the mellow, triple-cream Mt. Tam and *bocconcini* (small balls of fresh mozzarella)—are produced at a creamery an hour's drive north of the city. These and other carefully chosen artisanal cheeses and dairy products, including a luscious, freshly made crème fraîche, round out the selection at the in-town store. ✉ *Ferry Building Marketplace, 1 Ferry Bldg. #17, at foot of Market St., Embarcadero* ☎ *415/362–9354* 🌐 *www.cowgirlcreamery.com.*

McEvoy Ranch

FOOD/CANDY | This is the only retail outpost of this Sonoma County ranch, a producer of outstanding organic, extra-virgin olive oil. **■ TIP→ If you stop by in fall or winter, don't miss the Olio Nuovo, the days-old green oil produced during the harvest.** ✉ *Ferry Building Marketplace, 1 Ferry Bldg. #16, at foot of Market St., Embarcadero* ☎ *415/291–7224* 🌐 *www.mcevoyranch.com.*

Recchiuti Confections

FOOD/CANDY | Michael and Jacky Recchiuti began making otherworldly chocolates in San Francisco in 1997, using traditional European techniques. Now considered among the best confectioners in the world, they stock their store here (there's also a smaller one in the Dogpatch neighborhood) with their full chocolate line, including several unique items inspired by the surrounding gourmet markets. ✉ *Ferry Building Marketplace, 1 Ferry Bldg., Suite 30, Embarcadero at foot of Market St., Embarcadero* ☎ *415/834–9494* 🌐 *www.recchiuti.com.*

Whiskey Rhyme

The Italianate Hotaling building survived the disastrous 1906 quake and fire—a miracle considering the thousands of barrels of inflammable liquid inside. A plaque on the side of the structure repeats a famous query: "If, as they say, god spanked the town for being over frisky, why did he burn the churches down and save Hotaling's whiskey?"

TOYS

Exploratorium

TOYS | FAMILY | The educational gadgets and gizmos sold here are of the super-clever variety that kids won't know they're learning while playing. Space- and dinosaur-related games are popular, as are science videos and optical illusion gifts. ✉ *Piers 15, at Embarcadero at Green St., Embarcadero* ☎ *415/528–4390* 🌐 *www.exploratorium.edu.*

Activities

BOATING AND SAILING

Rendezvous Charters

BOATING | This operator offers individually ticketed trips on large sailing yachts, including sunset sails ($60) and Sunday brunch cruises on a schooner ($60). Ticketed trips tend to close from mid-October through March (although they continue to do private chartered sails throughout the year), so call in advance to confirm availability. ✉ *Pier 40, Suite 4, South Beach Harbor, Embarcadero* ☎ *415/543–7333* 🌐 *www.rendezvouscharters.com.*

Alcatraz as Native Land

In the 1960s, Native Americans attempted to reclaim Alcatraz, citing an 1868 treaty that granted Native Americans any surplus federal land. Their activism crested in 1969, when several dozen Native Americans began a 19-month occupation, supported by public opinion and friendly media.

The group offered to buy the island from the government for $24 worth of beads and other goods—exactly what Native Americans had been paid for Manhattan in 1626. In their "Proclamation to the Great White Father and His People," the group laid out the 10 reasons why Alcatraz was suitable for an Indian reservation "by the white man's own standards," among them: "There is no industry and so unemployment is very great," and "The soil is rocky and nonproductive, and the land does not support game." Federal agents removed the last holdouts in 1971, but each Thanksgiving Native Americans and others gather on the island to commemorate the takeover. In 2013 the park service restored the protesters' fading graffiti on the water tower, and today's visitors are still greeted with the huge message: "Indians Welcome. Indian Land."

Financial District

During the latter half of the 19th century, when San Francisco was a brawling, extravagant gold-rush town, today's Financial District was underwater. Yerba Buena Cove reached all the way up to Montgomery Street, and what's now Jackson Square was the heart of the Barbary Coast, bordering some of the roughest wharves in the world. These days, Jackson Square is a genteel and upscale neighborhood wedged between North Beach and the Financial District, but buried below Montgomery Street lies a remnant of these wild days: more than 100 ships abandoned by frantic crews and passengers caught up in gold fever lie under the foundations of buildings here.

The Financial District of the 21st century is a decidedly less exciting affair, and safer, too: no one's going to slip you a Mickey and ship you off to Shanghai. It's all office towers packed with mazes of cubicles now, and folks in suits and "office casual" fill the sidewalks at lunchtime. When the sun sets, this quarter empties out fast. The few sights here will appeal mainly to gold-rush history enthusiasts; others can safely steer clear.

Sights

Jackson Square Historic District

NEIGHBORHOOD | This was the heart of the Barbary Coast of the Gay '90s—the 1890s, that is. Although most of the red-light district was destroyed in the fire that followed the 1906 earthquake, the remaining old redbrick buildings, many of them now occupied by advertising agencies, law offices, and antiques firms, retain hints of the romance and rowdiness of San Francisco's early days.

With its gentrified gold rush–era buildings, the 700 block of **Montgomery Street** just barely evokes the Barbary Coast days, but this was a colorful block in the 19th century and on into the 20th. Writers Mark Twain and Bret Harte were among the contributors to the spunky *Golden Era* newspaper, which occupied No. 732 (now part of the building at No. 744).

Restored 19th-century brick buildings line Hotaling Place, which connects Washington and Jackson Streets. The lane is named for the **A.P. Hotaling Company whiskey distillery** (*451 Jackson St., at Hotaling Pl.*), the largest liquor repository on the West Coast in its day. The exceptional City Guides (*415/557–4266, www.sfcityguides.org*) Gold Rush City walking tour covers this area and brings its history to life. ✉ *Bordered by Columbus Ave., Broadway, and Washington and Sansome Sts., San Francisco.*

Market Street buildings

BUILDING | The street, which bisects the city at an angle, has consistently challenged San Francisco's architects. One of the most intriguing responses to this challenge sits diagonally across Market Street from the Palace Hotel. The tower of the **Hobart Building** (No. 582) combines a flat facade and oval sides and is considered one of Willis Polk's best works in the city. East on Market Street is Charles Havens's triangular **Flatiron Building** (Nos. 540–548), another classic solution. At Bush Street, the **Donahue Monument** holds its own against the skyscrapers that tower over the intersection. This homage to waterfront mechanics, which survived the 1906 earthquake (a famous photograph shows Market Street in ruins around the sculpture), was designed by Douglas Tilden, a noted California sculptor. The plaque in the sidewalk next to the monument marks the spot as the location of the San Francisco Bay shoreline in 1848. Telltale nautical details such as anchors, ropes, and shells adorn the gracefully detailed **Matson Building** (No. 215), built in the 1920s for the shipping line Matson Navigation. ✉ *Between New Montgomery and Beale Sts., Financial District.*

Transamerica Pyramid

BUILDING | It's neither owned by Transamerica nor is it a pyramid, but this 853-foot-tall obelisk *is* the most photographed of the city's high-rises. Excoriated in the design stages as "the world's largest architectural folly," the icon was quickly hailed as a masterpiece when it opened in 1972. Today it's probably the city's most recognized structure after the Golden Gate Bridge. Visit the small, street-level visitor center to see the virtual view from the top, watch videos about the building's history, and perhaps pick up a T-shirt. **TIP→ A fragrant redwood grove along the east side of the building, replete with benches and a cheerful fountain, is a placid patch in which to unwind.** ✉ *600 Montgomery St., Financial District* 🌐 *www.pyramidcenter.com.*

Wells Fargo Bank History Museum

MUSEUM | There were no formal banks in San Francisco during the early years of the gold rush, and miners often entrusted their gold dust to saloon keepers. In 1852, Wells Fargo opened its first bank in the city on this spot, and the company soon established banking offices in mother-lode camps throughout California. At the fun two-story museum, you can pick up a free ticket and climb aboard a stagecoach—the projected driver will tell you about the ride and the scenery passing by on the wall—or take the reins and experience a trip out west. Have your picture taken in front of the gorgeous red Concord stagecoach (collect your souvenir photo at the desk), the likes of which carried passengers from St. Joseph, Missouri, to San Francisco in just three weeks during the 1850s. The museum also displays samples of nuggets and gold dust from mines, an old telegraph machine on which you can practice sending codes, and tools the '49ers used to coax the precious mineral from the ground. ✉ *420 Montgomery St., Financial District* ☎ *415/396–2619* 🌐 *www.wellsfargohistory.com* 🎫 *Free.*

Restaurants

The center of commerce, with some very good restaurants (housed in old Barbary Coast buildings), FiDi caters to the business elite with prices to match, but engineers and software developers looking for a fast lunch head to modest Indian and Chinese places, as well as superb sandwich shops.

Barbacco

$$ | ITALIAN | The busy sister restaurant to neighboring Perbacco offers affordable small Italian plates, such as the chef's salumi selection and chicken thighs *alla cacciatora*, as well as plenty of Italian wines to explore by the glass. Financial District workers crowd in to the chic Milanese-style room for lunch or happy hour at the communal tables and long counter. **Known for:** regional Italian food; quality food in casual setting; curated wine list. *Average main: $19 ✉ 220 California St., Financial District ☎ 415/955–1919 🌐 www.barbaccosf.com ⏲ Closed Sun. No lunch Sat.*

Café Claude

$$$ | FRENCH | Francophiles congregate here for that *je ne sais quoi,* right down to the delicious croque monsieur, escargots, steak tartare, and coq au vin, especially Thursday through Sunday nights for live jazz. If you think this place looks straight out of Paris, it mostly is: the banquettes, the zinc bar, the light fixtures, and cinema posters were shipped from a defunct café in the City of Light to this atmospheric downtown alley. **Known for:** French bistro food; live jazz; Continental vibe. *Average main: $26 ✉ 7 Claude La., Financial District ☎ 415/392–3505 🌐 www.cafeclaude.com ⏲ No lunch Sun.*

Cotogna

$$$ | ITALIAN | The draw at this urban trattoria—just as in demand as its fancier big sister, Quince, next door—is chef Michael Tusk's flavorful, rustic, seasonally driven Italian cooking, such as the irresistible raviolo di ricotta, filled with warm house-made ricotta and topped with an egg yolk, and bistecca alla Fiorentina. The look is comfortably chic, with wood tables, quality stemware, and fantastic Italian wines by the bottle and glass. **Known for:** rustic Italian; fantastic wine list; chic space. *Average main: $27 ✉ 490 Pacific Ave., Financial District ☎ 415/775–8508 🌐 www.cotognasf.com ⏲ No lunch Sun.*

Kokkari Estiatorio

$$$$ | GREEK | Satisfy your craving for outstanding Greek taverna food—albeit at steak-house prices—from a dizzying selection of *mezethes* (small plates) such as stuffed grape leaves to main courses that showcase Athenian standards like moussaka, lemon-oregano chicken, and notable grilled lamb chops. There's a lively after-work scene in this chic farmhouse setting with wood beamed ceilings, a roaring wood oven, and candlelight. **Known for:** Greek cuisine and hospitality; inviting rustic-chic space; semolina custard wrapped in phylo. *Average main: $37 ✉ 200 Jackson St., Financial District ☎ 415/981–0983 🌐 www.kokkari.com ⏲ No lunch weekends.*

Michael Mina

$$$$ | MIDDLE EASTERN | The flagship outpost for this acclaimed chef remains a beacon of refined dining, with a Middle Eastern-inspired menu that includes luxurious renditions of Yemenite-style beef rib eye and grilled lamb with harissa and merguez sausage. Dinner is a six-course prix-fixe-only affair, while lunch is the time to sample the mastery of Mina at a fraction of the price. **Known for:** expensive prix-fixe menu; white-tablecloth dining; innovative, masterful cuisine. *Average main: $195 ✉ 252 California St., Financial District ☎ 415/397–9222 🌐 www.michaelmina.net ⏲ No lunch weekends.*

Perbacco

$$$ | ITALIAN | From the complimentary basket of skinny, brittle breadsticks to the pappardelle with short rib ragu, Chef Staffan Terje's entire menu is a delectable paean to northern Italy. With a long marble bar and open kitchen, this brick-lined two-story space oozes big-city charm, attracting business types and Italian food aficionados with such standouts as the house-made cured meats (Terje makes some of the city's finest salumi), burrata with seasonal vegetables, and delicate *agnolotti dal plin* (pasta stuffed with meat and cabbage). **Known for:** pasta stuffed with meat and cabbage; house-made cured meats; authentic Northern Italian cuisine. *Average main: $31 ✉ 230 California St., Financial District ☎ 415/955–0663 🌐 www.perbaccosf.com 🕓 Closed Sun. No lunch Sat.*

Quince

$$$$ | MODERN AMERICAN | To enjoy Michael Tusk's three-Michelin-starred contemporary Californian cuisine, you'll have to splurge on a 9- to 12-course chef's tasting menu, but you'll be rewarded with seasonal items such as *agnolottini* with squab and broccoli *di cicco* and chantenay carrots with ash butter. The 1,400-bottle-strong wine list is top-notch, but can get pricey (a steep corkage fee means you won't save much by bringing your own bottle), and the seamless service is both refined and welcoming. **Known for:** award-winning prix-fixe menu; highly seasonal ingredients; strong wine list. *Average main: $295 ✉ 470 Pacific Ave., Financial District ☎ 415/775–8500 🌐 www.quincerestaurant.com 🕓 Closed Sun. No lunch.*

The Ramen Bar

$ | RAMEN | Acclaimed chef Michael Mina has gotten on the ramen train with a big assist from Tokyo native and chef Ken Tominaga, and their FiDi collaboration is a popular lunchtime spot known as much for fast service as for Tokyo-style noodles—the light, casual setting has sit-down service only at dinner. The menu also veers into sushi roll and poke bowl territory, and prices tend to add up; this is not your strip-mall ramen joint. **Known for:** Tokyo-style noodles; poke bowl; elevated ramen. *Average main: $14 ✉ 101 California St., Financial District ☎ 415/684–1570 🌐 www.theramenbar.com 🕓 Closed weekends.*

Tadich Grill

$$$ | SEAFOOD | Locations and owners have changed more than once since this old-timer started as a coffee stand on the waterfront in 1849, but the crowds keep coming. Try to snag one of the private booths (complete with a bell to summon the crusty, white-coated waiters) and sample seafood—always the name of the game here—such as the Dungeness crab cocktail, crab Louie, and *cioppino* stew during crab season (usually November to June) and oysters Rockfeller, seafood curry, and iconic San Francisco sand dabs year-round. **Known for:** seafood focus; crab dishes; dedicated following. *Average main: $30 ✉ 240 California St., Financial District ☎ 415/391–1849 🌐 www.tadichgrill.com 🕓 Closed Sun.*

Wayfare Tavern

$$$ | AMERICAN | This energetic and upscale American tavern owned by TV chef and personality Tyler Florence is rich with turn-of-the-20th-century Americana, including brick walls, comfortable booths, and a billiards room and has an approachable menu that also tips its hat to tradition—and comfort. Deviled eggs, fresh seafood, and the decadent burger and fried chicken are particular standouts. **Known for:** comfort food; stand-out burger; lively scene (upstairs is quieter). *Average main: $29 ✉ 558 Sacramento St., Financial District ☎ 415/722–9060 🌐 www.wayfaretavern.com.*

Yank Sing

$$ | **CHINESE** | **FAMILY** | This bustling teahouse serves some of San Francisco's best dim sum to office workers on weekdays and boisterous families on weekends, and the take-out counter makes a meal on the run a satisfying compromise when office duties—or touring—won't wait. The several dozen varieties prepared daily include both the classic and the creative; steamed pork buns, shrimp dumplings, scallion-skewered prawns tied with bacon, and basil seafood dumplings are among the many delights, and the Shanghai soup dumplings are perfection. **Known for:** classic dim sum; Shanghai soup dumplings; energetic room. *Average main: $18 49 Stevenson St., Financial District 415/541–4949 www.yanksing.com No dinner.*

Hotels

The large hotels here lure business travelers with some of the city's finest luxury accommodations—with hefty price tags to boot. With public transportation, Union Square, the Ferry Building, Chinatown, and North Beach a short walk away, leisure travelers find this area a good base as well.

Galleria Park Hotel

$$$ | **HOTEL** | Renovated in 2017, the Galleria Park manages to be both hip and welcoming, with modern touches on historical bones and smallish guest rooms with all the technological amenities modern travelers require. **Pros:** convenient location one block from BART; complimentary wine at daily Wine Hour; in-house Gaspar French brasserie. **Cons:** small rooms and bathrooms; city noise; hefty required fee for extras like Wi-Fi, morning coffee, fitness room. *Rooms from: $339 191 Sutter St., Financial District 415/781–3060, 800/792–9639 www.galleriapark.com 177 rooms No meals.*

Hilton San Francisco Financial District

$$ | **HOTEL** | **FAMILY** | Business travelers patronize this hoppin' Hilton, which is overdue for an update, for its airy guest rooms and large work desks, but even in high season the weekend rates drop significantly, luring leisure travelers. **Pros:** abundant parking; bay and city views; great location at intersection of FiDi, Chinatown, and North Beach. **Cons:** congested downtown area; property needs sprucing up; feels very corporate. *Rooms from: $339 750 Kearny St., Financial District 415/433–6600 sanfranciscohiltonhotel.com 543 rooms No meals.*

Le Méridien San Francisco

$$$$ | **HOTEL** | The stylishly contemporary Le Méridien scores well on both form and function, with compelling artwork throughout the lobby and guest rooms outfitted with polished granite sinks, wall-size San Francisco maps, and handy in-room safes. **Pros:** spacious rooms, many with good views; interesting artwork throughout; accommodating staff. **Cons:** after dark this Financial District neighborhood grows sleepy; restaurant and bar merely adequate; high rates during major conventions. *Rooms from: $425 333 Battery St., Financial District 415/296–2900 lemeridiensanfrancisco.com 360 rooms No meals.*

Loews Regency San Francisco

$$$$ | **HOTEL** | **FAMILY** | Every room has spectacular city and bay views at this business-centric hotel, which occupies the top 11 floors in one of San Francisco's tallest buildings; glass-enclosed sky bridges with amazing vistas to themselves connect the hotel's two towers, and rooms all have binoculars. **Pros:** spectacular "bridge-to-bridge" views; among the city's most comfortable beds; seasonal rooftop bar. **Cons:** in a business area that's quiet at night and on weekends; pricey; coffeemakers only upon request. *Rooms from: $540*

Continued on page 171

ALCATRAZ

"They made that place purely for punishment, where men would rot. It was designed to systematically destroy human beings . . . Cold, gray, and lonely, it had a weird way of haunting you—there were those dungeons that you heard about, but there was also the city . . . only a mile and a quarter away, so close you could almost touch it. Sometimes the wind would blow a certain way and you could smell the Italian cooking in North Beach and hear the laughter of people, of women and kids. That made it worse than hell."

—Jim Quillen, former Alcatraz inmate

Gripping the rail as the ferryboat pitches gently in the chilly breeze, you watch formidable Alcatraz rising ahead. Imagine making this trip shackled at the ankle and waist, the looming fortress on the craggy island ahead, waiting to swallow you whole. Thousands of visitors come every day to walk in the footsteps of Alcatraz's notorious criminals. The stories of life and death on "the Rock" may sometimes be exaggerated, but it's almost impossible to resist the chance to wander the cellblock that tamed the country's toughest gangsters and saw daring escape attempts of tremendous desperation.

LIFE ON THE ROCK

The federal penitentiary's first warden, James A. Johnston, was largely responsible for Alcatraz's (mostly false) hell-on-earth reputation. A tough but relatively humane disciplinarian, Johnston strictly limited the information flow to and from the prison when it opened in 1934. Prisoners' letters were censored, newspapers and radios were forbidden, and no visits were allowed during a convict's first three months in the slammer. Understandably, imaginations ran wild on the mainland.

A LIFE OF PRIVILEGE

Monotony was an understatement on Alcatraz; the same precise schedule was kept daily. The rulebook stated, "You are entitled to food, clothing, shelter, and medical attention. Anything else you get is a privilege." These privileges, from the right to work to the ability to receive mail, were earned by following the prison's rules. A relatively minor infraction meant losing privileges. A serious breach, like fighting, brought severe punishments like time in the Hole (a.k.a. the Strip Cell, since the prisoner had to strip) or the Oriental (an absolutely dark, silent cell with a hole in the ground for a toilet).

THE SPAGHETTI RIOT

Johnston knew that poor food was one of the major causes of prison riots, so he insisted that Alcatraz serve the best chow in the prison system. But the next warden at Alcatraz slacked off, and in 1950, one spaghetti meal too many sent the inmates over the edge. Guards deployed tear gas to subdue the rioters.

A PRISONER'S DAY

6:30 am: Wake-up call. Prisoners get up, get dressed, and clean cells.

6:50 am: Prisoners stand at cell doors to be counted.

7:00 am: Prisoners march single-file to mess hall for breakfast.

7:20 am: Prisoners head to work or industries detail; count.

9:30 am: 8-minute break; count.

11:30 am: Count; prisoners march to mess hall for lunch.

12:00 pm: Prisoners march to cells; count; break in cells.

12:20 pm: Prisoners leave cells, march single-file back to work; count.

2:30 pm: 8-minute break; count.

4:15 pm: Prisoners stop work, two counts.

4:25 pm: Prisoners march into mess hall and are counted; dinner.

4:45 pm: Prisoners return to cells and are locked in.

5:00 pm: Prisoners stand at their doors to be counted.

8:00 pm: Count.

9:30 pm: Count; lights out.

12:01 am–5 am: Three counts.

INFAMOUS INMATES

Fewer than 2,000 inmates ever did time on the Rock; though they weren't necessarily the worst criminals, they were definitely the worst prisoners. Most were escape artists, and others, like Al Capone, had corrupted the prison system from the inside with bribes.

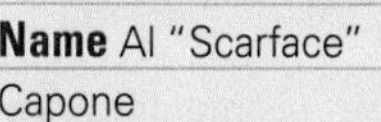

Name Al "Scarface" Capone

On the Rock 1934–1939

In for Tax evasion

Claim to fame Notorious Chicago gangster and bootlegger who arranged the 1929 St. Valentine's Day Massacre.

Hard fact Capone was among the first transfers to the Rock and arrived smiling and joking. He soon realized the party was over. Capone endured a few stints in the Hole and Warden Johnston's early enforced-silence policy; he was also stabbed by a fellow inmate. The gangster eventually caved, saying "it looks like Alcatraz has got me licked," thus cementing the prison's reputation.

Name Robert "The Birdman" Stroud

On the Rock 1942–1959

In for Murder, including the fatal stabbing of a prison guard

Claim to fame Subject of the acclaimed but largely fictitious 1962 film *Birdman of Alcatraz.*

Hard fact Stroud was actually known as the "Bird Doctor of Leavenworth." While incarcerated in Leavenworth prison through the 1920s and 30s, he became an expert on birds, tending an aviary and writing two books. The stench and mess in his cell discouraged the guards from searching it—and finding Stroud's homemade still. His years on the Rock were birdless.

Name George "Machine Gun" Kelly

On the Rock 1934–1951

In for Kidnapping

Claim to fame Became an expert with a machine gun at the urging of his wife, Kathryn. Kathryn also encouraged his string of bank robberies and the kidnapping for ransom of oilman Charles Urschel. While stashed in Leavenworth on a life sentence, Kelly boasted that he would escape and then free Kathryn. That got him a one-way ticket to Alcatraz.

Hard fact Was an altar boy on Alcatraz and was generally considered a model prisoner.

NO ESCAPE

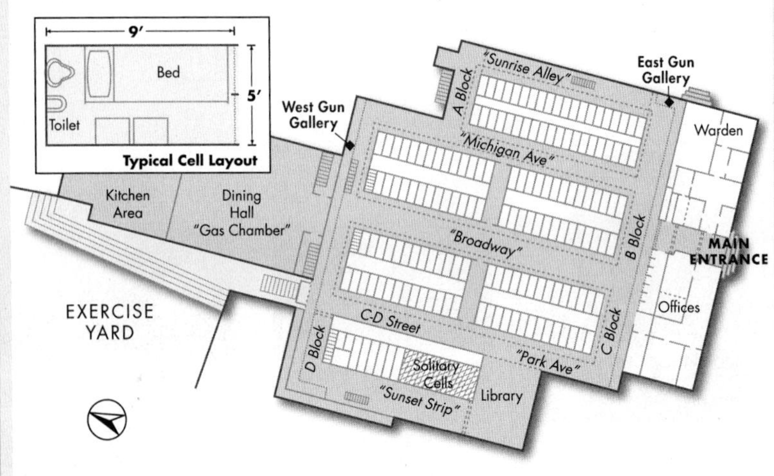

Alcatraz was a maximum-security federal penitentiary with one guard for every three prisoners. The biggest deterrent to escape, though, was the 1.4 miles of icy bay waters separating the Rock from the city. Only a few prisoners made it off the island, and only one is known to have survived. And that story about the shark-infested waters? There are sharks in the bay, but they're not the man-eating kind.

Bloodiest Attempt: In 1946, six prisoners hatched a plan to surprise a guard, seize weapons, and escape through the recreation yard. They succeeded up to a point, arming themselves and locking several guards into cells, but things got ugly when the group couldn't find the key that opened the door to the prison yard. Desperate, they opened fire on the trapped guards. Warden Johnston called in the Marines, who shelled the cell house for two days in the so-called Battle of Alcatraz. Three ringleaders were killed in the fighting; two were executed for murder; and one, who was just 19 years old, got 99 years slapped on to his sentence.

Craftiest Attempt: Over six months, three convicts stole bits and pieces from the kitchen and machine shop to make drills and digging pieces. They used these basic tools to widen a vent into the utility corridor. They also gathered bits of cardboard, toilet paper, and hair from the prison's barbershop to make crude models of their own heads. Then, like teenagers sneaking out, they put the decoy heads in their cots and walked away—up the pipes in the utility corridor to the roof, then down a drainpipe to the ground. They set sail in a raft made from prison raincoats, and are officially presumed dead.

Most Anticlimactic: In 1962, one prisoner spent an entire year loosening the bars in a window. Then he slipped through and managed to swim all the way to Fort Point, near the Golden Gate Bridge. He promptly fell asleep there and was found an hour later by some teenagers.

6 TIPS FOR ESCAPING TO ALCATRAZ

"Broadway," once the cell blocks' busiest corridor.

1. Buy your ticket in advance. Visit the website for Alcatraz Cruises (☎415/981–7625 🌐www.alcatrazcruises.com) to scout out available departure times for the ferry. Prepay by credit card—the ticket price covers the boat ride and the audio tour—and print your ticket at home. Bring it to Pier 33 up to an hour before sailing and experience just a touch of schadenfreude as you overhear attendants tell scores of too-late passengers that your tour is sold out.

2. Dress smart. Bring that pullover you packed to ward off the chill from the boat ride and Alcatraz Island. Also: sneakers. Some Alcatraz guides are fanatical about making excellent time.

3. Go for the evening tour. You'll get even more out of the experience if you do it at night. The evening tour has programs not offered during the day, the bridge-to-bridge view of the city twinkles at night, and your "prison experience" will be amplified as darkness mournfully falls while you shuffle around the cell block.

4. Unplug and go against the flow. If you miss a cue on the excellent audio tour and find yourself out of synch, don't sweat it—use it as an opportunity to switch off the tape and walk against the grain of the people following the tour. No one will stop you if you walk back through a cell block on your own, taking the time to listen to the haunting sound of your own footsteps on the concrete floor.

5. Be mindful of scheduled and limited-capacity talks. Some programs only happen once a day (the schedule is posted in the cell house). Certain talks have limited capacity seating, so keep an eye out for a cell house staffer handing out passes shortly before the start time.

6. Talk to the staff. One of the island's greatest resources is its staff, who practically bubble over with information. Pick their brains, and draw them out about what they know.

PRACTICALITIES

Visitors at the Alcatraz dock waiting to depart "Uncle Sam's Devil's Island."

GETTING THERE

All cruises are operated by Alcatraz Cruises, the park's authorized conces -sionaire.

TIMING

The boat ride to Alcatraz is only about 15 minutes long, but you should allow about three hours for your entire visit. The delightful F-line vintage streetcars are the most direct public transit to the dock; on weekdays the 10-Townsend bus will get you within a few blocks of Pier 33.

FOOD

The prisoners might have enjoyed good food on Alcatraz, but you won't—unless you pack a picnic. Food is not available on the island, so be sure to stock up before you board the boat. Sandwich fare is available at Alcatraz Landing, at Pier 33, and the Ferry Building's bounty is just a 20-minute walk from Pier 33. In a pinch, you can also pony up for the underwhelming snacks on the boat.

STORM TROOPER ALERT!

When he was filming *Star Wars*, George Lucas recorded the sound of Alcatraz's cell doors slamming shut and used the sound bite in the movie whenever Darth Vader's star cruiser closed its doors.

KIDS ON THE ROCK

Parents should be aware that the audio tour, while engaging and worthwhile, includes some startlingly realistic sound effects. (Some children might not get a kick out of the gunshots from the Battle of Alcatraz—or the guards' screams, for that matter.) If you stay just one minute ahead in the program, you can always fast forward through the violent moments on your little one's audio tour.

✉ *222 Sansome St., Financial District* ☎ *415/276–9888, 844/271–6289* 🌐 *www.loewshotels.com/regency-san-francisco* 🛏 *155 rooms* 🍽 *No meals.*

★ Omni San Francisco Hotel

$$$$ | **HOTEL** | In a 1926 Florentine Renaissance–style structure that once housed banks and other financial enterprises, the Omni draws travelers seeking historical flavor and a downtown location. **Pros:** immaculate rooms; historical flavor; good weekend rates. **Cons:** fee for in-room Wi-Fi; expensive restaurant; not much to do in immediate area at night and on weekends. $ *Rooms from: $375* ✉ *500 California St., Financial District* ☎ *415/677–9494* 🌐 *www.omnisanfrancisco.com* 🛏 *362 rooms* 🍽 *No meals.*

Nightlife

Not surprisingly, the nightlife scene here revolves around suits recovering from extended workdays or still trying to seal the deal. Wiggle in among the shop talkers and enjoy a stiff martini.

BARS

The Hidden Vine

WINE BARS—NIGHTLIFE | True to its name, this cozy wine bar is in a little alley (just north of Market Street) and the location is part of the appeal, but the wines and amuse-bouches make it truly worthwhile. A jumble of velvet chairs and love seats fills the space, and the owner, who serves most nights, acts as your sommelier. The space also features its very own bocce court. ✉ *408 Merchant St., at Battery St., Financial District* ☎ *415/674–3567* 🌐 *www.thehiddenvine.com.*

Pagan Idol

BARS/PUBS | Giving the Tonga Bar a run for its money as the kitchiest tiki bar in town, Pagan Idol features a secret back room complete with erupting volcano, giant tikis, and a starry night sky. The folks from Bourbon & Branch are behind this faux pirate ship, so even if the cocktails are served in goofy tiki glasses with paper umbrellas—even if they're on fire—rest assured they're top-shelf and on the money. Expect live music Tuesday through Thursday. ✉ *375 Bush St., near Kearney St., Financial District* ☎ *415/985–6375* 🌐 *www.paganidol.com.*

Rickhouse

BARS/PUBS | An after-work FiDi crowd fills this brick-walled and dimly lit speakeasy, revered for its extensive whiskey menu and curated list of seasonal cocktails. It's a beautiful space with barrels aplenty, an evening oasis in a neighborhood that traditionally rolls up the sidewalks at sunset. ✉ *246 Kearney St., near Bush St., Financial District* ☎ *415/398–2827* 🌐 *www.rickhousebar.com.*

COMEDY

Punchline

COMEDY CLUBS | A launch pad for the likes of Jay Leno and Whoopi Goldberg, this place books some of the nation's top talents. Headliners have included Dave Chappelle, Margaret Cho, and Jay Mohr. No one under 18 is admitted. ✉ *444 Battery St., between Clay and Washington Sts., Financial District* ☎ *415/397–7573* 🌐 *www.punchlinecomedyclub.com.*

Performing Arts

CONCERTS

42nd Street Moon

MUSIC | This group produces delightful "semistaged" concert performances of rare chestnuts from Broadway's golden age of musical theater, such as *L'il Abner* and *The Boys From Syracuse.* ✉ *Gateway Theatre, 215 Jackson St., Financial District* ☎ *415/255–8207* 🌐 *www.42ndstmoon.org.*

Gateway Theatre

MUSIC | The Gateway Theatre hosts most 42nd Street Moon shows as well as shows by Theatre Rhinoceros. ✉ *215 Jackson St., between Front and Battery Sts., Financial District* ☎ *415/788–7469* 🌐 *42ndstmoon.org/gateway.*

Noontime Concerts at Old St. Mary's Cathedral

MUSIC | This Gothic Revival church, completed in 1872 and rebuilt after the 1906 earthquake, hosts a notable—and free—chamber-music series on Tuesday at 12:30. ✉ *660 California St., Financial District* ☎ *415/777–3211* 🌐 *www.noontimeconcerts.org.*

THEATER

Theatre Rhinoceros

THEATER | Celebrating 40 years of queer theater in 2017, Theatre Rhinoceros showcases gay and lesbian performers and playwrights at the Gateway Theatre. ✉ *Financial District* ☎ *800/838–3006 tickets, 415/552–4100 offices* 🌐 *www.therhino.org.*

Shopping

The FiDi doesn't top anyone's list of great San Francisco shopping neighborhoods, but some major chains do business amid the office towers, and the narrow lanes and side streets hold a few clothing boutiques and a great bookshop.

BOOKS

William Stout Architectural Books

BOOKS/STATIONERY | Architect William Stout began selling books out of his apartment 25 years ago. Today the store is a source for Bay Area professionals looking for serious-minded tomes on architecture and design. Head down into the basement for beautifully illustrated coffee-table books. Stout is the sole distributor of the popular IDEO method cards, which offer and inspire design solutions. ✉ *804 Montgomery St., between Gold and Jackson Sts., Financial District* ☎ *415/391–6757* 🌐 *www.stoutbooks.com* ⏲ *Closed Sun.*

Chapter 8

THE MARINA AND THE PRESIDIO

Updated by
Trevor Felch

Sights	Restaurants	Hotels	Shopping	Nightlife
★★★★☆	★★★☆☆	★★★☆☆	★★★★☆	★★☆☆☆

THE GOLDEN GATE BRIDGE

Two red towers reach into the sky, floating above the mist like ghost ships on foggy days. If there's one image that instantly conjures San Francisco, it's the majestic Golden Gate Bridge, one of the most recognizable sights in the world.

Spanning the Golden Gate—the mouth of the San Francisco Bay, after which the bridge was named—between San Francisco and pastoral Marin County, the bridge has won both popular and critical acclaim, including being named one of the seven wonders of the modern world. With its simple but powerful art-deco design, the 1.7-mile suspension span and its 750-foot towers were built to withstand winds of more than 100 mph. It's also not a bad place to be in an earthquake: designed to sway almost 28 feet, the Golden Gate Bridge (unlike the Bay Bridge) was undamaged by the 1989 Loma Prieta quake. If you're on the bridge when it's windy, stand still and you can feel it swaying a bit.

Lincoln Blvd. near Doyle Dr. and Fort Point, Presidio, 415/921–5858, www.goldengatebridge.org

Pedestrians: Mar.–Oct., daily 5 am–9 pm; Nov.–Feb., daily 5 am–6:30 pm; hrs change with daylight saving time. Bicyclists: daily 24 hrs.

A DAY OVER THE BAY

Crossing the Golden Gate Bridge under your own power is a sensation that's hard to describe. Especially as you approach midspan, hovering more than 200 feet above the water makes you feel as though you're outside of time—exhilarating, a little scary (be careful taking selfies since the wind can steal phones!), definitely chilly. From the bridge's eastern-side walkway, the only side pedestrians are allowed on, you can take in the San Francisco skyline and the bay islands; look west for the wild hills of the Marin Headlands, the curving coast south to Lands End, and the Pacific Ocean. On sunny days, sailboats dot the water, and brave windsurfers test the often-treacherous tides beneath the bridge. A vista point on the Marin County side provides a spectacular city panorama. The views are fantastic however you cross—by foot, bicycle, or motorized vehicle—but driving or cycling will allow you to fully appreciate the bridge from multiple vantage points in and around the Presidio.

THE MAN WHO BUILT THE BRIDGE

In the early 1900s, San Francisco was behind the times. Sure, the city had the engineering marvel of the cable car and hundreds of streetcar lines, but as the largest U.S. city served mainly by ferries, this town needed a bridge. Enter Joseph Strauss, a structural engineer, dreamer, and poet who promised that not only could he build a bridge, but he could also do it on the cheap. At 5 feet 3 inches tall, Strauss was a force of nature. He worked tirelessly over the next 20-odd years, first as a bridge booster and then overseeing its design and construction.

If you want to ride across the bridge and avoid the crowds, bike early or on a weekday.

The iconic orange bridge is often enveloped by clouds of swirling fog knon as "Karl."

Though the final structure bore little resemblance to his original plan, Strauss guarded his legacy jealously, refusing to recognize the seminal contributions of engineer Charles A. Ellis. In 2007, the Golden Gate Bridge District finally recognized Ellis's role, though Strauss, who died less than a year after opening day in 1937, would doubtless be pleased with the inscription on his statue, which stands sentry in the southern parking lot: "The Man Who Built the Bridge."

VISITING THE BRIDGE TODAY

The bridge has been standing for three-quarters of a century, but the visitor's experience got an upgrade to coincide with the 75th-anniversary celebration in 2012. You can grab a snack at the art deco–style Bridge Café. The recently erected Bridge Pavilion sells attractive, high-quality souvenirs and has a small display of historical artifacts: look for an original brush used to paint the bridge. At the outdoor exhibits, you can see the bridge rise before your eyes on hologram panels, learn about the features that make it art deco, and read about the personalities behind its design and construction. City Guides offers free walking tours of the bridge every Thursday and Sunday at 11 am.

NEIGHBORHOOD SNAPSHOT

PLANNING YOUR TIME

Walking across the Golden Gate Bridge takes about an hour round-trip, but leave some time to take in the view on the other side. If you aren't in a hurry, plan to spend at least two to three hours in the Presidio, and be sure to allow 15 minutes to stroll around the stunning Palace of Fine Arts. In a pinch, make a 30- to 45-minute swing-through for the views. Shoppers can burn up an entire day browsing the Marina's Chestnut Street and Cow Hollow's Union Street. Weekends are liveliest, while Mondays are quiet, since some shops close.

TOP REASONS TO GO

■ **Golden Gate Bridge:** Get a good look at the iconic span from the Presidio, then bundle up and walk over the water.

■ **Shop Cow Hollow and the Marina:** Browse hip boutiques and lavish antiques shops on Union Street, Cow Hollow's main drag. Then head north to Chestnut Street.

■ **Palace of Fine Arts:** Bring a picnic to this movingly beautiful faux-Greek remnant of the 1915 Panama-Pacific International Exposition and travel back in time to the city's post-earthquake-and-fire coming-out party.

■ **Crissy Field:** Join jogging, cycling, and kitesurfing locals along this beautifully restored strip of sand and marshland where the bay laps the shore, a stone's throw from the Golden Gate Bridge.

■ **Presidio wanderings:** Lace up your walking shoes and follow one of the wooded trails; the city will feel a hundred miles away.

GETTING THERE

For those without wheels, the free year-round shuttle PresidiGo, which runs two routes through the Presidio every half hour, is a dream. Pick up the shuttle at the transit center at Lincoln Boulevard and Graham Street.

QUICK BITES

■ **Dynamo Donut & Coffee.** This tiny kiosk on the Marina's yacht harbor is the perfect spot to grab a pick-me-up before a stroll to the Palace of Fine Arts or along the beach. The doughnuts by a former Foreign Cinema pastry chef are universally terrific, from the vanilla bean standby to chocolate star anise, and there's locally roasted coffee for an extra prehike jolt. **Known for:** creative doughnuts; excellent gluten-free doughnuts; pick-me-up for frozen Marina tourists. ✉ *110 Yacht Rd., Marina* ☎ *415/920–1978* 🌐 *www.dynamodonut.com* ⊗ *Closed Mon.–Thurs.*

■ **Greens to Go.** The take-out counter of the famous vegetarian restaurant carries mouthwatering pre-made salads, sandwiches, and soups. Eat at picnic tables outside or head up a steep flight of stairs to a grassy park with splendid Marina views. **Known for:** vegetarian sandwiches; gorgeous bay views. ✉ *Fort Mason, Bldg. A, Marina* ☎ *415/771–6330* 🌐 *www.greensrestaurant.com.*

Yachts bob at their moorings, satisfied-looking folks jog along the Marina Green, and multimillion-dollar homes overlook the bay in the picturesque, if somewhat sterile, Marina neighborhood. Does it all seem a bit too perfect? Well, it got this way after the hard knock of Loma Prieta—the current pretty face was put on after hundreds of homes collapsed in the 1989 earthquake. Just west of this waterfront area is a more natural beauty: the Presidio. Once a military base, this beautiful, sprawling park is mostly green space, with hills, woods, and the marshlands of Crissy Field.

The Marina

Well-funded postcollegiates and the nouveau riche flooded the Marina after the 1989 Loma Prieta earthquake had sent many residents running for more-solid ground, changing the tenor of this formerly low-key neighborhood. The number of yuppie coffee emporiums skyrocketed, a bank became a Williams-Sonoma store, and the local grocer gave way to a Pottery Barn. On weekends a young, fairly homogeneous, well-to-do crowd floods the cafés and bars. (Some things don't change—even before the quake, the Marina Safeway was a famed pickup place for straight singles, hence the nickname "Dateway.") South of Lombard Street is the Marina's affluent neighbor, Cow Hollow, whose main drag, Union Street, has some of the city's best boutique shopping and a good selection of restaurants and cafés. Joggers and kite-flyers head to the Marina Green, the strip of lawn between the yacht club and the mansions of Marina Boulevard.

Sights

Fort Mason Center

ARTS VENUE | Originally a depot for the shipment of supplies to the Pacific during World War II, the fort was converted into a cultural center in 1977. Here you can find the vegetarian restaurant Greens and shops, galleries, and performance spaces.

The **Museo Italo-Americano** (*Bldg. C, 415/673–2200, museoitaloamericano.org, Tues.–Sun. noon–4*) is a small gallery that hosts one exhibit at a time, worth a glance if you're already at Fort Mason.

The temporary exhibits downstairs at the **SFMOMA Artists Gallery** (*Bldg. A, 415/441–4777, www.sfmoma.org/artists-gallery, weekdays 9–5*) can be great, but head upstairs and check out the paintings, sculptures, prints, and photographs for sale or rent. You won't find a Picasso or a Rembrandt, but where else can you get a $50,000 work of art to hang on your wall for $400 (a month)?

From March to October, Friday evening at Fort Mason mean **Off the Grid** *(offthegridsf.com)*; the city's food-truck gathering happens at locations around town, and this is one of the oldest and most popular. ✉ *Buchanan St. and Marina Blvd., Marina* ☎ *415/345–7500 event information* 🌐 *www.fortmason.org.*

★ Palace of Fine Arts

BUILDING | At first glance this stunning, rosy rococo palace seems to be from another world, and indeed, it's the sole survivor of the many tinted-plaster structures (a temporary classical city of sorts) built for the 1915 Panama-Pacific International Exposition, the world's fair that celebrated San Francisco's recovery from the 1906 earthquake and fire. The expo buildings originally extended about a mile along the shore. Bernard Maybeck designed this faux-Roman classic beauty, which was reconstructed in concrete and reopened in 1967. A victim of the elements, the Palace required a piece-by-piece renovation that was completed in 2008.

The pseudo-Latin language adorning the Palace's exterior urns continues to stump scholars. The massive columns (each topped with four "weeping maidens"), great rotunda, and swan-filled lagoon have been used in countless fashion layouts, films, and wedding photo shoots. After admiring the lagoon, look across the street to the house at 3460 Baker Street. If the maidens out front look familiar, they should—they're original casts of the "garland ladies" you can see in the Palace's colonnade. ✉ *3301 Lyon St., at Beach St., Marina* ☎ *415/563–6504* 🎫 *Free.*

Wave Organ

PUBLIC ART | **FAMILY** | Conceived by environmental artist Peter Richards and fashioned by master stonecutter George Gonzales, this unusual wave-activated acoustic sculpture gives off subtle harmonic sounds produced by seawater as it passes through 25 tubes. The sound is loudest at high tide. The granite and marble used for walkways, benches, and alcoves that are part of the piece were salvaged from a gold rush–era cemetery. ✉ *North of Marina Green at end of jetty by Yacht Rd., park in lot north of Marina Blvd. at Lyon St., Marina.*

Restaurants

On a sunny day, the Marina is perhaps one of the most cheerful places in the city, with sweeping views of Marin and the Golden Gate Bridge and plenty of joggers and bicyclists. Residents tend to be a mix of the just-graduated who are still very much into the nightclub scene. Mixed in are the affluent of the spectacular waterfront properties who hit Chestnut Street after dark for good food.

A16

$$$ | **ITALIAN** | Named after a highway that runs through Southern Italy, this trattoria specializes in the food from that region, done very, very well. The menu is stocked with pizza and rustic pastas like *maccaronara* with *ragu napoletana* and house-made salted ricotta, as well as entrées like roasted chicken with sage salsa verde. **Known for:** equally noteworthy pastas and pizzas; one of the city's best Italian wine lists; meatball Mondays. Ⓢ *Average main: $36* ✉ *2355 Chestnut St., Marina* ☎ *415/771–2216* 🌐 *www.a16pizza.com* 🕒 *No lunch Mon.–Thurs.*

Bistro Aix

$$$ | BISTRO | In a neighborhood full of trendy minichains, this over two decades-old Californian-French spot is the calm elder statesmen for the often rowdy Marina. The food is unfussy (perfect duck leg confit cassoulet; house-smoked salmon and potato galette) and doesn't try to be anything overly ambitious, yet everything is consistently on the mark. **Known for:** honest bistro cooking with quality ingredients; rear courtyard with beautiful olive tree; warm, romantic atmosphere. Ⓢ *Average main: $26* ✉ *3340 Steiner St., Marina* ✣ *Between Chestnut St. and Lombard St.* ☎ *415/202–0100* 🌐 *www.bistroaix.com* 🕒 *Closed Sun.*

Causwells

$$ | AMERICAN | There are two personalities to Chestnut Street's sleek grown-up diner—the double-stack burger that draws burgerhounds from dozens of miles away and the rest of the honest, spruced up comfort food menu. Start with homemade ricotta and a bountiful salad, then go straight after the burger and jerk chicken with creamed corn, before concluding with the must-try doughnut bread pudding. **Known for:** the Americana burger; excellent wine list full of lesser known regions; kitchen open until midnight on weekends. Ⓢ *Average main: $25* ✉ *2346 Chestnut St., Marina* ☎ *415/447–6081* 🌐 *www.causwells.com.*

Greens

$$$ | VEGETARIAN | Owned and operated by the San Francisco Zen Center, this legendary vegetarian restaurant gets some of its fresh produce from the center's organic Green Gulch Farm. Despite the lack of meat, hearty dishes from chef Annie Somerville—such as green squash curry and chestnut fettucine with chanterelle mushrooms—really satisfy. **Known for:** unbeatable views; superb vegetarian food; pizza at lunch. Ⓢ *Average main: $25* ✉ *Bldg. A, Fort Mason, 2 Marina Blvd., Marina* ☎ *415/771–6222* 🌐 *www.greensrestaurant.com* 🕒 *No lunch Mon.*

Isa

$$ | FRENCH | Beyond Isa's tiny storefront dining room is a heated, candlelit patio that consistently draws couples on date night, ladies night out, and groups of friends celebrating birthdays. The extensive menu of French-inspired tapas is known for its flat-iron steak, potato-wrapped sea bass, and veal-sweetbreads-and-mushroom fricassee but unfortunately the menu hasn't changed much in recent years and feels a bit tired. Ⓢ *Average main: $22* ✉ *3324 Steiner St., Marina* ☎ *415/567–9588* 🌐 *www.isarestaurant.com* 🕒 *No lunch.*

Tacolicious

$$ | MEXICAN | Tacos and tequila draw a young and energetic crowd to this perennial hot spot. Tables are topped with chips and guacamole, and platters of tortillas bursting with carnitas or shot-and-a-beer braised chicken. **Known for:** playful tacos; potent drinks; festive atmosphere. Ⓢ *Average main: $15* ✉ *2250 Chestnut St., Marina* ☎ *415/649–6077* 🌐 *www.tacolicious.com.*

Hotels

Marina is where the beautiful (and rich) go to see and be seen. Luxe B&Bs can be found here, but also reasonably priced motor inns whose enticements might include kitchenettes or free parking. The proximity to boutiques, eateries, and happening bars, as well as Crissy Field and the Presidio, make this area a popular choice.

Cow Hollow Motor Inn and Suites
$$ | HOTEL | FAMILY | The suites at this modern motel resemble typical San Francisco apartments and are more spacious than average, featuring big living rooms, one or two bedrooms, hardwood floors, sitting and dining areas, marble wood-burning fireplaces, and fully equipped kitchens. **Pros:** free covered parking in building for one vehicle; good value; easy walking distance to restaurants and bars. **Cons:** not much personality; standard rooms face a loud street; average decor. *Rooms from: $148 ✉ 2190 Lombard St., Marina ☎ 415/921–5800 🌐 www.cowhollowmotorinn.com 130 rooms No meals.*

Marina Inn
$ | B&B/INN | There's nothing fancy about this inn that occupies a four-story 1924 structure, but you're coming here for the price, not the decor or the housekeeping. **Pros:** affordable; 15-minute walk to Fisherman's Wharf; close to Marina and Union Street restaurants and shops. **Cons:** rooms facing street can be noisy; maintenance and housekeeping issues; must park on street (difficult) or at garage a few blocks away. *Rooms from: $149 ✉ 3110 Octavia St., at Lombard St., Marina ☎ 415/928–1000, 800/274–1420 🌐 www.marinainn.com 40 rooms Breakfast.*

Marina Motel
$ | HOTEL | Bougainvillea, fuchsia, and other foliage real and trompe l'oeil add color and verve to this 1939 motor court operated by the granddaughters of the original owners;when everything's in bloom and hummingbirds flit through the quiet courtyard the mood is magical. **Pros:** within walking distance of Marina District restaurants, bars, and shops; quiet courtyard rooms; strong value. **Cons:** loud rooms facing Lombard; no a/c (usually not a problem in the Marina); rooms look a bit dated. *Rooms from: $170 ✉ 2576 Lombard St., Marina ☎ 415/921–9406, 800/346–6118 🌐 www.marinamotel.com 39 rooms No meals.*

Nightlife

BARS

California Wine Merchant
WINE BARS—NIGHTLIFE | Part cluttered shop, part cozy bar, Chestnut Street's marquee wine destination is a longtime favorite for grabbing a glass or three. Wines featured always come from some of the state's most highly regarded vintners of all sizes and celebrity status. The neighborhood has many wine bars, but this is where the locals go when the focus is on the wine itself. *✉ 2113 Chestnut St., Marina ☎ 415/567–0646 🌐 www.californiawinemerchant.com.*

The Interval at Long Now
BARS/PUBS | Even many locals don't realize that the Fort Mason Center is home to one of the city's most impressive and scene-free cocktail bars. As part of the Long Now Foundation, a nonprofit devoted to long-term thinking, the cocktails reflect that commitment to finding innovative ways to serve tried-and-true libations. The Navy Gimlet with clarified lime juice is a modern day San Francisco classic. *✉ 2 Marina Blvd., Landmark Bldg. A, Marina ☎ 415/496–9187 🌐 www.theinterval.org.*

COMEDY

BATS Improv
COMEDY CLUBS | In addition to teaching workshops in improvisation, this renovated warehouse stages performances such as "Improvised Shakespeare" and "Spontaneous Broadway." The quality varies, but tickets are reasonably priced, usually $15–$20. *✉ Bayfront Theater, Fort Mason Center, Bldg. B, 3rd fl., at Marina Blvd. and Buchanan St., Marina ☎ 415/474–6776 🌐 www.improv.org.*

Performing Arts

THEATER

Magic Theatre

THEATER | Once Sam Shepard's favorite showcase, the pint-size Magic presents works by rising American playwrights such as Matthew Wells, Karen Hartman, and Claire Chafee. ✉ *Fort Mason, Bldg. D, Laguna St. at Marina Blvd., Marina* ☎ *415/441–8822* 🌐 *www.magictheatre.org.*

Cow Hollow

Between old-money Pacific Heights and the well-heeled, postcollegiate Marina lies comfortably upscale Cow Hollow. The neighborhood's name harks back to the 19th-century dairy farms whose owners eked out a living here despite the fact that there was more sand than grass. A patch of grass remains a scarce commodity in this mostly residential area, but Cow Hollow does have one heck of a commercial strip, centered around Union Street. To get a feel for this accessible bastion of affluence, stroll down Union. Browse the cosmetics and jewelry stores, snazzy clothing boutiques, and shops selling home decor for every taste (if not budget), then rest your feet at one of the many good restaurants or sidewalk cafés.

Sights

Octagon House

HOUSE | This eight-sided home sits across the street from its original site on Gough Street; it's one of two remaining octagonal houses in the city (the other is on Russian Hill), and the only one open to the public. White quoins accent each of the eight corners of the pretty blue-gray exterior, and a colonial-style garden completes the picture. The house is full of antique American furniture, decorative arts (paintings, silver, rugs), and documents from the 18th and 19th centuries, including the contents of a time capsule left by the original owners in 1861 that was discovered during a 1950s renovation. A deck of Revolutionary-era hand-painted playing cards takes an anti-monarchist position: in place of kings, queens, and jacks, the American upstarts substituted American statesmen, Roman goddesses, and Indian chiefs. Note that the home is only open on the second Sunday, and second and fourth Thursday of each month (closed all January). ✉ *2645 Gough St., near Union St., Cow Hollow* ☎ *415/441–7512* 🌐 *nscda-ca.org/octagon-house/* 🎟 *Free, donations encouraged.*

Vedanta Society Old Temple

RELIGIOUS SITE | A pastiche of colonial, Queen Anne, Moorish, and Hindu opulence, lavender with turrets battling red-top onion domes, and Victorian detailing everywhere, this 1905 structure is considered the first Hindu temple in the West. Vedanta, an underlying philosophy of Hinduism, maintains that all religions are paths to one goal. ✉ *2963 Webster St., Cow Hollow* ☎ *415/922–2323* 🌐 *www.sfvedanta.org.*

Wedding Houses

HOUSE | These identical white double-peak homes (joined in the middle) were erected in the late 1870s or early 1880s by dairy rancher James Cudworth as wedding gifts for his two daughters, down the street from his own house at 2040 Union Street. These days the buildings house a bar and a restaurant. ✉ *1980 Union St., Cow Hollow.*

Restaurants

★ Atelier Crenn

$$$$ | **MODERN FRENCH** | Dinner at the spectacularly inventive flagship of San Francisco's most celebrated chef of the moment, Dominique Crenn, starts with the presentation of a poem. Each course is described by a line in the

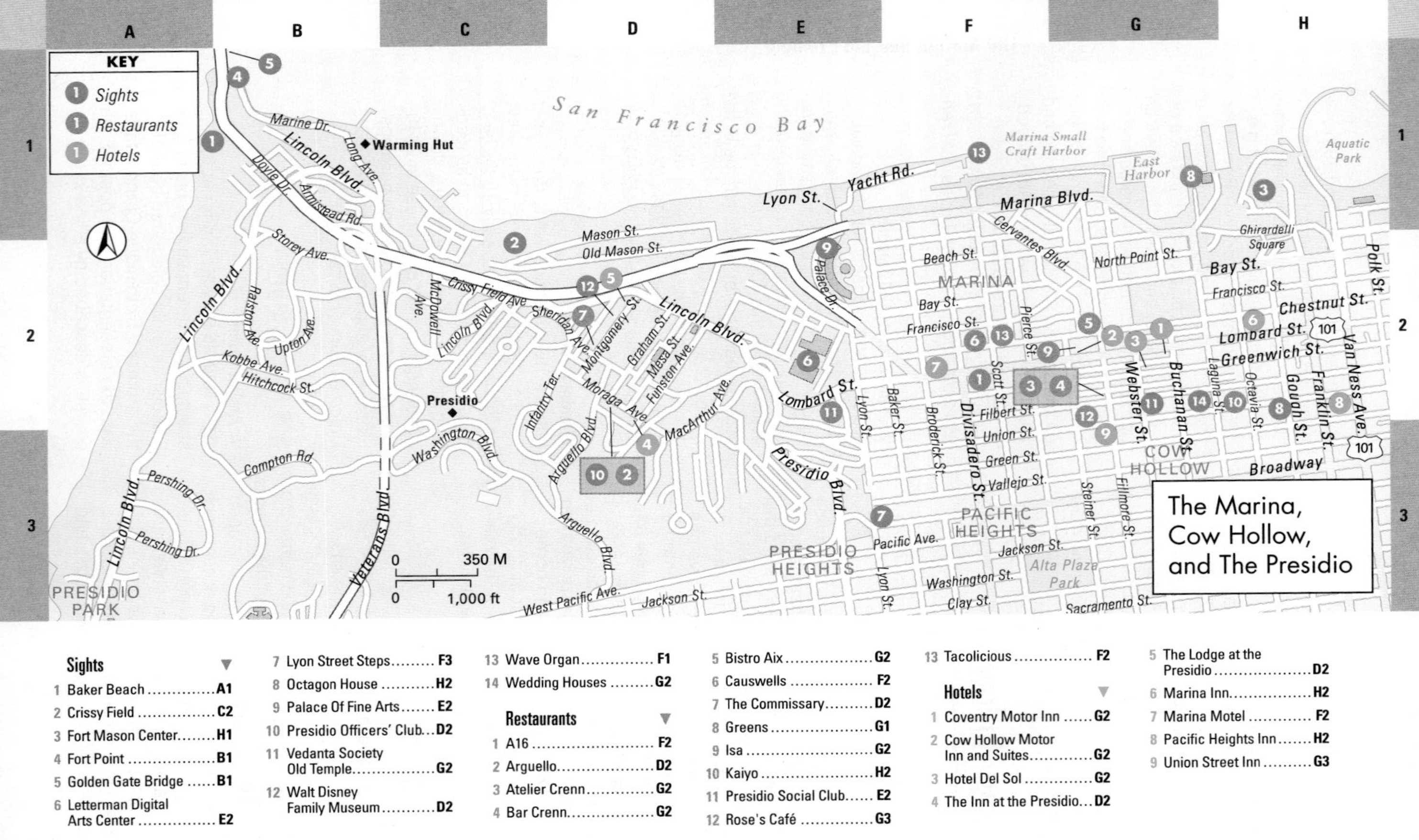

Sights

1 Baker Beach A1
2 Crissy Field C2
3 Fort Mason Center H1
4 Fort Point B1
5 Golden Gate Bridge B1
6 Letterman Digital Arts Center E2
7 Lyon Street Steps F3
8 Octagon House H2
9 Palace Of Fine Arts E2
10 Presidio Officers' Club D2
11 Vedanta Society Old Temple G2
12 Walt Disney Family Museum D2
13 Wave Organ F1
14 Wedding Houses G2

Restaurants

1 A16 ..... F2
2 Arguello D2
3 Atelier Crenn G2
4 Bar Crenn G2
5 Bistro Aix G2
6 Causwells F2
7 The Commissary D2
8 Greens G1
9 Isa G2
10 Kaiyo H2
11 Presidio Social Club E2
12 Rose's Café G3
13 Tacolicious F2

Hotels

1 Coventry Motor Inn G2
2 Cow Hollow Motor Inn and Suites G2
3 Hotel Del Sol G2
4 The Inn at the Presidio D2
5 The Lodge at the Presidio D2
6 Marina Inn H2
7 Marina Motel F2
8 Pacific Heights Inn H2
9 Union Street Inn G3

poem, so the "Hidden beneath the bluffs" might be whole grilled Monterey abalone with a purée of its own liver and a grilled mussel sauce. **Known for:** extraordinary, whimsical tasting menu; stratospheric prices; hip-elegant atmosphere. *Average main: $335* ✉ *3127 Fillmore St., Cow Hollow* ☎ *415/440–0460* 🌐 *www.ateliercrenn.com* ⏲ *Closed Sun. and Mon.*

Just up the hill from the Marina—and slightly quieter with more young families—is Cow Hollow. Union Street is the main strip, dense with restaurants, cafés, and boutiques that mostly cater to the trendy A-list crowd. Wander even farther up the hills and you'll be in the thick of the manses of Pacific Heights.

Bar Crenn

$$$ | **FRENCH** | Dominique Crenn's sumptuous salon decked out with fur-draped bar stools, chandeliers, and lush velvet drapes is really a bar only in name. Yes, there's a bar pouring outstanding wines and it's possible to graze on warm gougères and oysters. **Known for:** Versailles-style furnishings; eggshell filled with bone marrow custard, topped with caviar; fine Champagne. *Average main: $36* ✉ *3131 Fillmore St., Cow Hollow* ☎ *415/440–0460* 🌐 *www.barcrenn.com* ⏲ *Closed Sun. and Mon.*

Kaiyo

$$$ | **PERUVIAN** | San Francisco has a handful of Peruvian restaurants, but this uber hip Union Street spot is the first "Nikkei" cuisine (Japanese-Peruvian) restaurant for diners to explore. Skip the pedestrian *pollo a la brasa* and have fun sampling around the *tiraditos* and sushi rolls. **Known for:** creative pisco cocktails; smoked duck and shaved foie gras sushi; street art murals in bathrooms. *Average main: $18* ✉ *1838 Union St., Cow Hollow* ☎ *415/525–4804* 🌐 *www.kaiyosf.com* ⏲ *Closed Mon.*

Don't Look Down!

Armed only with helmets, safety harnesses, and painting equipment, a full-time crew of 38 painters keeps the Golden Gate Bridge clad in International Orange. Contrary to a favorite bit of local lore, they don't actually sweep on an entire coat of paint from one end of the bridge to the other, but instead scrape, prime, and repaint small sections that have rusted from exposure to the elements.

Rose's Café

$$$ | **ITALIAN** | **FAMILY** | Although it's open morning until night, this cozy café is most synonymous with brunch. Sleepy-headed locals turn up for delights like the smoked ham, fried egg, and gruyère breakfast sandwich and the French toast bread pudding with caramelized apples. **Known for:** pizzas for the morning and night; house-baked goods; brunch lines. *Average main: $28* ✉ *2298 Union St., Cow Hollow* ☎ *415/775–2200* 🌐 *www.rosescafesf.com.*

Hotels

Upscale urbanites toting iPhones and gazillion-dollar strollers call Cow Hollow home. Visitors will appreciate the array of boutiques lining Union Street, the world-class eateries, and the winning B&Bs and stylish motor inns catering to in-the-know travelers.

Coventry Motor Inn

$$ | **HOTEL** | **FAMILY** | Among the many motels on busy Lombard Street, this is one of the cleanest and quietest, and the unusually spacious rooms have quality beds and well-lighted dining and work areas that make this a favorite for those looking for comfort without a

Park It Here

Since 2010, San Francisco has been reclaiming parking spaces and turning them into parklets, tiny parks open to the public. These dot the city—more than three dozen and counting—from mobile, red-metal containers with built-in benches and plantings to Powell Street's eight-section high-design aluminum parklet. The Mission has the highest concentration, mostly along Valencia Street, but one of the most creative—an old Citroën van turned into seating and planters—is in front of the Rapha bike shop on Filbert near Fillmore in Cow Hollow. And even if everyone in that parklet in front of a café is clutching a to-go cup, remember these are public spaces; look for the "Public Parklet" sign and grab a seat. For a parklet map, visit *pavementtoparks.org.*

hefty price tag. **Pros:** good value; free parking in building; spacious rooms. **Cons:** busy street; few amenities; far from downtown sights. *Rooms from: $178 1901 Lombard St., Cow Hollow 415/567–1200 www.coventrymotorinn.com 69 rooms No meals.*

Hotel Del Sol

$$ | HOTEL | FAMILY | This rejuvenated beach-theme 1950s motor lodge is centrally located for exploring the Marina and Presidio. **Pros:** nearby places to eat and shop; heated pool; cheery design. **Cons:** fitness center is off-site; exterior walkways could use sprucing up; parking fee high for this area where there's often no charge. *Rooms from: $169 3100 Webster St., Cow Hollow 415/921–5520, 877/433–5765 www.jdvhotels.com/hotel-del-sol 57 rooms Breakfast.*

Pacific Heights Inn

$ | HOTEL | Rooms are unassuming and simple (some would say basic) at this two-story motor court near the busy intersection of Union and Van Ness, but the building is well maintained with wrought-iron railings and benches, hanging plants, and pebbled exterior walkways facing the parking lot. **Pros:** some kitchenettes; free parking; close walk to the Marina shopping and dining areas. **Cons:** can be noisy; crowded parking area; basic. *Rooms from: $109 1555 Union St., Cow Hollow 415/776–3310, 800/523–1801 www.pacificheightsinn.com 28 rooms, 12 suites Breakfast.*

★ Union Street Inn

$$$ | B&B/INN | Antiques, unique artwork, and such touches as candles, fresh flowers, wineglasses, and fine linens make rooms in this green-and-cream 1902 Edwardian popular with honeymooners and those looking for a romantic getaway with an English countryside ambience. **Pros:** personal service; excellent full breakfast; beautiful secret garden. **Cons:** parking is pricey; two-night minimum stay on weekends; no elevator. *Rooms from: $249 2229 Union St., Cow Hollow 415/346–0424 www.unionstreetinn.com 6 rooms Breakfast.*

Nightlife

In between the Marina and Pacific Heights, this small yet affluent neighborhood has a similar scene to the bordering Marina district but without the hefty price tags.

BARS

Balboa Cafe

BARS/PUBS | Here you'll spy young (thirty-something) and upwardly mobile former frat boys and sorority girls munching on tasty burgers served sandwich-style on a baguette—considered by some to be the best in town. Martinis are proper and stiff, and the wine list is one of the neighborhood's best. ✉ *3199 Fillmore St., at Greenwich St., Cow Hollow* ☎ *415/921–3944* 🌐 *www.balboacafe.com.*

The Black Horse London Pub

BARS/PUBS | Barely seven stools fit in San Francisco's smallest bar. Plus, there are just as many bottled beers (no taps) as seats and be sure to bring some cash since credit cards aren't accepted. It's as bare-bones as it gets but there's sports on TV, a fun dice game, and most importantly a neighborhood camaraderie that is increasingly hard to find. ✉ *1514 Union St., Cow Hollow* 🌐 *www.blackhorselondon.com.*

Perry's

BARS/PUBS | One of San Francisco's oldest singles bars still packs 'em in. You can dine on great hamburgers (and a stellar Reuben) as well as more substantial fare while gabbing about the 49ers with the well-scrubbed, khaki-clad, baseball-cap-wearing crowd. It's just as known for the plaid tablecloths as it is for the always fun, lively crowd. ✉ *1944 Union St., at Laguna St., Cow Hollow* ☎ *415/922–9022* 🌐 *www.perryssf.com.*

West Coast Wine & Cheese

WINE BARS—NIGHTLIFE | Whether you're in the mood for a Mendocino County rosé or an Oregon pinot noir, as the name suggests, you'll find it at this narrow, sleek locals' favorite. The kitchen isn't much more than a stovetop, but does some pretty impressive work beyond cheese and charcuterie. Take advantage of the ability to order half pours and sample more wines. ✉ *2165 Union St., Cow Hollow* ☎ *415/376–9720* 🌐 *www.westcoastsf.com.*

 Shopping

Quaint, busy, and sophisticated, the former dairy pastures of yesteryear are a fashion and home-decor hot spot today.

CLOTHING

Marmalade

CLOTHING | Filled with bright dresses and patterned tops, this Cow Hollow beacon of style has a real Californian feel. Designers both local and from Southern California are represented, and the owner and her staff are happy to help you match things, including earrings and sweaters and jeans and simple T-shirts. ✉ *1843 Union St., between Octavia and Laguna Sts., Cow Hollow* ☎ *415/757–8614.*

FOOD AND DRINK

The Caviar Company

FOOD/CANDY | "The Caviar Sisters" Petra and Saskia Bergstein created this sustainability-minded brand that developed a cult following among caviar connoisseurs and chefs in the Bay Area. Their chic above-street level boutique on Union Street allows the public to pick out some of the finest caviar products in town—and feel good about it. ✉ *1954 Union St., Cow Hollow* ☎ *415/300–0299* 🌐 *www.thecaviarco.com* ⏲ *Closed Mon.*

Ginger Elizabeth Chocolates

FOOD/CANDY | **FAMILY** | A Sacramento chocolatier with a nationally known name expanded to San Francisco in 2018. It's already a marquee destination for macarons or a box of chocolate bonbons with atypical flavors like sweet cream chai and buttermilk lime. ✉ *3108 Fillmore St., Cow Hollow* ☎ *415/671–7113* 🌐 *www.gingerelizabeth.com* ⏲ *Closed Mon. and Tues.*

PlumpJack Wines

WINE/SPIRITS | Cow Hollow's go-to wine boutique is much more than "the wine shop" co-founded by Governor Gavin Newsom more than a decade ago. A small selection of imported wines complements the well-priced, well-stocked collection of hard-to-find California wines here, combining for one of the city's strongest wine rosters. Noe Valley has a sister store. ✉ *3201 Fillmore St., at Greenwich St., Cow Hollow* ☎ *415/346–9870* 🌐 *www.plumpjackwines.com.*

Wrecking Ball Coffee Roasters

FOOD/CANDY | The Instagram set knows this Wi-Fi-free, almost seating-free Union Street roaster and café as the place with the pineapple wallpaper. Everyone enjoys some of the finest lattes and espresso shots around, usually to-go, but sometimes enjoyed on the low bench in front of that famous wallpaper. ✉ *2271 Union St., Cow Hollow* ☎ *415/638–9227* 🌐 *www.wreckingballcoffee.com.*

FURNITURE, HOUSEWARES, AND GIFTS

Topdrawer

BOOKS/STATIONERY | This Japanese store sells everything from high-quality bento boxes to fine Tokyo-made pens and lots more colorful stationary and journals. ✉ *1840 Union St., between Octavia and Laguna Sts., Cow Hollow* ☎ *415/771–1108* 🌐 *www.kolo.com.*

SPAS

Spa Radiance

SPA/BEAUTY | Elegant but casual Spa Radiance specializes in facials and draws the occasional celebrity. Try the warm cocoa butter body treatment, or the "Mother Nature's Kiss" spa escape—an organic detox facial followed by a warm lavender salt scrub and hot stone massage. ✉ *3011 Fillmore St., between Union and Filbert Sts., Cow Hollow* ☎ *415/346–6281* 🌐 *www.sparadiance.com.*

TOYS AND GADGETS

ATYS

CAMERAS/ELECTRONICS | Gadgets and home accessories with a sleek modern design are imported from all over Europe and Japan. Among the eye-catching items are levitating lights and French knives made of actual Golden Gate Bridge steel. ✉ *2149B Union St., between Fillmore and Webster Sts., Cow Hollow* ☎ *415/441–9220* 🌐 *www.atysdesign.com.*

Presidio

At the foot of the Golden Gate Bridge, one of city residents' favorite in-town getaways is the 1,400-plus-acre Presidio, which combines accessible nature-in-the-raw with a window into the past. For more than 200 years and under the flags of three nations—Spain, Mexico, and the United States—the Presidio served as an army post, but in 1995 the U.S. Army officially handed over the keys to the National Park Service. The keys came without sufficient federal funding, though, and it seemed the Presidio would be sold piecemeal to developers.

An innovative plan combining public and private monies and overseen by the Presidio Trust, the federal agency created to run the park, was hatched to help the Presidio become self-sufficient, which it did in 2013. The trust has found paying tenants such as George Lucas's Industrial Light and Magic, the Walt Disney Family Museum, and a few thousand lucky San Franciscans who live in restored army housing. Now this spectacular corner of the city—surrounded by sandy beaches and rocky shores, and with windswept hills of cypress dotted with historical buildings—is a thriving urban park and technically a "national park" (it's part of the Golden Gate National Recreation Area). The Presidio has superb views (be sure to visit Inspiration Point and the cemetery for the most striking ones) and some of the best hiking and biking areas in San Francisco; even a drive through this lush area is a treat. Start your visit at the Presidio Visitor Center (210 Lincoln Blvd., 415/561–4323) then enjoy a day of exploring.

Sights

★ Baker Beach

BEACH—SIGHT | FAMILY | West of the Golden Gate Bridge is a mile-long stretch of soft sand beneath steep cliffs, beloved for its spectacular views and laid-back vibe (read: you'll see naked people here on the northernmost end). Its isolated location makes it rarely crowded, but many San Franciscans know that there is no better place to take in the sunset than this beach. Kids love climbing around the old Battery Chamberlin. This is truly one of those places that inspires local pride. ✉ *Baker Beach, Presidio* ✣ *Accessed from Bowley St. off Lincoln Blvd.* 🌐 *www.parksconservancy.org/parks-baker-beach.*

Crissy Field

BEACH—SIGHT | FAMILY | One of the most popular places for San Franciscans to get fresh air is a stretch of restored marshland along the sand of the bay. Kids on bikes, folks walking dogs, and joggers share the paved path along the shore, often winding up at the Warming Hut, a combination café and fun gift store at the end of the path, for a hot chocolate in the shadow of the Golden Gate Bridge. Midway along the Golden Gate Promenade that winds along the shore is the Gulf of the Farallones National Marine Sanctuary Visitor Center, where kids can get a close-up view of small sea creatures and learn about the rich ecosystem offshore. Alongside the main green of Crissy Field, there are several renovated airplane hangars and warehouses that are now home to the likes of rock-climbing gyms, an air trampoline park, and a craft brewery. ✉ *Crissy Field, Presidio* 🌐 *www.presidio.gov/places/crissy-field.*

Fort Point

MILITARY SITE | FAMILY | Dwarfed today by the Golden Gate Bridge, this brick fortress constructed between 1853 and 1861 was designed to protect San Francisco from a Civil War sea attack that never materialized. It was also used as a coastal-defense fortification post during World War II, when soldiers stood watch here. This National Historic Site is now a sprawling museum of military memorabilia. The building, which surrounds a lonely, windswept courtyard, has a gloomy air and is suitably atmospheric. It's usually chilly, too, so bring a jacket. The top floor affords a unique angle on the bay. **■ TIP→ Take care when walking along the front side of the building, as it's slippery, and the waves have a dizzying effect.**

On the days when Fort Point is staffed (on Friday and weekends), guided group tours and cannon drills take place. The popular, guided candlelight tours, available only in winter, book up in advance, so plan ahead. Living-history days take place throughout the year, when Union soldiers perform drills, a drum-and-fife band plays, and a Civil War–era doctor shows his instruments and describes his surgical technique (gulp). ✉ *Marine Dr. off Lincoln Blvd., Presidio* ☎ *415/556–1693* 🌐 *www.nps.gov/fopo* 🎫 *Free* ⏲ *Closed Mon.–Thurs.*

★ Golden Gate Bridge

BRIDGE/TUNNEL | With its simple but powerful art-deco design, the 1.7-mile suspension span that connects San Francisco and Marin County was built to withstand winds of more than 100 mph. It's also not a bad place to be in an earthquake: designed to sway almost 28 feet, the Golden Gate Bridge (unlike the Bay Bridge) was undamaged by the 1989 Loma Prieta quake. If you're walking on the bridge when it's windy, stand still and you can feel it swaying a bit.

The Presidio with Kids

If you're in town with children (and you have a car), the sprawling, bayside Presidio offers enough kid-friendly diversions for one very full day. Start off at **Julius Kahn Park,** on the Presidio's southern edge, which has a disproportionate number of structures that spin. Swing by George Lucas's **Letterman Digital Arts Center** to check out the Yoda fountain; then head to the **Immigrant Point Lookout** on Washington Boulevard, with views of the bay and the ocean. Children love the pet cemetery, with its sweet, leaning headstones; it's near the stables, where you might glimpse some of the park police's equestrian members. Older kids might enjoy a stop at the **Walt Disney Family Museum** (✉ *104 Montgomery St.* ☎ *415/345–6800*) to see the model of Disneyland and a replica of the ambulance jeep Walt Disney drove during World War I. The last stop is **Crissy Field,** where kids can ride bikes, skate, or run along the beach and clamber over the rocks; the view of the Golden Gate Bridge from below is captivating. Two nature centers here have fun, hands-on exhibits for kids. Finally, stop by the **Warming Hut,** at the western end of Crissy Field, for sandwiches and hot chocolate. You can also do a version of this day using the PresidiGo shuttle, but you'll need to adapt your route according to the shuttle stops.

Crossing the Golden Gate Bridge under your own power is exhilarating—a little scary, and definitely chilly. From the bridge's eastern-side walkway, the only side pedestrians are allowed on, you can take in the San Francisco skyline and the bay islands; look west for the wild hills of the Marin Headlands, the curving coast south to Lands End, and the Pacific Ocean. On sunny days, sailboats dot the water, and brave windsurfers test the often-treacherous tides beneath the bridge. A vista point on the Marin County side provides a spectacular city panorama.

A structural engineer, dreamer, and poet named Joseph Strauss worked tirelessly for 20 years to make the bridge a reality, first promoting the idea of it and then overseeing design and construction. Though the final structure bore little resemblance to his original plan, Strauss guarded his legacy jealously, refusing to recognize the seminal contributions of engineer Charles A. Ellis. In 2007, the Golden Gate Bridge district finally recognized Ellis's role, though Strauss, who died less than a year after opening day in 1937, would doubtless be pleased with the inscription on his statue, which stands sentry in the southern parking lot: "The Man Who Built the Bridge."

You won't see it on a T-shirt, but the bridge is perhaps the world's most publicized suicide platform, with an average of one jumper about every 10 days. Signs on the bridge refer the disconsolate to special telephones, and officers patrol the walkway and watch by security camera to spot potential jumpers. A suicide barrier, an unobtrusive net not unlike the one that saved 19 workers during the bridge's construction, is expected to be completed in 2020.

While at the bridge, you can grab a healthy snack at the art deco–style Bridge Café. The Bridge Pavilion sells attractive, high-quality souvenirs and has a small display of historical artifacts. At the outdoor exhibits, you can see the bridge rise before your eyes on hologram panels, learn about the features that make it art deco, and read about the personalities behind its design and construction. City Guides offers free walking tours of the bridge every Thursday and Sunday at 11 am. ✉ *Lincoln Blvd. near Doyle Dr. and Fort Point, Presidio* ☎ *415/921–5858* 🌐 *www.goldengatebridge.org* 🎫 *Free.*

Letterman Digital Arts Center

BUILDING | FAMILY | Bay Area filmmaker George Lucas's 23-acre **Letterman Digital Arts Center,** a digital studio "campus," along the eastern edge of the land, is exquisitely landscaped and largely open to the public. If you have kids in tow or are a *Star Wars* fan yourself, make the pilgrimage to the **Yoda Fountain** (Letterman Drive at Dewitt Road), between two of the arts-center buildings, then take your picture with the life-size Darth Vader statue in the lobby, open to the public on weekdays. ✉ *1 Letterman Dr., Presidio* 🌐 *www.presidio.gov/letterman-digital-arts-center.*

Lyon Street Steps

VIEWPOINT | Get ready for a stairs workout—and a spectacularly rewarding view at the top—when tackling the 332 steps at the eastern edge of the Presidio. There will likely be no shortage of exercise seekers huffing and puffing up the steps, but feel free to conquer the climb slowly. The trimmed hedge landscaping is worthy of its own visit, but there's no doubt that the view of the Presidio forests and the bay are the reason these steps are a top attraction. ✉ *2545 Lyon St., Presidio Heights* ✣ *Between Green St. and Pacific Ave.*

Presidio Officers' Club

MILITARY SITE | An excellent place to begin a historical tour of the Presidio, the Officers' Club offers a walk through time from the Presidio's earliest days as the first nonnative outpost in present-day San Francisco to more than a century as a U.S. army post. Start with the excellent short film about life here from the time of the Ohlone to the present, then peruse the displays of artifacts including uniforms and weaponry. Head back downstairs to the Mesa Room, where you can literally see layers of history: part of the painstakingly preserved original adobe wall from the 1790s, the brick fireplace from the 1880s commander's office, and the mission revival fireplace from the 1930s billiard room. Excavation of the Presidio continues: outside, a canopy covers the Presidio Archaeology Field Station, where you can watch archaeologists at work from May to September. ✉ *50 Moraga Ave., Presidio* ☎ *415/561–4400* 🌐 *www.presidio.gov/officers-club* 🎫 *Free* ⏲ *Closed Mon.*

Walt Disney Family Museum

MUSEUM | This beautifully refurbished brick barracks house is a tribute to the man behind Mickey Mouse, the Disney Studios, and Disneyland. The smartly organized displays include hundreds of family photos, and well-chosen videos play throughout. Disney's legendary attention to detail becomes particularly evident in the cels and footage of *Fantasia, Sleeping Beauty,* and other animation classics. "The Toughest Period in My Whole Life" exhibit sheds light on lesser-known bits of history: the animators' strike at Disney Studios, the films Walt Disney made for the U.S. military during World War II, and his testimony before the House Un-American Activities Committee during its investigation of Communist influence in Hollywood. The liveliest exhibit and the largest gallery documents the creation of Disneyland with a fun, detailed model of what Disney imagined the park would be. Teacups spin, the Matterhorn looms, and that world-famous castle leads the way to Fantasyland. You won't be the first to leave humming "It's a Small World." In the final gallery, titled simply "December 15, 1966," a series of sweet cartoons chronicles the world's reaction to Disney's sudden death. ✉ *Main Post, 104 Montgomery*

Art in the Presidio

Fans of Andy Goldsworthy, the Scottish artist famed for his work with natural elements, will have a field day in the Presidio: the park contains four of his creations, all using materials reclaimed from the Presidio. *Spire*, created in 2008, is a 100-foot-high sculpture that reaches toward the sky in a grove near the Arguello Gate. Made of the trunks of 37 Monterey cypress trees cut down during reforestation work at the Presidio, it's currently surrounded by saplings that will one day be a forest. Near the intersection of Presidio Boulevard and West Pacific Avenue, Goldsworthy created *Wood Line* in 2011. Felled eucalyptus weave lines through a cypress grove in a work that the artist says "draws the place." In 2013, Goldsworthy moved inside for the installation *Tree Fall*, located in the Presidio's Powder Magazine. He covered a tree trunk and dome above it, suspended above the historic structure's walls, with clay from the Presidio, which cracked into lovely patterns. The work is open for viewing weekends 10–4. In 2014, Goldsworthy created *Earth Wall* in a wall around the patio at the Officers' Club. He collected curved eucalyptus branches from the site, affixed them in a sphere on the side of the concrete wall, then added a rammed-earth layer to the entire wall, burying the wood while thickening the wall. When it had dried, he used a chisel to reveal the ball, essentially excavating it in a nod to the layers of history at the Presidio. Free guided 3-mile walks that take in all of Goldsworthy's Presidio works; contact the Presidio Trust (415/561–4257) for information on dates.

St., off Lincoln Blvd., Presidio ☎ 415/345–6800 🌐 www.waltdisney.org 🎫 $25 ⏲ Closed Tues.

Restaurants

Arguello

$$ | MODERN MEXICAN | FAMILY | Whether enjoying shrimp tacos at lunch on the beautiful, intimate patio or a perfect margarita with a host of small plates at the bar for a casual dinner, celebrated chef Traci Des Jardins' Californian-Mexican restaurant always hits the right notes. Tortillas and salsas are made in-house, and the tequila and mezcal selection is one of the deepest in San Francisco. **Known for:** intimate outdoor patio; superb pozole verde; various lunch tacos. $ *Average main: $23 ✉ 50 Moraga St., Presidio ✣ In Presidio Officers' Club ☎ 415/561–3650 🌐 www.arguellosf.com ⏲ Closed Mon. No dinner Tues. and Sun.*

The Commissary

$$$ | SPANISH | Order a Spanish brandy riff on a Negroni and a few tapas, then get ready for one of the city's top Spanish dining experiences right by the Walt Disney Museum. Chef-owner Traci Des Jardins and her team does a fantastic job incorporating local produce and Bay Area spirit to tapas bar classics like patatas bravas and warm cheese fritters. **Known for:** large format steak dishes; excellent, simple desserts; terrific wine and sherry program but ugly stemless wine glasses. $ *Average main: $35 ✉ 101 Montgomery St., Presidio ☎ 415/561–3600 🌐 www.thecommissarysf.com ⏲ Closed Sun.*

Presidio Social Club

$$$ | **AMERICAN** | **FAMILY** | Set in an old barracks building at the eastern edge of the Presidio, American comfort classics meet seasonal California cooking. Like the military base/national park itself, the restaurant has a blend of the nostalgic past and the trendy present (beef liver and onions; ahi tuna poke and crisp eggplant fries). **Known for:** weekend brunch; PSC meat loaf; barrel-aged cocktails. *Average main: $24 ✉ 563 Ruger St., Presidio ☎ 415/885–1888 🌐 www.presidiosocialclub.com.*

Hotels

Long heralded as the place where upscale San Franciscans come to play, the Presidio has a few worthy lodgings, among them a fancy inn occupying former officer's quarters and a sleek lodge in a renovated barracks building. Though there are just a handful of restaurants and nightlife options are nonexistent, the Presidio's historic cachet, wealth of hiking trails, and gorgeous bay-view beaches entice tourists and locals alike, the latter escaping downtown for a restful staycation.

The Inn at the Presidio

$$$ | **B&B/INN** | **FAMILY** | Built in 1903 and opened as a hotel in 2012, this two-story, Georgian Revival–style structure once served as officers' quarters but now has 26 guest rooms—most of them suites—complete with gas fireplaces and modern-meets-salvage-store finds such as wrought-iron beds, historic black-and-white photos, and Pendleton blankets. **Pros:** beautifully designed rooms; peaceful, away from the frenetic city feel; Presidio's hiking and biking trails, Disney museum, and other attractions. **Cons:** lack of noise blocking because of old building; no elevator; challenging to get a taxi/ride-share. *Rooms from: $310 ✉ 42 Moraga Ave., Presidio ☎ 415/800–7356 🌐 www.innatthepresidio.com 26 rooms Breakfast.*

★ The Lodge at the Presidio

$$$ | **B&B/INN** | The Presidio's hotel population doubled in 2018 with the opening of its second boutique accommodation, a slightly more upscale sibling to The Inn at the Presidio. **Pros:** gorgeous and spacious rooms; charming staff; feels like a vacation from the city within the city. **Cons:** traffic noise is fairly loud in rooms facing Golden Gate Bridge; isolated from many attractions; prices are similar to downtown. *Rooms from: $275 ✉ 105 Montgomery St., Presidio ☎ 415/561–1234 🌐 www.presidiolodging.com/lodge-at-the-presidio 42 rooms Free Breakfast.*

Chapter 9

9

THE WESTERN SHORELINE

Updated by
Denise M. Leto

Sights	Restaurants	Hotels	Shopping	Nightlife
★★★☆☆	★★★☆☆	☆☆☆☆☆	☆☆☆☆☆	☆☆☆☆☆

NEIGHBORHOOD SNAPSHOT

MAKING THE MOST OF YOUR TIME

Despite low-lying fog and often biting chill, the premier sights of the Western Shoreline are outdoors—gorgeous hiking trails and sandy stretches of coastline. Bundle up and start off on the Coastal Trail, which passes by the Legion of Honor. Continue west to catch the sunset from the Cliff House or the Beach Chalet. If you don't want to do the entire 3-mile hike, you can spend an hour touring the museum, catch the stunning views just below it, and head to the beach.

TOP REASONS TO GO

■ **Lands End:** Head down the gorgeous Coastal Trail near the Cliff House; you'll quickly find yourself in a forest with unparalleled views of the Golden Gate Bridge.

■ **Toast the sunset at the Beach Chalet:** Top off a day of exploring with a cocktail overlooking Ocean Beach.

■ **Legion of Honor museum:** Tear yourself away from the spectacular setting and eye-popping view and travel back to 18th-century Europe through the paintings, drawings, and porcelain collected here.

■ **Ocean Beach:** Wrap up warm and stroll along the strand on a brisk, cloudy day and you'll feel like a gritty local. Then thaw out over a bowl of steaming pho in the Richmond.

■ **Old-time San Francisco:** Wandering among the ruins of the Sutro Baths below the Cliff House, close your eyes and imagine vintage San Francisco: the monumental baths, popular amusement park Playland at the Beach, and that great, old, teetering, Victorian Cliff House of days gone by.

GETTING THERE

■ To reach the Western Shoreline from downtown by Muni light rail, take the N–Judah to Ocean Beach or the L–Taraval to the zoo. From downtown by bus, take the 38–Geary, which runs all the way to 48th and Point Lobos Avenues, just east of the Cliff House. Along the Western Shoreline, the 18–46th Avenue runs between the Legion of Honor and the zoo (and beyond).

Few American cities provide a more intimate and dramatic view of the power and fury of the surf attacking the shore than San Francisco does along its wild Western Shoreline. From Lincoln Park in the north, along Ocean Beach from the Richmond south to the Sunset, a different breed of San Franciscan chooses to live in this area: surfers who brave the heaviest fog to ride the waves; writers who seek solace and inspiration in this city outpost; and dog lovers committed to giving their pets a good workout each day.

The Richmond

In the mid-19th century, the western section of town just north of Golden Gate Park was known as the Outer Lands, covered in sand dunes and seen fit for cemeteries and little else. Today it's the Richmond, comprised of two distinct neighborhoods: the Inner Richmond, from Arguello Boulevard to about 20th Avenue, and the Outer Richmond, from 20th to the ocean. Clement Street, packed with solid dining options, from French to Burmese, and with numerous Chinese groceries, is the Inner Richmond's favorite commercial strip. The street makes for great strolling and even better eating. The Outer Richmond has its share of restaurants—most along Geary Boulevard, some along Clement—including the city's highest concentration of Russian eateries and bakeries. But this mostly residential neighborhood is about the foggy hinterlands that stretch west to the coast: dramatic Lincoln Park with Golden Gate views, the Cliff House, and often-chilly, uncrowded Ocean Beach.

From Lands End in Lincoln Park you have some of the best views of the Golden Gate—the name was given to the opening of San Francisco Bay long before the bridge was built—and the Marin Headlands. From the historic Cliff House south to the sprawling San Francisco Zoo, the Great Highway and Ocean Beach run along the western edge of the city (south of Golden Gate

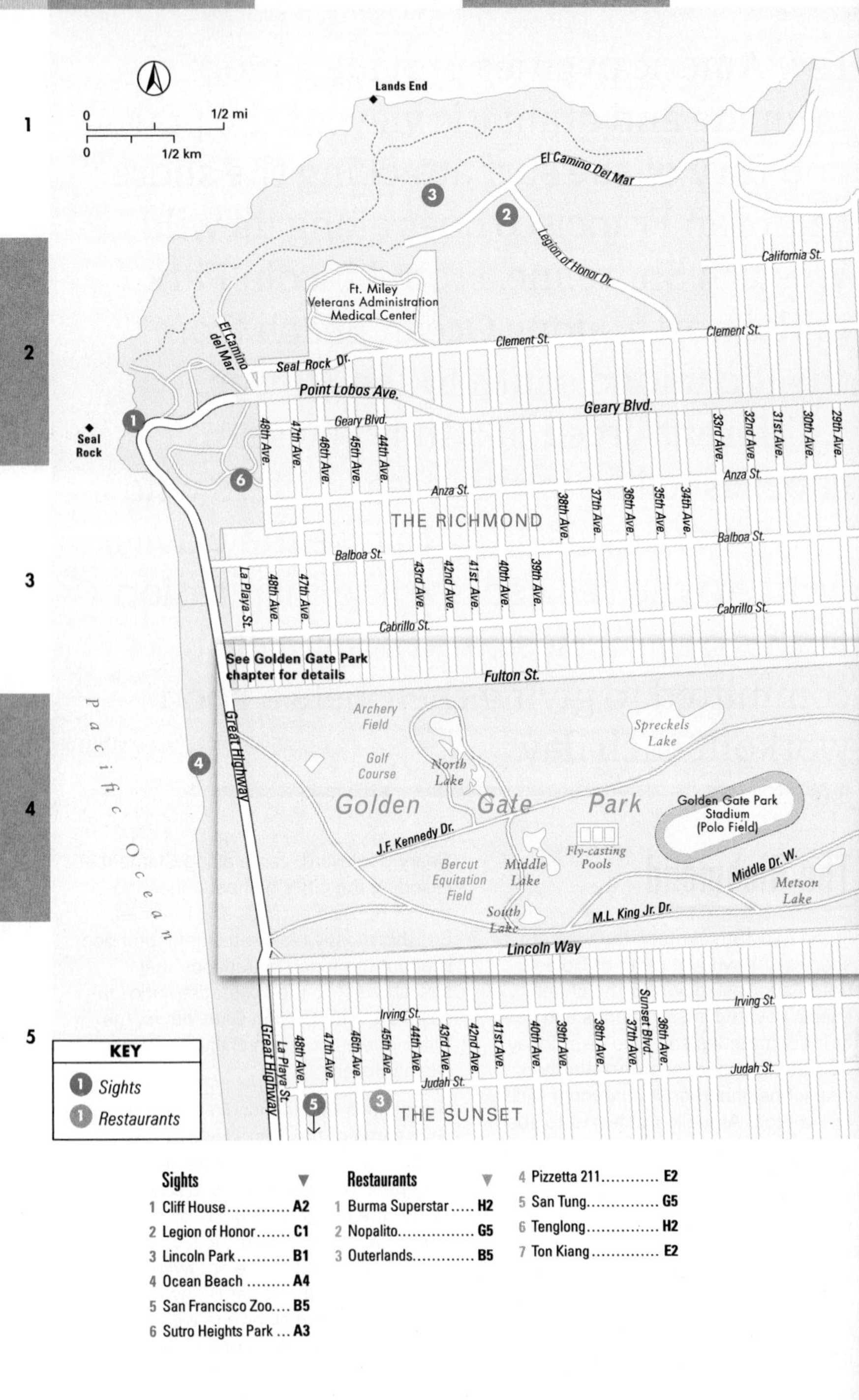

Sights

1 Cliff House **A2**
2 Legion of Honor **C1**
3 Lincoln Park **B1**
4 Ocean Beach **A4**
5 San Francisco Zoo.... **B5**
6 Sutro Heights Park ... **A3**

Restaurants

1 Burma Superstar **H2**
2 Nopalito................ **G5**
3 Outerlands............. **B5**
4 Pizzetta 211............ **E2**
5 San Tung............... **G5**
6 Tenglong................ **H2**
7 Ton Kiang **E2**

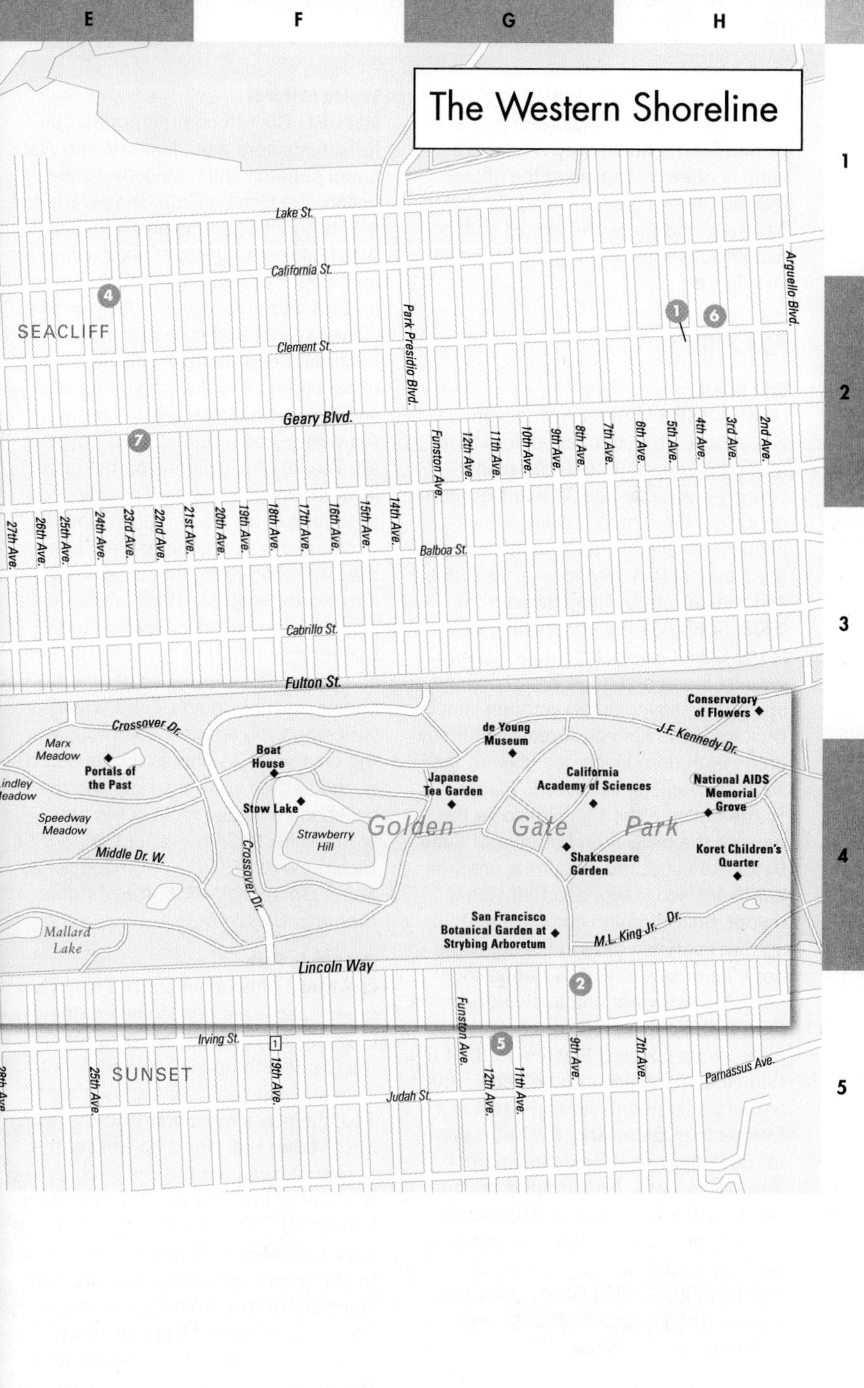

E
F
G
H
1
2
3
4
5
The Western Shoreline
Lake St.
California St.
Clement St.
Geary Blvd.
Balboa St.
Cabrillo St.
Fulton St.
Lincoln Way
Irving St.
Judah St.
Parnassus Ave.
Arguello Blvd.
Park Presidio Blvd.
SEACLIFF
SUNSET
Funston Ave.
12th Ave.
11th Ave.
10th Ave.
9th Ave.
8th Ave.
7th Ave.
6th Ave.
5th Ave.
4th Ave.
3rd Ave.
2nd Ave.
27th Ave.
26th Ave.
25th Ave.
24th Ave.
23rd Ave.
22nd Ave.
21st Ave.
20th Ave.
19th Ave.
18th Ave.
17th Ave.
16th Ave.
15th Ave.
14th Ave.
28th Ave.
Conservatory of Flowers
J.F. Kennedy Dr.
de Young Museum
Crossover Dr.
Marx Meadow
Portals of the Past
Boat House
Japanese Tea Garden
California Academy of Sciences
National AIDS Memorial Grove
Lindley Meadow
Stow Lake
Speedway Meadow
Strawberry Hill
Golden Gate Park
Middle Dr. W.
Shakespeare Garden
Koret Children's Quarter
Mallard Lake
San Francisco Botanical Garden at Strybing Arboretum
M.L. King Jr. Dr.

Park, you're in the Sunset). If you're here in winter or spring, keep your eyes peeled for migrating gray whales. The wind is often strong along the shoreline, summer fog can blanket the ocean beaches, and the water is cold and too dangerous for swimming. Don't forget your jacket!

Sights

Cliff House

LOCAL INTEREST | Spectacular ocean views have been bringing diners to its several restaurants for more than a century—you can see 30 miles or more on a clear day. Three buildings have occupied this site—today owned by the National Park Service—since 1863, and the current building dates from 1909. Sitting on the observation deck is the **Giant Camera,** a camera obscura with its lens pointing skyward housed in a cute yellow-painted wooden shack. Built in the 1940s and threatened many times with demolition, it's now on the National Register of Historic Places. To the north of the Cliff House lie the ruins of the once grand glass-roof **Sutro Baths**. Adolph Sutro, eccentric onetime San Francisco mayor and Cliff House owner, built the bath complex in 1896, so that everyday folks could enjoy the benefits of swimming. Six enormous baths—freshwater and seawater—more than 500 dressing rooms, and several restaurants covered 3 acres north of the Cliff House and accommodated 25,000 bathers. Likened to Roman baths in a European glass palace, the baths were for decades a favorite destination of San Franciscans. The complex fell into disuse after World War II, was closed in 1952, and burned down (under questionable circumstances) during demolition in 1966. ✉ *1090 Point Lobos Ave., Richmond* ☎ *415/386–3330* 🌐 *www.cliffhouse.com* 🎫 *Free.*

Legion of Honor

MUSEUM | Built to commemorate Californian soldiers who died in World War I, and set atop cliffs overlooking the ocean, the Golden Gate Bridge, and the Marin Headlands, this beautiful Beaux Arts building in Lincoln Park displays an impressive collection of 4,000 years of ancient and European art. A pyramidal glass skylight in the entrance court illuminates the lower-level galleries, which exhibit prints and drawings, English and European porcelain, and ancient Assyrian, Greek, Roman, and Egyptian art. The 20-plus galleries on the upper level display the permanent collection of European art (paintings, sculpture, decorative arts, and tapestries) from the 14th century to the present day. The noteworthy Auguste Rodin collection includes two galleries devoted to the master and a third with works by Rodin and other 19th-century sculptors. An original cast of Rodin's *The Thinker* welcomes you as you walk through the courtyard. As fine as the museum is, the setting and view outshine the collection and also make a trip here worthwhile. ✉ *34th Ave. at Clement St., Richmond* ☎ *415/750–3600* 🌐 *legionofhonor.famsf.org* 🎫 *$15, free 1st Tues. of month* ⏲ *Closed Mon.*

★ **Lincoln Park**

CITY PARK | Although many of the city's green spaces are gentle and welcoming, Lincoln Park is a wild, 275-acre park in the Outer Richmond with windswept cliffs and panoramic views. The Coastal Trail, the park's most dramatic one, leads out to **Lands End**; pick it up west of the Legion of Honor (at the end of El Camino del Mar) or from the parking lot at Point Lobos and El Camino del Mar. Time your hike to hit Mile Rock at low tide, and you might catch a glimpse of two wrecked ships peeking up from their watery graves. ⚠ **Be careful if you hike here; landslides are frequent, and people have fallen into the sea by standing too close to the edge of a crumbling bluff top.**

Visitors enjoy the rough beauty of the Pacific from the Cliff House.

Lincoln Park's 18-hole golf course is on land that in the 19th century was the Golden Gate Cemetery. In 1900 the Board of Supervisors voted to ban burials within city limits, and all but two city cemeteries (at Mission Dolores and the Presidio) were moved to Colma, a small town just south of San Francisco. When digging has to be done in the park, bones occasionally surface again. ✉ *Entrance at 34th Ave. at Clement St., Richmond.*

Ocean Beach

BEACH—SIGHT | Stretching 3 miles along the western side of the city from the Richmond to the Sunset, this sandy swath of the Pacific coast is good for jogging or walking the dog—but not for swimming. The water is so cold that surfers wear wet suits year-round, and riptides are strong—drownings are not infrequent. As for sunbathing, it's rarely warm enough here; think meditative walking instead of sun worshipping.

Paths on both sides of the Great Highway lead from Lincoln Way to Sloat Boulevard (near the zoo); the beachside path winds through landscaped sand dunes, and the paved path across the highway is good for biking and in-line skating (though you have to rent bikes elsewhere). The **Beach Chalet** restaurant and brewpub is across the Great Highway from Ocean Beach, about five blocks south of the Cliff House. **Amenities:** parking (no fee); showers; toilets. **Best for:** solitude; sunset; walking. ✉ *Along Great Hwy. from Cliff House to Sloat Blvd. and beyond, San Francisco.*

Sutro Heights Park

CITY PARK | Crows and other large birds battle the heady breezes at this cliff-top park on what were once the grounds of the home of Adolph Sutro, an eccentric mining engineer and former San Francisco mayor. An extremely wealthy man, Sutro may have owned about 10% of San Francisco at one point, but he couldn't buy good taste: a few remnants of his gaudy, faux-classical statue collection still stand (including the lions at what was the main gate). Monterey cypresses and Canary Island palms dot the park, and photos on placards depict what things looked like before the house burned down in 1896, from the greenhouse to the ornate carpet-bed designs.

All that remains of the main house is its foundation. Climb up for a sweeping view of the Pacific Ocean and the Cliff House below (which Sutro owned), and try to imagine what the perspective might have been like from one of the upper floors. San Francisco City Guides (*415/557–4266, www.sfcityguides.org*) runs a free Saturday tour of the park that starts at 2 (meet at the lion statue at 48th and Point Lobos Avenues). ✉ *Point Lobos and 48th Aves., Richmond.*

Restaurants

The Richmond encompasses the land on the north side of Golden Gate Park, running to the ocean's edge. As for architecture eye-candy, there isn't much, but this is the land of authentic Asian food, particularly in the Inner Richmond, known as the new Chinatown, covering Clement Street from about 2nd to 13th Avenues. On the main thoroughfares of Clement, Balboa, and Geary Streets, you'll find bargain dim sum, Burmese, Korean barbecue, and noodle soups of all persuasions.

Burma Superstar

$ | **ASIAN** | Locals make the trek to the "Avenues" for this perennially crowded spot's flavorful, well-prepared Burmese food, including its extraordinary signature tea leaf salad, a combo of spicy, salty, crunchy, and sour that is mixed table-side. The modestly decorated, no-reservations restaurant is small and lines can be long during peak times, so leave your number and wait for the call or walk a couple blocks east to B-Star, owned by the same people but often less crowded and with a welcoming patio. **Known for:** tea leaf salad; samusa soup; long lines. $ *Average main: $15* ✉ *309 Clement St., Richmond* ☎ *415/387–2147* 🌐 *www.burmasuperstar.com.*

Pizzetta 211

$$ | **PIZZA** | This shoebox-size spot puts together thin-crust pies topped with the kinds of ingredients that are worth the constant wait (they don't take reservations). Almost half the menu changes on a biweekly basis, while the tomato-basil-and-mozzarella pizza, the Sardinian-cheese-pine-nut-and-rosemary pie, and the San Marzano-tomato-sauce-wild-arugula-and-mascarpone pizza are dependable favorites. **Known for:** thin-crust pies; long lines; short constantly changing menu. $ *Average main: $16* ✉ *211 23rd Ave., Richmond* ☎ *415/379–9880* 🌐 *www.pizzetta211.com* ⏲ *Closed Tues.*

Tenglong

$ | **CHINESE** | This tidy space lures plenty of locals with remarkably friendly service and dry chicken wings, fried in garlic and roasted red peppers, as well as honey-walnut prawns, thinly sliced Mongolian beef, spicy seafood noodle soup, and *dan dan* noodles. Run by two former restaurant owners from Hong Kong, it specializes in mostly Southern-style Chinese like Cantonese and has a few Sichuan specialties, too. **Known for:** Cantonese food; chicken wings; local hot spot. $ *Average main: $14* ✉ *208 Clement St., Richmond* ☎ *415/666–3515* ⏲ *Closed Tues.*

★ Ton Kiang

$$ | **CHINESE** | **FAMILY** | Rarely found in this country and even obscure to many Chinese, the lightly seasoned Hakka cuisine of southern China is the hallmark of this local favorite, featuring dishes such as salt-baked chicken, braised stuffed tofu, steamed fresh bacon with dried mustard greens, and clay pots of meats and seafood. Ton Kiang opens in the morning for dim sum, serving delicate dumplings and steamed buns; a small selection of

dim sum is available at night, too. **Known for:** Hakka cuisine; delicious dim sum; Shanghai dumplings. *Average main: $18* *5821 Geary Blvd., Richmond* *415/752–4440* *Closed Wed.*

The nightlife in these practical, comfy neighborhoods centers more on reasonably priced restaurants—including Clement Street's good Chinese, Thai, Burmese, and Vietnamese ones—than on bars and nightclubs. What bar scene there is, you'll find low-key and welcoming. Fierce waves and mesmerizing sunsets are just a few of the reasons to make your way to the district's western reaches.

BARS

★ Cliff House

BARS/PUBS | Sure, it's the site of many high-school prom dates, and you could argue that the food and drinks are overpriced, but this is our pick if you must choose just one oceanfront restaurant/bar—its historical value is undeniable, and the views are terrific. The best window seats are reserved for diners, but there's a small upstairs lounge where you can watch gulls sail high above the vast blue Pacific. *1090 Point Lobos, at Great Hwy., Richmond* *415/386–3330* *cliffhouse.com.*

MUSIC CLUBS

The Plough and Stars

MUSIC CLUBS | This decidedly unglamorous pub, where crusty old-timers swap stories over pints of Guinness, is the city's best bet for traditional Irish music. Bay Area musicians (and, once in a while, big-name bands) perform every night except Monday. Talented locals gather to play on Tuesday and Sunday *seisiúns,* informal "sessions" where musicians sit around a table and drink and eat while chiming in; anyone skilled at Irish traditional music can join in. *116 Clement St., at 2nd Ave., Richmond* *415/751–1122* *theploughandstars.com.*

BOOKS

★ Green Apple Books

BOOKS/STATIONERY | This local favorite with a huge used-book department also carries new books in every field. It's known for its history room and rare-books collection. Two doors down, at 520 Clement Street, is a fiction annex that also sells CDs, DVDs, comic books, and graphic novels. *506 Clement St., at 6th Ave., Richmond* *415/387–2272* *www.greenapplebooks.com.*

The Sunset

Hugging the southern edge of Golden Gate Park and built atop the sand dunes that covered much of western San Francisco into the 19th century, the Sunset is made up of two distinct neighborhoods—the popular Inner Sunset, from Stanyan Street to 19th Avenue, and the foggy Outer Sunset, from 19th to the beach. The Inner Sunset is perhaps the perfect San Francisco "suburb": not too far from the center of things, reachable by public transit, and home to main streets—Irving Street and 9th Avenue just off Golden Gate Park—packed with excellent dining options, with Asian food particularly well represented. Long the domain of surfers and others who love the laid-back beach vibe and the fog, the slow-paced Outer Sunset finds itself newly on the radar of locals, with high-quality cafés and restaurants and quirky shops springing up along Judah Street between 42nd and 46th Avenues. The zoo is the district's main tourist attraction.

Sights

San Francisco Zoo

ZOO | FAMILY | Occupying prime oceanfront property, the San Francisco Zoo touts itself as a wildlife-focused recreation center that inspires visitors to become conservationists. Integrated exhibits group different species of animals from the same geographic areas together in enclosures that don't look like cages. More than 250 species reside here, including endangered species such as the snow leopard, Sumatran tiger, grizzly bear, and a Siberian tiger. The zoo's superstar exhibit is Grizzly Gulch, where orphaned grizzly bear sisters Kachina and Kiona enchant visitors with their frolicking and swimming. The Mexican Gray Wolf grotto houses three males: David Bowie, Jerry Garcia, and Prince. The Lemur Forest has four varieties of the bug-eyed, long-tailed primates from Madagascar. African Kikuyu grass carpets the circular outer area of Gorilla Preserve, one of the largest and most natural gorilla habitats of any zoo in the world. Other popular exhibits include Penguin Island, Koala Crossing, and the African Savanna exhibit. The 6-acre Children's Zoo has about 300 mammals, birds, and reptiles, plus a huge playground, a restored 1921 Dentzel carousel, and a mini–steam train. ✉ *Sloat Blvd. and 47th Ave., Sunset* ☎ *415/753–7080* 🌐 *www.sfzoo.org* 🎟 *$22, $1 off with Muni transfer (take Muni L–Taraval streetcar from downtown).*

Restaurants

The Sunset neighborhood encompasses the land south of Golden Gate Park, running all the way to the ocean's edge, and has a surf-town or small-town vibe. It's known for its fog, yes, but also bargain eats (UCSF is here) that range from pizzas and salads to Eritrean *injera* (flatbread) and Chinese dumplings, concentrated along Irving Street.

Nopalito

$$ | MEXICAN | An upscale take on Mexican featuring local, sustainable, and fresh ingredients is on the menu at this sleek, popular neighborhood spot just off the park, the second outpost of the Nopa favorite. Highlights include the pozole, anything with mole, and carnitas locals cross the city for, all of which you can enjoy on the front or back patio on sunny days, but be prepared for a wait almost anytime. **Known for:** carnitas worth waiting for; focus on freshness; Mexican beyond the taqueria. [$] *Average main: $22* ✉ *1224 9th Ave., Sunset* ☎ *415/233–9966* 🌐 *nopalitosf.com.*

Outerlands

$$$ | MODERN AMERICAN | As infamous for its lines as it is famous for its brunch, this cozy, wood-paneled restaurant serves food that is thoroughly Northern California, from the granola with goat's milk yogurt to the avocado toast drizzled with Meyer lemon vinaigrette. The cast-iron grilled cheese sandwich is legendary, and dinner also offers plenty of charm ... just make sure you have some time on your hands—and layers to ward off the Sunset chill while you wait. **Known for:** brunch; cast-iron grilled cheese; long waits. [$] *Average main: $27* ✉ *4001 Judah St., Sunset* ☎ *415/661–6140* 🌐 *outerlandssf.com.*

San Tung

$ | CHINESE | FAMILY | The food of China's northeastern province of Shandong is the draw at this bare-bones storefront restaurant where specialties include steamed dumplings—shrimp and leek dumplings are the most popular—and hand-pulled noodles, in soup or stir-fried. Parents and kids regularly fight over platters of dry-fried chicken wings, a cult dish in the city. **Known for:** chicken wings with cult following; steamed dumplings; long waits. [$] *Average main: $15* ✉ *1031 Irving St., Sunset* ☎ *415/242–0828* 🌐 *www.santung.net* 🕓 *Closed Wed.*

Nightlife

BARS

The Riptide

BARS/PUBS | A cozy cabin bar that's the perfect finale for beachgoers, Riptide is a surfer favorite, but you don't have to own a board to feel at home. You'll find classic beers and good food, all at wallet-friendly prices. There's live music most nights, often country, bluegrass, honky-tonk, and open mike. Many tourists fooled by San Francisco's version of summer end up warming their popsicle toes at the bar's fireplace. Sunday features a bacon Bloody Mary, great for hangovers. ✉ *3639 Taraval St, Sunset* ☎ *415/681–8433* 🌐 *www.riptidesf.com.*

Golden Gate Park

Jogging, cycling, skating, picnicking, going to a museum, checking out a concert, dozing in the sunshine ... Golden Gate Park is the perfect playground for fast-paced types, laid-back dawdlers, and everyone in between. More than 1,000 acres, stretching from the Haight all the way to the windy Pacific coast, the park is a vast patchwork of woods, trails, lakes, lush gardens, sports facilities, museums—even a herd of bison. You can hit the highlights in a few hours, but it would literally take days to fully explore the entire park.

Nightlife

Often shrouded by the city's famous fog and always scented by crisp eucalyptus, Golden Gate Park provides a suitably mellow nightlife experience.

BARS

Beach Chalet

BARS/PUBS | This restaurant-microbrewery, on the second floor of a historic building filled with 1930s Works Project Administration murals, has a stunning view of the Pacific Ocean, so you may want to time your visit to coincide with the sunset. **TIP→ Arrive at least 30 minutes before sunset to beat the dinner crowd.** The American bistro food is decent, the house brews are rich and flavorful, and there's a good selection of California wines by the glass. ✉ *1000 Great Hwy., near John F. Kennedy Dr., Golden Gate Park* ☎ *415/386–8439* 🌐 *www.beachchalet.com.*

Park Chalet Coastal Beer Garden

BARS/PUBS | You'll feel like you're in a cabin in the woods as you relax in an Adirondack chair under a heat lamp, enclosed by the greenery of Golden Gate Park. In addition to serving pub food such as burgers, salads, steaks, and fish-and-chips, the brewery churns out its own beer. On sunny spring and summer weekend days, there's live music on the lawn. The Park Chalet shares a building with the Beach Chalet—but it isn't waterside, so you won't freeze if it's overcast. ✉ *1000 Great Hwy., near John F. Kennedy Dr., Golden Gate Park* ☎ *415/386–8439* 🌐 *www.parkchalet.com.*

Activities

BOATING AND SAILING

Stow Lake

BOATING | If you prefer calm freshwater, you can rent rowboats and pedal boats at Stow Lake in Golden Gate Park. Remember to bring bread for the ducks. **TIP→ The lake is open daily from 10 to 5 for boating, rentals stop one hour before closing.** ✉ *50 Stow Lake Dr. E, off John F. Kennedy Dr., Golden Gate Park* ☎ *415/386–2531* 🌐 *stowlakeboathouse.com.*

HIKING

Golden Gate National Recreation Area (GGNRA)

HIKING/WALKING | **FAMILY** | This huge, protected area encompasses the San Francisco coastline, the Marin Headlands, and Point Reyes National Seashore, perhaps one of the most beautiful places on the planet. It's veined with hiking trails, including the spectacular Coastal Trail at Lands End, and guided walks are offered in some places. You can find current schedules at visitor centers at Lands End, in the Presidio, and in the Marin Headlands; they're also online at *www.nps.gov/goga.* ✉ *Bldg. 201, Fort Mason, San Francisco* ☎ *415/561–3000* 🌐 *www.nps.gov/goga, www.parksconservancy.org.*

Golden Gate Promenade
BICYCLING | This great walk passes through Crissy Field, taking in marshlands, kite-flyers, beachfront, and windsurfers, with the Golden Gate Bridge as a backdrop. The 4.3-mile walk is flat and easy—it should take less than two hours round-trip. If you begin at Aquatic Park, you'll end up practically underneath the bridge at Fort Point Pier. ■ TIP→ **If you're driving, park at Fort Point and do the walk from west to east.** It can get blustery, even when it's sunny, so be sure to layer. ✉ *San Francisco* 🌐 *www.presidio.gov.*

Chapter 10

GOLDEN GATE PARK

A GREEN RETREAT

Stretching more than 1,000 acres from the ocean to the Haight, Golden Gate Park is a place to slow down and smell the eucalyptus. Stockbrokers and gadget-laden parents stroll the Music Concourse, while speedy tattooed cyclists and wobbly, training-wheeled kids cruise along shaded paths. Stooped seniors warm the garden benches, hikers search for waterfalls, and picnickers lounge in the Rhododendron Dell. San Franciscans love their city streets, but the park is where they come to breathe.

PLANNING A PARK VISIT

ORIENTATION

The park breaks down naturally into three chunks. The eastern end attracts the biggest crowds with its cluster of blockbuster sights. It's also the easiest place to dip into the park for a quick trip. Water hobbyists come to the middle section's lake-speckled open space. Sporty types head west to the coastal end for its soccer fields, golf course, and archery range. This windswept western end is the park's least visited and most naturally landscaped part.
⏲ Daily 6 am—10 pm
🌐 www.sfrecpark.org.

WALKING TOURS

San Francisco Botanical Garden (☎ 415/661–1316) has free botanical tours every day (admission not included). Tours start near the main gate daily at 1:30 pm. Additional tours meet at the Friend Gate (at the northern entrance) Apr.–Sept., Fri.–Sun. at 2 pm.

San Francisco City Guides (☎ 415/557–4266) offers free year-round tours of the eastern end and the western end of the park and two different tours of the Japanese Tea Garden.

BEST TIMES TO VISIT

Time of day: It's best to arrive early at the Conservatory of Flowers, the de Young Museum, and the Japanese Tea Garden to avoid crowds. At sunset, the only place to be is the park's western end, watching the sun dip into the Pacific.

Time of year: Visit during the week if you can. The long, Indian summer days of September and October are the warmest times to visit, and many special weekend events are held then.

Blooms: The rhododendrons bloom between February and May. The Queen Wilhelmina Tulip Garden blossoms in February and March. Cherry trees in the Japanese Tea Garden bloom in April, and the Rose Garden is at its best from mid-May to mid-June, in the beginning of July, and during September

(opposite) Conservatory of Flowers. (top left) The San Francisco Botanical Garden in bloom.

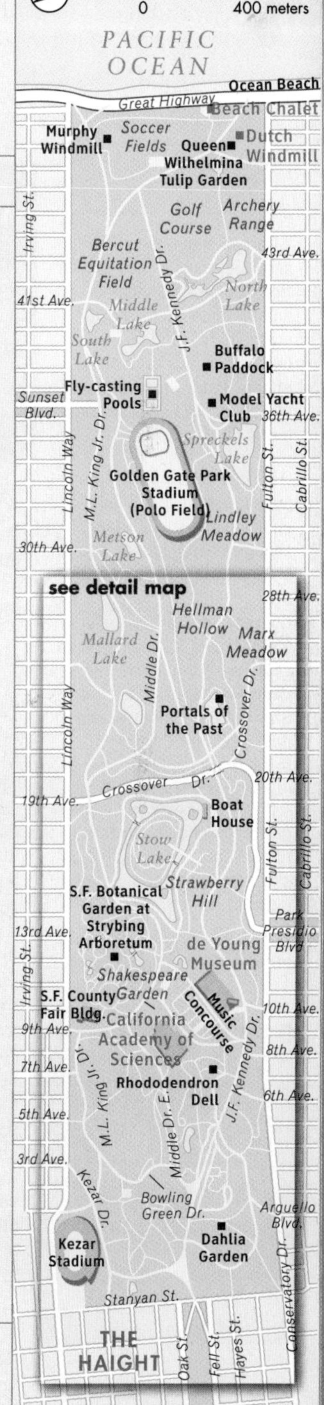

TIPS

- Carry a map—the park's sightlines usually prevent you from using city landmarks as reference points. Posted maps are few and far between, and they're often out of date. Paths aren't always clear, so stick to well-marked trails.
- In Golden Gate Park, free public restrooms are fairly common and mostly clean, especially around the eastern end's attractions. Facilities are available behind the Conservatory of Flowers or in the de Young Museum at the sculpture garden and café patio. Farther west, behind Stow Lake's boathouse and near the Koret Children's Quarter are facilities.
- Check out www.goldengate-park.com for a calendar of park events. This unofficial site also has maps and parking info.

BEST WAYS TO SPEND YOUR TIME

The park stretches 3 miles east to west and is a half-mile wide, so it's possible to cover the whole thing in a day—by car, public transportation, bike, or even on foot. But to do so might feel more like a forced march than a pleasure jaunt. Weigh your time and your interests, choose your top picks, then leave at least an extra hour to just enjoy being outdoors.

Two hours: Swing by the exquisite Conservatory of Flowers for a 20-minute peek, then head to the de Young Museum. Spend a few minutes assessing its controversial exterior and perhaps glide through some of the galleries before heading to the observation tower for a panoramic view of the city. Cross the music concourse to the spectacular Academy of Sciences.

Half day: Spend a little extra time at the sights described above, then head to the nearby Japanese Tea Garden to enjoy its perfectionist landscape. Next, cross the street to the San Francisco Botanical Garden at Strybing Arboretum and check out the intriguing Primitive Garden. If you brought supplies, this is a great place for a picnic; you can also grab lunch at the de Young Café.

Full day: After the half-day tour (above) continue on to the children's playground if you have kids in tow. Once your little ones see the playground's tree house–like play structures and climbing opportunities, you may be here for the rest of the day. Alternatively, make your way to the serene National AIDS Memorial Grove. Then head west, stopping at Stow Lake to climb Strawberry Hill. Wind up at the Beach Chalet for a sunset drink.

(top) Amateur musicians entertain passersby. (middle) Sundays are ideal biking days. (bottom) The meandering paths are perfect for strolling.

GETTING AROUND THE PARK

WALKING

The most convenient entry point is on the eastern edge at Stanyan Street, continuing into the park on JFK Drive, which points you directly toward the Conservatory of Flowers. It's a 10-minute walk there; allow another 10–15 minutes to reach the California Academy of Sciences, de Young Museum, Japanese Tea Garden, and San Francisco Botanical Garden. Stow Lake is another 10 minutes west from these four sights.

BY BIKE

The park is fantastic for cycling, especially on Sunday when cars are barred from John F. Kennedy Drive. Biking the park round-trip is about a 7-miles trip, which usually takes 1–2 hours. The route down John F. Kennedy Drive takes you past the prettiest, well-maintained sections of the park on a mostly flat circuit. The most popular route continues all the way to the beach. Keep in mind that the ride is downhill toward the ocean, uphill heading east.

BY CAR

If you have a car, you'll have no trouble hopping from sight to sight. (But remember, the main road, John F. Kennedy Drive, is closed to cars on Sunday.) Parking within the park is often free and is usually easy to find especially beyond the eastern end. On Sundays or anytime the eastern end is crowded, head for the residential streets north of the park or the underground parking lot; enter on 10th and Fulton (northern edge of the park) or MLK and Concourse (in the park).

BY SHUTTLE

The free Golden Gate Park shuttle runs 9–6 weekends and holidays. It loops through the park every 15–20 minutes, stopping at 14 sights from McLaren Lodge to the Dutch Windmill. If you're driving, leave your car in the free spaces along Ocean Beach (Great Highway between Lincoln and Fulton) and wait at the green shuttle stop sign.

(top) Water lilies adorn the Japanese Tea Garden.

WHERE TO RENT

Parkwide Bike Rentals & Tours (☎ *415/671–8989*). The only rental shop in the park is behind the band-shell on the music concourse. For an extra $10 you can return your bike to the Embarcadero/ Ferry Building, the Marina, or Union Square. **Golden Gate Park Bike & Skate** (✉ *3038 Fulton St.* ☎ *415/668–1117*). On the northern edge of the park; good deals on rentals. **San Francisco Bicycle Rentals** (✉ *425 Jefferson St.* ☎ *415/922–4537*). Customers rave about excellent service and good deals at this Fisherman's Wharf outfit. **Bike and Roll** (✉ *2800 Leavenworth St.* ☎ *415/229–2000*). This business operates out of Fisherman's Wharf, North Beach, and the Embarcadero, but you can take their bikes to the park, too.

BEST PLACES TO PICNIC ON WEEKENDS

- Lawn in front of the Conservatory of Flowers.
- By the pond in the San Francisco Botanical Garden.
- The benches overlooking the Rustic Bridge at Stow Lake.
- Rhododendron Dell.

DON'T-MISS SIGHTS

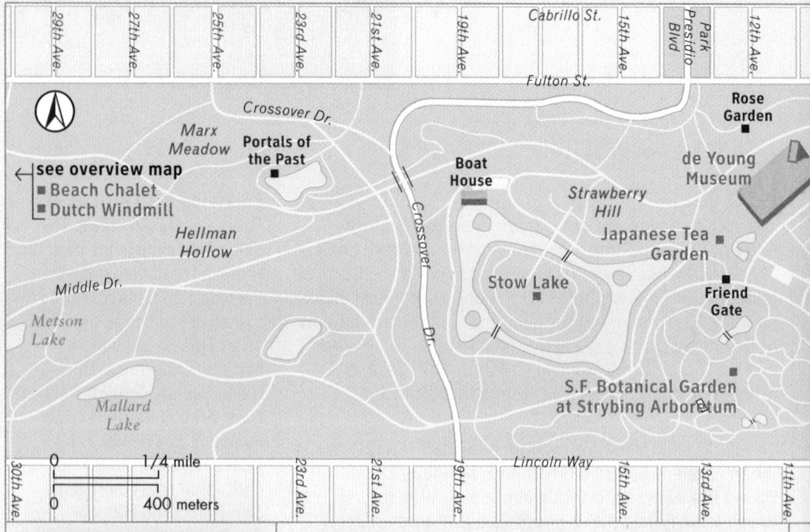

Conservatory of Flowers

✉ John F. Kennedy Dr. at Conservatory Dr.

☎ 415/666–7001

$9, free 1st Tues. of month

⏲ Tues.–Sun. 9–5; 10–4:30 in winter

🌐 www.conservatoryofflowers.org

CONSERVATORY OF FLOWERS

Whatever you do, be sure to at least drive by the Conservatory of Flowers—it's just too darn pretty to miss. The gorgeous, white-framed, 1878 glass structure is topped with a 14-ton glass dome. Stepping inside the giant greenhouse is like taking a quick trip to the rainforest; it's humid, warm, and smells earthy. The undeniable highlight is the Aquatic Plants section, where lily pads float and carnivorous plants dine on bugs to the sounds of rushing water. On the east side of the conservatory (to the right as you face the building), cypress, pine, and redwood trees surround the **Dahlia Garden,** which blooms in summer and fall. To the west is the **Rhododendron Dell,** which contains 850 varieties, more than any other garden in the country. It's a favorite local Mother's Day picnic spot.

STOW LAKE

Russian seniors feed the pigeons, kids watch turtles sunning themselves, and joggers circle this placid body of water, Golden Gate Park's largest lake. Early park superintendent John McLaren may have snarked that manmade Stow Lake was "a shoestring around a watermelon," but for more than a century visitors have come to walk its paths and bridges, paddle boats, and climb Strawberry Hill (the "watermelon"). Cross one of the bridges—the 19th-century stone bridge on the southwest side is lovely—and ascend the hill; keep your eyes open for the waterfall and an elaborate Chinese Pavilion.

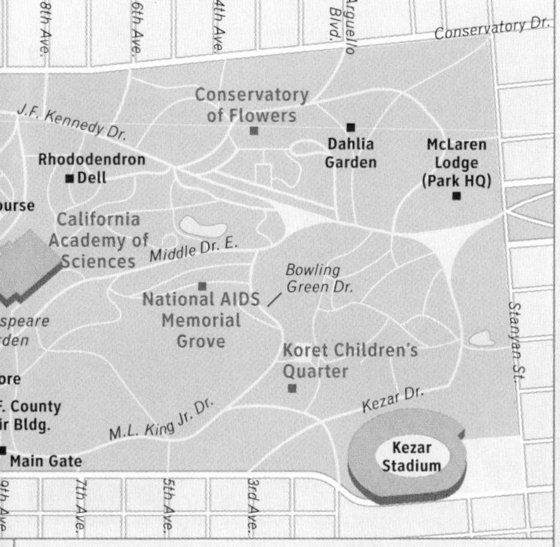

Stow Lake

✉ Off John F. Kennedy Dr.
☎ Boat rental 415/752–0347
⏲ Boat rentals daily 10–4

San Francisco Japanese Tea Garden

✉ Hagiwara Tea Garden Dr.
☎ 415/752–4227
🎟 $9, free Mon., Wed., and Fri. with entry by 10 am
⏲ Mar.–Oct., daily 9–6; Nov.–Feb., daily 9–4:45
🌐 www.japaneseteagardensf.com

SAN FRANCISCO JAPANESE TEA GARDEN

As you amble through the manicured landscape, past Japanese sculptures and perfect miniature pagodas, over ponds of huge, ancient carp, you may be transported to a more peaceful plane. Or maybe the shrieks of kids clambering over the almost vertical "humpback" bridges will keep you firmly in the here and now. Either way, this garden is one of those tourist spots that's truly worth a stop (a half-hour will do). And at 5 acres, it's large enough that you'll always be able to find a bit of serenity, even when the tour buses drop by. **■ TIP→ The garden is especially lovely in April, when the cherry blossoms are in bloom.**

KORET CHILDREN'S QUARTER

The country's first public children's playground reopened in 2007 after a spectacular renovation, with wave-shaped climbing walls, old-fashioned cement slides, and a 20-plus-foot rope climbing structure that kids love and parents fear. Thankfully, one holdover is the beautiful, handcrafted 1912 Herschell-Spillman Carousel. The lovely stone Sharon Building, next to the playground, offers kids' art classes. Bring a picnic or pick up grub nearby on 9th Avenue and you could spend the entire day here. Be aware that the playground, which has separate areas for toddlers and bigger kids, is unenclosed and sightlines can be obstructed.

Koret Children's Quarter

✉ Bowling Green Dr., off Martin Luther King Jr. Dr
☎ 415/831–2700
🎟 Playground free, carousel $2, kids 6–12 $1
⏲ Playground daily dawn–dusk; carousel Memorial Day–Labor Day, daily 10–4:30, Labor Day–Memorial Day, Fri.–Sun. 10–4:30.

DE YOUNG MUSEUM

✉ 50 Hagiwara Tea Garden Dr.

☎ 415/750–3600

🌐 deyoung.famsf.org

🎟 $15; free 1st Tues. of month

🕒 Tues.–Sun. 9:30–5:15

TIPS

■ Admission at the de Young is good for same-day admission to the Legion of Honor and vice-versa.

■ The de Young is famous these days first and foremost for its striking and controversial building and tree-topping tower. These are accessible to the public for free, so if it's not the art you're interested in seeing, save the cost of admission and head up the elevator to 360-degree views from the glass-walled observation floor.

■ When it's time for a nosh, head to the de Young Café and dine in the lovely outdoor sculpture garden on tableware fit for MOMA.

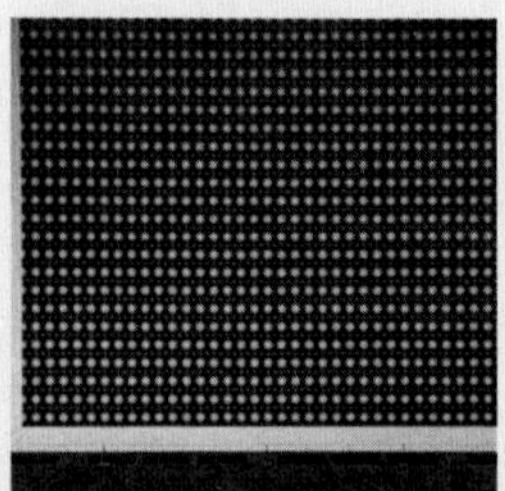

Everyone in town has a strong opinion about the de Young. Some adore the striking copper facade, while others grimace and hope that the green patina of age will mellow the effect. The building almost overshadows the museum's respected collection of American, African, and Oceanic art.

HIGHLIGHTS

Head through the sprawling concourse level and begin your visit on the upper level, where you'll find textiles; art from Africa, Oceana, and New Guinea; and highlights of the 20th-century American painting collection (such as Wayne Thiebaud, John Singer Sargent, Winslow Homer, and Richard Diebenkorn). These are the don't-miss items, so take your time. Then head back downstairs to see art from the Americas and contemporary work.

The de Young has had some major international coups, scoring exhibits such as Tutankhamun and the Golden Age of the Pharoahs; Van Gogh, Gaugin, Cezanne, and Beyond: Post-Impressionist Masterpieces from the Musée d'Orsay; and Picasso: Masterpieces from the Musée National Picasso, Paris. Be sure to check for traveling exhibits while you're visiting. Recent shows have included the stunning Jean Paul Gaultier exhibition (extra fees apply).

CALIFORNIA ACADEMY OF SCIENCES

With its native plant–covered living roof, retractable ceiling, three-story rain forest, gigantic planetarium, living coral reef, and frolicking penguins, the Cal Academy is one of the city's most spectacular treasures. Dramatically designed by Renzo Piano, it's an eco-friendly, energy-efficient adventure in biodiversity and green architecture. The roof's large mounds and hills mirror the local topography, and Piano's audacious design completes the dramatic transformation of the park's Music Concourse. Moving away from a restrictive role as a backward-looking museum that catalogued natural history, the new academy is all about sustainability and the future, but you'll still find those beloved dioramas in African Hall.

HIGHLIGHTS

By the time you arrive, hopefully you've decided which shows and programs to attend, looked at the academy's floorplan, and designed a plan to cover it all in the time you have. And if not, here's the quick version: Head left from the entrance to the wooden walkway over otherworldly rays in the Philippine Coral Reef, then continue to the Swamp to see Claude, the famous albino alligator. Swing through African Hall and gander at the penguins, take the elevator up to the living roof, then return to the main floor and get in line to explore the Rainforests of the World, ducking free-flying butterflies and watching for other live surprises. You'll end up below ground in the Amazonian Flooded Rainforest, where you can explore the academy's other aquarium exhibits. Phew.

- 55 Music Concourse Dr.
- 415/379–8000
- www.calacademy.org
- $40, free one Sun. per quarter, $3 off for visitors who walk, bike, or take public transit.
- Mon.–Sat. 9:30–5, Sun. 11–5

TIPS

- The academy often hosts gaggles of schoolchildren. Arrive early and allow plenty of time to wait in line.
- Plan ahead: check Planetarium show times, animal feeding times, etc, before you arrive.
- Visitors complain about the high cost of food here; consider bringing a picnic.
- Free days are tempting, but the tradeoff includes extremely long lines and the possibility that you won't get in.
- With antsy kids, visit Early Explorers Cove and use the academy's in-and-out privileges to run around outside.
- Take time to examine the structure itself, from denim insulation to weather sensors.

ALSO WORTH SEEING

San Francisco Botanical Garden at Strybing Arboretum

Beach Chalet

Dutch Windmill

SAN FRANCISCO BOTANICAL GARDEN AT STRYBING ARBORETUM

One of the best picnic spots in a very picnic-friendly park, the 55-acre arboretum specializes in plants from areas with climates similar to that of the Bay Area. Walk the Eastern Australian garden to see tough, pokey shrubs and plants with cartoon-like names, such as the hilly-pilly tree. Kids gravitate toward the large shallow fountain and the pond with ducks, turtles, and egrets. Free tours meet at the main gate daily at 1:30. ✉ *Enter park at 9th Ave. at Lincoln Way P415/661–1316 wwww.sfbotanicalgarden.org* 🎫 *$9* ⏲ *Mar.–Sept., daily 9–7; Oct.–early Nov. and Feb.–Mar., daily 9–5. Nov.–Jan., daily 9–4.*

NATIONAL AIDS MEMORIAL GROVE

This lush, serene 7-acre grove was conceived as a living memorial to the disease's victims. Coast live oaks, Monterey pines, coast redwoods, and other trees flank the grove. There are also two stone circles, one recording the names of the dead and their loved ones, the other engraved with a poem. Free 20-minute tours are available some Saturdays. ✉ *Middle Dr. E, west of tennis courts* ☎ *415/765–0497 wwww.aidsmemorial.org.*

BEACH CHALET

Hugging the park's western border, this 1925 Willis Polk–designed structure houses gorgeous depression-era murals of familiar San Francisco scenes, while verses by local poets adorn niches here and there. Stop by the ground-floor visitors center on your way to indulge in a microbrew upstairs, ideally at sunset. ✉ *1000 Great Hwy.* ☎ *415/386–8439 restaurant* 🌐 *www.beachchalet.com* ⏲ *Restaurant Mon.–Thurs. 9 am–10 pm, Fri. 9 am–11 pm, Sat. 8 am–11 pm, Sun. 8 am–10 pm.*

DUTCH WINDMILL

It may not pump water anymore, but this carefully restored windmill, built in 1903 to irrigate the park, continues to enchant visitors. The Queen Wilhelmina Tulip Garden here is a welcoming respite, particularly lovely during its February and March bloom. The Murphy Windmill is just south of the Dutch Windmill and has a refurbished copper dome; swing by for an interesting comparison. ✉ *Northwest corner of park* ☎ *No phone* ⏲ *Dawn–dusk.*

Chapter 11

THE HAIGHT, THE CASTRO, AND NOE VALLEY

Updated by
Andrea Powell

Sights	Restaurants	Hotels	Shopping	Nightlife
★☆☆☆☆	★★★☆☆	★☆☆☆☆	★★★☆☆	★★★☆☆

NEIGHBORHOOD SNAPSHOT

PLANNING YOUR TIME

The Upper Haight is only a few blocks long, and although there are plenty of shops and amusements, an hour or so should be enough unless you're into vintage shopping. Many restaurants here cater to the morning-after crowd, so this is a great place for brunch. With the prevalence of panhandling in this area, you may be most comfortable here during the day.

The Castro, with its fun, adult-theme storefronts, invites unhurried exploration; allot at least 60 to 90 minutes. Visit in the evening to check out the lively nightlife, or in the late morning—especially on weekends—when the street scene is hopping.

A loop through Noe Valley takes about an hour. With its popular breakfast spots and cafés, this neighborhood is a good place for a morning stroll. After you've filled up, browse the shops along 24th and Church Streets.

TOP REASONS TO GO

■ **Castro Theatre:** Take in a film at this gorgeous throwback and join the audience shouting out lines, commentary, and songs. Come early and let the Wurlitzer set the mood.

■ **Sunday brunch in the Castro:** Recover from Saturday night (with the entire community) at one of the area's favorite brunch spots.

■ **Vintage shopping in the Haight:** Find the perfect 1930s afternoon dress at Relic Vintage, a pristine faux-leopard coat at Held Over, or the motorcycle jacket of your dreams at Buffalo Exchange.

■ **24th Street stroll:** Take a leisurely ramble down lovable Noe Valley's main drag, lined with unpretentious cafés, comfy eateries, and cute one-of-a-kind shops.

QUICK BITES

■ **Flywheel Coffee Roasters.** Family-owned, this light-filled café with a view of Golden Gate Park roasts its beans in-house for a great cuppa. **Known for:** cold brew; vegan options. ✉ *672 Stanyan St., Haight* ☎ *415/682–4023* 🌐 *www.flywheelcoffee.com.*

■ **Lovejoy's Tea Room.** The tearoom is a homey jumble, with its lace-covered tables, couches, and mismatched chairs set among the antiques for sale. High tea and cream tea are served, along with traditional English-tearoom "fayre." **Known for:** high tea; comfy atmosphere. ✉ *1351 Church St., at Clipper St., Noe Valley* ☎ *415/648–5895* 🌐 *www.lovejoystearoom.com.*

GETTING THERE

■ F-line trolleys serve the Castro; Muni light rail K-Ingleside, L-Taraval, M-Ocean View, and T-Third trains stop at Castro station; and the J–Church serves the Castro and Noe Valley. The 7–Haight/Noriega bus from Market Street and the 6–Haight-Parnassus from Market serve the Haight. If on foot, know that the hill between the Castro and Noe Valley is steep.

These distinct neighborhoods wear their personalities large and proud, and all are perfect for just strolling around. Like a slide show of San Franciscan history, you can move from the Haight's residue of 1960s counterculture to the Castro's connection to 1970s and '80s gay life to 1990s gentrification in Noe Valley. Although historic events thrust the Haight and the Castro onto the international stage, both are anything but stagnant—they're still dynamic areas well worth exploring.

The Haight

During the 1960s the siren song of free love, peace, and mind-altering substances lured thousands of young people to the Haight, a neighborhood just east of Golden Gate Park. By 1966 the area had become a hot spot for rock artists, including the Grateful Dead, Jefferson Airplane, and Janis Joplin. Some of the most infamous flower children, including Charles Manson and People's Temple founder Jim Jones, also called the Haight home.

Today the '60s message of peace, civil rights, and higher consciousness has been distilled into a successful blend of commercialism and progressive causes: the Haight Ashbury Free Clinic, founded in 1967, survives at the corner of Haight and Clayton, while throwbacks like Bound Together Bookstore (the anarchist book collective), the head shop Pipe Dreams, and a bevy of tie-dye shops all keep the Summer of Love alive in their own way. The Haight's famous political spirit—it was the first neighborhood in the nation to lead a freeway revolt, and it continues to resist chain stores—survives alongside some of the finest Victorian-lined streets in the city.

Sights

Buena Vista Park

CITY PARK | If you can manage the steep climb, this eucalyptus-filled park has great city views. Dog walkers and homeless folks make good use of the park, and the playground at the top is popular with kids and adults alike. Be sure to scan the stone rain gutters lining many of

Hippie History

The eternal lure for twentysome-things, cheap rent, first helped spawn an indelible part of SF's history and public image. In the early 1960s young people started streaming into the sprawling, inexpensive Victorians in the area around the University of San Francisco, earnestly seeking a new era of communal living, individual empowerment, and expanded consciousness.

Golden Gate Park's Panhandle, a green strip on the Haight's northern edge, was their gathering spot—the site of protests, concerts, food giveaways, and general hanging out. In 1967, George Harrison strolled up the park's Hippie Hill, borrowed a guitar, and played for a while before being recognized. He led the crowd, Pied Piper–style, into the Haight.

A Hippie State of Mind

At first the counterculture was all about sharing and taking care of one another—a good thing, considering most hippies were either broke or had renounced money. The daily free "feeds" in the Panhandle were a staple for many. The Diggers, an anarchist street-theater group, were known for handing out bread shaped like the big coffee cans they baked it in.

At the time, the U.S. government, Harvard professor Timothy Leary, a Stanford student named Ken Kesey, and the kids in the Haight were all experimenting with LSD. Acid was legal, widely available, and usually given away for free. At Kesey's all-night parties, called "acid tests," a buck got you a cup of "electric" Kool-Aid, a preview of psychedelic art, and an earful of the house band, the Grateful Dead. When LSD was made illegal in 1966, the kids responded by staging a Love Pageant Rally, where they dropped acid tabs en masse and rocked out to Janis Joplin and the Dead.

The Peak of the Party

Things crested early in 1967, when between 10,000 and 50,000 people ("depending on whether you were a policeman or a hippie," according to one hippie) gathered at the Polo Field in Golden Gate Park for the Human Be-In of the Gathering of the Tribes. Allen Ginsberg and Timothy Leary spoke, the Dead and Jefferson Airplane played, and people costumed with beads and feathers waved flags, clanged cymbals, and beat drums. A parachutist dropped onto the field, tossing fistfuls of acid tabs to the crowd. America watched via satellite, gape-mouthed—it was every conservative parent's nightmare.

Burn Out

Later that year, thousands heeded Scott McKenzie's song "San Francisco," which promised "For those who come to San Francisco, Summer-time will be a love-in there." The Summer of Love swelled the Haight's population from 7,000 to 75,000; people came both to join in and to ogle. But degenerates soon joined the gentle people, heroin replaced LSD, crime became rampant, and the Haight began a fast slide.

Hippies will tell you the Human Be-In was the pinnacle of their scene, while the Summer of Love was a media creation that turned their movement into a monster. Still, the idea of that fictional summer lingers, and to this day draws pilgrims from all over the world.

the park's walkways for inscribed names and dates; these are the remains of gravestones left unclaimed when the city closed the Laurel Hill cemetery around 1940. A new pit stop includes a portable toilet and disposal for used needles and condoms; definitely avoid the park after dark, when these items are left behind. ✉ *Haight St. between Lyon St. and Buena Vista Ave. W, Haight.*

Haight-Ashbury Intersection

NEIGHBORHOOD | On October 6, 1967, hippies took over the intersection of Haight and Ashbury Streets to proclaim the "Death of Hip." If they thought hip was dead then, they'd find absolute confirmation of it today, what with the only tie-dye in sight on the famed corner being Ben & Jerry's storefront. ✉ *Haight.*

Restaurants

Haight-Ashbury was home base for the country's famed 1960s counterculture, and its café scene still reflects that colorful past.

Over time, the Haight has become two distinct neighborhoods. The Upper Haight is an energetic commercial stretch from Masonic Avenue to Stanyan Street, where head shops and tofu-burger joints still thrive.

Meanwhile, the modestly gritty Lower Haight has emerged as a lively bohemian quarter of sorts, with mostly ethnic eateries lining the blocks between Webster and Pierce Streets.

Cha Cha Cha

$$ | **CARIBBEAN** | Boisterous Cha Cha Cha serves island cuisine, a mix of Cajun, Southwestern, and Caribbean influences. The decor at this Haight Street institution is Technicolor tropical plastic, and the food is hot and spicy. **Known for:** Haight staple; cajun shrimp; ceviche. $ *Average main: $20* ✉ *1801 Haight St., at Shrader St., Haight* ☎ *415/386–7670* 🌐 *www.cha3.com.*

Parada 22

$$ | **PUERTO RICAN** | A small, colorful space sandwiched between larger restaurants on either side, Parada 22 serves up heaping plates of Puerto Rican cuisine—think plantains, seafood, and slow-roasted pork. This still being the Haight, there's plenty of vegetarian fare on offer, and the yuca fries will be devoured by everyone. **Known for:** home-style Puerto Rican cuisine; marinated meats and vegetables; lunch specials. $ *Average main: $17* ✉ *1805 Haight St., near Shrader St., Haight* ☎ *415/750–1111* 🌐 *parada22.com.*

Uva Enoteca

$$ | **ITALIAN** | This casual Italian wine bar hits all the right notes. The mood is convivial, the food is solid, and there's plenty of wine—more than 15 by the glass and a long list of bottles. **Known for:** simple but delicious dining; variety of wines by the glass; Italian food. $ *Average main: $17* ✉ *568 Haight St., Haight* ☎ *415/829–2024* 🌐 *www.uvaenoteca.com* ⏲ *No lunch weekdays.*

Hotels

★ **Metro Hotel**

$ | **HOTEL** | These tiny rooms, with simple yet modern decor and equipped with private, if small, bathrooms, are within walking distance to the lively Haight, Hayes Valley, Panhandle, NoPa, and Castro neighborhoods. **Pros:** can't beat the price; out-of-downtown location; friendly staffers. **Cons:** small rooms and bathrooms; street noise; no elevator. $ *Rooms from: $107* ✉ *319 Divisadero St., Hayes Valley* ☎ *415/861–5364* 🌐 *www.metrohotelsf.com* *24 rooms* *No meals.*

Nightlife

The hippie joints that made the Haight famous may be long gone, but this neighborhood retains a countercultural vibe. Beer connoisseurs should head directly to the Toronado or Magnolia.

Two Haights

The Haight is actually composed of two distinct neighborhoods: the Lower Haight runs from Divisadero to Webster; the Upper Haight, immediately east of Golden Gate Park, is the part people tend to call Haight-Ashbury (and the part that's covered here). San Franciscans come to the Upper Haight for the myriad vintage clothing stores concentrated in its few blocks, bars with character, restaurants where huge breakfast portions take the edge off a hangover, and Amoeba Music, the best place in town for new and used CDs and vinyl. The Lower Haight is an equally lively, stretch with several well-loved pubs and a smattering of niche music shops.

BARS

The Alembic

BARS/PUBS | This dark-wood and low-lit space has a certain swagger that is at once charming and classy. It serves full meals but is also a good choice for cocktails and small plates—the jerk-spiced duck hearts, deviled eggs, and gems salad are all winners. ■ **TIP→ Carnivores: check out the bone-marrow plate.** ✉ *1725 Haight St., at Cole St., Haight* ☎ *415/666–0822* 🌐 *www.alembicsf.com.*

Magnolia Brewing Company

BREWPUBS/BEER GARDENS | Known for its food as much as its beers, Magnolia is a San Francisco institution, thanks in part to its prime location one block away from the famous Haight-Ashbury intersection. Come for the smoked trout croquettes, falafel salad, and famed burgers, or just grab any one of the over a dozen beers on tap, many made right there in the in-house brewery. ✉ *1398 Haight St., Haight* ✣ *At Masonic St.* ☎ *415/864–7468* 🌐 *magnoliabrewing.com.*

Noc Noc

BARS/PUBS | A cross between a Tim Burton film and an Oingo Boingo album, this funky cavelike bar has been making every day Halloween since 1986. Noc Noc's bartenders serve up about 20 or so beers on tap ("No Bud, No Coors, No PBR" proclaims the menu) sake (even unfiltered), and unique twists on traditional drinks, like the Snake Bite, a blend of lager and cider. The house DJ plays acid jazz, industrial, and ambient tunes. When the nearby Toronado gets too busy, head over here. ✉ *557 Haight St., near Steiner St., Haight* ☎ *415/861–5811* 🌐 *nocnocs.com.*

★ **Toronado**

BARS/PUBS | You come to one of the city's most popular dive bars for one thing and one thing only: the reasonably priced beers, about four dozen of them on tap. The menu, which runs along the upper wall, will put a kink in your neck as you try to decide. The bar opens in the late morning and has a good-size crowd by early afternoon, so show up early to sit at one of the highly coveted tables. Just make sure to bring cash, they don't accept credit cards. ■ **TIP→ Don't worry about eating beforehand. It's okay to bring in or order in outside food.** ✉ *547 Haight St., near Fillmore St., Haight* ☎ *415/863–2276* 🌐 *www.toronado.com.*

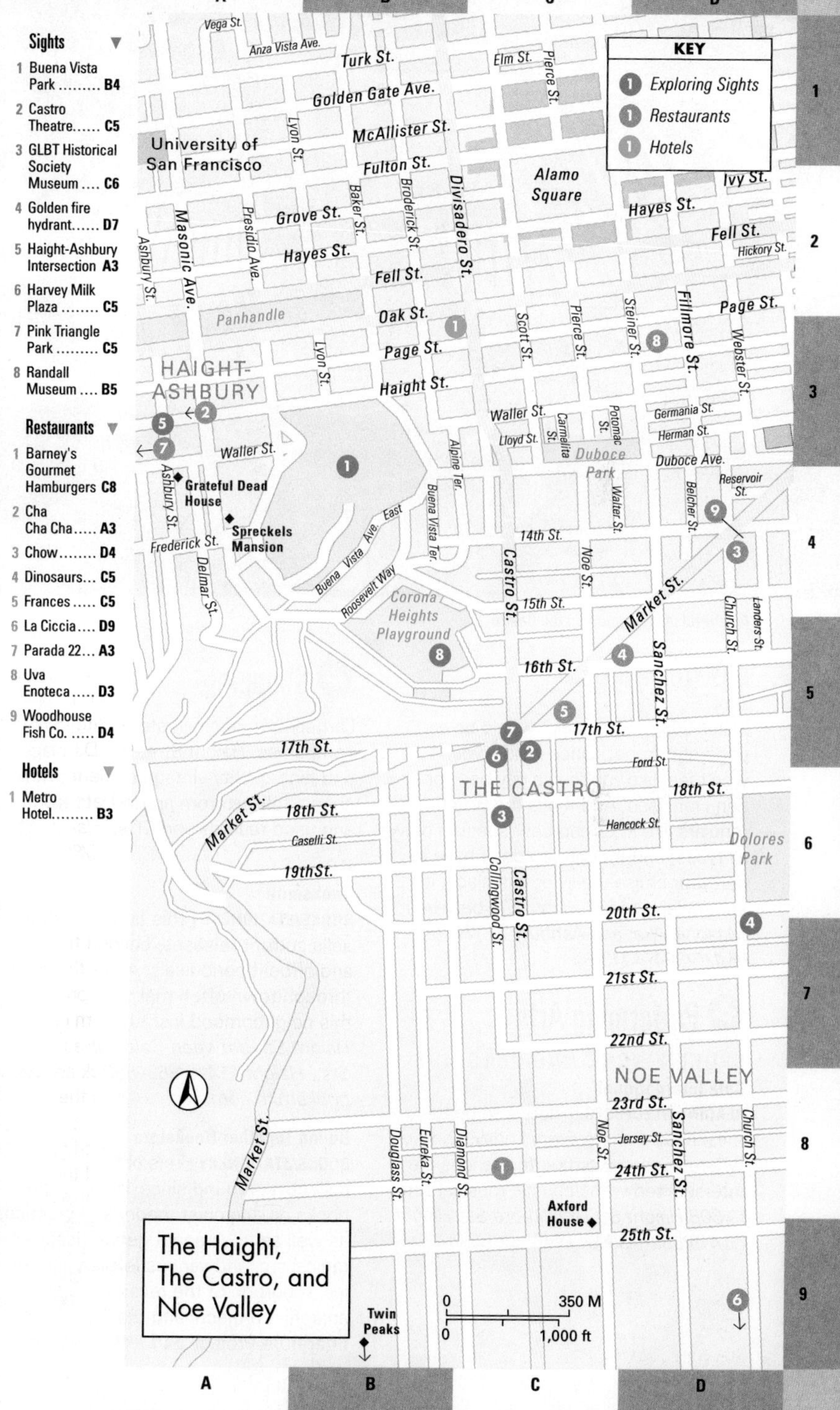
The Haight, The Castro, and Noe Valley
Sights
1 Buena Vista Park B4
2 Castro Theatre...... C5
3 GLBT Historical Society Museum C6
4 Golden fire hydrant...... D7
5 Haight-Ashbury Intersection A3
6 Harvey Milk Plaza C5
7 Pink Triangle Park C5
8 Randall Museum B5
Restaurants
1 Barney's Gourmet Hamburgers C8
2 Cha Cha Cha..... A3
3 Chow......... D4
4 Dinosaurs... C5
5 Frances C5
6 La Ciccia.... D9
7 Parada 22... A3
8 Uva Enoteca..... D3
9 Woodhouse Fish Co. D4
Hotels
1 Metro Hotel......... B3
KEY
Exploring Sights
Restaurants
Hotels
A
B
C
D
1
2
3
4
5
6
7
8
9
Vega St.
Anza Vista Ave.
Turk St.
Elm St.
Pierce St.
Golden Gate Ave.
McAllister St.
Lyon St.
University of San Francisco
Fulton St.
Alamo Square
Ivy St.
Hayes St.
Fell St.
Hickory St.
Grove St.
Baker St.
Broderick St.
Divisadero St.
Masonic Ave.
Presidio Ave.
Ashbury St.
Hayes St.
Fell St.
Panhandle
Oak St.
Page St.
Scott St.
Pierce St.
Steiner St.
Fillmore St.
Page St.
Webster St.
HAIGHT-ASHBURY
Lyon St.
Haight St.
Waller St.
Carmelita St.
Potomac St.
Germania St.
Herman St.
Lloyd St.
Alpine Ter.
Duboce Park
Duboce Ave.
Waller St.
Ashbury St.
Grateful Dead House
Spreckels Mansion
Buena Vista Ave. East
Buena Vista Ter.
Reservoir St.
Belcher St.
Walter St.
14th St.
Frederick St.
Delmar St.
Roosevelt Way
Castro St.
Noe St.
Market St.
Church St.
Landers St.
15th St.
Corona Heights Playground
16th St.
Sanchez St.
17th St.
17th St.
Ford St.
THE CASTRO
18th St.
Market St.
18th St.
Hancock St.
Caselli St.
19thSt.
Dolores Park
Collingwood St.
Castro St.
20th St.
21st St.
22nd St.
NOE VALLEY
23rd St.
Market St.
Douglass St.
Eureka St.
Diamond St.
Noe St.
Jersey St.
Sanchez St.
Church St.
24th St.
Axford House
25th St.
Twin Peaks
0
350 M
0
1,000 ft

A colorful mosaic mural in the Castro

GAY NIGHTLIFE

Trax

BARS/PUBS | "Laid-back" would be an understatement. Once inside, you won't feel like you're in a gay bar—or in San Francisco. And that's the way the regulars like it. Cheap beer specials draw all types, and though you don't have to don your cruise wear for this place, it's still social. ✉ *1437 Haight St., between Masonic Ave. and Ashbury St., Haight* ☎ *415/864–4213.*

Performing Arts

SPOKEN WORD AND READINGS

Cafe International

READINGS/LECTURES | There's an open-mike session here every Friday night, where spoken-word performances are interspersed with acoustic musical acts. ✉ *508 Haight St., at Fillmore St., Haight* ☎ *415/552–7390.*

Shopping

Largely free of chain stores or big companies, Haight Street is *the* place to find high-quality vintage clothing, funky shoes, folk art from around the world, and used records and CDs.

BOOKS

Booksmith

BOOKS/STATIONERY | This fine bookshop sells current releases, children's titles, and offbeat periodicals. Authors passing through town often make a stop at this neighborhood institution. ✉ *1644 Haight St., between Cole and Clayton Sts., Haight* ☎ *415/863–8688* 🌐 *www.booksmith.com.*

Bound Together Bookstore

BOOKS/STATIONERY | This old-school collective, around since 1976, stocks books on anarchist theory and practice, as well as titles about gender issues, radicalism, and various left-leaning topics. A portion of the revenue supports anarchist projects and the Prisoners' Literature Project. ✉ *1369 Haight St.,* *between Masonic and Central Aves., Haight* ☎ *415/431–8355* 🌐 *boundtogetherbooks.wordpress.com.*

CLOTHING: MEN AND WOMEN

Buffalo Exchange

CLOTHING | Men and women can find fashionable, high-quality, used clothing at this national chain. Among the items: Levi's, leather jackets, sunglasses, and novelty jewelry. It's also known for its costume offerings and more offbeat items. ✉ *1555 Haight St., between Clayton and Ashbury Sts., Haight* ☎ *415/431–7733* 🌐 *www.buffaloexchange.com.*

Held Over

CLOTHING | The extensive collection of clothing from the 1920s through 1980s is organized by decade, saving those looking for flapper dresses from having to wade through lime-green polyester sundresses of the '70s. Shoes, hats, handbags, and jewelry complete the different looks. ✉ *1543 Haight St., between Ashbury and Clayton Sts., Haight* ☎ *415/864–0818.*

MUSIC

★ Amoeba Music

MUSIC STORES | With well over a million new and used CDs, DVDs, and records at bargain prices, this warehouselike offshoot of the Berkeley original carries titles you likely can't find on Amazon. No niche is ignored—from electronica and hip-hop to jazz and classical—and the stock changes frequently. **■ TIP→ Weekly in-store performances attract large crowds.** ✉ *1855 Haight St., between Stanyan and Shrader Sts., Haight* ☎ *415/831–1200* 🌐 *www.amoeba.com.*

SHOES

John Fluevog

SHOES/LUGGAGE/LEATHER GOODS | The trendy but sturdily made footwear for men and women is among the best in the city. Club girls go gaga over the wacky heels, handing over a pretty penny. They have another small store near Union Square, at 253 Grant Avenue. ✉ *1697 Haight St., near Cole St., Haight* ☎ *415/436–9784* 🌐 *www.fluevog.com.*

The Castro

The brash and sassy Castro district—the social, political, and cultural center of San Francisco's thriving gay (and, to a much lesser extent, lesbian) community—stands at the western end of Market Street. This neighborhood is one of the city's liveliest and most welcoming, especially on weekends. Streets teem with folks out shopping, pushing political causes, heading to art films, and lingering in bars and cafés. It's also one of the city's most expensive neighborhoods to live in, with an influx of tech money exacerbating an identity crisis that's been simmering for a couple of decades. But you'll still see hard-bodied men in painted-on T-shirts cruising the cutting-edge clothing and novelty stores, and pairs of all genders and sexual persuasions hold hands. Brightly painted, intricately restored Victorians line the streets here, making the Castro a good place to view striking examples of the architecture San Francisco is famous for.

Sights

★ Castro Theatre

ARTS VENUE | Here's a classic way to join in a beloved Castro tradition: grab some popcorn and catch a flick at this 1,500-seat art-deco theater; built in 1922, it's the grandest of San Francisco's few remaining movie palaces. The neon marquee, which stands at the top of the Castro strip, is the neighborhood's great landmark. The Castro was the fitting host of 2008's red-carpet preview of Gus Van Sant's film *Milk*, starring Sean Penn as openly gay San Francisco supervisor Harvey Milk. The theater's elaborate Spanish baroque interior

The Early Days of Gay San Francisco

San Francisco's gay community has been a part of the city since its earliest days. As a port city and a major hub during the 19th-century gold rush, San Francisco became known for its sexual openness along with all of its other liberalities. But a major catalyst for the rise of a gay community was World War II.

Stationed in San Francisco

During the war, hundreds of thousands of servicemen cycled through "Sodom by the Sea," and for most, San Francisco's permissive atmosphere was an eye-opening experience. The army's "off-limits" lists of forbidden establishments unintentionally (but effectively) pointed the way to the city's gay bars. When soldiers were dishonorably discharged for homosexual activity, many stayed on.

Making the City Home

Scores of these newcomers found homes in what was then called Eureka Valley. When the war ended, the predominantly Irish-Catholic families in that neighborhood began to move out, heading for the 'burbs. The new arrivals snapped up the Victorians on the main drag, Castro Street.

Beginning of the Movement

The establishment pushed back. In the 1950s, San Francisco's police chief vowed to crack down on "perverts," and the city's gay, lesbian, bisexual, and transgender residents lived in fear of getting caught in police raids. (Arrest meant being outed in the morning paper.) But harassment helped galvanize the community. The Daughters of Bilitis lesbian organization was founded in the city in 1955; the gay male Mattachine Society, started in Los Angeles in 1950, followed suit with a San Francisco branch.

The Tide Begins to Turn

By the mid-1960s these clashing interests gave the growing gay population a national profile. The police upped their policy of harassment but overplayed their hand. In 1965 they dramatically raided a New Year's benefit event, and the tide of public opinion began to turn. The police were forced to appoint the first-ever liaison to the gay community. Local gay organizations began to lobby openly. As one gay participant noted, "We didn't go back into the woodwork."

The 1970s and Harvey Milk

The 1970s—thumping disco, raucous street parties, and gay bashing—were a tumultuous time for the gay community. Thousands from across the country flocked to San Francisco's gay scene. Eureka Valley had more than 60 gay bars, the bathhouse scene in SoMa (where the leather crowd held court) was thriving, and graffiti around town read "Save San Francisco—Kill a Fag." When the Eureka Valley Merchants Association refused to admit gay-owned businesses in 1974, camera shop owner Harvey Milk founded the Castro Valley Association, and the neighborhood's new moniker was born. Milk was elected to the city's Board of Supervisors in 1977, its first openly gay official (and the inspirational figure for the Oscar-winning film *Milk*).

is fairly well preserved. Before many shows the theater's pipe organ rises from the orchestra pit and an organist plays pop and movie tunes, usually ending with the Jeanette McDonald standard "San Francisco" (go ahead, sing along). The crowd can be enthusiastic and vocal, talking back to the screen as loudly as it talks to them. Flicks such as *Who's Afraid of Virginia Woolf?* take on a whole new life, with the assembled beating the actors to the punch and fashioning even snappier comebacks for Elizabeth Taylor. There are often family-friendly sing-alongs to classics like *Mary Poppins*, as well as the occasional niche film festival. ✉ *429 Castro St., Castro* ☎ *415/621–6120* 🌐 *www.castrotheatre.com.*

GLBT Historical Society Museum

MUSEUM | The small, two-gallery Gay, Lesbian, Bisexual, and Transgender (GLBT) Historical Society Museum, the first of its kind in the United States, presents multimedia exhibits from its vast holdings covering San Francisco's queer history. In the main gallery, you might hear the audiotape Harvey Milk made for the community in the event of his assassination; explore artifacts from "Gayborhoods," lost landmarks of the city's gay past; or flip through a memory book with pictures and thoughts on some of the more than 20,000 San Franciscans lost to AIDS. Though certainly not for the faint of heart (those offended by sex toys and photos of lustily frolicking naked people may, well, be offended), the museum offers an inside look at these communities so integral to the fabric of San Francisco life. ✉ *4127 18th St., near Castro St., Castro* ☎ *415/621–1107* 🌐 *www.glbthistory.org* 🎫 *$5.*

Harvey Milk Plaza

HISTORIC SITE | An 18-foot-long rainbow flag, the symbol of gay pride, flies above this plaza named for the man who electrified the city in 1977 by being elected to its Board of Supervisors as an openly gay candidate. In the early 1970s Milk had opened a camera store on the block of Castro Street between 18th and 19th Streets. The store became the center for his campaign to open San Francisco's social and political life to gays and lesbians.

The liberal Milk hadn't served a full year of his term before he and Mayor George Moscone, also a liberal, were shot in November 1978 at City Hall. The murderer was a conservative ex-supervisor named Dan White, who had recently resigned his post and then became enraged when Moscone wouldn't reinstate him. Milk and White had often been at odds on the board, and White thought Milk had been part of a cabal to keep him from returning to his post. Milk's assassination shocked the gay community, which became infuriated when the infamous "Twinkie defense"—that junk food had led to diminished mental capacity—resulted in a manslaughter verdict for White. During the so-called White Night Riot of May 21, 1979, gays and their allies stormed City Hall, torching its lobby and several police cars.

Sister Act!

If you're lucky enough to happen upon a cluster of cheeky overdressed nuns while in the Castro, meet the legendary Sisters of Perpetual Indulgence. They're decked out in white face-paint, glitter, and fabulous jewels. Renowned for their wit and charity fund-raising bashes, the Sisters—Sister MaryMae Himm, Sister Bella de Ball, Sister Flora Good Thyme, and the gang—are the pinnacle of Castro color.

Castro and Noe Walk

The Castro and Noe Valley are both neighborhoods that beg to be walked—or ambled through, really, without time pressure or an absolute destination. Hit the Castro first, beginning at **Harvey Milk Plaza** under the gigantic rainbow flag. If you're going on to Noe Valley, first head east down **Market Street** for the cafés, bistros, and shops, then go back to **Castro Street** and head south, past the glorious art-deco **Castro Theatre**, checking out boutiques and cafés along the way (Cliff's Variety, at 479 Castro Street, is a must). To tour Noe Valley, go east down **18th Street** to Church (at Dolores Park), and then either strap on your hiking boots and head south over the hill or hop the J–Church to **24th Street**, the center of this rambling neighborhood.

Milk, who had feared assassination, left behind a tape recording in which he urged the community to continue the work he had begun. His legacy is the high visibility of gay people throughout city government; a bust of him was unveiled at City Hall on his birthday in 2008, and the 2008 film *Milk* gives insight into his life. ✉ *Southwest corner of Castro and Market Sts., Castro.*

Pink Triangle Park

MEMORIAL | On a median near the Castro's huge rainbow flag stands this memorial to the gay people whom the Nazis forced to wear pink triangles. Fifteen triangular granite columns, one for every 1,000 gays, lesbians, bisexual, and transgender people estimated to have been killed during and after the Holocaust, stand in a grassy triangle—a reminder of the gay community's past and ongoing struggle for civil rights. ✉ *Corner of Market, Castro, and 17th Sts., Castro.*

Randall Museum

MUSEUM | **FAMILY** | One of the best things about visiting this free nature museum for kids may be its tremendous views of San Francisco. Younger kids who are still excited about petting a rabbit, touching a snakeskin, or seeing a live hawk will enjoy a trip here. The museum sits beneath a hill variously known as Red Rock, Museum Hill, and, correctly, Corona Heights; hike up the steep but short trail for great, unobstructed city views. ✉ *199 Museum Way, off Roosevelt Way, Castro* ☎ *415/554–9600* 🌐 *www.randallmuseum.org* 🎟 *Free.*

Restaurants

The Castro neighborhood, the epicenter of the city's gay community, is chockablock with restaurants and bars. Market Street between Church and Castro Streets is a great stretch for people-watching and café- or bistro-hopping.

Chow

$ | **AMERICAN** | **FAMILY** | This consistently popular and consciously unpretentious, funky-yet-savvy diner serves standards like hamburgers, pizzas, and spaghetti with meatballs, all treated with culinary respect. More budget-friendly than some of the area's other options, it has built its reputation on honest and approachable fare. **Known for:** diner-style food; good value; fresh ingredients.

$ Average main: $15 ✉ 215 Church St., Castro ☎ 415/552–2469 🌐 www.chow-foodbar.com.

Dinosaurs

$ | **VIETNAMESE** | Most folks think of the Tenderloin or the Richmond for Vietnamese sandwiches, but this small Castro storefront serves up exceptionally fresh bánh mì and rockin' spring rolls. Service is quick, and a couple of tables take in the scene on Market Street. **Known for:** bánh mì; vegetarian options; smoothies and iced coffee. $ *Average main: $8* ✉ *2275 Market St., near 16th St., Castro* ☎ *415/503–1421* 🌐 *eatdinosaurs.com.*

Frances

$$$ | **MODERN AMERICAN** | Still one of the hottest tickets in town, chef Melissa Perello's simple, sublime restaurant is a consummate date-night destination. Perello's seasonal California-French cooking is its own enduring love affair. **Known for:** seasonal menu; neighborhood gem; tough reservation. $ *Average main: $34* ✉ *3870 17th St., Castro* ☎ *415/621–3870* 🌐 *www.frances-sf.com* ⏲ *Closed Mon. No lunch.*

Woodhouse Fish Co.

$$ | **SEAFOOD** | **FAMILY** | New Englanders hungry for a lobster roll fix need look no further than this super-friendly spot, where the rolls are utterly authentic and accompanied with slaw and fries. Seafood fans will find plenty else to love on the menu, which is stocked with everything from cioppino to crab melts. **Known for:** fresh seafood; dollar oysters on Tuesday; legendary lobster roll. $ *Average main: $19* ✉ *2073 Market St., Castro* ☎ *415/437–2722* 🌐 *www.woodhousefish.com.*

Nightlife

The gay district is as outrageous as one might expect, if not more so. Leather daddies, costumed club kids, and those who defy recently passed "no nudity" laws are among the characters you'll stumble across day or night. The party never seems to stop at popular Badlands.

BARS

Blackbird

BARS/PUBS | This neighborhood hangout tries too hard to be hip and cool, but it's a lot of fun. The crowd is less casual than others in the Castro, though no one will judge you for wearing Chuck Taylors. Blackbird serves up a good selection of craft beers, along with seasonal cocktails. ✉ *2124 Market St., at Church St., Castro* ☎ *415/503–0630* 🌐 *www.blackbirdbar.com.*

Lucky 13

BARS/PUBS | Greasers, hipsters, Betty Page wannabes, anyone looking for a good beer in the Castro, and assorted other patrons make Lucky 13 a fun place indeed. The drink prices are reasonable, the beer selection is huge, and the jukebox is well-stocked with something for everyone. The best seats are upstairs overlooking the crowd. Bring cash, they don't accept credit cards. ✉ *2140 Market St., near Church St., Castro* ☎ *415/487–1313.*

GAY NIGHTLIFE

Badlands

BARS/PUBS | Shirts off! If a sweaty muscle sandwich sounds like your idea of a good time, head to Badlands, where serious party boys come to grind to throbbing music on a packed dance floor. The lines can be ridiculous on weekends; those in the know go on Wednesday or Thursday. Tight-teed patrons range from twenties to forties. ✉ *4121 18th St., between Castro and Collingwood Sts., Castro* ☎ *415/626–9320* 🌐 *www.sfbadlands.com.*

The Café

BARS/PUBS | Always comfortable and often packed with a mixed gay, lesbian, and straight crowd, this is a place where you can dance to house or disco music, shoot pool, or meet guys in their

Gay and Lesbian Nightlife

In the days before the gay liberation movement, bars were more than mere watering holes—they also served as community centers where members of a mostly underground minority could network and socialize. In the 1960s the bars became hotbeds of political activity; by the 1970s other social opportunities had become available to gay men and lesbians, and the bars' importance as centers of activity decreased.

Old-timers may wax nostalgic about the vibrancy of pre-AIDS, 1970s bar life, but you can still have plenty of fun. The one difference is the one-night-a-week operation of some of the best clubs, which may cater to a different (sometimes straight) clientele on other nights. This type of club tends to come and go, so it's best to pick up one of the two main gay papers to check the latest happenings.

Bay Area Reporter. The weekly *Bay Area Reporter* covers gay and lesbian events in its entertainment pages and calendar and has a nightlife website (🌐 *www.ebar.com*).

San Francisco Bay Times. The biweekly *Bay Times* (🌐 *www.sfbaytimes.com*) runs features and extensive calendar listings of lesbian and gay events.

For a place known as a gay mecca, San Francisco has always suffered from a surprising drought of lesbian bars. The Café is probably the most lesbian-friendly Castro bar, though you'll find queer gals (and many more queer guys) at the Mint and Q Bar, too.

twenties at the bar. The outdoor deck—a rarity—makes it a favorite destination for smokers. There's a small weekend cover; expect a line to get in. ✉ *2369 Market St., near 17th St., Castro* ☎ *415/779–3171* 🌐 *www.cafesf.com.*

Midnight Sun

BARS/PUBS | One of the Castro's longest-running bars is popular with the polo-shirt-and-khakis crowd and has giant video screens playing the latest music videos, as well as episodes of shows like *Will and Grace* and *Queer Eye*. ✉ *4067 18th St., at Castro St., Castro* ☎ *415/861–4186* 🌐 *midnightsunsf.com.*

Moby Dick

BARS/PUBS | A quintessential neighborhood watering hole outfitted with a pool table and pinball machines has TV screens playing pop videos and music. A giant fish tank sits over the bar, giving shy types a place to rest their gaze while taking a shot of liquid courage. Casually dressed couples and guys with nothing to prove frequent this place, but there's pickup potential, too. Like many smaller dive bars, it's cash only. ✉ *4049 18th St., at Hartford St., Castro* ☎ *415/294–0731.*

Pilsner Inn

BARS/PUBS | Casual and comfortable—yet still hip and cruise-y—this is the type of neighborhood joint you quickly claim as your own. Kick back with a pint on the fantastic year-round patio (it's covered), and enjoy eye candy of the thirtysomething variety (ranging from conservative yuppie guys to Mission emo boys). Pilsner Inn is technically a sports bar, which means it has a pool table and TVs tuned to local games. ✉ *225 Church St., at Market St., Castro* ☎ *415/621–7058* 🌐 *www.pilsnerinn.com.*

Performing Arts

DANCE

RAWdance CONCEPT Series

DANCE | A modern-day salon is made for both dance aficionados and those just ballet-curious. The semiregular series takes place in a small and awkward space, but it's perfect for making new friends. The choreography is colorful and "outside the lines" of your usual dance troupe. In true bohemian spirit, admission is pay-what-you-can, and sometimes food is served as well. ✉ *105 Sanchez St., Haight* ☎ *415/686–0728* 🌐 *www.rawdance.org.*

Shopping

The neighborhood that's often called the gay capital of the world is also a major shopping destination for all travelers. It's filled with men's clothing boutiques and home-accessories stores. And if you're looking for something kitschy to shock your Aunt Martha back home, you've come to the right place.

CLOTHING

Rolo

CLOTHING | Selling hard-to-find men's denim, sportswear, shoes, and accessories with a distinct European influence, this store includes clothes designed by Fred Perry, Eton, and Tre Noir. There's another location in SoMa at 1301 Howard Street. ✉ *2351 Market St., near Castro St., Castro* ☎ *415/431–4545* 🌐 *www.rolo.com.*

JEWELRY AND COLLECTIBLES

Brand X Antiques

JEWELRY/ACCESSORIES | The vintage jewelry, mostly from the early part of the 20th century, includes a wide selection of estate pieces and objets d'art. With rings that range in price from $5 to a couple thousand, there's something for everyone. Hours can vary, so it's best to call ahead before visiting. ✉ *570 Castro St., between 18th and 19th Sts., Castro* ☎ *415/626–8908.*

Noey Valley

There's no better way to stick out like a sore thumb/tourist than to mispronounce the Noe Valley as "No" Valley. Look like a local and pronounce it "NOH -ee" Valley.

Noe Valley

This upscale but relaxed enclave just south of the Castro is among the city's most desirable places to live, with laid-back cafés, kid-friendly restaurants, and comfortable, old-time shops along Church Street and 24th Street, its main thoroughfares. You can also see remnants of Noe Valley's agricultural beginnings: Billy Goat Hill (at Castro and 30th Streets), a wild-grass hill often draped in fog and topped by one of the city's best rope-swinging trees, is named for the goats that grazed here right into the 20th century.

Sights

Golden fire hydrant

LOCAL INTEREST | When all the other fire hydrants went dry during the fire that followed the 1906 earthquake, this one kept pumping. Noe Valley and the Mission District were thus spared the devastation wrought elsewhere in the city, which explains the large number of prequake homes here. Every year on April 18 (the anniversary of the quake), folks gather here to share stories about the earthquake, and the famous hydrant gets a fresh coat of gold paint. ✉ *Church and 20th Sts., southeastern corner, across from Dolores Park, Noe Valley.*

Off the Beaten Path

Twin Peaks. Windswept and desolate Twin Peaks yields sweeping vistas of San Francisco and the neighboring East and North Bay counties. You can get a real feel for the city's layout here, but you'll share it with busloads of other admirers; in summer, arrive before the late-afternoon fog turns the view into pea soup. To drive here, head west from Castro Street up Market Street, which eventually becomes Portola Drive. Turn right (north) on Twin Peaks Boulevard and follow the signs to the top. Muni Bus 37–Corbett heads west to Twin Peaks from Market Street. Catch this bus above the Castro Street Muni light-rail station on the island west of Castro at Market Street. ✉ *Noe Valley.*

Restaurants

Barney's Gourmet Hamburgers
$ | AMERICAN | FAMILY | The Noe Valley location of this family-friendly California burger chain offers a cozy indoor-outdoor dining area, the latter really a patio encased in glass windows for watching foot traffic along 24th Street. The menu is loaded with fancier versions of diner classics—think the "gastropub" burger with a fried egg, blackened potato chips, and a pretzel bun, or the "maui waui," with a teriyaki glaze and grilled pineapple. **Known for:** diverse menu selection; vegetarian options; milk shakes. $ *Average main: $14* ✉ *4138 24th St., near Castro St., Noe Valley* ☎ *415/282–7770* 🌐 *www.barneyshamburgers.com.*

★ **La Ciccia**
$$$ | ITALIAN | This charming neighborhood trattoria is the only restaurant in the city exclusively serving Sardinian food. The island's classics are all represented—octopus stew in a spicy tomato sauce; spaghetti with *bottariga* (cured roe); and macaroni with sea urchin and cured tuna heart. **Known for:** Sardinian food; industry favorite; extensive wine list. $ *Average main: $28* ✉ *291 30th St., at Church St., Noe Valley* ☎ *415/550–8114* 🌐 *www.laciccia.com* ⏲ *Closed Sun. and Mon. No lunch.*

Shopping

Just south of the Castro on 24th Street, largely residential Noe Valley is an enclave of fancy-food stores, bookshops, women' and children's clothing boutiques, and specialty gift stores.

BOOKS

Omnivore Books on Food
BOOKS/STATIONERY | Love to eat? Love to read? Then this place is paradise. The shelves are bursting with books on growing and cooking food. The store stocks cookbooks on such diverse subjects as colonial Jamaican and Victorian England cuisine or 1940s creole cooking. And if you're after a signed first edition by Julia Child or James Beard, you'll find that, too. ✉ *3885 Cesar Chavez St., at Church St., Noe Valley* ☎ *415/282–4712* 🌐 *www.omnivorebooks.com.*

CLOTHING

Ambiance

CLOTHING | A well-loved destination for fashion-conscious locals, this is a fun place to find 1920s-inspired dresses, velvet scarves, and dangling silver jewelry. The store has some jaw-dropping sales. There are additional locations on Union, Haight, and Irving Streets. ✉ *3979 24th St., between Sanchez and Noe Sts., Noe Valley* ☎ *415/647–5800* 🌐 *www.ambiancesf.com.*

Small Frys

CLOTHING | **FAMILY** | The colorful cottons carried here are mainly for infants, with some articles for older children. Brands include many Californian and French labels, including Petite Lem, Kanz, and Pommes. There's a sizable section of San Francisco-theme gear and books, and a few shelves of organic and eco-friendly toys as well as whimsical finger puppets round out the selection. ✉ *3985 24th St., near Noe St., Noe Valley* ☎ *415/648–3954* 🌐 *www.smallfrys.com.*

Two Birds

CLOTHING | A fresh place to find a lacy top or a soft pair of jeans, Two Birds stocks Freda Salvador, Ulla Johnson, and Smythe. Staying in touch with their city roots, owners Susanna Taylor and Audrey Yang carry sleek jewelry, handbags, and dresses by local designers, too. ✉ *1309 Castro St., between Jersey and 24th Sts., Noe Valley* ☎ *415/285–1840* 🌐 *www.2birds1store.com.*

FURNITURE, HOUSEWARES, AND GIFTS

Wink SF

GIFTS/SOUVENIRS | Cards, toasters, aprons, books, candles, and a wide selection of SF-theme items line the shelves. You'll also find fridge magnets, wisdom-spouting bags, and bakery-shape pencil erasers. And if you've misplaced your water bottle, the shop stocks a rainbow of colors. ✉ *4107 24th St., at Castro St., Noe Valley* ☎ *415/401–8881* 🌐 *www.winksf.com.*

HANDICRAFTS AND FOLK ART

Xela Imports

JEWELRY/ACCESSORIES | Africa, Southeast Asia, Europe, and Central America are the sources for the handicrafts sold at Xela (pronounced *shay*-la). They include jewelry, masks, religious icons, and decorative wall hangings. ✉ *3925 24th St., between Sanchez and Noe Sts., Noe Valley* ☎ *415/695–1323* 🌐 *xelaimports.com.*

Chapter 12

MISSION DISTRICT, DOGPATCH, BERNAL HEIGHTS, AND POTRERO HILL

Updated by
Denise M. Leto

Sights	Restaurants	Hotels	Shopping	Nightlife
★★☆☆☆	★★★★★	☆☆☆☆☆	★★★☆☆	★★★★★

NEIGHBORHOOD SNAPSHOT

TOP REASONS TO GO

■ **Bar-hop:** Embrace your inner (or not-so-inner) hipster. Grab a cocktail at Trick Dog, whose mixologists mix up some of the Mission's finest drinks, then peruse the highball menu at the retro-chic Beehive or stop by the Chapel, where live music often accompanies the cocktails.

■ **Chow down on phenomenal, cheap ethnic food:** Keen appetites and thin wallets will meet their match here. Just try to decide between deliciously fresh burritos, garlicky falafel, thin-crust pizza, savory samosas, and more.

■ **One-of-a-kind shopping:** Barter for buried treasure at 826 Valencia and its Pirate Supply Store, then hop next door and say hello to the giraffe's head at the mad taxidermy–cum–garden store hodgepodge that is Paxton Gate.

■ **Vivid murals:** Check out dozens of energetic, colorful public artworks in alleyways and on building exteriors.

■ **Hang out in Dolores Park:** Join Mission locals and their dogs on this hilly expanse of green that has a glorious view of downtown and, if you're lucky, the Bay Bridge. On sunny days the whole neighborhood comes out to play.

PLANNING YOUR TIME

A walk that includes Mission Dolores and the neighborhood's murals takes about two hours. If you plan to go on a mural walk with the Precita Eyes organization, or if you're a window-shopper, add at least another hour. The Mission is a neighborhood that sleeps in. In the afternoon and evening, the main drags—Mission, Valencia, and 24th Streets—really come to life.

From Sunday through Tuesday it's relatively quiet here, especially in the evening—a great time to get a café table with no wait. Dogpatch is liveliest during the week, midday to evening, when businesses are hopping. On weekends, this neighborhood relaxes at home.

GETTING THERE

■ After climbing the hills downtown, you'll find the Mission to be welcomingly flat. BART's two Mission District stations drop you right in the heart of the action. Get off at 16th Street for Mission Dolores and the shopping, nightlife, and restaurants of the Valencia Corridor or 24th Street to see the neighborhood murals and the increasingly trendy Calle 24 district. Parking can be a drag, especially on weekend evenings. If you're heading out in the evening, take a taxi. Dogpatch is well served by the T-Third Muni line, and the 22nd Street Caltrain station is nearby.

The Mission has a number of distinct personalities: it's the Latino neighborhood, where working-class folks raise their families and where gangs occasionally clash; it's the hipster hood, where tattooed and pierced twenty- and thirtysomethings hold court in the coolest cafés and bars in town; it's a culinary epicenter, with the strongest concentration of destination restaurants and affordable ethnic cuisine; it's the face of gentrification, where high-tech money prices out longtime commercial and residential renters; and it's the artists' quarter, where murals adorn literally blocks of walls long after the artists have moved to cheaper digs.

It's also the city's equivalent of the Sunshine State—this neighborhood's always the last to succumb to fog. The Mission has ceded the title of neighborhood with the most buzz to Dogpatch, another flat swath on the far side of Potrero Hill. Here artists and industry share space, restaurants draw diners from far-flung neighborhoods, and the city's largest stock of houses that survived the 1906 quake surround a thriving commercial strip with creative flair.

Mission District

Packed with destination restaurants, hole-in-the-wall ethnic eateries, and hip watering holes—plus taquerías, pupuserías, and produce markets—one of the city's hottest hoods strikes an increasingly precarious balance between cutting-edge hot spot and working-class enclave. With longtime businesses being forced out by astronomical rents and city agencies coming together with community groups to create an action plan to

Did You Know?

San Francisco is chockablock with murals—around 2,000—and the Mission District is the epicenter of all the artistic fervor.

reverse gentrification in the neighborhood, the Mission is in flux once again, a familiar state for almost 100 years.

The eight blocks of Valencia Street between 16th and 24th Streets—what's become known as the Valencia Corridor—typify the Mission District's diversity. Businesses on the block between 16th and 17th Streets, for instance, include an upscale Peruvian restaurant, a tattoo parlor, a Belgian eatery beloved for its fries, the yuppie-chic bar Blondie's, a handful of funky home-decor stores, a pizzeria, a Vietnamese kitchen, a trendy Italian place, a sushi bar, bargain and pricey thrift shops, and the Puerto Alegre restaurant, a near dive with pack-a-punch margaritas locals revere. As prices rise, this strip has lost some of its edge as even international publications proclaim its hipness. At the same time, nearby Mission Street is morphing from a down-at-the-heels row of check-cashing parlors, dollar stores, and residential hotels into overflow for the Valencia Corridor's restaurant explosion. Meanwhile, 24th Street has become the Calle 24 Latino Cultural District in an attempt to protect the mostly Latino-owned businesses that have served this thriving neighborhood for decades.

Italian and Irish in the early 20th century, the Mission became heavily Latino in the late 1960s, when immigrants from Mexico and Central America began arriving. Since the 1970s, groups of muralists have transformed walls and storefronts into canvases, creating art accessible to everyone. Following the example set by the Mexican liberal artist and muralist Diego Rivera, many of the Latino artists address political and social justice issues in their murals. More recently, artists of varied backgrounds, some of whom simply like to paint on a large scale, have expanded the conversation.

The actual conversations you'll hear on the street these days might unfold in Chinese, Vietnamese, Arabic, and other tongues of the non-Latino immigrants who began settling in the Mission in the 1980s and 1990s, along with a young bohemian crowd enticed by cheap rents and the burgeoning arts-and-nightlife scene. These newer arrivals made a diverse and lively neighborhood even more so, setting the stage for the Mission's current hipster cachet. With the neighborhood flourishing, rents have gone through the roof, but the Mission remains scruffy in patches, so as you plan your explorations, take into account your comfort zone.

■ TIP→ **Be prepared for homelessness and drug use around the BART stations, prostitution along Mission Street, and raucous bar-hoppers along the Valencia Corridor. The farther east you go, the sketchier the neighborhood gets.**

Sights

Balmy Alley murals

PUBLIC ART | Mission District artists have transformed the walls of their neighborhood with paintings, and Balmy Alley is one of the best-executed examples. Many murals adorn the one-block alley, with newer ones continually filling in the blank spaces. In 1971, artists began teaming with local children to create a space to promote peace in Central America, community spirit, and (later) AIDS awareness; since then dozens of artists have added their vibrant works. ⚠ **Be alert here: the 25th Street end of the alley adjoins a somewhat dangerous area.** ✉ *24th St. between and parallel to Harrison and Treat Sts., alley runs south to 25th St., Mission District.*

Clarion Alley murals

PUBLIC ART | Inspired by the work in Balmy Alley, a new generation of muralists began creating a fresh alley-cum-gallery here in 1992. The works by the loosely connected artists of the Clarion Alley Mural Project (CAMP) represent a broad range of styles and imagery, such as an exuberant, flowery exhortation to Tax the

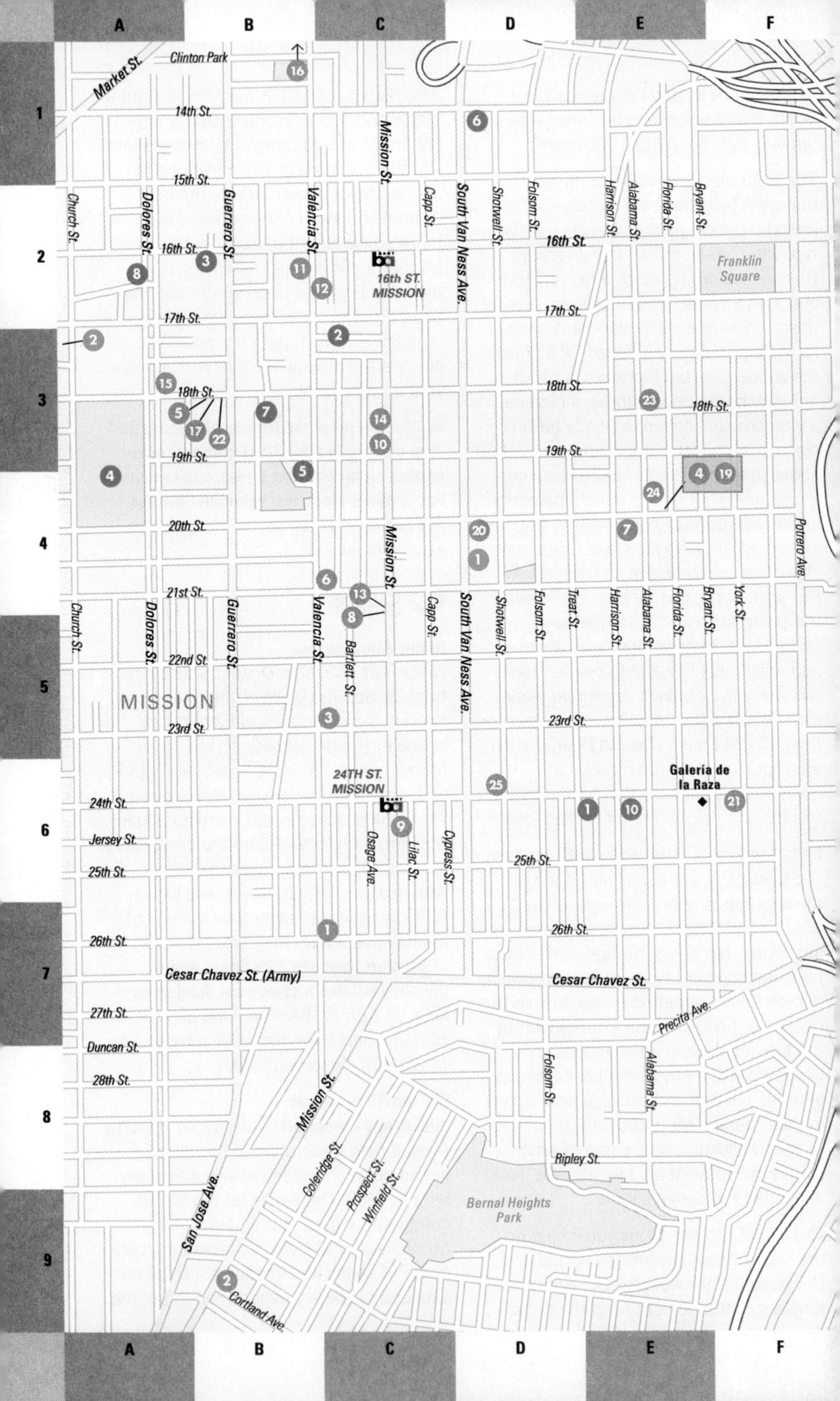

A
B
C
D
E
F
1
2
3
4
5
6
7
8
9
Market St.
Clinton Park
14th St.
15th St.
16th St.
17th St.
18th St.
19th St.
20th St.
21st St.
22nd St.
23rd St.
24th St.
Jersey St.
25th St.
26th St.
Cesar Chavez St. (Army)
27th St.
Duncan St.
28th St.
Church St.
Dolores St.
Guerrero St.
Valencia St.
Mission St.
Capp St.
South Van Ness Ave.
Shotwell St.
Folsom St.
Harrison St.
Alabama St.
Florida St.
Bryant St.
Franklin Square
16th ST. MISSION
24TH ST. MISSION
Bartlett St.
Osage Ave.
Lilac St.
Cypress St.
Treat St.
York St.
Potrero Ave.
MISSION
Galería de la Raza
Cesar Chavez St.
Precita Ave.
Ripley St.
Bernal Heights Park
San Jose Ave.
Coleridge St.
Prospect St.
Winfield St.
Cortland Ave.

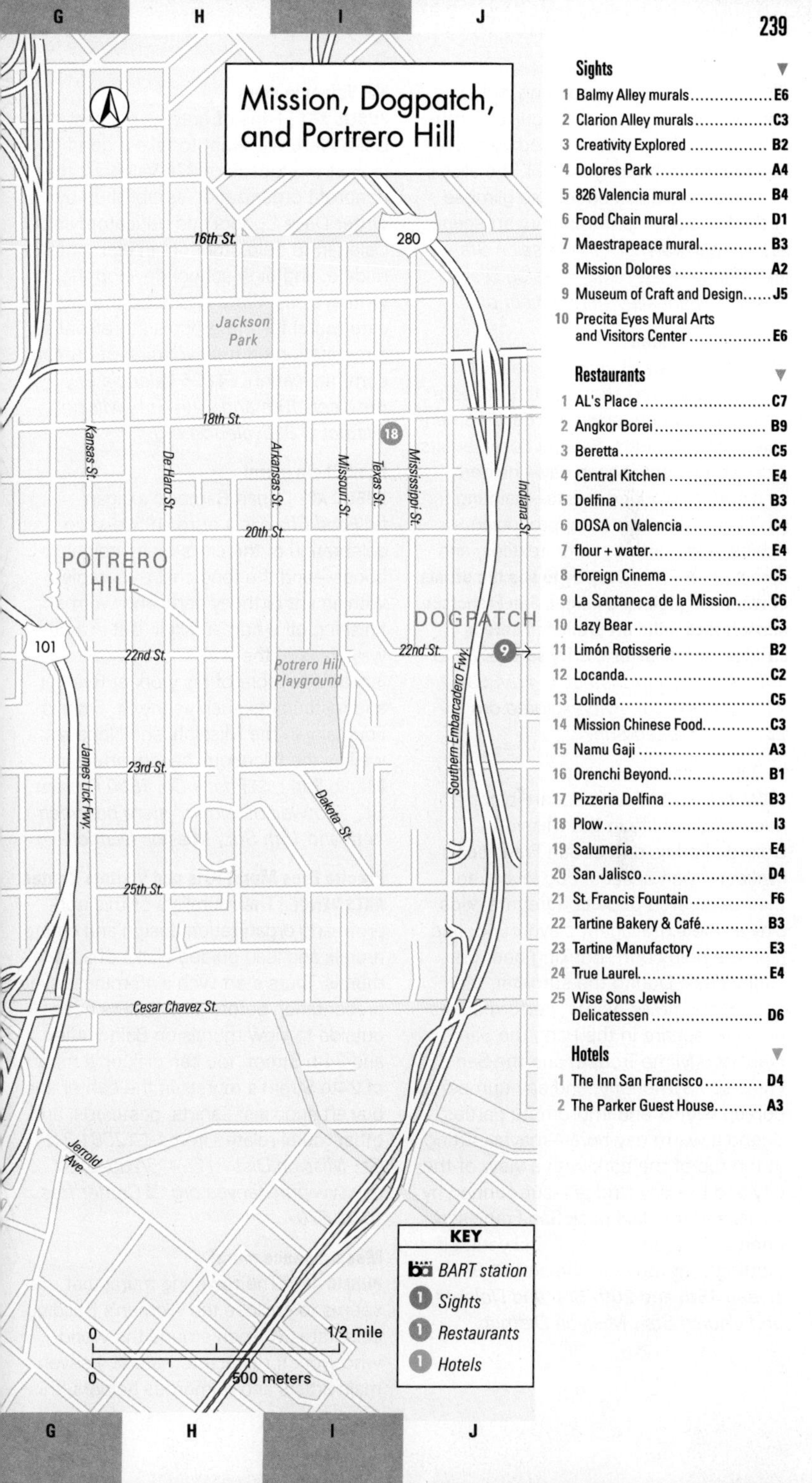

Sights

1 Balmy Alley murals....E6
2 Clarion Alley murals....C3
3 Creativity Explored....B2
4 Dolores Park....A4
5 826 Valencia mural....B4
6 Food Chain mural....D1
7 Maestrapeace mural....B3
8 Mission Dolores....A2
9 Museum of Craft and Design....J5
10 Precita Eyes Mural Arts and Visitors Center....E6

Restaurants

1 AL's Place....C7
2 Angkor Borei....B9
3 Beretta....C5
4 Central Kitchen....E4
5 Delfina....B3
6 DOSA on Valencia....C4
7 flour + water....E4
8 Foreign Cinema....C5
9 La Santaneca de la Mission....C6
10 Lazy Bear....C3
11 Limón Rotisserie....B2
12 Locanda....C2
13 Lolinda....C5
14 Mission Chinese Food....C3
15 Namu Gaji....A3
16 Orenchi Beyond....B1
17 Pizzeria Delfina....B3
18 Plow....I3
19 Salumeria....E4
20 San Jalisco....D4
21 St. Francis Fountain....F6
22 Tartine Bakery & Café....B3
23 Tartine Manufactory....E3
24 True Laurel....E4
25 Wise Sons Jewish Delicatessen....D6

Hotels

1 The Inn San Francisco....D4
2 The Parker Guest House....A3

Rich, and a lesbian celebration including donkey heads, skirts, and Donald Trump with hair of flames bookended by a white hooded figure holding a gavel. The alley's murals offer a quick but dense glimpse at the Mission's contemporary art scene. ✉ *Between Valencia and Mission Sts. and 17th and 18th Sts., Mission District* 🌐 *www.clarionalleymuralproject.org.*

Creativity Explored

COLLEGE | Joyous, if chaotic, creativity pervades the workshops of this art-education center and gallery for developmentally disabled adults. Several dozen adults work at the center each day—guided by a staff of working artists—painting, working in the darkroom, producing videos, and crafting prints, textiles, and ceramics. **TIP→ Drop by to see the artists at work and pick up a unique San Francisco masterpiece—the art produced here is striking, and some of it is for sale.** ✉ *3245 16th St., Mission District* ☎ *415/863–2108* 🌐 *www.creativityexplored.org* 🎫 *Free* ⏲ *Closed Sun.*

★ **Dolores Park**

LOCAL INTEREST | A two-square-block microcosm of life in the Mission, Dolores Park is one of San Francisco's liveliest green spaces: dog lovers and their pampered pups congregate, kids play at the extravagant playground, and hipsters hold court, drinking beer on sunny days. During the summer, the park hosts movie nights; performances by Shakespeare in the Park, the San Francisco Mime Troupe, and the San Francisco Symphony; and any number of pop-up events and impromptu parties. Spend a warm day here—maybe sitting at the top of the park with a view of the city and the Bay Bridge—surrounded by locals and that laid-back San Francisco energy, and you may well find yourself plotting your move to the city. ✉ *Between 18th and 20th Sts. and Dolores and Church Sts., Mission District.*

826 Valencia mural

PUBLIC ART | Fans of graphic novelist Chris Ware will want to take a good look at the facade of 826 Valencia, the nonprofit organization established by writer Dave Eggers and educator Nínive Calegari to help students in elementary, middle, and high school develop their writing skills. Ware designed the intricate mural for the group's storefront as a meditation on the evolution of human communication. ✉ *826 Valencia St., between 19th and 20th Sts., Mission District* 🌐 *826valencia.org.*

Food Chain mural

PUBLIC ART | Brian Barneclo's gigantic *Food Chain* is a retro, 1950s-style celebration of the city's many neighborhoods—and the food chain—complete with an ant birthday party and worms finishing off a human skull. But in a cute way. Fans of the well-known local muralist can see more of his work at Rye bar and restaurants such as the St. Francis Fountain, in the Mission, and Nopa (as well as the Facebook headquarters in Menlo Park). ✉ *Foods Co, 1800 Folsom St., Shotwell St. side of store between 14th and 15th Sts., Mission District.*

Precita Eyes Mural Arts and Visitors Center

ARTS VENUE | The muralists of this nonprofit arts organization design and create murals and lead guided walks of area murals. Tours start with a 45-minute slide presentation before participants head outside to view murals on Balmy Alley and 24th Street. You can pick up a map of 24th Street's murals at the center and buy art supplies, T-shirts, postcards, and other mural-related items. ✉ *2981 24th St., Mission District* ☎ *415/285–2287* 🌐 *www.precitaeyes.org* 🎫 *Center free, tours $20.*

Maestrapeace mural

PUBLIC ART | The towering mural that seems to enclose the Women's Building celebrates women around the world who work for peace. Created by seven main artists and numerous helpers, this

Vivid public art provides a backdrop for the Mission District.

is one of the city's don't-miss murals. If the building's open, you can pick up a key to the mural's figures and symbols and mural T-shirts and souvenirs. ✉ *Women's Bldg., 3543 18th St., between Valencia and Guerrero Sts., Mission District* ☎ *415/431–1180* 🌐 *womensbuilding.org.*

Mission Dolores

RELIGIOUS SITE | Two churches stand side by side here, including the small adobe **Mission San Francisco de Asís,** which, along with the Presidio's Officers' Club, is the oldest standing structure in San Francisco. Completed in 1791, it's the sixth of the 21 California missions founded by Franciscan friars in the 18th and early 19th centuries. Its ceiling depicts original Ohlone Indian basket designs, executed in vegetable dyes. The tiny chapel includes frescoes and a hand-painted wooden altar.

There's a hidden treasure here, too, a mural forgotten and rediscovered over more than 200 years. In 2004 an archaeologist and an artist crawled along the ceiling's rafters and opened a trapdoor behind the altar in an attempt to finally document the mission's original mural, painted with natural dyes by Native Americans in 1791. The centuries have taken their toll, so the team photographed the 20-by-22-foot mural and began digitally restoring the photographic version. Among the images is a dagger-pierced Sacred Heart of Jesus.

The small museum here covers the mission's founding and history, and the pretty little cemetery—which appears in Alfred Hitchcock's film *Vertigo*—contains the graves of mid-19th-century European immigrants. The remains of an estimated 5,000 Native Americans who died at the mission lie in unmarked graves. Services are held in both the old mission and next door in the handsome multidome basilica. ✉ *Dolores and 16th Sts., Mission District* ☎ *415/621–8203* 🌐 *www.missiondolores.org* 🎫 *Suggested donation $7.*

San Francisco on Film

With its spectacular cityscape, atmospheric fog, and a camera-ready iconic bridge, it's little wonder that San Francisco has been the setting for hundreds of films. While you're running around town, you might have the occasional sense of déjà vu, sparked by a scene from a Hitchcock or Clint Eastwood thriller. *Here are a few of the city's favorite cinematic sites:*

- *Zodiac*, a 2007 drama about a legendary Bay Area serial killer, filmed scenes at the real-life locations where victims were gunned down. It also re-created the *San Francisco Chronicle* offices, but down south in L.A.

- City Hall shows up in the Clint Eastwood cop thrillers *Dirty Harry* and *Magnum Force*, and is set aflame in the James Bond flick *A View to a Kill*. Its interior became a nightclub for Robin Williams's *Bicentennial Man* and a courthouse in *Tucker: The Man and His Dream*.

- Streets in Russian Hill, Potrero Hill, and North Beach were used for the supreme car-chase sequence in *Bullitt*. The namesake detective, played by Steve McQueen, lived in Nob Hill at 1153–57 Taylor Street. And the "King of Cool" did much of his own stunt driving, thank you very much.

- Brocklebank Apartments, at Mason and Sacramento Streets in Nob Hill, appears in several films, most notably as the posh residence of Kim Novak in Alfred Hitchcock's *Vertigo*. Other key *Vertigo* locations include the cemetery of Mission Dolores and the waterfront at Fort Point.

- The great Bogie-and-Bacall noir film *Dark Passage* revolves around the art-deco apartment building at 1360 Montgomery Street and the nearby Filbert Steps.

- Dashiell Hammett's *Thin Man* characters, Nick and Nora Charles, do much of their sleuthing in the city, especially in films like *After the Thin Man*, in which the base of Coit Tower stands in as the entrance to the Charles' home.

- North Beach's Tosca Café, at 242 Columbus Avenue, is the bar where Michael Douglas unwinds in *Basic Instinct*.

- The Hilton Hotel at 333 O'Farrell Street became the "Hotel Bristol," the scene of much of the mayhem caused by Barbra Streisand in *What's Up, Doc?*

- At 2640 Steiner Street in Pacific Heights is the elegant home that Robin Williams infiltrates while disguised as a nanny in *Mrs. Doubtfire*.

- The Castro of the 1970s comes alive in *Milk*, Gus Van Sant's film starring Sean Penn as slain San Francisco supervisor Harvey Milk.

- And, of course, there are plenty of movies about the notorious federal prison on Alcatraz Island, including Burt Lancaster's redemption drama *Birdman of Alcatraz*, Clint Eastwood's suspenseful *Escape from Alcatraz*, the goofy *So I Married an Axe Murderer*, and the Sean Connery and Nicolas Cage action flick, *The Rock*.

Restaurants

You'll never go hungry here, in San Francisco's most jam-packed restaurant neighborhood. From dirt-cheap taquerias to hip tapas joints, city dwellers know this sector as the go-to area for a great meal. The Valencia Street corridor has been particularly hot, opening new restaurants at a milestone pace, with many declaring this to be the best food neighborhood in the city.

AL's Place

$$ | **MODERN AMERICAN** | AL is chef Aaron London, and his place is a sunny, white-washed corner spot that serves inventive, Michelin-starred vegetable-forward cooking. London's menu changes frequently, but some dishes, like lightly cured trout and grits with seasonal produce, stick around, and the fries have a cult following. **Known for:** seasonal cooking; inventive vegetable-heavy menu; fries with cult following. *Average main: $18 1499 Valencia St., Mission 415/416–6136 www.alsplacesf.com Closed Mon. and Tues. No lunch.*

Angkor Borei

$ | **CAMBODIAN** | Lemongrass and softly sizzling chilies perfume this modest neighborhood favorite, opened by Cambodian refugees in the late 1980s. The menu includes an array of curries, salads of squid or cold noodles with ground fish, and lightly curried fish mousse cooked in a banana leaf basket, as well as plenty of vegetarian selections, but the friendly service can be languid, so don't stop here when you're in a hurry. **Known for:** Cambodian food; variety of curries; modest neighborhood vibe. *Average main: $11 3471 Mission St., Bernal Heights 415/550–8417 Closed Wed. No lunch Sun.*

Beretta

$$ | **ITALIAN** | A young crowd flocks to this perennially popular neighborhood favorite with a simple formula: excellent cocktails, affordable Italian food, and late dining until 1 am. The long room with tin ceiling and bare-wood tables is casual and smart but loud, the pizzas respect their Italian heritage (thin crusts, traditional and contemporary toppings), and the antipasti are an appealing mix of vegetables (cauliflower with capers), fish (a light fritto misto), and artisanal salumi . **Known for:** thin-crust pizza; excellent cocktails; lively and loud crowd. *Average main: $18 1199 Valencia St., Mission District 415/695–1199 www.berettasf.com No lunch weekdays.*

★ Central Kitchen

$$$ | **MODERN AMERICAN** | Californian cuisine in all of its freshness is on display in this offshoot of flour + water, where you might taste charred brussels sprouts with fermented scallions and fish sauce, or one of chef Thomas McNaughton's famous pastas. A planked-and-concrete tea-light strung courtyard, with a retractable awning, shares space with Salumeria (a deli and larder) and Trick Dog (an energetic cocktail bar). **Known for:** famous pasta dishes; family-style dining; pretty courtyard. *Average main: $24 3000 20th St., Mission District 415/826–7004 www.centralkitchensf.com No lunch.*

★ Delfina

$$$ | **ITALIAN** | Crowds are a constant fixture at Craig and Annie Stoll's cultishly adored Northern Italian spot, where aluminum-topped tables are squeezed into an urban interior, with hardwood floors and a tile bar that seems to radiate with happiness. Deceptively simple, exquisitely flavored dishes include the signature spaghetti with plum tomatoes and consistently great roast chicken, and the panna cotta is best in class. **Known for:** signature spaghetti with plum tomatoes; long waits; much-lauded panna cotta. *Average main: $24 3621 18th St., Mission District 415/552–4055 www.delfinasf.com No lunch.*

★ DOSA on Valencia

$$ | **INDIAN** | Aside from the large, thin savory namesake pancake, this cheerful temple of South Indian cuisine also prepares curries, *uttapam* (open-face pancakes), and various starters, breads, rice dishes, and chutneys. Dosa fillings range from traditional potatoes, onions, and cashews to green chilies and cilantro, and other popular menu options include mango fish curry, roasted masala lamb shank, and Indian street-food additions such as *vada pav* (a vegetarian slider). **Known for:** Southern Indian food; Indian street-food dishes; tasty curries. *Average main: $18 995 Valencia St., at 21st St., Mission District 415/642–3672 www.dosasf.com No lunch weekdays.*

flour + water

$$$ | **ITALIAN** | This handsome and boisterous hot spot with slate-gray walls, sturdy wooden tables, and a taxidermy cabinet in the bathroom is synonymous with pasta, though its blistery thin-crust Neapolitan pizzas are also top notch, but the grand experience here is the seven-course pasta-tasting menu (extra for wine pairings). The homemade rutabaga tortelli with candy cap mushrooms is a crowd-pleaser, as is the toasted sourdough rigatoni. **Known for:** difficult-to-get reservations; delicious pizzas and pastas; noisy scene. *Average main: $25 2401 Harrison St., Mission District 415/826–7000 www.flourandwater.com No lunch.*

Foreign Cinema

$$$ | **MODERN AMERICAN** | **FAMILY** | Classic films are projected on a wall in a large inner courtyard in this hip, loftlike space while you're served stellar seasonal California cooking, and weekend brunch brings throngs fighting for a spot on the patio for some of the city's best egg dishes and Bloody Marys. Avid filmgoers should keep in mind that the main event here is the food, such as perfectly shucked oysters on the half shell, warm brandade, house-cured sardines, bavette steak, and sesame fried chicken. **Known for:** seasonal and flavorful California cooking; date night; weekend brunch. *Average main: $30 2534 Mission St., Mission District 415/648–7600 www.foreigncinema.com No lunch weekdays.*

La Santaneca de la Mission

$ | **LATIN AMERICAN** | **FAMILY** | The El Salvadorans who live in the Mission head to this friendly, family-run place for *pupusas,* cornmeal rounds stuffed with meat, cheese, and beans. The kitchen also makes the more unusual rice-flour pupusa, as well as other dishes popular in Central America, including seafood soup, tamales, and *chicharrones* (fried pork skins) with yucca. **Known for:** classic Salvadoran fare; variety of pupusas; good value. *Average main: $7 2815 Mission St., Mission District 415/285–2131 No credit cards Closed Wed.*

Lazy Bear

$$$$ | **MODERN AMERICAN** | There's no end to the buzz around chef David Barzelay's 14-plus-course prix-fixe modern American dinners, which might include sweet pea custard lamb with dates, or charred onion broth with country ham. An ode to the Western lodge, the two-level dining room, which includes a fireplace, charred wood walls, wooden rafters, and tables made of American elm, hosts what is essentially a dinner party for 40, with cocktails and bites enjoyed upstairs and dinner downstairs at two communal tables. **Known for:** hot-ticket often resold; communal dining; dinner party setup. *Average main: $185 3416 19th St., Mission District 415/874–9921 www.lazybearsf.com Closed Sun. and Mon. No lunch.*

Limón Rotisserie

$$ | **PERUVIAN** | **FAMILY** | Cooks in Peru and Ecuador have long argued over which country invented ceviche, but most diners at Limón would probably line up with the Peruvians after eating the myriad delicious versions served here. Almost everything is served family-style at this restaurant with five locations, but the flavorful marinated roasted chicken gets an especially big nod (a whole chicken is a popular to-go item). **Known for:** Peruvian ceviche; marinated roasted chicken; creative cocktails. *Average main: $18 ✉ 524 Valencia St., Mission District ☎ 415/252–0918 ⊕ www.limon-rotisserie.com.*

Locanda

$$$ | ITALIAN | The owners of lauded Delfina channel the culinary traditions of Rome at this lively osteria, where the bar stools are constantly occupied and carbs get glorious treatment: chewy *pizza bianca* is an addictive starter, while peppery and creamy *tonnarelli cacio e pepe* is a signature. Finely made cocktails arrive at dark-wood tables on a candlelit tray, and white wall tiles from iconic local makers, Heath Ceramics, which lend a Mission vibe. **Known for:** delicious pasta and antipasti; busy bar; cool Mission vibe. *Average main: $27 ✉ 557 Valencia St., Mission District ☎ 415/863–6800 ⊕ www.locandasf.com ⊗ Closed Mon. and Tues. No lunch weekdays.*

Lolinda

$$ | ARGENTINE | Argentine fare, a convivial atmosphere, and good bartenders help explain the appeal of this contemporary steak house in a sceney two-level former nightclub space with two bars and a rooftop neighbor (El Techo) that offers captivating views—it's no surprise that the crowd swings young and noisy. Don't miss the chicken empanadas with flaky pastry and a slight sweetness. **Known for:** modern Argentine food; lively scene; tasty cocktails. *Average main: $22 ✉ 2518 Mission St., Mission District ☎ 415/550–6970 ⊕ www.lolindasf.com ⊗ No lunch.*

Mission Chinese Food

$ | CHINESE | While the setting is somewhat one-star, the food draws throngs for its bold, cheerfully inauthentic riffs on Chinese cuisine made with quality meats and ingredients, including the fine and super-fiery kung pao pastrami, salt cod fried rice with mackerel confit, and sour chili chicken. Some of the food spikes hot (mapo tofu) while milder dishes (Westlake rice porridge) are homey and satisfying. **Known for:** kung pao pastrami; salt cod fried rice; to-go spot due to long waits. *Average main: $16 ✉ 2234 Mission St., Mission District ☎ 415/863–2800 ⊕ www.missionchinesefood.com ⊗ No lunch Tues. and Wed.*

Namu Gaji

$$ | KOREAN FUSION | FAMILY | At a primo location across from Dolores Park, chef Dennis Lee serves innovative, satisfying dishes inspired both by Korean tradition and Northern Californian ingredients such as mushrooms accompanied by tofu and ricotta, and a burger anointed with pickled daikon and bacon jam. Delicate items, like shiitake dumplings, are plentiful, vegan options abound, and many of the ingredients come from the restaurant's own farm. **Known for:** innovative Korean cuisine; stonepot serving dishes; local ingredients. *Average main: $19 ✉ 499 Dolores St., Mission District ☎ 415/431–6268 ⊕ www.namusf.com ⊗ Closed Mon. No lunch Tues.*

Orenchi Beyond

$ | RAMEN | After years of heading an hour down the peninsula to satisfy their ramen cravings at Orenchi Santa Clara, San Franciscans now have their own Mission location—with a hipster slant, but the namesake ramen bowl still boasts the *tonkotsu* broth base that cooks for 18 hours, and chewy noodles that attract the harshest of critics. The space is airy and geometric, service is quick and friendly, and the wait is remedied (slightly) by the small front bar that sells sakes and beers. **Known for:** authentic ramen; long waits; hip vibe. *Average main: $15 ✉ 174 Valencia St., at Duboce, Mission District ☎ 415/431–3971 ⊕ www.orenchi-beyond.com.*

Pizzeria Delfina

$$ | PIZZA | FAMILY | As one of the contenders for the city's best pizza, this offshoot of Delfina is known for perfectly blistered thin crusts and near-constant crowds, as well as super-fresh salads and antipasti. The European-style pizzeria, sandwiched between Tartine Bakery and Delfina, has a few sidewalk tables that can be sublime on a nice day, or you can order takeout and carry the pizza to Dolores Park. **Known for:** European-style pizzeria; sidewalk seating; long waits for pizza to go. *Average main: $18 ✉ 3611 18th St., Mission District ☎ 415/437–6800 ⊕ www.pizzeriadelfina.com ⊗ No lunch Tues.*

Salumeria

$ | DELI | When chef Thomas McNaughton isn't hosting dinner guests at Central Kitchen, that restaurant's courtyard turns into a casual hangout for lunch goers who order from a day menu at this larder and deli that includes a half-dozen sandwiches, salads, and daily specials. The pasta salad is made with famed flour + water pasta (another McNaughton enterprise), the salumi is made in-house, and you can provision up here, as the place also serves as a specialty grocer. **Known for:** tasty sandwiches and salads; courtyard hangout; grocery. *Average main: $13 ✉ 3000 20th St., Mission District ☎ 415/471–2998 ⊕ salumeriasf.com ⊗ No dinner.*

SanJalisco

$ | MEXICAN | FAMILY | This colorful old-time, sun-filled, family-run restaurant has been a neighborhood favorite for more than 30 years, and not only because it serves breakfast all day—though the hearty *chilaquiles* hit the spot. On weekends, adventurous eaters may opt for *birria,* a spicy barbecued goat stew, or *menudo,* a tongue-searing soup made from beef tripe, complemented by beer and sangria. **Known for:** breakfast all day; beef-tripe menudo; delicious sangria. *Average main: $13 ✉ 901 S. Van Ness Ave., Mission District ☎ 415/648–8383.*

St. Francis Fountain

$ | DINER | For an old-fashioned soda or homemade ice cream, stop into the St. Francis Fountain and candy store, a hipster haven in a very hip neighborhood. Breakfast, burgers, sandwiches, and salads are also on the menu at this San Francisco institution, open since 1918. *Average main: $11 ✉ 2801 24th St., at York St., Mission District ☎ 415/826–4200 ⊕ www.stfrancisfountainsf.com ⊗ No dinner.*

★ Tartine Bakery & Café

$ | BAKERY | Chad Robertson is America's first modern cult baker, and this tiny Mission District outpost is where you'll find his famed loaves of tangy country bread, beloved pastries like croissants and morning buns, and near-constant lines out the door—good luck finding a seat. They're longest in the morning when locals (and plenty of tourists) need a pastry punch to start the day, and at 3:30 pm when the famed loaves emerge—and quickly sell out. **Known for:** bread with cult following; delicious pastries; long lines. *Average main: $10 ✉ 600 Guerrero St., at 18th St., Mission District ☎ 415/487–2600 ⊕ www.tartinebakery.com ⊗ No dinner.*

Tartine Manufactory

$$$$ | MODERN AMERICAN | FAMILY | At this sunny, cathedral-like space in the Heath Ceramics building, you'll find Chad Robertson's bread and Liz Prueitt's pastries, but also breakfast, lunch, and dinner, with seasonal salads front and center, as well as a porchetta sandwich that tends to sell out early. As with the original bakery, you can expect to spend some time in line—and to be rewarded for your troubles. **Known for:** Chad Robertson's bread; Liz Prueitt's pastries; seasonal salads. *Average main: $28 ✉ 595 Alabama St., Mission District ☎ 415/757–0007 ⊕ www.tartinemanufactory.com.*

Coffee Break

Blue Bottle Coffee. North Beach may have the highest coffee profile, but fantastic brews can be found all over town. Tear yourself away from Columbus Avenue and head to Hayes Valley's Blue Bottle Coffee, a modest kiosk where the organic beans (no more than two days from the roaster) are ground for each cup and the espresso is automatically *ristretto*—a short shot. (Although traditionalists stick with the long lines at the quirky kiosk, a few years ago Blue Bottle opened a "proper café" downtown in Mint Plaza, and there's another location in the Ferry Plaza Marketplace.) *315 Linden St., near Gough St., 415/252-7535.*

Café du Soleil. In the Lower Haight, sun seekers grab an outside table at Café du Soleil and sip bowls of café au lait with their morning croissant. *200 Fillmore St., at Waller St., 415/934-8637.*

Farley's. While you're sipping your inky strong cup at friendly Farley's, a neighborhood institution on sunny Potrero Hill, you can play chess, check out the eclectic magazine selection, or catch up on the local gossip. *1315 18th St., at Texas St., 415/648-1545.*

Four Barrel Coffee. Coffee aficionados should also head down Valencia Street to Four Barrel Coffee for excellent house-roasted coffee in a fun and funky space, packed with Mission hipsters, cyclists, and artists (be sure to look at the selection of Dynamo donuts as well). *375 Valencia St., between 14th and 15th Sts., 415/252-0800.*

Mojo Bicycle Café. If you're a serious bicyclist and serious about coffee, the funky Mojo Bicycle Café, in the increasingly hip North of the Panhandle neighborhood, is the place for you. You can down an espresso made from locally roasted fair-trade beans, tuck into a great sandwich, and either buy or admire a beautiful new bike or get the one you're riding fixed. *639A Divisadero St., between Grove and Hayes Sts., 415/440-2338.*

Red's Java House. And anyone looking for a real cup of joe in a bare-bones pine shack should join the savvy dock workers, carpenters, and young suits at the more-than-80-years-old Red's Java House, where the coffee typically follows a cheeseburger and a Bud and the gorgeous view of the East Bay is priceless. *Pier 30, between Embarcadero and Bryant St., 415/777-5626.*

Ritual Coffee Roasters. In the Mission District, the owners of the popular Ritual Coffee Roasters have plunked their roaster in the back of the café, so you know where your beans—usually single-origin, rather than a blend—were roasted when you order your espresso or drip coffee. *1026 Valencia St., between 21st and 22nd Sts., 415/641-1024.*

True Laurel

$$ | **MODERN AMERICAN** | A great Plan B for those who didn't book far enough ahead to score a table at Lazy Bear, this excellent cocktail bar and small-plates restaurant by the same people offers intriguing combinations and endless conversation starters in a cool modern setting. Menu standouts include the Dungeness-crab-and-aged-cheddar fondue and fried hen-of-the-woods mushrooms, while don't-misses on the cocktail side include the Top Dawg, a house-fermented sparkling concoction, and aquavit-based A-Dilla. **Known for:** equal focus on food and cocktails; unusual ingredients; innovative combinations. *Average main: $24* *753 Alabama St., Mission District* *415/341–0020* *truelaurelsf.com* *No lunch.*

★ **Wise Sons Jewish Delicatessen**

$ | **DELI** | **FAMILY** | The order of the day (and night) at this simple deli counter decorated with old family portraits is Jewish comfort food made with new-wave sensibilities: the pastrami and corned beef are hormone- and antibiotic-free. Breakfast, with bialy egg sandwiches and challah French toast, is served all day, and no one can stop gushing about the pastrami delicately smoked and heaped between two slabs of house-baked rye. **Known for:** contemporary Jewish cuisine; pastrami on rye; breakfast all day. *Average main: $14* *3150 24th St., at Shotwell St., Mission District* *415/787–3354* *wisesonsdeli.com* *No dinner Sun.*

The Inn San Francisco

$$$ | **B&B/INN** | For decades this Italianate Victorian mansion decked out in ornate poster beds, opulent Oriental rugs, and precious Victorian artifacts has welcomed visitors to the vibrant Mission District. **Pros:** charming antiques; location on city's sunny side; free street parking. **Cons:** neighborhood can be sketchy at night; some rooms are a tight squeeze; a couple of rooms lack a private bath. *Rooms from: $245* *943 S. Van Ness Ave., Mission District* *415/641–0188, 800/359–0913* *www.innsf.com* *21 rooms* *Breakfast.*

★ **The Parker Guest House**

$$$ | **B&B/INN** | Two yellow 1909 Edwardian houses enchant travelers wanting an authentic San Francisco experience; dark hallways and steep staircases lead to bright earth-toned rooms with private tiled baths (most with tubs), comfortable sitting areas, and cozy linens. **Pros:** handsome affordable rooms; just steps from Dolores Park and the vibrant Castro District on a Muni line; elaborate gardens. **Cons:** stairs can be challenging for those with limited mobility; parking can be difficult if garage is full; standard rooms are a little tight. *Rooms from: $249* *520 Church St., Mission District* *415/621–4139* *parkerguesthouse.com* *21 rooms* *Breakfast.*

Once a vibrant mix of Latino street culture and twentysomething dot-com action, the Mission is defined these days by its hipster crowd. This neighborhood rarely sleeps.

BARS

ABV

BARS/PUBS | One of the city's top cocktail bars offers elevated small plates—think pork belly with peanut mole, burgers, and meat and cheese boards—until 1 am to pair with the excellent cocktail menu, which features such favorites as the Mumbai Mule with saffron vodka. A knowledgeable and friendly staff serves a hipster crowd that knows their drinks in a smart modern setting, with hard surfaces, bar-stool seating, and a giant mural. The sidewalk tables are popular on sunny days. *3174 16th St., near Guerrero St., Mission District* *415/400–4748* *www.abvsf.com.*

Elixir

BARS/PUBS | The cocktails are well crafted and affordable at the city's second-oldest saloon location—various watering holes have operated on this site since 1858. **TIP→ Sunday's do-it-yourself Bloody Mary bar is a local favorite.** ✉ *3200 16th St., at Guerrero St., Mission District* ☎ *415/552–1633* 🌐 *www.elixirsf.com.*

★ El Rio

MUSIC CLUBS | A dive bar in the best sense, El Rio has a calendar chock-full of events, from free bands and films to Salsa Sunday (seasonal), all of which keep Mission kids coming back. Bands play several nights a week, and there are plenty of other events. No matter what day you attend, expect to find a diverse gay-straight crowd. When the weather's warm, the large patio out back is especially popular, and the midday dance parties are *the* place to be. ✉ *3158 Mission St., between César Chavez and Valencia Sts., Mission District* ☎ *415/282–3325* 🌐 *www.elriosf.com.*

The Knockout

BARS/PUBS | In a grungy but hip section of the Mission, the king of dive bars (with requisite cheap bottled beer and photo booth) is popular with the discerning hipsters who dare to venture south of César Chavez Street. There's usually a cover for bands or DJs on weekends, but it's never more than $10. Bingo on Thursday keeps it real. An added bonus for trekking out to the southern edge of the Mission: some of the city's best taquerías are nearby. ✉ *3223 Mission St., at Valencia St., Mission District* ☎ *415/550–6994* 🌐 *www.theknockoutsf.com.*

Laszlo

BARS/PUBS | Attached to the Foreign Cinema restaurant, Laszlo is a cavernous, classy space with an open, bi-level design; movies are projected onto the walls. Dim lighting, candles, and an upscale selection of cocktails and single malts make it suitable for romance, but the loud music and cacophonic levels of conversation keep it lively. DJs spin most nights after 9. ✉ *2526 Mission St., between 21st and 22nd Sts., Mission District* ☎ *415/401–0810* 🌐 *www.laszlo-bar.com.*

Nihon Whiskey Lounge

BARS/PUBS | Whiskey lovers *need* to check this place out, if only to drool over the 150 or so bottles behind the bar. Nihon attracts a super-swank, youngish crowd for decent (if pricey) Japanese tapas; the whiskeys pair with sushi surprisingly well. The dramatic lighting, close quarters, and blood-red tuffets make the bar more suitable for romance than business. ✉ *1779 Folsom St., near 14th St., Mission District* ☎ *415/552–4400* 🌐 *dajanigroup.net/establishments/nihon-whisky-lounge.*

Rite Spot Cafe

BARS/PUBS | A Mission tradition for more than 50 years, this classy and casual charmer is like a cabaret club in an aging mobster's garage. Quirky lounge singers and other musicians entertain most nights. A small menu of affordable sandwiches and Italian food beats your average bar fare. Rite Spot is in a mostly residential and somewhat desolate part of the Mission, so you may feel like you're entering a no-man's-land. ✉ *2099 Folsom St., at 17th St., Mission District* ☎ *415/552–6066* 🌐 *www.ritespotcafe.net.*

Urban Putt

THEMED ENTERTAINMENT | It may be kid-friendly during the day, but this 14-hole indoor miniature golf course really lights up at night. The bar features cocktails inspired by Bay Area attractions, as does the fairway, so you'll be putting through the Transamerica Pyramid and those famous Painted Ladies. And Urban Putt is complete with theme park cuisine, such as corn dogs and organic soft-serve ice cream. Those seeking more substantial eats should head upstairs to the restaurant. ✉ *1096 S. Van Ness Ave., at 22nd St., Mission District* ☎ *415/341–1080* 🌐 *www.urbanputt.com.*

Zeitgeist

BARS/PUBS | It's a dive but one of the city's best beer bars—there are almost 50 on tap—a great place to relax with a cold one or an ever-popular Bloody Mary in the large "garden" (there's not much greenery) on a sunny day. Burgers and brats are available, and if you own a trucker hat, a pair of Vans, and a Pabst Blue Ribbon T-shirt, you'll fit right in. ✉ *199 Valencia St., at Duboce Ave., Mission District* ☎ *415/255–7505.*

GAY NIGHTLIFE

Martuni's

BARS/PUBS | A mixed crowd enjoys cocktails in the semi-refined environment of this piano bar where the Castro, the Mission, and Hayes Valley intersect; variations on the martini are a specialty. In the intimate back room a pianist plays nightly, and patrons take turns boisterously singing show tunes. Martuni's often gets busy after symphony and opera performances—Davies Hall and the Opera House are both within walking distance. **■ TIP→ The Godiva Chocolate Martini is a crowd favorite.** ✉ *4 Valencia St., at Market St., Mission District* ☎ *415/241–0205.*

MUSIC CLUBS

Bottom of the Hill

MUSIC CLUBS | This is a great live-music dive—in the best sense of the word—and truly the epicenter of Bay Area indie rock. The club has hosted some great acts over the years, including the Strokes and the Throwing Muses. Rap and hip-hop acts occasionally make it to the stage. ✉ *1233 17th St., at Texas St., Potrero Hill* ☎ *415/621–4455* 🌐 *www.bottomofthehill.com.*

Performing Arts

Joe Goode Performance Group

DANCE | Physicality and high-flying style are the hallmarks of this original group, a blend of modern dance and theater. Works include narrative, video projections, and song, and succeed at being both poignant and funny. ✉ *401 Alabama St., Mission* ☎ *415/561–6565* 🌐 *www.joegoode.org.*

Shopping

The aesthetic of the hipsters and artist types who reside in the Mission contribute to the individuality of shopping here. These night owls keep the city's best thrift stores, vintage-furniture shops, alternative bookstores, and increasingly, small clothing boutiques afloat. As the Mission gentrifies though, bargain hunters find themselves trekking farther afield in search of truly local flavor.

ANTIQUES

Grand Central Station Antiques

ANTIQUES/COLLECTIBLES | This large, three-story space stocks mostly 19th- and early-20th-century European and American storage pieces—armoires, highboys, buffets, and the occasional barrister bookcase—with an emphasis on the small and practical. Service is affable. ✉ *360 Bayshore Blvd., Bernal Heights* ☎ *415/252–8155* 🌐 *www.gcsantiques.com.*

BOOKS

Dog Eared Books

BOOKS/STATIONERY | An eclectic group of shoppers—gay and straight, fashionable and practical—wanders the aisles of this pleasantly ramshackle bookstore. The diverse stock, about 85% of it used, includes quirky selections like local zines, vintage children's books, and remaindered art books. A bin of free books just outside the front door is fun to browse. ✉ *900 Valencia St., at 20th St., Mission District* ☎ *415/282–1901* 🌐 *www.dogearedbooks.com.*

CLOTHING: MEN AND WOMEN

Lemon Twist

CLOTHING | A fashionable family affair: Dannette Scheib is known for her inspired details, such as her signature tulle petticoats that go underneath her A-line skirts. Her husband Eric's T-shirts capture an urban essence in a simply stenciled telephone-pole design. ■ TIP→ **If you see a print you like on the workshop table in back, she's happy to make you a custom piece at no additional charge and ship it to you back home.** ✉ *3418 25th St., Mission District* ☎ *415/297–2423* 🌐 *lemontwist.net.*

Schauplatz

CLOTHING | A narrow store on a hip Mission block, Schauplatz sells vintage clothing from the 1920s to the 1980s. Some of the dramatic women's wear—go-go boots, pillbox hats, faux Chanel suits—is suitable for street wear or dress-up, depending on your style, while the menswear tends more toward fashionably retro jackets and button-up shirts from the classic to the gaudy. ✉ *791 Valencia St., at 19th St., Mission District* ☎ *415/864–5665* ⏲ *Closed Tues.*

FURNITURE, HOUSEWARES, AND GIFTS

★ Paxton Gate

GIFTS/SOUVENIRS | Elevating gardening to an art, this serene shop offers beautiful earthenware pots, amaryllis and narcissus bulbs, decorative garden items, and coffee-table books such as *An Inordinate Fondness for Beetles.* The collection of taxidermy and preserved bugs provides more unusual gift ideas. A couple of storefronts away is too-cute Paxton Gate Curiosities for Kids, jam-packed with retro toys, books, and other stellar finds. ✉ *824 Valencia St., between 19th and 20th Sts., Mission District* ☎ *415/824–1872* 🌐 *www.paxtongate.com.*

Therapy

GIFTS/SOUVENIRS | In addition to fun housewares, downright silly soap-on-a-rope, and stationery that leans toward the retro, this local company sells smart San Francisco- and California-theme linens, decor, and accessories that make great souvenirs. ✉ *545 Valencia St., between 16th and 17th Sts., Mission District* ☎ *415/865–0981* 🌐 *www.shopattherapy.com.*

TOYS AND GADGETS

826 Valencia

TOYS | FAMILY | The brainchild of local author Dave Eggers is primarily a center established to help kids with their writing skills via writing programs and storytelling events. But the storefront is also "San Francisco's only independent pirate supply store," a quirky space filled with eye patches, spyglasses, and other pirate-themed paraphernalia. Eggers's quarterly journal, *McSweeney's,* and other publications are available here. Proceeds benefit the writing center. ✉ *826 Valencia St., between 18th and 19th Sts., Mission District* ☎ *415/642–5905* 🌐 *826valencia.org.*

Dogpatch

East of the Mission District and Potrero Hill and a short T-Third Muni light-rail ride from SoMa, the Dogpatch neighborhood has been on the rise for the last decade. Red-hot galleries have hit a critical mass, decamping from aging Union Square and even New York to fill the Minnesota Street Project, a giant warehouse of art space; the Museum of Craft and Design is another neighborhood anchor. Artisans, designers, and craftspeople eager to protect the area's historical industrial legacy have all moved here in recent years, providing a solid customer base for shops, boutique restaurants, and artisanal food producers (but no grocery store or bank). At or near the intersection of 3rd and 22nd Streets, you'll find neighborhood breakfast favorite Just for You Café, locally sourced Italian food at sunny yellow Piccino, and small-batch organic ice cream at Mr. and Mrs. Miscellaneous.

Sights

Museum of Craft and Design

MUSEUM | Right at home in this once-industrial neighborhood now bursting with creative energy, this small, four-room space—definitely a quick view—mounts temporary art and design exhibitions. The focus might be sculpture, metalwork, furniture, or jewelry—or industrial design, architecture, or other topics. The MakeArt Lab gives kids (and grownups) the opportunity to create their own exhibit-inspired work, and the beautifully curated shop sells tempting textiles, housewares, jewelry, and other well-crafted items. *✉ 2569 3rd St., near 22nd St., Dogpatch ☎ 415/773–0303 🌐 sfmcd.org 🎟 $8, free 1st Tues. of month ⏲ Closed Mon.*

Portrero Hill

Tucked between two freeways east of the Mission and south of SoMa, warm and sunny Potrero Hill is a laid-back, family-friendly neighborhood that can feel a place apart from the rest of the city. Most of the action happens around 18th and Connecticut Streets. With fantastic views from its slopes; some good shops, restaurants, and bars; and the longtime music club Bottom of the Hill, Potrero Hill is a neighborhood attractive to locals but still off the tourist radar.

Restaurants

Plow

$$ | MODERN AMERICAN | FAMILY | The breakfast lines are as constant as the excellent fluffy lemon-ricotta pancakes, scrambles, and biscuits served at this neighborhood favorite, a former architect's studio. The atmosphere is also winning—bright and pastoral, with rustic wood floors and huge windows—and the Little Plowers menu dishes out smaller-portioned pancakes, French toast, and grilled cheese. **Known for:** in-demand breakfast; Little Plowers menu; long lines. *$ Average main: $17 ✉ 1299 18th St., Potrero Hill ☎ 415/821–7569 🌐 www.eatatplow.com ⏲ No dinner.*

Shopping

ART GALLERIES

Catharine Clark Gallery

ART GALLERIES | Although nationally known artists—like Masami Teraoka and Andy Diaz Hope—display their sculptures, paintings, photographs, and installation artwork here, emerging artists with a Bay Area connection get the spotlight, among them Chester Arnold and Josephine Taylor. *✉ 248 Utah St., Potrero Hill ☎ 415/399–1439 🌐 cclarkgallery.com ⏲ Closed Sun. and Mon.*

FURNITURE, HOUSEWARES, AND GIFTS

★ **Heath Ceramics**

CERAMICS/GLASSWARE | Founded in Sausalito in 1948, Heath offers sleek, glossy tiles for the home, newly spun dinnerware in rich earth colors, locally inspired cookbooks, and simple bamboo spoons stand stacked on shelves and tables at their factory showroom. **TIP→ This is worth a stop if you're interested in seeing how plates and bowls are made.** Nearby Blue Bottle Coffee serves coffee and light snacks for people and dogs. *✉ 2900 18th St., at Florida St., Potrero Hill ☎ 415/361–5552 🌐 www.heathceramics.com.*

HANDICRAFTS AND FOLK ART

Collage Gallery

CRAFTS | The studio-gallery showcases handmade purses, painted candlesticks, jewelry, and other items by Bay Area artists. There are also a few small antiques, such as charming Westclox alarm clocks. *✉ 1345 18th St., between Missouri and Texas Sts., Potrero Hill ☎ 415/282–4401 🌐 www.collage-gallery.com ⏲ Closed Mon.*

Chapter 13

PACIFIC HEIGHTS AND JAPANTOWN

Updated by
Trevor Felch

Sights	Restaurants	Hotels	Shopping	Nightlife
★★☆☆☆	★★★☆☆	★☆☆☆☆	★★★☆☆	★★☆☆☆

SAN FRANCISCO'S ARCHITECTURE

California Academy of Sciences

San Francisco's architecture scene underwent a dramatic growth spurt in the first decade of the new millennium. Boldface international architects spearheaded major projects like the de Young Museum, the California Academy of Sciences, and the Contemporary Jewish Museum. And with those additions came heated local debates.

The development flurry is thrown into sharp relief by the previous decades spent carefully preserving the city's historic buildings. Genteel Victorian homes are a city signature, and this residential legacy is fiercely protected.

Residents aren't shy about voicing opinions on the "starchitect" plans, either. As high-profile designs unfold and new condo neighborhoods break ground, criticism will surely escalate. One thing that gratifies everyone: the impressive advances made in eco-friendly building practices that are a recurring theme in the new, prominent building projects.

SAN FRANCISCO MUSEUM OF MODERN ART (SFMOMA)

Renowned Swiss architect Mario Botta's first shot at designing a museum resulted in the distinctive, sturdy geometrical forms that reflected his signature style. Here a black-and-white cylindrical tower anchors the brick structure. Botta called the huge, slanted skylight the "city's eye, like the Cyclops." A new wing, designed by Snøhetta, opened in 2016, adding more than 100,000 square feet of gallery and public space.

DE YOUNG MUSEUM OF FINE ART

Love it or hate it, the structure is a must-see destination in Golden Gate Park. After the original Egyptian-revival edifice was deemed seismically unsafe, the Pritzker-winning Swiss team Herzog & de Meuron won the commission to rebuild. Their design's copper facade and, in particular, the 144-foot observation tower—a twisted parallelogram grazing the treetops—drew fire from critics, who compared the design to a "rusty aircraft carrier." But the copper hue is mellowing with age, and the panoramic view from the ninth-floor observation deck is a hit.

CALIFORNIA ACADEMY OF SCIENCES

An eco-friendly, energy-efficient adventure in biodiversity, Renzo Piano's audacious design for this natural history museum comes equipped with a rain forest, a planetarium, skylights, and a retractable ceiling over the central courtyard. But it's the "living roof," covered in native plants, that generates the most comment.

MISSION BAY, RINCON HILL, AND THE TRANSBAY DISTRICT

San Francisco's cityscape is undergoing tremendous change, especially moving south from Market Street along the waterfront. Glass-sheathed, condo-crammed high-rises are taking over what was a working-class area of warehouses and lofts, led by Oracle Park, the Giants' baseball ballpark. The first phase of an ultramodern Transbay Terminal with a rooftop park opened in 2018, as did the soaring Salesforce Tower, now San Francisco's tallest building. A blocky new University of California, San Francisco (UCSF) Campus Conference Center by Mexican architect Ricardo Legorreta has changed the landscape of nearby Mission Bay as has the Warriors new waterfront home, the Chase Center basketball arena and entertainment complex.

PRESIDIO

The development of this parkland continues at a relatively slow pace. Its historic military-base buildings are being put to new uses—everything from a printing press to a spa. Additions include a digital arts center by George Lucas, a Walt Disney Museum, and the hip Inn at the Presidio and Lodge at the Presidio boutique hotels.

San Francisco Victorian homes

de Young Museum of Fine Art

NEIGHBORHOOD SNAPSHOT

TOP REASONS TO GO

■ **Chic shopping on Fillmore Street:** Browse the superfine shops along Pacific Heights' main drag.

■ **Picnic with a view at Lafayette Park:** Gather supplies along Fillmore Street and climb to the top of this park. It's surrounded by grand homes and has a sweeping view of the city.

■ **Asian shops galore in the Japan Center:** Grab an adorable taiyaki (a fish-shape cone filled with soft serve ice cream) or browse the wonderful Kinokuniya Bookstore and the tea implements at Asakichi.

■ **Spa serenity at Kabuki Springs:** Enter the peaceful lobby and prepare to be transported at the Japanese-style communal baths.

■ **See how the other half lives:** Check out the grand, historic homes along the tree-lined streets of Pacific Heights.

GETTING THERE

Steep streets in Pacific Heights make for impressive views and rough walking; unless you're in decent shape, consider taking a car or taxi to this neighborhood.

The only public transit that runs through the area is the bus. For Pacific Heights proper, take the 12–Folsom to its terminus at Van Ness and Pacific Avenues and walk west. For shopping on Fillmore Street, catch the 1–California or the 22–Fillmore bus.

PLANNING YOUR TIME

Give yourself an hour to wander Fillmore Street, more if you're planning to have a meal here or picnic in Lafayette or Alta Plaza park. Checking out the stunning homes in Pacific Heights is best done by car, unless you have serious stamina; a half hour should be enough.

Shops and restaurants are the highlights of Japantown, so plan a daytime visit for a meal and some window-shopping; lunchtime is ideal.

QUICK BITES

■ **b Patisserie.** Your search for the perfect *kouign-amann* (a traditional glazed, butter-enriched Breton pastry made of croissant dough) ends here. Seasonal varieties of that specialty in this buzzy, immaculate Pacific Heights café from baking wizard Belinda Leong include black sesame and pear, but you can't go wrong with the chocolate or plain standbys. **Known for:** gorgeous pastries, cakes and tarts; sandwiches across the street at sister establishment B. on the Go; perfect baguettes. ✉ *2821 California St., Pacific Heights* ✣ *At Divisadero St.* ☎ *415/440–1700* 🌐 *bpatisserie.com* ⏲ *Closed Mon.*

■ **Crown & Crumpet Tea Stop Cafe.** In the lobby of the New People building, this little tea shop looks like a little girl's fantasy, with pretty flowered and polka-dotted tablecloths and fancy settings. Stop in for a warm panini or salad, or have high tea with scones, crumpets, and finger sandwiches. **Known for:** high tea; crumpets; cuteness. ✉ *New People, 1746 Post St., Japantown* ☎ *415/771–4252* 🌐 *crownandcrumpet.com.*

Pacific Heights and Japantown are something of an odd couple: privileged, old-school San Francisco and the workaday commercial center of Japanese American life in the city, stacked virtually on top of each other. The sprawling, extravagant mansions of Pacific Heights gradually give way to the more modest Victorians and unassuming housing tracts of Japantown. The most interesting spots in Japantown huddle in the Japan Center, the neighborhood's two-block centerpiece, and along Post Street. You can find plenty of authentic Japanese treats in the shops and restaurants.

Pacific Heights

Pacific Heights defines San Francisco's most expensive and dramatic real estate. Grand Victorians line the streets, mansions and town houses are priced in the millions, and there are magnificent views from almost any point in the neighborhood. Old money and new, personalities in the limelight and those who prefer absolute media anonymity live here, and few outsiders see anything other than the pleasing facades of Queen Anne charmers, English Tudor imports, and baroque bastions. Nancy Pelosi and Dianne Feinstein, Larry Ellison, and Gordon Getty all own impressive homes here, but not even pockets as deep as those can buy a large garden—space in the city is simply at too much of a premium. Luckily, two of the city's most spectacular parks are located in the area. The boutiques and restaurants along Fillmore Street, which range from glam to funky, are a draw for the whole city as well.

Pacific Heights and Japantown
A
B
C
D
E
F
1
2
3
4
5
6
7
8
9
Lombard St.
Moulton St.
COW HOLLOW
Greenwich St.
Pixley St.
Laguna St.
Baker St.
Broderick St.
Filbert St.
Union St.
Green St.
Valleja St.
Scott St.
Pierce St.
Steiner St.
Fillmore St.
Webster St.
Buchanan St.
Broadway
Pacific Ave.
Jackson St.
WEBSTER ST. HISTORIC DISTRICT
Walnut St.
Presidio Ave.
Washington St.
Clay St.
Sacramento St.
Perine Pl.
California St.
Locust St.
Laurel St.
Lyon St.
Pine St.
Wilmot St.
Divisadero St.
Bush St.
JAPANTOWN
Sutter St.
Euclid Ave.
Masonic Ave.
Post St.
Wood St.
Emerson St.
Geary Blvd.
O'Farrell St.
Ellis St.
Anza St.
Barcelona
Encanto Ave.
Fortuna Ave.
Josephs Ave.
Vega St.
Turk St.
Elm St.
Golden Gate Ave.
ALAMO SQUARE HISTORIC DISTRICT
Fulton St.
Alamo Square
Grove St.
Hayes St.
Fell St.
Oak St.
Clayton St.
Ashbury St.
Panhandle
Page St.
Haight St.
Waller St.
Germania S
0
1/4 mile
400 meters

Sights

1 Alamo Square Park E8
2 Alta Plaza Park E3
3 Atherton House G4
4 Broadway estates E2
5 Buchanan Mall G6
6 Cathedral of Saint Mary of The Assumption H5
7 Haas-Lilienthal House H3
8 Japan Center F5
9 Kabuki Springs & Spa F5
10 Lafayette Park G3
11 Laguna Street Victorians G4
12 New People F5
13 Two Italianate Victorians H3
14 Whittier Mansion G3

Restaurants

1 Avery F5
2 Che Fico D7
3 4505 Burgers & BBQ D8
4 Marufuku Ramen F5
5 Merchant Roots F6
6 Mifune Don G5
7 The Mill D8
8 Nopa C8
9 Nopalito D8
10 Octavia G4
11 Out the Door E4
12 The Progress F5
13 Roam Artisan Burgers E4
14 Sorrel B4
15 SPQR E4
16 Spruce A4
17 State Bird Provisions F5

Hotels

1 Hotel Drisco C3
2 Hotel Kabuki G5
3 Hotel Majestic H4
4 Kimpton Buchanan Hotel F4
5 Laurel Inn B4
6 Queen Anne Hotel G4

A Pacific Heights Walk

Start at **Broadway and Webster Street,** where four notable estates stand within a block of one another. Two are on the north side of Broadway west of the intersection, one is on the same side to the east, and the last is half a block south on Webster. Head south down Webster and hang a right onto Clay to **Alta Plaza Park,** or skip the park and turn left on Jackson to the **Whittier Mansion,** at Jackson and Laguna Streets. Head south down Laguna and cross Washington Street to **Lafayette Park.** Walk on Washington along the edge of the park, past the formal French **Spreckels Mansion** at the corner of Octavia Street, and continue east two more blocks to Franklin Street. Turn left (north); halfway down the block stands the handsome **Haas-Lilienthal House.** Head back south on Franklin Street, stopping to view a handsome Georgian style residence (1735 Franklin St.) and the Queen Anne style Coleman House with a gorgeous purple stained glass window on the home's north side (1701 Franklin St.). At California Street, turn right (west) to see two **Italianate Victorians** and the **Atherton House.** Continue west to Laguna Street and turn left (south); past Pine Street sits a sedate block of **Laguna Street Victorians.**

Sights

★ Alta Plaza Park

CITY PARK | FAMILY | Golden Gate Park's longtime superintendent, John McLaren, designed the nearly 12-acre park in the early 1900s, modeling its steep south-facing terracing on that of the Grand Casino in Monte Carlo, Monaco. From the top you can see Marin to the north, downtown to the east, Twin Peaks to the south, and Golden Gate Park to the west. **■ TIP→ Kids love the many play structures at the large, enclosed playground at the top; dogs love the off-leash area in the parks southeast corner.** ⊠ *Bordered by Clay, Steiner, Jackson, and Scott Sts., Pacific Heights.*

Atherton House

HOUSE | The somewhat quirky design of this Victorian-era house incorporates Queen Anne, Stick-Eastlake, and other architectural elements. Many claim the house—now apartments—is haunted by the ghosts of its 19th-century residents, who (supposedly) regularly whisper, glow, and generally cause a mild fuss. ⊠ *1990 California St., Pacific Heights.*

Broadway estates

BUILDING | Broadway uptown, unlike its garish North Beach stretch, has plenty of prestigious addresses. The three-story palace at 2222 Broadway, which has an intricately filigreed doorway, was built by Comstock silver-mine heir James Flood and later donated to a religious order. The Convent of the Sacred Heart purchased the **Grant House** at 2220 Broadway. These two buildings, along with a Flood property at 2120 Broadway, are used as private school buildings today. A gold-mine heir, William Bourn II, commissioned Willis Polk to build the nearby brick mansion at 2550 Webster Street. Two blocks away, movie fans will surely recognize the "Mrs. Doubtfire" apartment at Broadway and Steiner (2640 Steiner St.). It's the home where Robin Williams donned his disguise as a lovable British nanny in the beloved 1993 comedy. ⊠ *Pacific Heights.*

Haas-Lilienthal House

HOUSE | A small display of photographs on the bottom floor of this elaborate, gray 1886 Queen Anne house makes clear that despite its lofty stature and striking, round third-story tower, the house was modest compared with some of the giants that fell victim to the 1906 earthquake and fire. San Francisco Heritage, a foundation to preserve San Francisco's architectural history, operates the home, whose carefully kept rooms provide a glimpse into late-19th-century life through period furniture, authentic details (antique dishes in the kitchen built-in), and photos of the Haas family who occupied the house for three generations until 1972. ■ **TIP→ You can admire hundreds of gorgeous San Francisco Victorians from the outside, but this is the only one that's open to the public, and it's worth a visit.** Volunteers conduct one-hour house tours three days a week, and informative two-hour walking tours of Pacific Heights on Sunday afternoon (call or check website for schedule). ✉ *2007 Franklin St., between Washington and Jackson Sts., Pacific Heights* ☎ *415/441–3004* 🌐 *www.haaslilienthalhouse.org* 🎫 *Tours $10.*

Lafayette Park

CITY PARK | FAMILY | Clusters of trees dot this four-block-square oasis for sunbathers and dog-and-Frisbee teams. On the south side of the park, squat but elegant **2151 Sacramento,** a private condominium, is the site of a home occupied by Sir Arthur Conan Doyle in the late 19th century. Coats of arms blaze in the front stained-glass windows. Meanwhile, the park's northern border is anchored by the stately Spreckels Mansion, built originally for sugar heir Adolph Spreckels and his wife, Alma. It is now the 55-room home of celebrated romance novelist Danielle Steele. Giant, immaculately trimmed hedges hide most of the mansion from public view—and have been quite the topic of debate among locals for many years. The park itself is a lovely neighborhood space, where Pacific Heights residents laze in the sun or exercise their pedigreed canines while gazing at downtown's skyline or the Bay and Marin County hills in the distance to the north. ✉ *Bordered by Laguna, Gough, Sacramento, and Washington Sts., Pacific Heights.*

Laguna Street Victorians

HISTORIC SITE | On the west side of the 1800 block of Laguna Street, these oft-photographed houses cost between $2,000 and $2,600 when they were built in the 1870s. No bright colors here, though—most of the paint jobs are in soft beiges or pastels. ✉ *Between Bush and Pine Sts., Pacific Heights.*

Two Italianate Victorians

HOUSE | Two Italianate Victorians stand out on the 1800 block of California. The beauty at 1834, the Wormser-Coleman house, was built in the 1870s. Coleman bought the lot next door, giving this property an unusually spacious yard for the city, even in this luxurious neighborhood. ✉ *1818 and 1834 California St., Pacific Heights.*

Whittier Mansion

HOUSE | With a Spanish-tile roof and scrolled bay windows on all four sides, this is one of the most elegant 19th-century houses in the state. Unlike other grand mansions lost in the 1906 quake, the Whittier Mansion was made of solid Arizona sandstone, so only a chimney toppled over during the disaster. Built by William Franklin Whittier, the founder of (what became) PG&E, the house served as the German consulate during the Nazi period. Legend has it that the house is haunted. ✉ *2090 Jackson St., Pacific Heights.*

Restaurants

Pacific Heights may well be one of the city's better-known neighborhoods, thanks to Hollywood movies and jaw-dropping mansions. More down-to-earth, and down the hill, is Lower Pac Heights, which attracts professionals and postgrads who flock to Fillmore Street's bustling eateries. Neighboring Presidio Heights has a handful of upscale dining favorites on Sacramento Street.

Did You Know?

These soft-color Victorian homes in Pacific Heights are closer to the original hues sported back in the 1900s. It wasn't until the 1960s that the bold, electric colors now seen around San Francisco gained popularity. Before that, the most typical house paint color was a standard gray.

★ Octavia

$$$ | MODERN AMERICAN | Regardless of the time of year, Melissa Perello's (Frances) second and more upscale restaurant is a perennial favorite for diners seeking out what "California cuisine" really tastes like. The warm, immaculate dining room is a perfect setting for edgier dishes like the popular chilled squid ink noodles starter, along with more comforting produce-driven small plates and entrées. **Known for:** exciting preparations with peak-of-season produce; spicy deviled egg starter; truly professional service. *Average main: $32* *1701 Octavia St., Lower Pacific Heights* *At Bush St.* *415/408–7507* *www.octavia-sf.com.*

Out the Door

$$ | VIETNAMESE | FAMILY | A casual offshoot of Charles Phan's Slanted Door, this spot is actually where locals prefer to go for his version of Vietnamese cooking. The look is chic and simple, with an open kitchen, a communal table, counter seating, and an eclectic crowd. **Known for:** Phan classics; comforting bowls of pho; family-friendly vibe. *Average main: $24* *2232 Bush St., Lower Pacific Heights* *By Fillmore St.* *415/923–9575* *www.outthedoors.com.*

Roam Artisan Burgers

$ | BURGER | FAMILY | All the burgers at this laid-back spot are responsibly sourced, and the beef is 100% grass-fed. Choose a patty (beef, bison, vegetarian, elk, or turkey), then choose a preset "style," or invent your own from the many creative toppings. **Known for:** creative burgers; popular with families; the "fry-fecta" trio of fries style for a side. *Average main: $11* *1923 Fillmore St., Pacific Heights* *415/800–7801* *www.roamburgers.com.*

Sorrel

$$$ | MODERN AMERICAN | After a long run as one of San Francisco's most important dining pop-ups, Alex Hong's refined Californian-Italian cooking finally found a permanent home in 2018. And, what a gorgeous home it is in swanky Laurel Heights! **Known for:** exemplary pastas; dry-aged duck for two; upscale dinner party vibe. *Average main: $33* *3228 Sacramento St., Presidio Heights* *415/525–3765* *www.sorrelrestaurant.com* *Closed Sun. and Mon.*

★ SPQR

$$$ | ITALIAN | Brought to you by the same team that operates the Marina's wildly popular A16, SPQR is a modern Italian spot known for Chef Matthew Accarrino's inventive, seasonal cooking. You'll find always tempting antipasti, superlative pastas like mustard capellini with guinea hen ragu, and a trio of hearty secondi. **Known for:** inventive pastas; learning about obscure Italian wine regions; chicken liver mousse antipasti. *Average main: $32* *1911 Fillmore St., Pacific Heights* *Near Bush St.* *415/771–7779* *www.spqrsf.com* *No lunch weekdays.*

Spruce

$$$ | MODERN AMERICAN | This elegant, grown-up restaurant caters to an older crowd who sink happily into its oversized faux ostrich leather chairs. The food is equally refined with ingredients often sourced from the restaurant's farm south of the city and charcuterie made in-house. **Known for:** a beloved burger on an English muffin bun; giant chocolate chip cookies; well-heeled regulars sipping expensive French wine. *Average main: $40* *3640 Sacramento St., Pacific Heights* *415/931–5100* *www.sprucesf.com.*

Hotels

A chic neighborhood—albeit a trek from downtown and many attractions—Pacific Heights pleases celebs, honeymooners, and other travelers with tony B&Bs and boutique properties.

★ **Hotel Drisco**

$$$$ | **HOTEL** | Pretend you're a denizen of one of San Francisco's wealthiest residential neighborhoods while you stay at this understated, elegant 1903 Edwardian hotel. **Pros:** terrific recent renovation of rooms and public spaces; great service and many amenities; quiet residential retreat. **Cons:** not an easy walk to nearby restaurants and bars; room prices are as steep as nearby hill; no complimentary chauffeur service in the afternoon or evening. *Rooms from: $499 ✉ 2901 Pacific Ave., Pacific Heights ☎ 415/346–2880, 800/634–7277 ⊕ www.hoteldrisco.com 64 rooms Breakfast.*

Hotel Majestic

$$ | **HOTEL** | Open in 1902, the five-story Majestic is the city's oldest continually operating hotel; its elegant lobby is a graceful haven of antique chandeliers, plush Victorian chairs, and antiquarian French books. **Pros:** nicely upgraded classic hotel; spacious rooms; rates are often a good value. **Cons:** bus ride or 20-minute walk to downtown; old style won't appeal to all guests; Wi-Fi is free but sometimes spotty. *Rooms from: $218 ✉ 1500 Sutter St., Pacific Heights ☎ 415/441–1100, 800/869–8966 ⊕ www.thehotelmajestic.com 58 rooms No meals.*

Laurel Inn

$$ | **HOTEL** | **FAMILY** | The blue-and-tan facade of this small hotel, punctuated on two sides by garage entrances, hints at its 1963 motor-inn origins, yet the spacious rooms, renovated in 2017, feel modern. **Pros:** spacious and stylish; family- and pet-friendly rooms; excellent bar. **Cons:** no a/c; isolated from much of the city; additional fee for gym or spa. *Rooms from: $229 ✉ 444 Presidio Ave., Pacific Heights ☎ 415/567–8467, 800/552–8735 ⊕ www.jdvhotels.com/hotels/california/san-francisco-hotels/laurel-inn 49 rooms Breakfast.*

Queen Anne Hotel

$$ | **B&B/INN** | Built in the 1890s as a girls' finishing school, this Victorian mansion has a large parlor and guest rooms with such touches as painted cherub murals and, in some, wood-burning fireplaces. **Pros:** lots of design character; library/salon areas will invite you to linger; old-time vibe that is hard to find in SF. **Cons:** 20-minute walk to downtown; no restaurant or gym; some guests complain of stuffy, airless rooms. *Rooms from: $179 ✉ 1590 Sutter St., Pacific Heights ✣ At Octavia St. ☎ 415/441–2828 ⊕ www.queenanne.com 48 rooms Breakfast.*

Nightlife

The Snug

BARS/PUBS | Open since late 2017, this Lower Pac Heights bar is exactly the welcoming yet refined drinking destination the well-heeled and fun-loving neighborhood needed. It's the rare bar that emphasizes clever cocktails, in-high demand local craft beer and smartly selected wine in equal parts. Come hungry, as well, because elevated takes on bar bites like seabream poke and fresh-from-the-tandoor sesame naan with shiitake mushroom hummus are created by a chef formerly at some of the country's gastronomic heavyweights (Benu, Alinea). *✉ 2301 Fillmore St., Lower Pacific Heights ✣ Near Clay St. ⊕ www.thesnugsf.com.*

Shopping

With grocery and hardware stores sitting alongside local clothing ateliers and international designer outposts, Pacific Heights' streets manage to mix small-town America with big-city glitz. After you've splurged on a cashmere sweater or a hand-blown glass vase, snag an outdoor seat at Peet's or The Grove; it's the perfect way to pass an afternoon watching the parade of old money, new money, dogs, and strollers.

BOOKS

Browser Books

BOOKS/STATIONERY | **FAMILY** | One of the city's most beloved independent bookstores resides quietly among the chic fashion boutiques lining Fillmore Street. Opened in 1976, all ages will find ample choices for their next reading material from contemporary fiction to children's books to a large selection of Buddhist Dharma literature. ✉ *2195 Fillmore St., Lower Pacific Heights* ☎ *415/567–8027* 🌐 *www.browserbookstore.com.*

CLOTHING

Crossroads Trading Company

CLOTHING | These stores buy, sell, and trade men's and women's new and used clothing, some of it vintage. Previously owned designer items are the specialty at this location. ✉ *1901 Fillmore St., at Bush St., Pacific Heights* ☎ *415/775–8885* 🌐 *www.crossroadstrading.com.*

Elizabeth Charles

CLOTHING | Feeding and fueling the city's obsession with international designers, this intimate boutique stocks Caroline Constas, Kinder Aggugini, Isabel Marant, and Timo Weiland, with an emphasis on the very finest fabrics. ✉ *2056 Fillmore St., between California and Pine Sts., Pacific Heights* ☎ *415/440–2100* 🌐 *www.elizabeth-charles.com.*

FOOD AND DRINK

D&M Wines and Liquors

WINE/SPIRITS | At first glance this family-owned business appears to be just another neighborhood liquor store, but it's actually a rare and wonderful specialist. In a city obsessed with wine, these spirits devotees distinguish themselves by focusing on rare, small-production Armagnac and Calvados brandy, and Champagne. Be sure to look up from the bottles and admire the stained-glass lamp shades, too. ✉ *2200 Fillmore St., at Sacramento St., Pacific Heights* ☎ *415/346–1325* 🌐 *dandm.com.*

★ Verve Wine

WINE/SPIRITS | Wine nerds will fall in love with this trendy, upscale destination from one of the country's few Master Sommeliers, Dustin Wilson. High-quality, smaller producers from prominent and lesser known regions share wall space in this exceptionally organized boutique. ✉ *Verve Wine, 2358 Fillmore St., Lower Pacific Heights* ✣ *Between Washington St. and Jackson St.* ☎ *415/896–4935* 🌐 *www.vervewine.com/about/san-francisco.*

FURNITURE, HOUSEWARES, AND GIFTS

Dash Lane

HOUSEHOLD ITEMS/FURNITURE | From longtime landscape designer Katherine Webster, gorgeous outdoor furnishings and accessories are the theme of this beautiful Presidio Heights showroom. While alfresco entertaining is the prominent theme, many of the goods from boutique luxury labels like Janus et Cie and DEDON work just as well indoors. ✉ *3352 B Sacramento St., Presidio Heights* ✣ *Upstairs from street level at orange door* ☎ *415/757–0794* 🌐 *www.dashlanesf.com.*

Nest

GIFTS/SOUVENIRS | A cross between a Parisian antiques show and a Jamaican flea market, this store could get even the most monochrome New Yorker excited about color. You can turn up the volume on your SF souvenirs with vibrant handmade quilts, Chan Luu jewelry, Les Indiennes hand-blocked cotton fabrics, and M. Sasek's cheerfully illustrated book *This is San Francisco.* ✉ *2300 Fillmore St., at Clay St., Pacific Heights* ☎ *415/292–6199* 🌐 *www.nestsf.com.*

Sue Fisher King Company

GIFTS/SOUVENIRS | When Martha Stewart or the buyers at Williams-Sonoma need inspiration, they come to see how Sue has set her sprawling table or dressed her stately bed. (Her specialty is opulent linens for every room.) And when Pacific Heights residents are looking for an impeccable hostess or bridal gift, they come by for a hand-embroidered velvet pillow or a piece of Nicholas Newcomb Hudson Valley pottery. ✉ *3067 Sacramento St., between Baker and Broderick Sts., Pacific Heights* ☎ *415/922–7276* 🌐 *www.suefisherking.com.*

JEWELRY AND COLLECTIBLES

Goldberry Jewelers

JEWELRY/ACCESSORIES | The former longtime girlfriend of Bob Dylan, Margie Rogerson opened this store to showcase her platinum-only designs. While she carries a large selection of engagement rings, her specialty is colored stones: rubies, sapphires, and emeralds. Their colors really sparkle against the background of this all white and Lucite space. By appointment only. ✉ *3516 Sacramento St., between Laurel and Locust Sts., Pacific Heights* ☎ *415/921–4389* 🌐 *www.goldberry.com.*

Japantown

Though still the spiritual center of San Francisco's Japanese American community, Japantown feels somewhat adrift. The Japan Center mall, for instance, comes across as rather sterile, and whereas Chinatown is densely populated and still largely Chinese, Japantown struggles to retain its unique character.

Also called Nihonmachi, Japantown is centered on the southern slope of Pacific Heights, north of Geary Boulevard between Fillmore and Laguna Streets. The Japanese community in San Francisco started around 1860; after the 1906 earthquake and fire many of these newcomers settled in the Western Addition. By the 1930s they had opened shops, markets, meeting halls, and restaurants and established Shinto and Buddhist temples. But during World War II the area was virtually gutted when many of its residents, including second- and third-generation Americans, were forced into so-called relocation camps. During the 1960s and 1970s redevelopment further eroded the neighborhood, and most Japanese Americans now live elsewhere in the city.

Still, when several key properties in the neighborhood were sold in 2007, a group rallied to "save Japantown," and some new blood finally infused the area with energy: Robert Redford's Sundance corporation revived the Kabuki Theatre; the local, hip hotel group Joie de Vivre took over the Hotel Kabuki; and the J-Pop Center, New People, brought Japanese pop culture and a long-missing youthful vibe. ■ **TIP→ Japantown is a relatively safe area, but the Western Addition, south of Geary Boulevard, can be dangerous even during the daytime. Also avoid going too far west of Fillmore Street on either side of Geary.**

Sights

★ Buchanan Mall

LOCAL INTEREST | **FAMILY** | The shops lining this open-air mall are geared more toward locals—travel agencies, electronics shops—but there are some fun Japanese-goods stores here, too. Start your exploration with some fabulous *mochi* (a soft, sweet Japanese rice confection) at **Benkyodo Company** (*1747 Buchanan St., 415/922–1244, www.benkyodocompany.com*), a local legend who has been in business since 1906 and still feels like a time warp. It's easy to spend hours among the fabulous origami and craft papers at **Paper Tree** (*1743 Buchanan St., 415/921–7100, paper-tree.com*). After shop browsing, have a seat on the steps around local artist Ruth Asawa's twin origami-style fountains, which sit in the middle of the mall. Wrap up a visit with lunch at **Hinodeya Ramen** (*1737 Buchanan St., 415/757–0552*), serving lighter dashi (clear-broth) ramen, a rarity in the city. ✉ *Buchanan St. between Post and Sutter Sts., Japantown.*

Japan Center

HISTORIC SITE | **FAMILY** | Cool and curious trinkets, noodle houses and sushi joints, a destination bookstore, and a peek at Japanese culture high and low await at this 5-acre complex designed in 1968 by noted American architect Minoru Yamasaki. The Japan Center includes the shop- and restaurant-filled Kintetsu and Kinokuniya buildings; the excellent Kabuki Springs & Spa; the Hotel Kabuki; and the AMC Kabuki reserved-seating cinema/ restaurant complex.

The Kinokuniya Bookstore, in the Kinokuniya Building, has an extensive selection of Japanese-language books, *manga* (graphic novels), books on design, English-language translations, and books on Japanese topics. Just outside, follow the Japanese teenagers to Pika Pika, where you and your friends can step into a photo booth and then use special effects and stickers to decorate your creation. On the bridge connecting the buildings, check out Shige Antiques for *yukata* (lightweight cotton kimonos) for kids and lovely silk kimonos, and Asakichi and its tiny incense shop for tinkling wind chimes and display-worthy teakettles. Continue into the Kintetsu Building for a selection of Japanese restaurants.

Between the West Mall and the East Mall are the five-tier, 100-foot-tall **Peace Pagoda** and the Peace Plaza, where seasonal festivals are held. The pagoda, which draws on the 1,200-year-old tradition of miniature round pagodas dedicated to eternal peace, was designed in the late 1960s by Yoshiro Taniguchi to convey the "friendship and goodwill" of the Japanese people to the people of the United States. ✉ *Bordered by Geary Blvd. and Fillmore, Post, and Laguna Sts., Japantown* 🌐 *www.japancentersf.com.*

★ **Kabuki Springs & Spa**

SPA—SIGHT | This serene spa is one Japantown destination that draws locals from all over town, from hipster to grandma, Japanese American or not. Balinese urns decorate the communal bath area of this house of tranquility.

The extensive service menu includes facials, salt scrubs, and mud and seaweed wraps, in addition to massage. You can take your massage in a private room with a bath or in a curtained-off area.

The communal baths ($30) contain hot and cold tubs, a large Japanese-style bath, a sauna, a steam room, and showers. Bang the gong for quiet if your fellow bathers are speaking too loudly. The clothing-optional baths are open for men only on Monday, Thursday, and Saturday; women bathe on Wednesday, Friday, and Sunday. Bathing suits are required on Tuesday, when the baths are coed.

Men and women can reserve private rooms daily. ✉ *1750 Geary Blvd., Japantown* ☎ *415/922–6000* 🌐 *www.kabukisprings.com.*

New People

ARTS VENUE | The younger generation's counterpart to the Japan Center, this fresh shopping center combines a cinema, a tea parlor, and shops with a successful synergy. The downstairs cinema shows classic and cutting-edge Asian (largely Japanese) films and is home to the San Francisco Film Society. Upstairs you can peruse Japanese pop-culture items and anime-inspired fashion, like handmade, split-toe shoes at Sou Sou. The latest addition is an immersive live puzzle "escape room". ✉ *1746 Post St., Japantown* 🌐 *www.newpeopleworld.com.*

Restaurants

The epicenter of Japantown, which covers about six city blocks, may well be the Japan Center Mall, with several restaurants dishing out ramen, donburi, and sushi. There's also a glut of karaoke bars, sushi shops, and ramen restaurants along Buchanan Street's pedestrian way, between Post and Sutter.

Marufuku Ramen
$$ | **RAMEN** | Hakata style *tonkotsu* (pork) or extra intense chicken *paitan* ramen are the specialty of this modern looking Japan Center restaurant that serves what many San Franciscans consider the city's finest bowl of ramen. As a result, long lines can be daunting, but luckily prospective guests can join an online wait list. **Known for:** rich bowls of ramen; more "al dente" style noodles; lively, contemporary vibe. *Average main: $13* ✉ *1581 Webster St. #235, Japantown* ✥ *In Kinokuniya Bldg.* ☎ *415/872–9786* ⊕ *www.marufukuramen.com* ⏲ *Closed Mon.*

Mifune Don
$ | **JAPANESE** | **FAMILY** | Homemade thin soba and thick udon, served either or hot cold with various toppings, are the stars of this low-key, charming restaurant with a wooden facade that looks like it was imported directly from the countryside. Seating is at wooden tables, where diners of every age can be heard slurping down big bowls of traditional Japanese combinations. **Known for:** bowls of noodles; savory Japanese pancakes (okonomiyaki); bargain lunch deals. *Average main: $12* ✉ *22 Peace Plaza, Suite 560, Japantown* ✥ *2nd fl. of East Mall* ☎ *415/346–1993* ⏲ *Closed Tues.*

Hotels

Though a slight trek from downtown, the bustling Japantown neighborhood pleases travelers who appreciate the neighborhood's cuisine or seek proximity to events at the historic Fillmore music venue.

Hotel Kabuki
$$$ | **HOTEL** | Parent company Joie de Vivre Hotels poured $32 million into the two-year long renovation project of this pagoda-style Japantown retreat—and the now finished results are indeed beautiful. **Pros:** serene environment; excellent fitness center; terrific bar and virtuous "small farms" breakfast. **Cons:** pesky guest amenity fee; in-room thermostat is confusing; rooms don't block outside noise. *Rooms from: $249* ✉ *1625 Post St., at Laguna St., Japantown* ☎ *415/922–3200* ⊕ *www.jdvhotels.com/hotel-kabuki* *225 rooms* *No meals.*

Kimpton Buchanan Hotel
$$ | **HOTEL** | Local designer Nicole Hollis created a mildly opulent apartmentlike feel in the Kimpton Buchanan's rooms and public areas. **Pros:** nicely sized rooms; away from downtown bustle yet still convenient; complimentary yoga mats in rooms, bicycles at front desk. **Cons:** too far from the action for some travelers; annoying to join hotel rewards club in order to have free Wi-Fi; closet and toiletries storage space is limited in cheaper rooms. *Rooms from: $208* ✉ *1800 Sutter St., Japantown* ☎ *415/921–4000, 855/454–4644* ⊕ *www.thebuchananhotel.com* *131 rooms* *No meals.*

Shopping

Unlike shops in the ethnic enclaves of Chinatown, North Beach, and the Mission, the 5-acre Japan Center (✉ *Bordered by Laguna, Fillmore, and Post Sts. and Geary Blvd.*) is under one roof. The three-block complex includes a reasonably priced public garage and three shop-filled buildings. Especially worthwhile are the West Mall and Kinokuniya buildings, where shops sell things like bonsai trees, tapes and records, jewelry, antique kimonos, *tansu* (Japanese chests), electronics, and colorful glazed dinnerware and teapots.

BOOKS

Kinokuniya Bookstore

BOOKS/STATIONERY | The selection of English-language books about Japanese culture—everything from medieval history to origami instructions—is one of the finest in the country. Kinokuniya is the city's biggest seller of Japanese-language books. Dozens of glossy Asian fashion magazines attract the young and trendy; the manga and anime books and magazines are wildly popular, too. ✉ *Kinokuniya Bldg., 1581 Webster St., at Geary Blvd., Japantown* ☎ *415/567–7625* 🌐 *www.kinokuniya.com/us.*

Western Addition

Part of the Western Addition, the Lower Fillmore in its post–World War II heyday was known as the Harlem of the West for its profusion of jazz night spots, where such legends as Billie Holliday, Duke Ellington, and Charlie Parker would play. These days the neighborhood tries to maintain its African American core and its link to that heritage; one success is the annual Fillmore Jazz Festival in June. More live music rings at the Fillmore Auditorium, made famous in the 1960s by Bill Graham and the iconic bands he booked there, and at the blues-centric Boom Boom Room.

The larger Western Addition, traditionally one of the city's most diverse neighborhoods, struggles in some areas with poverty and gang violence. And yet the same neighborhood includes the trendy Divisadero dining-rich corridor, and Alamo Square and its iconic Painted Ladies.

Sights

★ **Alamo Square Park**

CITY PARK | **FAMILY** | Whether you've seen them on postcards or on the old TV show "Full House," the colorful "Painted Ladies" Victorians are one of San Francisco's world renowned icons. The signature view of them with the downtown skyline in the background is from the east side of this hilly park that reopened in 2017 after an extensive renovation. Tourists love the photo opportunities, but locals also adore the park's tennis courts, dog-playing area, and ample picnic area—with great views, of course. After taking plenty of photos, swing by the park's northwest corner and admire the William Westerfeld House (1198 Fulton St.), a splendid five-story late-19th-century Victorian mansion. ✉ *Western Addition* ✣ *Between Steiner St., Hayes St., Fulton St., and Hayes St.*

Cathedral of Saint Mary of the Assumption

RELIGIOUS SITE | Residing at the prominent intersection of two busy thoroughfares (Geary Blvd. and Gough St.), there's no missing this striking cathedral and its sweeping contemporary design. Opened in 1971, Italian architects Pietro Belluschi and Pier Luigi Nervi intended to create a spectacular cathedral that reflects the Catholic faith and modern technology. It was controversial at first, yet now is applauded for its grand, curving roof that rises to a height of 190 feet, meeting to form a cross. Don't miss the ceiling's intricate stained glass work. The cathedral is open daily for visitors other than during mass times and usually has docents on duty in the late morning hours. ✉ *1111 Gough St., Western Addition* ✣ *At Geary St.* 🌐 *smcsf.org.*

Restaurants

This is a patchwork of culturally and economically diverse neighborhoods bordering the Lower Haight, the Fillmore District, and Japantown, and the neighborhood reflects that diversity with Italian, Japanese, and Indian restaurants housed in 1950s-era and Victorian buildings in the span of a couple of city blocks. Some of San Francisco's hottest tables, from morning to late night, can be found on the busy Fillmore and Divisadero commercial corridors.

Avery

$$$$ | **MODERN AMERICAN** | With caviar bumps, a cheese course in buckwheat tartlet form and dazzling crispy shrimp "aebelskivers" (Danish beignet), the solo debut of wunderkind chef Rodney Wages is definitely not your average proper fine dining destination. Then again, with its triple digit price tags and liberal use of luxe ingredients, it very much fits right into the exclusive San Francisco lavish spectacle dining club. **Known for:** captivating tasting menu with distinct Japanese influences; minimalist elegant decor; strong sake roster. *Average main: $130* *1552 Fillmore St., Western Addition* *By Geary St.* *415/817–1187* *www.averysf.com* *Closed Mon. and Tues.*

Che Fico

$$$ | **MODERN ITALIAN** | This red hot Divisadero spot on the second floor of a revamped auto body shop was San Francisco's biggest restaurant debut of 2018. In a city full of Italian restaurants, it sets itself apart with homemade charcuterie, antipasti, pastas and pizza that effortlessly blur the line between modern and traditional. **Known for:** pineapple pizza; hard-to-get reservations; Roman Jewish specialties. *Average main: $$28* *838 Divisadero St., Western Addition* *415/416–6959* *www.chefico.com* *Closed Sun. and Mon.*

4505 Burgers & BBQ

$$ | **BARBECUE** | The smoker works overtime from noon to night at this hipster-chic barbecue shack, churning out an array of succulent meats that can be had by the plate, the pound, or as a sandwich. Every plate comes with two sides, and you should certainly make the frankaroni one of them. **Known for:** smoked meats; decadent sides; self-named "Best Damn Cheeseburger". *Average main: $17* *705 Divisadero St., Western Addition* *Between Grove St. and Fulton St.* *415/231–6993* *www.4505burgersandbbq.com.*

Merchant Roots

$$ | **CAFÉ** | It's hard to look past the vintage pasta machine by the sidewalk window, cranking out fresh pastas all day. However, the Fillmore café/craft grocer is so much more than pastas with salads, sandwiches, baked goods, and a noteworthy wine shop in the back. **Known for:** chocolate chip cookies; excellent pasta; photogenic chocolate cannolis. *Average main: $13* *1365 Fillmore St., Western Addition* *530/574–7365* *www.merchantroots.com* *Closed Sun. and Mon.*

★ The Mill

$ | **BAKERY** | "Four-dollar toast" is a phrase used around San Francisco referring to gentrification—and it was inspired by this sundrenched, Wi-Fi-less café. It's a project between one of the city's leading bakers, Josey Baker (yes, that's really his last name and profession!), and the Mission's Four Barrel Coffee. **Known for:** toast in various forms; stellar loaves of bread; a precious, postyoga vibe. *Average main: $8* *736 Divisadero St., Western Addition* *415/345–1953* *www.themillsf.com.*

★ Nopa

$$$ | **AMERICAN** | This is the good-food granddaddy of the hot corridor of the same name (it's hard to tell which came first—Nopa the restaurant or NoPa the North of the Panhandle neighborhood).

The Cali-rustic fare here draws dependable crowds regardless of the night. **Known for:** high-quality comforting food with smart twists; actually good food after 11 pm; a constant and diverse crowd. *Average main: $27* ✉ *560 Divisadero St., Western Addition* ☎ *415/864–8643* 🌐 *www.nopasf.com* ⏲ *No lunch weekdays.*

Nopalito

$$$ | MEXICAN | FAMILY | Those in the mood for a fresh take on both common and seldom seen Mexican dishes will adore Nopa's nearby little sibling. All the tortillas are made from organic house-ground *masa* (dough), and Mexico's peppers find their way into many of the spice-filled offerings. **Known for:** excellent Mexican food; hearty bowl of pork shoulder filled pozole rojo; any drink consisting tequila or mezcal. *Average main: $24* ✉ *306 Broderick St., Western Addition* ☎ *415/437–0303* 🌐 *www.nopalitosf.com.*

The Progress

$$$ | MODERN AMERICAN | The second, grander restaurant from the chef-owners of State Bird Provisions is one of the city's most perennially underrated restaurants thanks to the constant spotlight on its older sibling. Its lofty, bustling setting within an early-20th-century theater is reason enough to visit the Fillmore destination. **Known for:** edgy, lively Californian cuisine; superb cocktails; artistic bar and dining room design. *Average main: $32* ✉ *1525 Fillmore St., Western Addition* ☎ *415/673–1294* 🌐 *www.theprogress-sf.com* ⏲ *No lunch.*

★ **State Bird Provisions**

$$$ | MODERN AMERICAN | It's more or less impossible to nab a reservation for a normal dinner hour at husband-and-wife Stuart Brioza and Nicole Krasinski's game-changing restaurant. But once you nab a golden ticket for one of the 80 dining room and chef counter seats, you'll be rewarded with fascinating bites served from roving carts and an à la carte printed menu. **Known for:** dim sum–style dining; long lines at opening time; "State Bird" namesake buttermilk fried quail. *Average main: $23* ✉ *1529 Fillmore St., Western Addition* ☎ *415/795–1272* 🌐 *www.statebirdsf.com* ⏲ *No lunch.*

Nightlife

Boom Boom Room

MUSIC CLUBS | One of San Francisco's liveliest music spots is this Fillmore blues favorite, opened in 1997 by the "King of Boogie" John Lee Hooker. The club has a fun blend of blues, funk and hip-hop shoes most nights of the week. ✉ *1601 Fillmore St., Western Addition* ✣ *At Geary Blvd.* ☎ *415/673–8000* 🌐 *www.boomboomroom.com.*

Fat Angel

BARS/PUBS | Part of San Francisco knows this intimate, dimly lit Fillmore spot as the unofficial waiting room for State Bird Provisions. However, its many regulars know this gastropub is one of the finest craft beer bars in the entire city. Belgian beers and hard-to-find west coast small batch brews share space on the tap list and bottle roster. On the food front, spicy mac 'n' cheese and SF's best chicken pot pie are crowd favorites for soaking up multiple rounds. ✉ *1740 O'Farrell St., Western Addition* ✣ *Near Fillmore St.* ☎ *415/525–3013* 🌐 *www.fatangelsf.com.*

The Fillmore

MUSIC CLUBS | From the Counting Crows to Jimi Hendrix, this legendary auditorium dating back to 1912 has seen it all. It remains one of San Francisco's essential concert destinations for a variety of music styles. Check out the fun rock poster collection upstairs before the show and enjoy complimentary apples after the show—a fun tradition for Fillmore concertgoers. ✉ *1805 Geary Blvd., Western Addition* ✣ *At Fillmore St.* ☎ *415/346–6000* 🌐 *www.thefillmore.com.*

Horsefeather

BARS/PUBS | Creative produce-driven cocktails and a chic, low-key vibe make this Divisadero drinking destination a locals' frequent top choice for a fun night out. The always interesting (but never too bizarre) cocktails range from a breezy "California Cooler" with celery juice to the rum and whiskey based "Breakfast Punch" featuring clarified Cinnamon Toast Crunch-infused milk. Weekend brunch is excellent as is the delightfully messy double cheeseburger. As an added bonus, the kitchen stays open until 1 am nightly. ✉ *528 Divisadero St., Western Addition* ☎ *415/817–1939* 🌐 *www.horsefeatherbar.com.*

Indian Paradox

WINE BARS—NIGHTLIFE | This festive, tiny Divisadero wine bar is hardly your average "wine bar." Cheese and charcuterie plates are swapped out here for Indian street food and chaat. With an eye-catching bar background made of milk crates and murals of the colorful delivery trucks in India, it also certainly doesn't like your typical wine bar. Most of all, the quirky but beautiful wines work wonders with the exciting small bites offered à la carte or in a very reasonably priced tasting menu. ✉ *258 Divisadero St., Western Addition* ☎ *415/593–5386* 🌐 *www.indianparadoxsf.com.*

Chapter 14

THE BAY AREA

Updated by
Monique Peterson

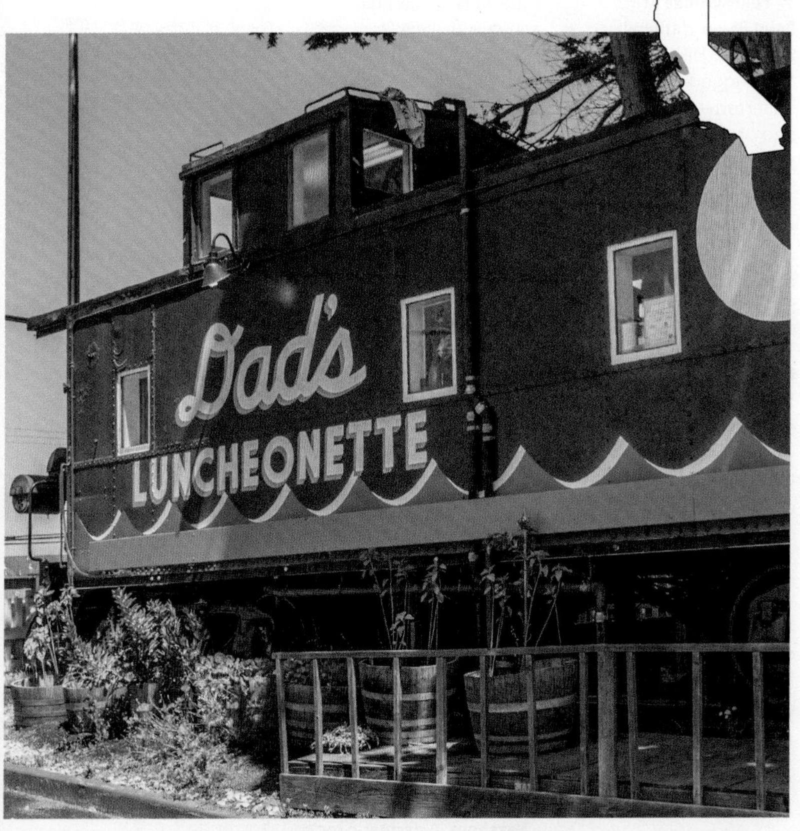

Sights	Restaurants	Hotels	Shopping	Nightlife
★★★★☆	★★★★☆	★★☆☆☆	★★☆☆☆	★★★★☆

WELCOME TO THE BAY AREA

TOP REASONS TO GO

★ **Bite into the "Gourmet Ghetto":** Eat your way through this area of North Berkeley, starting with a slice of perfect pizza from Cheese Board Pizza (just look for the line).

★ **Find solitude at Point Reyes National Seashore:** Hike beautifully rugged—and often deserted—beaches at one of the most beautiful places on Earth, period.

★ **Sit on a dock by the bay:** Admire the beauty of the Bay Area from the rocky, picturesque shores of Sausalito or Tiburon.

★ **Go barhopping in Oakland's hippest hood:** Spend an evening swinging through the watering holes of Uptown, Oakland's artsy-hip and fast-rising corner of downtown.

★ **Walk among giants:** Walking into Muir Woods, a mere 12 miles north of the Golden Gate Bridge, is like entering a cathedral built by God.

1 **Berkeley.** Independent bookstores, excellent coffee spots, and thousands of cyclists.

2 **Oakland.** A diverse, multifaceted city with a lively arts, nightlife, and food scene.

3 **The Marin Headlands.** Stretching from the Golden Gate Bridge to Muir Beach, these headlands offer spectacular views.

4 **Sausalito.** This Marin County city has stunning views and a bohemian feel.

5 **Tiburon.** This scenic, quaint town has lots of good dining and hiking and a more low-key vibe than Sausalito.

6 **Mill Valley.** A superb natural setting with a lively downtown area.

7 **Muir Woods National Monument.** Home to some of the most majestic redwoods in the world—some more than 250 feet tall.

8 **Mt. Tamalpais State Park.** Next to Muir Woods National Monument, this park offers views of the entire Bay Area and the Pacific Ocean to the west.

9 **Muir Beach.** A quiet beach has a distinctly local feel.

10 **Stinson Beach.** An expansive stretch of beach and a town with a nonchalant surfer vibe.

11 **Point Reyes National Seashore.** A dramatic rocky coastline with miles of sandy beaches.

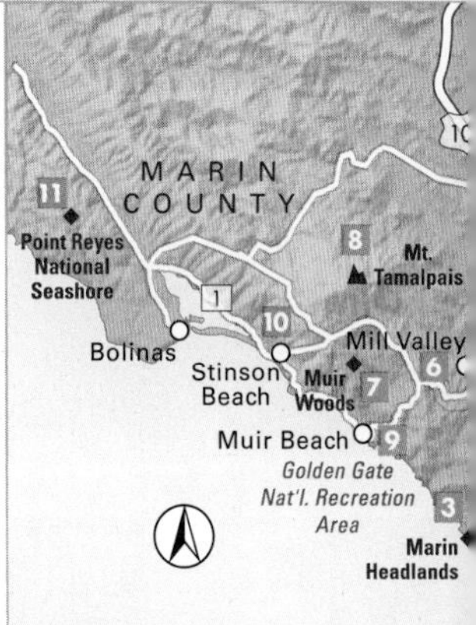

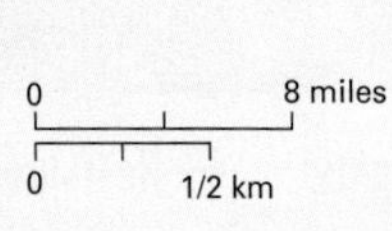

San Pablo Bay
San Rafael
Richmond
El Cerrito
Briones Regional Park
Tilden Regional Park
Four Corners
Walnut Creek
Mt. Diablo State Park
Marin City
Tiburon
Angel Island
Sausalito
Golden Gate Br.
Berkeley
Redwood Regional Park
THE EAST BAY
Oakland
San Francisco
San Francisco Bay
San Leandro
Oakland International Airport
Daly City
Dublin
South San Francisco
Hayward
San Francisco International Airport
Pacifica
Burlingame
San Mateo
Union City
Foster City
Montara
Belmont
Fremont
Moss Beach
San Francisco Bay National Wildlife Refuge
Purisima Creek Redwoods Open Space Preserve
Redwood City
Half Moon Bay
Palo Alto
Stanford University
Milpitas
SANTA CRUZ MTS.
Mountain View
Santa Clara
Pescadero
San Jose
TO AÑO NUEVO STATE RESERVE
TO BIG BASIN REDWOODS STATE PARK
580
80
24
1
2
280
101
880
680
82
92
84
35
237
85
5

It's rare for a metropolis to compete with its suburbs for visitors, but the view from any of San Francisco's hilltops shows that the Bay Area's temptations extend far beyond the city limits. East of the city are the energetic urban centers of Berkeley and Oakland. Famously radical Berkeley is also comfortably sophisticated, while Oakland has an arts and restaurant scene so hip that it pulls San Franciscans across the bay. To the north is Marin County with its dramatic coastal beauty and chic, affluent villages.

MAJOR REGIONS

The East Bay. The college town of Berkeley has long been known for its liberal ethos, stimulating university community (and perhaps even more stimulating coffee shops), and activist streak. But these days, the lively restaurant and arts scenes are luring even those who wouldn't be caught dead in Birkenstocks. Meanwhile, life in the diverse, harbor-front city of Oakland is strongly defined by a turbulent history. Today, progressive Oakland is an incubator for artisans of all kinds, and the thriving culinary and art scenes are taking off.

Marin County. Marin is considered the prettiest of the Bay Area counties, primarily because of its wealth of open space. Anchored by water on three sides, the county is mostly parkland, including long stretches of undeveloped coastline. The picturesque small towns here—Sausalito, Tiburon, Mill Valley, and Bolinas among them—may sometimes look rustic, but most are in a dizzyingly high tax bracket.

Planning

When to Go

As with San Francisco, you can visit the rest of the Bay Area any time of year, and it's especially nice in late spring and fall. Unlike San Francisco, though, the surrounding areas are reliably sunny in summer—it gets hotter as you head inland. Even the rainy season has its charms, as otherwise golden hills turn a rich green and wildflowers become plentiful. Precipitation is usually the heaviest between November and

March. Berkeley is a university town, so it's easier to navigate the streets and find parking near the university between semesters, but there's also less buzz around town.

Getting Here and Around

Seamless travel from train to ferry to bus with one fare card is possible—and often preferable to driving on congested freeways and over toll bridges. For trips from one city to the next across the bay, take a tip from locals and save time and money with a Clipper card. They work with BART, MUNI, buses, and ferries. **■ TIP→ Order a Clipper card before you travel:** 🌐 *www.clippercard.com.*

BART TRAVEL

Using public transportation to reach Berkeley or Oakland is ideal. The under- and aboveground BART (Bay Area Rapid Transit) trains make stops in both cities as well as other East Bay destinations. Trips to either take about a half hour one-way from the center of San Francisco. BART does not serve Marin County.

CONTACTS BART. ☎ *510/465–2278* 🌐 *www.bart.gov.*

BOAT AND FERRY TRAVEL

For sheer romance, nothing beats the ferry; there's service from San Francisco to Sausalito, Tiburon, and Larkspur in Marin County, and to Alameda and Oakland in the East Bay.

The Golden Gate Ferry crosses the bay to Larkspur and Sausalito from San Francisco's Ferry Building (✉ *Market St. and the Embarcadero*). Blue & Gold Fleet ferries depart daily for Sausalito and Tiburon from Pier 41 at Fisherman's Wharf; weekday commuter ferries leave from the Ferry Building for Tiburon. The trip to either Sausalito or Tiburon takes from 25 minutes to an hour. Purchase tickets from terminal vending machines.

The Angel Island–Tiburon Ferry sails to the island daily from April through October and on weekends the rest of the year.

The San Francisco Bay Ferry runs several times daily between San Francisco's Ferry Building or Pier 41 and Oakland's Jack London Square by way of Alameda. The trip lasts from 25 to 45 minutes, and leads to Oakland's waterfront shopping and restaurant district. Purchase tickets on board.

BOAT AND FERRY LINES Angel Island–Tiburon Ferry. ☎ *415/435–2131* 🌐 *www.angelislandferry.com.* **Blue & Gold Fleet.** ☎ *415/705–8200* 🌐 *www.blueandgold-fleet.com.* **Golden Gate Ferry.** ☎ *415/921–5858* 🌐 *www.goldengateferry.org.* **San Francisco Bay Ferry.** ☎ *707/643–3779, 877/643–3779* 🌐 *sanfranciscobayferry.com.*

BUS TRAVEL

Golden Gate Transit buses travel north to Sausalito, Tiburon, and elsewhere in Marin County from the Transbay Temporary Terminal (located at Howard and Main, two blocks south of Market) and other points in San Francisco. For Mt. Tamalpais State Park and West Marin (Stinson Beach, Bolinas, and Point Reyes Station), take any route to Marin City and then transfer to the West Marin Stagecoach. San Francisco Muni buses primarily serve the city, though the 76X does cross the Golden Gate and end at the Marin Headlands Visitors Center on weekends. **■ TIP→ Several other bus options exist for local and regional travel throughout the Bay Area, including Amtrak, Greyhound, California Shuttle, and more (www.bayareatransit.net/regional).**

Though less speedy than BART, more than 30 AC Transit bus lines provide service to and from the Transbay Temporary Terminal and throughout the East Bay, even after BART shuts down. The F and FS lines will get you to Berkeley, while lines C, P, B, and O take you to Oakland and Piedmont.

BUS LINES AC Transit. ☎ *510/891–4777* 🌐 *www.actransit.org.* **Golden Gate Transit.** ☎ *511* 🌐 *www.goldengatetransit.org.* **SamTrans.** ☎ *800/660–4287* 🌐 *www.samtrans.com.* **San Francisco Muni.** ☎ *311* 🌐 *www.sfmta.com.* **West Marin Stagecoach.** ☎ *511* 🌐 *www.marintransit.org.*

CAR TRAVEL

To reach the East Bay from San Francisco, take Interstate 80 East across the San Francisco–Oakland Bay Bridge. For U.C. Berkeley, merge onto Interstate 580 West and take Exit 11 for University Avenue. For Oakland, merge onto Interstate 580 East. To reach downtown, take Interstate 980 West from Interstate 580 East and exit at 14th Street. Travel time varies depending on traffic, but should take about 30 minutes (or more than an hour if it's rush hour).

For all points in Marin, head north on U.S. 101 and cross the Golden Gate Bridge. Sausalito, Tiburon, the Marin Headlands, and Point Reyes National Seashore are all accessed off U.S. 101. The scenic coastal route, Highway 1, also called Shoreline Highway and Panoramic for certain stretches, can be accessed off U.S. 101 as well. Follow this road to Muir Woods, Mt. Tamalpais State Park, Muir Beach, Stinson Beach, and Bolinas. From Bolinas, you can continue north on Highway 1 to Point Reyes.

Restaurants

The Bay Area is home to many popular and innovative restaurants, such as Chez Panisse in Berkeley and Commis in Oakland—for which reservations must be made well in advance. There are also countless casual but equally tasty eateries to test out; expect an emphasis on organic seasonal produce, locally raised meats, craft cocktails, and curated wine menus. Marin's dining scene trends toward the sleepy side, so be sure to check hours ahead of time. *Restaurant reviews have been shortened. For full information, visit Fodors.com.*

Hotels

With a few exceptions, hotels in Berkeley and Oakland tend to be standard-issue, but many Marin hotels package themselves as cozy retreats. Summer in Marin is often booked well in advance, despite weather that can be downright chilly. Check for special packages during this season. *Hotel reviews have been shortened. For full information, visit Fodors.com.*

WHAT IT COSTS			
$	**$$**	**$$$**	**$$$$**
RESTAURANTS			
under $16	$16–$22	$23–$30	over $30
HOTELS			
under $150	$150–$199	$200–$250	over $250

Tours

★ Best Bay Area Tours
Morning and afternoon tours of Muir Woods and Sausalito include at least 90 minutes in the redwoods before heading on to Sausalito. On returning to the city, tours make a scenic stop in the Marin Headlands to enjoy fantastic views. Knowledgeable guides lead small tours in comfortable vans, and hotel pickup is included, though park entrance is not. Another tour option includes a visit to Muir Woods and Wine Country exploration. ☎ *877/705–8687* 🌐 *bestbayareatours.com* 🎫 *From $60.*

Berkeley

2 miles northeast of Bay Bridge.

Berkeley is the birthplace of the Free Speech Movement, the radical hub of the 1960s, the home of arguably the nation's top public university, and a frequent site of protests and political movements. The city of 115,000 is also a culturally diverse breeding ground for social trends, a bastion of the counterculture, and an important center for Bay Area writers, artists, and musicians. Berkeley residents, students, and faculty spend hours nursing coffee concoctions while they read, discuss, and debate at the dozens of cafés that surround campus. It's the quintessential university town, with numerous independent bookstores, countless casual eateries, myriad meetups, and thousands of cyclists.

Oakland may have Berkeley beat when it comes to ethnic diversity and cutting-edge arts, but unless you're accustomed to sipping hemp milk lattes while planning a protest prior to yoga, you'll likely find Berkeley charmingly offbeat.

GETTING HERE AND AROUND

BART is the easiest way to get to Berkeley from San Francisco. Exit at the Downtown Berkeley station, and walk a block up Center Street to get to the western edge of campus. AC Transit buses F and FS lines stop near the university and 4th Street shopping. By car, take Interstate 80 East across the Bay Bridge, merge onto Interstate 580 West, and take the University Avenue exit through downtown Berkeley or take the Ashby Avenue exit and turn left on Telegraph Avenue. Once you arrive, explore on foot. Berkeley is very pedestrian-friendly.

ESSENTIALS

VISITOR INFORMATION Koret Visitor Center. ✉ *2227 Piedmont Ave., at California Memorial Stadium, Downtown* ☎ *510/642–5215* 🌐 *visit.berkeley.edu.* **Visit Berkeley.** ✉ *2030 Addison St., Suite 102, Downtown* ☎ *510/549–7040, 800/847–4823* 🌐 *www.visitberkeley.com.*

Sights

BAMPFA (Berkeley Art Museum and Pacific Film Archive)

MUSEUM | This combined art museum and repertory movie theater and film archive contains more than 19,000 works of art and 16,000 films and videos. Art works span five centuries and include modernist notables Mark Rothko, Jackson Pollock, David Smith and Hans Hofmann. The Pacific Film Archive specializes in international films and offers regular screenings, programs, and performances. ✉ *2155 Center St., Downtown* ☎ *510/642–0808* 🌐 *bampfa.org* 🎟 *$13; free 1st Thurs. of month* ⏲ *Closed Mon. and Tues.*

Fourth Street

NEIGHBORHOOD | Once an industrial area, this walkable stretch of Fourth Street north of University Avenue has transformed into the busiest few blocks of refined shopping and eating in Berkeley. For lovers of design, curated taste experiences, artful living, and fashion, the vibrant district boasts more than 70 shops, specialty stores, cafes, and restaurants. See creation and inspiration at Castle in the Air, Builders Booksource, and The Stained Glass Garden, or sip a "live roast" at Artis, where you can watch small batch coffee roasting in progress. ✉ *4th St. between University Ave. and Virginia St.* 🌐 *www.fourth-street.com.*

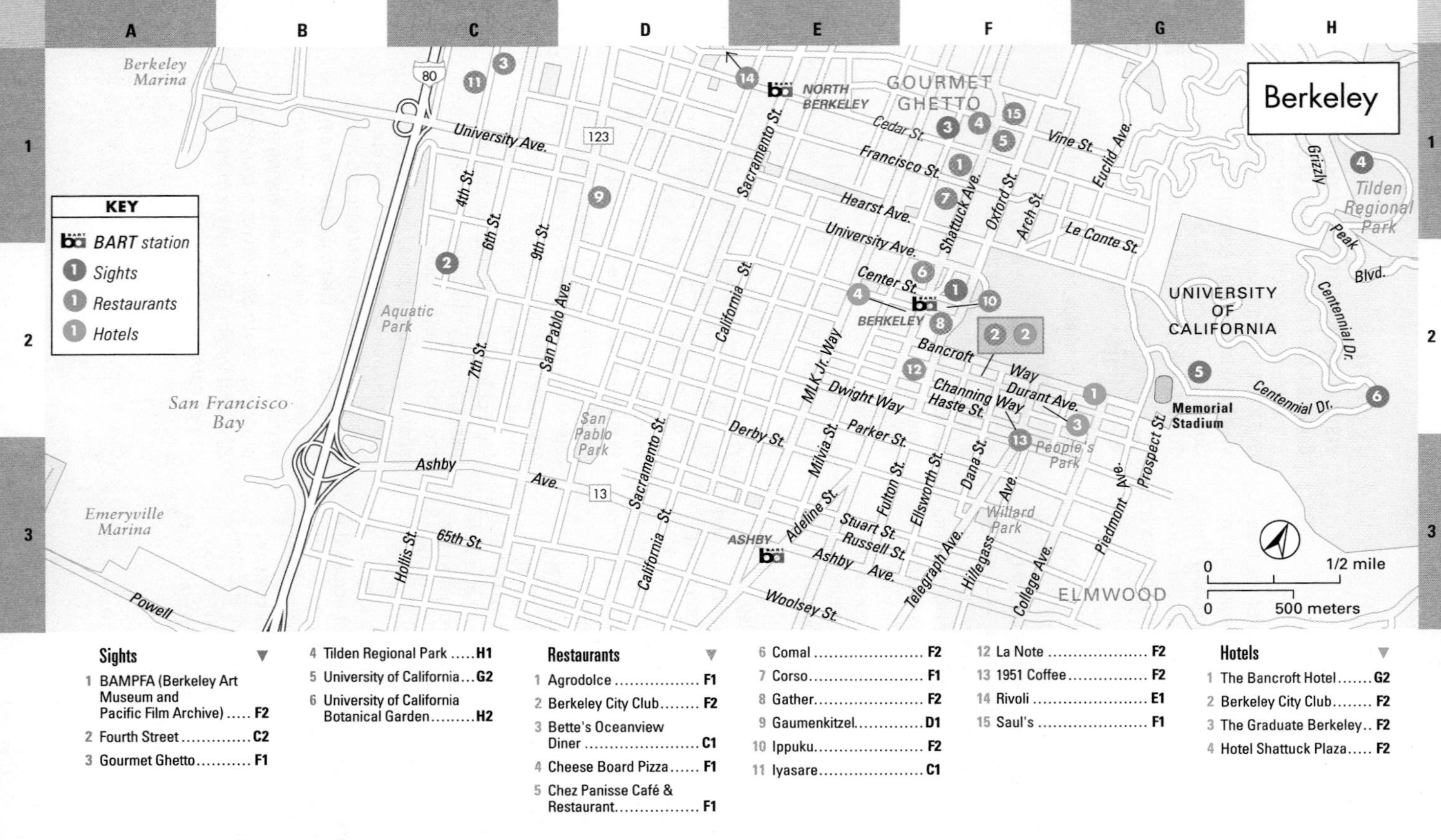

Sights

1 BAMPFA (Berkeley Art Museum and Pacific Film Archive) F2
2 Fourth Street C2
3 Gourmet Ghetto F1
4 Tilden Regional Park H1
5 University of California ... G2
6 University of California Botanical Garden H2

Restaurants

1 Agrodolce F1
2 Berkeley City Club F2
3 Bette's Oceanview Diner C1
4 Cheese Board Pizza F1
5 Chez Panisse Café & Restaurant F1
6 Comal F2
7 Corso F1
8 Gather F2
9 Gaumenkitzel D1
10 Ippuku F2
11 Iyasare C1
12 La Note F2
13 1951 Coffee F2
14 Rivoli E1
15 Saul's F1

Hotels

1 The Bancroft Hotel G2
2 Berkeley City Club F2
3 The Graduate Berkeley .. F2
4 Hotel Shattuck Plaza F2

★ Gourmet Ghetto

NEIGHBORHOOD | The success of Alice Water's Chez Panisse defined California cuisine and attracted countless food-related enterprises to a stretch of Shattuck Avenue now known as the Gourmet Ghetto. Foodies will do well here poking around the shops, grabbing a quick bite, or indulging in a feast.

César (*1515 Shattuck*) wine bar provides afternoon tapas and late-night drinks, while the **Epicurious Garden** (*1509–1513 Shattuck*) food stands sell everything from sushi to gelato. A small terraced garden winds up to the **Imperial Tea Court**, a Zen-like teahouse rife with imports and tea ware.

Across Vine, the **Vintage Berkeley** (*2113 Vine*) wine shop offers regular tastings and reasonably priced bottles within the walls of a historic former pump house. Coffee lovers can head to the original **Peet's Coffee & Tea** at the corner of Walnut and Vine (*2124 Vine*).

South of Cedar Street, the **Local Butcher Shop** (*No. 1600*) sells locally sourced meat and hearty sandwiches of the day. For high-end food at takeout prices, try the salads, sandwiches, and signature potato puffs at **Grégoire**, around the corner on Cedar Street (*No. 2109*). **Masse's Pastries** (*No. 1469 Shattuck*) is a museum of edible artwork. We could go on, but you get the idea. ⊠ *Shattuck Ave. between Delaware and Rose Sts., North Berkeley* 🌐 *www.gourmetghetto.org.*

★ Tilden Regional Park

NATIONAL/STATE PARK | **FAMILY** | Stunning bay views, a scaled-down steam train, and a botanic garden that boasts the nation's most complete collection of California plant life are the hallmarks of this 2,000-acre park in the hills just east of the U.C. Berkeley campus. The garden's visitors center offers tours, as well as information about Tilden's other attractions, including its picnic spots, Lake Anza swimming site, golf course, and hiking trails (the paved **Nimitz Way**, at Inspiration Point, is a popular hike with wonderful sunset views). **■ TIP→ Children love Tilden's interactive Little Farm and vintage carousel.** ⊠ *Tilden Regional Park, 2501 Grizzly Peak Blvd., Tilden Park* ☎ *510/544–2747 park office* 🌐 *www.ebparks.org/parks/tilden* *Free parking and botanic garden.*

A Tasting Tour

For an unforgettable foodie experience, book a **Culinary Walking Tour** with Edible Excursions (*415/806–5970, www.edibleexcursions.net*). Come hungry for knowledge and noshing. Tours ($110) take place on Thursday at 11 and Saturday at 10.

University of California

COLLEGE | Known simply as "Cal," the founding campus of California's university system is one of the leading intellectual centers in the United States and a major site for scientific research. Chartered in 1868, the university sits on 178 oak-covered acres split by Strawberry Creek; it's bound by Bancroft Way to the south, Hearst Avenue to the north, Oxford Street to the west, and Gayley Road to the east. Campus highlights include bustling and historic **Sproul Plaza** (*Bancroft Way and Sather Rd.*), the seven floors and 61-bell carillon of **Sather Tower** (*Campanile Esplanade*), the nearly 3 million artifacts in the **Phoebe A. Hearst Museum of Anthropology** (Kroeber Hall), hands-on **Lawrence Hall of Science** (*1 Centennial Dr.*), the vibrant 34-acre **Botanical Gardens** (*200 Centennial Dr.*), and the historic **Hearst Greek Theatre** (*2001 Gayley Rd.*), the classic outdoor amphitheater designed by John Galen Howard. ⊠ *Downtown* ☎ *510/642–6000* 🌐 *www.berkeley.edu.*

The University of California is the epicenter of Berkeley's energy and activism.

University of California Botanical Garden
GARDEN | **FAMILY** | Thanks to Berkeley's temperate climate, more than 10,000 types of plants from all corners of the world flourish in the 34-acre University of California Botanical Garden. Free garden tours are given regularly with paid admission. Benches and shady picnic tables make this a relaxing place for a snack with a breathtaking view. ✉ *200 Centennial Dr., Downtown* ☎ *510/643–2755* 🌐 *botanicalgarden.berkeley.edu* 🎫 *$12* ⏲ *Closed 1st Tues. every month.*

Restaurants

Dining in Berkeley may be low-key when it comes to dress, but it's top-of-class in quality, even in less-refined spaces. Late diners beware: Berkeley is an "early to bed" kind of town.

Agrodolce
$$ | **ITALIAN** | **FAMILY** | Angelo D'Alo's family brings Sicilian flavors and their love for preparing them freshly to the heart of the Gourmet Ghetto, where black-and-white photos and Italian home decor add to the old-world atmosphere. The menu features local, sustainable, and organic ingredients in such dishes as house-made orecchiette, seafood risotto, and free-range *pollo scarpariello*. **Known for:** braised pork pappardelle; homemade sauces; antipasti specialties. 💲 *Average main: $17* ✉ *1730 Shattuck Ave., North Berkeley* ☎ *510/848–8748* 🌐 *www.agrodolceberkeley.com* ⏲ *Closed Tues.*

Bette's Oceanview Diner
$ | **DINER** | **FAMILY** | Checkered floors, vintage burgundy booths, and an old-time jukebox set the scene at this retro-chic diner in the heart of Berkeley's fashionable 4th Street shopping district. The wait for a seat at breakfast can be quite long; luckily Bette's To Go is always an option. **Known for:** soufflé pancakes; poached egg specialties; meat loaf and gravy. 💲 *Average main: $13* ✉ *1807 4th St., near Delaware St., 4th Street* ☎ *510/644–3230* 🌐 *www.bettesdiner.com* ⏲ *No dinner.*

★ Cheese Board Pizza

$ | **PIZZA** | A jazz combo entertains the line that usually snakes down the block outside Cheese Board Pizza; it's that good. The cooperatively owned takeout spot and restaurant draws devoted customers with the smell of just-baked garlic on the pie of the day. **Known for:** vegetarian pizza by the slice or slab; live music performances; green sauce. *Average main: $11 1504–1512 Shattuck Ave., at Vine St., North Berkeley 510/549–3183 cheeseboardcollective.coop/pizza Pizza closed Sun. and Mon., bakery closed Sun.*

★ Chez Panisse Café & Restaurant

$$$$ | **MODERN AMERICAN** | Alice Waters's legendary eatery is known for its locally sourced ingredients, formal prix-fixe menus, and personal service, while its upstairs café offers simpler fare in a more casual setting. Both menus change daily and legions of loyal fans insist that Chez Panisse lives up to its reputation. **Known for:** sustainably sourced meats; inventive use of seasonal ingredients; attention to detail. *Average main: $125 1517 Shattuck Ave., at Vine St., North Berkeley 510/548–5525 restaurant, 510/548–5049 café www.chezpanisse.com Closed Sun. No lunch in restaurant.*

★ Comal

$ | **MODERN MEXICAN** | Relaxed yet trendy, Comal's cavernous indoor dining space and intimate back patio and fire pit draw a diverse, decidedly casual crowd for creative Oaxacan-inspired fare and well-crafted cocktails. The modern Mexican menu centers on small dishes that lend themselves to sharing and are offered alongside more than 100 tequilas and mezcals. **Known for:** margaritas and mezcal; house-made chicharrones; wood-fired entrées. *Average main: $16 2020 Shattuck Ave., near University Ave., Downtown 510/926–6300 www.comalberkeley.com No lunch.*

Corso

$$$ | **MODERN ITALIAN** | This lively spot serves up a seasonal menu of excellent Tuscan cuisine and Italian wines in a sparse but snazzy space. The open kitchen dominates a room, which includes closely spaced tables and festive flickering candles. **Known for:** handcrafted pastas; house-cured salumi; daily butcher's specials. *Average main: $24 1788 Shattuck Ave., at Delaware St., North Berkeley 510/704–8004 www.corsoberkeley.com No lunch.*

Gather

$$$ | **MODERN AMERICAN** | All things local, organic, seasonal, and sustainable reside harmoniously under one roof at Gather. This haven for vegans, vegetarians, and carnivores alike is a vibrant, well-lit space that boasts funky light fixtures, shiny wood furnishings, and banquettes made of recycled leather belts. **Known for:** heirloom varietals; wood-fired pizzas; house-made liqueurs. *Average main: $24 2200 Oxford St., at Allston Way, Downtown 510/809–0400 www.gatherrestaurant.com.*

Gaumenkitzel

$$ | **GERMAN** | **FAMILY** | This convivial locale for organic, slow-food German fare is also the spot for the Bay Area's best variety of German beers. With dishes like spätzle and caramelized onions, house-made *brezel* with bratwurst, *jägerschnitzel* with braised red cabbage, and pan-fried rainbow trout, this kitchen puts a fresh stamp on traditional German favorites. **Known for:** German wine and beer selection; house-made German breads; fresh, sustainable ingredients. *Average main: $20 2121 San Pablo Ave., Downtown 510/647–5016 www.gaumenkitzel.net Closed Mon.*

★ Ippuku

$$$ | **JAPANESE** | More Tokyo street chic than standard sushi house, this *izakaya*—the Japanese equivalent of a bar with appetizers—is decked with bamboo-screen booths. Servers pour an

impressive array of sakes and *shōchū* and serve up surprising fare. **Known for:** shōchū selection; charcoal-grilled yakitori skewers; selection of small dishes. 💲 *Average main: $28* ✉ *2130 Center St., Downtown* ☎ *510/665–1969* 🌐 *www.ippukuberkeley.com* ⏲ *Closed Mon. No lunch.*

Iyasare

$$$ | JAPANESE | Reservations are recommended at this 4th Street hot spot where the outdoor seating is ideal for people-watching and the Japanese country food is uniquely prepared. Locals come back for seasonally changing eclectic dishes made with a blend of local ingredients, such as burdock root tempura and ume-cured sashimi or miso-bell pepper puree with Dungeness crab. **Known for:** Japanese whiskey and specialty sakes; donburi and small plates; cured salads. 💲 *Average main: $23* ✉ *1830 4th St., 4th Street* ☎ *510/845–8100* 🌐 *iyasare-berkeley.com.*

★ La Note

$$ | FRENCH | A charming taste of Provence in a 19th-century locale with stone floors, country tables, and a seasonal flowering patio, La Note's rustic French food is as thoughtfully prepared as the space is lovely. Enjoy breakfast and brunch outdoors with fresh crusty breads and pastries, eggs *Lucas* with house roasted tomatoes, and lemon gingerbread pancakes or romantic dinners with mussels *mouclade,* ratatouille, and homemade fondue. **Known for:** sandwiches; house-made Merguez sausage; brioche pan perdu. 💲 *Average main: $18* ✉ *2377 Shattuck Ave., Downtown* ✣ *Between Channing and Durant* ☎ *510/843–1525* 🌐 *www.lanoterestaurant.com* ⏲ *Closed for dinner Sun.–Wed.*

1951 Coffee

$ | CAFÉ | Taking its name from the 1951 Refugee Convention at which the United Nations first set guidelines for refugee protections, 1951 Coffee Company is a nonprofit coffee shop inspired and powered by refugees. In addition to crafting high-caliber coffee drinks and dishing out local pastries and savory bites, this colorful café also serves as an inspiring advocacy space and training center for refugees. Just three blocks south of campus, it's a favorite meet-up spot for locals and students alike. **Known for:** 1951 hand-roasted blends; Third Culture Bakery Mochi doughnuts and muffins; chai latte. 💲 *Average main: $7* ✉ *2410 Channing Way, at Dana St., Downtown* ☎ *510/280–6171* 🌐 *1951coffee.com.*

Rivoli

$$$$ | MODERN AMERICAN | Italian-inspired dishes using fresh California ingredients star on a menu that changes regularly. Inventive offerings are served in a Zen-like modern dining room with captivating views of the lovely back garden. **Known for:** line-caught fish and sustainably sourced meats; curated wine list; thoughtfully combined ingredients. 💲 *Average main: $32* ✉ *1539 Solano Ave., at Neilson St., North Berkeley* ☎ *510/526–2542* 🌐 *www.rivolirestaurant.com* ⏲ *No lunch.*

★ Saul's

$ | AMERICAN | FAMILY | High ceilings and red-leather booths add to the friendly, retro atmosphere of Saul's deli, a Berkeley institution that is well known for its homemade celery tonic sodas and enormous sandwiches made with Acme bread. Locals swear by the pastrami sandwiches, stuffed-cabbage rolls, and challah French toast. **Known for:** hand-rolled organic bagels; matzo ball soup; Niman Ranch grass-fed beef and Monterey Fish Company seafood. 💲 *Average main: $16* ✉ *1475 Shattuck Ave., near Vine St., North Berkeley* ☎ *510/848–3354* 🌐 *www.saulsdeli.com.*

Famed Berkeley restaurant Chez Panisse focuses on seasonal local ingredients.

Hotels

For inexpensive lodging, investigate University Avenue, west of campus. The area can be noisy, congested, and somewhat dilapidated, but it does include a few decent motels and chain properties. All Berkeley lodgings are strictly mid-range.

The Bancroft Hotel

$$ | HOTEL | This eco-friendly boutique hotel—across from the U.C. campus—is quaint, charming, and completely green. **Pros:** closest hotel in Berkeley to U.C. campus; friendly staff; many rooms have good views. **Cons:** some rooms are quite small; despite renovation, the building shows its age with thin walls; no elevator. *Rooms from: $160 2680 Bancroft Way, Downtown 510/549–1000, 800/549–1002 toll-free bancrofthotel.com 22 rooms Breakfast.*

★ **Berkeley City Club**

$$$ | HOTEL | Moorish design and Gothic architecture meet modern amenities at this historic locale steps from campus, arts, and eateries. **Pros:** art gallery and courtyard seating; laundry facilities; on-site salon and skin care. **Cons:** no nonservice pets allowed; limited, fee-only parking; no televisions in rooms. *Rooms from: $245 2315 Durant Ave., Downtown www.berkeleycityclub.com 38 rooms Free Breakfast.*

The Graduate Berkeley

$$$ | HOTEL | Fresh, colorful design and Bohemian flair set the tone at this historically renovated hotel just steps from campus and downtown eating, shopping, and entertainment. **Pros:** convenient location; pet-friendly; complimentary bikes. **Cons:** rooms can be noisy; rooms can be small; fee parking only. *Rooms from: $239 2600 Durant Ave., Downtown 510/845–8981 www.graduatehotels.com/berkeley 144 rooms No meals.*

★ **Hotel Shattuck Plaza**

$$$ | HOTEL | This historic boutique hotel sits amid Berkeley's downtown arts district, just steps from the U.C. campus and a short walk from the Gourmet

Ghetto. **Pros:** central location near public transit; special date night and B&B packages; modern facilities. **Cons:** public and street parking only; limited on-site fitness center; street-facing rooms may be loud. *Rooms from: $246* ✉ *2086 Allston Way, at Shattuck Ave., Downtown* ☎ *510/845–7300* 🌐 *www.hotelshattuck-plaza.com* *199 rooms* *No meals.*

Nightlife

★ The Freight & Salvage Coffeehouse

MUSIC CLUBS | For more than 50 years, the Freight has been a venue for some of the world's finest practitioners of folk, jazz, gospel, blues, world-beat, bluegrass, and storytelling. The nonprofit organization grew from an 87-seat coffee house to a thriving, 500-seat venue in the heart of Berkeley's Art District. Many tickets cost less than $30. ✉ *2020 Addison St., between Shattuck Ave. and Milvia St., Downtown* ☎ *510/644–2020* 🌐 *www.thefreight.org.*

★ Tupper & Reed

BARS/PUBS | Housed in the former music shop of John C. Tupper and Lawrence Reed, this music-inspired cocktail haven features a symphony of carefully crafted libations, which are mixed with live music performed by local musicians. The historic 1925 building features a balcony bar, cozy nooks, antique fixtures, a pool table, and romantic fireplaces. ✉ *2271 Shattuck Ave., at Kitteredge St., Downtown* ☎ *510/859–4472* 🌐 *www.tupperandreed.com.*

Performing Arts

Berkeley Repertory Theatre

THEATER | One of the region's most highly respected and innovative repertory theaters, Berkeley Rep performs the work of classic and contemporary playwrights. Well-known pieces such as *Tartuffe* and *Macbeth* mix with world premieres and edgier fare like Green Day's *American Idiot* and Lemony Snicket's *The Composer Is Dead.* The theater's complex is in the heart of downtown Berkeley's arts district, near BART's Downtown Berkeley station. ✉ *2025 Addison St., near Shattuck Ave., Downtown* ☎ *510/647–2949* 🌐 *www.berkeleyrep.org.*

Cal Performances

CONCERTS | Based out of U.C. Berkeley, this series runs from September through May. It features a varied bill of internationally acclaimed artists ranging from classical soloists to the latest jazz, world-music, theater, and dance ensembles. Past performers include Alvin Ailey American Dance Theater, the National Ballet of China, and Yo-Yo Ma. ✉ *101 Zellerbach Hall, Suite 4800, Dana St. and Bancroft Way, Downtown* ☎ *510/642–9988* 🌐 *calperformances.org.*

Shopping

★ Acci Gallery

ART GALLERIES | The Arts and Crafts Cooperative, Inc., a collective of Berkeley artists and artisans, has been a stalwart gallery and retail store showcasing ceramics, textiles, paintings, photography, jewelry, and various media for more than 60 years. Explore the amazing range of local talent in a well-lit historic space, and find truly one-of-a-kind gems to take home. ✉ *1652 Shattuck Ave., North Berkeley* ✣ *At Lincoln* ☎ *510/843–2527* 🌐 *www.accigallery.com.*

★ Amoeba Music

MUSIC STORES | Heaven for audiophiles and movie collectors, this legendary Berkeley favorite is *the* place to head for new and used CDs, vinyl, cassettes, VHS tapes, Blu-ray discs, and DVDs. The massive and ever-changing stock includes thousands of titles for all music tastes, as well as plenty of Amoeba merch. There are branches in San Francisco and Hollywood, but this is the original. ✉ *2455 Telegraph Ave., at Haste St., Downtown* ☎ *510/549–1125* 🌐 *www.amoeba.com.*

Kermit Lynch Wine Merchant

WINE/SPIRITS | Credited with taking American appreciation of old-world wines to a higher level, this small shop is a great place to peruse as you educate your palate. The friendly salespeople will happily direct you to the latest French and Italian bargains. ✉ *1605 San Pablo Ave., at Cedar St.* ☎ *510/524–1524* 🌐 *www.kermitlynch.com* 🕙 *Closed Sun. and Mon.*

Moe's Books

BOOKS/STATIONERY | The spirit of Moe—the creative, cantankerous, cigar-smoking late proprietor—lives on in this world-famous four-story house of new and used books. Students and professors come here to browse the large selection, which includes literary and cultural criticism, art titles, and literature in foreign languages. ✉ *2476 Telegraph Ave., near Haste St., Downtown* ☎ *510/849–2087* 🌐 *www.moesbooks.com.*

Oakland

East of Bay Bridge.

In contrast to San Francisco's buzz and beauty and Berkeley's storied counterculture, Oakland's allure lies in its amazing diversity. Here you can find a Nigerian clothing store, a Gothic revival skyscraper, a Buddhist meditation center, and a lively salsa club, all within the same block.

Oakland's multifaceted nature reflects its colorful and tumultuous history. Once a cluster of Mediterranean-style homes and gardens that served as a bedroom community for San Francisco, the town had a major rail terminal and port city by the turn of the 20th century. Already a hub of manufacturing, Oakland became a center for shipbuilding and industry when the United States entered World War II. New jobs in the city's shipyards, railroads, and factories attracted thousands of laborers from across the country, including sharecroppers from the Deep South, Mexican Americans from the southwest, and some of the nation's first female welders. Neighborhoods were imbued with a proud but gritty spirit, along with heightened racial tension. In the wake of the civil rights movement, racial pride gave rise to militant groups like the Black Panther Party, but they were little match for the economic hardships and racial tensions that plagued Oakland. In many neighborhoods the reality was widespread poverty and gang violence—subjects that dominated the songs of such Oakland-bred rappers as the late Tupac Shakur. The highly publicized protests of the Occupy Oakland movement in 2011 and 2012 and the #BlackLivesMatter movement of 2014 and 2015 illustrate just how much Oakland remains a mosaic of its past.

Oakland's affluent reside in the city's hillside homes and wooded enclaves like Claremont, Piedmont, and Montclair, which provide a warmer, more spacious alternative to San Francisco, while a constant flow of newcomers ensures continued diversity, vitality, and growing pains. Many neighborhoods to the west and south of the city center have yet to be touched by gentrification, but a renovated downtown and vibrant arts scene has injected new energy into the city. Even San Franciscans, often loath to cross the Bay Bridge, come to Uptown and Temescal for the nightlife, arts, and restaurants.

Everyday life here revolves around the neighborhood. In some areas, such as Piedmont and Rockridge, you'd swear you were in Berkeley or San Francisco's Noe Valley. Along Telegraph Avenue just south of 51st Street, Temescal is littered with hipsters and pulsing with creative culinary and design energy. These are perfect places for browsing, eating, or relaxing between sightseeing trips to Oakland's architectural gems, rejuvenated waterfront, and numerous green spaces.

GETTING HERE AND AROUND

Driving from San Francisco, take Interstate 80 East across the Bay Bridge, then take Interstate 580 East to the Grand Avenue exit for Lake Merritt. To reach downtown and the waterfront, take Interstate 980 West from Interstate 580 East and exit at 12th Street; exit at 18th Street for Uptown. For Temescal, take Interstate 580 East to Highway 24 and exit at 51st Street.

By BART, use the Lake Merritt Station for the Oakland Museum and southern Lake Merritt; the Oakland City Center–12th Street Station for downtown, Chinatown, and Old Oakland; and the 19th Street Station for Uptown, the Paramount Theatre, and the north side of Lake Merritt.

By bus, take the AC Transit's C and P lines to get to Piedmont in Oakland. The O bus stops at the edge of Chinatown near downtown Oakland.

Oakland's Jack London Square is an easy hop on the ferry from San Francisco. Those without cars can take advantage of the free Broadway Shuttle, which runs from the Jack London Square to 27th Street via downtown on weekdays and Friday and Saturday nights.

Be aware of how quickly neighborhoods can change. Walking is generally safe downtown and in the Piedmont and Rockridge areas, but be mindful when walking west and southeast of downtown, especially at night.

SHUTTLE CONTACT Broadway Shuttle. 🌐 *www.oaklandca.gov.*

ESSENTIALS

VISITOR INFORMATION Visit Oakland. ✉ *481 Water St., near Broadway, Jack London Square* ☎ *510/839–9000* 🌐 *www.visitoakland.com.*

Sights

Lake Merritt

NATURE PRESERVE | This lagoon with its unique habitat for more than 100 bird species became the nation's first wildlife refuge in 1870. Today the 3.1-mile path around the lake is also a refuge for walkers, bikers, joggers, and nature lovers. **Lakeside Park** has **Children's Fairyland** (*699 Bellevue*) and the **Rotary Nature Center** (*600 Bellevue*), where monthly bird walks commence every fourth Wednesday. For views from the water, the **Lake Merritt Boating Center** (*568 Bellevue*) rents kayaks and rowboats (*www.lakemerritt.org*). Venetian gondolas cruise from the Oakland Boathouse (*$60 for 30 min. for 2;* 🌐 *gondolaservizio.com*).

On the lake's south side, the **Camron-Stanford House** (*1418 Lakeside Dr.*), is the last of the grand Victorians that once dominated the area; it's open Sundays for tours. Nearby bold **Oakland mural art** offers a more modern feast for the eyes (*between Madison and Webster Streets and 7th and 11th Sts.*).

The lake's necklace of lights adds allure for dinner-goers to the art deco **Terrace Room** (*1800 Madison St.*) or **Lake Chalet** (*1520 Lakeside Dr.*), as well as to a host of tasty spots along Grand Avenue, from **Enssaro** Ethiopian (*357a*) and Korean BBQ at **Jong Ga House** (*372*) to comfort gourmet at **Grand Lake Kitchen** (*576*). ✉ *Lake Merritt.*

★ Oakland Museum of California

MUSEUM | FAMILY | This museum, designed by Kevin Roche, is one of the country's quintessential examples of mid-century modern architecture. Explore the robust collection of nearly 2 million objects in three distinct galleries celebrating the state's history, natural sciences, and art. Listen to native species and environmental soundscapes in the Library of Natural Sounds and engage in stories of the state's past

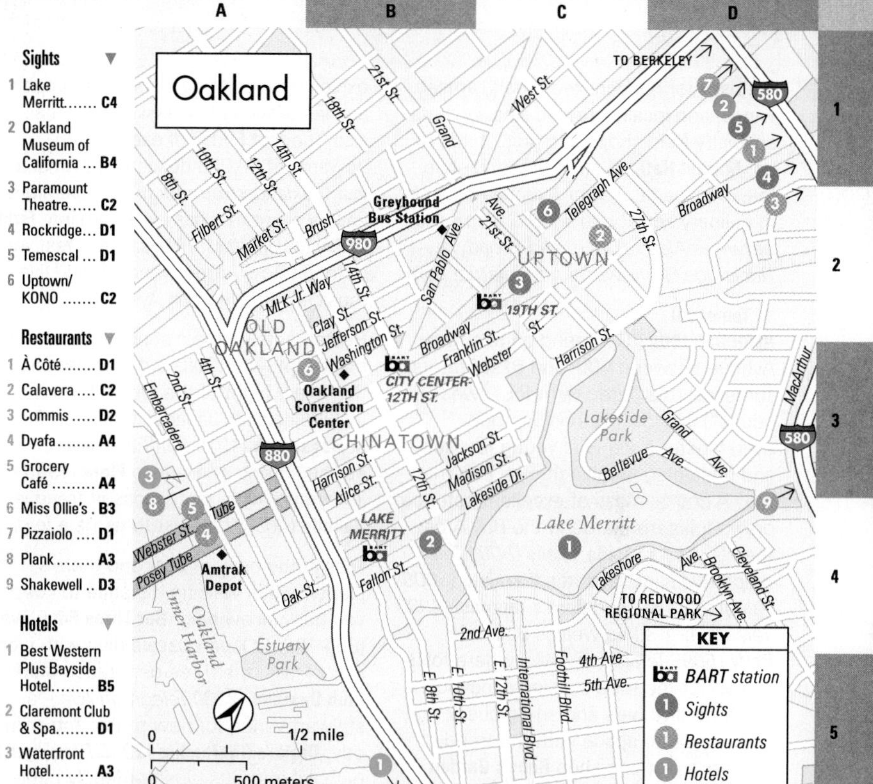

and future from Ohlone basket making to emerging technologies and current events. Not to be missed are the photographs from Dorothea Lange's personal archive and worthy collection of by Bay Area figurative painters including David Park and Joan Brown. Take a break at the Blue Oak café for seasonal dishes sourced from local ingredients. **TIP→ On Friday evening the museum gets lively, with live music, food trucks, and after-hours gallery access.** ✉ *1000 Oak St., at 10th St., Downtown* ☎ *510/318–8400, 888/625–6873 toll-free* 🌐 *museumca.org* 🎫 *$16, free 1st Sun. of month* ⏲ *Closed Mon. and Tues.*

★ Paramount Theatre

ARTS VENUE | A glorious art deco specimen, the Paramount operates as a venue for concerts and performances of all kinds, from the Oakland Symphony to Jerry Seinfeld and Elvis Costello. The popular classic movie nights start off with a 30-minute Wurlitzer concert. **TIP→ Docent-led tours, offered the first and third Saturday of the month, are fun and informative.** ✉ *2025 Broadway, at 20th St., Uptown* ☎ *510/465–6400* 🌐 *www.paramounttheatre.com* 🎫 *Tour $5.*

★ Rockridge

NEIGHBORHOOD | **FAMILY** | This fashionable upscale neighborhood is one of Oakland's most desirable places to live. Explore the tree-lined streets that radiate out from **College Avenue** just north and south of the Rockridge BART station for a look at California Craftsman bungalows at their finest. By day College Avenue between Broadway and Alcatraz Avenue is crowded with shoppers buying fresh flowers, used books, and clothing; by night the same folks are back for handcrafted meals, artisan wines, and locally brewed ales. With its specialty-food shops and quick bites to go, **Market Hall,** an airy European-style marketplace at Shafter Avenue, is a hub of culinary activity. ✉ *5655 College Ave., between Alcatraz Ave. and Broadway, Rockridge* 🌐 *www.rockridgedistrict.com.*

★ Temescal

NEIGHBORHOOD | Centering on Telegraph Avenue between 40th and 51st Streets, Temescal (the Aztec term for "sweat house") is a low-pretension, mon-eyed-hipster hood with young families and middle-aged folks thrown into the mix. A critical mass of excellent eateries draws folks from around the Bay Area; there's veteran **Doña Tomás** (*5004 Telegraph Ave.*) and favorites **Pizzaiolo** (*5008 Telegraph Ave.*) and **Rose's Taproom** (*4930 Telegraph Ave.*) as well as **Bakesale Betty** (*5098 Telegraph Ave.*), where folks line up for the fried-chicken sandwich. Old-time dive bars and smog-check stations share space with the trendy children's clothing shop **Ruby's Garden** (*5026 Telegraph Ave.*) and the stalwart **East Bay Depot for Creative Reuse** (*4695 Telegraph Ave.*), where you might find a bucket of buttons or 1,000 muffin wrappers among birdcages, furniture, lunch boxes, and ribbon.

Around the corner, **Temescal Alley** (*49th St.*), a tucked-away lane of tiny storefronts, crackles with the creative energy of local makers. Find botanical wonders at **Crimson Horticultural Rarities** (*No. 470*) or an old-fashioned straight-edge shave at **Temescal Alley Barbershop** (*No. 470B*). Don't miss grabbing a sweet scoop at **Curbside Creamery** (*No. 482*). ✉ *Telegraph Ave., between 40th and 51st Sts., Temescal* 🌐 *www.temescaldistrict.org.*

★ Uptown/KONO

NEIGHBORHOOD | Uptown and KONO (Koreatown-Northgate) is where nightlife and cutting-edge art merge. Dozens of galleries cluster around Telegraph Avenue and north of Grand Avenue into KONO, exhibiting everything from photography and installations to glasswork and fiber arts. The first Friday of each month, upwards of 50,000 descend for **Art Murmur** (*oaklandartmurmur.org*), a late-night gallery event that has expanded into **First Friday** (*oaklandfirstfridays.org*), a festival of food trucks, street vendors, and live music along Telegraph Avenue.

Restaurants with a distinctly urban vibe make Uptown/KONO a dining destination every night of the week. Favorites include eclectic Japanese-inspired fare at **Hopscotch** (*1915 San Pablo Ave.*), stylish cuisine at art-deco **Flora** (*1900 Telegraph Ave.*), tasty tapas at trendy **Duende** (*468 19th*), just to name a few.

Toss in the bevy of bars and there's plenty within walking distance to keep you busy all evening: **Bar Three Fifty-Five** (*355 19th St.*), an upscale dive with iconic cocktails; the three-generation **Stork Club Oakland** (*2330 Telegraph Ave.*), a stalwart venue for new music and comedy; **Drake's Dealership** (*2325 Broadway*), with its spacious hipster-friendly beer garden; and **Somar** (*1727 Telegraph Ave.*), a bar, music lounge, and art gallery in one. ✉ *Oakland* ✥ *Telegraph Ave. and Broadway from 14th to 27th Sts.*

Restaurants

À Côté

$$ | MEDITERRANEAN | This Mediterranean hot spot is all about seasonal small plates, cozy tables, family-style eating, and excellent wine. Heavy wooden tables, intimate dining nooks, natural light, and a heated patio make this an ideal destination for couples, families, and the after-work crowd. **Known for:** Pernod mussels; exquisite small plates; global and regional wine list. $ *Average main: $19* ✉ *5478 College Ave., at Taft Ave., Rockridge* ☎ *510/655–6469* 🌐 *acoterestaurant.com* ⏲ *No lunch.*

Calavera

$$$ | **MODERN MEXICAN** | This Oaxacan-inspired hot spot offers inventive and elevated plates in an industrial-chic space with lofty ceilings, warm wooden tables, exposed brick walls, and heated outdoor dining. Innovative cocktails like the salt-air margarita come from a beautiful bar with a library of more than 100 agaves. **Known for:** fresh ceviche; wide selection of tequilas and mezcal; carnitas tacos served in nixtamal heirloom corn tortillas. *Average main: $24 2337 Broadway, at 24th St., Uptown 510/338–3273 calaveraoakland.com Closed Mon.*

★ Commis

$$$$ | **AMERICAN** | A slender, unassuming storefront houses the first East Bay restaurant with a Michelin star (two of them, in fact). The room is minimalist and polished: nothing distracts from the artistry of chef James Syhabout, who creates a multicourse dining experience based on the season and his distinctive vision. **Known for:** inventive multicourse tasting menu; Michelin-winning execution; artful precision. *Average main: $165 3859 Piedmont Ave., at Rio Vista Ave., Piedmont 510/653–3902 commisrestaurant.com Closed Mon. and Tues. No lunch.*

Dyafa

$$$ | **MIDDLE EASTERN** | **FAMILY** | Reem Assil, one of the Bay Area's best chefs, brings Arabic heritage flavors to Jack London Square at Dyafa, where hot and cold *mezze* dishes such as Hummus Kawarma (served warm with lamb and cured lime) and *suhoon* dishes such as Musakhan (sumac-spiced chicken confit) are best shared family-style. Menus pair cocktails and wine flights with seasonally changing dishes for brunch, lunch, and dinner. **Known for:** freshly baked mana'eesh; house-made dips and pickles; Arabic-inspired cocktails. *Average main: $30 44 Webster St., Jack London Square 510/250–9491 www.dyafaoakland.com.*

Grocery Café

$$ | **BURMESE** | Home-style Burmese food may be one of the best kept secrets in the Jack London Square area, where the bright, cozy Grocery Café serves up savory street food like *khauk swe thoke* (rainbow noodle salad) alongside traditional favorites like *mohinga* (fish chowder soup) and mango chutney pork stew. Vegan and veggie house special tofu and vegetarian hinga soup are among the locals' favorites on the menu. **Known for:** tea leaf salad; pork belly thoke; coconut rice. *Average main: $19 90 Franklin St., Jack London Square.*

Miss Ollie's

$$ | **CARIBBEAN** | **FAMILY** | Centrally located in the city's historic district, Miss Ollie's is a colorful Afro-Caribbean gem in Swan's Market that packs in mouth-watering flavors. Daily lunch specialties include juicy, crispy fried chicken and waffles, braised oxtails, and creole doughnuts, while hearty dinner fare offers jerk chicken, island-style slow-cooked pork, split-pea and okra fritters, and exceptional pea and pumpkin soups. **Known for:** fried chicken; sweet plantains; jerk shrimp. *Average main: $17 901 Washington St., Old Oakland 510/285–6188 www.realmissolliesoakland.com.*

Pizzaiolo

$$$ | **ITALIAN** | **FAMILY** | Chez Panisse alum Charlie Hallowell helms the kitchen of this rustic-chic Oakland institution. Diners of all ages perch on wooden chairs with red-leather backs and nosh on farm-to-table Italian fare from a daily changing menu. **Known for:** seasonal wood-fired pizza; daily house-made breads; rustic California-Italian entrées. *Average main: $23 5008 Telegraph Ave., at 51st St., Temescal 510/652–4888 www.pizzaiolooakland.com No lunch.*

Plank

$$ | AMERICAN | FAMILY | Plank brings food and entertainment together in an expansive indoor-outdoor space with a waterfront view. Sip from more than 50 handcrafted local beers while playing bocce ball in the beer garden, lunch on Cuban sandwiches and Cajun mahi tacos during a bowling or billiards match, or try your hand at the arcade before biting into baby back ribs. **Known for:** fun outdoor space with fire pits; generous portions; games and activities. *Average main: $17 ✉ 98 Broadway, Jack London Square ☎ 510/817–0980 ⊕ www.plankoakland.com.*

★ **Shakewell**

$$$ | MEDITERRANEAN | Two *Top Chef* vets opened this stylish Lakeshore restaurant, which serves creative and memorable Mediterranean small plates in a lively setting that features an open kitchen, wood-fired oven, communal tables, and snug seating. As the name implies, well-crafted cocktails are shaken (or stirred) and poured with panache. **Known for:** wood-oven paella; Spanish and Mediterranean small plates; unique cocktails. *Average main: $26 ✉ 3407 Lakeshore Ave., near Mandana Blvd., Grand Lake ☎ 510/251–0329 ⊕ www.shakewelloakland.com ⏲ Closed Mon. No lunch Tues.*

Hotels

Best Western Plus Bayside Hotel

$$ | HOTEL | Sandwiched between the serene Oakland Estuary and an eight-lane freeway, this all-suites property has handsome accommodations with balconies or patios, many overlooking the water. **Pros:** attractive, budget-conscious choice; free parking; free shuttle to and from airport, Jack London Square, and downtown locations. **Cons:** few shops or restaurants in walking distance; freeway-side rooms can be loud; some rooms have no views or patios/balconies. *Rooms from: $189 ✉ 1717 Embarcadero, off I–880, at 16th St. exit ☎ 510/356–2450 ⊕ www.baysidehoteloakland.com 81 rooms Breakfast.*

★ **Claremont Club & Spa**

$$$$ | HOTEL | FAMILY | Straddling the Oakland–Berkeley border, this amenities-rich Fairmont property—which is more than 100 years old—beckons like a gleaming white castle in the hills. **Pros:** amazing spa; supervised child care; solid business amenities. **Cons:** parking is pricey; mandatory facilities charge; remote from shops or restaurants. *Rooms from: $338 ✉ 41 Tunnel Rd., at Ashby and Domingo Aves. ☎ 510/843–3000, 800/257–7544 reservations ⊕ www.fairmont.com/claremont-berkeley 276 rooms No meals.*

Waterfront Hotel

$$$ | HOTEL | FAMILY | This thoroughly modern, pleasantly appointed Joie de Vivre property sits among the many high-caliber restaurants of Jack London Square. **Pros:** complimentary wine-and-cheese hour weekdays; lovely views; free shuttle service to downtown. **Cons:** passing trains can be noisy on city side; parking is pricey; limited amenities. *Rooms from: $209 ✉ 10 Washington St., Jack London Square ☎ 510/836–3800 front desk, 888/842–5333 reservations ⊕ www.jdvhotels.com 145 rooms No meals.*

Nightlife

Back when rent was still relatively cheap, artists flocked to Oakland, giving rise to a cultural scene—visual arts, indie music, spoken word, film—that's still buzzing, especially in Uptown. Trendy new spaces pop up regularly and the beer-garden renaissance is already well-established. Whether you're a self-proclaimed beer snob or just someone who enjoys a cold drink on a sunny day, there's something for everyone. Oakland's nightlife scene is less crowded and more intimate than what you'll find in San Francisco. Music is just about everywhere, though the most popular venues are downtown.

BARS

★ Café Van Kleef

BARS/PUBS | Long before Uptown got hot, the late Peter Van Kleef was serving stiff fresh-squeezed greyhounds, telling tales about his collection of pop-culture mementos, and booking live music at Café Van Kleef, a funky café-bar that crackles with creative energy—there's still live music every weekend. This local favorite still serves some of the stiffest drinks in town. ✉ *1621 Telegraph Ave., between 16th and 17th Sts., Uptown* ☎ *510/763–7711* 🌐 *cafevankleef.net.*

★ Heinold's First and Last Chance Saloon

BARS/PUBS | Arguably California's longest continuously active saloon since it opened in 1884, this watering hole, built from the hull of a flat-bottomed sternwheeler, is the famous place where young Jack London got his start as a writer. Historic photos, artifacts, and turn-of-the-century curios hang from the crooked walls and ceilings, which have been atilt since the 1906 earthquake. Sit at the slanted bar for beers on tap and bottomless stories of Oakland history or take drinks outside and enjoy the marina view. ✉ *48 Webster St., Jack London Square* ☎ *510/839–6761* 🌐 *oaklandsaloon.com.*

The Layover Music Bar and Lounge

BARS/PUBS | Bright, bold, and unabashedly bohemian, this hangout filled with recycled furniture is constantly evolving because everything is for sale, from the artwork to the pillows, rugs, and lamps. The busy bar serves up signature organic cocktails, and live entertainment includes comedy shows, storytelling, and local DJs. ✉ *1517 Franklin St., near 15th St., Uptown* ☎ *510/834–1517* 🌐 *www.oaklandlayover.com.*

Make Westing

BARS/PUBS | Named for a short story by Oakland native Jack London, this sprawling industrial-chic space is always abuzz with hipsters playing bocce, the postwork crowd sipping old-fashioneds, or pretheater couples passing Mason jars of unexpected delectables like Cajun shrimp boil. The patio's your best bet for a conversation on a busy evening. ✉ *1741 Telegraph Ave., at 18th St., Uptown* ☎ *510/251–1400* 🌐 *makewesting.com.*

BREWPUBS AND BEER GARDENS

Beer Revolution

BREWPUBS/BEER GARDENS | Hard-core beer geeks: with hundreds of bottled beers and 50 taps, this craft beer and bottle shop is for you. When you're done salivating over the extensive beer lists, grab a table on the patio. ✉ *464 3rd St., at Broadway, Jack London Square* ☎ *510/452–2337* 🌐 *www.beer-revolution.com.*

Diving Dog Brewhouse

BARS/PUBS | The brewing scene is alive and hopping in Oakland, and among the dozens of stops on the Oakland Ale Trail, the Diving Dog is one craft locale where folks can brew their own alongside the masters (and bottle it in two-weeks' time). With more than 100 rare and unusual bottled beers and 30 flavors on tap, this modern space is an ideal place to improve your brew IQ and sample what's fresh before a show at the Fox or other Uptown venue. ✉ *1802 Telegraph Ave., Uptown* ☎ *510/306–1914* 🌐 *www.divingdogbrew.com.*

★ Lost & Found

BREWPUBS/BEER GARDENS | **FAMILY** | The diversions on the spacious, succulent-filled patio include ping-pong, cornhole, and communal tables full of chilled-out locals. The beer selection ranges from blue collar to Belgian, and a seasonal menu focuses on internationally inspired small bites. ✉ *2040 Telegraph Ave., at 21st St., Uptown*

510/763–2040 www.lostandfound510.com Closed Mon.

The Trappist

BREWPUBS/BEER GARDENS | Brick walls, dark wood, soft lighting, and a buzz of conversation set a warm and mellow tone inside this Old Oakland Victorian space that's been renovated to resemble a traditional Belgian pub. The setting (which includes two bars and a back patio) is definitely a draw, but the real stars are the artisan beers—more than 100 Belgian, Dutch, and North American brews. Light fare includes bar snacks and meat and cheese boards. *460 8th St., near Broadway, Old Oakland 510/238–8900 www.thetrappist.com.*

ROCK, POP, HIP-HOP, FOLK, AND BLUES CLUBS

Fox Theater

MUSIC CLUBS | This renovated 1928 theater, Oakland's favorite performance venue, is a remarkable feat of Mediterranean Moorish architecture and has seen the likes of Willie Nelson, Magnetic Fields, Rebelution, and B.B. King, to name a few. The venue boasts good sight lines, a state-of-the-art sound system, brilliant acoustics, and a restaurant and bar, among other amenities. *1807 Telegraph Ave., between 18th and 19th Sts., Uptown 510/302–2250 thefoxoakland.com.*

★ Yoshi's

MUSIC CLUBS | Opened in 1972 as a sushi bar, Yoshi's has evolved into one of the area's best jazz and live music venues. The full Yoshi's experience includes traditional Japanese and Asian fusion cuisine in the adjacent restaurant. *510 Embarcadero W, between Washington and Clay Sts., Jack London Square 510/238–9200 www.yoshis.com.*

Shopping

Pop-up shops and stylish, locally focused stores are scattered throughout the funky alleys of Old Oakland, Uptown, Rockridge, and Temescal, while the streets around Lake Merritt and Grand Lake offer more modest boutiques.

Maison d'Etre

GIFTS/SOUVENIRS | Close to the Rockridge BART station, this store epitomizes the Rockridge neighborhood's funky-chic shopping scene. Look for high-end housewares and impulse buys like whimsical watches, imported fruit-tea blends, and funky slippers. *5640 College Ave., at Keith Ave., Rockridge 510/658–2801 maisondetre.com.*

★ Oaklandish

CLOTHING | This is the place for Oaktown swag. What started in 2000 as a public art project of local pride has become a celebrated brand around the bay, and a portion of the proceeds from hip Oaklandish brand T-shirts and accessories supports grassroots nonprofits committed to bettering the local community. It's good-looking stuff for a good cause. *1444 Broadway, near 15th St., Uptown 510/251–9500 oaklandish.com.*

Viscera

JEWELRY/ACCESSORIES | Urban planning meets fashion in this atypical men's and women's boutique. With 3D printing technology and custom-made items in house, the creators behind this Oakland flagship brand achieve artful, innovative functionality in their American-made clothing, gifts, and accessories. Ask about their in-house DIY workshops. *1542 Broadway, Uptown 510/500–5376 shopviscera.com Closed Sun. and Mon. (open by appt. only).*

The Marin Headlands

Due west of the Golden Gate Bridge's northern end.

The term *Golden Gate* has become synonymous with the world-famous bridge, but it was first given to the narrow waterway that connects the Pacific and the San Francisco Bay. To the north of the Golden Gate Strait lies the Marin Headlands, part of the Golden Gate National Recreation Area (GGNRA), which boasts some of the area's most dramatic scenery.

GETTING HERE AND AROUND

Driving from San Francisco, head north on U.S. 101. Just after you cross the Golden Gate Bridge, take Exit 442 for Alexander Avenue. Keep left at the fork and follow signs for "San Francisco/U.S. 101 South", go through the tunnel under the freeway, and turn right up the hill. Muni bus 76X runs hourly from Sutter and Sansome Streets to the Marin Headlands Visitor Center on weekends and major holidays only.

Sights

★ Marin Headlands

NATIONAL/STATE PARK | **FAMILY** | The headlands stretch from the Golden Gate Bridge to Muir Beach. Photographers perch on the southern headlands for spectacular shots of the city and bridge. Equally remarkable are the views north along the coast and out to the ocean, where the Farallon Islands are visible on clear days.

The headlands' strategic position at the mouth of San Francisco Bay made them a logical site for military installations from 1890 through the Cold War. Today you can explore the crumbling concrete batteries where naval guns once protected the area. The headlands' main attractions are centered on Fts. Barry and Cronkhite, which are separated by Rodeo Lagoon and Rodeo Beach, a dark stretch of sand that attracts sand-castle builders and dog owners.

The visitor center is a worthwhile stop for its exhibits on the area's history and ecology, and kids enjoy the "please touch" educational sites and small play area inside. You can pick up guides to historic sites and wildlife, and get information about programming and guided walks. ✉ *Golden Gate National Recreation Area, Visitors Center, Fort Barry Chapel, Ft. Barry, Bldg. 948, Field and Bunker Rds., Fort Baker* ☎ *415/331–1540* 🌐 *www.nps.gov/goga/marin-headlands.htm* ⏲ *Closed Tues.*

Point Bonita Lighthouse

LIGHTHOUSE | **FAMILY** | A restored beauty that still guides ships to safety with its original 1855 refractory lens, the lighthouse anchors the southern headlands. Half the fun of a visit is the steep half-mile walk from the parking area through a rock tunnel, across a suspension bridge, and down to the lighthouse. Signposts along the way detail the bravado of surfmen, as the early lifeguards were called, and the tenacity of the "wickies," the first keepers of the light. **TIP→ Call about 90-minute full-moon tours.** ✉ *End of Conzelman Rd., Ft. Barry, Bldg. 948, Sausalito* ☎ *415/331–1540* 🌐 *www.nps.gov/goga/pobo.htm* ⏲ *Closed Tues.–Sat.*

Sausalito

2 miles north of Golden Gate Bridge.

Bougainvillea-covered hillsides and an expansive yacht harbor give Sausalito the feel of an Adriatic resort. The town sits on the northwestern edge of San Francisco Bay, where it's sheltered from the ocean by the Marin Headlands; the mostly mild weather here is perfect for strolling and outdoor dining. Nevertheless, morning fog and afternoon winds can roll over the hills without warning, funneling through the central part of Sausalito once known as Hurricane Gulch.

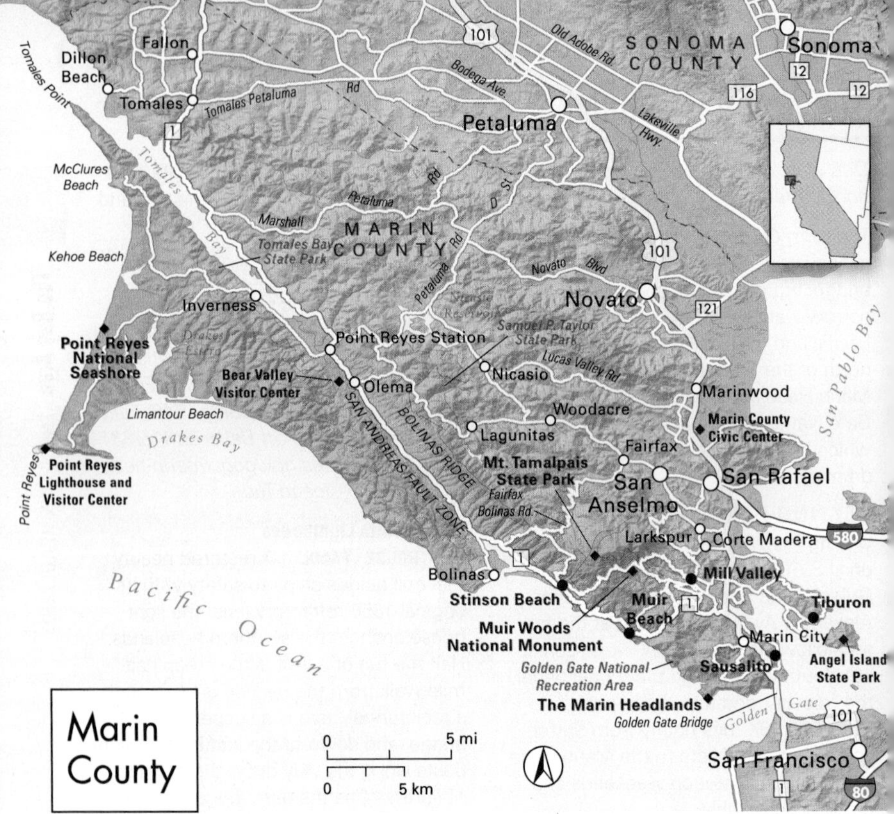

South of Bridgeway, which snakes between the bay and the hills, a waterside esplanade is lined with restaurants on piers that lure diners with good seafood and even better views. Stairs along the west side of Bridgeway and throughout town climb into wooded hillside neighborhoods filled with both rustic and opulent homes, while back on the northern portion of the shoreline, harbors shelter a community of more than 400 houseboats. As you amble along Bridgeway past shops and galleries, you'll notice the absence of basic services. Find them and more on Caledonia Street, which runs parallel to Bridgeway and inland a couple of blocks. While ferry-side shops flaunt kitschy souvenirs, smaller side streets and narrow alleyways offer eccentric jewelry and handmade crafts.

TIP→ The ferry is the best way to get to Sausalito from San Francisco; you get more romance (and less traffic) and disembark in the heart of downtown.

Sausalito developed its bohemian flair in the 1950s and '60s, when creative types, including artist Jean Varda, poet Shel Silverstein, and madam Sally Stanford, established an artists' colony and a houseboat community here (this is Otis Redding's "Dock of the Bay"). Both the spirit of the artists and the neighborhood of floating homes persist. For a close-up view of the quirky community, head north on Bridgeway, turn right on Gate Six Road, park where it dead-ends, and enter through the unlocked gates.

GETTING HERE AND AROUND

From San Francisco by car or bike, follow U.S. 101 north across the Golden Gate Bridge and take Exit 442 for Alexander

Avenue, just past Vista Point; continue down the winding hill to the water to where the road becomes Bridgeway. Golden Gate Transit buses will drop you off in downtown Sausalito, and the ferries dock downtown as well. The center of town is flat, with plenty of sidewalks and bay views. It's a pleasure and a must to explore on foot.

ESSENTIALS

VISITOR INFORMATION Sausalito Chamber of Commerce. ✉ *1913 Bridgeway* ☎ *415/331–7262* 🌐 *www.sausalito.org.*

Sights

The Marine Mammal Center

COLLEGE | FAMILY | This hospital for distressed, sick, and injured marine animals is a leading center for ocean conservancy in the Bay Area and the largest rehabilitation center of its kind. Dedicated to pioneering education, rehabilitation, and research, the center is free and open daily to the public. Tour the facilities and see how elephant seals, sea lions, and pups are cared for and meet the scientists who care for them. Bonus: you'll see some of the best views of the Marin Headlands and San Francisco Bay along the way. ✉ *2000 Bunker Rd., Fort Baker* ☎ *415/289–7325* 🌐 *www.marinemammalcenter.org* 🎫 *Guided tours $10.*

Sally Stanford Drinking Fountain

FOUNTAIN | There's an unusual historic landmark on the Sausalito Ferry Pier—a drinking fountain inscribed "Have a drink on Sally" in remembrance of Sally Stanford, the former San Francisco brothel madam who became Sausalito's mayor in the 1970s. Sassy Sally would have appreciated the fountain's eccentric attachment: a knee-level basin with the inscription "Have a drink on Leland," in memory of her beloved dog. ✉ *Sausalito Ferry Pier, Anchor St. at Humboldt St., off southwest corner of Gabrielson Park* 🌐 *www.oursausalito.com/sausalito-ferry-1.html.*

Sausalito Ice House Visitors Center and Museum

INFO CENTER | The local historical society operates this dual educational exhibit and visitor center, where you can get your bearings, learn some history, and find out what's happening in town. The artifacts of indigenous Miwok peoples and photography of turn-of-the-century Sausalito are worth a peek. ✉ *780 Bridgeway, at Bay St.* ☎ *415/332–0505* 🌐 *www.sausalitohistoricalsociety.com* ⏲ *Closed Mon.*

Viña del Mar Plaza and Park

PLAZA | The landmark Plaza Viña del Mar, named for Sausalito's sister city in Chile, marks the center of town. Adjacent to the parking lot and ferry pier, the plaza is flanked by two 14-foot-tall elephant statues, which were created for the San Francisco Panama–Pacific International Exposition in 1915. It also features a picture-perfect fountain that's great for people-watching. ✉ *Bridgeway and El Portal St.* 🌐 *www.oursausalito.com/parks-in-sausalito/vina-del-mar-park.html.*

Restaurants

Bridgeway Cafe

$ | CAFÉ | The view's the thing at this diner-café on the main drag across the road from the bay. People line up on weekends for great traditional breakfast fare and fresh café lunch items. **Known for:** all-day breakfast fare, including eggs Benedict; Mediterranean-inspired hummus and kabobs; generous burgers. 💲 *Average main: $14* ✉ *633 Bridgeway, at Princess St.* ☎ *415/332–3426* 🌐 *bridgewaycafe.com* ⏲ *No dinner.*

Fast Food Français

$$ | BISTRO | FAMILY | F3 puts a French twist on classic American fast food and dishes up some French nibbles, too, in this casual bistro. The same folks who started Le Garage branch out here with quick-bites like French onion burgers with cheddar fondue and double-cream mac and cheese among servings of Brussels sprouts chips, deviled eggs, and ratatouille. **Known for:** fries and frites; spacious locale; brunch. *Average main: $17 ✉ 39 Caledonia St. ☎ 415/887–9047 🌐 www.eatf3.com.*

★ Fish

$$ | SEAFOOD | FAMILY | Unsurprisingly, fish—specifically, fresh, sustainably caught fish—is the focus at this gleaming dockside fish house a mile north of downtown. Order at the counter—cash only—and then grab a seat by the floor-to-ceiling windows or at a picnic table on the pier, overlooking the yachts and fishing boats. **Known for:** taco plate; barbecued oysters; sustainably caught, fire-grilled entrées. *Average main: $21 ✉ 350 Harbor Dr., at Gate 5 Rd., off Bridgeway ☎ 415/331–3474 🌐 www.331fish.com No credit cards ☞ Cash only.*

★ Hamburgers Sausalito

$ | BURGER | Patrons queue up daily outside this tiny street-side shop for organic Angus beef patties that are made to order on a wheel-shaped grill. Brave the line (it moves fast) and take your food to the esplanade to enjoy fresh air and bayside views. **Known for:** legendary burgers; bay views; local following. *Average main: $9 ✉ 737 Bridgeway, at Anchor St. ☎ 415/332–9471 No dinner.*

Le Garage

$$$ | FRENCH | Brittany-born Olivier Souvestre serves traditional French bistro fare in a relaxed, bay-side setting that feels more sidewalk café than the converted garage that it is. The restaurant seats only 35 inside and 15 outside, so make reservations or arrive early. **Known for:** PEI mussels and house-cut fries; weekend brunch; balsamic-glazed Brussels sprouts. *Average main: $26 ✉ 85 Liberty Ship Way, Suite 109 ☎ 415/332–5625 🌐 www.legaragebistrosausalito.com ☞ No reservations for weekend brunch.*

Poggio

$$$ | ITALIAN | A hillside dining destination, Poggio serves modern Tuscan-style comfort food in a handsome, old-world-inspired space whose charm spills onto the sidewalks. An extensive and ever-changing menu, with ingredients sourced from their own garden and local farms, include house-made capellini, grilled fish, and wood-fired pizzas. **Known for:** fresh local ingredients and traditional Northern Italian dishes; rotisserie chicken with property-grown organic herbs and vegetables; lobster-roe pasta. *Average main: $30 ✉ 777 Bridgeway, at Bay St. ☎ 415/332–7771 🌐 www.poggiotrattoria.com.*

Sausalito Seahorse

$$$ | ITALIAN | Live music and dancing served alongside Tuscan seafood and pasta specialties make the Seahorse one of Sausalito's most spirited supper clubs. Sample an abundant antipasti menu and homemade focaccia on outdoor patios or enjoy the band inside with traditional seafood stew or lasagna classica. **Known for:** happy hour; Sunday salsa dancing; fun atmosphere. *Average main: $24 ✉ 305 Harbor Dr. ☎ 415/331 2899 🌐 www.sausalitoseahorse.com.*

★ Sushi Ran

$$$ | JAPANESE | Sushi aficionados swear that this tiny, stylish restaurant—in business for more than three decades—is the Bay Area's best option for raw fish, but don't overlook the excellent Pacific Rim fusions, a melding of Japanese ingredients and French cooking techniques. Book in advance or expect a wait, which you can soften by sipping one of the bar's 30 by-the-glass sakes. **Known for:** fish imported from Tokyo's famous Tsukiji market; local miso-glazed black cod; outstanding sake and wine list. *Average main: $30 ✉ 107 Caledonia St., at Pine St. ☎ 415/332–3620 🌐 www.sushiran.com No lunch weekends.*

Taste of Rome
$ | **ITALIAN** | **FAMILY** | From early morning espresso and frittatas to late night wine and marsalas, there's something just right at the Taste of Rome any time of day. With spacious indoor and outdoor seating and a bountiful menu of fresh and homemade Italian specialties, it's easy to see why this family-owned café is beloved among locals. **Known for:** coffee drinks; desserts; house-made pasta. *Average main: $16 ✉ 1000 Bridgeway ☎ 415/332–7660 🌐 tasteofrome.co.*

Venice Gourmet Deli & Pizza
$ | **ITALIAN** | The Italian deli sandwiches, pizzas made daily, and a shop filled with gourmet delectables, wines, kitchenware, and local flavor here have enticed tastebuds along picturesque Bridgeway for more than 50 years. Enjoy a meal alfresco at the sidewalk tables, or take a picnic a few steps away to Yee Toch Chee Park for a waterside bite. **Known for:** picnic perfect sandwiches; service and quality from family owners; plentiful selections. *Average main: $13 ✉ 625 Bridgeway ☎ 415/332–3544 🌐 www.venicegourmet.com.*

Hotels

Hotel Sausalito
$$$$ | **HOTEL** | Handcrafted furniture and tasteful original art and reproductions give this Mission Revival-style inn the feel of a small European hotel. **Pros:** some rooms have harbor or park views; central location; vouchers to nearby Cafe Tutti provided. **Cons:** no room service; most rooms are small; daily public parking fee. *Rooms from: $240 ✉ 16 El Portal, at Bridgeway ☎ 415/332–0700 🌐 www.hotelsausalito.com 16 rooms No meals.*

The Inn Above Tide
$$$$ | **B&B/INN** | The balconies at the Inn Above Tide literally hang over the water, and each of its rooms has a "perfect 10" view that takes in wild Angel Island as well as the city lights across the bay. **Pros:** generous continental breakfast; free bikes to tour the area; in-room spa services available. **Cons:** costly daily parking; some rooms are on the small side; ferry-side rooms can be noisy. *Rooms from: $415 ✉ 30 El Portal ☎ 415/332–9535, 800/893–8433 🌐 www.innabovetide.com 33 rooms Breakfast.*

Shopping

Studio 333 Downtown
ART GALLERIES | There's always something new, interesting, and eye-catching on display at this storefront, including curated collections of handcrafted gifts, housewares, jewelry, and accessories by more than 40 Bay Area artisans. Visit the original art gallery and event space on 333 Caledonia for more delightful creations. *✉ 803 Bridgeway ☎ 415/332–5483 🌐 www.studio333downtown.com.*

Tiburon

7 miles north of Sausalito, 11 miles north of Golden Gate Bridge.

On a peninsula that was named Punta de Tiburon (Shark Point) by 18th-century Spanish explorers, this beautiful Marin County community retains the feel of a village—it's more low-key than Sausalito—despite the encroachment of commercial establishments from the downtown area. The harbor faces Angel Island across Raccoon Strait, and San Francisco is directly south across the bay—which means the views from the decks of harbor restaurants are major attractions. Since 1884, when the San Francisco and North Pacific Railroad relocated their ferry terminal facilities to the harbor town, Tiburon has centered on the waterfront. **TIP→ The ferry is the most relaxing (and fastest) way to get here, and allows you to skip traffic and parking problems.**

GETTING HERE AND AROUND

Blue & Gold Fleet ferries travel between San Francisco and Tiburon daily. By car, head north from San Francisco on U.S. 101 and get off at CA 131/Tiburon Boulevard/East Blithedale Avenue (Exit 447). Turn right onto Tiburon Boulevard and drive just over 4 miles to downtown. Golden Gate Transit serves downtown Tiburon from San Francisco; watch for changes during evening rush hour. Tiburon's Main Street is made for wandering, as are the footpaths that frame the water's edge.

ESSENTIALS

VISITOR INFORMATION Tiburon. ✉ *Town Hall, 1505 Tiburon Blvd.* ☎ *415/435–7373* 🌐 *www.destinationtiburon.org.*

Sights

Angel Island State Park

NATIONAL/STATE PARK | **FAMILY** | One of the Bay's best secrets in plain sight, its largest natural island was once a favored camp for Coast Miwok (later for the U.S. Army to protect San Francisco Bay), and is now a natural wildlife habitat and historic park favored by bikers, hikers, and picnickers. Thirteen miles of roads and trails from the perimeter up to Mt. Livermore (788 feet/240 meters) offer magnificent panoramic views. The 12-minute ferry ride to Angel Island from Tiburon ($15 round-trip) includes the cost of the park. **■ TIP→ To see the sites by bike, rent on the island (angelisland.com/bicycles) or in Tiburon at Pedego Electric Bikes (10 Main Street).** ✉ *Angel Island* ✣ *Accessible only by public ferry or private boat* ☎ *415/435–1915* 🌐 *www.parks.ca.gov.*

Ark Row

STORE/MALL | **FAMILY** | The second block of Main Street is known as historic Ark Row and has a tree-shaded walk lined with antiques, restaurants, and specialty stores. The quaint stretch gets its name from the 19th-century ark houseboats that floated in Belvedere Cove before being beached and transformed into stores. **■ TIP→ If you're curious about architectural history, the Tiburon Heritage & Arts Commission has a self-guided walking-tour map, available online and at local businesses.** ✉ *Ark Row, Main St., south of Juanita La.* 🌐 *tiburonheritageandarts.org.*

Old St. Hilary's Landmark and John Thomas Howell Wildflower Preserve

NATURE PRESERVE | The architectural centerpiece of this attraction is a stark-white 1888 Carpenter Gothic church that overlooks the town and the bay from its hillside perch. Surrounding the church, which was dedicated as a historical monument in 1959, is a wildflower preserve that's spectacular in May and June, when the rare Tiburon paintbrush or black jewelflower blooms. Expect a steep walk uphill to reach the preserve. The Landmarks Society will arrange guided tours by appointment. **■ TIP→ The hiking trails behind the landmark wind up to a peak that has views of the entire Bay Area.** ✉ *201 Esperanza St., off Mar West St. or Beach Rd.* ☎ *415/435–1853* 🌐 *landmarkssociety.com/landmarks/st-hilarys/* ⊗ *Church closed Mon.–Sat. and Nov.–Mar.*

Railroad and Ferry Depot Museum

HISTORIC SITE | A short waterfront walk from the ferry landing, this free museum in Shoreline Park is a well-preserved time capsule of the city's industrial history, complete with working trains. The landmark building has a detailed scale model of Tiburon and its 43-acre rail yard at the turn of the 20th century when the city served as a major railroad and ferry hub for the San Francisco Bay. The Depot House Museum on the second floor showcases a restoration of the stationmaster's living quarters. ✉ *1920 Paradise Dr.* ☎ *415/435–1853* 🌐 *landmarkssociety.com/landmarks/railroad-ferry-museum* ⊗ *Closed Nov.–Mar; Mon. and Tues.*

Restaurants

Caffe Acri

$ | **CAFÉ** | This Italian espresso bar and café at the end of the Tiburon Ferry dock is a sweet spot to enjoy a leisurely breakfast or lunch with a cup of locally roasted coffee while waiting for the ferry. In addition to daily-baked pastries and desserts, the menu ranges from omelets and toasted sandwiches to smoothies and farm fresh salads. **Known for:** desserts; espresso drinks; soups and paninis. *Average main: $9 ✉ 1 Main St. ☎ 415/435–8515 🌐 www.caffeacri.com.*

Luna Blu

$$$ | **SICILIAN** | Friendly, informative staff serve Sicilian-inspired seafood in this lively sliver of an Italian restaurant just a stone's throw from the ferry. Take a seat on the heated patio overlooking the bay, or cozy up with friends on one of the high-sided booths near the bar. **Known for:** sustainably caught seafood and local, organic ingredients; homemade pastas; rock crab bisque. *Average main: $26 ✉ 35 Main St. ☎ 415/789–5844 🌐 lunablurestaurant.com ⏲ Closed Tues. No lunch weekdays.*

New Morning Cafe

$$ | **AMERICAN** | **FAMILY** | Omelets, scrambles, and pancakes are served all day long at this homey triangular bay-side café with sunny outdoor seating. If you're past morning treats, this locals' go-to brunch spot offers many soups, salads, and sandwiches, best enjoyed at picnic tables. **Known for:** hearty American breakfast fare; fresh-squeezed orange juice; sour cream waffles. *Average main: $14 ✉ 1696 Tiburon Blvd., near Juanita La. ☎ 415/435–4315 ⏲ No dinner.*

Salt & Pepper

$$ | **AMERICAN** | **FAMILY** | This bright and welcoming American bistro on Ark Row is known for its seafood starters and salads (think: oyster poppers, crab stacks, and steamers) as well as shareable dishes and burgers, chops, and ribs. The airy, rustic space has a pleasant café-like atmosphere that makes it easy to stay and consider the organic ice cream sundaes and banana splits for dessert. **Known for:** clam chowder; kabocha squash and vegetable curry; Mongolian pork chops. *Average main: $21 ✉ 38 Main St. ☎ 415/435–3594 🌐 www.saltandpeppertiburon.com.*

Sam's Anchor Cafe

$$$ | **AMERICAN** | Open since 1920, this casual dockside restaurant, rife with plastic chairs and blue-checked oilcloths, is the town's most famous eatery. Most people flock to the deck for beers, views, sunsets, and exceptionally tasty seafood. **Known for:** raw bar; pink lemonade and margarita "bowls"; hurricane fries. *Average main: $25 ✉ 27 Main St. ☎ 415/435–4527 🌐 www.samscafe.com.*

Servino Ristorante

$$ | **SOUTHERN ITALIAN** | **FAMILY** | This family-owned eatery specializes in southern Italian recipes including lobster agnolotti, seafood stew, pork sausage fondue, and pizza made with local, sustainable ingredients. With spacious indoor and outdoor seating and waterfront views, the scene is cozy and welcoming even in cooler weather, when there's heated patio dining. **Known for:** alfresco dining; wines from Italy and California; black truffle raviolacci. *Average main: $22 ✉ 9 Main St. ☎ 415/435–2676 🌐 www.servino.com.*

Waypoint Pizza

$ | **PIZZA** | **FAMILY** | A nautical theme and a tasty "between the sheets" pizza-style sandwich are signatures of this creative pizzeria, which is housed in the 19th-century landmark building that was once home to the Pioneer Boat House and is now owned by two sailing aficionados. Booths are brightened with blue-checked tablecloths, and a playful air is added by indoor deck chairs and a picnic table complete with umbrella. **Known for:**

pizza-style sandwiches; wild shrimp pesto pizza; soft-serve organic ice cream. *Average main: $13* *15 Main St.* *415/435–3440* *www.waypointpizza.com* *Closed Tues.*

Hotels

Waters Edge Hotel

$$$$ | **B&B/INN** | Checking into this stylish downtown hotel feels like tucking away into an inviting retreat by the water—the views are stunning and the lighting is perfect. **Pros:** complimentary wine and cheese for guests every evening; restaurants/sights are steps away; free bike rentals for guests. **Cons:** downstairs rooms lack privacy and balconies; paid self-parking; fitness center is off-site. *Rooms from: $299* *25 Main St., off Tiburon Blvd.* *415/789–5999, 877/789–5999* *www.marinhotels.com* *23 rooms* *Breakfast.*

Mill Valley

2 miles north of Sausalito, 4 miles north of Golden Gate Bridge.

Chic and woodsy Mill Valley has a dual personality. Here, as elsewhere in the county, the foundation is a superb natural setting. Virtually surrounded by parkland, the town lies at the base of Mt. Tamalpais and contains dense redwood groves traversed by countless creeks. But this is no lumber camp. Smart restaurants and chichi boutiques line streets that have been roamed by more rock stars than one might suspect.

The rustic village flavor isn't a modern conceit, but a holdover from the town's early days as a center for the lumber industry. In 1896, the Mt. Tamalpais Scenic Railroad—dubbed "The Crookedest Railroad in the World" because of its curvy tracks—began transporting visitors from Mill Valley to the top of Mt. Tam and down to Muir Woods, and the town soon became a vacation retreat for city slickers. The trains stopped running in the 1930s, as cars became more popular, but the old railway depot still serves as the center of town: the 1929 building has been transformed into the popular Depot Bookstore & Cafe, at 87 Throckmorton Avenue.

The small downtown area has the constant bustle of a leisure community; even at noon on a Tuesday, people are out shopping for fancy cookware, eco-friendly home furnishings, and boutique clothing.

GETTING HERE AND AROUND

By car from San Francisco, head north on U.S. 101 and get off at CA 131/Tiburon Boulevard/East Blithedale Avenue (Exit 447). Turn left onto East Blithedale Avenue and continue west to Throckmorton Avenue; turn left to reach Depot Plaza, then park. Golden Gate Transit buses serve Mill Valley from San Francisco. Once here, explore the town on foot.

Off the Beaten Path

Marin County Civic Center. A wonder of arches, circles, and skylights just 10 miles north of Mill Valley, the Civic Center was Frank Lloyd Wright's largest public project and has been designated a national and state historic landmark, as well as a UNESCO World Heritage Site. One-hour docent-led tours leave from the café on the second floor Wednesday and Friday morning at 10:30. *3501 Civic Center Dr., off N. San Pedro Rd., San Rafael* *415/473–3762 visitor services office* *www.marincounty.org/depts/cu/tours* *Free admission; $10 tour fee.*

ESSENTIALS

VISITOR INFORMATION Mill Valley Chamber of Commerce and Visitor Center. *85 Throckmorton Ave.* *415/388–9700* *www.millvalley.org.*

Sights

Lytton Square

PLAZA | FAMILY | Mill Valley locals congregate on weekends to socialize in the coffeehouses and cafés near the town's central square, but it bustles most of the day. The Mill Valley Book Depot and Cafe at the hub of it all is the place to grab a coffee and sweet treat while reading or playing a game of chess. Shops, restaurants, and cultural venues line the nearby streets. *Miller and Throckmorton Aves.*

★ Mill Valley Lumber Yard

HISTORIC SITE | FAMILY | The Mill Valley Lumber Yard, once a vital center of the region's logging industry, is now a vibrant micro village of craftsfolk, bakers, makers and their boutiques and restaurants. The preserved brick-red historic structures are hard to miss along Miller Avenue, and with plenty of parking in the area, plus picnic tables and outdoor space, it's well worth a visit. *129 Miller Ave.* *millvalleylumberyard.com.*

Old Mill Park

CITY PARK | FAMILY | To see one of the numerous outdoor oases that make Mill Valley so appealing, follow Throckmorton Avenue a quarter mile west from Lytton Square to Old Mill Park, a shady patch of redwoods that shelters a playground and reconstructed sawmill and hosts September's annual Mill Valley Arts Festival. From the park, Cascade Way winds its way past creekside homes to the trailheads of several forest paths. *Throckmorton Ave. and Cascade Dr.* *www.millvalleyrecreation.org.*

Restaurants

Avatar's Restaurant

$ | INDIAN | The lines can get long at this hole-in-the-wall kitchen, where Indian curries are served burrito style while you wait (note: it's cash only). Punjabi burritos or rice plates come with savory lamb, chicken, fish, vegetarian, and vegan ingredients flavored with seasonal fruit chutneys, tamarind sauce, and aromatic blends. **Known for:** curried pumpkin; smoked eggplant; lassi drinks. *Average main: $8* *15 Madrona St.* *415/381–8293* *avatars-restaurant-mill-valley.sites.tablehero.com* *No credit cards.*

Boo Koo

$ | ASIAN | Southeast Asian street food with a local flair is fired up in this hip and modern street cafe, where there's outdoor seating and a 10-tap bar. Summer rolls, satays, and skewers complement pho and wok specialties. **Known for:** green curry noodles; mint salad; Asian Brussels sprouts. *Average main: $11* *25 Miller Ave.* *415/888–8303* *eatbookoo.com.*

Buckeye Roadhouse

$$$$ | AMERICAN | House-smoked meats and fish, grilled steaks, classic salads, and decadent desserts bring locals and visitors back again and again to this 1937 lodge-style roadhouse. Enjoy a Marin martini at the cozy mahogany bar or sip local wine beside the river-rock fireplace. **Known for:** oysters bingo; chili-lime "brick" chicken; ribs and chops. *Average main: $35* *15 Shoreline Hwy., off U.S. 101* *415/331–2600* *www.buckeyeroadhouse.com.*

Bungalow 44

$$$ | AMERICAN | An open, well-lit space with booths and countertop seating from which diners can watch the cooks in action sets the scene at this lively eatery, which serves contemporary Californian cuisine and inventive cocktails. A 2018 remodel revitalized the decor as well as the menu, with its focus on locally sourced veggies and seafood. **Known for:** $1 oyster daily happy hour; tuna carpaccio; kickin' fried chicken. *Average main: $25* ✉ *44 E. Blithedale Ave., at Sunnyside Ave.* ☎ *415/381–2500* 🌐 *www.bungalow44.com* ⏲ *No lunch.*

The Dipsea Cafe

$$ | **AMERICAN** | **FAMILY** | Named after the 7-mile trail that winds from Mill Valley to Stinson Beach, this bustling diner serves hearty breakfast favorites, sandwiches, salads, and Mediterranean-inspired lunch plates. Locals crowd the checkered tables, bright yellow booths, and a shiny wooden counter and stools. **Known for:** weekend brunches; huevos rancheros; Mediterranean gyros, calamari, and souvlaki. *Average main: $18* ✉ *200 Shoreline Hwy.* ☎ *415/381–0298* 🌐 *www.dipseacafe.com* ⏲ *No dinner.*

Equator Coffees and Teas

$ | **CAFÉ** | This is the prime spot for a pick-me-up (and people-watching) over a picturesque view of downtown Mill Valley and Mount Tam. The owners are as serious about coffee as they are about social responsibility, from their fair-chain single-origin beans and organic loose teas down to locally recycled metal decor. **Known for:** espresso and cappuccino drinks; breakfast sandwiches; strawberry and chocolate waffles. *Average main: $9* ✉ *2 Miller Ave.* ☎ *415/383–1651* 🌐 *www.equatorcoffees.com/pages/mill-valley-1.*

La Ginestra

$$ | **ITALIAN** | **FAMILY** | In business since 1964, La Ginestra—named for the flowers that grow on Mt. Vesuvius, the owners' homeland—is a Mill Valley institution renowned for its no-pretense, family-style Italian meals and impressive wine list. The Sorrento Bar, off the dining room, serves up a delectable array of bar bites, pizzas, and sweets to enjoy while sipping wines and cocktails inspired by the Aversa's family's homeland. **Known for:** handmade pasta and gnocchi; ravioli; daily fish and small plates. *Average main: $19* ✉ *127 Throckmorton Ave., off Miller Ave.* ☎ *415/388–0224* 🌐 *www.laginestramv.com* ⏲ *No lunch. Closed Mon.*

Piazza D'Angelo

$$ | **ITALIAN** | **FAMILY** | In the heart of downtown, busy D'Angelo's is known for its authentic and fresh pastas; there even are gluten-free options. Another draw is the scene, especially in the lounge area, which hosts a lively cocktail hour that serves food until 10 or 11 pm—late for Mill Valley. **Known for:** fresh seafood; homemade pasta; tiramisu. *Average main: $20* ✉ *22 Miller Ave., off Throckmorton* ☎ *415/388–2000* 🌐 *www.piazzadangelo.com.*

★ **Pizza Molina**

$ | **CONTEMPORARY** | A cozy and clean aesthetic, a convivial vibe, and impeccable pizza from a wood-fired oven are central to this neighborhood spot. Chef Justin Bruckert spent months developing the perfect dough with just the right texture, pliability, and flavor as a base for the freshest seasonal ingredients. **Known for:** wood-fired pizzas; housemade meatballs; local beers on tap. *Average main: $16* ✉ *17 Madrona St., between Lovell and Throckmorton Aves.* ☎ *415/383–4200* 🌐 *www.pizzamolina.com* ⏲ *No lunch.*

Playa

$$ | **MODERN MEXICAN** | Modern Mexican farm-to-table creations and inspired cocktails are the focus of this festive indoor-outdoor space that's popular for its fire pit, made-to-order masa station, and happy hour. An open kitchen serves up locally sourced, organic, and sustainable dishes like ceviche and flautas, grilled octopus tacos, and braised pork tortas. **Known for:** taco Tuesdays; rare tequilas and mezcals; moles and salsas. *Average main: $18* ✉ *41 Throckmorton Ave.* ☎ *415/384–8871* 🌐 *www.playamv.com.*

Vasco
$ | **ITALIAN** | This lovely corner restaurant, with its wood-fired pizza, wine bar, and live music in the evening, has serious neighborhood charm. Authentic Italian specialties include chicken marsala and calamari steak. **Known for:** great atmosphere; tiramisu; pizzas. *Average main: $16 ✉ 106 Throckmorton Ave. ☎ 415/381–3343 🌐 vascorestaurantmillvalley.com.*

Hotels

Acqua Hotel
$$$ | **HOTEL** | Astride Richardson Bay, this stylish boutique hotel has modern, elegant rooms decorated in soft Zen-like color schemes. **Pros:** evening wine service; free parking and Wi-Fi; hearty breakfast buffet. **Cons:** next to freeway; traffic audible in rooms facing east; not much within walking distance. *Rooms from: $229 ✉ 555 Redwood Hwy., off U.S. 101 ☎ 415/388–9353 🌐 www.marinhotels.com 49 rooms Breakfast.*

Mill Valley Inn
$$$$ | **B&B/INN** | The only hotel in downtown Mill Valley is comprised of one of the area's first homes, the Creek House, with smart-looking Victorian rooms, and two small cottages tucked in a grove beyond a creek. **Pros:** steps from local shops and restaurants; some rooms have balconies, soaking tubs, and fireplaces; free mountain bikes. **Cons:** limited room service; dark in winter because of surrounding trees; some rooms are not accessible via elevator. *Rooms from: $369 ✉ 165 Throckmorton Ave., near Miller Ave. ☎ 415/389–6608, 855/334–7946 🌐 www.marinhotels.com 25 rooms Breakfast.*

Mountain Home Inn
$$$ | **B&B/INN** | Abutting 40,000 acres of state and national parks, this airy wooden inn sits on the skirt of Mt. Tamalpais, where you can follow hiking trails all the way to Stinson Beach. **Pros:** amazing terrace and views; peaceful, remote setting; cooked-to-order breakfast. **Cons:** nearest town is a 12-minute drive away; restaurant can get crowded on sunny weekend days; no on-site fitness option. *Rooms from: $210 ✉ 810 Panoramic Hwy., at Edgewood Ave. ☎ 415/381–9000 🌐 www.mtnhomeinn.com 10 rooms Breakfast.*

Nightlife

BREWPUS AND BEERGARDENS

Mill Valley Beerworks
BREWPUBS/BEER GARDENS | A great place to rest your feet after shopping or hiking, this neighborhood taproom serves a rotating selection of local and imported drafts and bottles alongside choice house brews on tap. A simple menu of small plates includes locally sourced cheeses and enticing salads. Weekend brunches include fresh recipes like strawberry pepper scones or polenta with roasted beets along with Verve coffee. *✉ 173 Throckmorton Ave. ☎ 415/888–8218 🌐 millvalleybeerworks.com.*

MUSIC VENUES

Sweetwater Music Hall
MUSIC CLUBS | With the help of part-owner Bob Weir of the Grateful Dead, this renowned nightclub and café reopened in a historic Masonic Hall in 2012. Famous as well as up-and-coming bands play on most nights, and local stars such as Bonnie Raitt and Huey Lewis have been known to stop in for a pickup session. *✉ 19 Corte Madera Ave., between Throckmorton and Lovell Aves. ☎ 415/388–3850, 877/987–6487 tickets 🌐 www.sweetwatermusichall.com.*

Performing Arts

★ **Throckmorton Theatre**
ART GALLERIES—ARTS | The restored cinema and vaudeville house in Mill Valley is a vibrant cultural hub in the region and is known for fostering exceptional arts and

Did You Know?

The gorgeous old-growth redwood trees in Muir Woods are often enveloped in fog, which provides the moisture to help them survive the dry summers.

education. The darling playhouse seats upwards of 260 and features live theater, Tuesday night comedy, and concerts. Two smaller street-side halls, the Tivoli and Crescendo feature free classical concerts on Wednesdays, along with Sunday evening sessions, jazz performances, and new art exhibits every month. ✉ *142 Throckmorton Ave.* ☎ *415/383–9611* 🌐 *throckmortontheatre.org.*

Shopping

Mill Valley Market

FOOD/CANDY | FAMILY | This family-owned market has been the go-to stop for specialty foods, grocery, deli, and hot food since 1929. Known for their notable beer and wine selection alongside a variety of local and organic produce and healthy grab-and-go foods, this is an ideal stop to prepare for a picnic or to seek out gourmet gifts like imported chocolates and 100-year-old balsamic vinegars. ✉ *12 Corte Madera Ave.* ☎ *415/388–3222* 🌐 *millvalleymarket.com.*

Muir Woods National Monument

12 miles northwest of the Golden Gate Bridge.

Climbing hundreds of feet into the sky, *Sequoia sempervirens* are the tallest living things on Earth—some are more than 1,800 years old. One of the last remaining old-growth stands of these redwood behemoths, Muir Woods is nature's cathedral: imposing, awe-inspiring, reverence-inducing, and not to be missed.

Though much of California's 2 million acres of redwood forest were lost to the logging industry, this area was saved from destruction by William and Elizabeth Kent, who purchased the land in 1905, and later gifted it to the federal government. Theodore Roosevelt declared the space a national monument in 1908 and Kent named it after naturalist John Muir, whose environmental campaigns helped establish the national park system.

GETTING HERE AND AROUND

If you drive to Muir Woods on a weekend or during peak season, expect to find epic traffic jams around the tiny parking areas and adjacent roads. Do yourself a favor and take a shuttle if you can. Reservations are required for parking, so plan ahead. Marin Transit's Route 66 Muir Woods shuttle (*$3 round-trip* 🌐 *www.marintransit.org*) provides weekend and seasonal transport from the Sausalito ferry landing, as well as Marin City, on a seasonal schedule. Private bus tours run year-round. To drive directly from San Francisco by car, take U.S. 101 north across the Golden Gate Bridge to Exit 445B for Mill Valley/Stinson Beach, then follow signs for Highway 1 north and Muir Woods.

Sights

★ **Muir Woods National Monument**

NATIONAL/STATE PARK | FAMILY | Nothing gives perspective like walking among old-growth redwoods. The nearly 560 acres of Muir Woods National Monument contain some of the most majestic redwoods in the world—some more than 250 feet tall.

Part of the Golden Gate National Recreation Area, Muir Woods is a pedestrian's park. The popular 2-mile main trail begins at the park headquarters and provides easy access to streams, ferns, azaleas, and redwood groves. Summer weekends can prove busy, so for a little serenity, consider taking a more challenging route, such as the **Dipsea Trail** , which climbs west from the forest floor to soothing views of the ocean and the Golden Gate Bridge. For a complete list of trails, which vary in difficulty and distance, check with rangers.

Picnicking and camping aren't allowed, and neither are pets. Crowds can be large, especially from May through October, so try to come early in the morning or late in the afternoon. The **Muir Woods Visitor Center** has books and exhibits about redwood trees and the woods' history as well as the latest info on trail conditions; the **Muir Woods Trading Company** serves hot food, organic pastries, and other tasty snacks, and the gift shop offers plenty of souvenirs.

■ TIP→ **Muir Woods has no cell service or Wi-Fi, so plan directions and communication ahead of time.** ✉ *1 Muir Woods Rd., off Panoramic Hwy., Mill Valley* ☎ *415/561–2850 park information, 511 Marin transit* 🌐 *www.nps.gov/muwo* 🎫 *$15; free on government holidays.*

Mt. Tamalpais State Park

13 miles northwest of Golden Gate Bridge.

The view of Mt. Tamalpais from all around the bay can be a beauty, but that's nothing compared to the views *from* the mountain, which range from jaw-dropping to spectacular and take in San Francisco, the East Bay, the coast, and beyond—on a clear day, all the way to the Farallon Islands, 25 miles away.

GETTING HERE AND AROUND

By car, take U.S. 101 north across the Golden Gate Bridge and Exit 445B for Mill Valley/Stinson Beach. Continue north on Highway 1, which will turn into Panoramic Highway. By bus, take Golden Gate Transit to Marin City; in Marin City transfer to the West Marin Stagecoach, Route 61, and get off at Pantoll Ranger Station (☎ *415/226–0855* 🌐 *www.marintransit.org/stage.html*). Once here, the only way to explore is on foot or by bike.

Sights

★ Mt. Tamalpais State Park

NATIONAL/STATE PARK | **FAMILY** | Although the summit of Mt. Tamalpais is only 2,571 feet high, the mountain rises practically from sea level, dominating the topography of Marin County. Adjacent to Muir Woods National Monument, Mt. Tamalpais State Park affords views of the entire Bay Area and the Pacific Ocean to the west. The name for the sacred mount comes from the Coast Miwok tribe and means "west hill," though some have tied it to a folktale about the "sleeping maiden" in the mountain's profile. For years the 6,300-acre park has been a favorite destination for hikers. There are more than 200 miles of trails, some rugged but many developed for easy walking through meadows, grasslands, and forests and along creeks. Mt. Tam, as it's called by locals, is also the birthplace (in the 1970s) of mountain biking, and today many spandex-clad bikers whiz down the park's winding roads.

The park's major thoroughfare, Panoramic Highway, snakes its way up from U.S. 101 to the **Pantoll Ranger Station** and then drops down to the town of Stinson Beach. Pantoll Road branches off the highway at the station, connecting up with Ridgecrest Boulevard. Along these roads are numerous parking areas, picnic spots, scenic overlooks, and trailheads. Parking is free along the roadside, but there's an $8 fee (cash or check only) to park at the ranger station and additional charges for walk-in campsites and group use.

The **Mountain Theater,** also known as the Cushing Memorial Amphitheatre, is a natural 4,000-seat amphitheater that was reconstructed with stone by the Civilian Conservation Corps in the 1930s. It has showcased summer "Mountain Plays" since 1913.

The **Rock Spring Trail** starts at the Mountain Theater and gently climbs for 1½ miles to the **West Point Inn,** which was once a stop on the Mt. Tam railroad route. Relax at a picnic table and stock up on water before forging ahead, via Old Railroad Grade Fire Road and the Miller Trail, to Mt. Tam's Middle Peak, which is another 1½–2 miles depending on route.

Starting from the Pantoll Ranger Station, the precipitous **Steep Ravine Trail** brings you past stands of coastal redwoods and, in the springtime, small waterfalls. Take the connecting **Dipsea Trail** to reach the town of Stinson Beach and its swath of golden sand. **TIP→ If you're too weary to make the 3½-mile trek back up, Marin Transit Bus 61 takes you from Stinson Beach back to the ranger station.** ✉ *Pantoll Ranger Station, 3801 Panoramic Hwy., at Pantoll Rd.* ☎ *415/388–2070* 🌐 *www.parks.ca.gov.*

Muir Beach

12 miles northwest of Golden Gate Bridge, 6 miles southwest of Mill Valley.

Except on the sunniest of weekends, Muir Beach is relatively quiet, but the drive here is a scenic adventure.

GETTING HERE AND AROUND

A car is the best way to reach Muir Beach. From Highway 1, follow Pacific Way southwest ¼ mile.

Sights

Green Gulch Farm Zen Center

FARM/RANCH | Giant eucalyptus trees frame the long and winding road that leads to this tranquil Buddhist practice center. Meditation programs, tea instruction, gardening classes, and various other workshops and events take place here; there's also an extensive organic farm. Visitors are welcome to roam the property and walk through the gardens that reach down toward Muir Beach. Public Sunday programs are especially geared toward visitors. ✉ *1601 Shoreline Hwy., at Green Gulch Rd.* ☎ *415/383–3134 welcome center* 🌐 *www.sfzc.org* 🎫 *Free.*

Beaches

Muir Beach

BEACH—SIGHT | **FAMILY** | Small but scenic, this beach—a rocky patch of shoreline off Highway 1 in the northern Marin Headlands—is a good place to stretch your legs and gaze out at the Pacific. Locals often walk their dogs here; families and cuddling couples come for picnicking and sunbathing. At the northern end of the beach are waterfront homes (and occasional nude sunbathers) and at the other are the bluffs of the Golden Gate National Recreation Area. A land bridge connects directly from the parking lot to the beach, as well as a short trail that leads to a scenic overlook and connects to other coastal paths. There are no lifeguards on duty and the currents can be challenging so swimming is not advised. **Amenities:** parking (free); toilets. **Best for:** solitude; sunsets; hiking. ✉ *100 Pacific Way, off Shoreline Hwy.* 🌐 *www.nps.gov/goga/planyourvisit/muirbeach.htm.*

Hotels

Pelican Inn

$$$ | **B&B/INN** | From its slate roof to its whitewashed plaster walls, this inn looks so Tudor that it's hard to believe it was built in the 1970s, but the Pelican is English to the core, with its cozy upstairs guest rooms (no elevator), draped half-tester beds, a sun-filled solarium, and bangers and grilled tomatoes for breakfast. **Pros:** five-minute walk to beach; great bar and restaurant; peaceful setting. **Cons:** 20-minute drive to nearby attractions; rooms are quite small and rustic; workout and steam room access not on-site. 💲 *Rooms from: $224* ✉ *10 Pacific Way, off Hwy. 1* ☎ *415/383–6000* 🌐 *www.pelicaninn.com* *7 rooms* 🍽 *Breakfast.*

Stinson Beach

20 miles northwest of Golden Gate Bridge.

This laid-back hamlet is all about the beach, and folks come from all over the Bay Area to walk its sandy, often windswept shore. Ideal day trip: a morning hike at Mt. Tam followed by lunch at one of Stinson's unassuming eateries and a leisurely beach stroll.

GETTING HERE AND AROUND

If you're driving, take U.S. 101 to the Mill Valley/Stinson Beach/Highway 1 exit and follow the road west and then north. By bus, take Golden Gate Transit to Marin City and then transfer to the West Marin Stagecoach (61) for Bolinas.

Stinson Beach

BEACH—SIGHT | FAMILY | When the fog hasn't rolled in, this expansive stretch of sand is about as close as you can get in Marin to the stereotypical feel of a Southern California beach. There are several clothing-optional areas, among them a section south of Stinson Beach called Red Rock Beach. ⚠ **Swimming at Stinson Beach can be dangerous; the undertow is strong, and shark sightings, though infrequent, have occurred; lifeguards are on duty May–September.** On any hot summer weekend, roads to Stinson are packed and the parking lot fills, so factor this into your plans. The town itself—population 600, give or take—has a nonchalant surfer vibe, with a few good eating options and pleasant hippie-craftsy browsing. **Amenities:** food and drink; lifeguards (summer); parking (free); showers; toilets. **Best for:** nudists; sunset; surfing; swimming; walking, windsurfing. ✉ *Hwy. 1, 1 Calle Del Sierra* ☎ *415/868–0942 lifeguard tower* 🌐 *www.stinsonbeachonline.com* ☞ *No pets allowed on national park section of beach.*

Parkside Cafe

$$$ | AMERICAN | FAMILY | The Parkside is popular for its 1950s beachfront snack bar, but the adjoining café, coffee bar, marketplace, and bakery shouldn't be missed either. A full menu serves up fresh ingredients, local seafood, wood-fired pizzas, and just-baked breads. **Known for:** espresso and pastry bar; fish-and-chips; rustic house-made breads. Ⓢ *Average main: $27* ✉ *43 Arenal Ave., off Shoreline Hwy.* ☎ *415/868–1272* 🌐 *www.parksidecafe.com.*

 Hotels

Sandpiper Lodging

$$ | B&B/INN | FAMILY | Recharge, rest, and enjoy the local scenery at this ultrapopular lodging that books up months, even years, in advance. **Pros:** beach chairs, towels, and toys provided; lush gardens with BBQ; minutes from the beach and town. **Cons:** walls are thin; limited amenities; charge for roll-away beds and extra persons. Ⓢ *Rooms from: $185* ✉ *1 Marine Way, off Arenal Ave.* ☎ *415/868–1632* 🌐 *www.sandpiperstinsonbeach.com* *11 rooms* *No meals.*

Point Reyes National Seashore

Bear Valley Visitor Center is 14 miles north of Stinson Beach.

With sandy beaches stretching for miles, a dramatic rocky coastline, a gem of a lighthouse, and idyllic, century-old dairy farms, Point Reyes National Seashore is one of the most varied and strikingly beautiful corners of the Bay Area.

GETTING HERE AND AROUND

From San Francisco, take U.S. 101 north, head west at Sir Francis Drake Boulevard (Exit 450B) toward San Anselmo, and

Did You Know?

The majestic Point Reyes National Seashore offers many attractions for nature lovers: hiking, bird-watching, camping, or whale-watching, depending on the season. But flower picking isn't an approved activity; the wildflowers here are protected.

follow the road just under 20 miles to Bear Valley Road. From Stinson Beach or Bolinas, drive north on Highway 1 and turn left on Bear Valley Road. If you're going by bus, take one of several Golden Gate Transit buses to Marin City; in Marin City transfer to the West Marin Stagecoach (you'll switch buses in Olema). Once at the visitor center, the best way to get around is on foot.

Sights

Bear Valley Visitor Center

INFO CENTER | FAMILY | A life-size elephant seal model dominates the center's engaging exhibits about the wildlife, history, and ecology of the Point Reyes National Seashore. The rangers at the barnlike facility are fonts of information about beaches, whale-watching, hiking trails, and camping. Restrooms are available, as well as trailhead parking and a picnic area with barbecue grills. Winter hours may be shorter and summer weekend hours may be longer; call or check the website for details. ✉ *Bear Valley Visitor Center, 1 Bear Valley Visitor Center Access Rd., west of Hwy. 1, off Bear Valley Rd., Point Reyes Station* ☎ *415/464–5100* 🌐 *www.nps.gov/pore/planyourvisit*.

★ Duxbury Reef

NATURE PRESERVE | FAMILY | Excellent tide pooling can be had along the 3-mile shoreline of Duxbury Reef; it's the most extensive tide pool area near Point Reyes National Seashore, as well as one of the largest shale intertidal reefs in North America. Look for sea stars, barnacles, sea anemones, purple urchins, limpets, sea mussels, and the occasional abalone. But check a tide table (*tidesandcurrents.noaa.gov*) or the local papers if you plan to explore the reef—it's accessible only at low tide. The reef is a 30-minute drive from the Bear Valley Visitor Center. Take Highway 1 south from the center, turn right at Olema–Bolinas Road (keep an eye peeled; the road is easy to miss), left on Horseshoe Hill Road, right on Mesa Road, left on Overlook Drive, and then right on Elm Road, which dead-ends at the Agate Beach County Park parking lot. ✣ *At Duxbury Point, 1 mile west of Bolinas* 🌐 *www.ptreyes.org/activities/tidepools*.

Palomarin Field Station & Point Reyes Bird Observatory

NATURE PRESERVE | FAMILY | Birders adore Point Blue Conservation Science, which maintains the Palomarin Field Station and the Point Reyes Bird Observatory (PRBO) that are located in the southernmost part of Point Reyes National Seashore. The Field Station, open daily from sunrise to sunset, has excellent interpretive exhibits, including a comparative display of real birds' talons. The surrounding woods harbor some 200 bird species. As you hike the quiet trails through forest and along ocean cliffs, you're likely to see biologists banding birds to aid in the study of their life cycles. ■ **TIP→ Visit Point Blue's website for detailed directions and to find out when banding will occur.** ✉ *999 Mesa Rd., Bolinas* ☎ *415/868–0655 field station, 707/781–2555 headquarters* 🌐 *www.pointblue.org*.

★ Point Reyes National Seashore

NATIONAL/STATE PARK | FAMILY | One of the Bay Area's most spectacular treasures and the only national seashore on the West Coast, the 71,000-acre Point Reyes National Seashore encompasses hiking trails, secluded beaches, and rugged grasslands as well as Point Reyes itself, a triangular peninsula that juts into the Pacific. The town of **Point Reyes Station** is a one-main-drag affair with some good places to eat and gift shops that sell locally made and imported goods.

When explorer Sir Francis Drake sailed along the California coast in 1579, he allegedly missed the Golden Gate and San Francisco Bay, but he did land at what he described as a convenient harbor. In 2012 the federal government conceded a centuries-long debate and officially recognized Drake's Bay, which flanks the point on the east, as that harbor, designating the spot a National Historic Landmark and silencing competing claims in the 433-year-old controversy. Today Point Reyes's hills and dramatic cliffs attract other kinds of explorers: hikers, whale-watchers, and solitude seekers.

The infamous San Andreas Fault runs along the park's eastern edge and up the center of Tomales Bay; take the short **Earthquake Trail** from the visitor center to see the impact near the epicenter of the 1906 earthquake that devastated San Francisco. A half-mile path from the visitor center leads to **Kule Loklo,** a reconstructed Miwok village that sheds light on the daily lives of the region's first inhabitants. From here, trails also lead to the park's hike-in campgrounds (no car camping).

■ TIP→ **In late winter and spring, take the short walk at Chimney Rock, just before the lighthouse, to the Elephant Seal Overlook.** Even from the cliff, the male seals look enormous as they spar, growling and bloodied, for resident females.

You can experience the diversity of Point Reyes's ecosystems on the scenic **Coast Trail,** which starts at the Palomarin Trailhead, just outside Bolinas. From here, it's a 3-mile trek through eucalyptus groves and pine forests and along seaside cliffs to beautiful and tiny Bass Lake. To reach the Palomarin Trailhead, take Olema–Bolinas Road toward Bolinas, turn right on Mesa Road, follow signs to Point Blue Conservation Science, and then continue until the road dead-ends.

The 4.7-mile-long (one-way) **Tomales Point Trail** follows the spine of the park's northernmost finger of land through a Tule Elk Preserve, providing spectacular ocean views from the high bluffs. Expect to see elk, but keep your distance from the animals. To reach the moderately easy hiking trail, take Sir Francis Drake Boulevard through the town of Inverness; when you come to a fork, veer right to stay on Pierce Point Road and continue until you reach the parking lot at Pierce Point Ranch. ✉ *Bear Valley Visitor Center, 1 Bear Valley Visitor Center Access Rd., west of Hwy. 1, off Bear Valley Rd., Point Reyes Station* ☎ *415/464–5100* 🌐 *www.nps.gov/pore.*

Restaurants

Café Reyes

$$ | PIZZA | FAMILY | Sunny patio seating, hand-tossed pizza, and organic local ingredients are the selling points of this laid-back café. The semi-industrial dining room, which is built around a brick oven, features glazed concrete floors, warm-painted walls, and ceilings high enough to accommodate full-size market umbrellas. **Known for:** wood-fired pizza; Drake's Bay fresh oysters; outdoor patio dining. $ *Average main: $16* ✉ *11101 Hwy. 1, Point Reyes Station* ☎ *415/663–9493* 🌐 *cafe-reyes.com* ⊗ *Closed Mon. and Tues.*

Due West

$$$ | AMERICAN | Award-winning chef Jonathan Pfluege brings local, sustainable culinary provisions to this classic Point Reyes tavern, a popular horse and wagon stop since the 1860s. The seasonal menu includes American classics from burgers and brick-roasted chicken to seafood specialties like Dungeness crab chowder and oysters fried, grilled, or freshly shucked. **Known for:** artisanal cheese plate; steak frites; regional wine list. $ *Average main: $24* ✉ *10021 Coastal Hwy. 1, Olema* ☎ *415/663–1264* 🌐 *olemahouse.com/dine.*

★ Hog Island Oyster Co. Marshall Oyster Farm & the Boat Oyster Bar

$$$ | **SEAFOOD** | **FAMILY** | Take a short trek north on Highway 1 to the gritty mecca of Bay Area oysters—the Hog Island Marshall Oyster Farm. For a real culinary adventure, arrange to shuck and barbecue your own oysters on one of the outdoor grills (all tools supplied, reservations required), or for the less adventurous, the Boat Oyster Bar is an informal outdoor café that serves raw and BBQ oysters, local snacks, and tasty beverages. **Known for:** fresh, raw, and BBQ oysters; picnic grills; Hog Shack shellfish to go. *Average main: $24 20215 Shoreline Hwy. 415/663–9218 hogislandoysters.com/locations/marshall Oyster Bar closed Tues.–Thurs. No dinner.*

★ Osteria Stellina

$$ | **ITALIAN** | Chef-owner Christian Caiazzo's menu of "Point Reyes Italian" cuisine puts an emphasis on showcasing hyperlocal ingredients like Marin-grown kale and Sonoma cheese. Pastas, pizzas, and a handful of entrées are served in a rustic-contemporary space with a raw bar that serves local oysters all day long. **Known for:** locally sourced produce and seafood; fresh oysters; inventive pizzas. *Average main: $22 11285 Hwy. 1, at 3rd St., Point Reyes Station 415/663–9988 www.osteriastellina.com.*

★ Side Street Kitchen

$ | **AMERICAN** | **FAMILY** | Rotisserie meats and veggies sourced from local farms steal the show at this former mid-century truck stop and diner. It's a go-to for tri-tip and pork belly sandwiches or house-seasoned roasted chicken, best eaten family style with a host of salads, sides, and butterscotch pudding. **Known for:** cold smoked seafood and rotisserie chicken; dog-friendly outdoor patio; apple fritters. *Average main: $16 60 4th St., Point Reyes Station 415/663–0303 sidestreet-prs.com No dinner.*

Sir and Star at the Olema

$$$$ | **AMERICAN** | With lovely garden views, creative and cryptically named dishes, and upscale-rustic decor that somehow incorporates taxidermied animals, this historic roadhouse (located within the Olema Inn) elicits both rants and raves, often from diners sharing the same table. The locally focused menu of California cuisine changes seasonally; a special prix fixe is offered by reservation on Saturday evening. **Known for:** great atmosphere; small plates; Saturday Chef's Meal. *Average main: $35 10000 Sir Francis Drake Blvd., at Hwy. 1, Olema 415/663–1034 sirandstar.com Closed Mon.–Wed. No lunch.*

Station House Cafe

$$ | **AMERICAN** | In good weather, hikers fresh from the park fill the Station House's lovely outdoor garden as well as its homey indoor tables, banquettes, and bar stools, so prepare for a wait. The community-centric eatery is locally focused and serves a blend of modern and classic California dishes comprised of organic seasonal ingredients, sustainable hormone-free meats, and wild-caught seafood. **Known for:** signature popovers; hearty breakfast items; local fresh seafood. *Average main: $22 11180 Hwy. 1, at 2nd St., Point Reyes Station 415/663–1515 www.stationhousecafe.com Closed Wed.*

Stinson Beach Breakers Cafe

$$$ | **AMERICAN** | Hard to miss along the tiny stretch of Main Street, this café is an easy prebeach destination for coffee and griddle specialties or postsurf bar bites and cocktails on the heated patio in the afternoon. Beach cottage hardwood floors and a wood stove add to the warmth of the rustic seaside interior, while a mountain view and fire pit adds to the deck. **Known for:** hearty egg breakfast dishes with a Latin twist; fresh oysters; fish tacos. *Average main: $23 3465 Hwy. 1, Stinson*

Beach ☎ *415/868–2002* 🌐 *stinsonbeachcafe.com* ⏲ *Closed Tues. and Wed., Nov.–Mar.*

Hotels

★ Olema House

$$$$ | B&B/INN | FAMILY | Once a historic 1860s stagecoach stopover, this renovated, luxurious getaway offers just as many reasons to stay on property—with its views of Mt. Wittenberg—as to explore the 71,000 acres of national seashore just steps away. **Pros:** lush garden; convenient parking and horse hitching; friendly and informative staff. **Cons:** steps to some rooms may be steep; street-facing rooms above restaurant may be noisy; Wi-Fi and cell service may be spotty. 💲 *Rooms from: $300* ✉ *10021 Coastal Hwy. 1, Olema* ☎ *415/663–9000* 🌐 *olemahouse.com* 🛏 *25 rooms* 🍽 *Free Breakfast.*

Shopping

★ Cowgirl Creamery

LOCAL SPECIALTIES | FAMILY | In this former hay barn, a couple of Berkeley foodies (from Chez Panisse and Bette's Oceanview Diner) started their original creamery for artisanal cheeses. In addition to more than 200 specialty cheeses—local, regional, and international—you'll find Tomales Bay Foods offerings featuring West Marin farm wares. Cowgirl Creamery cheeses harness flavors unique to Point Reyes, such as their award-winning Red Hawk and Mt Tam made from Straus Family Dairy milk. Sample seasonal cheeses and see how the cheese is made or order a hot mac and cheese at the cantina and stay for a bite at the picnic tables. Abundant deli items, gourmet goodies, and wine selections make it easy to pack a picnic for the beach or a hike here. ✉ *80 4th St., Point Reyes Station* ☎ *415/663–9335* 🌐 *www.cowgirlcreamery.com/pt-reyes-shop-creamery* ⏲ *Closed Mon. and Tues.*

Gospel Flat Farm Stand

OUTDOOR/FLEA/GREEN MARKETS | FAMILY | This combination art gallery, farm stand, and flower shop captures the true essence of the area, with its dedication to community and bounty of local organic vegetables, fruits, and eggs. A must-see when passing through the Bolinas and Olema area, the self-serve site is open 24 hours. What makes it truly special is that the entire stand operates on the honor system. Weigh and log your produce, and slip your payment (cash or check) in the box. The local art on exhibit adds to the allure of this roadside treasure. ✉ *140 Olema-Bolinas Rd., Bolinas* ☎ *415/858–4730* 🌐 *gospelflatfarm.com.*

★ Toby's Feed Barn

LOCAL SPECIALTIES | FAMILY | The heart of the community since 1942, this barn has a bounty of local gifts and produce, plus an art gallery, yoga studio, and Toby's Coffee Bar for espresso drinks and sell-out pastries. See and hear what's happening locally, catch a live band, and explore the garden. The internationally renowned all local, all organic Point Reyes Farmers' Market is held here on Saturday for 20 weeks during the growing season. ✉ *11250 Hwy. 1, Point Reyes Station* ☎ *415/663–1223* 🌐 *tobysfeedbarn.com.*

Chapter 15

NAPA AND SONOMA

Updated by
Daniel Mangin

Sights ★★★★★ | Restaurants ★★★★★ | Hotels ★★★★☆ | Shopping ★★★☆☆ | Nightlife ★★★☆☆

WELCOME TO NAPA AND SONOMA

TOP REASONS TO GO

★ **Touring wineries:** Let's face it: this is the reason you're here, and the range of excellent sips to sample would make any oenophile (or novice drinker, for that matter) giddy.

★ **Biking:** Gentle hills and vineyard-laced farmland make Napa and Sonoma perfect for combining leisurely back-roads cycling with winery stops.

★ **Browsing the farmers' markets:** Many towns in Napa and Sonoma have seasonal farmers' markets, each rounding up an amazing variety of local produce.

★ **A meal at The French Laundry:** Chef Thomas Keller's Yountville restaurant is one of the country's best. The mastery of flavors and attention to detail are subtly remarkable.

★ **Viewing the art:** Several wineries, among them the Hess Collection in Napa, The Donum Estate in Sonoma, and Hall St. Helena, display museum-quality artworks indoors and on their grounds..

The Napa and Sonoma valleys run parallel, northwest to southeast , and are separated by the Mayacamas Mountains. Southwest of Sonoma Valley are several other important viticultural areas in Sonoma county, including the Dry Creek, Alexander, and Russian River Valleys. The Carneros, which spans southern Sonoma and Napa counties, is just north of San Pablo Bay.

1 **Napa.**

2 **Yountville.**

3 **Oakville.**

4 **Rutherford.**

5 **St. Helena.**

6 **Calistoga.**

7 **Sonoma.**

8 **Glen Ellen.**

9 **Kenwood.**

10 **Healdsburg.**

11 **Geyserville**

12 **Forestville.**

13 **Guerneville**

14 **Sebastopol.**

15 **Santa Rosa.**

16 **Petaluma.**

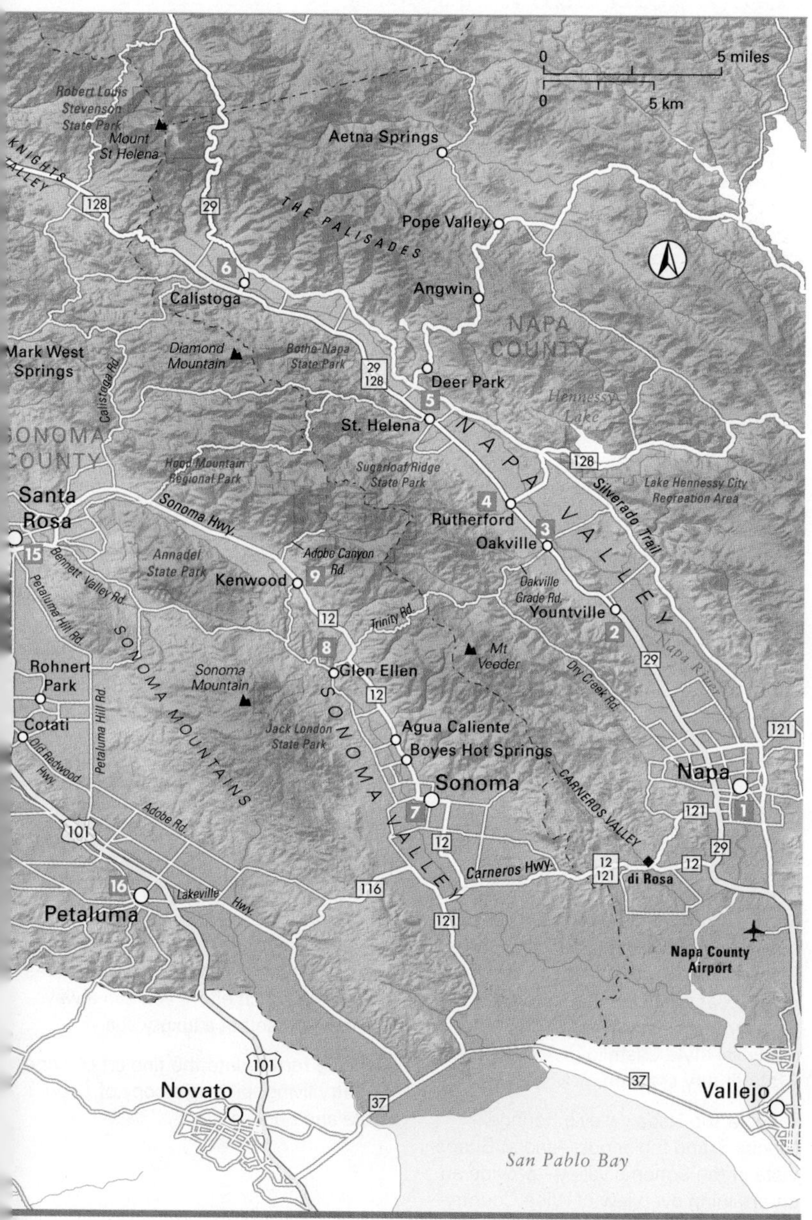

0
5 miles
0
5 km
Robert Louis Stevenson State Park
Mount St Helena
KNIGHTS VALLEY
128
29
Aetna Springs
THE PALISADES
Pope Valley
Angwin
NAPA COUNTY
6
Calistoga
Mark West Springs
Calistoga Rd.
Diamond Mountain
Bothe-Napa State Park
29
128
Deer Park
Hennessy Lake
5
St. Helena
NAPA VALLEY
SONOMA COUNTY
Hood Mountain Regional Park
Sugarloaf Ridge State Park
128
Silverado Trail
Lake Hennessy City Recreation Area
Santa Rosa
Sonoma Hwy.
4
Rutherford
3
Oakville
15
Bennett Valley Rd.
Annadel State Park
Adobe Canyon Rd.
Kenwood
9
Oakville Grade Rd.
Yountville
2
Petaluma Hill Rd.
12
Trinity Rd.
Napa River
SONOMA MOUNTAINS
8
Mt Veeder
29
Rohnert Park
Sonoma Mountain
Glen Ellen
Dry Creek Rd.
12
Cotati
Old Redwood Hwy.
Petaluma Hill Rd.
Jack London State Park
Agua Caliente
Boyes Hot Springs
121
SONOMA VALLEY
Sonoma
CARNEROS VALLEY
Napa
121
1
7
Adobe Rd.
101
12
29
Carneros Hwy.
12
121
di Rosa
12
16
Lakeville Hwy
116
Petaluma
121
Napa County Airport
101
37
Novato
37
Vallejo
San Pablo Bay

In California's premier wine region, the pleasures of eating and drinking are celebrated daily. It's easy to join in at famous wineries and rising newcomers off country roads, or at trendy in-town tasting rooms. Chefs transform local ingredients into feasts, and gourmet groceries sell perfect picnic fare. Yountville, Healdsburg, and St. Helena have small-town charm as well as luxurious inns, hotels, and spas, yet the natural setting is equally sublime, whether experienced from a canoe on the Russian River or the deck of a winery overlooking endless rows of vines.

The Wine Country is also rich in history. In Sonoma you can explore California's Spanish and Mexican pasts at the Sonoma Mission, and the origins of modern California wine making at Buena Vista Winery. Some wineries, among them St. Helena's Beringer and Rutherford's Inglenook, have cellars or tasting rooms dating to the late 1800s. Calistoga is a flurry of late-19th-century Steamboat Gothic architecture, though the town's oldest-looking building, the medieval-style Castello di Amorosa, is a 21st-century creation.

Tours at the Napa Valley's Beringer, Mondavi, and Inglenook—and at Buena Vista in the Sonoma Valley—provide an entertaining overview of Wine Country history. The tour at the splashy visitor center at St. Helena's Hall winery will introduce you to 21st-century wine-making technology, and over in Glen Ellen's Benziger Family Winery you can see how its vineyard managers apply biodynamic farming principles to grape growing. At numerous facilities you can play winemaker for a day at seminars in the fine art of blending wines. If that strikes you as too much effort, you can always pamper yourself at a luxury spa.

To delve further into the fine art of Wine Country living, pick up a copy of *Fodor's Napa and Sonoma*.

MAJOR REGIONS

Napa Valley. With more than 500 wineries and many of the biggest brands in the business, the Napa Valley is the Wine Country's star. With a population of about 79,000, Napa, the valley's largest town, lures with its cultural attractions and (relatively) reasonably priced accommodations. A few miles farther north, compact **Yountville** is densely packed with top-notch restaurants and hotels, and **Rutherford** and **Oakville** are renowned for their Cabernet Sauvignon–friendly soils. Beyond them, **St. Helena** teems with elegant boutiques and restaurants, and casual **Calistoga**, known for spas and hot springs, has the feel of an Old West frontier town.

The Sonoma Valley. The birthplace of modern California wine making—Count Aragon Haraszthy opened Buena Vista Winery here in 1857—Sonoma Valley seduces with its unpretentious attitude and pastoral landscape. Tasting rooms, restaurants, and historic sites, among the latter the last mission established in California by Franciscan friars, abound near Sonoma Plaza. Beyond downtown Sonoma, the wineries and attractions are spread out along gently winding roads. Sonoma County's half of the Carneros District lies within Sonoma Valley, whose other towns of note include Glen Ellen and Kenwood. Sonoma Valley tasting rooms are often less crowded than those in Napa or northern Sonoma County, especially midweek, and the vibe here, though sophisticated, is definitely less sceney.

Planning

When to Go

High season extends from April through October. In summer, expect the days to be hot and dry, the roads filled with cars, and traffic heavy at the tasting rooms. Hotel rates are highest during the height of harvest, in September and October. Then and in summer book lodgings well ahead. November, except for Thanksgiving week, and December before Christmas are less busy. The weather in Napa and Sonoma is pleasant nearly year-round. Daytime temperatures average from about 55°F during winter to the 80s in summer, when readings in the 90s and higher are common. April, May, and October are milder but still warm. The rainiest months are usually from December through March.

Getting Here and Around

AIR TRAVEL

Wine Country regulars often bypass San Francisco and Oakland and fly into Santa Rosa's Charles M. Schulz Sonoma County Airport (STS), which receives direct flights from San Diego, Las Vegas, Los Angeles, Phoenix, Portland, and Seattle. The airport is 15 miles from Healdsburg. ■ TIP→ **Alaska Airlines allows passengers flying out of STS to check up to one case of wine for free.**

BUS TRAVEL

Bus travel is an inconvenient way to explore the Wine Country, though it is possible. Take Golden Gate Transit from San Francisco to connect with Sonoma County Transit buses. VINE connects with BART commuter trains in the East Bay and the San Francisco Bay Ferry in Vallejo *(see Ferry Travel, below)*. VINE buses serve the Napa Valley.

CAR TRAVEL

A car is the most convenient way to navigate Napa and Sonoma. If you're flying into the area, it's almost always easiest to pick up a car at the airport. You'll also find rental companies in major Wine Country towns. A few rules to note: Smartphone use for any purpose is prohibited, including mapping applications unless the device is mounted to a car's windshield or dashboard and can be activated with a single swipe or finger tap. A right turn after stopping at a red light is legal unless posted otherwise.

If you base yourself in the Napa Valley towns of Napa, Yountville, or St. Helena, or in Sonoma County's Healdsburg or Sonoma, you can visit numerous tasting rooms and nearby wineries on foot or by bicycle on mostly flat terrain. The free Yountville trolley loops through town, and ride-sharing is viable there and in Napa. Sonoma County sprawls more, but except for far west the public transit and ride-sharing generally work well.

■ TIP→ If you're wine tasting, either select a designated driver or be careful of your wine intake—the police keep an eye out for tipsy drivers.

From San Francisco to Napa: Cross the Golden Gate Bridge, then go north on U.S. 101. Head east on Highway 37 toward Vallejo, then north on Highway 121, aka the Carneros Highway. Turn left (north) when Highway 121 runs into Highway 29.

From San Francisco to Sonoma: Cross the Golden Gate Bridge, then go north on U.S. 101, east on Highway 37 toward Vallejo, and north on Highway 121. When you reach Highway 12, take it north to the town of Sonoma. For Sonoma County destinations north of Sonoma Valley stay on U.S. 101, which passes through Santa Rosa and Healdsburg.

From Berkeley and Oakland: Take Interstate 80 north to Highway 37 west, then on to Highway 29 north. For the Napa Valley, continue on Highway 29; to reach Sonoma County, head west on Highway 121.

Restaurants

Farm-to-table Modern American cuisine is the prevalent style in the Napa Valley and Sonoma County, but this encompasses both the delicate preparations of Thomas Keller's highly praised The French Laundry and the upscale comfort food served throughout the Wine Country. The quality (and hype) often means high prices, but you can also find appealing, inexpensive eateries, especially in the towns of Napa, Calistoga, Sonoma, and Santa Rosa, and many high-end delis prepare superb picnic fare. At pricey restaurants you can save money by having lunch instead of dinner. With a few exceptions (noted in individual restaurant listings), dress is informal. *Restaurant reviews have been shortened. For full information, visit Fodors.com.*

Hotels

The fanciest accommodations are concentrated in the Napa Valley towns of Yountville, Rutherford, St. Helena, and Calistoga; Sonoma County's poshest lodgings are in Healdsburg. The spas, amenities, and exclusivity of high-end properties attract travelers with the means and desire for luxury living. The cities of Napa and Santa Rosa are the best bets for budget hotels and inns, but even at a lower price point you'll still find a touch of Wine Country glamour. On weekends, two- or even three-night minimum stays are commonly required at smaller lodgings. Book well ahead for stays at such places during the busy summer or fall season. If your party will include travelers under age 16, inquire about policies regarding younger guests; some smaller lodgings discourage (or discreetly forbid) children. *Hotel reviews have been shortened. For full information, visit Fodors.com.*

What It Costs

	$	$$	$$$	$$$$
RESTAURANTS				
	under $16	$16–$22	$23–$30	over $30
HOTELS				
	under $200	$200–$300	$301–$400	over $400

Napa

46 miles northeast of San Francisco.

After many years as a blue-collar burg detached from the Wine Country scene, the Napa Valley's largest town (population about 80,000) has evolved into one of its shining stars. Masaharu Morimoto and other chefs of note operate restaurants here, swank hotels and inns can be found downtown and beyond, and the nightlife options include the West Coast edition of the famed Blue Note jazz club. A walkway that follows the Napa River has made downtown more pedestrian-friendly, and the Oxbow Public Market, a complex of high-end food purveyors, is popular with locals and tourists. The nearby CIA at Copia, operated by the Culinary Institute of America, hosts cooking demonstrations and other activities open to the public and has a shop and a restaurant. If you establish your base in Napa, plan on spending at least a half day strolling the downtown district.

GETTING HERE AND AROUND

Downtown Napa lies a mile east of Highway 29—take the 1st Street exit and follow the signs. Ample parking, much of it free for the first three hours and some for the entire day, is available on or near Main Street. Several VINE buses serve downtown and beyond.

Sights

Artesa Vineyards & Winery

WINERY/DISTILLERY | From a distance the modern, minimalist architecture of Artesa blends harmoniously with the surrounding Carneros landscape, but up close its pools, fountains, and large outdoor sculptures make a vivid impression. So, too, do the wines: mostly Chardonnay and Pinot Noir but also Cabernet Sauvignon, sparkling, and limited releases like Albariño and Tempranillo. You can sample wines without a reservation in the Foyer Bar, but one is required for single-vineyard flights and food pairings. The latter can be enjoyed in the light-filled Salon Bar or outside on a terrace with views of estate and neighboring vineyards and, on a clear day, San Francisco. ✉ *1345 Henry Rd., Napa* ✣ *Off Old Sonoma Rd. and Dealy La.* ☎ *707/224–1668* 🌐 *www.artesawinery.com* 🎫 *Tastings from $35, tour $45 (includes tasting).*

★ **Ashes & Diamonds**

WINERY/DISTILLERY | Barbara Bestor's sleek white design for this appointment-only winery's glass-and-metal tasting space evokes midcentury modern architecture and with it the era and wines before the Napa Valley's rise to prominence. Two much-heralded pros lead the wine-making team assembled by record producer Kashy Khaledi: Steve Matthiasson, known for his classic, restrained style and attention to viticultural detail, and Diana Snowden Seysses, who draws on experiences in Burgundy, Provence, and California. Bordeaux varietals are the focus, most notably Cabernet Sauvignon and Cabernet Franc but also the white blend of Sauvignon Blanc and Sémillon and even the rosé (of Cabernet Franc). With a label designer who was also responsible for a Jay-Z album cover and interiors that recall the *Mad Men* in Palm Springs story arc, the pitch seems unabashedly to millennials, but the wines, low in alcohol and with higher acidity (good for aging), enchant connoisseurs

Continued on page 334

WINE
TASTING in
NAPA and
SONOMA

Whether you're a serious wine collector making your annual pilgrimage to Nothern California's Wine Country or a newbie who doesn't know the difference between a Merlot and Mourvèdre but is eager to learn, you can have a great time touring Napa and Sonoma wineries. Your gateway to the wine world is the tasting room, where staff members are happy to chat with curious guests.

(opposite page) Carneros vineyards in autumn, Napa Valley. (top) Pinot Gris grapes. (bottom) Bottles from Far Niente winery.

VISITING WINERIES

Tasting rooms range from the grand to the humble, offering everything from a few sips of wine to in-depth tours of facilities and vineyards. Many are open for drop-in visits, usually daily from around 10 am to 5 pm. Others require guests to make reservations. First-time visitors frequently enjoy the history-oriented tours at Charles Krug and Inglenook, or ones at Mondavi and J Vineyards that highlight the process as well. The environments at some wineries reflect their founders' other interests: art and architecture at Artesa and Hall St. Helena, movie making at Francis Ford Coppola, and medieval history at the Castello di Amorosa.

Many wineries describe their pourers as "wine educators," and indeed some of them have taken online or other classes and have passed an exam to prove basic knowledge of appellations, grape varietals, vineyards, and wine-making techniques. The one constant, however, is a deep, shared pleasure in the experience of wine tasting. To prepare you for winery visits, we've covered the fundamentals: tasting rooms, fees and what to expect, and the types of tours wineries offer.

Fees. In the past few years, tasting fees have skyrocketed. Most Napa wineries charge $25 or $30 to taste a few wines, though $40, $50, or even $75 fees aren't unheard of. Sonoma wineries are often a bit cheaper, in the $15 to $35 range, and you'll still find the occasional freebie.

Some winery tours are free, in which case you're usually required to pay a separate fee if you want to taste the wine. If you've paid a fee for the tour—generally from $20 to $40—your wine tasting is usually included in that price.

MAKING THE MOST OF YOUR TIME

(top) Sipping and swirling in the DeLoach tasting room. (bottom) Learning about barrel aging at Robert Mondavi Winery.

- **Call ahead.** Some wineries require reservations to visit or tour. It's wise to check before visiting.

- **Come on weekdays.** Especially between June and October, try to visit on weekdays to avoid traffic-clogged roads and crowded tasting rooms. For more info on the best times of year to visit, see this chapter's Planner.

- **Get an early start.** Tasting rooms are often deserted before 11 am or so, when most visitors are still lingering over a second cup of coffee. If you come early, you'll have the staff's undivided attention. You'll usually encounter the largest crowds between 3 and 5 pm.

- **Schedule strategically.** Visit appointment-only wineries in the morning and ones that allow walk-ins in the afternoon. It'll spare you the stress of being "on time" for later stops.

- **Hit the Trail.** Beringer, Mondavi, and other high-profile wineries line heavily trafficked Highway 29, but the going is often quicker on the Silverado Trail, which runs parallel to the highway to the east. You'll find famous names here, too, among them the sparkling wine house Mumm Napa Valley, but the traffic is often lighter and sometimes the crowds as well.

Domaine Carneros.

AT THE BAR

In most tasting rooms, you'll be handed a list of the wines available that day. The wines will be listed in a suggested tasting order, starting with the lightest-bodied whites, progressing to the most intense reds, and ending with dessert wines. If you can't decide which wines to choose, tell the server what types of wines you usually like and ask for a recommendation.

The server will pour you an ounce or so of each wine you select. As you taste it, feel free to take notes or ask questions. Don't be shy—the staff are there to educate you about the wine. If you don't like a wine, or you've simply tasted enough, feel free to pour the rest into one of the dump buckets on the bar.

TOURS

Tours tend to be the most exciting (and the most crowded) in September and October, when the harvest and crushing are underway. Tours typically last from 30 minutes to an hour and give you a brief overview of the winemaking process. At some of the older wineries, the tour guide might focus on the history of the property.

■ **TIP→** If you plan to take any tours, wear comfortable shoes, since you might be walking on wet floors or dirt or gravel pathways or stepping over hoses or other equipment.

MONEY-SAVING TIPS

■ Many hotels and B&Bs distribute coupons for free or discounted tastings to their guests—don't forget to ask.

■ If you and your travel partner don't mind sharing a glass, servers are happy to let you split a tasting.

■ Some wineries will refund all or part of the tasting fee if you buy a bottle. Usually one fee is waived per bottle purchased, though sometimes you must buy two or three.

■ Almost all wineries will also waive the fee if you join their wine club program. However, this typically commits you to buying a certain number of bottles on a regular basis, so be sure you really like the wines before signing up.

Preston of Dry Creek bottles only estate-grown grapes.

TOP 2-DAY ITINERARIES

First-Timer's Napa Tour

Start: **Oxbow Public market, Napa.** Get underway by browsing the shops selling wines, spices, locally grown produce, and other fine foods, for a taste of what the Wine Country has to offer.

Inglenook, Rutherford. The tour here is a particularly fun way to learn about the history of Napa winemaking—

and you can see the old, atmospheric, ivy-covered château.

Frog's Leap, Rutherford. Friendly, unpretentious, and knowledgeable staff makes this place great for wine newbies. (Make sure you get that reservation lined up.)

Dinner and Overnight: **St. Helena.** Splurge at Meadowood Napa Valley and you won't need to leave the property for an extravagant din-

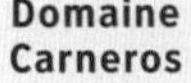

di Rosa Preserve

121

12

Old Sonoma Rd.

Oxbow Public Market

Napa

29

NAPA COUNTY

Yountville

Far Niente

Oakville

Rober
Monda

Silverado Trail

Stag's Leap Wine Cellars

Wine Buff's Tour

Start: **Stag's Leap Wine Cellars, Yountville, Napa.** Famed for its Cabernet Sauvignon and Bordeaux blends.

Silver Oak, Oakville. Schedule a tour of this celebrated winery and taste the flagship Cabernet Sauvignon.

Mumm Napa, Rutherford. Come for the bubbly—which is available in a variety of tastings—stay for the photography exhibits.

Dinner and Overnight: **Yountville.** Have dinner at one of the Thomas Keller restaurants. Splurge at Bardessono; save at Maison Fleurie.

Next Day: **Robert Mondavi, Oakville.** Spring for the reserve room tasting so you can sip the top-of-the-line wines, especially the Cabernet Sauvignon. Head across Highway 29 to the Oakville Grocery to pick up a picnic lunch.

ner at its restaurant. Save at El Bonita Motel with dinner at Gott's.

Next Day: Poke around St. Helena's shops, then drive to Yountville for lunch.

di Rosa, Napa.
Call ahead to book a one- or two-hour tour of the acres of gardens and galleries, which are chock-full of thousands of works of art.

Domaine Carneros, Napa.
Toast your trip with a glass of outstanding bubbly.

Far Niente, Oakville.
You have to make a reservation and the fee for the tasting and tour is steep, but the payoff is an especially intimate winery experience. You'll taste excellent Cabernet and Chardonnay, then end your trip on a sweet note with a dessert wine.

Sonoma Backroads

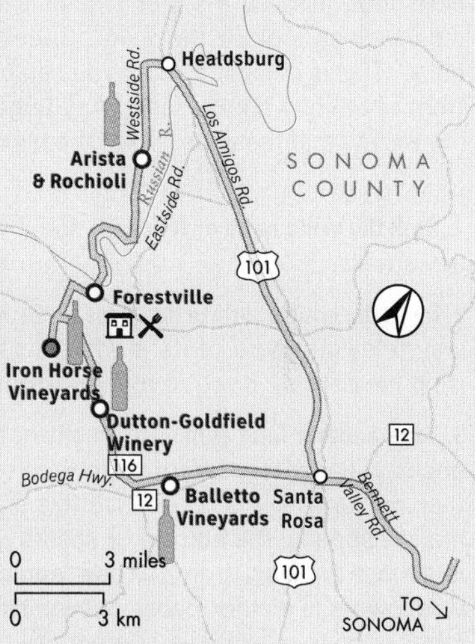

Start: **Iron Horse Vineyards, Russian River Valley.**
Soak up a view of vine-covered hills and Mount St. Helena while sipping a sparkling wine or Pinot Noir at this beautifully rustic spot.

Dutton-Goldfield Winery, Russian River Valley.
A terrific source for Pinot Noir and Chardonnay, the stars of this valley.

Dinner and Overnight: **Forestville.** Go all out with a stay at the Farmhouse Inn, whose award-winning restaurant is one of the best in all of Sonoma.

Next Day: **Westside Road, Russian River Valley.**
This scenic route, which follows the river, is crowded with worthwhile wineries like Arista and Rochioli—but it's not crowded with visitors. Pinot fans will find a lot to love. Picnic at either winery and enjoy the view.

Balletto Vineyards, Santa Rosa. End on an especially relaxed note with a walk through the vineyards and a patio tasting.

WINE TASTING 101

TAKE A GOOD LOOK.

Hold your glass by the stem, raise it to the light, and take a close look at the wine. Check for clarity and color. (This is easiest to do if you can hold the glass in front of a white background.) Any tinge of brown usually means that the wine is over the hill or has gone bad.

BREATHE DEEP.

1. Sniff the wine once or twice to see if you can identify any smells.

2. Swirl the wine gently in the glass. Aerating the wine this way releases more of its aromas. (It's called "volatilizing the esters," if you're trying to impress someone.)

3. Take another long sniff. You might notice that experienced wine tasters spend more time sniffing the wine than drinking it. This is because this step is where the magic happens. The number of scents you might detect is almost endless, from berries, apricots, honey, and wildflowers to leather, cedar, or even tar. Does the wine smell good to you? Do you detect any "off" flavors, like wet dog or sulfur?

AT LAST! TAKE A SIP.

1. Swirl the wine around your mouth so that it makes contact with all your taste buds and releases more of its aromas. Think about the way the wine feels in your mouth. Is it watery or rich? Is it crisp or silky? Does it have a bold flavor, or is it subtle? The weight and intensity of a wine are called its body.

2. Hold the wine in your mouth for a few seconds and see if you can identify any developing flavors. More complex wines will reveal many different flavors as you drink them.

SPIT OR SWALLOW.

The pros typically spit, since they want to preserve their palate (and sobriety!) for the wines to come, but you'll find that swallowers far outnumber the spitters in the winery tasting rooms. Whether you spit or swallow, notice the flavor that remains after the wine is gone (the finish).

Swirl

Sniff

Sip

DODGE THE CROWDS

To avoid bumping elbows in the tasting rooms, look for wineries off the main drags of Highway 29 in Napa and Highway 12 in Sonoma. The back roads of the Russian River, Dry Creek, and Alexander valleys, all in Sonoma, are excellent places to explore. In Napa, try the northern end. Also look for wineries that are open by appointment only; they tend to schedule visitors carefully to avoid a big crush at any one time.

HOW WINE IS MADE

1. CRUSHING
Harvested grapes go into a stemmer-crusher, which separates stems from fruit and crushes the grapes to release "free-run" juice.

2. PRESSING
Remaining juice is gently extracted from grapes. Usually done by pressing grapes against the walls of a tank with an inflatable bladder.

3. FERMENTING
Extracted juice (and also grape skins and pulp, when making red wine) goes into stainless-steel tanks or oak barrels to ferment. During fermentation, sugars convert to alcohol.

4. AGING
Wine is stored in stainless-steel or oak casks or barrels, or sometimes in concrete vessels, to develop flavors.

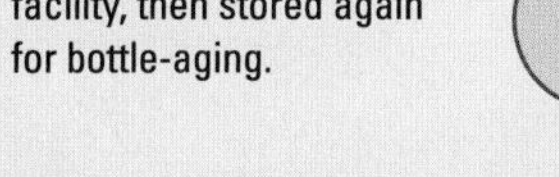

5. RACKING
Wine is transferred to clean barrels; sediment is removed. Wine may be filtered and fined (clarified) to improve its clarity, color, and sometimes flavor.

6. BOTTLING
Wine is bottled either at the winery or at a special facility, then stored again for bottle-aging.

WHAT'S AN APPELLATION?

American Viticultural Area (AVA) or, more commonly, an appellation. What can be confusing is that some appellations encompass smaller subappellations. The Rutherford, Oakville, and Mt. Veeder AVAs, for instance, are among the Napa Valley AVA's 15 subappellations. Wineries often buy grapes from outside their AVA, so their labels might reference different appellations. A winery in the warmer Napa Valley, for instance, might source Pinot Noir grapes from the cooler Russian River Valley, where they grow better. The appellation listed on a label always refers to where a wine's grapes were grown, not to where the wine was made.

By law, if a label bears the name of an appellation, 85% of the grapes must come from it.

Napa Valley
KEY
1 Sights
Mount St Helena
Robert Louis Stevenson State Park
Knights Valley
The Palisades
Aetna Springs
Pope
Pope Valley
Howell Mtn Rd.
Angwin
Angwin Airport
Chalk Hill Rd.
Franz Valley Rd.
Tubbs Ln.
Calistoga
Dunaweal Ln.
Larkmead Ln.
Petrified Forest Rd.
Mark West Springs
Diamond Mountain
Bothe-Napa State Park
Deer Park
Sanitarium Rd.
Bale Grist Mill State Historic Park
St. Helena
Pope
Silverado Trail
Napa
Fulton
Fulton Rd.
Piner Rd.
Guerneville Rd.
Santa Rosa
Santa Rosa Creek
Sebastopol Hwy.
Sonoma County
Hood Mountain Regional Park
Sugarloaf Ridge State Park
Sonoma Hwy
Adobe Canyon Rd.
Bald Mountain
Rutherford
Mt St. John
Oakville Grade Rd.
Annadel State Park
Kenwood
Petaluma Hill Rd.
Trinity Rd.
Mt Veeder
Bennett Valley Rd.
Sonoma Valley
Glen Ellen
Valley of the Moon
Stony Point Rd.
Rohnert Park
Sonoma Mountain
Sonoma Mountains
Jack London State Park
Agua Caliente
Boyes Hot Springs
Arnold Dr.
Roblar Rd.
Cotati
Old Redwood Hwy.
Sonoma
Napa Rd.
Adobe Rd.
Bodega Ave.
Petaluma
Lakeville Hwy.
Bonness Rd.
Carneros Hwy.
Laguna Lake
Novato
Black Point
29
128
101
12
116
121
21
22
23
26
27
28
29
30
31
32
33
34
35
36
37
38
39
40
41

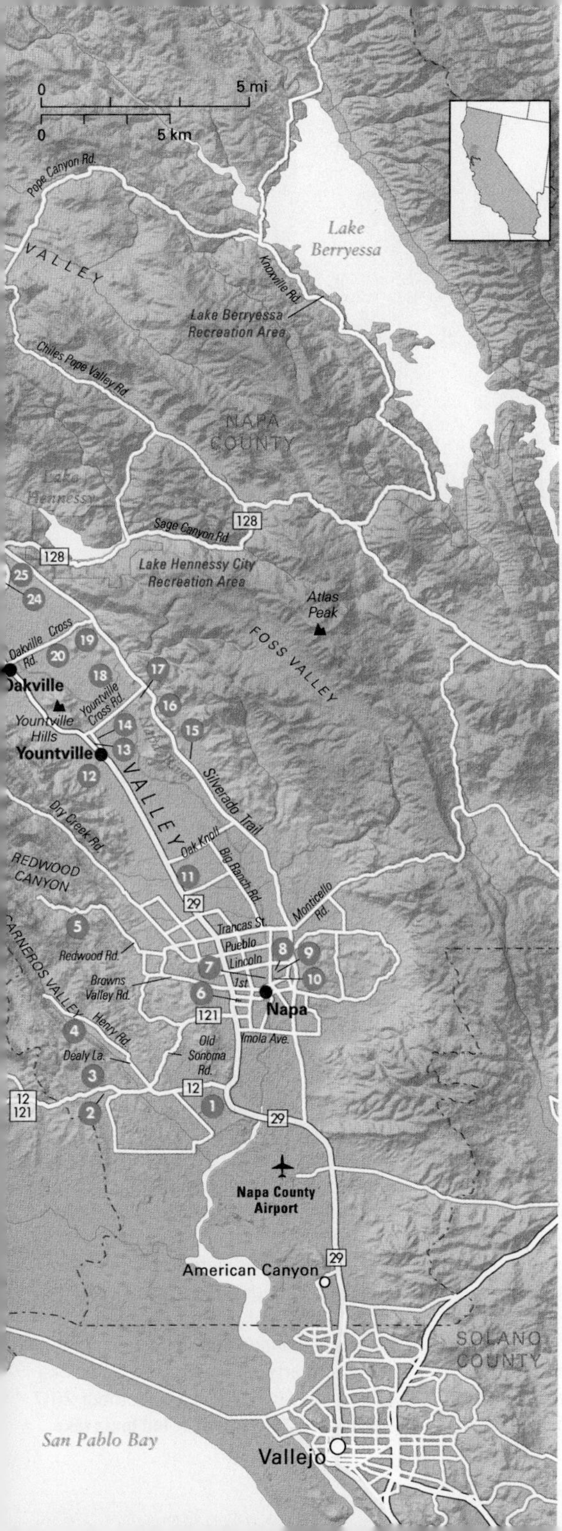

Sights

- Artesa Vineyards & Winery 4
- Ashes & Diamonds 11
- B Cellars 19
- Beringer Vineyards 33
- Ca' Toga Galleria d'Arte 39
- Castello di Amorosa 37
- Charles Krug Winery 32
- Chateau Montelena 40
- CIA at Copia 9
- Cliff Lede Vineyards 17
- Culinary Institute of America at Greystone 34
- di Rosa Center for Contemporary Art 3
- Domaine Carneros 2
- Domaine Chandon 12
- Etude Wines 1
- Far Niente 21
- Frank Family Vineyards 36
- Frog's Leap 24
- Goosecross Cellars 18
- Hall St. Helena 29
- Hess Collection 5
- Honig Vineyard & Winery 26
- Inglenook 23
- Joseph Phelps Vineyards 31
- Mad Fritz Brewing Co. 30
- Mumm Napa 25
- Napa Valley Distillery. 6
- Napa Valley Wine Train 8
- Oxbow Public Market 10
- Prager Winery & Port Works .. 28
- Pride Mountain Vineyards 35
- The Prisoner Wine Company .. 27
- RH Yountville 13
- Robert Mondavi Winery 22
- Robert Sinskey Vineyards 16
- Silver Oak 20
- St Clair Brown Winery & Brewery 7
- Stag's Leap Winery 15
- Stewart Cellars 14
- Tamber Bey Vineyards 41
- Venge Vineyards 38

Wine and contemporary art find a home at di Rosa.

of all stripes. ✉ *4130 Howard La., Napa ✥ Off Hwy. 29* ☎ *707/666–4777* 🌐 *ashes-diamonds.com* 🎫 *Tastings from $40.*

★ CIA at Copia

COLLEGE | Full-fledged foodies and the merely curious achieve gastronomical bliss at the Culinary Institute of America's Oxbow District campus, its facade brightened since 2018 by a wraparound mural inspired by the colorful garden that fronts the facility. A restaurant, a shop, a museum, and the Vintners Hall of Fame—not to mention classes and demonstrations involving food-and-wine pairings, sparkling wines, ancient grains, cheeses, pasta, and sauces—make this a spend-a-half-day-here sort of place. One well-attended class for adults explores the Napa Valley's history through eight glasses of wine, and children join their parents for Family Funday workshops about making mac and cheese and nutritious lunches. Head upstairs to the Chuck Williams Culinary Arts Museum. Named for the founder of the Williams-Sonoma kitchenwares chain, it holds a fascinating collection of cooking, baking, and other food-related tools, tableware, gizmos, and gadgets, some dating back more than a century. ✉ *500 1st St., Napa ✥ Near McKinstry St.* ☎ *707/967–2500* 🌐 *www.ciaatcopia.com* 🎫 *Facility free, demonstrations and classes from $15.*

di Rosa Center for Contemporary Art

MUSEUM | The late Rene di Rosa assembled an extensive collection of artworks created by Northern California artists from the 1960s to the present, displaying them on this 217-acre Carneros District property surrounded by Chardonnay and Pinot Noir vineyards. Two galleries at opposite ends of a 35-acre lake show works from the collection and host temporary exhibitions, and the Sculpture Meadow behind the second gallery holds a few dozen large outdoor pieces. As 2019 dawned, di Rosa's residence, previously a highlight of a visit here, remained closed as conservation efforts continued to restore artworks damaged by smoke during the Wine Country's October 2017 wildfires. ■ **TIP→ Docent-led tours take**

place daily at 11 and 1. ✉ *5200 Sonoma Hwy./Hwy. 121, Napa* ✥ *Near Duhig Rd.* ☎ *707/226–5991* 🌐 *www.dirosaart.org* 🎫 *$18* ⏲ *Closed Mon. and Tues.*

★ Domaine Carneros

WINERY/DISTILLERY | A visit to this majestic château is an opulent way to enjoy the Carneros District—especially in fine weather, when the vineyard views are spectacular. The château was modeled after an 18th-century French mansion owned by the Taittinger family. Carved into the hillside beneath the winery, the cellars produce sparkling wines reminiscent of those made by Taittinger, using only Los Carneros AVA grapes. The winery sells flights and glasses of its sparklers, Chardonnay, Pinot Noir, and other wines. Enjoy them all with cheese and charcuterie plates, caviar, or smoked salmon. Seating is in the Louis XV–inspired salon or on the terrace overlooking the vines. The tour covers traditional methods of making sparkling wines. Tours and tastings are by appointment only. ✉ *1240 Duhig Rd., Napa* ✥ *At Hwy. 121* ☎ *707/257–0101, 800/716–2788* 🌐 *www.domainecarneros.com* 🎫 *Tastings from $12, tour $50.*

Etude Wines

WINERY/DISTILLERY | You're apt to see or hear hawks, egrets, Canada geese, and other wildlife on the grounds of Etude, known for sophisticated Pinot Noirs. Although the winery and its light-filled tasting room are in Napa County, the grapes for its flagship Carneros Estate Pinot Noir come from the Sonoma portion of Los Carneros, as do those for the rarer Heirloom Carneros Pinot Noir. Hosts pour Chardonnay, Pinot Blanc, Pinot Noir, and other wines daily at the tasting bar and in good weather on the patio. Carneros, Sonoma Coast, Willamette Valley, Santa Barbara County, and New Zealand Pinots, all crafted by winemaker Jon Priest, are compared at Study of Pinot Noir sessions (reservations required). **■ TIP→ Etude also excels at single-vineyard Napa Valley Cabernets; these can be sampled by appointment at seated tastings overlooking the production facility.** ✉ *1250 Cuttings Wharf Rd., Napa* ✥ *1 mile south of Hwy. 121* ☎ *707/257–5782* 🌐 *www.etudewines.com* 🎫 *Tastings from $25.*

Hess Collection

WINERY/DISTILLERY | About 9 miles northwest of Napa, up a winding road ascending Mt. Veeder, this winery is a delightful discovery. The limestone structure, rustic from the outside but modern and airy within, contains Swiss owner Donald Hess's world-class art collection, including large-scale works by contemporary artists such as Andy Goldsworthy, Anselm Kiefer, and Robert Rauschenberg. Cabernet Sauvignon is a major strength, with Chardonnays, Albariño, and Grüner Veltliner among the whites. Tastings outdoors in the garden and the courtyard take place from spring to fall, with cheese or nuts and other nibbles accompanying the wines. **■ TIP→ Among the wine-and-food pairings offered year-round, most of which involve a guided tour of the art collection, is a fun one showcasing locally made artisanal chocolates.** ✉ *4411 Redwood Rd., Napa* ✥ *West off Hwy. 29 at Trancas St./Redwood Rd. exit* ☎ *707/255–1144* 🌐 *www.hesscollection.com* 🎫 *Tastings from $25, art gallery free.*

Napa Valley Distillery

WINERY/DISTILLERY | Entertaining educators keep the proceedings light and lively at this distillery, which bills itself as Napa's first since Prohibition. NVD makes gin, rum, whiskey, and the flagship grape-based vodka, along with brandies and barrel-aged bottled cocktails that include Manhattans (the top seller), mai tais, and negronis. Visits, always by appointment, begin with a tasting upstairs in the "art deco speakeasy with a tiki twist" Grand Salon, where lesson number one is how to properly sip spirits (spoiler: don't swirl your glass like you would with wine).

Back downstairs in the production facility, you'll learn the basics of alcohol and distilling. **TIP→ If you just want to sample the wares, the distillery operates a tasting bar in the main Oxbow Public Market building.** ✉ *2485 Stockton St., Napa ⊕ Off California Blvd.* ☎ *707/265-6272* 🌐 *www.napadistillery.com* 🎟 *Tastings $30* ⏲ *Closed Wed.*

Napa Valley Wine Train

TOUR—SIGHT | Guests on this Napa Valley attraction, a fixture since 1989, ride the same rails along which, from the 1860s to the 1930s, trains transported passengers as far north as Calistoga's spas and hauled wine and other agricultural freight south toward San Francisco. The rolling stock includes restored Pullman railroad cars and a two-story Vista Dome car with a curved glass roof that travel a leisurely, scenic route between Napa and St. Helena. Patrons on the Quattro Vino tour enjoy a four-course lunch and tastings at four wineries, with stops at one or more wineries incorporated into other tours. Some rides involve no winery stops, and themed trips are scheduled throughout the year. **TIP→ It's best to make this trip during the day, when you can enjoy the vineyard views.** ✉ *1275 McKinstry St., Napa ⊕ Off 1st St.* ☎ *707/253-2111, 800/427-4124* 🌐 *www.winetrain.com* 🎟 *From $149.*

★ **Oxbow Public Market**

MARKET | The market's two dozen stands provide an introduction to Northern California's diverse artisanal food products. Swoon over decadent charcuterie at the Fatted Calf (great sandwiches, too), slurp oysters at Hog Island, or chow down on vegetarian, duck, or salmon tacos at C Casa. You can sample wine (and cheese) at the Oxbow Cheese & Wine Merchant, ales at Fieldwork Brewery's taproom, and barrel-aged cocktails at the Napa Valley Distillery. Napa Bookmine is among the few nonfood vendors here. **TIP→ If you don't mind eating at the counter, you can select a steak at the Five Dot Ranch meat stand and pay $10 above market price ($14 with two sides) to have it grilled on the spot, a real deal for a quality slab.** ✉ *610 and 644 1st St., Napa ⊕ At McKinstry St.* 🌐 *www.oxbowpublicmarket.com.*

Stags' Leap Winery

WINERY/DISTILLERY | A must for history buffs, this winery was established in 1893 in a bowl-shaped micro valley at the base of the Stags Leap Palisades. Three years earlier its original owners erected the Manor House, which reopened in 2016 after restoration of its castlelike stone facade and redwood-paneled interior. The home, whose open-air porch seems out of a flapper-era movie set, hosts elegant, appointment-only seated tastings of equally refined wines by the Bordeaux-born Christophe Paubert. Estate Cabernet Sauvignons, Merlot, and Petite Sirah, one bottling of the last varietal from vines planted in 1929, are the calling cards. Paubert also makes a blend of these three red grapes, along with Viognier, Chardonnay, and rosé. Some tastings take place on the porch, others inside; all require an appointment and include a tour of the property and tales of its storied past. ✉ *6150 Silverado Trail, Napa ⊕ ¾ mile south of Yountville Cross Rd.* ☎ *707/257-5790* 🌐 *stagsleap.com* 🎟 *Tastings from $65.*

★ **St. Clair Brown Winery & Brewery**

WINERY/DISTILLERY | Tastings at this women-run "urban winery"—and, since 2017, nanobrewery—a few blocks north of downtown take place in an intimate, light-filled greenhouse or a colorful culinary garden. Winemaker Elaine St. Clair, well regarded for stints at Domaine Carneros and Black Stallion, produces elegant wines—crisp yet complex whites and smooth, French-style reds whose stars include Cabernet Sauvignon and Syrah. While pursuing her wine-making degree, St. Clair also studied brewing; a few of her light-, medium-, and full-bodied brews are always on tap. You can taste the wines or beers by the glass or flight or enjoy them paired with appetizers that might include pork rillette with pickled tomatoes from the garden or addictive almonds roasted with rosemary, lemon zest, and lemon olive oil. Tuesday and Wednesday visits are by appointment only. ✉ *816 Vallejo St., Napa* ✣ *Off Soscol Ave.* ☎ *707/255–5591* 🌐 *www.stclairbrown.com* *Tastings from $12 flights, from $4 by the glass.*

Restaurants

★ Compline

$$$ | MODERN AMERICAN | The full name of the three-in-one enterprise masterminded by master sommelier Matt Stamp and restaurant wine vet Ryan Stetins is Compline Wine Bar, Restaurant, and Merchant, and indeed you can just sip wine or purchase it here. The place evolved into a hot spot, though, for its youthful vibe and chef Yancy Windsperger's eclectic small and large plates that might include poached egg and polenta or gnocchi vegetable Bolognese. **Known for:** youthful vibe; by-the-glass wines; knowledgeable staff. $ *Average main: $25* ✉ *1300 1st St., Suite 312, Napa* ☎ *707/492–8150* 🌐 *complinewine.com* ⊙ *Closed Tues.*

Grace's Table

$$$ | ECLECTIC | A dependable, varied, three-squares-a-day menu makes this modest corner restaurant occupying a brick-and-glass storefront many Napans' go-to choice for a simple meal. Iron-skillet corn bread with lavender honey and butter shows up at all hours, with chilaquiles scrambled eggs a breakfast favorite, savory fish tacos a lunchtime staple, and cassoulet and roasted young chicken popular for dinner. **Known for:** congenial staffers; good beers on tap; eclectic menu focusing on France, Italy, and the Americas. $ *Average main: $24* ✉ *1400 2nd St., Napa* ✣ *At Franklin St.* ☎ *707/226–6200* 🌐 *www.gracestable.net.*

Gran Eléctrica

$$ | MEXICAN | A neon sign toward the back of Gran Eléctrica translates to "badass bar," but the same goes for the restaurant and its piquant lineup of *botanas* (snacks), tacos, tostadas, quesadillas, entrées, and sides. Ceviche tostadas, fish and carnitas tacos, the chile relleno, and duck-confit mole are among the year-round favorites, with dishes like grilled street-style corn with chipotle mayo appearing in-season. **Known for:** zippy decor; outdoor patio; tequila and mescal flights, specialty cocktails. $ *Average main: $19* ✉ *1313 Main St., Napa* ✣ *Near Clinton St.* ☎ *707/258–1313* 🌐 *www.granelectrica.com/about-napa* ⊙ *No lunch Mon.–Sat.*

★ La Toque

$$$$ | MODERN AMERICAN | Chef Ken Frank's La Toque is the complete package: his imaginative French cuisine, served in a formal brown-hued dining space, is complemented by a wine lineup that earned the restaurant a coveted *Wine Spectator* Grand Award. Signature dishes that might appear on the prix-fixe four- or five-course tasting menu include rösti potato with Kaluga caviar, Angus beef tenderloin with grilled king trumpet mushrooms, and New York strip loin with Fiscalini cheddar pearl tapioca and Rutherford red-wine sauce. **Known for:** chef's table menu for entire party; astute wine pairings; vegetarian tasting menu. $ *Average main: $110* ✉ *Westin Verasa Napa, 1314 McKinstry St., Napa* ✣ *Off Soscol Ave.* ☎ *707/257–5157* 🌐 *www.latoque.com* ⊙ *No lunch.*

★ Miminashi

$$$ | JAPANESE | Japanese *izakaya*—gastropubs that serve appetizers downed with sake or cocktails—inspired chef Curtis Di Fede's buzz-worthy downtown Napa restaurant, where two peaks in the slatted poplar ceiling echo Shinto and Buddhist temple designs. Ramen, fried rice, and yakitori anchor the menu, whose highlights include wok-fried edamame and the ooh-inspiring *okonomiyaki* pancake with bacon, cabbage, and dried fermented tuna flakes; wines and sakes selected by Jessica Pinzon, formerly of Thomas Keller's Yountville restaurants Bouchon and Ad Hoc, further elevate Di Fede's dishes. **Known for:** distinctive design; wine and sake selection; soft-serve ice cream for dessert and from to-go window. *Average main: $29 ✉ 821 Coombs St., Napa ✥ Near 3rd St. ☎ 707/254–9464 🌐 miminashi.com ⏲ No lunch.*

Morimoto Napa

$$$$ | **JAPANESE** | *Iron Chef* star Masaharu Morimoto is the big name behind this downtown Napa restaurant where everything is delightfully overdone, right down to the desserts. Organic materials such as twisting grapevines above the bar and rough-hewn wooden tables seem simultaneously earthy and modern, creating a fitting setting for the gorgeously plated Japanese fare, from sashimi served with grated fresh wasabi to elaborate concoctions that include sea-urchin carbonara made with Inaniwa udon noodles. **Known for:** elaborate concoctions; gorgeous plating; chef's choice omakase menu (from $130). *Average main: $37 ✉ 610 Main St., Napa ✥ At 5th St. ☎ 707/252–1600 🌐 www.morimotonapa.com.*

Oenotri

$$$ | **ITALIAN** | Often spotted at local farmers' markets and his restaurant's gardens, Oenotri's ebullient chef-owner and Napa native Tyler Rodde is ever on the lookout for fresh produce to incorporate into his rustic southern-Italian cuisine. His restaurant, a brick-walled contemporary space with tall windows and wooden tables, is a lively spot to sample house-made salumi and pastas, thin-crust pizzas, and entrées that might include roasted squab, Atlantic salmon, or pork sausage. **Known for:** fresh ingredients; Margherita pizza with San Marzano tomatoes; lively atmosphere. *Average main: $27 ✉ 1425 1st St., Napa ✥ At Franklin St. ☎ 707/252–1022 🌐 www.oenotri.com.*

★ Torc

$$$$ | **MODERN AMERICAN** | *Torc* means "wild boar" in an early Celtic dialect, and owner-chef Sean O'Toole, who formerly helmed kitchens at top Manhattan, San Francisco, and Yountville establishments, occasionally incorporates the restaurant's namesake beast into his eclectic offerings. A recent menu featured sea urchin with Persian melon carpaccio, Maine-lobster risotto, and veal sweetbreads with sweet and sour tomatoes, all prepared by O'Toole and his team with style and precision. **Known for:** gracious service; specialty cocktails; Bengali sweet-potato pakora and deviled-egg appetizers. *Average main: $36 ✉ 1140 Main St., Napa ✥ At Pearl St. ☎ 707/252–3292 🌐 www.torcnapa.com ⏲ Closed Tues. No lunch weekdays.*

★ ZuZu

$$$ | **SPANISH** | At festive ZuZu the focus is on cold and hot tapas, paella, and other Spanish favorites often downed with cava or sangria. Regulars revere the paella, made with Spanish *bomba* rice, and small plates that might include grilled octopus, garlic shrimp, jamón Ibérico, and white anchovies with sliced egg and rémoulade on grilled bread. **Known for:** singular flavors and spicing; Latin jazz on the stereo; sister restaurant La Taberna three doors south for beer, wine, and bar bites. *Average main: $30 ✉ 829 Main St., Napa ✥ Near 3rd St. ☎ 707/224–8555 🌐 www.zuzunapa.com ⏲ No lunch weekends.*

Hotels

★ Andaz Napa

$$$ | **HOTEL** | Part of the Hyatt family, this boutique hotel with an urban-hip vibe has spacious, luxurious rooms with flat-screen TVs, laptop-size safes, and white-marble bathrooms stocked with

high-quality bath products. **Pros:** proximity to downtown restaurants, theaters, and tasting rooms; access to modern fitness center; complimentary beverage upon arrival; complimentary snacks and nonalcoholic beverages in rooms. **Cons:** parking can be a challenge on weekends; unremarkable views from some rooms; expensive on weekends in high season. *Rooms from: $306* ✉ *1450 1st St., Napa* ☎ *707/687–1234* 🌐 *andaznapa.com* *141 rooms* *No meals.*

★ Archer Hotel Napa

$$$ | **HOTEL** | A hybrid of New York City and Las Vegas glamour infused downtown Napa with the 2018 completion of this five-story hotel ideal for travelers seeking design pizzazz, a see-and-be-seen atmosphere, and a slate of first-class amenities. **Pros:** restaurants and room service by chef Charlie Palmer; Sky & Vine rooftop bar; views from upper-floor rooms (especially south and west). **Cons:** not particularly rustic; expensive in high season; occasional service, hospitality lapses. *Rooms from: $374* ✉ *1230 1st St., Napa* ☎ *707/690–9800, 855/437–9100* 🌐 *archerhotel.com/napa* *183 rooms* *No meals.*

★ Carneros Resort & Spa

$$$$ | **RESORT** | Freestanding board-and-batten cottages with rocking chairs on each porch are simultaneously rustic and chic at this luxurious property made even more so by a $6.5 million makeover. **Pros:** cottages have lots of privacy; beautiful views from hilltop pool and hot tub; heaters on private patios. **Cons:** long drive to upvalley destinations; least expensive accommodations pick up highway noise; pricey pretty much year-round. *Rooms from: $600* ✉ *4048 Sonoma Hwy./Hwy. 121, Napa* ☎ *707/299–4900, 888/400–9000* 🌐 *www.carnerosresort.com* *100 rooms* *No meals.*

★ The Inn on First

$$ | **B&B/INN** | Guests gush over the hospitality at this inn whose painstakingly restored 1905 mansion facing 1st Street contains five rooms, with five additional accommodations, all suites, in a building behind a secluded patio and garden. **Pros:** full gourmet breakfast by hosts-with-the-most owners; gas fireplaces and whirlpool tubs in all rooms; away from downtown but not too far. **Cons:** no TVs; owners "respectfully request no children"; lacks pool, fitness center, and other amenities of larger properties. *Rooms from: $220* ✉ *1938 1st St., Napa* ☎ *707/253–1331* 🌐 *www.theinnonfirst.com* *10 rooms* *Breakfast.*

★ Inn on Randolph

$$ | **B&B/INN** | A few calm blocks from the downtown action on a nearly 1-acre lot with landscaped gardens, the Inn on Randolph—with a Gothic Revival–style main house and its five guest rooms plus five historic cottages out back—is a sophisticated haven celebrated for its gourmet gluten-free breakfasts and snacks. **Pros:** quiet residential neighborhood; spa tubs in cottages and two main-house rooms; romantic setting. **Cons:** a bit of a walk from downtown; expensive in-season; weekend minimum-stay requirement. *Rooms from: $299* ✉ *411 Randolph St., Napa* ☎ *707/257–2886* 🌐 *www.innonrandolph.com* *10 rooms* *Breakfast.*

Nightlife

Blue Note Napa

MUSIC CLUBS | The famed New York jazz room's West Coast club hosts national headliners such as Brian McKnight, Dee Dee Bridgewater, and Coco Montoya, along with local talents such as Lavay Smith & Her Red Hot Skillet Lickers. There's a full bar, and you can order a meal or small bites from the kitchen. ✉ *Napa Valley Opera House, 1030 Main St., Napa* ✣ *At 1st St.* ☎ *707/880–2300* 🌐 *www.bluenotenapa.com.*

Cadet Wine + Beer Bar

WINE BARS—NIGHTLIFE | Cadet plays things urban-style cool with a long bar, high-top tables, an all-vinyl soundtrack, and a low-lit, generally loungelike feel. When they opened their bar, the two owners described their outlook as "unabashedly pro-California," but their wine-and-beer lineup circles the globe. The crowd here is youngish, the vibe festive. ✉ *930 Franklin St., Napa* ⊕ *At end of pedestrian alley between 1st and 2nd Sts.* ☎ *707/224–4400* 🌐 *www.cadetbeerandwinebar.com.*

Yountville

9 miles north of the town of Napa.

These days Yountville is something like Disneyland for food lovers. You could stay here for a week and not exhaust all the options—several of them owned by The French Laundry's Thomas Keller—and the tiny town is full of small inns and high-end hotels that cater to those who prefer to walk (not drive) after an extravagant meal. It's also well located for excursions to many big-name Napa wineries, especially those in the Stags Leap District, from which big, bold Cabernet Sauvignons helped make the Napa Valley's wine-making reputation.

GETTING HERE AND AROUND

Downtown Yountville sits just off Highway 29. Approaching from the south take the Yountville exit—from the north take Madison—and proceed to Washington Street, home to the major shops and restaurants. Yountville Cross Road connects downtown to the Silverado Trail, along which many noted wineries do business. The free Yountville Trolley serves the town daily 10 am–7 pm (on-call service until 11 except on Sunday).

Sights

★ Cliff Lede Vineyards

WINERY/DISTILLERY | Inspired by his passion for classic rock, owner and construction magnate Cliff Lede named the blocks in his Stags Leap District vineyard after hits by the Grateful Dead and other bands. The vibe at his efficient, high-tech winery is anything but laid-back, however. Cutting-edge agricultural and enological science informs the vineyard management and wine making here. Architect Howard Backen designed the winery and its tasting room, where Lede's Sauvignon Blanc, Cabernet Sauvignons, and other wines, along with some from sister winery FEL, which produces much-lauded Anderson Valley Pinot Noirs, are poured. **TIP→ Walk-ins are welcome at the tasting bar, but appointments are required for the veranda outside and a nearby gallery that displays rock-related art.** ✉ *1473 Yountville Cross Rd., Yountville* ⊕ *Off Silverado Trail* ☎ *707/944–8642* 🌐 *cliffledevineyards.com* 🎫 *Tastings from $35.*

Domaine Chandon

WINERY/DISTILLERY | On a knoll shaded by ancient oak trees, this French-owned maker of sparkling wines claims one of Yountville's prime pieces of real estate. Chandon is best known for bubbles, but the still wines—among them Cabernet Sauvignon, Chardonnay, and Pinot Noir—are also worth a try. You can sip by the flight or by the glass at the bar, or begin there and sit at tables in the lounge and return to the bar as needed; in good weather, tables are set up outside. Bottle service is also available. ✉ *1 California Dr., Yountville* ⊕ *Off Hwy. 29* ☎ *707/204–7530, 888/242–6366* 🌐 *www.chandon.com* 🎫 *Tastings from $10.*

Goosecross Cellars

WINERY/DISTILLERY | When Christi Coors Ficeli purchased this boutique winery in 2013 and commissioned a new barnlike tasting space, she and her architect had one major goal: bring the outside in. Large retractable west-facing windows open up behind the tasting bar to idyllic views of Cabernet vines—in fine weather, guests on the outdoor deck can practically touch them. Goosecross makes Chardonnay and Pinot Noir from

Carneros grapes, but the soul of this cordial operation is its 12-acre estate vineyard, its 10 planted acres mostly Cabernet Sauvignon and Merlot with some Cabernet Franc and Petit Verdot. The Cab and Merlot are the stars, along with the Aeros Bordeaux-style blend of the best estate grapes. Aeros isn't usually poured, but a Howell Mountain Petite Sirah with expressive tannins (there's also a Howell Mountain Cabernet) often is. Visits to Goosecross are by appointment only. ✉ *1119 State La., Yountville* ✣ *Off Yountville Cross Rd.* ☎ *707/944–1986* 🌐 *www.goosecross.com* 🎫 *Tastings from $40.*

RH Yountville

MUSEUM | Gargantuan crystal chandeliers, century-old olive trees, and strategically placed water features provide visual and aural continuity at Restoration Hardware's quadruple-threat food, wine, art, and design compound. An all-day café fronts two steel, glass, and concrete home-furnishings galleries, with a bluestone walkway connecting them to a reboot of the Ma(i)sonry wine salon. Inside a two-story 1904 manor house constructed from Napa River stone and rechristened The Wine Vault at the Historic Ma(i)sonry Building, it remains an excellent tasting choice. Classic and Connoisseur flights focus on small-lot Napa and Sonoma bottlings; hosts at Collector tastings pour Napa Valley wines by elite winemakers like Heidi Barrett and Philippe Melka. In good weather, some tastings take place in outdoor living rooms where patrons can also enjoy coffee, tea, or wine by the glass or bottle. Walk-ins are welcome, but reservations are recommended (and wise on weekends in-season). ✉ *6725 Washington St., Yountville* ✣ *At Pedroni St.* ☎ *707/339–4654* 🌐 *www.restorationhardware.com* 🎫 *Tastings from $50.*

★ **Robert Sinskey Vineyards**

WINERY/DISTILLERY | Although the winery produces a well-regarded Stags Leap Cabernet Sauvignon, two Bordeaux-style red blends (Marcien and POV), and white wines, Sinskey is best known for its intense, brambly Carneros District Pinot Noirs. All the grapes are grown in organic, certified biodynamic vineyards. The influence of Robert's wife, Maria Helm Sinskey—a chef and cookbook author and the winery's culinary director—is evident during the tastings, which are accompanied by a few bites of food with each wine. ■ **TIP→ The Perfect Circle Tour, offered daily, takes in the winery's gardens and ends with a seated pairing of food and wine. Even more elaborate, also by appointment, is the five-course Chef's Table pairing of seasonal dishes with current and older wines.** ✉ *6320 Silverado Trail, Napa* ✣ *At Yountville Cross Rd.* ☎ *707/944–9090* 🌐 *www.robertsinskey.com* 🎫 *Tastings from $40, tours (with tastings) from $95.*

★ **Stewart Cellars**

WINERY/DISTILLERY | Three stone structures meant to mimic Scottish ruins coaxed into modernity form this complex that includes public and private tasting spaces, a bright outdoor patio, and a hip, independently run café. The attention to detail in the ensemble's design mirrors that of the wines, whose grapes come from coveted vineyards, most notably all six of the Beckstoffer Heritage Vineyards, among the Napa Valley's most historic sites. Although Cabernet is the focus, winemaker Blair Guthrie, with input from consulting winemaker Paul Hobbs, also makes Sauvignon Blanc, Chardonnay, Pinot Noir, and Merlot. ■ **TIP→ On sunny days this is a good stop around lunchtime, when you can order a meal from the café and a glass of wine from the tasting room—for permit reasons this must be done separately—and enjoy them on the patio.** ✉ *6752 Washington St., Yountville* ✣ *Near Pedroni St.* ☎ *707/963–9160* 🌐 *www.stewartcellars.com* 🎫 *Tastings from $30.*

Restaurants

★ Ad Hoc

$$$$ | **MODERN AMERICAN** | At this low-key dining room with zinc-top tables and wine served in tumblers, superstar chef Thomas Keller offers a single, fixed-price, nightly menu that might include smoked beef short ribs with creamy herb rice and charred broccolini or sesame chicken with radish kimchi and fried rice. Ad Hoc also serves a small but decadent Sunday brunch, and Keller's Addendum annex, in a separate small building behind the restaurant, sells boxed lunches to go (beyond moist buttermilk fried chicken) from Thursday to Saturday except in winter. **Known for:** casual cuisine at great prices for a Thomas Keller restaurant; don't-miss buttermilk-fried-chicken night; streetside outdoor seating. *Average main: $55* ✉ *6476 Washington St., Yountville* ✣ *At Oak Circle* ☎ *707/944–2487* 🌐 *www.adhocrestaurant.com* ⏲ *No lunch Mon.–Sat.; no dinner Tues. and Wed.* ☞ *Call day ahead to find out next day's menu.*

★ Bistro Jeanty

$$$ | **FRENCH** | Escargots, cassoulet, *daube de boeuf* (beef stewed in red wine), and other French classics are prepared with the utmost precision at this country bistro whose lamb tongue and other obscure delicacies delight daring diners. Regulars often start with the rich tomato soup in a flaky puff pastry before proceeding to sole meunière or coq au vin, completing the French sojourn with a lemon meringue tart or other authentic desserts. **Known for:** traditional preparations; oh-so-French atmosphere; European wines. *Average main: $29* ✉ *6510 Washington St., Yountville* ✣ *At Mulberry St.* ☎ *707/944–0103* 🌐 *www.bistrojeanty.com.*

★ Bouchon Bistro

$$$$ | **FRENCH** | The team that created The French Laundry is also behind this place, where everything—the lively and crowded zinc-topped bar, the elbow-to-elbow seating, the traditional French onion soup—could have come straight from a Parisian bistro. Pan-seared rib eye with béarnaise and mussels steamed with white wine, saffron, and Dijon mustard—both served with crispy, addictive fries—are among the perfectly executed entrées. **Known for:** bistro classics; raw bar; Bouchon Bakery next door. *Average main: $32* ✉ *6534 Washington St., Yountville* ✣ *Near Humboldt St.* ☎ *707/944–8037* 🌐 *www.bouchonbistro.com.*

Ciccio

$$ | **MODERN ITALIAN** | The ranch of Ciccio's owners, Frank and Karen Altamura, supplies some of the vegetables and herbs for the modern Italian cuisine prepared in the open kitchen of this remodeled former grocery store. Seasonal growing cycles dictate the menu, with fried-seafood appetizers (calamari, perhaps, or softshell crabs), a few pasta dishes, bavette steak with red-wine jus, and pancetta pizzas among the frequent offerings. **Known for:** Negroni bar; prix-fixe chef's dinner; mostly Napa Valley wines, some from owners' winery. *Average main: $19* ✉ *6770 Washington St., Yountville* ✣ *At Madison St.* ☎ *707/945–1000* 🌐 *www.ciccionapavalley.com* ⏲ *Closed Mon. and Tues. No lunch* ☞ *No reservations, except for prix-fixe chef's dinner (required; for 2–10 guests).*

★ The French Laundry

$$$$ | **AMERICAN** | An old stone building laced with ivy houses chef Thomas Keller's destination restaurant. Some courses on the two prix-fixe menus, one of which highlights vegetables, rely on luxe ingredients such as *calotte* (cap of the rib eye) while other courses take humble elements like carrots or fava beans and elevate them to art; many courses offer "supplements"—sea urchin, for instance, or black truffles. **Known for:** signature starter "oysters and pearls"; intricate flavors; superior

wine list. *Average main: $325* ✉ *6640 Washington St., Yountville* *At Creek St.* ☎ *707/944–2380* ⊕ *www.frenchlaundry.com* *No lunch Mon.–Thurs.* *Jacket required* *Reservations essential wks ahead.*

Mustards Grill

$$$ | **AMERICAN** | Cindy Pawlcyn's Mustards Grill fills day and night with fans of her hearty cuisine, equal parts updated renditions of traditional American dishes—what Pawlcyn dubs "deluxe truck stop classics"—and fanciful contemporary fare. Barbecued baby back pork ribs and a lemon-lime tart piled high with brown-sugar meringue fall squarely in the first category, with sweet corn tamales with tomatillo-avocado salsa and wild mushrooms representing the latter. **Known for:** roadhouse setting; convivial mood; hoppin' bar. *Average main: $28* ✉ *7399 St. Helena Hwy./Hwy. 29, Napa* *1 mile north of Yountville* ☎ *707/944–2424* ⊕ *www.mustardsgrill.com.*

★ **Protéa Restaurant**

$$ | **LATIN AMERICAN** | A meal at Yountville's The French Laundry motivated Puerto Rico–born Anita Cartagena to pursue a career as a chef, which she did for several years at nearby Ciccio and elsewhere before opening this perky storefront serving Latin-inspired multiculti fast-food cuisine. What's in season and the chef's whims determine the order-at-the-counter fare, but Puerto Rican rice bowls (often with pork), empanadas, and sweet-and-sour ramen stir-fries make regular appearances. **Known for:** patio and rooftop seating; beer and wine lineup; eager-to-please staff. *Average main: $16* ✉ *6488 Washington St., Yountville* *At Oak Circle* ☎ *707/415–5035* ⊕ *www.proteayv.com* *Closed Wed.*

Redd Wood

$$ | **ITALIAN** | Chef Richard Reddington's casual restaurant specializes in thin-crust wood-fired pizzas and contemporary variations on Italian classics. With potato–and–green garlic soup, pizzas such as the sausage with a blend of goat cheese and mozzarella, and the pork chop entrée enlivened in fall by persimmon, Redd Wood does for Italian comfort food what nearby Mustards Grill does for the American version: it spruces it up but retains its innate pleasures. **Known for:** industrial decor; easygoing service; lunch through late-night menu. *Average main: $22* ✉ *North Block Hotel, 6755 Washington St., Yountville* *At Madison St.* ☎ *707/299–5030* ⊕ *www.redd-wood.com.*

Hotels

★ **Bardessono**

$$$$ | **RESORT** | Tranquillity and luxury with a low carbon footprint are among the goals of this ultragreen wood, steel, and glass resortlike property in downtown Yountville, but there's nothing spartan about its accommodations, arranged around four landscaped courtyards. **Pros:** large rooftop lap pool; in-room spa treatments; smooth service. **Cons:** expensive; limited view from some rooms; a bit of street traffic on hotel's west side. *Rooms from: $700* ✉ *6526 Yount St., Yountville* ☎ *707/204–6000* ⊕ *www.bardessono.com* *62 rooms* *No meals.*

Maison Fleurie

$$ | **B&B/INN** | A stay at this comfortable, reasonably priced inn, said to be the oldest hotel in the Napa Valley, places you within walking distance of Yountville's fine restaurants. **Pros:** smallest rooms a bargain; outdoor hot tub and pool; free bike rental. **Cons:** breakfast room can be crowded at peak times; some rooms pick up noise from nearby Bouchon Bakery; hard to book in high season. *Rooms from: $229* ✉ *6529 Yount St., Yountville* ☎ *707/944–2056* ⊕ *www.maisonfleurienapa.com* *13 rooms* *Breakfast.*

Napa Valley Lodge

$$ | **HOTEL** | Clean rooms in a convenient motel-style setting draw travelers willing to pay more than at comparable lodgings in the city of Napa to be within walking distance of Yountville's tasting rooms, restaurants, and shops. **Pros:** clean rooms; filling continental breakfast; large pool area. **Cons:** no elevator; lacks amenities of other Yountville properties; pricey on weekends in high season. *Rooms from: $280* ✉ *2230 Madison St., Yountville* ☎ *707/944–2468, 888/944–3545* 🌐 *www.napavalleylodge.com* *55 rooms* *Breakfast.*

★ **North Block Hotel**

$$$$ | **HOTEL** | A two-story boutique property near downtown Yountville's northern edge, the North Block attracts sophisticated travelers who appreciate its clever but unpretentious style and offhand luxury. **Pros:** extremely comfortable beds; attentive service; room service by Redd Wood restaurant. **Cons:** outdoor areas get some traffic noise; weekend minimum-stay requirement; rates soar on high-season weekends. *Rooms from: $425* ✉ *6757 Washington St., Yountville* ☎ *707/944–8080* 🌐 *northblockhotel.com* *20 rooms* *No meals.*

Vintage House

$$$ | **RESORT** | Part of the 22-acre Estate Yountville complex—other sections include sister lodging Hotel Villagio and the shops and restaurants of V Marketplace—this downtown hotel consists of two-story brick buildings along verdant landscaped paths shaded by mature trees. **Pros:** aesthetically pleasing accommodations; private patios and balconies; secluded feeling yet near shops, tasting rooms, and restaurants. **Cons:** highway noise audible in some exterior rooms; very expensive on summer and fall weekends; weekend minimum-stay requirement. *Rooms from: $355* ✉ *6541 Washington St., Yountville* ☎ *707/944–1112* 🌐 *www.vintagehouse.com* *80 rooms* *Breakfast.*

Activities

BALLOONING

Napa Valley Aloft

BALLOONING | Between 8 and 12 passengers soar over the Napa Valley in balloons that launch from downtown Yountville. Rates include preflight refreshments and a huge breakfast. ✉ *V Marketplace, 6525 Washington St., Yountville* ✣ *Near Mulberry St.* ☎ *707/944–4400, 855/944–4408* 🌐 *www.nvaloft.com* *From $200.*

BIKING

Napa Valley Aloft

BALLOONING | Between 8 and 12 passengers soar over the Napa Valley in balloons that launch from downtown Yountville. Rates include preflight refreshments and a huge breakfast. ✉ *V Marketplace, 6525 Washington St., Yountville* ✣ *Near Mulberry St.* ☎ *707/944–4400, 855/944–4408* 🌐 *www.nvaloft.com* *From $200.*

Napa Valley Bike Tours

BICYCLING | With dozens of wineries within 5 miles, this shop makes a fine starting point for guided and self-guided vineyard and wine-tasting excursions. The outfit also rents bikes. ✉ *6500 Washington St., Yountville* ✣ *At Mulberry St.* ☎ *707/944–2953* 🌐 *www.napavalleybiketours.com* *From $124 (½-day guided tour).*

Shopping

Hunter Gatherer

CLOTHING | A Napa Valley play on the classic general store, Colby Hallen's high-end lifestyle shop sells women's clothing and accessories from designers such as Frēda Salvador and Emerson Fry. She carries some men's items, too, along with everything from ceramic flasks and small gifts and cards to artisanal honey and Vintner's Daughter Active Botanical Serum face oil. ✉ *6795 Washington St., Bldg. B, Yountville* ✣ *At Madison St.* 🌐 *www.huntergatherernapavalley.com.*

V Marketplace

SHOPPING CENTERS/MALLS | This two-story redbrick market, which once housed a winery, a livery stable, and a brandy distillery, now contains clothing boutiques, art galleries, a chocolatier, and food, wine, and gift shops. Celebrity chef Michael Chiarello operates a restaurant (Bottega), a tasting room for his wines, and Ottimo, with pizza, fresh mozzarella, and other stands plus retail items. Show some love to the shops upstairs, especially Knickers and Pearls (lingerie and loungewear) and Lemondrops (kids' clothing and toys). ✉ *6525 Washington St., Yountville* ✢ *Near Mulberry St.* ☎ *707/944–2451* 🌐 *www.vmarketplace.com.*

SPAS

B Spa Therapy Center

SPA/BEAUTY | Many of this spa's patrons are Bardessono Hotel guests who take their treatments in their rooms' large, customized bathrooms—all of them equipped with concealed massage tables—but the main facility is open to guests and nonguests. An in-room treatment popular with couples starts with massages in front of the fireplace and ends with a tea bath and a split of sparkling wine. The two-hour Yountville Signature treatment, which can be enjoyed in-room or at the spa, begins with a shea-butter-enriched sugar scrub, followed by a Chardonnay grapeseed oil massage and a hydrating hair-and-scalp treatment. The spa engages massage therapists skilled in Swedish, Thai, and several other techniques. In addition to massages, the services include facials and other skin-care treatments. ✉ *Bardessono Hotel, 6526 Yount St., Yountville* ✢ *At Mulberry St.* ☎ *707/204–6050* 🌐 *www.bardessono.com/spa* 🎫 *Treatments from $165.*

Oakville

2 miles northwest of Yountville.

A large butte that runs east–west just north of Yountville blocks the cooling fogs from the south, facilitating the myriad microclimates of the Oakville AVA, home to several high-profile wineries.

GETTING HERE AND AROUND

Driving along Highway 29, you'll know you've reached Oakville when you see the Oakville Grocery on the east side of the road. You can reach Oakville from the Sonoma County town of Glen Ellen by heading east on Trinity Road from Highway 12. The twisting route, along the mountain range that divides Napa and Sonoma, eventually becomes the Oakville Grade. The views on this drive are breathtaking, though the continual curves make it unsuitable for those who suffer from motion sickness.

Sights

B Cellars

WINERY/DISTILLERY | The chefs take center stage in the open-hearth kitchen of this boutique winery's hospitality house, and with good reason: creating food-friendly wines is B Cellars's raison d'être. Visits to the Oakville facility—all steel beams, corrugated metal, and plate glass yet remarkably cozy—begin with a tour of the winery's culinary garden and in some cases also the caves. Most guests return to the house to sample wines paired with small bites, with some visitors remaining in the caves for exclusive tastings of Cabernet Sauvignons from several historic vineyards of Andy Beckstoffer, a prominent grower. Kirk Venge, whose fruit-forward style well suits the winery's food-oriented approach, crafts these and other wines, among them red and white blends and single-vineyard Cabernets from other noteworthy vineyards. All visits here are strictly by appointment. ✉ *703 Oakville Cross*

Rd., Oakville ✥ West of Silverado Trail ☎ 707/709–8787 🌐 www.bcellars.com 🎫 Tastings from $65.

Far Niente

WINERY/DISTILLERY | Hamden McIntyre, a prominent winery architect of his era also responsible for Inglenook and what's now the Culinary Institute of America at Greystone, designed the centerpiece 1885 stone winery here. Abandoned in the wake of Prohibition and only revived beginning in 1979, Far Niente now ranks as one of the Napa Valley's most beautiful properties. Guests participating in the main tour and tasting learn some of this history while strolling the winery and its aging caves. The trip completed, hosts pour the flagship wines, a Chardonnay and a Cabernet Sauvignon blend. The tasting session concludes with Dolce, a late-harvest Sémillon and Sauvignon Blanc wine. Two shorter tastings, one highlighting older vintages, the other showcasing the output of affiliated wineries, dispense with the tour. **■ TIP→ Aged and rare Cabernets from the Far Niente wine library are served at Cave Collection tastings.** ✉ *1350 Acacia Dr., Oakville ✥ Off Oakville Grade Rd. ☎ 707/944–2861 🌐 www.farniente.com 🎫 Tastings from $80; tour and tasting $80.*

Robert Mondavi Winery

WINERY/DISTILLERY | The graceful arch at the center of the winery's mission-style building frames the lawn and the vineyard behind, inviting a stroll under the arcades. You can head for one of the walk-in tasting rooms, but if you've not toured a winery before, the 75-minute Signature Tour and Tasting is a good way to learn about enology and the late Robert Mondavi's role in California wine making. Those new to tasting should consider the 45-minute Wine Tasting Basics experience. Serious wine lovers can opt for the Exclusive Cellar tasting, during which a server pours and explains limited-production, reserve, and older vintages. The three-course Harvest of Joy Lunch and wine pairing starts with a tour. All visits except walk-in tastings require reservations. **■ TIP→ Well-attended concerts take place in summer on the lawn.** ✉ *7801 St. Helena Hwy./Hwy. 29, Oakville ☎ 888/766–6328 🌐 www.robertmondaviwinery.com 🎫 Tastings and tours from $25.*

★ Silver Oak

WINERY/DISTILLERY | The first review of this winery's Napa Valley Cabernet Sauvignon declared the debut 1972 vintage not all that good and, at $6 a bottle, overpriced. Oops. The celebrated Bordeaux-style Cabernet blend, still the only Napa Valley wine bearing its winery's label each year, evolved into a cult favorite, and Silver Oak founders Ray Duncan and Justin Meyer received worldwide recognition for their signature use of exclusively American oak to age the wines. At the Oakville tasting room, constructed out of reclaimed stone and other materials from a 19th-century Kansas flour mill, you can sip the current Napa Valley vintage, its counterpart from Silver Oak's Alexander Valley operation, and a library wine without an appointment. One is required for tours, private tastings, and food–wine pairings. ✉ *915 Oakville Cross Rd., Oakville ✥ Off Hwy. 29 ☎ 707/942–7022 🌐 www.silveroak.com 🎫 Tastings from $30, tours from $40 (includes tasting).*

Rutherford

2 miles northwest of Oakville.

With its singular microclimate and soil, Rutherford is an important viticultural center, with more big-name wineries than you can shake a corkscrew at. Cabernet Sauvignon is king here. The well-drained, loamy soil is ideal for those vines, and since this part of the valley gets plenty of sun, the grapes develop exceptionally intense flavors.

GETTING HERE AND AROUND

Wineries around Rutherford are dotted along Highway 29 and the parallel Silverado Trail north and south of Rutherford Road/Conn Creek Road, on which wineries can also be found.

Sights

★ Frog's Leap

WINERY/DISTILLERY | **FAMILY** | If you're a novice, the tour at Frog's Leap is a fun way to begin your education. You'll taste wines that might include Zinfandel, Merlot, Chardonnay, Sauvignon Blanc, and an estate-grown Cabernet Sauvignon. The winery includes a barn built in 1884, 5 acres of organic gardens, an eco-friendly visitor center, and a frog pond topped with lily pads. Reservations are required for all visits here. ■ TIP→ **The tour is recommended, but you can also just sample wines either inside or on a porch overlooking the garden.** ✉ *8815 Conn Creek Rd., Rutherford* ☎ *707/963–4704, 800/959–4704* 🌐 *www.frogsleap.com* 🎫 *Tastings from $25, tour $35.*

Honig Vineyard & Winery

WINERY/DISTILLERY | **FAMILY** | Sustainable farming is the big story at this family-run winery. The Eco Tour, offered seasonally, focuses on the Honig family's environmentally friendly farming and production methods, which include using biodiesel to fuel the tractors, monitoring water use in the vineyard and winery, and generating power for the winery with solar panels. The family produces only Sauvignon Blanc and Cabernet Sauvignon. By appointment, you can taste whites and reds at a standard tasting; the reserve tasting pairs single-vineyard Cabernets with small bites. ✉ *850 Rutherford Rd., Rutherford* ✣ *Near Conn Creek Rd.* ☎ *800/929–2217* 🌐 *www.honigwine.com* 🎫 *Tastings from $30, tour $45.*

★ Inglenook

WINERY/DISTILLERY | Filmmaker Francis Ford Coppola began his wine-making career in 1975, when he bought part of the historic Inglenook estate. Over the decades he reunited the original property acquired by Inglenook founder Gustave Niebaum, remodeled Niebaum's ivy-covered 1880s château, and purchased the rights to the Inglenook name. The Inglenook Experience, an escorted tour of the château, vineyards, and caves, ends with a seated tasting of wines paired with artisanal cheeses. Among the topics discussed are the winery's history and the evolution of Coppola's signature wine, Rubicon, a Cabernet Sauvignon–based blend. The Heritage Tasting, which also includes a Rubicon pour, is held in the opulent Pennino Salon. Reservations are required for some tastings and tours, and are recommended for all. ■ TIP→ **Walk-ins can sip wines by the glass or bottle at The Bistro, a wine bar with a picturesque courtyard.** ✉ *1991 St. Helena Hwy./Hwy. 29, Rutherford* ✣ *At Hwy. 128* ☎ *707/968–1100* 🌐 *www.inglenook.com* 🎫 *Tastings from $45, private experiences from $75.*

Mumm Napa

WINERY/DISTILLERY | In Mumm's light-filled tasting room or adjacent outdoor patio you can enjoy bubbly by the flight, but the sophisticated sparkling wines, elegant setting, and vineyard views aren't the only reasons to visit. An excellent gallery displays original Ansel Adams prints and presents temporary exhibitions by premier photographers. Winery tours cover the major steps in making sparklers. For a leisurely tasting of several vintages of the top-of-the-line DVX wines, book an Oak Terrace tasting. Reservations are required for this tasting and the tour; they're recommended for tastings inside or on the patio. ✉ *8445 Silverado Trail, Rutherford* ✣ *1 mile south of Rutherford Cross Rd.* ☎ *707/967–7700, 800/783–5826* 🌐 *www.mummnapa.com* 🎫 *Tastings from $25, tour $40 (includes tasting).*

Frog's Leap's picturesque country charm extends all the way to the white picket fence.

Restaurants

★ Restaurant at Auberge du Soleil

$$$$ | MODERN AMERICAN | Possibly the most romantic roost for dinner in all the Wine Country is a terrace seat at the Auberge du Soleil resort's illustrious restaurant, and the Mediterranean-inflected cuisine more than matches the dramatic vineyard views. The prix-fixe dinner menu, which relies mainly on local produce, might include crispy veal sweetbreads and chanterelles or prime beef pavé with hearts of palm, arugula pesto, and tomato confit. **Known for:** polished service; comprehensive wine list; over-the-top weekend brunch. *Ⓢ Average main: $120 ✉ Auberge du Soleil, 180 Rutherford Hill Rd., Rutherford ✣ Off Silverado Trail ☎ 707/963–1211, 800/348–5406 🌐 www.aubergedusoleil.com.*

★ Rutherford Grill

$$$ | AMERICAN | Dark-wood walls, subdued lighting, and red-leather banquettes make for a perpetually clubby mood at this Rutherford hangout whose patio, popular for its bar, fireplace, and rocking chairs, is open for full meal service or drinks and appetizers when the weather's right. Many entrées—steaks, burgers, fish, rotisserie chicken, and barbecued pork ribs—emerge from an oak-fired grill operated by master technicians. **Known for:** signature French dip sandwich and grilled jumbo artichokes; reasonably priced wine list with rarities; patio's bar, fireplace, and rocking chairs. *Ⓢ Average main: $30 ✉ 1180 Rutherford Rd., Rutherford ✣ At Hwy. 29 ☎ 707/963–1792 🌐 www.rutherfordgrill.com.*

Hotels

★ Auberge du Soleil

$$$$ | RESORT | Taking a cue from the olive-tree-studded landscape, this hotel with a renowned restaurant and spa cultivates a luxurious look that blends French and California style. **Pros:** stunning views over the valley; spectacular pool and spa areas; the most expensive suites are fit for a superstar. **Cons:** stratospheric prices; least expensive rooms get some noise from the bar and restaurant; weekend minimum-stay requirement. *Rooms from: $950 180 Rutherford Hill Rd., Rutherford 707/963–1211, 800/348–5406 www.aubergedusoleil.com 52 rooms Breakfast.*

St. Helena

2 miles northwest of Oakville.

Downtown St. Helena is the very picture of good living in the Wine Country: sycamore trees arch over Main Street (Highway 29), where visitors flit between boutiques, cafés, and storefront tasting rooms housed in sun-faded redbrick buildings. The genteel district pulls in rafts of tourists during the day, though like most Wine Country towns St. Helena more or less rolls up the sidewalks after dark.

The Napa Valley floor narrows between the Mayacamas and Vaca mountains around St. Helena. The slopes reflect heat onto the vineyards below, and since there's less fog and wind, things get pretty toasty. This is one of the valley's hottest AVAs, with midsummer temperatures often reaching the mid-90s. Bordeaux varietals are the most popular grapes grown here—especially Cabernet Sauvignon but also Merlot, Cabernet Franc, and Sauvignon Blanc.

GETTING HERE AND AROUND

Downtown stretches along Highway 29, called Main Street here. Many wineries lie north and south of downtown along Highway 29. More can be found off Silverado Trail, and some of the most scenic spots are on Spring Mountain, which rises southwest of town.

Sights

Beringer Vineyards

WINERY/DISTILLERY | Brothers Frederick and Jacob Beringer opened the winery that still bears their name in 1876. One of California's earliest bonded wineries, it is the oldest one in the Napa Valley never to have missed a vintage—no mean feat, given Prohibition. Frederick's grand Rhine House Mansion, built in 1884, serves as the reserve tasting room. Here, surrounded by Belgian art-nouveau hand-carved oak and walnut furniture and stained-glass windows, you can sample wines that include a limited-release Chardonnay, a few big Cabernets, and a Sauterne-style dessert wine. A less expensive tasting takes place in the original stone winery. Reservations are required for some tastings and recommended for tours. **TIP→ The one-hour Taste of Beringer tour of the property and sensory gardens surveys the winery's history and wine making and concludes with a seated wine-and-food pairing.** *2000 Main St./Hwy. 29, St. Helena Near Pratt Ave. 707/963–8989 www.beringer.com Tastings from $25, tours from $30.*

Charles Krug Winery

WINERY/DISTILLERY | A historically sensitive renovation of its 1874 Redwood Cellar Building transformed the former production facility of the Napa Valley's oldest winery into an epic hospitality center. Charles Krug, a Prussian immigrant, established the winery in 1861 and ran it until his death in 1892. Italian immigrants Cesare Mondavi and his wife, Rosa, purchased Charles Krug in 1943, and operated it with their sons Peter and Robert (who later opened his own winery). The winery, still run by Peter's family, specializes in small-lot Yountville and Howell Mountain Cabernet Sauvignons and makes Chardonnay, Merlot, Pinot Noir, Sauvignon Blanc, Zinfandel, and a Zinfandel port. The tour is by appointment only. *2800 Main St./Hwy. 29, St. Helena Across from Culinary Institute of America 707/967–2229 www.charleskrug.com Tastings $45, tour $75 (includes tasting).*

Culinary Institute of America at Greystone

COLLEGE | The West Coast headquarters of the country's leading school for chefs is in the 1889 Greystone Cellars, an imposing building once the world's largest stone winery. On the ground floor you can check out the quirky Corkscrew Museum and browse the Spice Islands Marketplace store, stocked with gleaming gadgets and many cookbooks. The Bakery Café by illy serves soups, salads, sandwiches, and baked goods. One-day and multiday cooking and beverage classes often take place. Students run the Gatehouse Restaurant, which serves dinner except during semester breaks. ✉ *2555 Main St./Hwy. 29, St. Helena* ☎ *707/967–1100* 🌐 *www.ciachef.edu/california* 🎫 *Museum free, tour $10; class prices vary.*

Hall St. Helena

WINERY/DISTILLERY | The Cabernet Sauvignons produced here are works of art and the latest in organic-farming science and wine-making technology. A glass-walled tasting room allows guests to see in action some of the high-tech equipment winemaker Steve Leveque employs to craft wines that also include Merlot, Cabernet Franc, and Sauvignon Blanc. Westward from the second-floor tasting area, rows of neatly spaced Cabernet vines capture the eye, and beyond them the tree-studded Mayacamas Mountains. The main guided tour takes in the facility, the grounds, and a restored 19th-century winery, passing artworks by John Baldessari, Jaume Plensa, and other contemporary talents. On Friday and weekends, tastings of limited-production Baca label Zinfandels take place. ■ **TIP→ Hall Rutherford, an appointment-only sister winery, provides an exclusive, elegant wine-and-food pairing atop a Rutherford hillside.** ✉ *401 St. Helena Hwy./Hwy. 29, St. Helena* ✣ *Near White La.* ☎ *707/967–2626* 🌐 *www.hallwines.com* 🎫 *Tastings from $30, tours from $40.*

★ **Joseph Phelps Vineyards**

WINERY/DISTILLERY | An appointment is required for tastings at the winery started by the late Joseph Phelps, but it's well worth the effort—all the more so after an inspired renovation of the main redwood structure, a classic of 1970s Northern California architecture. Known for wines crafted with grace and precision, Phelps does produce fine whites, but the blockbusters are red, particularly the Cabernet Sauvignon and the luscious-yet-subtle Bordeaux-style blend called Insignia. In good weather, one-hour seated tastings take place on a terrace overlooking vineyards and oaks. At 90-minute tastings as thoughtfully conceived as the wines, guests explore such topics as wine-and-cheese pairing, wine blending, and the role oak barrels play in wine making. Participants in the blending seminar mix the various varietals that go into the Insignia blend. ✉ *200 Taplin Rd., St. Helena* ✣ *Off Silverado Trail* ☎ *707/963–2745, 800/707–5789* 🌐 *www.josephphelps.com* 🎫 *Tastings and seminars from $75.*

★ **Mad Fritz Brewing Co.**

WINERY/DISTILLERY | #Beerpassion reigns at this St. Helena tap room where enthusiastic fans and palate-cleansing wine tourists stop to quaff small-lot lagers and ales crafted with a winemaker's sensibility. The goal of founder and master brewer Nile Zacherle, who, when he's not at the brewery, works at a Pritchard Hill winery, isn't merely to make great beers. He and his wife, Whitney Fisher, succeed at that, but they also create what they call "origin specific beers," with each label listing where the couple sourced every ingredient from hops to barley to water. The beers' label art and names, among them The Wind and the Sun and The Donkey and the Thistle, derive from a centuries-old *Aesop's Fables* edition. Along with the label's ingredients list is a summary of the bottling's fable and, in boldface, its moral. ✉ *1282B Vidovich Ave., St.*

Helena ✣ At Hwy. 29 ☎ 707/968–5097 🌐 www.madfritz.com 🎫 Tastings from $3 per pour.

Prager Winery & Port Works

WINERY/DISTILLERY | "If door is locked, ring bell," reads a sign outside the weathered-redwood tasting shack at this family-run winery known for red, white, and tawny ports. The sign, the bell, and the thousands of dollar bills tacked to the walls and ceilings inside are your first indications that you're drifting back in time with the old-school Pragers, who have been making regular and fortified wines in St. Helena since the late 1970s. Five members of the second generation, along with two spouses, run this homespun operation founded by Jim and Imogene Prager. In addition to ports the winery makes Petite Sirah and Sweet Claire, a late-harvest Riesling dessert wine. ✉ *1281 Lewelling La., St. Helena* ✣ *Off Hwy. 29* ☎ *707/963–7678* 🌐 *www.pragerport.com* 🎫 *Tastings $30 (includes glass).*

Pride Mountain Vineyards

WINERY/DISTILLERY | This winery 2,200 feet up Spring Mountain straddles Napa and Sonoma counties, confusing enough for visitors but even more complicated for the wine-making staff: government regulations require separate wineries and paperwork for each side of the property. It's one of several amusing Pride Mountain quirks, but winemaker Sally Johnson's "big red wines," including a Cabernet Sauvignon that earned 100-point scores from a major wine critic two years in a row, are serious business. At tastings and on tours you can learn about the farming and cellar strategies behind Pride's acclaimed Cabs (the winery also produces Syrah, a Cab-like Merlot, Viognier, and Chardonnay among others). The tour, which takes in vineyards and caves, also includes tastings of wine still in barrel. **■ TIP→ The views here are knock-your-socks-off gorgeous.** ✉ *4026 Spring Mountain Rd., St. Helena* ✣ *Off St. Helena Rd. (extension of Spring Mountain Rd. in Sonoma County)* ☎ *707/963–4949* 🌐 *www.pridewines.com* 🎫 *Tastings from $30* 🕐 *Closed Tues.*

The Prisoner Wine Company

WINERY/DISTILLERY | The iconoclastic brand opened an industrial-chic space with interiors by the wildly original Napa-based designer Richard Von Saal to showcase its flagship The Prisoner red blend. "Getting the varietals to play together" is winemaker Chrissy Wittmann's goal with that wine (Zinfandel, Cabernet Sauvignon, Petite Sirah, Syrah, Charbono) and siblings like the Blindfold white (Viognier, Roussanne, Chenin Blanc, Vermentino). Walk-in patrons can sip these and other selections in the Tasting Lounge, more hip hotel bar than traditional tasting room, or outside in the casual open-air The Yard. Southward in The Makery, private appointment-only experiences unfold, some involving boldly flavored plates the winery kitchen turns out. Several alcoves within The Makery contain products for sale inspired by the Wine Country. The Prisoner's tasting space is quite the party, for most of which a reservation is required. ✉ *1178 Galleron Rd., St. Helena* ✣ *At Hwy. 29* ☎ *707/967–3823, 877/283–5934* 🌐 *www.theprisonerwinecompany.com* 🎫 *Tastings from $45.*

Restaurants

Charter Oak

$$$ | **MODERN AMERICAN** | Executive chef Christopher Kostow prepares ornate swoonworthy haute cuisine at The Restaurant at Meadowood, but he and chef Katianna Hong take a simpler approach (fewer ingredients chosen for maximum effect) at this high-ceilinged, brown-brick downtown restaurant. On a recent menu the strategy translated into dishes like hearth-roasted ham with horseradish, black cod grilled in corn leaves, and cauliflower with raisins and brown butter. **Known for:** exceedingly fresh produce;

patio dining in brick courtyard; new chicken-wings appetizer recipe from high-profile restaurant each month. *Average main: $29* *1050 Charter Oak Ave., at Hwy. 29, St. Helena* *707/302–6996* *www.thecharteroak.com* *No lunch Mon.–Thurs.*

★ Cook St. Helena

$$$ | ITALIAN | A curved marble bar spotlit by contemporary art-glass pendants adds a touch of style to this downtown restaurant whose Northern Italian cuisine pleases with similarly understated sophistication. Mussels with house-made sausage in a spicy tomato broth, chopped salad with pancetta and pecorino, and the daily changing risotto are among the dishes regulars revere. **Known for:** top-quality ingredients; reasonably priced local and international wines; Cook Tavern two doors down for pizza and small plates. *Average main: $23* *1310 Main St., St. Helena* *Near Hunt Ave.* *707/963–7088* *www.cooksthelena.com.*

★ Farmstead at Long Meadow Ranch

$$$ | MODERN AMERICAN | Housed in a high-ceilinged former barn, Farmstead revolves around an open kitchen where executive chef Stephen Barber's team prepares meals with grass-fed beef and lamb, fruits and vegetables, and eggs, olive oil, wine, honey, and other ingredients from Long Meadow Ranch. Entrées might include wood-grilled trout with fennel, mushroom, onion and a bacon-mustard vinaigrette; Yukon potato gnocchi with wild mushrooms; or a wood-grilled heritage pork chop with jalapeño grits and chutney. **Known for:** Tuesday fried-chicken night; house-made charcuterie; seasonal cocktails. *Average main: $29* *738 Main St., St. Helena* *At Charter Oak Ave.* *707/963–4555* *www.longmeadowranch.com/eat-drink/restaurant.*

Goose & Gander

$$$ | MODERN AMERICAN | The pairing of food and drink at G&G is as likely to involve cool cocktails as wine. Main courses such as koji-poached sea bass, heritage-pork porterhouse, and dry-aged New York steak with black-lime and pink-peppercorn butter work well with starters that might include blistered shishito peppers and grilled Spanish octopus. **Known for:** intimate main dining room with fireplace; alfresco dining on patio in good weather; basement bar among Napa's best drinking spots. *Average main: $26* *1245 Spring St., St. Helena* *At Oak St.* *707/967–8779* *www.goosegander.com.*

Gott's Roadside

$ | AMERICAN | A 1950s-style outdoor hamburger stand goes upscale at this spot whose customers brave long lines to order breakfast sandwiches, juicy burgers, root-beer floats, and garlic fries. Choices not available a half century ago include the ahi tuna burger and the Vietnamese chicken salad. **Known for:** tasty (if pricey) 21st-century diner cuisine; shaded picnic tables (arrive early or late for lunch to get one); second branch at Napa's Oxbow Public Market. *Average main: $13* *933 Main St./Hwy. 29, St. Helena* *707/963–3486* *www.gotts.com* *Reservations not accepted.*

★ Press

$$$$ | MODERN AMERICAN | Few taste sensations surpass the combination of a sizzling steak and a Napa Valley red, a union the chef and sommeliers at Press celebrate with a reverence bordering on obsession. Grass-fed beef from celebrated California purveyor Bryan Flannery cooked on the cherry-and-almond-wood-fired grill is the star—especially the 38-ounce Porterhouse and the *côte de boeuf* bone-in rib eye, both dry-aged—but the cooks also prepare pork chops, free-range chicken, and fish. **Known for:** extensive wine cellar; impressive cocktails; casual-chic ambience. *Average main: $59* *587 St. Helena Hwy./Hwy. 29, St. Helena* *At White La.* *707/967–0550* *www.pressnapavalley.com* *Closed Tues. No lunch.*

★ The Restaurant at Meadowood
$$$$ | **MODERN AMERICAN** | Chef Christopher Kostow has garnered rave reviews—and three Michelin stars for several years running—for creating a unique dining experience. Patrons choosing the Tasting Menu option ($285 per person) enjoy their meals in the dining room, its beautiful finishes aglow with warm lighting, but up to four guests can select the Counter Menu ($500 per person) for the chance to sit in the kitchen and watch Kostow's team prepare the food ("the height of our vacation," said four recent guests). **Known for:** complex cuisine; first-class service; romantic setting. *Average main: $275 ✉ 900 Meadowood La., St. Helena ✣ Off Silverado Trail N ☎ 707/967–1205, 800/458–8080 ⊕ www.therestaurantatmeadowood.com ⊙ Closed Sun. and Mon. No lunch ☞ Jacket suggested but not required.*

Hotels

El Bonita Motel
$ | **HOTEL** | A classic 1950s-style neon sign marks the driveway to this well-run roadside motel that—when it isn't sold out—offers great value to budget-minded travelers. **Pros:** cheerful rooms; hot tub; microwaves and mini-refrigerators. **Cons:** road noise a problem in some rooms; noise in ground-floor rooms from second floor; lacks amenities of fancier properties. *Rooms from: $149 ✉ 195 Main St./Hwy. 29, St. Helena ☎ 707/963–3216, 800/541–3284 ⊕ www.elbonita.com ⇆ 52 rooms 🍽 Breakfast.*

Harvest Inn by Charlie Palmer
$$$ | **HOTEL** | Although this inn sits just off Highway 29, its patrons remain mostly above the fray, strolling 8 acres of gardens, enjoying views of the vineyards adjoining the property, partaking in spa services, and drifting to sleep in beds adorned with fancy linens and down pillows. **Pros:** garden setting; spacious rooms; near choice wineries, dining spots, and shops. **Cons:** some lower-price rooms lack elegance; high weekend rates; occasional service lapses. *Rooms from: $354 ✉ 1 Main St., St. Helena ☎ 707/963–9463, 800/950–8466 ⊕ www.harvestinn.com ⇆ 78 rooms 🍽 Breakfast.*

Ink House
$$$$ | **B&B/INN** | The goal of the Castellucci family, which lavishly refurbished an 1885 Italianate along Highway 29, is to provide "a curated luxury experience" in impeccably styled rooms with 11-foot ceilings and vineyard views out tall windows. **Pros:** panoramic views from the cupola; attention to detail; Elvis Presley slept here (but it wasn't this stylish). **Cons:** extremely pricey; lacks on-site pool, fitness center, spa; two bathrooms have showers only (albeit nice ones). *Rooms from: $500 ✉ 1575 St. Helena Hwy., St. Helena ☎ 707/968–9686 ⊕ www.inkhousenapavalley.com/inn ⇆ 4 rooms 🍽 Free Breakfast.*

Inn St. Helena
$$ | **B&B/INN** | A large room at this spiffed-up downtown St. Helena inn is named for author Ambrose Bierce *(The Devil's Dictionary)*, who lived in the main Victorian structure in the early 1900s, but sensitive hospitality and modern amenities are what make a stay worth writing home about. **Pros:** filling breakfast; outdoor porch and swing; convenient to shops, tasting rooms, restaurants. **Cons:** no pool, gym, room service, or other hotel amenities; two-night minimum on weekends (three with Monday holiday); per website "children 16 and older are welcome." *Rooms from: $279 ✉ 1515 Main St., St. Helena ☎ 707/963–3003 ⊕ www.innsthelena.com ⇆ 8 rooms 🍽 Breakfast.*

Las Alcobas Napa Valley
$$$$ | **HOTEL** | Upscale-casual luxury is the goal of this hillside beauty—part of the Starwood chain's Luxury Collection—next to Beringer Vineyards and six blocks north of Main Street shopping and dining. **Pros:** pool, spa, and fitness center; vineyard views from most rooms; chef Chris

Cosentino's Acacia House restaurant. **Cons:** pricey; per website no children under age 17 permitted; no self-parking. *Rooms from: $638* ✉ *1915 Main St., St. Helena* ☎ *707/963–7000* 🌐 *www.lasalcobasnapavalley.com* *68 rooms* *Breakfast.*

★ **Meadowood Napa Valley**
$$$$ | **RESORT** | Founded in 1964 as a country club, Meadowood evolved into an elite resort, a gathering place for Napa's wine-making community, and a celebrated dining destination. **Pros:** superb restaurant; all-organic spa; gracious service. **Cons:** very expensive; far from downtown St. Helena; weekend minimum-stay requirement. *Rooms from: $650* ✉ *900 Meadowood La., St. Helena* ☎ *707/963–3646, 800/458–8080* 🌐 *www.meadowood.com* *85 rooms* *No meals.*

Wine Country Inn
$$$ | **B&B/INN** | Vineyards flank the three buildings, containing 24 rooms, and five cottages of this pastoral retreat, where blue oaks, maytens, and olive trees provide shade, and gardens feature lantana (small butterflies love it) and lavender. **Pros:** staff excels at anticipating guests' needs; good-size swimming pool; vineyard views from most rooms. **Cons:** some rooms let in noise from neighbors; expensive in high season; weekend minimum-stay requirement. *Rooms from: $349* ✉ *1152 Lodi La., St. Helena* ✣ *East of Hwy. 29* ☎ *707/963–7077, 888/465–4608* 🌐 *www.winecountryinn.com* *29 rooms* *Breakfast.*

Nightlife

The Saint
WINE BARS—NIGHTLIFE | This high-ceilinged downtown wine bar benefits from the grandeur and gravitas of its setting inside a stone-walled late-19th-century former bank. Lit by chandeliers and decked out in contemporary style with plush sofas and chairs and Lucite stools at the bar, it's a classy, loungelike space to expand your enological horizons comparing the many small-lot Napa Valley wines on offer with their counterparts in France and beyond. There's live or DJ music some nights. ✉ *1351 Main St., St. Helena* ✣ *Near Adams St.* ☎ *707/302–5130* 🌐 *www.thesaintnapavalley.com.*

Calistoga

3 miles northwest of St. Helena.

With false-fronted, Old West–style shops and 19th-century inns and hotels lining its main drag, Lincoln Avenue, Calistoga comes across as more down-to-earth than its more polished neighbors. Don't be fooled, though. On its outskirts lie some of the Wine Country's swankest (and priciest) resorts and its most fanciful piece of architecture, the medieval-style Castello di Amorosa winery.

Calistoga was developed as a spa-oriented getaway from the start. Sam Brannan, a gold rush–era entrepreneur, planned to use the area's natural hot springs as the centerpiece of a resort complex. His venture failed, but old-time hotels and bathhouses—along with some glorious new spas—still operate. You can come for an old-school mud bath, or go completely 21st century and experience lavish treatments based on the latest innovations in skin and body care.

GETTING HERE AND AROUND

Highway 29 heads east (turn right) at Calistoga, where in town it is signed as Lincoln Avenue. If arriving via the Silverado Trail, head west at Highway 29/ Lincoln Avenue.

Sights

Ca' Toga Galleria d'Arte
MUSEUM | The boundless wit, whimsy, and creativity of the Venetian-born Carlo Marchiori, this gallery's owner-artist, finds expression in paintings,

watercolors, ceramics, sculptures, and other artworks. Marchiori often draws on mythology and folktales for his inspiration. A stop at this magical gallery might inspire you to tour Villa Ca' Toga, the artist's fanciful Palladian home, a tromp-l'oeil tour de force open for tours from May through October on Saturday morning only, by appointment. ✉ *1206 Cedar St., Calistoga* ✣ *Near Lincoln Ave.* ☎ *707/942–3900* 🌐 *www.catoga.com* ⏲ *Closed Tues. and Wed.*

Castello di Amorosa

WINERY/DISTILLERY | An astounding medieval structure complete with drawbridge and moat, chapel, stables, and secret passageways, the Castello commands Diamond Mountain's lower eastern slope. Some of the 107 rooms contain artist Fabio Sanzogni's replicas of 13th-century frescoes (cheekily signed with his website address), and the dungeon has an iron maiden from Nuremberg, Germany. You must pay for a tour to see most of Dario Sattui's extensive eight-level property, though with a basic tasting you'll have access to part of the complex. Bottlings of note include several Italian-style wines, including La Castellana, a robust "super Tuscan" blend of Cabernet Sauvignon, Sangiovese, and Merlot; and Il Barone, a deliberately big Cab primarily of Rutherford grapes. **TIP→ The 2½-hour Royal Food & Wine Pairing Tour by sommelier Mary Davidek (by appointment only) is among the Wine Country's best.** ✉ *4045 N. St. Helena Hwy./Hwy. 29, Calistoga* ✣ *Near Maple La.* ☎ *707/967–6272* 🌐 *www.castellodiamorosa.com* 🎫 *Tastings from $30, tours from $40 (include tastings).*

Chateau Montelena

WINERY/DISTILLERY | Set amid a bucolic northern Calistoga landscape, this winery helped establish the Napa Valley's reputation for high-quality wine making. At the pivotal Paris tasting of 1976, the Chateau Montelena 1973 Chardonnay took first place, beating out four white Burgundies from France and five other California Chardonnays, an event immortalized in the 2008 movie *Bottle Shock*. A 21st-century Napa Valley Chardonnay is always part of a Current Release Tasting—the winery also makes Sauvignon Blanc, Riesling, a fine estate Zinfandel, and Cabernet Sauvignon—or you can opt for a Limited Release Tasting focusing more on Cabernets. The walking Estate Tour takes in the grounds and covers the history of this stately property whose stone winery building was erected in 1888. Guests board a vehicle for the seasonal Vineyard Tour. Tours and some tastings require a reservation. ✉ *1429 Tubbs La., Calistoga* ✣ *Off Hwy. 29* ☎ *707/942–5105* 🌐 *www.montelena.com* 🎫 *Tastings from $30, tours from $50.*

Frank Family Vineyards

WINERY/DISTILLERY | As a former Disney film and television executive, Rich Frank knows a thing or two about entertainment, and it shows in the chipper atmosphere that prevails in the winery's bright-yellow Craftsman-style tasting room. The site's wine-making history dates from the 19th century, and portions of an original 1884 structure, reclad in stone in 1906, remain standing today. From 1952 until 1990, Hanns Kornell made sparkling wines on this site. Frank Family makes sparklers itself, but the high-profile wines are the Cabernet Sauvignons, particularly the Rutherford Reserve and the Winston Hill red blend. Tastings are mostly sit-down affairs, indoors, on the popular back veranda, or at picnic tables under 100-year-old elms. Reservations are required from Friday through Sunday; they're wise on other days, too. ✉ *1091 Larkmead La., Calistoga* ✣ *Off Hwy. 29* ☎ *707/942–0859* 🌐 *www.frankfamilyvineyards.com* 🎫 *Tastings from $40.*

Tamber Bey Vineyards

WINERY/DISTILLERY | Endurance riders Barry and Jennifer Waitte share their passion for horses and wine at their glam-rustic

All it needs is a fair maiden: Castello di Amorosa's re-created castle.

winery north of Calistoga. Their 22-acre Sundance Ranch remains a working equestrian facility, but the site has been revamped to include a state-of-the-art winery with separate fermenting tanks for grapes from Tamber Bey's vineyards in Yountville, Oakville, and elsewhere. The winemakers produce three Chardonnays and a Sauvignon Blanc, but the stars are several subtly powerful reds, including the flagship Oakville Cabernet Sauvignon and a Yountville Merlot. The top-selling wine, Rabicano, is a Cabernet Sauvignon-heavy blend that in a recent vintage contained the four other main Bordeaux red grapes: Malbec, Merlot, Petit Verdot, and Cabernet Franc. Visits here require an appointment. ✉ *1251 Tubbs La., Calistoga* ✣ *At Myrtledale Rd.* ☎ *707/942–2100* 🌐 *www.tamberbey.com* 🎫 *Tastings from $45.*

★ **Venge Vineyards**

WINERY/DISTILLERY | As the son of Nils Venge, the first winemaker to earn a 100-point score from the wine critic Robert Parker, Kirk Venge had a hard act to follow. Now a consultant to exclusive wineries himself, Kirk is an acknowledged master of balanced, fruit-forward Bordeaux-style blends. At his casual ranch-house tasting room you can sip wines that might include the estate Bone Ash Cabernet Sauvignon, an Oakville Merlot, and the Silencieux Cabernet, a blend of grapes from several appellations. With its views of the well-manicured Bone Ash Vineyard and, west across the valley, Diamond Mountain, the ranch house's porch would make for a magical perch even if Venge's wines weren't works of art in themselves. Tastings are by appointment only. ✉ *4708 Silverado Trail, Calistoga* ✣ *1½ miles south of downtown, near Dunaweal La.* ☎ *707/942–9100* 🌐 *www.vengevineyards.com* 🎫 *Tastings $45* 🕒 *Reservations recommended 3–4 wks in advance for weekend visits.*

Restaurants

★ **Evangeline**

$$$ | MODERN AMERICAN | The gas-lamp-style lighting fixtures, charcoal-black hues, and bistro cuisine at Evangeline evoke old New Orleans with a California twist. Executive chef Gustavo Rios, whose previous stops include Calistoga's Solbar and Yountville's Bouchon Bistro, puts a jaunty spin on dishes that might include shrimp étouffée, duck confit, or steak frites; the elaborate weekend brunch, with everything from avocado toast to buttermilk biscuits and sausage gravy, is an upvalley favorite. **Known for:** outdoor courtyard; palate-cleansing Sazeracs; addictive fried pickles. *Average main: $27 ✉ 1226 Washington St., Calistoga ✣ Near Lincoln Ave. ☎ 707/341–3131 🌐 www.evangelinenapa.com ⏲ No lunch weekdays.*

Sam's Social Club

$$$ | MODERN AMERICAN | Tourists, locals, and spa guests—some of the latter in bathrobes after treatments—assemble at this resort restaurant for breakfast, lunch, bar snacks, or dinner. Lunch options include pizzas, sandwiches, an aged-cheddar burger, and entrées such as chicken paillard, with the burger reappearing for dinner along with pan-seared Alaskan halibut, rib-eye steak frites, and similar fare, perhaps preceded by oysters and other cocktail-friendly starters. **Known for:** casual atmosphere; active patio scene; thin-crust lunch pizzas. *Average main: $28 ✉ Indian Springs Resort and Spa, 1712 Lincoln Ave., Calistoga ✣ At Wappo Ave. ☎ 707/942–4969 🌐 www.samssocialclub.com.*

★ **Solbar**

$$$$ | MODERN AMERICAN | As befits a restaurant at a spa resort, the sophisticated menu at Solbar is divided into "healthy, lighter dishes" and "hearty cuisine," with the stellar wine list's many half-bottle selections encouraging moderation, too. On the lighter side, seared black cod served with bok choy, ginger endive, and carrots, with heartier options recently including hibachi-grilled Wagyu rib eye with new potatoes. **Known for:** stylish dining room; festive outdoor patio; Sunday brunch. *Average main: $35 ✉ Solage Calistoga, 755 Silverado Trail, Calistoga ✣ At Rosedale Rd. ☎ 866/942–7442 🌐 solage.aubergeresorts.com/dine.*

Hotels

Calistoga Ranch

$$$$ | RESORT | Spacious cedar-shingle lodges throughout this posh wooded Auberge Resorts property have outdoor living areas—even the restaurant, spa, and reception space have outdoor seating and fireplaces. **Pros:** many lodges have private hot tubs on the deck; hiking trails on property; guests have reciprocal facility privileges at Auberge du Soleil and Solage Calistoga. **Cons:** indoor-outdoor concept works better in fine weather than in rain or cold; no self-parking; expensive. *Rooms from: $895 ✉ 580 Lommel Rd., Calistoga ☎ 707/254–2800, 855/942–4220 🌐 www.calistogaranch.com 52 lodges No meals.*

★ **Embrace Calistoga**

$$$ | B&B/INN | Extravagant hospitality defines the Napa Valley's luxury properties, but Embrace Calistoga takes the prize in the "small lodging" category. **Pros:** attentive owners; marvelous breakfasts; restaurants, tasting rooms, and shopping within walking distance. **Cons:** light hum of street traffic; no pool or spa; two-night minimum some weekends. *Rooms from: $309 ✉ 1139 Lincoln Ave., Calistoga ☎ 707/942–9797 🌐 embracecalistoga.com 5 rooms Breakfast.*

Indian Springs Resort and Spa

$$ | RESORT | Palm-studded Indian Springs—operating as a spa since 1862—ably splits the difference between laid-back and chic in accommodations that include lodge rooms, suites, 14 historic cottages, three stand-alone bungalows, and two houses. **Pros:** palm-studded grounds with outdoor seating areas; on-site Sam's Social Club restaurant; enormous mineral pool. **Cons:** lodge rooms are small; many rooms have showers but no tubs; two-night minimum on weekends (three with Monday holiday). *Rooms from: $279* *1712 Lincoln Ave., Calistoga* *707/942–4913* *www.indianspringscalistoga.com* *113 rooms* *No meals.*

★ Solage Calistoga

$$$$ | RESORT | The aesthetic at this 22-acre property, where health and wellness are priorities, is Napa Valley barn meets San Francisco loft: guest rooms have high ceilings, polished concrete floors, recycled walnut furniture, and all-natural fabrics in soothingly muted colors. **Pros:** great service; complimentary bikes; separate pools for kids and adults. **Cons:** vibe might not suit everyone; longish walk from some lodgings to spa and fitness center; expensive in-season. *Rooms from: $481* *755 Silverado Trail, Calistoga* *866/942–7442, 707/226–0800* *www.solagecalistoga.com* *89 rooms* *No meals.*

Shopping

Calistoga Pottery

CERAMICS/GLASSWARE | You might recognize the dinnerware and other pottery sold by owners Jeff and Sally Manfredi—their biggest customers are the area's inns, restaurants, and wineries. *1001 Foothill Blvd./Hwy. 29, Calistoga* *500 feet south of Lincoln Ave.* *707/942–0216* *www.calistogapottery.com* *Closed Sun.*

SPAS

Indian Springs Spa

SPA/BEAUTY | Even before Sam Brannan constructed a spa on this site in the 1860s, the Wappo Indians were building sweat lodges over its thermal geysers. Treatments include a Calistoga-classic, pure volcanic-ash mud bath followed by a mineral bath, after which clients are wrapped in a flannel blanket for a 15-minute cool-down session or until called for a massage if they've booked one. Intraceuticals oxygen-infusion facials are another specialty. Spa clients have access to the Olympic-size mineral-water pool, kept at 92°F in summer and a toasty 102°F in winter. *1712 Lincoln Ave., Calistoga* *At Wappo Ave.* *707/942–4913* *www.indianspringscalistoga.com/spa* *Treatments from $95.*

★ Spa Solage

This eco-conscious spa reinvented the traditional Calistoga mud-and-mineral-water regimen with the hour-long "Mudslide." The three-part treatment includes a mud body mask self-applied in a heated lounge, a soak in a thermal bath, and a power nap in a sound-vibration chair. The mud here, less gloppy than at other resorts, is a mix of clay, volcanic ash, and essential oils. Traditional spa services—combination Shiatsu-Swedish and other massages, full-body exfoliations, facials, and waxes—are available, as are yoga and wellness sessions. *755 Silverado Trail, Calistoga* *At Rosedale Rd.* *707/226–0825* *solage.aubergeresorts.com/spa* *Treatments from $110.*

Activities

Calistoga Bikeshop

BICYCLING | Options here include regular and fancy bikes that rent for $28 and up for two hours, and there's a self-guided Cool Wine Tour ($110) that includes tastings at three or four small wineries. *1318 Lincoln Ave., Calistoga* *Near Washington St.* *707/942–9687* *www.calistogabikeshop.net.*

Sonoma

14 miles west of Napa, 45 miles northeast of San Francisco.

One of the few towns in the valley with multiple attractions not related to food and wine, Sonoma has plenty to keep you busy for a couple of hours before you head out to tour the wineries. And you needn't leave town to taste wine. There are about three dozen tasting rooms within steps of the tree-filled Sonoma plaza, some of which pour wines from more than one winery. The valley's cultural center, Sonoma was founded in 1835 when California was still part of Mexico.

GETTING HERE AND AROUND

Highway 12 (signed as Broadway near Sonoma Plaza) heads north into Sonoma from Highway 121 and south from Santa Rosa into downtown Sonoma, where (signed as West Spain Street) it travels east to the plaza. Parking is relatively easy to find on or near the plaza, and you can walk to many restaurants, shops, and tasting rooms. Signs point the way to several wineries a mile or more east of the plaza.

Sights

Bedrock Wine Co.

WINERY/DISTILLERY | Wines, notably Zinfandel, celebrating Sonoma County's heritage vineyards are the focus of Bedrock, whose backstory involves several historical figures. Tastings take place in a home just east of Sonoma Plaza owned in the 1850s by General Joseph Hooker. By coincidence, Hooker planted grapes at what's now the estate Bedrock Vineyard a few miles away. General William Tecumseh Sherman was his partner in the vineyard (a spat over it affected their Civil War interactions), which newspaper magnate William Randolph Hearst's father, George, replanted in the late 1880s. Some Hearst vines still produce grapes. Current owner-winemaker Morgan Twain-Peterson learned about Zinfandel from his dad, Joel Peterson, who started Ravenswood Winery. **TIP→ The shaded patio out back faces the circa-1840 Blue Wing Inn, where Hooker often partied.** ✉ *General Joseph Hooker House, 414 1st St. E, Sonoma* ☎ *707/343–1478* 🌐 *www.bedrockwineco.com* *Tastings $30* *Closed Tues.*

Buena Vista Winery

WINERY/DISTILLERY | The birthplace of modern California wine making has been transformed into an entertaining homage to the accomplishments of the 19th-century wine pioneer Count Agoston Haraszthy. Tours pass through the original aging caves dug deep into the hillside by Chinese laborers, and banners, photos, and artifacts inside and out convey the history made on this site. The rehabilitated former press house (used for pressing grapes into wine), which dates to 1862, hosts the standard tastings. Chardonnay, Pinot Noir, several red blends, and a vibrant Petit Verdot are the strong suits here. **TIP→ The high-tech Historic Wine Tool Museum displays implements, some decidedly low-tech, used to make wine over the years.** ✉ *18000 Old Winery Rd., Sonoma* ✣ *Off E. Napa St.* ☎ *800/926–1266* 🌐 *www.buenavistawinery.com* *Tastings from $20; tours from $25.*

★ The Donum Estate

WINERY/DISTILLERY | Anne Moller-Racke, the founder of this prominent Chardonnay and Pinot Noir producer, calls herself a winegrower in the French *vigneron* tradition that emphasizes agriculture—selecting vineyards with the right soils, microclimates, and varietals, then farming with precision—over wine-making wizardry. The Donum Estate, whose white board-and-batten tasting room affords guests hilltop views of Los Carneros, San Pablo Bay, and beyond, farms two vineyards surrounding the structure, along with one in the Russian River Valley and another in Mendocino County's

Cloverdale
128
Cobb Mountain
175
Geyser Peak
Alexander Valley
Dutcher Creek Rd.
Lake Sonoma
Geysers Rd.
Black Mountain
101
1
2
Geyserville
3
Russian River
128
Pine Flat Rd.
Lake Sonoma Recreation Area
West Dry Creek Rd.
Dry Creek Rd.
Lytton Springs Rd.
5
6
Lytton
Alexander Valley Rd.
7
4
Dry Creek Rd.
Healdsburg Ave.
Knights Valley
128
Calyton
Chalk Hill Rd.
Healdsburg
Mill Creek Rd.
Westside Rd.
Los Amigos Rd.
Franz Valley Rd.
Austin Creek State Recreation Area
Russian River Valley
Eastside Rd.
20
9
Porter Creek Hwy.
Sweetwater Springs Rd.
Windsor
Mark West Springs
Armstrong Redwoods State Natural Reserve
8
10
Mark West Springs Rd.
Rio Nido
11
101
River Rd.
Main St.
Guerneville
Charles P. Schulz Sonoma County Airport
Fulton
Russian River
12
River Rd.
18
Sonoma County
116
Forestville
Olivet Rd.
Fulton Rd.
Piner Rd.
13
Monte Rio
116
19
14
15
Guerneville Rd.
Santa Rosa
Graton
Bohemian Hwy
Santa Rosa Creek
Hall Rd.
Willow Creek Rd.
Occidental Rd.
Bennett Valley
Graton Rd.
Sebastopol Hwy.
16
Occidental
17
12
Petaluma Hill Rd.
Sebastopol
Taylor Mtn
Coleman Valley Rd.
Bodega Hwy.
Freestone
Stony Point Rd.
Rohnert Park
Bodega Hwy.
Cunningham
Salmon Creek
Rd.
116
1
Bodega
Bodega Bay
Cotati
Valley Ford Cutoff
Roblar Rd.
Bay Hwy.
Valley Ford
Bloomfield
40
Bloomfield
Old Redwood Hwy.
101
Petaluma Valley Ford Rd.
Bodega Bay
1
Fallon
Two Rock
Bodega Ave.
Dillon Beach
Tomales
Marin County
0
4 mi
0
4 km
Point Reyes National Seashore
Tomales Bay
Laguna Lake

Sonoma County
KEY
1 Sights
Middletown
LAKE COUNTY
Butts Canyon Rd.
Mount St Helena
Robert Louis Stevenson State Park
Aetna Springs
THE PALISADES
Pope Valley
Calistoga
Angwin
Angwin Airport
Petrified Forest Rd.
Bothe-Napa State Park
Diamond Mountain
Calistoga Rd.
Deer Park
Silverado Trail
St. Helena
NAPA COUNTY
Hood Mountain Regional Park
Bald Mountain
Rutherford
Sonoma Hwy.
Adobe Canyon Rd.
Sugarloaf Ridge State Park
Oakville Grade Rd.
Annadel State Park
Kenwood
SONOMA VALLEY
Trinity Rd.
BENNETT VALLEY
Bennett Valley Rd.
Mt Veeder
Glen Ellen
Sonoma Mountain
VALLEY OF THE MOON
Gehricke Rd.
Jack London State Park
Agua Caliente
Arnold Dr.
Boyes Hot Springs
SONOMA MOUNTAINS
E. Napa St.
Sonoma
Adobe Rd.
Napa Rd.
Washington
Carneros Hwy.
Petaluma
Bonness Rd.
Lakeville Hwy

Sights

Anderson Valley. All the wines exhibit the "power yet elegance" that sealed the winery's fame in the 2000s. Tastings are by appointment only. ■ **TIP→ Large museum-quality outdoor sculptures by Anselm Kiefer, Lynda Benglis, Ai Weiwei, and three dozen other contemporary talents add a touch of high culture to a visit here.** ✉ *24500 Ramal Rd., Sonoma* ✣ *Off Hwy. 121/12* ☎ *707/732–2200* 🌐 *www.thedonumestate.com* 🎫 *Tastings $80.*

Gloria Ferrer Caves and Vineyards
WINERY/DISTILLERY | A tasting at Gloria Ferrer is an exercise in elegance: at tables inside the Spanish hacienda–style winery or outside on the terrace (no standing at the bar at Gloria Ferrer), you can take in vistas of gently rolling Carneros hills while sipping sparkling and still wines. The Chardonnay and Pinot Noir grapes from the surrounding vineyards are the product of old-world wine-making knowledge—the same family started the sparkling-wine maker Freixenet in 16th-century Spain—and contemporary soil management techniques and clonal research. The daily tour covers *méthode traditionelle* wine making, the Ferrer family's history, and the winery's vineyard sustainability practices. ✉ *23555 Carneros Hwy./Hwy. 121, Sonoma* ☎ *707/933–1917* 🌐 *www.gloriaferrer.com* 🎫 *Tastings from $9, tour with tasting $25.*

Gundlach Bundschu
WINERY/DISTILLERY | The Bundschu family, which has owned most of this property since 1858, makes reds that include Cabernet Franc, Cabernet Sauvignon, Merlot, and a Bordeaux-style blend of each vintage's best grapes. Gewürztraminer, Chardonnay, and two rosés are also in the mix. Parts of the 1870 stone winery where standard tastings unfold are still used for wine making. For a more comprehensive experience, book a cave tour, a Pinzgauer vehicle vineyard tour, or a Heritage Reserve pairing of limited-release wines with small gourmet bites. Some tastings and all tours are by appointment only. "Gun lock bun shoe" gets you close to pronouncing this winery's name correctly, though everyone here shortens it to Gun Bun. ✉ *2000 Denmark St., Sonoma* ✣ *At Bundschu Rd., off 8th St. E, 3 miles southeast of Sonoma Plaza* ☎ *707/938–5277* 🌐 *www.gunbun.com* 🎫 *Tastings from $20, tours $45 (includes tastings).*

Hanson of Sonoma Organic Vodka
WINERY/DISTILLERY | The Hanson family makes grape-based organic vodkas, one of them straightforward and four others infused with cucumbers, ginger, mandarin oranges, and habanero and other chili peppers. To produce these vodkas and a few seasonal offerings, white wine is made from three grape types and then distilled. The family pours its vodkas, which have racked up some impressive awards, in an industrial-looking tasting room heavy on the steel, with wood reclaimed from Deep South smokehouses adding a rustic note. Because you're in a tasting room rather than a bar, there's a limit to the amount poured, but it's sufficient to get to know the product. Book distillery tours through Hanson's website. ■ **TIP→ A popular tasting involves three vodka sips and a well-mixed cocktail.** ✉ *22985 Burndale Rd., Sonoma* ✣ *Off Carneros Hwy. (Hwy. 121)* ☎ *707/343–1805* 🌐 *hansonofsonoma.com* 🎫 *Tastings from $15; tours from $25 (includes tasting).*

★ **Patz & Hall**
WINERY/DISTILLERY | Sophisticated single-vineyard Chardonnays and Pinot Noirs are the trademark of this respected winery whose tastings take place in a fashionable single-story residence 3 miles southeast of Sonoma Plaza. It's a Wine Country adage that great wines are made in the vineyard—the all-star fields represented here include Hyde, Durell, and Gap's Crown—but winemaker James Hall routinely surpasses peers with access to the same fruit, proof that

discernment and expertise (Hall is a master at oak aging) play a role, too. You can sample wines at the bar and on some days on the vineyard-view terrace beyond it, but to learn how food-friendly these wines are, consider the Salon Tasting, at which they're paired with gourmet bites. Tastings are by appointment only. ✉ *21200 8th St. E, Sonoma* ✣ *Near Peru Rd.* ☎ *707/265–7700* 🌐 *www.patzhall.com* 🎟 *Tastings from $35.*

★ Scribe

WINERY/DISTILLERY | Andrew and Adam Mariani established Scribe in 2007 on land first planted to grapes in 1858 by Emil Dresel, a German immigrant. Dresel's claims to fame include cultivating Sonoma's first Riesling and Sylvaner, an achievement the brothers honor by growing both varietals on land he once farmed. Using natural wine-making techniques, they craft bright, terroir-driven wines from those grapes, along with Chardonnay, Pinot Noir, Syrah, and Cabernet Sauvignon. In restoring their property's 1915 mission revival–style hacienda, the brothers preserved various layers of history—original molding and light fixtures, for instance, but also fragments of floral-print wallpaper and 1950s newspapers. Now a tasting space, the hacienda served during Prohibition as a bootleggers' hideout, and its basement harbored a speakeasy. Tastings, which include meze plates whose ingredients come from Scribe's farm, are by appointment only. ✉ *2100 Denmark St., Sonoma* ✣ *Off Napa Rd.* ☎ *707/939–1858* 🌐 *scribewinery.com* 🎟 *Tastings from $60.*

Sonoma Mission

RELIGIOUS SITE | The northernmost of the 21 missions established by Franciscan friars in California, Sonoma Mission was founded in 1823 as Mission San Francisco Solano. These days it serves as the centerpiece of **Sonoma State Historic Park,** which includes several other sites in Sonoma and nearby Petaluma. Some early mission structures were destroyed, but all or part of several remaining buildings date to the era of Mexican rule over California. Worth a look are the **Sonoma Barracks,** a half block west of the mission at 20 East Spain Street, which housed troops under the command of General Mariano Guadalupe Vallejo, who controlled vast tracts of land in the region. **General Vallejo's Home,** a Victorian-era structure, is a few blocks west. ✉ *114 E. Spain St., Sonoma* ✣ *At 1st St. E* ☎ *707/938–9560* 🌐 *www.parks.ca.gov* 🎟 *$3, includes same-day admission to other historic sites.*

Restaurants

★ Cafe La Haye

$$$ | **AMERICAN** | In a postage-stamp-size open kitchen (the dining room, its white walls adorned with contemporary art, is nearly as compact), chef Jeffrey Lloyd turns out understated, sophisticated fare emphasizing seasonably available local ingredients. Chicken, beef, pasta, and fish get deluxe treatment without fuss or fanfare—the daily risotto special is always good. **Known for:** Napa-Sonoma wine list with French complements; signature butterscotch pudding dessert; owner Saul Gropman on hand to greet diners. 💲 *Average main: $24* ✉ *140 E. Napa St., Sonoma* ✣ *Just off Sonoma Plaza* ☎ *707/935–5994* 🌐 *www.cafelahaye.com* ⏲ *Closed Sun. and Mon. No lunch.*

El Dorado Kitchen

$$$ | **MODERN AMERICAN** | This restaurant owes its visual appeal to its clean lines and handsome decor, but the eye inevitably drifts westward to the open kitchen, where the chefs craft dishes full of subtle surprises. The menu might include ahi tuna tartare with wasabi tobiko caviar as a starter, with paella awash with seafood and dry-cured Spanish chorizo sausage among the entrées. **Known for:** subtle tastes and textures; truffle-oil fries with Parmesan; pot de crème and other desserts. $ *Average main: $27 ✉ El Dorado Hotel, 405 1st St. W, Sonoma ✣ At W. Spain St. ☎ 707/996–3030 🌐 eldoradokitchen.com.*

★ Girl & the Fig

$$$ | FRENCH | At this hot spot for inventive French cooking inside the historic Sonoma Hotel bar, you can always find a dish with owner Sondra Bernstein's signature figs on the menu, whether it's a fig-and-arugula salad or an aperitif blending sparkling wine with fig liqueur. Also look for duck confit, a burger with matchstick fries, and wild flounder meunière. **Known for:** Rhône-wines emphasis; artisanal cheese platters; croque monsieur and eggs Benedict at Sunday brunch. $ *Average main: $28 ✉ Sonoma Hotel, 110 W. Spain St., Sonoma ✣ At 1st St. W ☎ 707/938–3634 🌐 www.thegirlandthefig.com.*

★ Harvest Moon Cafe

$$$ | AMERICAN | Everything at this little restaurant with an odd, zigzagging layout is so perfectly executed and the vibe is so genuinely warm that a visit here is deeply satisfying. The ever-changing menu might include homey dishes such as hand-cut tagliatelle with sautéed mushrooms or panfried swordfish with herbed quinoa pilaf. **Known for:** friendly service; patio dining area; husband-and-wife chefs Nick and Jen Demarest. $ *Average main: $28 ✉ 487 1st St. W, Sonoma ✣ At W. Napa St. ☎ 707/933–8160 🌐 www.harvestmooncafesonoma.com ⏲ Closed Tues. No lunch.*

Oso Sonoma

$$$ | MODERN AMERICAN | Chef David Bush, who achieved national recognition for his food pairings at St. Francis Winery, owns this barlike small-plates restaurant whose menu evolves throughout the day. Lunch might see mole-braised pork-shoulder tacos or an achiote chicken sandwich, with dinner fare perhaps of steamed mussels, miso-glazed salmon, or poutine, all of it served in an 1890s structure, erected as a livery stable, that incorporates materials reclaimed from the building's prior incarnations. **Known for:** bar menu between lunch and dinner; smart beer and wine selections; Sonoma Plaza location. $ *Average main: $29 ✉ 9 E. Napa St., Sonoma ✣ At Broadway ☎ 707/931–6926 🌐 www.ososonoma.com ⏲ No lunch Mon.–Wed.*

Sunflower Caffé

$ | AMERICAN | Whimsical art and brightly painted walls set a jolly tone at this casual eatery whose assets include sidewalk seating with Sonoma Plaza views and the verdant patio out back. Omelets and waffles are the hits at breakfast, with the smoked duck *banh mi,* served on a toasted baguette with Sriracha aioli, a favorite for lunch. **Known for:** combination café, gallery, and wine bar; local cheeses and hearty soups; free Wi-Fi. $ *Average main: $14 ✉ 421 1st St. W, Sonoma ✣ At W. Spain St. ☎ 707/996–6645 🌐 www.sonomasunflower.com ⏲ No dinner.*

Hotels

Inn at Sonoma

$$ | B&B/INN | Little luxuries delight at this well-run inn ¼-mile south of Sonoma Plaza: wine and hors d'oeuvres are served every evening in the lobby, where a jar brims with cookies from noon to 8 pm and free beverages are always available. **Pros:** last-minute specials are a great deal; comfortable beds; good soundproofing blocks out Broadway street noise. **Cons:** on a busy street rather than right on the plaza; pet-friendly rooms book up quickly; some rooms on the small side. $ *Rooms from: $249 ✉ 630 Broadway, Sonoma ☎ 707/939–1340 🌐 www.innatsonoma.com 🛏 27 rooms 🍴 Breakfast.*

★ Ledson Hotel

$$$ | B&B/INN | With just six rooms the Ledson feels intimate, and the furnishings and amenities—down beds, mood lighting, gas fireplaces, whirlpool tubs, and balconies for enjoying breakfast or a glass of wine—stack up well against Wine Country rooms costing more, especially in high season. **Pros:** convenient Sonoma Plaza location; spacious, individually decorated rooms with whirlpool tubs; complimentary tasting at ground-floor Zina Lounge wine bar. **Cons:** maximum occupancy in all rooms is two people; children must be at least 12 years old; front rooms have plaza views but pick up some street noise. *Rooms from: $350 480 1st St. E, Sonoma 707/996–9779 www.ledsonhotel.com 6 rooms Free Breakfast.*

★ **MacArthur Place Hotel & Spa**
$$$ | **HOTEL** | Guests at this 7-acre boutique property five blocks south of Sonoma Plaza bask in ritzy seclusion in plush accommodations set amid landscaped gardens. **Pros:** verdant garden setting; tranquil spa; great for a romantic getaway. **Cons:** a bit of a walk from the plaza; some traffic noise audible in street-side rooms; pricey in high season. *Rooms from: $359 29 E. MacArthur St., Sonoma 707/938–2929, 800/722–1866 www.macarthurplace.com 64 rooms No meals.*

Sigh
WINE BARS—NIGHTLIFE | From the oval bar and walls the color of a fine Blanc de Blancs to retro chandeliers that mimic champagne bubbles, everything about this sparkling-wine bar's frothy space screams "have a good time." That owner Jayme Powers and her posse are trained in the fine art of *sabrage* (opening a sparkler with a saber) only adds to the festivity. **TIP→ Sigh opens at noon, so it's a good daytime stop, too.** *120 W. Napa St., Sonoma At 1st St. W 707/996–2444 www.sighsonoma.com.*

Shopping

Sonoma Plaza is a shopping magnet, with tempting boutiques and specialty food purveyors facing the square or within a block or two.

★ **Sonoma Valley Certified Farmers Market**
OUTDOOR/FLEA/GREEN MARKETS | To discover just how bountiful the Sonoma landscape is—and how talented its farmers and food artisans are—head to Depot Park, just north of the Sonoma Plaza, on Friday morning. This market is considered Sonoma County's best. *Depot Park, 1st St. W, Sonoma At Sonoma Bike Path 707/538–7023 www.svcfm.org.*

SPAS

Willow Stream Spa at Fairmont Sonoma Mission Inn & Spa
SPA/BEAUTY | By far the Wine Country's largest spa, the Fairmont resort's 40,000-square-foot facility provides every amenity you could possibly want, including pools and hot tubs fed by local thermal springs. The signature 2½-hour Sonoma Organic Lavender Kur and Facial includes a botanical body wrap, a full-body massage, and a facial. Couples seeking romance often request the treatment room with the two-person copper bathtub. *100 Boyes Blvd./Hwy. 12, Sonoma 2½ miles north of Sonoma Plaza 707/938–9000 www.fairmont.com/sonoma/willow-stream Treatments from $79.*

Glen Ellen

7 miles north of Sonoma.

Unlike its flashier Napa Valley counterparts, Glen Ellen eschews well-groomed sidewalks lined with upscale boutiques and restaurants, preferring instead its crooked streets, some with no sidewalks at all, shaded with stands of old oak trees. Jack London, who represents Glen Ellen's rugged spirit, lived in the area for many years; the town commemorates him with place names and nostalgic establishments. Hidden among sometimes-ramshackle buildings abutting Sonoma and Calabasas creeks are low-key shops and galleries worth poking through, and several fine dining establishments.

GETTING HERE AND AROUND

Craggy Glen Ellen epitomizes the difference between the Napa and Sonoma valleys. Whereas small Napa towns like St. Helena get their charm from upscale boutiques and restaurants lined up along well-groomed sidewalks, Glen Ellen's crooked streets are shaded with stands of old oak trees and occasionally bisected by the Sonoma and Calabazas creeks. Tucked among the trees of a narrow canyon, where Sonoma Mountain and the Mayacamas pinch in the valley floor, Glen Ellen looks more like a town of the Sierra foothills gold country than a Wine Country village.

Sights

Benziger Family Winery

WINERY/DISTILLERY | One of the best-known Sonoma County wineries sits on a sprawling estate in a bowl with 360-degree sun exposure, the benefits of which are explored on tram tours that depart several times daily. Guides explain Benziger's biodynamic farming practices and provide a glimpse of the extensive cave system. Choose from a regular tram tour or a more in-depth excursion that concludes with a seated tasting. Known for Chardonnay, Cabernet Sauvignon, Merlot, Pinot Noir, and Sauvignon Blanc, the winery is a beautiful spot for a picnic. ■ **TIP→ Reserve a seat on the tram tour through the winery's website or arrive early in the day on summer weekends and during harvest season.** ✉ *1883 London Ranch Rd., Glen Ellen* ✣ *Off Arnold Dr.* ☎ *888/490–2739* 🌐 *www.benziger.com* 🎫 *Tastings from $20, tours from $30 (includes tastings).*

★ **Jack London State Historic Park**

NATIONAL/STATE PARK | The pleasures are pastoral and intellectual at author Jack London's beloved Beauty Ranch, where you could easily spend the afternoon hiking some of the 30-plus miles of trails that loop through meadows and stands of oaks, redwoods, and other trees. Manuscripts and personal artifacts depicting London's travels are on view at the House of Happy Walls Museum, which provides an overview of the writer's life, literary passions, humanitarian and conservation efforts, and promotion of organic farming. A short hike away lie the ruins of Wolf House, which burned down just before London was to move in. Also open to visitors are a few outbuildings and the restored wood-framed cottage where London penned many of his later works. He's buried on the property. ■ **TIP→ Well-known performers headline the park's Broadway Under the Stars series, a hot ticket in summer.** ✉ *2400 London Ranch Rd., Glen Ellen* ✣ *Off Arnold Dr.* ☎ *707/938–5216* 🌐 *www.jacklondonpark.com* 🎫 *Parking $10 ($5 walk-in or bike), includes admission to museum; cottage $4.*

★ **Lasseter Family Winery**

WINERY/DISTILLERY | Immaculately groomed grapevines dazzle the eye at John and Nancy Lasseter's secluded winery, and it's no accident: Phil Coturri, Sonoma Valley's premier organic vineyard manager, tends them. Even the landscaping, which includes an insectary to attract beneficial bugs, is meticulously maintained. Come harvest-time, the wine-making team oversees gentle processes that transform the fruit into wines of purity and grace: a Sémillon–Sauvignon Blanc blend, two rosés, and Bordeaux and Rhône reds. Evocative labels illustrate the tale behind each wine. These stories are well told on tours that precede some tastings of wines, paired with local artisanal cheeses, in an elegant room whose east-facing window frames

Hitching a ride on the Benziger Family Winery tram tour

vineyard and Mayacamas Mountains views. Tastings, by the glass or flight, also take place on the winery's outdoor patio. All visits are by appointment only. ✉ *1 Vintage La., Glen Ellen* ✣ *Off Dunbar Rd.* ☎ *707/933–2814* 🌐 *www.lasseterfamilywinery.com* 🎫 *Tastings (some including tours) from $30.*

Loxton Cellars

WINERY/DISTILLERY | Back in the day when tasting rooms were low-tech and the winemaker often poured the wines, the winery experience unfolded pretty much the way it does at Loxton Cellars today. The personable Australia-born owner, Chris Loxton, who's on hand many days, crafts Zinfandels, Syrahs, a Pinot Noir, and a Cabernet Sauvignon, all quite good, and some regulars swear by the seductively smooth Syrah Port. You can sample a few current releases without an appointment, but one is needed to taste library- and limited-release wines. **■ TIP→ To learn more about Loxton's wine-making philosophy and practices, book a Walkabout tour (weekends only) of the vineyard and winery that's followed by a seated tasting.** ✉ *11466 Dunbar Rd., Glen Ellen* ✣ *At Hwy. 12* ☎ *707/935–7221* 🌐 *www.loxtonwines.com* 🎫 *Tastings from $15, tour $40.*

Restaurants

Fig Cafe

$$ | **FRENCH** | The compact menu at this cheerful bistro focuses on California and French comfort food—pot roast and duck confit, for instance, as well as thin-crust pizza. Steamed mussels are served with crispy fries, which also accompany the Chef's Burger (top sirloin with Gruyère), two of the many dependable dishes that have made this restaurant a downtown Glen Ellen fixture. **Known for:** daily three-course prix-fixe specials; no corkage fee; local winemakers pouring wines on Wednesday evening. $ *Average main: $19* ✉ *13690 Arnold Dr., Glen Ellen* ✣ *At O'Donnell La.* ☎ *707/938–2130* 🌐 *www.thefigcafe.com* ⏲ *No lunch.*

★ **Glen Ellen Star**

$$$ | **ECLECTIC** | Chef Ari Weiswasser honed his craft at The French Laundry, Daniel, and other bastions of culinary finesse, but at his Wine Country outpost he prepares haute-rustic cuisine, much of it emerging from a wood-fired oven that burns a steady 600°F. Crisp-crusted, richly sauced Margherita and other pizzas thrive in the torrid heat, as do tender whole fish entrées and vegetables roasted in small iron skillets. **Known for:** kitchen-view counter for watching chefs cook; prix-fixe Wednesday "neighborhood night" menu with free corkage; Weiswasser's sauces, emulsions, and spices. *Average main: $28 ✉ 13648 Arnold Dr., Glen Ellen ✣ At Warm Springs Rd. ☎ 707/343–1384 ⊕ glenellenstar.com ⊙ No lunch.*

Hotels

★ **Gaige House + Ryokan**

$$$ | **B&B/INN** | There's no other place in Sonoma or Napa quite like the Gaige House + Ryokan, which blends the best elements of a traditional country inn, a boutique hotel, and a longtime expat's classy Asian hideaway. **Pros:** short walk to Glen Ellen restaurants, shops, and tasting rooms; bottomless jar of cookies in the common area; full breakfasts, afternoon wine and appetizers. **Cons:** sound carries in the main house; the least expensive rooms are on the small side; oriented more toward couples than families with children. *Rooms from: $358 ✉ 13540 Arnold Dr., Glen Ellen ☎ 707/935–0237, 800/935–0237 ⊕ www.gaige.com 23 rooms Breakfast.*

★ **Olea Hotel**

$$$ | **B&B/INN** | The husband-and-wife team of Ashish and Sia Patel operate this boutique lodging that's at once sophisticated and down-home country casual, and the attention to detail impresses most visitors almost instantly, from the exterior landscaping, pool, and hot tub to the colors and surfaces in the guest rooms and public spaces. **Pros:** beautiful style; complimentary wine; chef-prepared breakfasts. **Cons:** minor road noise in some rooms; fills up quickly on weekends; weekend minimum-stay requirement. *Rooms from: $308 ✉ 5131 Warm Springs Rd., Glen Ellen ✣ West off Arnold Dr. ☎ 707/996–5131 ⊕ www.oleahotel.com 15 rooms Breakfast.*

Kenwood

4 miles north of Glen Ellen.

Tiny Kenwood consists of little more than a few restaurants, shops, tasting rooms, and a historic train depot, now used for private events. But hidden in this pretty landscape of meadows and woods at the north end of Sonoma Valley are several good wineries, most just off the Sonoma Highway. Varietals grown here at the foot of the Sugarloaf Mountains include Sauvignon Blanc, Chardonnay, Zinfandel, and Cabernet Sauvignon.

GETTING HERE AND AROUND

To get to Kenwood from Glen Ellen, head northeast on Arnold Drive and north on Highway 12. Sonoma Transit Bus 30 and Bus 38 serve Kenwood from Glen Ellen and Sonoma.

B Wise Vineyards Tasting Lounge

WINERY/DISTILLERY | The stylish roadside tasting room (walk-ins welcome) of this producer of small-lot reds sits on the valley floor, but B Wise's winery and vineyards occupy prime acreage high in the Moon Mountain District AVA. The winery made its name crafting big, bold Cabernets, including one from owner Brion Wise's estate, but in recent years has also focused on Pinot Noirs from Sonoma County and Oregon's Willamette Valley. Among the other stars in the uniformly excellent lineup is the Cabernet-heavy blend Trios, whose grapes, all from Wise's estate, include Merlot, Petit Verdot, Syrah, and Tannat. The winery also makes Chardonnay and a rosé of Pinot Noir that quickly sells out. A tasting here may whet your appetite for a visit to the estate, done by appointment only. ✉ *9077 Sonoma Hwy., Kenwood* ✣ *At Shaw Ave.* ☎ *707/282–9169* 🌐 *www.bwisevineyards.com* 🎫 *Tastings $20.*

Kunde Estate Winery & Vineyards

WINERY/DISTILLERY | On your way into Kunde you pass a terrace flanked by fountains, virtually coaxing you to stay for a picnic with views over the vineyard. Family owned for more than a century, Kunde prides itself on producing 100% estate wines from its 1,850-acre property, which rises 1,400 feet from the valley floor. Kunde's whites include several Chardonnays and a Sauvignon Blanc, with Cabernet Sauvignon, Merlot, and a Zinfandel from 1880s vines among the reds. ■ **TIP→ Make a reservation for the Mountain Top Tasting, a tour by luxury van that ends with a sampling of reserve wines.** ✉ *9825 Sonoma Hwy./Hwy. 12, Kenwood* ☎ *707/833–5501* 🌐 *www.kunde.com* 🎫 *Tastings from $15, grounds and cave tour free.*

St. Francis Winery

WINERY/DISTILLERY | Nestled at the foot of Mt. Hood, St. Francis has earned national acclaim for its wine-and-food pairings. With its red-tile roof and bell tower and views of the Mayacamas Mountains just to the east, the winery's California mission–style visitors center occupies one of Sonoma County's most scenic locations. The charm of the surroundings is matched by the mostly red wines, including rich, earthy Zinfandels from the Dry Creek, Russian River, and Sonoma valleys. Five-course pairings with small bites and wine—chicken medallions with Chardonnay, for instance, or a grilled lamb chop with Cabernet Franc—are offered from Thursday through Monday; pairings with cheeses and charcuterie are available daily. ✉ *100 Pythian Rd., Kenwood* ✣ *Off Hwy. 12* ☎ *707/538–9463, 888/675–9463* 🌐 *www.stfranciswinery.com* 🎫 *Tastings from $15.*

Restaurants

★ Salt & Stone

$$$ | MODERN AMERICAN | The menu at this upscale roadhouse with a sloping wood-beamed ceiling focuses on seafood (salt) and beef, lamb, chicken, duck, and other meats (stone), with many dishes in both categories grilled. Start with the classics, perhaps a martini and oysters Rockefeller, before moving on to well-plated contemporary entrées that might include crispy-skin salmon or duck breast, fish stew, or grilled rib-eye. **Known for:** suave cocktails including signature New York Sour; mountain-view outdoor seating area; Monday–Wednesday "Bistro Nights" three-course dinners. $ *Average main: $25* ✉ *9900 Sonoma Hwy., Kenwood* ✣ *At Kunde Winery Rd.* ☎ *707/833–6326* 🌐 *www.saltstonekenwood.com* ⏲ *No lunch Tues. and Wed.*

Hotels

Kenwood Inn and Spa

$$$$ | B&B/INN | Fluffy feather beds, custom Italian furnishings, and French doors in most cases opening onto terraces or balconies lend this inn's uncommonly spacious guest rooms a romantic air. **Pros:** large rooms; lavish furnishings; romantic setting. **Cons:** road or lobby noise in some rooms; expensive in high season; geared more to couples than families with children. $ *Rooms from: $489* ✉ *10400 Sonoma Hwy./Hwy. 12, Kenwood* ☎ *707/833–1293, 800/353–6966* 🌐 *www.kenwoodinn.com* 🛏 *29 rooms* 🍴 *Breakfast.*

Healdsburg

17 miles north of Santa Rosa.

Easily Sonoma County's ritziest town and the star of many a magazine spread or online feature, Healdsburg is located at the intersection of the Dry Creek Valley, Russian River Valley, and Alexander Valley AVAs. Several dozen wineries bear a Healdsburg address, and around downtown's plaza you'll find fashionable boutiques, spas, hip tasting rooms, and art galleries, and some of the Wine Country's best restaurants. Star chef Kyle Connaughton, who opened SingleThread Farms Restaurant to much fanfare, has motivated his counterparts all over town to up their game.

Especially on weekends, you'll have plenty of company as you tour the downtown area. You could spend a day just exploring the tasting rooms and shops surrounding Healdsburg Plaza, but be sure to allow time to venture into the surrounding countryside. With orderly rows of vines alternating with beautifully overgrown hills, this is the setting you dream about when planning a Wine Country vacation. Many wineries here are barely visible, often tucked behind groves of eucalyptus or hidden high on fog-shrouded hills. Country stores and roadside farm stands alongside relatively untrafficked roads sell just-plucked fruits and vine-ripened tomatoes.

GETTING HERE AND AROUND

Healdsburg sits just off U.S. 101. Heading north, take the Central Healdsburg exit to reach Healdsburg Plaza; heading south, take the Westside Road exit and pass east under the freeway. Sonoma County Transit Bus 60 serves Healdsburg from Santa Rosa.

Sights

★ Arista Winery

WINERY/DISTILLERY | Brothers Mark and Ben McWilliams own this winery specializing in small-lot Pinot Noirs that was founded in 2002 by their parents. The sons have raised the winery's profile in several ways, most notably by hiring winemaker Matt Courtney, who has earned high praise from the *Wine Spectator* and other publications for his balanced, richly textured Pinot Noirs. Courtney shows the same deft touch with Arista's Zinfandels, Chardonnays, and a Gewürztraminer. One tasting focuses on the regions from which Arista sources its grapes, another on small-lot single-vineyard wines. Visits are by appointment only. ■ TIP→ **Guests who purchase a bottle are welcome to enjoy it in the picnic area, near a Japanese garden that predates the winery.** ✉ *7015 Westside Rd.* ☎ *707/473–0606* 🌐 *www.aristawinery.com* 🎫 *Tastings from $35.*

Dry Creek Vineyard

WINERY/DISTILLERY | Sauvignon Blanc marketed as Fumé Blanc brought instant success to the Dry Creek Valley's first new winery since Prohibition, but this area stalwart established in 1972 receives high marks as well for its Zinfandels, Bordeaux-style red blends, and Cabernet Sauvignons. In the nautical-themed tasting room—Dry Creek has featured sailing vessels on its labels since the 1980s—you can choose an all–Sauvignon Blanc flight, an all-Zinfandel one, or a mix of these and other wines. A vineyard walk and an insectary garden enhance a visit to this historic producer, a fine place for a picnic under the shade of a magnolia and several redwood trees. ■ TIP→ **You can reserve a boxed lunch two days ahead through the winery, a time-saver on busy weekends.** ✉ *3770 Lambert Bridge Rd.* ✣ *Off Dry Creek Rd.* ☎ *707/433–1000, 800/864–9463* 🌐 *www.drycreekvineyard.com* 🎫 *Tastings from $15, tour $30.*

Gary Farrell Vineyards & Winery
WINERY/DISTILLERY | Pass through an impressive metal gate and wind your way up a steep hill to reach this winery with knockout Russian River Valley views from the elegant two-tiered tasting room and terrace outside. In 2017 *Wine Enthusiast Magazine* named a Gary Farrell Chardonnay wine of the year, one among many accolades for this winery known for sophisticated single-vineyard Chardonnays and Pinot Noirs. The private Exploration Tour & Tasting, which includes a winery tour and artisanal cheeses, provides a solid introduction. The quicker Elevation Tasting (no tour) takes place inside or on the terrace; the Inspiration Tasting, in a private salon, concentrates on gifted winemaker Theresa Heredia's Pinot Noirs. ■ **TIP→ All visits are by appointment, but same-day Elevation reservations are usually possible during the week.** ✉ *10701 Westside Rd.* ☎ *707/473–2909* 🌐 *www.garyfarrellwinery.com* 🎫 *Tastings from $35, tour $45.*

★ **Jordan Vineyard and Winery**
WINERY/DISTILLERY | A visit to this 1,200-acre property revolves around an impressive estate built in the early 1970s to replicate a French château. Founders Tom and Sally Jordan—their son, John, now runs the winery—erected the structure in part to emphasize their goal of producing Sonoma County Chardonnays and Cabernet Sauvignons to rival those in the Napa Valley and France itself. A seated Library Tasting of the current release of each varietal takes place in the château, accompanied by executive chef Todd Knoll's small bites. The tasting concludes with an older vintage Cabernet Sauvignon. The 90-minute Winery Tour & Tasting includes the above, plus a walk through part of the château. All visits are by appointment only. ■ **TIP→ For a truly memorable experience, splurge on the three-hour Estate Tour & Tasting, whose pièce de résistance is the Cabernet segment, which unfolds at a 360-degree vista point overlooking vines, olive trees, and countryside.** ✉ *1474 Alexander Valley Rd.* ✣ *1½ miles east of Healdsburg Ave.* ☎ *800/654–1213, 707/431–5250* 🌐 *www.jordanwinery.com* 🎫 *Library tasting $30, winery tour and tasting $40, estate tour and tasting $120* ⏲ *Closed Sun. Dec.–Mar.*

MacRostie Estate House
WINERY/DISTILLERY | A driveway off Westside Road curls through undulating vineyard hills to the steel, wood, and heavy-on-the-glass tasting space of this longtime Chardonnay and Pinot Noir producer. Moments after you've arrived and a host has offered a glass of wine, you'll already feel transported to a genteel, rustic world. Hospitality is clearly a priority here, but so, too, is seeking out top-tier grape sources—30 for the Chardonnays, 15 for the Pinots—among them Dutton Ranch, Bacigalupi, and owner Steve MacRostie's Wildcat. With fruit this renowned, current winemaker Heidi Bridenhagen downplays the oak and other tricks of her trade, letting the vineyard settings, grape clones, and vintage do the talking. Tastings, inside or on balcony terraces with views across the Russian River Valley, are all seated. ■ **TIP→ Reservations, required on weekends, are a good idea on weekdays, too.** ✉ *4605 Westside Rd.* ✣ *Near Frost Rd.* ☎ *707/473–9303* 🌐 *macrostiewinery.com* 🎫 *Tastings from $25.*

★ **Ridge Vineyards**
WINERY/DISTILLERY | Ridge stands tall among local wineries, and not merely because its 1971 Monte Bello Cab placed first in a 30th-anniversary rematch of the famous Judgment of Paris blind tasting of California and French reds. The winery built its reputation on Cabernet Sauvignons, Zinfandels, and Chardonnays of unusual depth and complexity, but you'll also find blends of Rhône varietals. Ridge makes wines using grapes from several California locales—including the Dry Creek Valley, Sonoma Valley, Napa Valley, and Paso Robles—but the focus

is on single-vineyard estate wines, such as the Lytton Springs Zinfandel from grapes grown near the tasting room. In good weather you can sit outside, taking in views of rolling vineyard hills while you sip. **TIP→ The $25 tasting includes a pour of the top-of-the-line Monte Bello Cabernet Sauvignon from Santa Cruz Mountains grapes.** ✉ *650 Lytton Springs Rd.* ✥ *Off U.S. 101* ☎ *408/867–3233* 🌐 *www.ridgewine.com/visit/lytton-springs* 🎫 *Tastings from $10, tours from $35.*

★ Silver Oak

WINERY/DISTILLERY | The views and architecture are as impressive as the wines at the Sonoma County outpost of the same-named Napa Valley winery. In 2018, six years after purchasing a 113-acre parcel with 73 acres planted to grapes, Silver Oak debuted its ultramodern, environmentally sensitive winery and glass-walled tasting pavilion. As in Napa, the Healdsburg facility produces just one wine each year: a robust, well-balanced Alexander Valley Cabernet Sauvignon aged in American rather than French oak barrels. The walk-in tasting includes the current Alexander Valley Cabernet and Napa Valley Bordeaux blend plus an older vintage. Tours, worth taking to experience the high-tech winery, are by appointment. The winery's chef prepares several courses (enough to serve as lunch) paired with library and current Cabernets plus two or more wines of sister operation Twomey Cellars, which produces Sauvignon Blanc, Pinot Noir, and Merlot. ✉ *7370 Hwy. 128* ☎ *707/942–7082* 🌐 *www.silveroak.com* 🎫 *Tastings from $20, tours and tastings from $30.*

Restaurants

★ Barndiva

$$$$ | **AMERICAN** | Music plays quietly in the background while servers ferry the inventive seasonal cocktails of this restaurant that abandons the homey vibe of many Wine Country spots for a more urban feel. Make a light meal out of yellowtail tuna crudo or Dungeness crab salad, or settle in for the evening with pan-seared king salmon with caviar and crème fraîche or sautéed rack of lamb with gnocchi. **Known for:** cool cocktails; stylish cuisine; open-air patio. $ *Average main: $34* ✉ *231 Center St.* ✥ *At Matheson St.* ☎ *707/431–0100* 🌐 *www.barndiva.com* ⊗ *Closed Mon. and Tues.*

Bravas Bar de Tapas

$$$ | **SPANISH** | Spanish-style tapas and an outdoor patio in perpetual party mode make this restaurant, headquartered in a restored 1920s bungalow, a popular downtown perch. Contemporary Spanish mosaics set a perky tone inside, but unless something's amiss with the weather, nearly everyone heads out back for flavorful croquettes, paella, jamón, *pan tomate* (tomato toast), duck egg with chorizo cracklings, grilled octopus, skirt steak, and crispy fried chicken. **Known for:** casual small plates; specialty cocktails, sangrias, and beer; sherry flights. $ *Average main: $27* ✉ *420 Center St.* ✥ *Near North St.* ☎ *707/433–7700* 🌐 *www.barbravas.com.*

Campo Fina

$$ | **ITALIAN** | Chef Ari Rosen showcases his contemporary-rustic Italian cuisine at this converted storefront that once housed a bar notorious for boozin' and brawlin'. Sandblasted red brick, satin-smooth walnut tables, and old-school lighting fixtures strike a retro note for a menu built around pizzas and gems such as Rosen's variation on his grandmother's tomato-braised chicken with creamy-soft polenta. **Known for:** outdoor patio and boccie court out of an Italian movie set; lunch sandwiches; wines from California and Italy. $ *Average main: $20* ✉ *330 Healdsburg Ave.* ✥ *Near North St.* ☎ *707/395–4640* 🌐 *www.campofina.com.*

★ Chalkboard

$$$ | **MODERN AMERICAN** | Unvarnished oak flooring, wrought-iron accents, and a vaulted white ceiling create a polished yet rustic ambience for executive chef Shane McAnelly's playfully ambitious small-plate cuisine. Starters such as pork-belly biscuits might seem frivolous, but the silky flavor blend—maple glaze, pickled onions, and chipotle mayo playing off feathery biscuit halves—signals a supremely capable tactician at work. **Known for:** festive happy hour; pasta "flights" (choose three or six styles); The Candy Bar dessert. *Average main: $30* *Hotel Les Mars, 29 North St.* *West of Healdsburg Ave.* *707/473–8030* *www.chalkboardhealdsburg.com.*

Costeaux French Bakery

$ | **FRENCH** | Breakfast, served all day at this bright-yellow French-style bakery and café, includes the signature omelet (sun-dried tomatoes, applewood-smoked bacon, spinach, and Brie) and French toast made from thick slabs of cinnamon-walnut bread. French onion soup, salad Niçoise, and smoked-duck, cranberry-turkey, and French dip sandwiches are among the lunch favorites. **Known for:** breads, croissants, and fancy pastries; quiche and omelets; front patio (arrive early on weekends). *Average main: $14* *417 Healdsburg Ave.* *At North St.* *707/433–1913* *www.costeaux.com* *No dinner.*

★ **SingleThread Farms Restaurant**

$$$$ | **ECLECTIC** | The seasonally oriented, multicourse Japanese dinners known as *kaiseki* inspired the prix-fixe vegetarian, meat, and seafood menu at the spare, elegant restaurant—redwood walls, walnut tables, mesquite-tile floors, muted-gray yarn-thread panels—of internationally renowned culinary artists Katina and Kyle Connaughton (she farms, he cooks). As Katina describes the endeavor, the 72 microseasons of their farm—5 acres at a nearby vineyard plus SingleThread's rooftop garden of fruit trees and microgreens—dictate Kyle's rarefied fare, prepared in a theatrically lit open kitchen. **Known for:** culinary precision; new online reservation slots released on first of month; impeccable wine pairings. *Average main: $275* *131 North St.* *At Center St.* *707/723–4646* *www.singlethreadfarms.com* *No lunch weekdays.*

★ **Valette**

$$$$ | **MODERN AMERICAN** | Northern Sonoma native Dustin Valette opened this homage to the area's artisanal agricultural bounty with his brother, who runs the high-ceilinged dining room, its playful contemporary lighting tempering the austerity of the exposed concrete walls and butcher-block-thick wooden tables. Charcuterie is an emphasis, but also consider the signature day-boat scallops *en croûte* (in a pastry crust) or dishes that might include Liberty duck breast with blackberry gastrique or Padrón-pepper-crusted Alaskan halibut. **Known for:** intricate cuisine; "Trust me" (the chef) tasting menu; well-chosen mostly Northern California wines. *Average main: $34* *344 Center St.* *At North St.* *707/473–0946* *www.valettehealdsburg.com* *No lunch.*

Hotels

★ **Harmon Guest House**

$$ | **HOTEL** | A boutique sibling of the h2hotel two doors away, this downtown delight debuted in late 2018 having already earned LEED Gold status for its eco-friendly construction and operating practices. **Pros:** rooftop bar's cocktails, food menu, and views; connecting rooms and suites; convenient to Healdsburg Plaza action. **Cons:** minor room-to-room noise bleed-through; room gadgetry may flummox some guests; minimum-stay requirements some weekends. *Rooms from: $264* *227 Healdsburg Ave.* *707/922–5262* *harmonguesthouse.com* *39 rooms* *Free Breakfast.*

★ **The Honor Mansion**

$$$ | **B&B/INN** | There's a lot to like about the photogenic Honor Mansion, starting with the main 1883 Italianate

Victorian home, the beautiful grounds, the elaborate breakfasts, and the home-away-from-home atmosphere. **Pros:** homemade sweets available at all hours; pool, putting green, and boccie, croquet, tennis, and basketball courts; secluded vineyard suites with indoor soaking tubs, outdoor hot tubs. **Cons:** almost a mile from Healdsburg Plaza; walls can seem thin; weekend minimum-stay requirement includes Thursday. *$ Rooms from: $380 ✉ 891 Grove St. ☎ 707/433–4277, 800/554–4667 🌐 www.honormansion.com ⏲ Closed 2 wks at Christmas ⇨ 13 rooms 🍴 Breakfast.*

Hotel Trio Healdsburg

$$ | **HOTEL** | Named for the three major wine appellations—the Russian River, Dry Creek, and Alexander valleys—whose confluence it's near, this Residence Inn by Marriott a mile and a quarter north of Healdsburg Plaza and its many restaurants and shops caters to families and extended-stay business travelers with spacious rooms equipped with full kitchens. **Pros:** cute robot room service; full kitchens; rooms sleep up to four or six. **Cons:** 30-minute walk to downtown; slightly corporate feel; pricey in high season. *$ Rooms from: $209 ✉ 110 Dry Creek Rd. ☎ 707/433–4000 🌐 www.hoteltrio.com ⇨ 122 rooms 🍴 Free Breakfast.*

★ **River Belle Inn**

$$ | **B&B/INN** | An 1875 Victorian with a storied past and a glorious colonnaded wraparound porch anchors this boutique property along the Russian River. **Pros:** riverfront location near a dozen-plus tasting rooms; cooked-to-order full breakfasts; attention to detail. **Cons:** about a mile from Healdsburg Plaza; minimum-stay requirement on weekends; lacks on-site pool, fitness center, and other amenities. *$ Rooms from: $250 ✉ 68 Front St. ☎ 707/955–5724 🌐 www.riverbelleinn.com ⇨ 12 rooms 🍴 Free Breakfast.*

★ **SingleThread Farms Inn**

$$$$ | **B&B/INN** | A remarkable Relais & Châteaux property a block north of Healdsburg Plaza, SingleThread is the creation of husband-and-wife team Kyle and Katina Connaughton, who operate the ground-floor destination restaurant and the four guest rooms and a suite above it. **Pros:** multicourse breakfast; in-room amenities from restaurant; rooftop garden. **Cons:** expensive year-round; no pool or fitness center (free passes provided to nearby facility with both); no spa, but in-room massages available. *$ Rooms from: $1000 ✉ 131 North St. ✥ At Center St. ☎ 707/723–4646 🌐 www.singlethreadfarms.com ⇨ 5 rooms 🍴 Breakfast.*

Shopping

ART GALLERIES

★ **Gallery Lulo**

ART GALLERIES | A collaboration between a local artist and jewelry maker and a Danish-born curator, this gallery presents changing exhibits of jewelry, sculpture, and objets d'art. *✉ 303 Center St. ✥ At Plaza St. ☎ 707/433–7533 🌐 www.gallerylulo.com.*

CRAFTS

★ **One World Fair Trade**

CRAFTS | Independent artisans in developing countries create the clothing, household items, jewelry, gifts, and toys sold in this bright, well-designed shop whose owners have a shrewd eye for fine craftsmanship. *✉ 353 Healdsburg Ave. ✥ Near North St. ☎ 707/473–0880 🌐 www.oneworldfairtrade.net.*

SPAS

★ **Spa Dolce**

SPA/BEAUTY | Owner Ines von Majthenyi Scherrer has a good local rep, having run a popular nearby spa before opening this stylish facility just off Healdsburg Plaza. Spa Dolce specializes in skin and body care for men and women, and waxing and facials for women. Curved white walls and fresh-cut floral arrangements set a subdued tone for such treatments as the exfoliating Hauschka body scrub, which combines organic brown sugar with scented oil. There's a romantic room for couples to enjoy massages for two. **TIP→ Many guests come just for the European-style facials, which range from a straightforward cleansing to an anti-aging peel.** ✉ *250 Center St.* ✣ *At Matheson St.* ☎ *707/433–0177* 🌐 *www.spadolce.com* 🎫 *Treatments from $60.*

Activities

BICYCLING

★ Wine Country Bikes

BICYCLING | This shop several blocks southeast of Healdsburg Plaza is perfectly located for single or multiday treks into the Dry Creek and Russian River valleys. Bikes, including tandems, rent for $39–$145 per day. One-day tours start at $139. **TIP→ The owner and staff can help with bicycling itineraries, including a mostly gentle loop, which takes in Westside Road and Eastside Road wineries and a rusting trestle bridge, as well as a more challenging excursion to Lake Sonoma.** ✉ *61 Front St.* ✣ *At Hudson St.* ☎ *707/473–0610, 866/922–4537* 🌐 *www.winecountrybikes.com.*

Geyserville

8 miles north of Healdsburg.

Several high-profile Alexander Valley AVA wineries, including the splashy Francis Ford Coppola Winery, can be found in the town of Geyserville, a small part of which stretches west of U.S. 101 into northern Dry Creek. Not long ago this was a dusty farm town, and downtown Geyserville retains its rural character, but the restaurants, shops, and tasting rooms along the short main drag hint at Geyserville's growing sophistication.

GETTING HERE AND AROUND

From Healdsburg, the quickest route to downtown Geyserville is north on U.S. 101 to the Highway 128/Geyserville exit. Turn right at the stop sign onto Geyserville Avenue and follow the road north to the small downtown. For a more scenic drive, head north from Healdsburg Plaza along Healdsburg Avenue. About 3 miles north, jog west (left) for a few hundred feet onto Lytton Springs Road, then turn north (right) onto Geyserville Avenue. In town the avenue merges with Highway 128. Sonoma County Transit Bus 60 serves Geyserville from downtown Healdsburg.

Sights

Francis Ford Coppola Winery

WINERY/DISTILLERY | **FAMILY** | The fun at what the film director calls his "wine wonderland" is all in the excess. You may find it hard to resist having your photo snapped standing next to Don Corleone's desk from *The Godfather* or beside other memorabilia from Coppola films (including some directed by his daughter, Sofia). A bandstand reminiscent of one in *The Godfather Part II* is the centerpiece of a large pool area where you can rent a changing room, complete with shower, and spend the afternoon lounging poolside, perhaps ordering food from the adjacent café. A more elaborate restaurant, Rustic, overlooks the vineyards. As for the wines, the excess continues in the cellar, where several dozen varietal wines and blends are produced. ✉ *300 Via Archimedes* ✣ *Off U.S. 101* ☎ *707/857–1400* 🌐 *www.franciscoppolawinery.com* 🎫 *Tastings free–$25, tours $50, pool pass from $40.*

★ Locals Tasting Room

WINERY/DISTILLERY | If you're serious about wine, Carolyn Lewis's tasting room alone is worth a trek 8 miles north of Healdsburg Plaza to downtown Geyserville. Connoisseurs who appreciate Lewis's ability to spot up-and-comers head here regularly to sample the output of a dozen or so small wineries, most without tasting rooms of their own. There's no fee for tasting—extraordinary for wines of this quality—and the extremely knowledgeable staff are happy to pour you a flight of several wines so you can compare, say, different Cabernet Sauvignons. *21023A Geyserville Ave. At Hwy. 128 707/857–4900 www.tastelocalwines.com Tastings free.*

★ Robert Young Estate Winery

WINERY/DISTILLERY | Panoramic Alexander Valley views unfold at Scion House, the stylish yet informal knoll-top tasting space this longtime Geyserville grower opened in 2018. The first Youngs began farming this land in the mid-1800s, raising cattle and growing wheat, prunes, and other crops. In the 1960s the late Robert Young, of the third generation, began cultivating grapes, eventually planting two Chardonnay clones now named for him. Grapes from them go into the Area 27 Chardonnay, noteworthy for the quality of its fruit and craftsmanship. The reds—small-lot Cabernet Sauvignons plus individual bottlings of Cabernet Franc, Malbec, Merlot, and Petit Verdot—shine even brighter. Tastings at Scion House, named for the fourth generation, whose members built on Robert Young's legacy and established the winery, are by appointment, but the winery accommodates walk-ins when possible. *5120 Red Winery Rd. Off Hwy. 128 707/431–4811 www.ryew.com Tastings from $25 Closed Tues.*

★ Zialena

WINERY/DISTILLERY | Sister-and-brother team Lisa and Mark Mazzoni (she runs the business, he makes the wines) debuted their small winery's first vintage in 2014, but their Italian-American family's Alexander Valley wine-making heritage stretches back more than a century. Mark—whose on-the-job teachers included the late Mike Lee of Kenwood Vineyards and Philippe Melka, a premier international consultant—specializes in smooth Zinfandel and nuanced Cabernet Sauvignon. Most of the grapes come from the 120-acre estate vineyard farmed by Lisa and Mark's father, Mike, who sells to Jordan and other big-name wineries. Other Zialena wines include a Sauvignon Blanc and Cappella, a Zin-based blend Lisa describes as "Mark's fun wine." Tastings take place in a contemporary stone, wood, and glass tasting room amid the family's vineyards. Tours, one focusing on production, the other on the vineyards, are by appointment only. *21112 River Rd. Off Hwy. 128 707/955–5992 www.zialena.com Tastings from $15, tours $50.*

Restaurants

Diavola Pizzeria & Salumeria

$$ | ITALIAN | A dining area with hardwood floors, a pressed-tin ceiling, and exposed-brick walls provides a fitting setting for the rustic cuisine at this Geyserville mainstay. Chef Dino Bugica studied with several artisans in Italy before opening this restaurant that specializes in pizzas pulled from a wood-burning oven and several types of house-cured meats, with a few salads and meaty main courses rounding out the menu. **Known for:** talented chef; smoked pork belly, pancetta, and spicy Calabrese sausage; casual setting. *Average main: $20 21021 Geyserville Ave. At Hwy. 128 707/814–0111 www.diavolapizzeria.com.*

Hotels

Geyserville Inn

$ | HOTEL | Clever travelers give the Healdsburg hubbub and prices the heave-ho but still have easy access to outstanding Dry Creek and Alexander Valley wineries from this modest, motel-like inn. **Pros:** outdoor pool; second-floor rooms in back have vineyard views; picnic area. **Cons:** rooms facing pool or highway can be noisy; not much style; some maintenance issues. *Rooms from: $179 21714 Geyserville Ave. 707/857–4343, 877/857–4343 www.geyservilleinn.com 41 rooms No meals.*

Forestville

13 miles southwest of Healdsburg.

To experience the Russian River AVA's climate and rusticity, follow the river's westward course to the town of Forestville, home to a highly regarded restaurant and inn and a few wineries producing Pinot Noir from the Russian River Valley and well beyond.

GETTING HERE AND AROUND

To reach Forestville from U.S. 101, drive west from the River Road exit north of Santa Rosa. From Healdsburg, follow Westside Road west to River Road and then continue west. Sonoma County Transit Bus 20 serves Forestville.

Sights

★ Hartford Family Winery

WINERY/DISTILLERY | Pinot Noir lovers appreciate the subtle differences in the wines Hartford's Jeff Stewart crafts from grapes grown in four Sonoma County AVAs, along with fruit from nearby Marin and Mendocino counties and Oregon. Stewart also makes highly rated Chardonnays and old-vine Zinfandels. If the weather's good and you've made a reservation, you can enjoy a flight of five or six wines on the patio outside the opulent main winery building. Indoors, at seated private library tastings, guests sip current and older vintages. **TIP→ Hartford also has a tasting room in downtown Healdsburg.** *8075 Martinelli Rd. Off Hwy. 116 or River Rd. 707/887–8030, 800/588–0234 www.hartfordwines.com Tastings from $25.*

Joseph Jewell Wines

WINERY/DISTILLERY | Micah Joseph Wirth and Adrian Jewell Manspeaker founded this winery whose name combines their middle ones. Pinot Noirs from the Russian River Valley and Humboldt County to the north are the strong suit. Wirth, who worked for seven years for vintner Gary Farrell, credits his interactions with Farrell's Russian River growers, among them the owners of Bucher Vineyard and Hallberg Ranch, with easing the winery's access to prestigious fruit. Manspeaker, a Humboldt native, spearheaded the foray into Pinot Noir grown in the coastal redwood country. Joseph Jewell's playfully rustic storefront tasting room in downtown Forestville provides the opportunity to experience what's unique about the varietal's next Northern California frontier. The bonuses: a Zinfandel from 1970s vines and two Chardonnays. *6542 Front St. 707/820–1621 www.josephjewell.com Tastings from $10, tours from $105 per couple ($500 tour is in a helicopter).*

Restaurants

Backyard

$$$ | **MODERN AMERICAN** | The folks behind this casually rustic modern American restaurant regard Sonoma County's farms and gardens as their "backyard" and proudly list their purveyors on the menu. Dinner entrées, which change seasonally, might include herb tagliatelle with goat sausage or chicken pot pie. **Known for:** buttermilk fried chicken with buttermilk biscuits to stay or go; poplar-shaded outdoor front patio in good weather; Monday locals'-night specials, plus live music. *Average main: $26 6566 Front St./Hwy. 116 At 1st St. 707/820–8445 backyardforestville.com Closed Tues.–Thurs.*

Russian River Valley AVA

As the Russian River winds its way from Mendocino to the Pacific Ocean, it carves out a valley that's a near-perfect environment for growing certain grape varietals. Because of the low elevation, sea fog pushes far inland to cool the soil, yet in summer it burns off, giving the grapes enough sun to ripen properly. Fog-loving Pinot Noir and Chardonnay grapes are king and queen in the Russian River Valley AVA, which extends from Healdsburg west to the town Guerneville. The namesake river does its part by slowly carving its way downward through many layers of rock, depositing a deep layer of gravel that in parts of the valley measures 60 or 70 feet. This gravel forces the roots of grapevines to go deep in search of water and nutrients. In the process, the plants absorb trace minerals that add complexity to the flavor of the grapes.

Hotels

★ The Farmhouse Inn
$$$$ | B&B/INN | With a farmhouse-meets-modern-loft aesthetic, this low-key but upscale getaway with a pale-yellow exterior contains spacious rooms filled with king-size four-poster beds, whirlpool tubs, and hillside-view terraces. **Pros:** fantastic restaurant; luxury bath products; full-service spa. **Cons:** mild road noise audible in rooms closest to the street; two-night minimum on weekends; pricey, especially during high season. *Rooms from: $545 7871 River Rd. 707/887–3300, 800/464–6642 www.farmhouseinn.com 25 rooms Breakfast.*

Activities

Burke's Canoe Trips
CANOEING/ROWING/SKULLING | You'll get a real feel for the Russian River's flora and fauna on a leisurely 10-mile paddle downstream from Burke's to Guerneville. A shuttle bus returns you to your car at the end of the journey, which is best taken from late May through mid-October and, in summer, on a weekday—summer weekends can be crowded and raucous. *8600 River Rd. At Mirabel Rd. 707/887–1222 www.burkescanoetrips.com $78 per canoe.*

Guerneville

7 miles northwest of Forestville, 15 miles southwest of Healdsburg.

Guerneville's tourist demographic has evolved over the years—Bay Area families in the 1950s, lesbians and gays starting in the 1970s, and these days a mix of both groups, plus techies and outdoorsy types—with coast redwoods and the Russian River always central to the town's appeal. The area's most famous winery is Korbel Champagne Cellars, established nearly a century and a half ago. Even older are the stands of trees that except on the coldest winter days make Armstrong Redwoods State Natural Reserve such a perfect respite from wine tasting.

GETTING HERE AND AROUND

To get to Guerneville from Healdsburg, follow Westside Road south to River Road and turn west. From Forestville, head west on Highway 116; alternatively, you can head north on Mirabel Road to River Road and then head west. Sonoma County Transit Bus 20 serves Guerneville.

Sights

★ Armstrong Redwoods State Natural Reserve
NATIONAL/STATE PARK | **FAMILY** | Here's your best opportunity in the western Wine Country to wander amid *Sequoia sempervirens,* also known as coast redwood trees. The oldest example in this 805-acre state park, the Colonel Armstrong Tree, is thought to be more than 1,400 years old. A half mile from the parking lot, the tree is easily accessible, and you can hike a long way into the forest before things get too hilly. ■ TIP→ **During hot summer days, Armstrong Redwoods's tall trees help the park keep its cool.** ⊠ *17000 Armstrong Woods Rd.* ✥ *Off River Rd.* ☎ *707/869–2958 for visitor center, 707/869–2015 for park headquarters* ⊕ *www.parks.ca.gov* *$8 per vehicle, free to pedestrians and bicyclists.*

Restaurants

★ boon eat+drink
$$$ | **MODERN AMERICAN** | A casual storefront restaurant on Guerneville's main drag, boon eat+drink has a menu built around small, "green" (salads and cooked vegetables), and main plates assembled for the most part from locally produced organic ingredients. Like many of chef-owner Crista Luedtke's dishes, the signature polenta lasagna—creamy ricotta salata cheese and polenta served on greens sautéed in garlic, all of it floating upon a spicy marinara sauce—deviates significantly from the lasagna norm but succeeds on its own merits. **Known for:** adventurous culinary sensibility; all wines from Russian River Valley; local organic ingredients. [$] *Average main: $23* ⊠ *16248 Main St.* ✥ *At Church St.* ☎ *707/869–0780* ⊕ *eatatboon.com* ⊙ *Closed Wed.*

Hotels

boon hotel+spa
$ | **HOTEL** | Redwoods, Douglas firs, and palms supply shade and seclusion at this lushly landscaped resort ¾ mile north of downtown Guerneville. **Pros:** memorable breakfasts; pool area and on-site spa; complimentary bikes. **Cons:** lacks amenities of larger properties; pool rooms too close to the action for some guests; can be pricey in high season. [$] *Rooms from: $195* ⊠ *14711 Armstrong Woods Rd.* ☎ *707/869–2721* ⊕ *boonhotels.com* *15 rooms* *Breakfast.*

Sebastopol

6 miles east of Occidental, 7 miles southwest of Santa Rosa.

A stroll through downtown Sebastopol—a town formerly known more for Gravenstein apples than for grapes but these days a burgeoning wine hub—reveals glimpses of the distant and recent past and perhaps the future, too. Many hippies settled here in the 1960s and 70s and, as the old Crosby, Stills, Nash & Young song goes, they taught their children well: the town remains steadfastly, if not entirely, countercultural.

GETTING HERE AND AROUND

Sebastopol can be reached from Occidental by taking Graton Road east to Highway 116 and turning south. From Santa Rosa, head west on Highway 12. Sonoma County Transit Buses 20, 22, 24, and 26 serve Sebastopol.

Sights

The Barlow
MARKET | A multibuilding complex on the site of a former apple cannery, The Barlow celebrates Sonoma County's "maker" culture with tenants who produce or sell wine, beer, spirits, crafts,

clothing, art, and artisanal food and herbs. Only club members and guests on the allocation waiting list can visit the anchor wine tenant, Kosta Browne, but MacPhail, Pax, and Friedeman have tasting rooms open to the public. Crooked Goat Brewing and Woodfour Brewing Company make and sell ales, and you can have a nip of vodka, gin, sloe gin, or wheat and rye whiskey at Spirit Works Distillery. A locally renowned mixologist teamed up with the duo behind nearby Lowell's and Handline restaurants to open Fern Bar, whose zero-proof (as in nonalcoholic) cocktails entice as much as the traditional ones. ✉ *6770 McKinley St.* ✥ *At Morris St., off Hwy. 12* ☎ *707/824–5600* 🌐 *www.thebarlow.net* 🎫 *Complex free; tasting fees at wineries, breweries, distillery.*

★ Dutton-Goldfield Winery

WINERY/DISTILLERY | An avid cyclist whose previous credits include developing the wine-making program at Hartford Court, Dan Goldfield teamed up with fifth-generation farmer Steve Dutton to establish this small operation devoted to cool-climate wines. Goldfield modestly strives to take Dutton's meticulously farmed fruit and "make the winemaker unnoticeable," but what impresses the most about these wines, which include Pinot Blanc, Chardonnay, Pinot Noir, and Zinfandel, is their sheer artistry. Among the ones to seek out are the Angel Camp Pinot Noir, from Anderson Valley (Mendocino County) grapes, and the Morelli Lane Zinfandel, from grapes grown on the remaining 1.8 acres of an 1880s vineyard Goldfield helped revive. Tastings often begin with Pinot Blanc, a white-wine variant of Pinot Noir, proceed through the reds, and end with a palate-cleansing Chardonnay. ✉ *3100 Gravenstein Hwy. N/Hwy. 116* ✥ *At Graton Rd.* ☎ *707/827–3600* 🌐 *www.duttongoldfield.com* 🎫 *Tastings from $20.*

★ Iron Horse Vineyards

WINERY/DISTILLERY | A meandering one-lane road leads to this winery known for its sparkling wines and estate Chardonnays and Pinot Noirs. The sparklers have made history: Ronald Reagan served them at his summit meetings with Mikhail Gorbachev; George H. W. Bush took some along to Moscow for treaty talks; and Barack Obama included them at official state dinners. Despite Iron Horse's brushes with fame, a casual rusticity prevails at its outdoor tasting area (large heaters keep things comfortable on chilly days), which gazes out on acres of rolling, vine-covered hills. Regular tours take place on weekdays at 10 am. Tastings and tours are by appointment only. ■ TIP→ **When his schedule permits, winemaker David Munksgard leads a private tour by truck at 10 am on Monday.** ✉ *9786 Ross Station Rd.* ✥ *Off Hwy. 116* ☎ *707/887–1507* 🌐 *www.ironhorsevineyards.com* 🎫 *Tastings $30, tours from $50 (includes tasting).*

Restaurants

Handline Coastal California

$ | **MODERN AMERICAN** | **FAMILY** | Lowell Sheldon and Natalie Goble, who also run a fine-dining establishment (Lowell's) a mile away, converted Sebastopol's former Foster's Freeze location into a 21st-century fast-food palace that won design awards for its rusted-steel frame and translucent panel-like windows. Their menu, a paean to coastal California cuisine, includes oysters raw and grilled, fish tacos, ceviches, tostadas, three burgers (beef, vegetarian, and fish), and, honoring the location's previous incarnation, chocolate and vanilla soft-serve ice cream for dessert. **Known for:** upscale comfort food; outdoor patio; sustainable seafood and other ingredients. 💲 *Average main: $14* ✉ *935 Gravenstein Hwy. S* ✥ *Near Hutchins Ave.* ☎ *707/827–3744* 🌐 *www.handline.com.*

★ **Ramen Gaijin**
$$ | JAPANESE | Inside a tall-ceilinged, brick-walled, vaguely industrial-looking space with reclaimed wood from a coastal building backing the bar, the chefs in Ramen Gaijin's turn out richly flavored ramen bowls brimming with crispy pork belly, woodear mushrooms, seaweed, and other well-proportioned ingredients. *Izakaya* (Japanese pub grub) dishes like *donburi* (meat and vegetables over rice) are another specialty, like the ramen made from mostly local proteins and produce. **Known for:** craft cocktails by renowned mixologist Scott Beattie, Japanese whiskeys; gluten-free, vegetarian dishes; pickle, karage (fried-chicken thigh), and other small plates. *Average main: $17 ✉ 6948 Sebastopol Ave. ✣ Near Main St. ☎ 707/827–3609 🌐 www.ramengaijin.com ⊗ Closed Sun. and Mon.*

Santa Rosa

6 miles east of Sebastopol, 55 miles north of San Francisco.

Urban Santa Rosa isn't as popular with tourists as many Wine Country destinations—which isn't surprising, seeing as there are more office parks than wineries within its limits. Nevertheless, this hardworking town is home to a couple of interesting cultural offerings and a few noteworthy restaurants and vineyards. The city's chain motels and hotels can be handy if you're finding that everything else is booked up, especially since Santa Rosa is roughly equidistant from Sonoma, Healdsburg, and the western Russian River Valley, three of Sonoma County's most popular wine-tasting destinations.

GETTING HERE AND AROUND

To get to Santa Rosa from Sebastopol, drive east on Highway 12. From San Francisco, cross the Golden Gate Bridge and continue north on U.S. 101. Santa Rosa's hotels, restaurants, and wineries are spread over a wide area; factor in extra time when driving around the city, especially during morning and evening rush hour. To get here from downtown San Francisco, take Golden Gate Transit Bus 101. Several Sonoma County Transit buses serve the city and surrounding area.

Sights

Balletto Vineyards
WINERY/DISTILLERY | A few decades ago Balletto was known for quality produce more than for grapes, but the new millennium saw vineyards emerge as the core business. About 90% of the fruit from the family's 650-plus acres goes to other wineries, with the remainder destined for Balletto's estate wines. The house style is light on the oak, high in acidity, and low in alcohol content, a combination that yields exceptionally food-friendly wines. On a hot summer day, sipping a Pinot Gris, rosé of Pinot Noir, or brut rosé sparkler on the outdoor patio can feel transcendent, but the superstars are the Chardonnays and Pinot Noirs. **TIP→ Look for the Teresa's unoaked and Cider Ridge Chardonnays and the Burnside Road, Sexton Hill, and Winery Block Pinots, but all the wines are exemplary—and, like the tastings, reasonably priced.** *✉ 5700 Occidental Rd. ✣ 2½ miles west of Hwy. 12 ☎ 707/568–2455 🌐 www.ballettovineyards.com Tastings $10.*

Charles M. Schulz Museum
MUSEUM | FAMILY | Fans of Snoopy and Charlie Brown will love this museum dedicated to the late Charles M. Schulz, who lived his last three decades in Santa Rosa. Permanent installations include a re-creation of the cartoonist's studio, and temporary exhibits often focus on a particular theme in his work. **TIP→ Children and adults can take a stab at creating cartoons in the Education Room.** *✉ 2301 Hardies La. ✣ At W. Steele La.*

☎ *707/579–4452* 🌐 *www.schulzmuseum.org* 🎫 *$12* ⏲ *Closed Tues. early Sept.–late May.*

★ Martinelli Winery

WINERY/DISTILLERY | In a century-old hop barn with the telltale triple towers, Martinelli has the feel of a traditional country store, but the sophisticated wines made here are anything but old-fashioned. The winery's reputation rests on its complex Pinot Noirs, Syrahs, and Zinfandels, including the Jackass Hill Vineyard Zin, made with grapes from 130-year-old vines. Noted winemaker Helen Turley set the Martinelli style—fruit-forward, easy on the oak, reined-in tannins—in the 1990s, and the current team continues this approach. You can sample current releases at a walk-in tasting at the bar or reserve space a couple of days ahead for a seated tasting on the vineyard-view terrace. Rarer and top-rated vintages are poured at appointment-only sessions. ✉ *3360 River Rd., Windsor* ✣ *East of Olivet Rd.* ☎ *707/525–0570, 800/346–1627* 🌐 *www.martinelliwinery.com* 🎫 *Tastings from $25.*

Safari West

NATURE PRESERVE | **FAMILY** | An unexpected bit of wilderness in the Wine Country, this preserve with African wildlife covers 400 acres. Begin your visit with a stroll around enclosures housing lemurs, cheetahs, giraffes, and rare birds like the brightly colored scarlet ibis. Next, climb with your guide onto open-air vehicles that spend about two hours combing the expansive property, where more than 80 species—including gazelles, cape buffalo, antelope, wildebeests, and zebras—inhabit the hillsides. ■ **TIP→ If you'd like to extend your stay, lodging in swank Botswana-made tent cabins is available.** ✉ *3115 Porter Creek Rd.* ✣ *Off Mark West Springs Rd.* ☎ *707/579–2551, 800/616–2695* 🌐 *www.safariwest.com* 🎫 *From $83.*

Restaurants

★ Bistro 29

$$$ | **FRENCH** | Chef Brian Anderson prepares steak frites, cassoulet, duck confit, and sautéed fish with precision at his perky downtown restaurant—rich-red walls, white tile floors, and butcher paper atop linen tablecloths set the mood—but the mixed-greens salad with Dijon vinaigrette best illustrates his understated approach: its local produce bursts with freshness, and the dressing delicately balances its savory and acidic components. Start with escargots or bay scallops with béchamel, finishing with beignets or orange crème brûlée for dessert. **Known for:** midweek prix-fixe menu; sweet and savory crepes; beer selection, Sonoma County and French wines. 💲 *Average main: $27* ✉ *620 5th St.* ✣ *Near Mendocino Ave.* ☎ *707/546–2929* 🌐 *www.bistro29.com* ⏲ *Closed Sun. and Mon. No lunch Sat.*

★ The Spinster Sisters

$$$ | **MODERN AMERICAN** | Modern, well-sourced variations on eggs Benedict and other standards are served at this concrete-and-glass hot spot's weekday breakfast and weekend brunch. Lunch might bring carrot soup, wilted kale salad, or a *banh mi* sandwich, with dinner consisting of shareable bites and small and large plates—think kimchi-and-bacon deviled eggs, vegetable *fritto misto,* and grilled hanger steak. **Known for:** local and international wines; happy hour (Tuesday–Friday 4 pm–6 pm) small bites; horseshoe-shaped bar a good perch for dining single, picking up gossip. 💲 *Average main: $26* ✉ *401 S. A St.* ✣ *At Sebastopol Ave.* ☎ *707/528–7100* 🌐 *thespinstersisters.com* ⏲ *No dinner Sun. and Mon.*

Hotels

Vintners Inn

$$ | HOTEL | With a countryside location, a sliver of style, and spacious rooms with comfortable beds, the Vintners Inn further seduces with a slew of amenities and a scenic vineyard landscape. **Pros:** John Ash & Co. restaurant; jogging path through the vineyards; online deals pop up year-round. **Cons:** occasional noise from adjacent events center; trips to downtown Santa Rosa or Healdsburg require a car; pricey on summer and fall weekends. *Rooms from: $295* *4350 Barnes Rd.* *707/575–7350, 800/421–2584* *www.vintnersinn.com* *78 rooms* *No meals.*

Petaluma

14 miles west of Sonoma, 39 miles north of San Francisco.

The first thing you should know about Petaluma is that this is a farm town—with more than 60,000 residents, a large one—and the residents are proud of it. Recent years have seen an uptick in the quality of Petaluma cuisine, fueled in part by the proliferation of local organic and artisanal farms and boutique wine production. With the 2018 approval of the Petaluma Gap AVA, the town even has its name on a wine appellation.

Petaluma's agricultural history reaches back to the mid-1800s, when General Mariano Vallejo established Rancho de Petaluma as the headquarters of his vast agrarian empire. From the late 1800s into the 1960s Petaluma marketed itself as the "Egg Capital of the World," and with production totals that peaked at 612 million eggs in 1946, the point was hard to dispute. Although a poultry processor remains Petaluma's second-largest employer, the town has diversified. The adobe, an interesting historical stop, was once the area's *only* employer, but these days its visitation figures are dwarfed by Lagunitas Brewing Company, whose free tour is a hoot. At McEvoy Ranch, which started out producing gourmet olive oil and now also makes wine, you can taste both products and tour parts of the farm.

GETTING HERE AND AROUND

Petaluma lies west of Sonoma and southwest of Glen Ellen and Kenwood. From Highway 12 or Arnold Drive, take Watmaugh Road west to Highway 116 west. Sonoma Transit buses (Nos. 30, 40, and 53) serve Petaluma from the Sonoma Valley. From San Francisco take U.S. 101 (or Golden Gate Transit Bus 101) north.

Sights

Keller Estate

WINERY/DISTILLERY | This boutique winery's guests discover why "wind to wine" is the Petaluma Gap AVA's slogan. The steady Pacific Ocean and San Pablo Bay breezes that mitigate the midday heat give the grapes thick "sailor's skin," heightening their tannins and flavor, says Ana Keller, whose parents planted vineyards three decades ago on former dairy fields. Keller Estate concentrates on Chardonnay, Pinot Noir, and Syrah. In good weather, tastings take place on a stone terrace shaded by umbrellas and flowering pear trees. Book a walking tour to see the property's cave, winery, vineyards, and olive trees, or go farther afield touring in a 1956 Mercedes van. **TIP→ The winery requires reservations for all tastings and tours, but same-day visits are usually possible if you call ahead.** *5875 Lakeville Hwy.* *At Cannon La.* *707/765–2117* *www.kellerestate.com* *Tastings $25, tours (with tastings) from $35* *Closed Tues. and Wed.*

★ Lagunitas Brewing Company

WINERY/DISTILLERY | These days owned by Heineken International, Lagunitas began as a craft brewery in Marin County in 1993 before moving to Petaluma in 1994. In addition to its large facility, the company operates a taproom, the Schwag Shop, and an outdoor beer garden that in good weather bustles even at midday. Guides leading the free weekday Tasting/Walking Tour, which starts with a flight of four beers, provide an irreverent version of the company's rise to international acclaim. An engaging tale involves the state alcohol board's sting operation commemorated by Undercover Investigation Shut-down Ale, one of several small-batch brews made here. **TIP→ The taproom closes on Monday and Tuesday, but tours take place and the gift shop stays open.** *1280 N. McDowell Blvd. ½ mile north of Corona Rd. 707/769–4495 lagunitas.com/taproom/petaluma Tour free Taproom closed Mon. and Tues.*

★ McEvoy Ranch

WINERY/DISTILLERY | The pastoral retirement project of the late Nan McEvoy after departing as board chair of the *San Francisco Chronicle,* the ranch produces organic extra virgin olive oil and Pinot Noir and other wines, the estate ones from the Petaluma Gap AVA. Some guests sip a few selections at the bar inside, but far better is to reserve an At Our Table Tasting of wines, oils, seasonal edibles from the organic gardens, and artisanal cheeses. In good weather these relaxing sessions unfold on a pond's-edge flagstone patio with views of alternating rows of Syrah grapes and mature olive trees. Walkabout Ranch Tours of four guests or more take in vineyards, gardens, a Chinese pavilion, and other sites. All visits require an appointment. *5935 Red Hill Rd. 6½ miles south of downtown 866/617–6779 www.mcevoyranch.com Tastings from $20, tour and tasting $95 Closed Mon. and Tues. No tour Sun.*

Restaurants

★ Central Market

$$$ | MODERN AMERICAN | A participant in the Slow Food movement, Central Market serves creative, upscale Cal-Mediterranean dishes—many of whose ingredients come from the restaurant's organic farm—in a century-old building with exposed brick walls and an open kitchen. The menu, which changes daily depending on chef Tony Najiola's inspiration and what's ripe and ready, might include tortilla soup or a buttermilk-fried halibut-cheeks starter, a slow-roasted-beets salad, pizzas and stews, and wood-grilled fish and meat. **Known for:** chef's tasting menus; superior wine list; historic setting. *Average main: $25 42 Petaluma Blvd. N Near Western Ave. 707/778–9900 www.centralmarketpetaluma.com Closed Wed. No lunch.*

★ Pearl

$$ | MEDITERRANEAN | Regulars of this southern Petaluma "daytime café" with indoor and outdoor seating rave about its Eastern Mediterranean–inflected cuisine—then immediately downplay their enthusiasm lest this 2018 arrival become more popular. The menu, divided into "smaller," "bigger," and "sweeter" options, changes often, but mainstays include buckwheat polenta, a lamb burger dripping with tzatziki (pickled fennel and yogurt sauce), and *shakshuka* (tomato-based stew with chickpeas, fava beans, and baked egg). **Known for:** weekend brunch; zippy beverage lineup; menu prices include gratuity. *Average main: $18 500 1st St. At G St. 707/559–5187 pearlpetaluma.com Closed Tues. No dinner.*

Index

D

E

F

X

Y

Z

Photo Credits

Front Cover: Huber Images/eStock Photo [Description: View from the Urban District of North Beach towards Transamerica Pyramid, San Francisco, California]. Back cover, from left to right: Jaspe/Dreamstime.com; Serrnovik/Dreamstime.com; Lunamarina/Dreamstime.com. Spine: holbox/Shutterstock. Interior from left to right: IM_photo/Shutterstock (1). travelview/Shutterstock (2). Pius Lee/Shutterstock (5). **Chapter 1:Experience San Francisco:** f11photo/Shutterstock (6-7). Scott Wilson / Alamy Stock Photo (8-9). Jill Krueger (9). Ekaterina Pokrovsky/shutterstock (9). Tetra Images, LLC / Alamy Stock Photo (10). Steve Wood/shutterstock (10). Pung/shutterstock (10). canyalcin/ shutterstock (10). Matt Boyle/shutterstock (11). Dan Henson/shutterstock (11). Della Huff/Alamy Stock Photo (12). Gene X Hwang/Orange Photography (12). Alex Zyuzikov/shutterstock (12). Maciej Bledowski/shutterstock (12). Zachary Frank / Alamy Stock Photo (13). TJ Muzeni (14). eye35 stock / Alamy Stock Photo (14). TJ Mueni (14). Courtesy of Tonga Room (14). dibrova/shutterstock (15). Engel Ching/shutterstock (15). Sundry Photography/shutterstock (16). Courtesy of Tartine Bakery (16). Paul Juser/shutterstock.com (16). Courtesy of Musée Mécanique (16). Matthew Kiernan / Alamy Stock Photo (17). Courtesy of Bluxome Street Winery (22). Courtesy of Boudin Bakery (22). Marc Fiorito - Gamma Nine Photography (22). Photo Copyright, Jack Hollingsworth (23). Courtesy of Blue Bottle Coffee (23). ESB Professional/Shutterstock (24). Jemny/Shutterstock (24). Jill Krueger (24). TJ Muzeni (24). MNStudio/Shutterstock (25). Eug Png/Shutterstock (25). Morenovel/Shutter-stock (25). kropic1/Shutterstock (25). Book Club of California (26). Alison Taggart-Barone/Parks Conservancy (26). Courtesy of Kabuki Springs & Spa (26). Courtesy of TreasureFest (26). JHVEPhoto/Shutterstock (27). canadastock/Shutterstock (35). Pius Lee/Shutterstock (37). San Francisco Municipal Railway Historical Archives (38). **Chapter 3:Union Square and Chinatown:** Victoria R/Shutterstock (63). TJ Muzeni (69). spatuletail/Shutterstock (82). CURAphotography/Shutterstock (83) Brett Shoaf Artistic Visuals (84). Arnold Genthe (Public Domain) (84). Library of Congress Prints and Photographs Division (85). Sandor Balatoni (85). Library of Congress (86). **Chapter 4: Soma and Civic Center:** Jill Krueger (89). **Chapter 5: Nob Hill and Russian Hill:** yhelfman/Shutterstock (117). **Chapter 6: North Beach**: Alix Kreil/ Shutterstock (131). randy andy/Shutterstock (135). **Chapter 7: On the Waterfront:** telesniuk/Shutterstock (143). IM_photo/Shutterstock (155). f11photo/Shutterstock (165). Daniel DeSlover/Shutterstock (166). Public Domain (167). POPPERFOTO/Alamy (167). Wikipedia (167). Eliza Snow/iStockphoto (169). Steve Rosset/Shutterstock (170). **Chapter 8: The Marina and the Presidio:** Jeremy Borkat/Shutterstock (173). CAN BALCIOGLU/Shutterstock (174). Steve Holderfield/Shutterstock (175). Zack Frank/Shutterstock (175). **Chapter 9: The Western Shoreline:** Robert Holmes (193). Chee-Onn Leong/Shutterstock (199). **Chapter 10: Golden Gate Park:** California Travel and Tourism Co. (205). Robert Holmes (206-208). Robert Holmes (208). Natalia Bratslavsky/iStockphoto (209). Robert Holmes (210-211). Jack Hollingsworth (211). Robert Holmes (211-212). Janet Fullwood (213). Donna & Andrew/Flickr (214). Andrew Zarivny/Shutterstock (214). Robert Holmes (214). **Chapter 11: The Haight, the Castro, and Noe Valley:** Michael Warwick/Shutterstock (215). Nickolay Stanev (222). **Chapter 12: Mission District, Dogpatch, Bernal Heights, and Potrero Hill:** Kārlis Dambrāns/Flickr, [CC BY 2.0] (233). Held Jürgen/age fotostock (236).Robert Holmes (241). **Chapter 13: Pacific Heights and Japantown:** Della Huff/Alamy Stock Photo (253). Janet Fullwood (254). Susanne Friedrich/iStockphoto (255). terraxplorer/iStockphoto (255). Rafael Ramirez Lee/iStockphoto (262). **Chapter 14: The Bay Area:** TJ Muzeni (273). Andrei Stanescu/Alamy Stock Photo (282). Nancy Hoyt Belcher/Alamy (285). topseller/Shutterstock (306). S. Greg Panosian/ iStockphoto (311). **Chapter 15: Napa and Sonoma:** Andrew Zarivny/Shutterstock (317). Robert Holmes (324-325). kevin miller/iStockphoto (325). Robert Holmes (326). Domaine Carneros (327). star5112/Flickr (327). Robert Holmes (328). Gundolf Pftoenhauer (328). Robert Holmes (329). Agence Images/Alamy (330). Cephas Picture Library/Alamy (330). PHILIPPE ROY/Alamy (330). Caphas Picture Library/Alamy (331). Napa Valley Conference Bureau (331). Wild Horse. Winery (Forrest L. Doud) (331). Panther Creek Cellars (Ron Kaplan) (331). Clos du Val (Marvin Collins) (331). Warren H. White (331) Warren H. White (334). Terry Joanis/Frog's Leap (348). Warren H. White (356). Robert Holmes (367).

*About Our Writers: All photos are courtesy of the writers.

*Every effort has been made to trace the copyright holders, and we apologize in advance for any accidental errors. We would be happy to apply the corrections in the following edition of this publication.

Notes

Notes

Notes

Fodor's SAN FRANCISCO

Publisher: Stephen Horowitz, *General Manager*

Editorial: Douglas Stallings, *Editorial Director*, Margaret Kelly, Jacinta O'Halloran, Amanda Sadlowski, *Senior Editors*; Kayla Becker, Alexis Kelly, Teddy Minford, Rachael Roth, *Editors*

Design: Tina Malaney, *Design and Production Director*, Jessica Gonzalez, *Graphic Designer;* Mariana Tabares, *Design & Production Intern*

Production: Jennifer DePrima, *Editorial Production Manager*, Carrie Parker, *Senior Production Editor*, Elyse Rozelle, *Production Editor;* Jackson Pranica, *Editorial Production Assistant*

Maps: Rebecca Baer, *Senior Map Editor*, David Lindroth, Mark Stroud (Moon Street Cartography), *Cartographers*

Photography: Jill Krueger, *Director of Photo;* Namrata Aggarwal, Ashok Kumar, Carl Yu, *Photo Editors;* Rebecca Rimmer, *Photo Intern*

Business & Operations: Chuck Hoover, *Chief Marketing Officer*, Robert Ames, *Group General Manager*, Tara McCrillis, *Director of Publishing Operations;* Victor Bernal, *Business Analyst*

Public Relations and Marketing: Joe Ewaskiw, *Senior Director Communications & Public Relations*; Esther Su, *Senior Marketing Manager;* Ryan Garcia, Thomas Talarico, Miranda Villalobos, *Marketing Specialists*

Fodors.com Jeremy Tarr, *Editorial Director;* Rachael Levitt, *Managing Editor*

Technology: Jon Atkinson, *Director of Technology;* Rudresh Teotia, *Lead Developer*, Jacob Ashpis, *Content Operations Manager*

Writers: Trevor Felch, Denise Leto, Daniel Mangin, Rebecca Flint Marx, Monique Peterson, Andrea Powell

Editor: Jacinta O'Halloran

Production Editor: Carrie Parker

Production Design: Liliana Guia

30th Edition

ISBN 978-1-64097-160-8

ISSN 1525–1829

Library of Congress Control Number 2018966978

PRINTED IN THE UNITED STATES OF AMERICA

10 9 8 7 6 5 4 3 2 1

About Our Writers

Trevor Felch is a lifelong Bay Area resident who has spent countless days catching his breath after climbing San Francisco's hills. He spends most of his time eating and drinking around San Francisco, then writing about those experiences for several local and national publications. When he isn't staring at a laptop or a bakery case full of sourdough loaves and croissants, he's usually swimming or preparing for the next half marathon (remember all those sourdough loaves and croissants?), exploring around town with his girlfriend's dog, or some other activity for soaking up the California sun.

Longtime Fodor's writer and editor **Denise M. Leto** roams the city out of sheer love for SF, peeking down overgrown alleyways and exploring tucked-away corners from the Tenderloin to the Richmond, and diligently inspecting every bakery along the way. When she's not exploring San Francisco, she can often be found camping in or hiking Northern California's spectacular parks—especially during mushroom season. For this edition, Denise updated the Union Square/Chinatown, North Beach, the Mission/Dogpatch, the Western Shoreline, and On the Waterfront chapters. She also wrote our special features on cable cars, Chinatown, Golden Gate Park, Alcatraz, and the Golden Gate Bridge.

Daniel Mangin has been a Fodor's Travel writer and editor for more than a quarter century. The writer of all three editions of Fodor's Napa and Sonoma, he also contributed to its predecessor, Fodor's InFocus Napa and Sonoma. As the editorial director of the Compass American Guides, Daniel was the series editor of California Wine Country. For Wine House Press he is the coauthor of the Napa and Sonoma edition of The California Directory of Fine Wineries and contributed to the directory's Central Coast edition. He has also written about wine and wineries for Marin Magazine, Make It Better Magazine, and other print and online outlets. A wine lover whose earliest visits to Napa and Sonoma predate the Wine Country lifestyle, Daniel is delighted by the evolution in wines, wine making, and hospitality. With several dozen wineries less than a half- hour's drive from home, he often finds himself transported as if by magic to a tasting room, communing with a sophisticated Cabernet or savoring the finish of a smooth Pinot Noir.

Rebecca Flint Marx is a Brooklyn-based journalist who writes mostly about food. Her James Beard Award-winning work has appeared in numerous publications and a few books. Born in Alabama, raised in Michigan, and now a steadfast New Yorker, she recently spent a few years living in San Francisco, which she covered for this edition.

Monique Peterson A Northern California native, writer and editor Monique Peterson navigates Bay Area cities and landscapes with ease to share her insights on favorite places and new experiences, from Lake Merritt to Point Reyes Station. For many years, Monique's wanderlust landed her in New York City writing and editing books about art, science, history, and nature for The Walt Disney Company, Discovery Channel School, and Random House. She is also co-founder of a regional writing guild (tell-tailors.com), where she leads fiction and nonfiction workshops when she's not hiking, biking, or pursuing new adventures.

Andrea Powell is an Oregon native who has lived in San Francisco since 2009. She previously worked at San Francisco magazine, covering city politics, education, and culture, and at *WIRED*, where she wrote about business, technology, and science. Now a freelance writer, she spends her free time roaming the city's 47 square miles on foot and trying to keep up with its ever-evolving restaurant scene, both passions that came in handy for this edition.

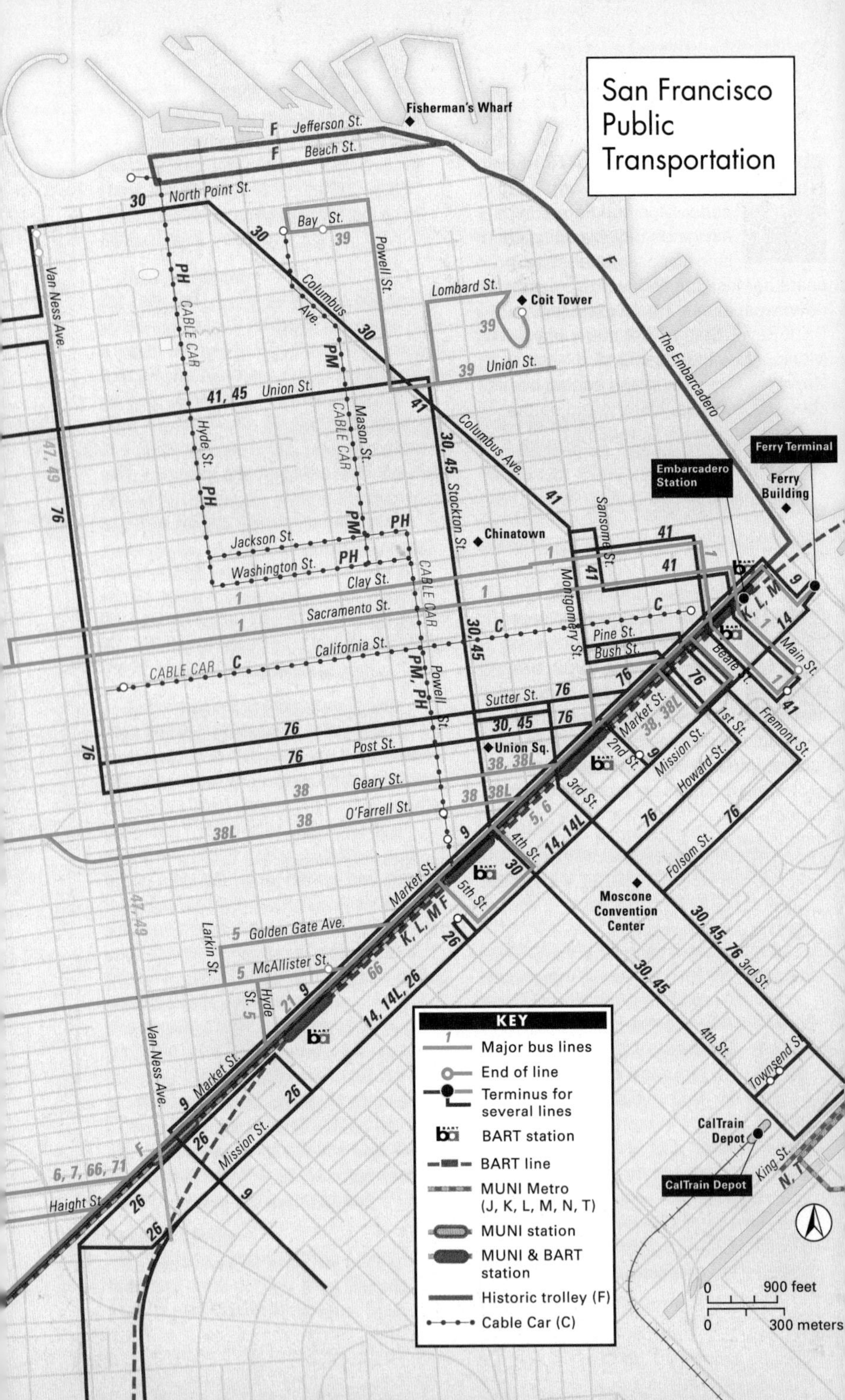
San Francisco Public Transportation
Fisherman's Wharf
Jefferson St.
Beach St.
North Point St.
Bay St.
Columbus Ave.
Powell St.
Lombard St.
Coit Tower
Union St.
The Embarcadero
Van Ness Ave.
CABLE CAR
Hyde St.
Mason St.
Stockton St.
Chinatown
Jackson St.
Washington St.
Clay St.
Sacramento St.
California St.
Sansome St.
Montgomery St.
Pine St.
Bush St.
Embarcadero Station
Ferry Terminal
Ferry Building
Beale St.
Main St.
Fremont St.
1st St.
2nd St.
3rd St.
4th St.
5th St.
Market St.
Mission St.
Howard St.
Folsom St.
Sutter St.
Post St.
Union Sq.
Geary St.
O'Farrell St.
Moscone Convention Center
Larkin St.
Golden Gate Ave.
McAllister St.
Hyde St.
Townsend St.
CalTrain Depot
King St.
Haight St.
KEY
Major bus lines
End of line
Terminus for several lines
BART station
BART line
MUNI Metro (J, K, L, M, N, T)
MUNI station
MUNI & BART station
Historic trolley (F)
Cable Car (C)
0 900 feet
0 300 meters